The Quality Movement & Organization Theory

The Quality Movement & Organization Theory

Robert E. Cole
W. Richard Scott

Editors

Sage Publications, Inc.
International Educational and Professional Publisher
Thousand Oaks ▪ London ▪ New Delhi

For information:

Sage Publications, Inc.
2455 Teller Road
Thousand Oaks, California 91320
E-mail: order@sagepub.com

Sage Publications Ltd.
6 Bonhill Street
London EC2A 4PU
United Kingdom

Sage Publications India Pvt. Ltd.
M-32 Market
Greater Kailash I
New Delhi 110 048 India

Printed in the United States of America

Library of Congress Cataloging-in-Publication Data

Cole, Robert E.
The quality movement and organization theory / by Robert E. Cole and
W. Richard Scott, editors.
    p. cm.
Includes bibliographical references and index.
ISBN 0-7619-1975-9 (cloth: acid-free paper)
ISBN 0-7619-1976-7 (pbk.: acid-free paper)
 1. Organizational change. 2. Industrial organization. 3. Industrial
management. I. Scott, W. Richard. II. Title.
  HD58.8 .C636 1999
  658.4'013—dc21   99-050512

This book is printed on acid-free paper.

00 01 02 03 04 05 06 7 6 5 4 3 2 1

Acquisition Editor:	Harry Briggs
Editorial Assistant:	MaryAnn Vail
Production Editor:	Sanford Robinson
Editorial Assistant:	Victoria Cheng
Designer:	Danielle Dillahunt
Typesetter:	Christina Hill
Indexer:	Cristina Haley

Contents

III. Stages and Processes in Quality Improvement

IV. Conditions and Contingencies Affecting Quality Development

Preface

The developmental history of this volume mirrors its twin aims. We seek to direct the attention of academic scholars to some of the new practices under way in work organizations so as to inform their theory and research and, at the same time, to encourage practitioners and applied researchers to make more use of existing concepts and theories of organizational change. Representatives from both of these constituencies played a part in the processes leading to this collection of chapters.

Scholarly interests were represented by the role played by the National Academy of Sciences, Commission on Behavioral and Social and Sciences and Education, which sponsored a series of workshops leading to the production of this volume. Scholarly as well as practitioner and applied research interests were reflected by the involvement of the Program on Transformation to Quality Organizations. This program is based on a collaboration between the National Science Foundation (NSF) and the Total Quality Leadership Steering Committee, a group composed of both executives from leading firms and university leaders that was organized to provide leadership in the development and deployment of quality concepts and methods in the United States. We briefly detail each strand.

National Academy of Sciences: Early Interest in Organizations and Organizational Change

The Commission on Behavioral and Social Sciences and Education (CBASSE) is one of the major divisions of the National Research Council (NRC), the principal operating agency of the National Academy of Sciences (NAS) and the National Academy of Engineering (National Research Council, 1993-1994). The CBASSE is the primary forum and governance body, overseeing behavioral and social science activities in all NRC activities. As a part of its mission, it regularly sponsors research panels, workshops, and conferences designed to strengthen and advance the disciplines within its domain as well as to seek ways to apply the knowledge and analytical tools of the social sciences to the nation's most pressing problems. Thus, although the NAS is primarily organized around scholarly interests, the NRC was created to facilitate the mobilization of these interests around more policy-relevant and applied interests.

Dr. Scott served on the CBASSE from 1990 to 1996 and helped to initiate a number of activities intended to stimulate theory, research, and application in organizational studies. Prior to this period, more microlevel foci had been pursued as organizational psychology was included in the projects initiated by the Committee on Techniques for the Enhancement of Human Performance, but there was little attention to organization-level phenomena. Beginning in the early 1990s, the Committee initiated three projects that recognized the importance of organizational as well as individual and interpersonal factors in technological change and productivity enhancement. The first linked engineering with social science expertise. Gerald Nadler, Professor of Engineering Management at the University of Southern California, and

Edward O. Laumann, Professor of Sociology at the University of Chicago, co-chaired a conference examining factors affecting the introduction and successful utilization of new technologies in organizations[1] (National Academy of Engineering and CBASSE, 1991). The second activity focused primary attention on organizational factors by examining the "productivity paradox," posing the question "Why are increases in individual productivity not reflected in measures of organizational productivity?" (Harris, 1994, p. 1). Douglas H. Harris, Senior Scientist at Anacapa Sciences, Inc., chaired a panel to examine "organizational linkages"—individual-work group-department-organization—as they affect individual and organizational productivity across a variety of settings.[2] A third study group was convened under the chairmanship of Jerome E. Singer, Professor in the Department of Medical and Clinical Psychology, Uniformed Services, University of Health Sciences, Bethesda, to examine the organizational context of individual and group performance. Topics examined by this group included organizational change and design, techniques for making organizations effective, organizational culture, leadership development, and interorganizational relations[3] (Druckman, Singer, & Van Cott, 1997).

In addition, two workshops were convened to highlight the complexity of controlling and assessing organizational change. The first of these was held at the Beckman Center in Irvine, California in 1993 to explore "Organizations and Purposive Change." The intent of this effort, chaired by Scott, was to identify a few key areas or themes and priority projects likely to contribute to improved organizational practice and to the further development of the science base.[4]

This activity was followed, in 1994, by a workshop focusing on "Improving the Effectiveness of Government," held in Washington, D.C., and chaired by Scott and economist Sidney G. Winter. This meeting brought together representatives from the National Performance Review Commission (the agency charged with "reinventing government"), key members of various federal agencies, and a collection of organizational scholars. Current reform initiatives under way were described and evaluated by governmental participants, and academics were asked to respond by placing the initiatives in historical and theoretical perspective.[5] It became obvious to academic participants that although there were some interesting change efforts under way in the public sector—many of them mimicking efforts to improve quality in private organizations—far stronger and more extensive change processes were under way outside the sphere of government.

As a consequence, when CBASSE members learned of the chance to become better informed about research already being conducted to evaluate change efforts in a wide range of organizations under the auspices of the National Science Foundation, they were eager to join forces. Before describing these efforts, however, it is appropriate to briefly detail the origins and early development of the Total Quality Leadership Steering Committee, which led to NSF involvement.

Evolution of Total Quality Leadership Steering Committee and National Science Foundation Involvement

The source of funding and inspiration for NSF involvement in this project had its origins in the formation of the Leadership Steering Committee, a loose-knit group of executives from leading firms and deans and presidents of universities. The participating companies had all initiated organizationwide efforts based on the principles of quality management to significantly improve their performance. This small group came together in 1989 for the first in a succession of annual meetings that came to be known as the Total Quality Forum. The objectives of the initiating executives were articulated by David Kearns, then Chief Executive Officer of Xerox, at the very first meeting. The business community wanted to work with the academic community because they depended on that community to provide the basic human capital needed to operate their organizations successfully. At the height of the Japanese competitive challenge in the late 1980s, there was a strong concern in the business community that universities were not providing these essential skills. In particular, executives believed that an understanding of "total quality" was one of those essential skills required for contemporary managers. The executives stressed the importance of preparing students who understood quality issues by getting quality topics into the curriculum, developing requisite skills, and working with the business community to establish quality as a major tool.

A turning point came at the conclusion of the 1991 Total Quality Forum. Under the leadership of Edwin Artzt, then Chairman of the Board and Chief Executive of Procter & Gamble, a leadership committee composed of executives from leading firms and universities was formed to ensure that the recommendations of the conference participants were implemented.[6] To that end, the Committee chartered six working councils to address the crucial issues necessary to move forward. One of those committees was the Total Quality Research Working Council, on which Cole served. One of the key recommendations of this group was that a research grant mechanism similar to the grant programs run by organizations such as the National Science Foundation be established to support research on quality improvement. The group also recommended that a large pool of funds be created to support this effort under the auspices of the leadership committee.

This recommendation was formally accepted by the Leadership Steering Committee (LSC) as outlined in *A Report of the Total Quality Leadership Steering Committee and Working Councils* (Leadership Steering Committee, 1992). The LSC agreed to support the formation of a pool of research funding and the creation of a process for administration of research grants. Funding was to be provided by the business community and an appropriate foundation, with in-kind support being provided by universities. The intent was to create funds sufficient to cover an initial period of 3 years.

The LSC supported this new research agenda in order to legitimate quality as a subject of academic research and to influence university curricula, particularly in schools of engineering and business. Based on the experience and prominence of the National Science Foundation

in supporting academic research, the LSC approached the NSF with the proposal to form a partnership. Conversations between representatives of the two organizations took place over the course of 1992-1993 and came to fruition in 1994 with the founding of the Transformation to Quality Organizations (TQO) program (Baba, 1999, p. 88). The American Society for Quality also became a partner in the program through its contributions of funding and expertise. In total, a 9-million-dollar research fund was created for 3 years. The name "Transformation to Quality Organizations" was chosen to communicate the message that the program encompassed a broad spectrum of research on organizational and technological changes related to quality improvement in organizations. The objectives of TQO's founders were to support research to increase the fundamental understanding of quality in organizations and to promote research projects and experiences to improve teaching, preparation of students, and management practice in the United States. In the effort to build a generalizable knowledge base and encourage broad applications of knowledge related to quality transformations in organizations, the TQO program aimed at promoting interdisciplinary and multidisciplinary research involving engineering, management, and the social sciences. An advisory committee—chaired by Ben Bethell, Senior Vice President of Human Resources at Procter & Gamble, and Cole at the University of California, Berkeley, and composed of private-sector executives and academics—was established to provide management oversight of the TQO program.[7]

Additional funding for the program came through two directorates within the NSF: Social, Behavioral and Economic Sciences, and Engineering. As of 1998, some 30 research grants had been made in five rounds of funding. The initial 3 years of funding was extended with additional funding for another 2 years, with the program expiring in 1998. At that time, the activities were institutionalized within the NSF by combining the TQO program and another existing program, Management of Technological Innovation (MOTI), to create the Innovation and Organizational Change Program.

As the advisory committee wrestled with the task of furthering the deployment of quality principles into university curricula, it observed that one of the most effective ways to achieve this end was to ensure that high-quality research was supported and disseminated to a broad scholarly constituency. If high-quality scholarly research could demonstrate and elaborate the importance and role of quality improvement principles, faculty would be more likely to incorporate these principles into their course offerings. Thus, when a proposal was made in 1997 to compile a book composed of the work of leading social scientists in the area of quality, the committee was very supportive.

Conjoint Activities: Steps Leading to the Development of This Volume

During the spring of 1995, Scott and Cole began to discuss possible ways in which activities under way at the CBASSE and NSF-TQO could be fruitfully combined. In particular, the intent from the outset was to use research efforts already occurring under the auspices of the NSF as a vehicle to stimulate theory development within a wider set of organizational scholars while ensuring that ongoing quality research was informed by existing theory. Related to the latter, TQO program staff hoped to identify new priority areas for research on quality (Baba, 1999, p. 87). To pursue these aims, we proposed to "bring together the smartest and best informed current researchers in the quality arena with their counterparts in the broader area of organizations studies." With the assistance of staff members from the CBASSE—in particular, Miron Straf, Director, Committee on National Statistics, CBASSE; and Marietta L. Baba, Program Director, Transformations to Quality Organizations Program, NSF—a workshop was organized under the auspices of the CBASSE. After careful preparation, a workshop on Improving Theory and Research on Quality Enhancement in Organizations was convened in Washington, D.C., in September 1996 with Cole and Scott as co-chairs.

The conference format involved the presentation of research reports by a set of invited investigators conducting research on quality initiatives, followed by critiques and commentaries by designated discussants.[8] The hope was to identify promising research-in-progress that, by dialogue and discussion, could be made even better, and, at the same time, to capture the attention of a set of generalist scholars that might be induced to reflect on the more general issues raised by the research presentations. To a considerable extent, this hope was realized, because genuine exchange occurred during the workshop (Wellens, Scott, & Cole, 1997), and the possibility of a set of publishable research reports and commentaries began to take shape.

To realize this possibility, however, it seemed essential to the organizers that a follow-up workshop be conducted—an occasion permitting selected participants to revise their research papers and commentaries, and, at the same time, inviting new scholars to participate in order to fill in missing topics and perspectives. The TQO Program at the NSF, under its new Program Director, James W. Dean, Jr., sponsored the follow-up workshop. The meeting took place in May 1997 at the Haas School of Business, University of California, Berkeley, and was again chaired by Cole and Scott.[9]

All research papers and commentaries accepted for publication in this volume were individually reviewed and critiqued by Cole or Scott in addition to the feedback that authors received during the two workshops. Throughout the rather lengthy gestation process for this volume, all contributors have been highly cooperative and responsive to suggestions.

Of the many individuals who have contributed time and energy to this project, we editors wish to single out two for particular thanks. Without the continuing support and encouragement of Myron Straf, Director of Committee on National Statistics at CBASSE, and James W. Dean, Jr., former Program Director of the Total Quality Organizations Program at the NSF, this effort to improve communication channels between basic and applied programs and researchers would not have been sustained and brought to completion with the publication of this volume.

W.R.S.
R.E.C.

Notes

1. Organizational scholars involved in the panel on organizational linkages were Paul A. Attewell, sociology, City University of New York; John P. Campbell, psychology, University of Minnesota; Jerome I. Elkind, Lexia Institute; Paul S. Goodman, Graduate School of Industrial Administration, Carnegie Mellon University; Sara B. Kiesler, Social and Decision Sciences, Carnegie Mellon University; Robert D. Prichard, psychology, Texas A&M; William A. Ruch, Decision and Information Systems, Arizona State; Benjamin Schneider, psychology, University of Maryland; D. Scott Sink, Virginia Polytechnic Institute; George L. Smith, Jr., Industrial and Systems Engineering, Ohio State; and David A. Whetten, Business Administration, University of Illinois.

2. The symposium planning committee included, in addition to Nadler and Laumann, Robert M. Anderson, Jr., Technical Education Operation, General Electric; Alden S. Bean, Management Studies, Lehigh University; Harvey Brooks, Technology and Public Policy, Harvard University; Robert L. Kahn, Institute for Social Research, University of Michigan; Sara B. Kiesler, Social and Decision Sciences, Carnegie Mellon University; and Scott, sociology, Stanford University.

3. In addition to Singer, study participants were Janice M. Beyer, Department of Management, University of Texas; Nicole W. Biggart, Department of Management and Sociology, University of California, Davis; W. Warner Burke, Department of Organization and Leadership, Teachers College, Columbia University; Kim S. Cameron, Department of Management, Brigham Young University; David L. DeVries, Kaplan DeVries, Inc., Greensboro, North Carolina; Paul F. Diehl, political science, University of Illinois; George P. Huber, management, University of Texas; Robert L. Kahn, Institute for Social Research, University of Michigan; James A. Wall, Jr., Department of Management, University of Missouri; Brig. General John M. Wattendort, Department of Behavioral Sciences and Leadership, West Point; Brig. General Myra H. Williamson, A&E Electronics, Arlington, Virginia; and Gary Yukl, Department of Management, State University of New York, Albany. CBASSE staff members were Daniel Druckman, Harold Van Cott, and Cindy Prince.

4. Academic participants were James N. Baron, Graduate School of Business, Stanford University; Robert D. Behn, Policy Sciences, Duke University; Nicole Biggart, School of Management and Sociology, University of California, Davis; Glenn CarToll, Haas School of Business, University of California, Berkeley; Gerald Davis, Kellogg School of Management, Northwestern University; Paul Goodman, School of Industrial Administration, Carnegie Mellon University; Sharon Lynn Kagan, Yale Bush Center, Yale University; Thomas Kochan, Sloan School of Management, MIT; Edward Lawler III, School of Business Administration, University of Southern California; William Morrill, Mathtech, Inc., Princeton, New Jersey; John Roberts, Graduate School of Business, Stanford University; Scott, sociology, Stanford University; and Mike Useem,

Wharton School and sociology, University of Pennsylvania. Cora Marrett represented the NSF, and NAS staff participants were Daniel Druckman and Miron Straf. Druckman provided staff support from the CBASSE.

5. Government participants were William Hinkle, Social Security Administration; Pamela Johnson, National Performance Review; Elaine Kamarck, Office of Vice President; Robert Knisely, Department of Transportation; and David Mathiasen, General Accounting Office. Participants from the National Science Foundation or the National Academy of Sciences/National Research Council were Hal Arkes, NSF; William Bainbridge, NSF; Michael Feuer, CBASSE; Lawrence McCray, National Academy of Engineering; Daniel Newlon, NSF; Miron Straf, CBASSE; Barbara Boyle Torrey, CBASSE; Alexandra Wigdor, CBASSE; and Suzanne Woolsey, NRC. Academic participants were Nicole Biggart, management and sociology, University of California, Davis; Thomas Cook, Research Triangle Institute, North Carolina; Walter W. Powell, sociology, University of Arizona; Scott, sociology, Stanford University; Barry Staw, organizational behavior, School of Business, University of California, Berkeley; and Sidney Winter, Wharton School, University of Pennsylvania. Staff support was provided by Janet S. Hansen and Michele L. Conrad, CBASSE.

6. Members of the Leadership Steering Committee were John Akers, Chairman of the Board, IBM; Paul Allaire, Chairman and Chief Executive Officer, Xerox Corporation; Edwin Artzt, Chairman and Chief Executive, Procter & Gamble; John Byme, President, Oregon State University; Livio DeSimone, Chairman and Chief Executive Officer, 3M; Meyer Feldberg, Dean, Graduate School of Business, Columbia University; Christopher Galvin, Senior Executive Vice President, Motorola Inc.; Roger Milliken, Chairman and Chief Executive Officer, Milliken & Company; C. Warren Neel, Dean, College of Business Administration, University of Tennessee at Knoxville; John Pepper, President, Procter & Gamble; Frank Rhodes, President, Cornell University; James Robinson III, Chairman and Chief Executive Officer, American Express Company; William Showalter, Dean, School of Engineering, University of Illinois; Donna Shalala, Chancellor, University of Wisconsin at Madison; Robert Stempel, Chairman, General Motors Corporation; Charles Vest, President, Massachusetts Institute of Technology; John White, Dean of Engineering, Georgia Institute of Technology; and B. Joseph White, University of Michigan.

7. Other members were Thomas Murrin, Dean of Business School, Duquesne University; Robert Osterhoff, Director of Corporate Quality, Xerox Corporation; David Luther, President of the American Society of Quality; Stanley Settles, Chair, Industrial and Systems Engineering, University of Southern California; and Marietta Baba (NSF Program Director). Baba was followed in this role by James W. Dean, Jr. Their able counterpart on the industry side was Gary Huysse, the Associate Director of Global Quality Improvement at Procter & Gamble.

8. Academic participants, in addition to Cole and Scott, were Soren Bisgaard-Frantzen, College of Engineering, University of Wisconsin; Kim Cameron, Marriott School of

Management, Brigham Young University; George Easton,
Goizueta School of Business, Emory University; Kathleen
Eisenhardt, Industrial Engineering and Management, Stan-
ford University; Barbara Flynn, Department of Manage-
ment, Iowa State University; Richard Hackman, Depart-
ment of Psychology, Harvard University; Tomoka Hamada,
Department of Anthropology, College of William and
Mary; Thomas Kochan, Sloan School of Management,
MIT; David Levine, Haas School of Business, University of
California, Berkeley; Nelson Repenning, Sloan School of
Management, MIT; Stanley Settles, Department of Indus-
trial and Systems Engineering, University of Southern Cali-
fornia; Kathryn Shaw, Graduate School of Industrial Engi-
neering, Carnegie Mellon University; Sim Sitkin, Fuqua
School of Business, Duke University; John Sterman, Sloan
School of Management, MIT; Kathleen Sutcliffe, School of
Business, University of Michigan; Karl Weick, School of
Business Administration, University of Michigan; and Sid-
ney Winter, Wharton School, University of Pennsylvania.
Staff participants from NSF were Marietta Baba and James
W. Dean, Jr., Transformation to Quality Organizations Pro-
gram; William Butz and Hilleary Everist, Social, Behav-
ioral and Economic Research Program; Rachelle Hollander,
Ethics Program; and Cora Marrett, Director of Social Sciences. Staff participants from the CBASSE were Daniel
Druckman and Janet Hansen, Division on Education, Labor
and Human Performance; and Miron Straf, Tracy Wellens,
and Karen Huie, Committee on National Statistics.

9. Academic participants, in addition to Cole and Scott,
were Kim Cameron, Marriott School of Management,
Brigham Young University; George Easton, Goizueta
School of Business, Emory University; Kathleen
Eisenhardt, Department of Industrial Engineering and Man-
agement, Stanford University; Tomoko Hamada, Depart-
ment of Anthropology, College of William and Mary; Linda
Kabollian, Kennedy School of Government, Harvard Uni-
versity; Thomas Kochan, Sloan School of Management,
MIT; David Levine, Haas School of Business, University of
California, Berkeley; John Paul McDuffie, Wharton
School, University of Pennsylvania; Kathryn Shaw, Gradu-
ate School of Industrial Administration, Carnegie Mellon

University; Sim Sitkin, Fuqua School of Business, Duke
University; John Sterman, System Dynamics Group, Sloan
School of Management, MIT; Kathleen Sutcliffe, School of
Business Administration, University of Michigan; Karl E.
Weick, School of Business Administration, University of
Michigan; and Sidney G. Winter, Wharton School, Univer-
sity of Pennsylvania. Gary Huysse, Associate Director of
Global Quality Improvement at Procter & Gamble, was
present as an industry representative. James W. Dean, Jr.,
Program Director for the TQO program at the NSF, pro-
vided staff support for this follow-up workshop.

References

Baba, M. (1999). Academic culture and the American quality movement: Linking fundamental research and quality practice. In M. Stahl (Ed.), *Perspectives in total quality.* Oxford, UK: Blackwell.

Druckman, D., Singer, J. E., & Van Cott, H. (1997). *Enhancing organizational performance.* Washington, DC:
National Academy Press.

Harris, D. H. (1994). *Organizational linkages: Understanding the productivity paradox.* Washington, DC: National
Academy Press.

Leadership Steering Committee. (1992). *A report of the Total Quality Leadership Steering Committee and
Working Councils.* Cincinnati, OH: Procter & Gamble.

National Academy of Engineering and CBASSE. (1991).
People and technology in the workplace. Washington,
DC: National Academy Press.

National Research Council. (1993-1994). *Commission on
Behavioral and Social Sciences and Education:
1993-1994.* Washington, DC: National Academy Press.

Wellens, T. R., Scott, W. R., & Cole, R. (Eds.). (1997). *Improving theory and research on quality enhancement in
organizations: Report of a workshop.* Washington, DC:
National Academy Press.

Introduction

The Quality Movement
and Organization Theory

W. RICHARD SCOTT
ROBERT E. COLE

This book is devoted to exploring the linkages between organization theory and research and the new ideas and practices related to quality improvement that spread across many types of organizations in the United States during the 1980s and 1990s. Although most of the chapters focus on a particular time (recent decades), place (the United States), and change vehicle (quality management practices), the broader concern is with the large and complex questions of how and why organizations change. This concern is enduring, not bounded by time or geography, and deals with issues much more general than any particular set of change strategies or tactics. We believe that there is much to be learned—by both researchers and practitioners—in viewing quality management as a recent important instance of change and bringing this movement into closer dialogue with the more general formulations and enduring concerns of organization theory.

Beginning in 1980 and continuing well into the 1990s, quality became a major issue for

American managers across a broad range of industries. Quality improvement rose to the top of management's agenda of "things to do," and it led to much talk as well as a large number of diverse, sometimes sustained, organizational initiatives. By contrast, throughout this period and up to the present time, students of organizations have either largely ignored these efforts or, if they took notice, have tended to dismiss them as yet another superficial and ephemeral fad. Far from being in the forefront of this major change movement, whether by guiding or assessing its development, organization scholars, for the most part, have remained aloof and skeptical.

This volume assembles a collection of chapters that constitutes important exceptions to the general pattern of neglect. They present the research and reflections of a handful of leading students of organizations who have elected to take notice of recent quality improvement efforts with the intent to better understand change processes in organizations and to place this work in a broader theoretical context. A few of the chapters were published previously, but we regarded them to be sufficiently insightful and influential to justify their reprinting in this collection. The remaining chapters, published here for the first time, are the fruits of a workshop process, described in the Preface, that was designed to bring researchers currently studying quality improvement efforts together with other organizational scholars who could reflect and comment on this research.

Thus, the new chapters are of two types. One group consists of empirical studies examining the who, what, and why of specific change efforts to improve quality. We believe that they exemplify some of the best contemporary efforts by researchers to illuminate what kinds of changes organizations are introducing and with what effects. They served to inform—but were also partially shaped by—discussion in the workshops because researchers took advantage of the opportunity to respond to comments and suggestions from their colleagues in revising their chapters for publication here. The second group consists of more reflective pieces written by other invited participants who elected to pursue a facet of the issues raised by the workshop discussion. Both the empirical studies and the more general chapters are intended to link this topic more closely to the broader arena of organization theory and research. To the extent that this connection is made, and continues to be deepened and extended, we believe that both theory and practice will benefit.

Potential Insights From Organization Theory

Organizational researchers have accorded much attention, particularly of late, to the topic of organization change. Although contemporary theorists differ as to whether to emphasize the internal or external sources of change, whether the principal mechanisms are adaptation or selection, or whether change is ubiquitous and easy or difficult and dangerous, few deny its interest or importance. Some regard organizational change as a somewhat distinctive area of research requiring its own theoretical frame-

works and explanatory ideas, but we insist that many mainstream theories make important predictions about change (see Barnett & Carroll, 1995). Thus, we begin by asking which theoretical frameworks or ideas are available that may be of assistance in explaining how organizations relate to changes of the type represented by the quality movement.

The introductory chapter by Dean and Bowen (Chapter 1) adopts the same general stance that we embrace by asking what theories can contribute to the understanding of quality (and vice versa). However, the arguments they examine are drawn largely from management theory rather than the broader perspectives associated with organization theory. They review leadership theories, human resources management, strategic quality planning, and information and analysis approaches. Their discussion of these ideas and their connections to practice are certainly instructive, but we wish to supplement their review with comments on some additional organizational theories that we believe to be relevant. We briefly consider contingency theory, resource dependence, evolutionary economics, organizational learning, organizational ecology, and institutional theory.

Contingency Theory

Originally developed by Lawrence and Lorsch (1967) and Thompson (1967), and elaborated by Galbraith (1973, 1977), among others, contingency theory was instrumental in ushering in the modern epoch of organization theory.[1] It did so in two senses. First, it was the first attempt to draw into organization theory insights from general systems theory emphasizing the importance of the environment in shaping organizational structures and processes (Katz & Kahn, 1966). Second, contingency theory represented an important break from the earlier dominant perspective of scientific management developed by Frederick Taylor (1911, 1947) by insisting that there was no one best way to organize. Rather, the design of organizations was, or, in the interest of fostering effectiveness, was supposed to be, *contingent* on environmental factors, in particular, the nature of work being performed and the wider task environment.

In applying these ideas, much depends on how the environment is conceived. Contingency theorists emphasized the importance of technical and production processes and, in particular, the kinds of information needed to adequately cope with the challenges and uncertainties posed by the tasks being performed. The basic thesis was that the greater the uncertainty and complexity of the work carried out and the greater the interdependency of the work processes, the greater the need for information by task performers and, hence, the larger the resources that needed to be devoted to information gathering and transmission (Galbraith 1973).

How does all this relate to quality improvement efforts? The most important connections concern the ways in which the quality movement changed managers' conception of what the environment was and how to relate to it. Earlier views generally stressed ways in which the organization could act to restrict and curtail the effect of the environment on the organization, in particular, by reducing the uncertainty confronted so that work processes could be simplified and routinized. Theorists such as Thompson stressed the utility of "buffering" techniques by means of which organizations could suppress or constrain environmental demands so as to increase predictability of resource flows and work processes within the technical core of the firm. Similarly, to the extent possible, the interdependence among work units was reduced, allowing departments to engage in batch production and minimize coordination with related units. In short, in the absence of strong competitive pressures, firms organized their production to reduce information-processing demands on workers and managers.

The emerging quality movement redefined the firm's environment by stressing that quality was to be determined by external customers rather than by internal quality control units; products were to satisfy consumers, not engineers. This redefinition of the environment—from passive consumer of outputs to active definer of satisfactory products and services—necessarily requires corresponding changes in the internal structure and operation of companies. Contingency theory, as a body of analytic propositions, predicts such changes. If the conception of the relevant environment undergoes change, then the organizational structure must be revised accordingly. And, in its more normative versions (e.g., Galbraith & Lawler, 1993), contingency theory has provided guidance to managers seeking to design structures capable of handling more complex tasks and processing larger amounts of information. Stinchcombe (1990), for example, asserts that the structure of organizations is determined by "their growth toward sources of news, news about the uncertainties that most affect their outcomes" (pp. 6-7). And, in their chapter in this volume (Chapter 14), Hargadon and Eisenhardt provide an apt illustration of how firms can develop internal structures that increase their information-processing capacity and speed of decision making to support high-quality work in a rapidly changing environment.

Resource Dependence

Whereas contingency theory focuses attention primarily on the structure of an organization and its suitability for handling the information-processing demands posed by the task demands confronted, resource dependence gives more attention to the interdependence of an organization with other organizations in its environment. Attention is shifted from the internal structure of a single organization to the nature of the relation between that organization—termed the "focal" organization—and its exchange partners and competitors. Interdependence may occur because participants' behaviors are affected, as in resource and information exchanges, or because the organization's outcomes are affected, such as through competition. In either case, resource dependence theorists argue that organizations are likely to take steps to reduce their dependence on other organizations by developing various types of governance structures. As Pfeffer and Salancik (1978) suggest, "The typical solution to problems of interdependence and uncertainty involves increasing coordination, which means increasing the mutual control over each other's activities" (p. 43). The interconnections of economic and political processes are highlighted. Because economic dependence gives rise to power asymmetries, economic problems stimulate political solutions. Coordinating strategies range from bargaining, contracting, and co-optation to the formation of joint ventures, alliances, mergers, and wider industry associations (see Pfeffer and Salancik, 1978; Scott, 1998).

Whereas there was no apparent direct communication between the developers of quality management ideas and the resource dependency theorists, there is obvious similarity and synergy between the two conceptions. In particular, both groups stress the arbitrary nature of an organization's boundaries, encouraging managers to take a broader view of production and marketing functions. Suppliers of raw materials and parts are viewed by both as integral parts of the firm's production process that should be nurtured and cultivated. Similarly, consumers are not just passive recipients of whatever goods or services the firms wants to dispense, but indispensable sources of information on needs and preferences that can become the basis for new products and services. There is an inevitable interdependency between firms and their suppliers and customers, and it is in the firm's long-term interest to develop close working partnerships with knowledgeable suppliers and perspicacious customers.

Evolutionary Economics

In his chapter, which is reprinted in this volume, Winter (Chapter 3) provides a thoughtful review of the similarities and associations between evolutionary economics, as developed by Nelson and Winter (1973, 1982), and quality management approaches. As Winter points out, the two approaches converge particularly in their view that the distinctive competence of an enterprise resides in the organizational routines carried out by those involved in producing its

goods and services. Attempts to improve these routines necessarily involve the active cooperation of these participants. Therein lies much of the difficulty of inducing organizational change.

Redundancy of information is seen as an asset. Evolutionary theorists emphasize that one major source of difficulty is that much of the knowledge of work routines in organizations possessed by workers is in the form of tacit knowledge. Workers cannot express in verbal form to others what they know and routinely do; in Polanyi's (1967) formulation, "we can know more than we can tell" (p. 4). Many of the specific procedures developed by quality advocates, such as quality circles, have as one of their functions to make explicit and share with others the competence that individual workers possess. Evolutionary theorists emphasize the informal, fragmented, and distributed character of knowledge in most organizations but are willing to entertain the possibility that more systematic and concerted efforts to improve work processes could well have major payoffs.

Whether or not managers can make continuous improvements in work processes is partly a matter of obtaining better information on what workers are currently doing, subjecting these procedures to testing and refinement, and then instilling in workers the new routines. But, as Hackman and Wageman (Chapter 2) and Kochan and Rubinstein (Chapter 17) emphasize, of equal or greater importance than improved information is engendering trust between workers and managers of the sort that the improvements achieved will benefit all parties. In a period when top management's attention seems to be focused almost exclusively on the interests of stockholders, securing the commitment of workers to quality improvement becomes problematic.

Organizational Learning

Closely related to the concerns of evolutionary economics is a body of work that focuses on why and how organizations change their capabilities. Organizational learning theorists accept the premise developed by evolutionary economists that organizational behavior is based on routines. These routines are organizational in the sense that they are independent of particular actors and persist in spite of turnover. According to Levitt and March (1988), these routines are "history-dependent": Organizations learn by "encoding inferences from history into routines that guide behavior" (p. 320). In addition, they are oriented to targets in that the lessons learned depend not only on the outcomes observed but also on which aspirations are held.

Organizations learn from their own direct experience as they attempt to decipher the relation between the behaviors carried out and the outcomes experienced. In his study of shop-floor problem solving in auto assembly plants, MacDuffie (Chapter 8) provides a detailed examination of how such learning can occur and which conditions facilitate improvement. What is learned will vary greatly from one experience to another and one organization to another because many factors affect outcomes. The nature of what happened and why is fraught with ambiguity, presenting what Weick (1995, and Chapter 7, this volume) describes as occasions for "sensemaking" (see also March, Sproull, & Tamuz, 1991). Organizations also learn from the experience of others—most often from others regarded as similar to themselves and as successful.

However, whether learning results in improved performance is not guaranteed. Organization learning theorists, more so than quality management advocates, emphasize the problematic nature of organizational change (March & Olsen, 1976). "Learning" refers to modifications in routines, but such changes are only infrequently associated with improved performance. Learning is frequently "superstitious"—organizations drawing incorrect inferences from history—and much learning involves attempts to mindlessly copy the activities of others regarded as superior. Even at best, the world is more complex than most organizational participants realize: "Organizations are collections of subunits learning in an environment that consists largely of other collections of learning subunits" (Levitt & March, 1988, p. 331). In such a world, it is difficult to decide what to learn and even more difficult to predict what will be the effects of such learning.

Learning theorists also raise questions about the suitability of conventional quality management approaches in situations involving high levels of uncertainty or ambiguity. Sutcliffe, Sitkin, and Browning (in Chapter 13) point out that a methodology that emphasizes the discovery of improved routines, which are then standardized and imposed on workers, may suppress further learning of the type needed in less structured situations. Such an "engineering" approach clearly involves learning, but "represents first-order rather than second-order learning (Argyris & Schon, 1978) in that it involves more effectively exploiting familiar skills in addressing known problems" rather than exploring new approaches leading to new types of skills (Sitkin, Sutcliffe, & Schroeder, 1994, p. 554; see also March, 1991). In these and other ways, learning theorists emphasize that organizational learning is both difficult and dangerous and that structural arrangements conducive to some types of learning may inhibit other valuable forms.

Organizational Ecology

Beginning in the late 1970s, organizational theorists began to employ arguments and models developed by biologists and urban sociologists to organizations. Hannan and Freeman (1977) and Aldrich (1979) suggested that collections of similar organizations, or "populations," could be viewed as experiencing change processes analogous to those associated with biological species. The arguments developed emphasized organizational inertia resistance to change posed by both internal commitments (e.g., the sunk costs of capital equipment and current employee skills) and external constraints (e.g., regulatory systems and commitments to suppliers and customers). Hence, it was argued, change is more likely to occur by environmental selection (as existing organizations fail and new organizations arise to take their place) than by adaptation (Hannan & Freeman, 1989). Shifting attention to the population level of analysis allows investigators to identify how much change is the result of organizational turnover versus the adaptation of existing organizations. The replacement of existing organizations by new types is particularly likely to be associated with the development of new technologies (e.g., Tushman & Anderson, 1986) and with major changes in the policy or regulatory environment of an industry (e.g., Scott, Ruef, Mendel, & Caronna, 1999).

Ecologists emphasize the importance of two design issues in examining organizational change: (a) attending to the experience of the full range of organizations or a given type, and (b) studying change over prolonged periods of time. Most existing studies of the quality movement do not conform to these criteria. None of the studies in this volume meets the first criterion. Some of them employ data from the *Fortune* 500; others target leading companies or selected cases to examine in detail processes of interest; but none collect the type of data that would allow us to generalize about all organizations within a given time frame or of a given type. The only study conducted to date of which we are aware that does target the full range of organizations within a selected population is the study by Westphal, Gulati, and Shortell (1997), which examines all community general medical surgical hospitals that responded to the National Quality Survey administered by the American Hospital Association. Such studies necessarily provide us with more insight into the full range of responses by organizations subject to the process of interest.

The second criterion emphasized by ecologists reminds us of the relatively brief time span during which the quality movement has been under way. One of the most useful services that organizational researchers can perform is to view this movement in its historical context and compare and contrast it with other, both similar and different, change efforts. Hackman and Wageman (Chapter 2), Cole (Chapter 4), and Kochan and Rubinstein (Chapter 17) all provide useful historical perspective.

Institutional Theory

An active area of theory and research in recent years emphasizes the ways in which organizations are influenced not only by their technical environments (resource flows and information required for task performance) but also by their institutional environments: cultural and cognitive frames, and rule and belief systems. Institutional theorists emphasize that organizations strive to achieve social "fitness"—legitimacy—as well as technological efficiency (DiMaggio & Powell, 1983; Meyer & Rowan, 1977).

Institutionalists come in many stripes and give varying emphasis to different facets of the institutional environment. Economists and some political scientists stress the importance of regulative systems—of governance structures, whether in the form of public laws or private corporate authority systems; sociologists, however, emphasize normative systems carried by informal, interpersonal relations or broader professional or craft associations. And, more recently, neoinstitutional theorists, primarily anthropologists and sociologists, have come to recognize the importance of cognitive and cultural belief systems that provide frameworks of common meaning and give structure and coherence to social behavior (see DiMaggio & Powell, 1991; Scott, 1995).

Cole (Chapter 4) employs a variety of institutional arguments in examining the adoption and spread of quality management ideas and practices in the United States during its formative stages. He points to the important role of cognitive processes ("sensemaking," in Weick's terms) as managers struggled to interpret what quality meant and to rethink the conventional trade-off between cost and quality. Cole's arguments underline the role of discourse—the transmission of ideas and information through interpersonal channels as well as the media—in bringing about change. Cole suggests, and other research has documented, how, over time, different types of agents and carriers come into play. For example, a study of discourse on quality circles in the business literature by Strang

(1997) found that during the early period (1977 to 1981), journalists and consultants dominated the talk about this innovation, whereas during the later period, 1987 to 1992, academics were the most prevalent voices. Consultants and journalists are in the business of touting the new, and they need to move on to different ideas or, at least, to new labels for describing how change and improvement is to be fostered. Academics are less driven by the novel and more attentive to evidence as to what works and why.

If reform efforts are sustained, it is often because they are supported by wider governance structures, whether in the form of public agencies or private trade and professional associations. For example, Cole (1989) has shown that reform efforts to encourage worker participation, such as quality circles, developed more rapidly and were sustained for longer periods in Japan than in Sweden, and in Sweden than in the United States, because societal infrastructures were stronger and more pervasive in the former countries. Later, normative frameworks such as the Baldrige Award competition have helped to encourage and sustain the quality movement in the United States (see Cole, Chapter 4; Easton and Jarrell, Chapter 10); that is, there evolved much stronger regulative, normative, and cognitive support structures in Japan and Sweden by industrial trade associations, unions, and government agencies.

However, institutional theory also recognizes that much social change is associated simply with the spread of new conceptions. The adoption of new ideas and values, the raising of consciousness, the attempt to keep up with the times and to reflect the "modern" ways—all are powerful levels of social change in societies committed to rationality and improvement (Meyer, 1994). These arguments suggest that some of the important effects of broad programs such as the quality movement may not be associated with the adoption of specific techniques and programs but may occur because of changes in the everyday meanings that managers, workers, and customers—across a broad range of organizations—associate with the idea of quality.

An important insight associated with institutional theory is that there will be differences between early and late adopters of an organizational innovation with respect to both determinants and consequences. Considering determinants, early adopters tend to exhibit different characteristics from late adopters. For example, studies reveal that organizations adopting administrative innovations, such as equal opportunity and affirmative action structures, were more likely to be closely associated with the public sector, large, unionized, and to have a personnel office in place (Dobbin, Sutton, Meyer, & Scott, 1993; Edelman, 1992). Research has also shown that organizations with relational ties (e.g., alliance partners or common board members) to other organizations that have adopted the innovation were more likely to themselves adopt the innovation (Burns & Wholey, 1993; Davis & Greve, 1997). Similar findings have been reported concerning the adoption of quality management practices by hospitals, with network ties operationalized as alliance partnerships (Westphal et al., 1997).

Turning to consequences, numerous theorists have suggested that early adopters will be more likely to embrace new practices because these practices are viewed as improving their effectiveness or efficiency, whereas later adopters will do so primarily because they seek to be in conformity with prevailing norms of practice (see Tolbert & Zucker, 1983). The results reported by Easton and Jarrell (Chapter 10) are consistent with this argument: Those firms judged to have achieved more advanced implementation of quality management practices were more likely to have adopted these practices earlier than other firms studied. Further evidence of the importance of timing comes from the research by Westphal and colleagues, who, in a study of more than 2,700 U.S. hospitals, found that the later the date at which the hospital adopted quality management practices, in relation to practices by other hospitals, the greater the level of their conformity to normative patterns of quality practice. Early adopters were more likely to adapt and customize quality management practices to their specific situation, whereas later adopters were more likely to simply embrace widely adopted practices (Westphal et al., 1997).

These examples suggest to us that institutional theory is particularly helpful in explaining why certain practice patterns and structures diffuse through a field of organizations as well as help to account for some of the differences in outcomes observed not only between adopters and nonadopters but also between early and late adopters.

More generally, we believe that these and other perspectives drawn from organization theory can contribute in important ways to understanding the quality movement and the ways in which it can serve as a vehicle of organizational change.

Having briefly reviewed some of the major organization theories and suggested some of the ways in which they might stimulate inquiry into the nature and pace of change in the quality movement, let us reverse the telescope and ask how the quality movement might aid the advancement of organization theory and our understanding of organizational change. In particular, what are the challenges posed by this set of developments?

Key Issues and Questions Raised by the Quality Movement

What are the questions raised by the recent quality movement, and how do they relate to the broader agenda of organization theory and research? Although each of the ensuing chapters addresses these questions in one way or another, we employ this introduction to signal—foreshadow and highlight—some of the issues we view as most significant.

- What was the impetus for the American quality movement? Where and when did these ideas develop? Who first proposed them, and which organizations pioneered in their adoption? Which forces fueled it, and which structures were created to advance and sustain it?

It is apparent that the movement began in selected manufacturing sectors that, in the late

1970s, became aware of the competitive threat posed by their Japanese competitors. In industries such as automobiles, steel, office machinery, machine tools, and a large number of electronics sectors, such as semiconductors, the Japanese onslaught rested on the development of cost-competitive products but also flowed from the use of quality superiority (particularly as measured by product reliability) as an effective strategy to expand market share in industry after industry. Manufacturing managers faced a major challenge in making sense of this novel exogenous threat from Japan. Cole (Chapter 4) documents the initial confusion and casting about for diagnoses and remedies that characterized the behavior of American managers, and Weick (Chapter 7) views their "thrownness" as an inevitable stage of the more general process of sensemaking. Managers knew that something was very wrong, that the survival of their organizations was at stake, but why this was the case and, more important, what they could do about it was very much in doubt.

Something very much akin to a social movement within industry arose to discover what was meant by quality and how firms should go about doing it. As quality caught on among U.S. manufacturing managers as a competitive issue, it was fueled by media attention, management conferences and seminars, and consultant activity. As the movement progressed, managers, consultants, professional and trade associations, and governmental agencies built infrastructural arrangements to spread both declarative and procedural knowledge (Cohen & Sproull, 1996) concerning the nature of the quality challenges and specific techniques and methodologies to meet them.

These developments appear to illustrate a more general trend characterizing the spread of ideas among organizational managers. Pascale (1990, pp. 19-20) has observed that managerial ideas began to become subject to fad-like processes after World War II. He attributes this development to the professionalization of management, which, in turn, rests on the premise that a set of generic concepts and approaches underlies managerial activity regardless of industry. Increasingly, we see a "commodification" of managerial techniques, allowing their pattern of diffusion to resemble that of packaged goods. Consultant firms, increasingly prominent during the post-World War II period, competed among themselves to drive a mass marketing of diverse managerial techniques, one fad following another in quick succession.

During the latter period of its development, the quality movement was fueled by efforts of the federal government to encourage adoption of quality practices. The principal mechanism used to stimulate interest in the private sector was the Baldrige Award, which encouraged companies to compete for the prize of being designated an award-winning enterprise. The quality movement came somewhat later to the public sector (see Kaboolian, Chapter 6), but it was given high-level visibility and support when Vice President Gore headed the effort to reinvent government, resulting in the National Performance Review Act of 1993.

Although one of many management movements, the quality movement stands out from the others during the past half-century for its longevity, dominating management's attention for almost two decades. This fact alone makes this movement worthy of social science interest.

- How are we to view the results of the quality movement? Was it successful in achieving its objectives? Why do the assessments of the business community appear to be at variance with those of academic researchers?

It is not possible at the present time to provide a definitive assessment of the results of the quality movement. One's views will necessarily depend on how broadly or narrowly the movement is defined. We observe an interesting dichotomy of interpretations of the meaning and lessons of the quality movement between academic observers and the management community. Whereas the former group tends to ignore or discount the significance of these quality improvement efforts, managers are more inclined to believe that significant changes occurred and palpable gains were achieved. What could account for these contradictory views?

Social scientists are trained to be skeptical—indeed, a useful definition of science is as a community of "organized skepticism." They seek precision in measuring activities and systematic and representative data in assessing outcomes. Although such safeguards are useful, they can also result in distortions of the phenomena being examined, particularly when broader and more diffuse forces are at work. In some cases, investigators have used very narrow interpretations of what constitutes quality practices, employing what is, in effect, a lazy use of the positivist research methodology. In the case of quality, this approach has led some researchers to see evidence of the quality movement's effects only if they can show the application, deployment, and contributions to improvement outcomes of specific, well-formed quality methodologies. Such scholars look for evidence of the use of specific quality methodologies in a prescribed fashion (e.g., use of the seven tools of effective problem solving). When such evidence is lacking, they point to the gap between quality rhetoric and reality, and they shift their attention to analyze the causes of that discrepancy (e.g., Zbaracki, 1994). Or, they contrast the weakness of the American efforts with what is perceived to be the robustness of Japanese practice (e.g., Easton & Jarrell, 1997). In either case, the quality initiative is judged to be ineffectual.

For their part, managers want to believe that what they do makes a difference, and they are more willing to settle for anecdotal evidence of effectiveness. (Some may even suggest that the researcher's prized "data" are only the plural of anecdote.) More important, they may embrace a broader perspective than researchers in identifying relevant organizational practices and defining related outcomes. As with many social movements, the quality effort is not readily linked to a well-identified, clearly specified set of ideas and practices (see Dean and Bowen, Chapter 1; Hackman and Wageman, Chapter 2) but, rather, appears as a loosely coupled collection of orientations and practices. And, in terms of outcomes, managers point not only to the enhanced quality levels attained in some areas of manufacturing but also to the improved cooperation between product designers and manufacturing groups, to an emphasis on continual improvement of organizational processes, and to heightened attention to and linkages with external customers. Although such emphases are not always correct and do not invariably lead to improvement in more specific outcome indicators, they represent important signs of organizational change.

Is it possible that some of the early, highly publicized failures identified by academic researchers, such as quality circles and the ubiquitous 14-point consultant programs, actually laid the groundwork for some of the later successes? If so, this would suggest that organizational researchers might well examine management "fads" in a broader time-and-space framework. It raises the intriguing question of whether and under what conditions management fads are compatible with organizational learning (see Cole, 1999).

We believe that students of organizational life will find much in the quality movement to arouse their curiosity. We need to give better and closer attention to the extent to which organizational changes made in the name of quality improvement actually produce the outcomes claimed by their advocates. Hackman and Wageman's review of the state of our knowledge about quality, conducted in the mid-1990s (see Chapter 2), found an abundance of shoddy research designs and scant convincing evidence for the claimed effects. What would more sophisticated research designs show? We provide one example of such a study in this volume. The study by Ichniowski and Shaw (Chapter 15) provides evidence regarding the effectiveness of quality management approaches in one branch of the steel industry.

Winter (Chapter 3) deftly summarizes the two points we seek to make. First, he asserts, "That quality management methods have produced positive results in some organizations is beyond dispute; that these methods are generally economically effective by conventional standards has not been demonstrated" (p. 92 of original). But second, and important, Winter's conclusion is that "quality management should be taken seriously" by the academic community (p. 90 of original).

- In what ways do the ideas associated with the quality movement contribute to and/or challenge our current understanding of organizational performance? Do the approaches proposed by quality reformers coincide or conflict with findings stemming from organizational research?

As Cole makes clear (Chapter 4), the quality movement had its origins as a practitioner-led movement in Japan. What little academic involvement there was came primarily from engineers who had only modest familiarity with Western social science. As the Japanese ideas were transported to American industry, again the movement was practitioner led, with American academics playing only a minor role. Indeed, as late as 1991, industry leaders issued a public call in *Harvard Business Review* for academics to give more attention to developments in quality management (Robinson et al., 1991). In contrast to other movements, such as strategic planning, in which American academics played a seminal developmental role (e.g., Porter, 1985), leadership in the quality movement has been dominated by consultants and practitioners.

As a consequence of these practitioner origins, quality leaders presented concepts like continuous improvement as ad hoc techniques. Yet these concepts have obvious links to work in operations research, systems theory, worker motivation, organizational learning, sensemaking, and many other streams of organization theory. For example, March (1991) has pointed to the trade-offs between exploitation of existing knowledge—continuing to do the things one knows how to do best—and exploration—investigating other approaches that may prove to be superior. And we can also ask whether there are ways to structure continuous improvement that allow participants to think about both simultaneously. Are there conditions under which the simultaneous pursuit of exploitation of existing routines and exploration of other ways of acting is more likely to occur? Sutcliffe, Sitkin, and Browning (Chapter 13) probe these questions. And, in a related discussion, Repenning and Sterman (Chapter 9) provide a careful analysis of work processes that support efforts to allow participants to simultaneously work harder and work smarter.

There seems little doubt that careful, systematic attention to the specifics of work processes can result in substantial improvement in performance. Small gains accumulate in an incremental way, and attending to the full range of processes contributing to the final output can sometimes reveal sources of problems that, if remedied, can produce large gains. MacDuffie (Chapter 8) provides a detailed illustration of such problem-solving processes observed in three auto assembly plants, emphasizing which conditions are associated with adaptive learning.

In some cases, quality leaders have advocated practices and policies at variance with the main lessons of organization theorists. For example, some quality gurus (e.g., Deming) have argued against providing material rewards for behavior advancing quality improvement. Most organizational research on the change process, while acknowledging implementation difficulties, stresses the importance of aligning incentives with desired organizational behavior (see Hackman and Wageman, Chapter 2). Because some companies have chosen to ignore the gurus' advice, we are provided with a natural laboratory for examining the effects of varying combinations of intrinsic and extrinsic rewards, as proposed by Levine and Shaw in Chapter 16.

One of the fundamental insights of the new approach to quality has been a recognition of the benefits achieved in moving from organizational activities directed to detecting error to those focused on preventing error. This reconception not only calls into question the earlier notion that quality control is a specialized function, but it also challenges the rationality of organizational designs privileging functional specialization over a concern for coordination and integration of functions across the entire commodity or service chain.

A related insight associated with the quality movement is the pivotal role of new product development in achieving high-quality performance. Organizational researchers have recently begun to recognize that in many industries, new product development is critical to organizational survival and renewal (Brown & Eisenhardt, 1995; Hargadon and Eisenhardt, Chapter 14). One theme intersecting research on new product development and the thinking of prevention-oriented quality improvement involves the time needed for new product development and its relationship to product quality. In the past, it was assumed that time to market (speed), critical in many industries, could be achieved only at the expense of quality (as measured particularly by product reliability and durability). Promoters of quality improvement argue that by using quality methodologies and eliminating waste, firms can both shorten time to market and achieve high quality. Research in the auto industry by Clark and Fujimoto (1991) supports such claims. The validity of these arguments is particularly important for high-technology firms with short product cycles, rapidly changing technologies, and, as a consequence, high levels of uncertainty.

Although the writing of quality gurus and promoters has, by and large, ignored the voluminous literature on employee participation in decision making (see Dean and Bowen, Chapter 1, and Hackman and Wageman, Chapter 2), a pervasive theme in the quality literature has been the importance of all-employee involvement in continuous process improvement. Although the evidence suggests that the rise in the utilization of employee involvement practices in industry in recent years went hand in hand with the rise of the quality initiatives of the 1980s and early 1990s (Lawler, Mohrman, & Ledford, 1995), there is ample opportunity for research into the relation between innovative human resource practices and the implementation of quality improvement technologies. Ichniowski and Shaw (Chapter 15) provide one useful model for such inquiry. Kochan and Rubinstein (Chapter 17) argue the value of employing a wider canvas, urging students of organizations to examine "how the combined effects of quality, human resource, and other organizational practices are producing fundamental transformations in American corporations."

A closely related issue is job security. It appears that the introduction of quality improvement into Japan from the 1960s through the 1980s was not generally associated with job loss. The large manufacturing firms were able to avoid laying off current job holders by using their cost competitiveness and their evolving quality superiority to greatly expand their markets while improving productivity. Thus, employees were not threatened by quality improvement and could respond quite positively to this initiative. In the United States, however, the rise of the quality movement in the 1980s and 1990s was often associated with downsizing initiatives that left employees feeling more ambivalent and suspicious of activities taken in the name of quality improvement. Workers who were asked to share their tacit knowledge at one phase of process improvement sometimes subsequently found themselves out of a job because fewer workers were required to execute the new programs. Enthusiasm and support for such improvements may vary greatly depending on one's location in the hierarchy: Senior managers may continue to extol the virtues of quality improvement efforts whose effects may be differently experienced by middle managers or production workers (Zbaracki, 1994).

- Do the ideas associated with the quality movement display sufficient coherence to be treated as a single phenomenon? Is the quality movement best viewed as a set of discrete techniques or methodologies, or as a complex collection of values and beliefs—an organizational culture? If the latter, how does one assess its presence and strength?

Rather diverse answers to these important questions have been offered. In this volume, Dean and Bowen (Chapter 1) propose that the quality movement is characterized by three principles—customer focus, continuous improvement, and teamwork, each of which is associated with a set of practices and more specific techniques. Contrary to the view of many, Dean and Bowen insist that this focus on total quality

is not simply a hodgepodge of slogans and tools; it is a set of mutually reinforcing principles, each of which is supported by a set of practices and techniques, and all of which are ultimately based on fulfilling customers' needs. (p. 396 of original)

Hackman and Wageman (Chapter 2) only partially agree with this positive appraisal. Although they concur that the underlying principles enunciated by the three founding authorities—Deming, Juran, and Ishikawa—do exhibit substantial agreement regarding the "key assumptions and practices" of quality management and that contemporary practice is "generally consistent" with the founders' ideas, they argue that a number of other practices are also employed by these organizations that were "specifically eschewed by the founders." (pp. 318-319 of original). As developed over time, quality ideas have begun to lose their distinctive flavor and to incorporate ingredients from other, different change paradigms, such as participative management and quality of worklife movements.

Winter (Chapter 3) acknowledges that a few key features have characterized recent quality improvement efforts. These include (a) a process orientation, stressing the centrality of production processes in contrast to characteristics of the products; (b) a focus on the customer as the final arbiter of quality; (c) an emphasis on the systematic application of tools to evaluate and improve work processes; and (d) the insistence that managers at all levels must take responsibility for quality improvement because it is they who must design the systems of production. Although these ideas are widely espoused, he asserts that they are less consistently applied, so that in practice, quality management is portrayed as a "promising innovation," or, "more accurately, it is a meta-innovation, a loose collection of heuristic methods for producing improvements in organizational routines" (p. 101 of original).

Although much scholarly attention focuses on the application of specific quality-enhancing techniques and their consequences, the quality movement, like any large-scale management movement, may be viewed as a broader complex of beliefs and values. Some managers and consultants came to speak of quality not as a product characteristic but as a generalized concept reflecting an organizational environment most conducive to enhanced performance. According to this view, the mere adoption of a collection of quality techniques cannot reasonably be expected to significantly improve organizational performance. Rather, one needs to make more fundamental changes in the basic premises, values, and commitments of participants: In short, a new quality culture is required (see Hamada, Chapter 12). Although a number of quality advocates have touted the benefits of creating such an organizational culture, there have been few attempts to measure its existence empirically and to assess its impact on performance. Cameron and Barnett (Chapter 11) report such research, pointing out that all organizations possess a quality culture—"a way of thinking about and defining quality"—but that most organizations settle for an "error detection" culture. Quality advocates have attempted to encourage the development of an "error prevention" culture, or even a "perpetually creative" culture. Beliefs and practices associated with these differing cultures are identified and assessed.

This work suggests that what quality is believed to be and how it is to be obtained varies over time and space. The quality movement, if it has done nothing else, has brought about major changes in the meaning of quality for many people, ranging from CEOs to managers to workers to clients and customers. Hamada (Chapter 12) suggests that the idea of quality continues to evolve. In Japan, it is increasingly being associated with attention to the quality of the environment.

Previewing the Contributions to This Volume

Although the contents of this volume may not address all of the useful questions and issues raised by the quality movement, they do tackle many of them and, we believe, extend our understanding of what has transpired in the United States in recent decades. And, like all thoughtful scholarship, the chapters pose many additional questions deserving of the attention of both practitioners and researchers.

Part I provides a set of foundational works that provides theoretical and historical background to the quality movement. We begin with the work of James Dean and David Bowen (Chapter 1), who review the relationship between management theory and total quality

management. They show how students of quality can benefit from theoretical perspective drawn from management, as well as how students of management can benefit from the insights flowing from the quality movement. Richard Hackman and Ruth Wageman (Chapter 2) assess the total quality movement through the writings of the movement's founders, noting their association with practices. They evaluate the coherence and distinctiveness of the movement and explore the ways in which researchers have failed to produce a full-fledged evaluation of quality management practices, with advice on which evaluation strategies make the most sense.

Sidney Winter (Chapter 3) provides a survey of quality management principles and practices and examines their connections to economic theory generally and evolutionary economic theory specifically. He notes the significant degree of overlap in the emphasis given by both evolutionary economics and quality management to organizational routines and the characterization of organizational capabilities. These three chapters, together with our own introductory survey, provide what we regard as a reasonable overview of the central principles and practices associated with the recent quality movement. They also survey the most relevant and potentially applicable theoretical approaches to understanding quality practices as they relate to organizational functioning and change.

Part II contains chapters dealing with the dynamics of the quality movement in America, examining the early years, the early experiences of some of the more advanced adopters, and the spread of the movement into the public sector. Robert Cole (Chapter 4) draws on various insights from organization theory to explore the initial reactions of managers to the Japanese quality threat of the early 1980s. He details the cognitive and institutional barriers that inhibited adaptive learning and reduced the ability of managers to develop effective responses. He shows the inertial patterns at work in organizations as many managers, when faced with exogenous threats they could not explain, continued to do more of the same. George Easton and Sherry Jarrell (Chapter 5) explore the patterns displayed by leading companies in deploying quality management programs, including the examination of the predeployment phase of sensemaking and consensus generation. They highlight the important role played by consultants and gurus, who provided usable interpretations of what was happening and models for making adaptive changes.

Linda Kaboolian (Chapter 6) characterizes the experiences of the public sector with quality improvement programs. She reviews some of the varied programs under way at all levels of government and highlights differences in implementation and evaluation between the private and public sectors. She also addresses the extent to which quality methods represent important sensemaking routines in public organizations, thereby creating meaning and legitimacy. Karl Weick (Chapter 7) extends these ideas, providing a comprehensive sensemaking analysis of total quality management. His approach is premised on the view that rationality is often retrospective and an account of actions previously taken rather than a predesigned course of action. Social actors engage in a continual process of socially constructing shared meanings. Quality improvement initiatives often fail when these ongoing interpretive practices are not taken into account. Weick sees organizing for continual improvement as the key element of quality management approaches, showing its consistency with a sensemaking perspective and its potential capacity to generate new insights and innovations.

Part III addresses general processes and stages associated with quality improvement. The first three chapters deal with evidence regarding performance improvement at both the micro and macro levels. John Paul MacDuffie (Chapter 8) provides a case study of "root cause" shop-floor problem solving at three auto assembly plants. His analysis captures the complexities of problem-solving activity, including varying conceptualization of problems, approaches to problems—as opportunities for learning versus liabilities to be avoided—and ways of thinking about process standardization. Nelson Repenning and John Sterman (Chapter 9) also pursue a microlevel research strategy, examining process improvement activities and

the ways in which they can sometimes operate at cross-purposes. Using two in-depth case studies, the authors develop a model that allows them to consider both technical and social processes, integrating physical structures of process improvement with theories of human cognition, learning, and organization to examine the intricacies of the dynamics of process improvement initiatives. Their work suggests that a full understanding of process improvement requires an integrated approach to the physical and behavioral dimensions.

At a more macro level, George Easton and Sherry Jarrell (Chapter 10) examine a sample of firms judged to be using advanced quality practices and compare their financial performance to overall market rates of return. They report a strong statistical association between deployment of TQM and improved financial performance in the 3 to 5 years following the initial deployment. The results are particularly strong for those firms judged to have adopted the most advanced quality practices.

Kim Cameron and Carole Barnett (Chapter 11) examine organizational quality as a cultural variable. They call into question the tendency of empirical researchers to focus on the tools and techniques that are implemented as opposed to the more fundamental changes in beliefs and assumptions about what quality is and how it is to be pursued. The authors propose a framework for identifying different types of quality cultures in organizations, and they investigate the relationship between these culture types and organizational performance. Tomoko Hamada (Chapter 12) reviews several conceptions of the nature and functions of organizational culture and then examines how the concept of a quality culture varies over time and space, focusing particular attention on recent development in Japanese management circles.

In Part IV, several chapters explore the contingencies influencing quality improvement efforts and the conditions affecting their success. Kathleen Sutcliffe, Sim Sitkin, and Larry Browning (Chapter 13) attempt to resolve an enduring issue in organization design to improve quality. One emphasis stresses pressure for continual improvement by focusing on the control of unwanted variance; traditional quality control tactics symbolize this approach. Another stresses the need to learn from the observed variance, which may provide clues to new and better ways of working. Thus, variance reduction control strategies are often pitted against flexible, open, learning-oriented processes. The authors suggest an integrative approach and seek to show the conditions under which organizations can response simultaneously to the need for both control and learning.

Just as control and learning are often treated as contradictory approaches demanding compromise, so speed and quality are similarly viewed widely as requiring trade-offs. Andrew Hargadon and Kathleen Eisenhardt (Chapter 14) challenge conventional wisdom and describe procedures and structures developed by successful companies seeking to combine rapid new product development with high-quality production methods. Their model is based on an underlying process of experiential learning, as managers in high-technology firms seek to cope with rapidly shifting markets and technologies.

The final three chapters all confront the reality that all organizations are both technical and social systems. Quality management must concern itself not only with technical know-how and finely honed production methods but also with human resource policies that provide appropriate incentives to sustain the energy and commitment of employees. Casey Ichniowski and Kathryn Shaw (Chapter 15) assess the effects of technical quality improvement (QI) and innovative human resource management (HRM) practices on production performance in a sample of steel finishing lines. They seek to determine the contribution that each of these clusters of practice makes to performance improvement. They conclude that although QI practices raise production quality, they have little effect on worker productivity; the latter is affected primarily by HRM practices. They also report different patterns of adoption in older "brownfield" than in the newer "greenfield" facilities. In the former, QI practices are usually adopted first, leading to the adoption of some participatory HRM practices. In the newer plants, QI practices are more likely to be embedded in a broader complex of HRM practices.

David Levine and Kathryn Shaw (Chapter 16) begin with the observation that the founders of the modern quality movement have typically emphasized the drawbacks of incentive pay schemes and called attention to the ways in which they could work to reduce quality. Consistent with this conclusion, many companies have given little or no attention to developing pay incentives that might support quality improvement efforts. The authors outline a theory of the interaction between quality improvement and incentive pay and discuss the conditions under which pay incentives are likely to be supportive of quality improvements.

Tom Kochan and Saul Rubinstein (Chapter 17) insist that if the quality movement is to have significant and lasting effects, it needs to be coupled with broader changes in the structure and operation of organizations—in particular, their human resource programs, production systems, labor management relations, and corporate governance arrangements. They suggest that the logic underlying quality improvement requires that quite fundamental changes occur in the status, power, and governance structures of organizations if all parties are to be willing and able to strive for continuous improvements. Their arguments, which call for quite fundamental changes in organizations as a condition for sustaining the quality movement, are usefully contrasted with those of Hackman and Wageman (Chapter 2), who suggest that quality management approaches were adopted by U.S. companies *because* they were viewed as being consistent with the maintenance of managerial prerogatives and the existing organizational power structure.

This debate, along with the many others we have previewed, serves to underline the principle assumption motivating the preparation of this volume: namely, that the quality movement raises quite fundamental questions about the nature of organizations and organizational change that should be of concern to all thoughtful organizational scholars and practitioners.

Note

1. Contingency theory is partially included in and closely related to the "information and analysis" managerial perspectives described by Dean and Bowen (Chapter 1).

References

Aldrich, H. E. (1979). *Organizations and environments.* Englewood Cliffs, NJ: Prentice Hall.

Argyris, C., & Schon, D. A. (1978). *Organizational learning: A theory of action perspective.* Reading, MA: Addison-Wesley.

Barnett, W. P., & Carroll, G. R. (1995). Modeling internal organizational change. *Annual Review of Sociology, 21,* 217-236.

Brown, S., & Eisenhardt, K. (1995). Product development: Past research, present findings and future directions. *Academy of Management Review, 20,* 343-378.

Burns, L. R., & Wholey, D. R. (1993). Adoption and abandonment of matrix management programs: Effects of organizational characteristics and interorganizational networks. *Academy of Management Journal, 36,* 106-138.

Clark, K., & Fujimoto, T. (1991). *Product development performance: Strategy, organization, and management in the world auto industry.* Cambridge, MA: Harvard Business School Press.

Cohen, M., & Sproull, L. (Eds.). (1996). *Organizational learning.* Thousand Oaks, CA: Sage.

Cole, R. E. (1989). *Strategies for learning: Small group activities in American, Japanese and Swedish industry.* Berkeley: University of California Press.

Cole, R. E. (1999). *Managing quality fads: How American business learned to play the quality game.* New York: Oxford University Press.

Davis, G. F., & Greve, H. R. (1997). Corporate elite networks and governance changes in the 1980s. *American Journal of Sociology, 103,* 1-37.

DiMaggio, P. J., & Powell, W. W. (1983). The iron cage revisited: Institutional isomorphism and collective rationality in organizational fields. *American Sociological Review, 48,* 147-160.

DiMaggio, P. J., & Powell, W. W. (1991). Introduction. In W. W. Powell & P. J. DiMaggio (Eds.), *The new institutionalism in organizational analysis* (pp. 1-38). Chicago: University of Chicago Press.

Dobbin, F. R., Sutton, J. R., Meyer, J. W., & Scott, W. R. (1993). Equal opportunity law and the construction of internal labor markets. *American Journal of Sociology, 99,* 396-427.

Easton, G., & Jarrell, S. (1997, January). *Strategic quality planning: Analysis of factors driving effectiveness.* Paper presented at the National Science Foundation Design and Manufacturing Grantees' Conference, Seattle, WA.

Edelman, L. B. (1992). Legal ambiguity and symbolic structures: Organizational mediation of civil rights law. *American Journal of Sociology, 97,* 1531-1576.

Galbraith, J. R. (1973). *Designing complex organizations.* Reading, MA: Addison-Wesley.

Galbraith, J. R. (1977). *Organization design.* Reading, MA: Addison-Wesley.

Galbraith, J. R., & Lawler, E. E., III. (Eds.). (1993). *Organizing for the future: The new logic for managing complex organizations.* San Francisco: Jossey-Bass.

Hannan, M. T., & Freeman, J. (1977). The population ecology of organizations. *American Journal of Sociology, 82,* 929-964.

Hannan, M. T., & Freeman, J. (1989). *Organizational ecology.* Cambridge, MA: Harvard University Press.

Katz, D., & Kahn, R. L. (1966). *The social psychology of organizations.* New York: Wiley.

Lawler, E. E., III, Mohrman, S., & Ledford, G. (1995). *Creating high performance organizations.* San Francisco: Jossey-Bass.

Lawrence, P. R., & Lorsch, J. W. (1967). *Organization and environment: Managing differentiation and integration.* Boston: Graduate School of Business Administration, Harvard University.

Levitt, B., & March, J. G. (1988). Organizational learning. *Annual Review of Sociology, 14,* 319-340.

March, J. G. (1991). Exploration and exploitation in organizational learning. *Organization Science, 2,* 71-87.

March, J. G., & Olsen, J. P. (1976). *Ambiguity and choice in organizations.* Bergen, Norway: Universitetsforlaget.

March, J. G., Sproull, L. S., & Tamuz, M. (1991). Learning from samples of one or fewer. *Organization Science, 2,* 1-13.

Meyer, J. W. (1994). Rationalized environments. In W. R. Scott & J. W. Meyer (Eds.), *Institutional environments and organizations: Structural complexity and individualism* (pp. 28-54). Thousand Oaks, CA: Sage.

Meyer, J. W., & Rowan, B. (1977). Institutionalized organizations: Formal structure as myth and ceremony. *American Journal of Sociology, 83,* 340-363.

Nelson, R. R., & Winter, S. G. (1973). Toward an evolutionary theory of economic capabilities. *American Economic Review, 63,* 440-449.

Nelson, R. R., & Winter, S. G. (1982). *An evolutionary theory of economic change.* Cambridge, MA: Belknap.

Pascale, R. (1990). *Managing on the edge.* New York: Simon & Schuster.

Pfeffer, J., & Salancik, G. R. (1978). *The external control of organizations.* New York: Harper & Row.

Polanyi, M. (1967). *The tacit dimension.* Garden City, NY: Doubleday.

Porter, M. E. (1985). *Competitive strategy: Techniques for analyzing industries and competitors.* New York: Free Press.

Robinson, J. D., III, Akers, J. F., Artzt, E. L., Poling, H. A., Galvin, R. W., & Allaire, P. A. (1991). An open letter: TQM on the campus. *Harvard Business Review, 69*(6), 94-95.

Scott, W. R. (1995). *Institutions and organizations.* Thousand Oaks, CA: Sage.

Scott, W. R. (1998). *Organizations: Rational, natural and open systems* (4th ed.). Upper Saddle River, NJ: Prentice Hall.

Scott, W. R., Ruef, M., Mendel, P., & Caronna, C. A. (1999). *Institutional change and organizations: Transformation of a healthcare field.* Chicago: University of Chicago Press.

Sitkin, S. B., Sutcliffe, K. M., & Schroeder, R. G. (1994). Distinguishing control from learning in total quality management: A contingency perspective. *Academy of Management Review, 19,* 537-564.

Stinchcombe, A. L. (1990). *Information and organizations.* Berkeley: University of California Press.

Strang, D. (1997, August). *Cheap talk: Managerial discourse on quality circles as an organizational innovation.* Paper presented at the annual meeting of the American Sociological Association, Toronto.

Taylor, F. W. (1911). *The principles of scientific management.* New York: Harper.

Taylor, F. W. (1947). *Scientific management.* New York: Harper & Brothers.

Thompson, J. D. (1967). *Organizations in action.* New York: McGraw-Hill.

Tolbert, P. S., & Zucker, L. G. (1983). Institutional sources of change in the formal structure of organizations: The diffusion of civil service reform, 1880-1935. *Administrative Science Quarterly, 28,* 22-39.

Tushman, M. L., & Anderson, P. (1986). Technological discontinuities and organizational environments. *Administrative Science Quarterly, 31,* 439-465.

Weick, K. E. (1995). *Sensemaking in organizations.* Thousand Oaks, CA: Sage.

Westphal, J. D., Gulati, R., & Shortell, S. M. (1997). Customization or conformity? An institutional and network perspective on the content and consequences of TQM adoption. *Administrative Science Quarterly, 42,* 366-394.

Zbaracki, M. (1994). *The rhetoric and reality of total quality management.* Unpublished doctoral dissertation, Department of Industrial Engineering and Management, Stanford University.

PART I

Questions and Concerns From Organization Theory: Three Foundational Papers

Chapter 1

Management Theory and Total Quality

Improving Research and Practice Through Theory Development

JAMES W. DEAN, JR.
DAVID E. BOWEN

Our goal in this article, and in this special issue as a whole,[1] is to stimulate the development of theory on total quality. We pursue our goal in this article as follows. First, we present the rationale for a theory-development forum on total quality (TQ). Second, we provide an overview of the principles, practices, and techniques associated with TQ. Third, we explore the relationship between the principles of TQ and those of management theory, using the Malcolm Baldrige National Quality Award criteria as a bridge between the two areas. Finally, we develop suggestions for theory building and research, and we indicate how the articles in this issue serve this end. We hope that our efforts will contribute to both the relevance and theoretical rigor of management research as well as to the effectiveness of management practice.

Why a Theory-Development Forum on Total Quality?

Like previous forums, this one was undertaken to stimulate theory development and research in a specific area. We believe greater research attention should be devoted to TQ for several reasons. First, it has generated a tremendous amount of interest in many sectors of the economy—manufacturing, service, health care, education, and government—and in many countries around the world (Ernst & Young and American Quality Foundation, 1992; Lawler, Mohrman, & Ledford, 1992). It is difficult to identify any major organization in which quality issues are not on management's agenda. Furthermore, many of the leaders of these organizations have begun to question why management research and education have not yet incorpo-

AUTHORS' NOTE: Reprinted with permission of Academy of Management, PO Box 3020, Briar Cliff Manor, NY 10510-8020. *Management Theory and Total Quality: Improving Research and Practice Through Theory Development,* J. Dean & D. Bowen, Academy of Management Review, Vol. 19, No. 3 (1994). Reproduced by permission of the publisher via Copyright Clearance Center, Inc.

rated TQ to any great degree (Robinson et al., 1991). Given its importance in practice, we risk losing our credibility as management theorists by ignoring TQ in our research.

Second, TQ appears to cover a great deal of the same ground as management theory. Although they may use different terms, managers pursuing TQ are concerned with strategy, information processing, leadership, and many other topics that are well within our domain. Even though there is certainly a faddish element in the current attention being devoted to TQ, the issues it encompasses are fundamental to understanding and managing organizations. Thus, theoretical attention devoted to these issues will be valuable regardless of the future status of the TQ movement.

Third, theory development on total quality should benefit both researchers and practitioners. It should help to stimulate empirical research, as researchers may be reluctant to conduct research based on the consulting-oriented frameworks currently available. TQ researchers also will be much more productive if there is a theoretical base upon which they can draw. The premium on theory development is particularly high for TQ because its interdisciplinary nature means that it often transcends the boundaries of existing theories. Thus, it is unlikely that existing theories will be sufficiently broad based to support research on TQ.

Theory development is likely to serve the needs of practitioners as well. TQ initiatives often do not succeed, but as yet there is little theory available to explain the differences between successful and unsuccessful efforts. Moreover, experienced managers recognize that currently available approaches often are organizationally and politically naive. Management theorists have the capability to develop frameworks that incorporate the accumulated knowledge about organizations and, thus, can better guide TQ implementation (e.g., Reger, Gustafson, DeMarie, & Mullane, this issue).

In summary, total quality is a ubiquitous organizational phenomenon that has been given little research attention. This forum was created to publish articles that make substantial progress in building theory about customer-focused organizations. We hope that it will create a critical mass of thinking about TQ that will provide a useful reference for researchers and eventually benefit managers attempting to improve organizational effectiveness.

An Overview of Total Quality

Despite thousands of articles in the business and trade press, total quality remains a hazy, ambiguous concept. The differences among frameworks proposed by writers such as Deming, Juran, and Crosby have no doubt contributed to this confusion. Deming's (1986) framework emphasizes the systemic nature of organizations, the importance of leadership, and the need to reduce variation in organizational processes (Anderson, Rungtusanatham, & Schroeder, this issue). Juran's (1989) framework involves three sets of activities—quality planning, control, and improvement—and emphasizes the use of statistical tools to eliminate defects. Crosby (1979) focused on reducing cost through quality improvement and stressed that both high- and low-end products can have high quality. Beyond these differences, the variety and continuing evolution of techniques being practiced under the rubric of TQ makes it difficult to maintain a clear conception of its meaning. Indeed, the meaning of the term *quality* itself is still being debated (Reeves & Bednar, this issue).

Due to this ambiguity, TQ has come to function as a sort of Rorschach test, to which people's reactions vary as a function of their own beliefs and experiences. TQ is seen by some as an extension of scientific management, by others in terms of systems theory, and by still others as an altogether new paradigm for management (Spencer, this issue). To help resolve this ambiguity, we present an overview of TQ that captures its most important features.

We see TQ as a philosophy or an approach to management that can be characterized by its principles, practices, and techniques. Its three principles are customer focus, continuous improvement, and teamwork, and most of what has been written about TQ is explicitly or im-

TABLE 1.1 Principles, Practices, and Techniques of Total Quality

	Customer Focus	Continuous Improvement	Teamwork
Principles	Paramount importance of providing products and services that fulfill customer needs; requires organizationwide focus on customers	Consistent customer satisfaction can be attained only through relentless improvement of processes that create products and services	Customer focus and continuous improvement are best achieved by collaboration throughout an organization as well as with customers and suppliers
Practices	Direct customer contact Collecting information about customer needs Using information to design and deliver products and services	Process analysis Reengineering Problem solving Plan/do/check/act	Search for arrangements that benefit all units involved in a process Formation of various types of teams Group skills training
Techniques	Customer surveys and focus groups Quality function deployment (translates customer information into product specifications)	Flowcharts Pareto analysis Statistical process control Fishbone diagrams	Organizational development methods such as the nominal group technique Team-building methods (e.g., role clarification and group feedback)

plicitly based on these principles. Each principle is implemented through a set of practices, which are simply activities such as collecting customer information or analyzing processes. The practices are, in turn, supported by a wide array of techniques (i.e., specific step-by-step methods intended to make the practices effective [see Dean & Evans, 1994, for an overview]). This conception of total quality is summarized in Table 1.1.

The first and most important principle is customer focus. The goal of satisfying customers is fundamental to TQ and is expressed by the organization's attempt to design and deliver products and services that fulfill customer needs. The rationales for this principle are the beliefs that customer satisfaction is the most important requirement for long-term organizational success and that this satisfaction requires that the entire organization be focused on customers' needs. Practices exemplifying customer focus include promoting direct contact with customers, collecting information about customers' expectations, and disseminating this information within the organization. Techniques used to accomplish these activities include customer surveys and more elaborate methods such

as quality function deployment (Hauser & Clausing, 1988).

These practices and techniques also can be applied to internal customers (i.e., those whose work depends on prior work by others in the organization). For example, line managers, who rely upon the human resources department to supply staffing and training services, can be surveyed to assess whether their needs are being met.

The second principle, continuous improvement, means a commitment to constant examination of technical and administrative processes in search of better methods. Underlying this principle are the concept of organizations as systems of interlinked processes and the belief that by improving these processes, organizations can continue to meet the increasingly stringent expectations of their customers. Relevant practices include process analysis and reengineering. Many techniques, including flow charts and statistical process control, are associated with this principle.

Teamwork—collaboration between managers and nonmanagers, between functions, and between customers and suppliers—is the third TQ principle. The first type of teamwork is based on the familiar assumption that nonmanagerial employees can make important contributions to organizations when they have the power and necessary preparation. Teamwork among functions is based on the notion that organizations as systems cannot be effective if subunits emphasize their own outcomes over those of others. The principle of teamwork with customers and suppliers is based on the perceived benefits (e.g., synergy, loyalty) of partnerships.

Teamwork practices include identifying the needs of all groups and organizations involved in decision making, trying to find solutions that will benefit everyone involved, and sharing responsibility and credit (Ciampa, 1991). Often such practices are promoted by forming teams (e.g., cross-functional problem-solving teams) that draw together various organizational units. Team-building techniques such as role clarification and group feedback are associated with this principle.

These three principles relate closely to one another. Continuous improvement is undertaken to achieve customer satisfaction, and it is most effective when driven by customer needs. Because the processes targeted for continuous improvement transcend hierarchical, functional, and organizational boundaries, teamwork is essential. Thus, TQ is not simply a hodgepodge of slogans and tools; it is a set of mutually reinforcing principles, each of which is supported by a set of practices and techniques, and all of which are ultimately based on fulfilling customers' needs.

Total Quality and Management Theory

Before trying to develop theories of total quality, we should first examine TQ's relationship with *existing* management theories, so as to establish a point of departure for theorizing. Specifically, we need to question our premise that there is considerable conceptual overlap between TQ and management theory. Can meaningful comparisons be made between TQ concepts and management theory? How similar are the topics addressed and the recommendations made in the two areas? We will address each of these questions in turn.

Global Comparisons of Total Quality and Management Theory

Total quality is an approach to management that has evolved from a narrow focus on statistical process control to encompass a variety of technical and behavioral methods for improving organizational performance. Management theory is a multidisciplinary academic field whose links to practice are controversial (e.g., Astley & Zammuto, 1992; Barley, Meyer, & Gash, 1988; Hambrick, 1994). Do the two share enough common ground to be meaningfully related to one another?

Perhaps the fundamental difference between TQ and management theory is in their audiences. Whereas TQ is aimed at managers, management theory is directed to researchers, with the expectation that ideas relevant to practitioners will, through teaching or perhaps consulting, eventually find them. Given this difference in audiences, the language used in the two literatures differs substantially (cf. Spencer, this issue). This difference in audiences results in two other differences.

First, TQ is inherently cross-functional. In a single article on TQ, it is not unusual to find references to marketing, product design, operations, and human resource management. Management theory *as a field* is multidisciplinary, but individual theories and articles tend to be discipline bound. Second, given its mission to improve organizational performance, TQ is almost completely prescriptive in orientation. Deming's well-known 14 points, for example, are actually imperative statements, such as "drive out fear." Management theory, in contrast, is concerned with understanding, not just improving, organizations. Some management theories are prescriptive; others simply describe relationships among organizational characteristics.

When management theory *is* prescriptive, its prescriptions tend to be contingent (i.e., sensitive to variation in the organizational context). TQ recommendations tend to be context independent and, therefore, implicitly universal (Spencer, this issue). There is little attention in TQ devoted to the boundary conditions for TQ applicability or even how variation in organizational settings might be reflected in TQ implementation (Sitkin, Sutcliffe, & Schroeder, this issue).

Given these differences between TQ and management theory, is there a basis for comparing them? In a word, yes. As TQ has outgrown its statistical origins, it has evolved into a set of prescriptions for organizational effectiveness. As Ciampa (1991: 13) put it, TQ is "another chapter in the ongoing search for a formula for organizational excellence." Whereas some of TQ's prescriptions are outside the bounds of management theory, many are not. Management theory is also, among other things, a source of implicit and explicit prescriptions for organizational success. Thus, the two systems of thought can be compared on the basis of their area of overlap: recommendations for organizational effectiveness.

Topic-Specific Comparisons of Total Quality and Management Theory

We have chosen the content areas that comprise the Malcolm Baldrige National Quality Award as the basis for comparing the prescription of TQ and management theory. The Baldrige Award was created by the U.S. government in 1987 to recognize quality excellence and to stimulate quality improvement in American industry (Garvin, 1991). It is given annually to manufacturers, service companies, and small businesses, and currently it is being extended to include health care and educational organizations. The Baldrige categories are *leadership, information and analysis, strategic quality planning, human resource development and management, management of process quality,* and *customer focus and satisfaction* (Award Criteria, Malcolm Baldrige National Quality Award, 1994). (We have excluded the quality and operational results category because it is simply an assessment of effectiveness.)

There are several advantages to using the Baldrige criteria. First, the conceptual framework underlying the award addresses the principal domains of TQ. Second, it has been repeatedly updated by a team of experts to reflect current thinking on TQ. Third, the award framework is not limited to a single quality perspective (e.g., Deming's or Juran's), but rather it incorporates a diversity of viewpoints.

We will draw from the accumulated writings on TQ as the source of our TQ prescriptions. For each of the areas represented by the Baldrige Award, we will assess the extent to which the area is addressed by management theory and the similarity of prescriptions offered by the two fields. Because a diverse set of voices is heard in both fields, often we will be able to state only in general terms the similarity of prescriptions between them. Nevertheless, this comparison should allow the reader to develop an overall impression of the relationships between total quality and management theory. An overview of these relationships is presented in Figure 1.1. Based on our analysis, we will place quality/management prescriptions into one of three categories: those in which *TQ is virtually identical to management theory;* those in which *TQ practice should be informed by management theory;* and those in which *new directions in management theory are suggested by TQ.*

Leadership

The TQ domain of leadership is covered extensively in the management literature, and the prescriptions offered by the two areas are very similar (see Figure 1.1). TQ advocates emphasize the activities of *senior* leadership in terms much like transformational leadership theory (Bass, 1985; Burns, 1978; Tichy & Devanna, 1986). Writers on both TQ and transformational leadership stress the communication and reinforcement of values and the articulation and implementation of a vision. In TQ, this entails aligning organizational members' values with quality values of customer focus, continuous improvement, and teamwork.

The focus on *senior* leadership, however, implies that transactional leadership theory appears irrelevant to TQ practice. The domain of transactional leadership covers contingencies surrounding follower-leader exchange as well as leadership style (e.g., initiating structure and

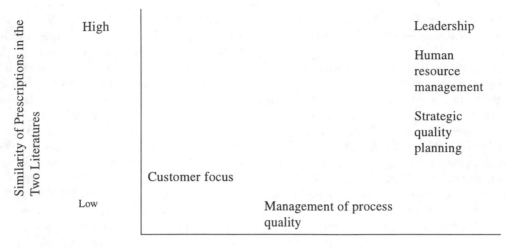

Figure 1.1. Treatment of TQ in the Management Literature

consideration) (e.g., Podsakoff, Todor, & Skov, 1982). Transactional leadership emphasizes the workgroup level, in contrast to TQ's focus on the more global level of organizations or major subunits. Dean and Evans (1994) suggested that this difference in focus occurs because TQ advocates emphasize empowerment at lower levels. Further, Waldman (this issue) speculates that transactional leadership may encourage the short-term, individually based goal setting denounced in TQ.

Overall, the description of leadership's role in TQ appears to take both sides of the "does-leadership-make-a-difference" issue that appears in the literature. The TQ perspective that senior leadership is critical for organizational success (e.g., Deming, 1986; Juran, 1989) contrasts with Pfeffer's (1977) argument that leadership is irrelevant to most organizational outcomes. Ironically, Pfeffer's argument rests on a *situation*-based approach that claims factors outside the leader's control affect business outcomes more than anything a leader might do. This sounds similar to Deming's own perspective that system factors matter more than individual differences in explaining *worker* effectiveness (cf. Waldman, this issue).

TQ, however, appears to assign far less importance to leadership's role further down the hierarchy. In this case, TQ has a "substitutes-for-leadership" flavor, in which various

characteristics of subordinates, tasks, and organizations take the place of many leadership behaviors (Kerr & Jermier, 1978). Certainly, TQ emphasizes subordinate training and organizational formalization, two characteristics presented as possible substitutes for instrumental leadership. Overall, then, firms implementing TQ may be provocative sites for studying the relevance of leadership.

Human Resource Management (HRM)

This TQ domain is covered extensively in management theory. The two areas exhibit considerable similarity in their prescriptions, but conflict substantially on a few points (see Figure 1.1). The HRM areas identified by the Baldrige Award criteria are frequently appearing topics in the management literature: human resource planning, employee involvement, employee education and training, employee performance and recognition, and employee well-being and satisfaction. More broadly, all of the content areas of total quality contain human resources implications (Hart & Schlesinger, 1991), so that the TQ domain covered by the HRM-focused management literature even reaches beyond the HRM category, per se. Given the enormous size of the HRM domain in both TQ and the management theory literature, and their extensive overlap, we can describe only a few of the many similarities and differences in prescriptions. We do this by the individual HRM areas that appear in the Baldrige Award.

Human resource planning and management. In the Baldrige criteria, this TQ domain includes developing an overall HRM plan for selection, employee involvement, training, performance management, and employee recognition that is aligned with company strategy. Strategic HRM has been well covered by management theory in recent years (e.g., Fombrun, Tichy, & Devanna, 1984; Wright & McMahan, 1992).

Employee selection, as part of the overall HRM mix, receives much less attention in TQ than in management theory. In the Baldrige criteria, for example, selection appears only as a subcomponent in "planning," unlike other HRM processes (e.g., education and training), which appear not only in planning, but also as separate HRM category line items. Furthermore, a recent study of HRM practices in Baldrige Award-winning companies found that although many HRM practices had changed in the shift from a traditional HRM perspective to a TQ-based HRM perspective, selection processes had remained relatively unchanged (Blackburn & Rosen, 1993). In contrast, selection has a prominent position in management theory and continues as a heavily researched subject.

The limited attention selection receives in TQ reflects TQ's overall emphasis on the situation, more so than the person, as a determinant of employee effectiveness (Dobbins, Cardy, & Carson, 1991). In the context of the person-situation controversy, "person" advocates believe that selection, which identifies individual differences that predict performance, is the key HRM practice; "situationists" stress training, reward, and socialization practices as aspects of strong situations that can overwhelm the influence of individual differences (Chatman, 1989).

Models of hiring for person-organization fit (Bowen, Ledford, & Nathan, 1991; Rynes & Gerhart, 1990) would appear to be well matched to the TQ perspective that the overall work setting heavily influences work performance. This model differs from conventional approaches by focusing on the selection of a "whole" person (i.e., not just technical skills, but also personality traits and needs) who will fit not only specific job requirements, but also the unique characteristics of the overall organization. When hiring for person-organization fit, an organization acknowledges the effect of the system on performance and even takes advantage of it (Dobbins et al., 1991). Isolated cases have been reported of TQ-oriented firms adapting innovative selection techniques to achieve person-environment fit (Schuler & Harris, 1991). In fact, increasing numbers of TQ-oriented firms may be open to alternative selection models, as indicated by Snell and Dean's (1992) finding that a sample of manufacturing firms practicing TQ were more selective in their hiring practices for employees in the quality area.

Employee involvement. The approaches in TQ to involvement and empowerment are similar to early work on "System 4" organizations (Likert, 1967), which emphasized empowered workgroups and collaborative teams, and Theory Y (McGregor, 1960), which assumed employees were motivated and capable of doing good work on their own (Dean & Evans, 1994). TQ practices directed at granting employees more autonomy and skill variety on the job match the job characteristics model (Hackman & Oldham, 1980), which, according to some research, better predicts quality than quantity of work as an outcome (Pasmore, Frances, Haldeman, & Shani, 1982). The contributions that teams can make to enhance involvement have long been recognized (Trist & Bamforth, 1952); even cross-functional teams appear in the literature (McCann & Galbraith, 1981). More recently, the concept of empowerment has been elaborated in the scholarly literature (Conger & Kanungo, 1988; Thomas & Velthouse, 1990).

The management literature, however, presents some of these practices within a contingency perspective, in contrast to the universalistic prescriptions of TQ. For example, the relationship between redesign of jobs and quality work as an outcome is moderated by growth need strength—in theory (Hackman & Oldham, 1980) and in research (Berlinger, Glick, & Rodgers, 1988). Additionally, the effectiveness of involvement and empowerment strategies have been presented as contingent upon such factors as business strategy, the nature of the relationship with customers, technology, and environment (Bowen & Lawler, 1992b; Lawler, 1988). Relatedly, the research does not promise universal performance returns from participative decision making, as TQ proponents tend to do (Cotton, Vollrath, Froggatt, Lengnick-Hall, & Jennings, 1988).

A very different point of view on the overall similarity between how TQ and management theory treat employee involvement is found in the argument that TQ is really a modern repackaging of Taylorism (Boje, 1993; Hetrick & Boje, 1992; Spencer, this issue). Employee involvement is said to be a masquerade for getting workers to self-Taylorize their own jobs, and that teams are really a source of tighter, more oppressive control than hierarchy. A far less extreme, but related, point is found in Lawler's (1994) observation that research and writing on employee involvement emphasizes job enrichment and employee discretion, whereas TQ efforts stress work simplification.

Employee education and training. This domain is covered extensively in management theory, and the prescriptions of the two areas are similar. Indeed, TQ practitioners appear to implement techniques such as training evaluation and systematic needs analysis (Blackburn & Rosen, 1993) and comprehensive training in a broad range of skills (Snell & Dean, 1992), which have been long prescribed in the literature but slighted in practice.

The two areas offer similar prescriptions for career management, but for different reasons. Both reframe career progression and success away from vertical, and toward horizontal, movement. The rationale of TQ is to help employees acquire a systems orientation via cross-functional career moves and horizontal reassignments (Bowen & Lawler, 1992a). In the careers literature, the logic is that vertical channel blockage from the baby-boomer cohort has led to career plateauing that requires lateral/horizontal solutions (Bardwick, 1986; Driver, 1988; Hall & Richter, 1990).

Employee performance and recognition. This TQ domain is extensively covered in management theory, but the two areas offer different approaches to performance appraisal and compensation, reflecting the controversy about whether person or system factors are the primary influence upon performance (cf. Waldman, this issue).

Traditional HRM research (and practice) in performance appraisal emphasizes the impact of individual differences (i.e., the person) on performance and assumes that the assessment of individual differences in performance is meaningful. TQ advocates, most notably Deming, maintain that performance is due mainly to system factors beyond an individual's control and that, consequently, individual performance appraisals should be abolished. Less extreme TQ advocates argue that if appraisals are done, they should be done on a gross instrument with the majority of workers receiving an average rating (Dobbins et al., 1991).

For employee rewards in TQ, Deming advocated abandoning the individual-based incentive pay systems that have long occupied an important place in HRM research and practice. He argued that these plans represent another case of management focusing on the person instead of the system and that piece-rate incentive plans also reinforce a short-term, *quantity*-oriented focus inconsistent with continuous quality improvement (Dobbins et al., 1991). Although TQ-oriented firms increasingly are adopting reward-system innovations (Blackburn & Rosen, 1993; Lawler et al., 1992; Snell & Dean, in press), these innovations are drawn more from management theory on employee involvement and compensation than from TQ writings, which do not say much about financial rewards (Lawler, 1994). TQ does stress the importance of recognition rewards, which have received virtually no research attention in management theory.

Employee well-being and satisfaction. TQ advocates appear to give more weight to the importance of employee satisfaction in organizational effectiveness than do HRM researchers, who focus on performance per se (Cardy & Dobbins, 1993). The assumption of TQ advocates is that employee satisfaction is needed to support continuous improvement and customer satisfaction. They also appear to assume a strong correlation between job satisfaction and performance, but management researchers find only a modest relationship (Iaffaldano & Muchinsky, 1985).

Summary of HRM. The HRM domain in TQ has been covered extensively in the management literature, and similar prescriptions are found in the areas of employee involvement, training, and career management. However, there also are significantly different prescriptions in the areas of selection, performance appraisal, and compensation. These differences are embedded in the issue of person versus system determinants of work performance (Dobbins et al., 1991; Waldman, this issue), which is an important area for future HRM research. Because performance is certain to be an interaction of the two, an issue for both research and practice is whether raters can separate person and system factors in performance appraisal and compensation (Dobbins et al., 1991).

Strategic Quality Planning

This category addresses

business planning and deployment of plans, with special focus on customer and operational performance requirements. [It] stresses that customer-driven quality and operational performance excellence are key strategic business issues which need to be an integral part of overall business planning.

The first item in this category is "how the company develops and deploys customer-focused strategy," and the second, "effective translation of plans . . . to specific requirements for work units and suppliers" (Award Criteria, Malcolm Baldrige National Quality Award, 1994: 7).

Strategic quality planning (SQP) has been given much attention by management theorists, insofar as it overlaps considerably with the area of strategic management. The TQ perspective on strategy deals extensively with business unit strategy (how to compete for a set of customers) but is generally silent on corporate strategy (how to decide which customers to compete for). The prescriptions of the two fields differ considerably (see Figure 1.1).

The role of quality in business strategy. Perhaps the most fundamental difference between the TQ and management theory perspectives is in the role of quality in strategy. The Award Criteria, Malcolm Baldrige National Quality Award summarize the TQ perspective that "customer-driven quality [is a] key strategic business issue which needs to be an integral part of overall business planning" (1994: 6). Belohlav (1993a) argued that quality directly influences a firm's competitive position, thereby constraining the set of strategies available to the firm and, thus, its competitive viability.

Other TQ advocates have elevated quality's role to the point of arguing that TQ *transcends* strategy. Schonberger (1992a: 81) claimed that TQ "can effectively govern much of what conventionally required executive-level strategic planning." In other words, if an organization is continuously improving quality, other strategic considerations are of secondary interest at best. This position may be based on the idea that improving quality drives improvements on other sources of competitive advantage, particularly cost (e.g., Belohlav, 1993b), a position for which there is some empirical support (Phillips, Chang, & Buzzell, 1983).

This position is in sharp contrast to the traditional treatment of quality in the strategy literature. From the management theory standpoint, quality is a potentially important source of competitive advantage, but only one among many. For example, quality is one basis on which a firm can pursue a differentiation strategy, but such a strategy also can be based on factors such as speed, safety, and convenience (Porter, 1985; Stalk & Hout, 1990). Furthermore, although quality is important for firms that are pursuing a low-cost strategy, its role is limited to ensuring that efforts to achieve the low-cost position do not compromise quality to the point where customers do not consider the firm's products comparable to higher priced offerings (Porter, 1985). Finally, high quality does not ensure competitive success; marketing issues such as timing and technical standards can undermine even the finest of products.

To some extent, the degree of conflict between these perspectives depends on the definition of quality one adopts (cf. Reeves & Bednar, this issue). If quality is defined as meeting or exceeding customer expectations, it can be seen as comprising virtually *any* source of differentiation. Thus, it is not surprising that researchers using a similar definition of quality have concluded that quality is the most important factor in predicting profitability (Buzzell & Gale, 1987). When quality is more narrowly defined (e.g., performance of products, presence of features), strategy scholars have a harder time accepting the grandiose role for quality proposed by TQ advocates. Clearly, both conceptual and empirical work will be needed to sort out the differences among the various TQ and management theory positions on the role of quality in strategy.

The importance of strategy implementation. TQ proponents strongly emphasize strategy implementation, or deployment, as it is often called in this literature. For example, Juran (1989) emphasized the involvement of all parts of the organization in implementing quality plans as part of his quality planning-control-improvement trilogy. The importance of strategy implementation also is clearly recognized in the Baldrige Award framework because deployment is an integral aspect of the SQP category.

The best-known TQ approach to strategy implementation is *hoshin kanri,* a Japanese term translated as policy deployment (Akao, 1991; Imai, 1986; King, 1989). In this approach, top managers annually develop strategic priorities (e.g., improved quality, better safety) for their firm. These priorities are then deployed throughout the organization, with progressively

more detailed plans for achieving them established at each level. This ensures, at least in theory, that all of the improvement efforts in a prioritized area are consistent and focused on the policy goals of top management.

In contrast, theorists generally have emphasized strategic content over strategic process, and the strategy formulation process over strategy implementation. Strategy scholars have certainly not ignored implementation (e.g., Bourgeois & Brodwin, 1984; Floyd & Wooldridge, 1992; Guth & Macmillan, 1986; Hrebeniak & Joyce, 1984; Skivington & Daft, 1991). Nevertheless, strategy researchers are mostly concerned with what strategies allow firms to compete effectively or how these strategies are chosen, rather than how they can be effectively implemented.

TQ's emphasis on strategy implementation represents a challenge to the priorities of strategic management scholars. There is little evidence to justify the relative lack of research attention to strategy implementation. In fact, some observers wonder whether in some environments implementation might actually be *more* important than formulation (Egelhoff, 1993). If strategy implementation is crucial to organizational performance, then strategy scholars should intensify their efforts toward development of strategy implementation theories. One important research issue is the relative effectiveness of the essentially top-down implementation models prevalent in TQ and the consensus-oriented models found in management theory (e.g., Floyd & Wooldridge, 1992).

Strategic focus. The focus of strategy from the TQ viewpoint is simple: Strategy consists of understanding what customers want and aligning the organization with a set of plans to deliver it to them (e.g., Schonberger, 1992a). From this perspective, one would expect the strategies of organizations in the same industry to converge, as each seeks to focus more closely than the others on the same customer needs.

We know, however, that different groups of firms often successfully utilize different strategies in the same industry (e.g., Cool, 1993; Ketchen, Thomas, & Snow, 1993; Lewis, 1990; Miles & Snow, 1978). This finding implies both that there are multiple ways to satisfy customer needs and that individual firms are unlikely to be all things to all customers. Moreover, the presence of multiple strategies suggests that strategy must be responsive not only to customer needs, but also to the core strengths and weaknesses of the organization (e.g., Hall, 1993; Prahalad & Hamel, 1990; Schoemaker, 1992). The idea that strategies are viable only if they can be effectively implemented by the organization is well established in the strategic literature. It should be reflected in a more nearly comprehensive understanding of strategy among managers subscribing to TQ.

Strategic process. A final difference between the TQ and strategic management perspectives concerns their respective approaches to strategic process. From a TQ standpoint, the processes of strategy formulation and implementation are no different from any other business or operational process (e.g., billing, injection molding), which is to say that they should be continuously subjected to analysis and improvement. This is exemplified by the Baldrige criteria, in which points are awarded for "how the company evaluates and improves (1) its planning process and (2) [the deployment of] plan requirements to work units" (Award Criteria, Malcolm Baldrige National Quality Award, 1994: 18).

Strategic management researchers, in contrast, have devoted little attention to the improvement of strategic processes. Rather, the literature has been focused on explaining variation in these processes in terms of size, structure, and so on (e.g., Egelhoff, 1982; Fredrickson & Iaquinto, 1989; Miller & Friesen, 1983). This difference in perspectives raises an interesting question. If strategic processes are indeed a product of relatively stable organizational conditions, how likely is it that firms will be able to change them? Are TQ advocates naive and unrealistic in insisting on

continuous improvement in strategic processes, or are strategy researchers insufficiently optimistic about top managers' capacity to practice it? Some aspects of organizations are relatively easy to change, others nearly impossible (Hannan & Freeman, 1984). Where do strategic processes fit?

Information and Analysis

This area is concerned with the "scope, management, and use of data and information to maintain a customer focus, to drive quality excellence, and to improve . . . performance" (Award Criteria, Malcolm Baldrige National Quality Award, 1994: 16). "Decision making based on fact" is the mantra for this aspect of the TQ philosophy, which emphasizes the collection and analysis of information about customer needs, operational problems, and the success of improvement attempts. Many popular TQ techniques (e.g., cause-and-effect analysis, Pareto charts) are aimed at helping organizations to process information effectively. In sum, the TQ literature suggests that organizations that consistently collect and analyze information will be more successful than those that do not.

Management theorists have worked extensively in the area of information and analysis (see Figure 1.1). Management theory topics that overlap considerably with this category include decision making and information processing. In fact, the TQ prescription to scrupulously collect and analyze data in order to enhance organizational effectiveness is quite similar to the well-known rational model of decision making (e.g., Langley, 1989). In contrast to this similarity in coverage between the two fields, the similarity of their recommendations is quite low. We are hampered in making a direct comparison between the prescriptions of the two fields because so much of the management theory in this area is descriptive. Some prescriptive theories do exist, however, and other theories have prescriptive implications.

Many organizational theorists would agree that, in general, information processing is related to organizational effectiveness (e.g., Daft & Weick, 1984; Galbraith, 1977). For example, Thomas, Clark, and Gioia (1993) and Smith, Grimm, Gannon, and Chen (1991) related information processing to performance in the hospital and airline industries, respectively. Several themes in the research literature, however, comprising a less optimistic view of how information is actually used in organizations, complicate the link between analysis and performance.

First, organization members' judgments about a situation may be more strongly influenced by the people with whom they interact than by their own direct experience with the data (Rice & Aydin, 1991; Salancik & Pfeffer, 1978; Zalesny & Ford, 1991). Second, analysis of information often serves political rather than rational motives: Extensive analysis may be used to bolster predetermined conclusions, rather than to discover an effective approach to a problem (Pettigrew, 1973; Pfeffer, 1981). Third, analysis is often conducted solely to create the appearance of a rational process, in hopes of legitimizing whatever course of action is eventually pursued (DiMaggio & Powell, 1983; Feldman & March, 1981; Langley, 1989). Finally, people's limited information-processing ability suggests that decision makers will always be working with simplified definitions of situations, and the choices they make will be at best satisfactory (March & Simon, 1958). In light of these findings, management theorists would be reluctant to predict that extensive analysis of information will necessarily lead to high performance.

Even more problematic, however, are findings that suggest that the sort of analysis advocated by TQ can actually *inhibit* effectiveness. For example, Fredrickson (1984) found that although comprehensive decision making was positively related to performance in the highly stable paint industry, it was negatively related to performance in the highly unstable forest products industry. Other researchers have concluded that rational, comprehensive information processing is of limited usefulness or even counterproductive under conditions in which multiple problem definitions are possible, goals are ambiguous, or uncertainty is great (Daft & Lengel,

1986; Daft, Sormunen, & Parks, 1988; Lord & Maher, 1990; March & Olsen, 1976). Ironically, as TQ moves from the buffered technical core of manufacturing toward use in research, marketing, and customer service activities, such conditions are more likely.

In summary, management theorists see information processing as useful in general but potentially irrelevant or even hazardous in specific situations. Researchers since March and Simon (1958), however, have devoted little effort to developing realistic *prescriptions* for organizational decision making and information processing. Thus, we are in the uncomfortable position of believing that the prescriptions of total quality are overly simplistic but having little with which to replace them. Though some progress has been made (e.g., Eisenhardt, 1989; Gales, Porter, & Mansour-Cole, 1991; Schweiger, Sandberg, & Rechner, 1989), the need for prescriptive theories of decision making and information processing represents an important research opportunity (Eisenhardt & Zbaracki, 1992).

Management of Process Quality

This category deals with how design, operational, and support processes are designed and improved. It includes such items as how benchmarking is used to improve performance and how the quality of suppliers' products and services is ensured. As noted previously, continuous process improvement is fundamental to TQ; an organization could hardly practice TQ while ignoring it. However, as Figure 1.1 indicates, management theorists have devoted only a moderate degree of coverage to topics in this category, and the similarity of prescriptions between the two areas is low.

The core ideas behind this facet of TQ are that organizations are sets of interlinked processes, and that improvement of these processes is the foundation of performance improvement. Deming's (1986) quality-improvement framework in particular dwells extensively on the understanding and improvement of processes (Anderson et al., this issue). Deming saw sets of interlinked processes as systems, and his treatment of organizational systems is generally consistent with the use of this term in management theory (Spencer, this issue).

For some time, however, the intellectual turf represented by this category has been abandoned by management theorists, and it is currently occupied by industrial engineers. The work of Taylor (1911) is downplayed by management scholars, due partly to his failure to incorporate psychological and sociological constructs into his models of performance. The Hawthorne experiments (e.g., Mayo, 1933) are generally looked upon by management theorists as a turning point at which behavioral factors permanently (if somewhat inadvertently) took center stage in performance models. From our current vantage point, attempts to improve performance through process change are guilty by association with a simplistic management-centered and efficiency-obsessed conception of organizations and management.

Management theorists may, however, have gone too far in emphasizing sociobehavioral over process and technical factors in explaining variation in performance. Some organizations have experienced dramatic performance improvements through process redesign or reengineering (e.g., Hammer & Champy, 1993; Stewart, 1993). Such efforts certainly call into play constructs with which management scholars are familiar (e.g., job design, organizational change), but with the exception of the socio-technical systems school of thought (e.g., Trist & Bamforth, 1952), management researchers have rarely extended their theories to include both social and technical aspects of organizational and process design. The lesson of the Hawthorne studies should have been that *both* of these aspects are important for organizational success. The challenge to management theory is to reclaim a part of our heritage that has been lost.

Customer Focus and Satisfaction

Management theory has been criticized for ignoring the role of customers in organizations (e.g., Peters & Waterman, 1982). Customer focus and satisfaction receive little coverage in the management literature, and within that coverage there is some similarity in the prescriptions of TQ and management theory (see Figure 1.1). The word *customer* rarely appears in journal article titles, management textbook indexes, or session titles at the Academy of Management meetings. Because customer focus is the central principle of TQ, its essential absence in management theory represents a fundamental difference in the orientation of the two areas. Customer focus in TQ obliges organizations to deal with such issues as assessment of customer expectations and organizational performance in meeting them, customer relationship management, and commitment to customers. The customer is omnipresent in the practice of TQ. In fact, this category has the highest weighting in the Baldrige criteria.

Management theory, in contrast, still looks very much as Peters and Waterman described it over 10 years ago. Why? The answer may lie in Danet's (1981) observation that organizational theorists view organizations from the top down (management's perspective) or from the inside out (employee's perspective) but rarely from the outside in (customer's perspective). The resource dependence perspective (RDP) (Pfeffer & Salancik, 1978) offers a possible counter to Danet's observation, given its focus on how organizations obtain the resources they need from the environment. However, the RDP is very different from TQ, in that it deals with the demands of *many* entities in the environment, whereas TQ focuses almost exclusively on customers; also, RDP emphasizes gaining control over these environmental entities, whereas TQ stresses satisfying customer requirements to both parties' advantage (Dean & Evans, 1994).

In the TQ perspective, the "customer" is the next organization in the customer-supplier chain as well as the ultimate individual customer. TQ theorists advocate organization-level customer-supplier relationships based on *trust* to avoid the monitoring costs incurred under conditions of mutual suspicion. Customer-supplier relationships, though perhaps not covered in management theory per se, are covered somewhat by the literature on forms of voluntary interfirm cooperation, such as strategic alliances (Borys & Jemison, 1989; Parkhe,

1993; Ring & Van de Ven, 1992). Management theorists, however, tend to treat trust-based cooperation as more complicated and less universally desirable than do TQ advocates. For example, the transaction costs paradigm emphasizes the propensity of partners to behave opportunistically to exploit one another (Williamson, 1985), although some have argued that the paradigm overstates this propensity (e.g., Hill, 1990).

Customers as individual consumers have become an explicit and visible focus in emerging management theory on service organizations. It is difficult to ignore the role of these customers in organizational analysis because they are often physically present within organizational boundaries (e.g., restaurant diners, hospital patients), even co-producing the services they consume (e.g., bussing their own tables). The intangibility of many services (e.g., consulting, entertaining) also makes quality measurement dependent on customers' perceptions, because conformance to physical specifications is less measurable than with manufactured goods (Reeves & Bednar, this issue).

The services literature offers *customer*-focused treatments of organizational theory (Mills, 1986), organizational behavior (Bowen & Schneider, 1988), operations management (Chase, 1978, 1981), HRM (Schneider & Bowen, 1992), and strategic management (Nayyar, 1990). TQ-type perspectives on customer relationships can be found in the ideas of establishing relational markets under conditions of goal congruence (Bowen & Jones, 1986), managing customers as "partial employees" in the co-production of the services they consume (Bowen, 1986; Mills, Chase, & Marguiles, 1983; Mills & Morris, 1986), involving customers in the design of organizational practices to gain their commitment (Ulrich, 1989), and exchanging emotion and contesting control in the employee-customer encounter (Rafaeli, 1989a, 1989b; Rafaeli & Sutton, 1990).

Relative to the assessment of customer satisfaction, research on how customer perceptions of service quality are correlated with employee perceptions of service quality and organizational practices falls into this domain (Schlesinger & Zornitsky, 1991; Schneider & Bowen, 1985; Schneider, Parkington, & Buxton, 1980; Tornow & Wiley, 1991). Overall, though, research on customer satisfaction remains in the domain of marketing, in which recent work has attempted to differentiate between the constructs of customer satisfaction and customer perceptions of service quality (Oliver, 1993).

As a final observation, it is ironic that within management theory, customer focus emerged most visibly in services, whereas within TQ, customer focus emerged, and is still most common, in manufacturing. This is changing as TQM moves more and more into the service sector (Schonberger, 1992b). At the same time, customer focus has begun to find its way into management theories of manufacturing, providing a theoretical framework for analyzing customer-service orientations (Bowen, Siehl, & Schneider, 1989) and a discussion of the various roles customers can fill in what has been termed the *service factory* (Chase & Garvin, 1989).

Discussion and Conclusion

Summary of Implications for Research and Practice

We have covered a great deal of ground in our examination of the relationship between total quality and management theory. At this point, we would like to summarize the implications for research and practice of our analysis, which fall into three categories: areas in which management theory and TQ are essentially identical, areas in which management theory could and should improve the practice of total quality, and areas in which TQ raises questions that theorists should address.

TQ consistent with management theory. We identified a number of areas in which the TQ perspective is based to a great extent on management theory. These include top-management leadership and human resource practices such as employee involvement, the use of teams, training needs analysis and evaluation, and career management. The close correspondence between TQ and management theory prescriptions in the HRM area may reflect that HRM research has greater "instrumental" value (Pelz, 1978) than does research in other management areas (Astley & Zammuto, 1992). Another factor may be that the TQ movement legitimized the efforts of HRM professionals to adopt the prescriptions of management theory, consistent with an institutionalization perspective (Meyer & Rowan, 1977; Scott, 1987). Whatever explains the correspondence, the fact that it exists is reassuring in light of the questions raised about the relevance of management theory.

TQ should be informed by management theory. We also identified a number of areas in which the TQ perspective must be seen as incomplete or simply incorrect in light of extensive management research. In such areas, the implementation of TQ, and the practice of management in general, would be enhanced by incorporating the insights of management theory. These implications for practice include:

1. Managers should beware of overreliance on formal analysis of information, especially in ambiguous and political settings.
2. Strategy formulation must include careful assessment of organizational strengths and weaknesses, not just customer expectations.
3. Selection should play a bigger role among HR practices in organizations practicing TQ, especially with respect to assessing person-organization fit.
4. Customer-supplier relationships and employee involvement and empowerment initiatives should be designed using a contingency approach, rather than assumed to be universally appropriate.

TQ suggests new directions for management theory. Finally, there are a number of areas in which the TQ perspective suggests interesting and important research questions. These include areas that have not been emphasized by management theory and areas in which our traditional perspectives have been called into question by trends in management practice. These include:

1. Can TQ be considered a substitute for leadership?
2. What is the role of quality in competitive strategy?
3. Can strategy formulation processes be improved? How?
4. What are the relative contributions of person and system factors to performance?

Areas in which theory development is clearly needed, encompassing any number of such specific questions, include prescriptions for information processing, strategy implementation, process improvement, and customer focus and satisfaction.

Note

1. All references to "this issue" are to the special issue of the journal from which this chapter is reprinted.

References

Akao, Y. (Ed.). 1991. *Hoshin kanri: Policy deployment for successful TQM*. Portland, OR: Productivity Press.

Award Criteria, Malcolm Baldrige National Quality Award. 1994. Washington, DC: United States Department of Commerce, National Institute of Standards and Technology.

Astley, W. G., & Zammuto, R. 1992. Organization science, managers, and language games. *Organization Science*, 3: 443-460.

Bardwick, J. M. 1986. *The plateauing trap*. New York: Amacon.

Barley, S. R., Meyer, G. W., & Gash, D. C. 1988. Cultures of culture: Academics, practitioners and the pragmatics of normative control. *Administrative Science Quarterly*, 33: 24-60.

Bass, B. M. 1985. *Leadership and performance beyond expectations*. New York: Free Press.

Belohlav, J. A. 1993a. Developing the quality organization. *Quality Progress*, 26(10): 119-122.

Belohlav, J. A. 1993b. Quality, strategy, and competitiveness. *California Management Review*, 35(3): 55-67.

Berlinger, L. R., Glick, W. H., & Rodgers, R. C. 1988. Job enrichment and performance improvement. In J. P. Campbell & R. J. Campbell (Eds.), *Productivity in organizations: New perspectives from industrial and organi-*

zational psychology: 219-254. San Francisco: Jossey-Bass.

Blackburn, R., & Rosen, B. 1993. Total quality and human resources management: Lessons learned from Baldrige award-winning companies. *Academy of Management Executive,* 7(3): 49-66.

Boje, D. M. 1993. *Toyota: Deconstructing our 21st-century organizations.* Paper presented at the Annual Meeting of the International Academy of Business Disciplines, New Orleans, LA.

Borys, B., & Jemison, D. B. 1989. Hybrid arrangements as strategic alliances: Theoretical issues in organizational combinations. *Academy of Management Review,* 14: 234-249.

Bourgeois, L. J., III, & Brodwin, D. R. 1984. Strategic implementation: Five approaches to an elusive phenomenon. *Strategic Management Journal,* 5: 241-264.

Bowen, D. E. 1986. Managing customers as human resources in service organizations. *Human Resource Management,* 25: 371-384.

Bowen, D. E., & Jones, G. R. 1986. A transaction cost analysis of service organization-customer exchange. *Academy of Management Review,* 11: 428-441.

Bowen, D. E., & Lawler, E. E. III. 1992a. Total quality-oriented human resources management. *Organizational Dynamics,* Spring: 29-41.

Bowen, D. E., & Lawler, E. E. III. 1992b. The empowerment of service workers: What, why, how, and when. *Sloan Management Review,* 33(3): 31-39.

Bowen, D. E., Ledford, G. E., & Nathan, B. N. 1991. Hiring for the organization, not the job. *Academy of Management Executive,* 5(4): 35-51.

Bowen, D. E., & Schneider, B. 1988. Services marketing and management: Implications for organizational behavior. In B. M. Staw & L. L. Cummings (Eds.), *Research in organizational behavior,* vol. 10: 43-80. Greenwich, CT: JAI Press.

Bowen, D. E., Siehl, C., & Schneider, B. 1989. A framework for analyzing customer service orientations in manufacturing. *Academy of Management Review,* 14: 75-95.

Burns, J. M. 1978. *Leadership.* New York: Harper & Row.

Buzzell, R. D., & Gale, B. T. 1987. *The PIMS principles.* New York: Free Press.

Cardy, R. L., & Dobbins, G. H. 1993. *Human resource management in a total quality organizational environment: Shifting from a traditional to a TQHRM approach.* Working paper, Arizona State University, Tempe.

Chase, R. B. 1978. Where does the customer fit in a service operation? *Harvard Business Review,* 56(6): 137-142.

Chase, R. B. 1981. The customer contact approach to services: Theoretical bases and practical extensions. *Operations Research,* 29: 698-706.

Chase, R. B., & Garvin, D. 1989. The service factory. *Harvard Business Review,* 67(4): 61-76.

Chatman, J. A. 1989. Improving interactional organizational research: A model of person-organization fit. *Academy of Management Review,* 14: 333-349.

Ciampa, D. 1992. *Total quality: A user's guide for implementation.* Reading, MA: Addison-Wesley.

Conger, J. A., & Kanungo, R. 1988. The empowerment process: Integrating theory and practice. *Academy of Management Review,* 13: 471-482.

Cool, K. 1993. Rivalry, strategic groups and firm profitability. *Strategic Management Journal,* 14: 47-59.

Cotton, J. L., Vollrath, D. A., Froggatt, K. L., Lengnick-Hall, M. L., & Jennings, K. R. 1988. Employee participation: Diverse forms and different outcomes. *Academy of Management Review,* 13: 8-22.

Crosby, P. B. 1979. *Quality is free: The art of making quality certain.* New York: New American Library.

Daft, R. L., & Lengel, R. H. 1986. Organizational information requirements, media richness, and structural design. *Management Science,* 32: 554-571.

Daft, R. L., Sormunen, J., & Parks, D. 1988. Chief executive scanning, environmental characteristics, and company performance: An empirical study. *Strategic Management Journal,* 9: 129-139.

Daft, R. L., & Weick, K. E. 1984. Toward a model of organizations as interpretation systems. *Academy of Management Review,* 9: 284-295.

Danet, B. 1981. Client-organization relationships. In P. C. Nystrom & W. H. Starbuck (Eds.), *Handbook of organizational design:* 382-428. New York: Oxford University Press.

Dean, J. W., Jr., & Evans, J. R. 1994. *Total quality: Management, organization, and strategy.* St. Paul, MN: West.

Deming, W. E. 1986. *Out of the crisis.* Cambridge: Massachusetts Institute of Technology Press.

DiMaggio, P. J., & Powell, W. W. 1983. The iron cage revisited: Institutional isomorphism and collective rationality in organizational fields. *American Sociological Review,* 48: 147-160.

Dobbins, G. H., Cardy, R. L., & Carson, K. P. 1991. Examining fundamental assumptions: A contrast of person and system approaches to human resources management. In G. Ferris (Ed.), *Research in personnel and human resource management,* vol. 4: 1-38. Greenwich, CT: JAI Press.

Driver, M. J. 1988. Careers: A review of personal and organizational research. In C. L. Cooper & I. Robertson (Eds.), *International Review of Psychology,* 295-277. London: Wiley.

Egelhoff, W. G. 1982. Strategy and structure in multinational corporations: An information-processing approach. *Administrative Science Quarterly,* 27: 435-458.

Egelhoff, W. G. 1993. Great strategy or great strategy implementation—Two ways of competing in global markets. *Strategic Management Journal,* 34: 37-50.

Eisenhardt, K. M. 1989. Making fast decisions in high-velocity environments. *Academy of Management Journal,* 32: 543-577.

Eisenhardt, K. M., & Zbaracki, M. J. 1992. Strategic decision making. *Strategic Management Journal,* 13: 17-37.

Ernst & Young and American Quality Foundation. 1992. *International quality study: Top line findings.* New York: Authors.

Feldman, M. A., & March, J. G. 1981. Information in organizations as signal and symbol. *Administrative Science Quarterly,* 26: 171-186.

Floyd, S. W., & Wooldridge, B. 1992. Managing strategic consensus: The foundation of effective implementation. *Academy of Management Executive,* 6(4): 27-39.

Fombrun, C. J., Tichy, N. M., & Devanna, M. A. 1984. *Strategic human resource management.* New York: Wiley.

Fredrickson, J. W. 1984. The comprehensiveness of strategic decision processes: Extension, observations, future directions. *Academy of Management Journal,* 27: 445-466.

Fredrickson, J. W., & Iaquinto, A. L. 1989. Inertia and creeping rationality in strategic decision processes. *Academy of Management Journal,* 32: 516-542.

Galbraith, J. R. 1977. *Organization design.* Reading, MA: Addison-Wesley.

Gales, L., Porter, P., & Mansour-Cole, D. 1991. Innovation project technology, information processing, and performance: A test of the Daft and Lenger conceptualization. *Journal of Engineering and Technology Management,* 9: 303-338.

Garvin, D. A. 1991. How the Baldrige award really works. *Harvard Business Review,* 69(6): 80-93.

Guth, W., & MacMillan, I. 1986. Strategy implementation versus middle management self-interest. *Strategic Management Journal,* 7: 313-328.

Hackman, J. R., & Oldham, G. R. 1980. *Work redesign.* Reading, MA: Addison-Wesley.

Hall, D. T., & Richter, J. 1990. Career gridlock: Baby boomers hit the wall. *Academy of Management Executive,* 4(3):7-22.

Hall, R. 1993. A framework linking intangible resources and capabilities to sustainable competitive advantage. *Strategic Management Journal,* 14: 607-618.

Hambrick, D. C. 1994. 1993 Presidential address: What if the Academy actually mattered? *Academy of Management Review,* 19: 11-16.

Hammer, M., & Champy, J. 1993. *Reengineering the corporation: A manifesto for business revolution.* New York: HarperCollins.

Hannan, M. T., & Freeman, J. 1984. Structural inertia and organizational change. *American Sociological Review,* 49: 149-164.

Hart, C., & Schlesinger, L. 1991. Total quality management and the human resource professional: Applying the Baldrige framework to human resources. *Human Resource Management,* 30: 433-454.

Hauser, J. R., & Clausing, D. 1988. The house of quality. *Harvard Business Review,* 66(3): 63-73.

Hetrick, W. P., & Boje, D. M. 1992. Organization and the body: Post-Fordist dimensions. *Journal of Organizational Change Management,* 5: 48-57.

Hill, C. W. L. 1990. Cooperation, opportunism, and the invisible hand: Implications for transaction cost theory. *Academy of Management Review,* 15: 500-513.

Hrebeniak, L., & Joyce, W. 1984. *Implementing strategy.* New York: Macmillan.

Iaffaldano, M. T., & Muchinsky, P. M. 1985. Job satisfaction and job performance: A meta-analysis. *Psychological Bulletin,* 97: 251-273.

Imai, M. 1986. *Kaizen: The key to Japan's competitive success.* New York: McGraw-Hill.

Juran, J. A. M. 1989. *Juran on leadership for quality.* New York: Free Press.

Kerr, S., & Jermier, J. M. 1978. Substitutes for leadership: Their meaning and measurement. *Organizational Behavior and Human Decision Processes,* 22: 375-403.

Ketchen, D. J., Jr., Thomas, J. B., & Snow, C. C. 1993. Organizational configurations and performance: A comparison of theoretical approaches. *Academy of Management Journal,* 36: 1278-1313.

King, B. 1989. *Hoshin planning: The developmental approach.* Methuen, MA: GOAL/QPC.

Langley, A. 1989. In search of rationality: The purposes behind the use of formal analysis in organizations. *Administrative Science Quarterly,* 34: 598-631.

Lawler, E. E. III. 1988. Choosing an involvement strategy. *Academy of Management Executive,* 2: 197-204.

Lawler, E. E. III. 1994. Total quality management and employee involvement: Are they compatible? *Academy of Management Executive,* 8(1): 68-76.

Lawler, E. E. III, Mohrman, S. A., & Ledford, G. E. 1992. *Employee involvement and total quality management.* San Francisco: Jossey-Bass.

Lewis, P. 1990. The linkage between strategy, strategic groups, and performance in the U.K. retail grocery industry. *Strategic Management Journal,* 11: 385-397.

Likert, R. 1967. *The human organization.* New York: McGraw-Hill.

Lord, R. G., & Maher, K. J. 1990. Alternative information-processing models and their implications for theory, research, and practice. *Academy of Management Review,* 15: 9-28.

March, J. G., & Olsen, J. P. 1976. *Ambiguity and choice in organizations.* Bergen, Norway: Universitetsforlaget.

March, J. G., & Simon, H. A. 1958. *Organizations.* New York: Wiley.

Mayo, G. E. 1933. *The human problems of an industrial society* (2nd ed.). New York: Macmillan.

McCann, J. E., & Galbraith, J. R. 1981. Interdepartmental relations. In P. C. Nystrom & W. H. Starbuck (Eds.), *Handbook of organizational design,* 2: 60-84. New York: Oxford University Press.

McGregor, D. 1960. *The human side of enterprise.* New York: McGraw-Hill.

Meyer, J. W., & Rowan, B. 1977. Institutional organizations: Formal structure as myth and ceremony. *American Journal of Sociology,* 83: 340-363.

Miles, R., & Snow, C. 1978. *Organizational strategy, structure and process.* New York: McGraw-Hill.

Miller, D., & Friesen, P. H. 1983. Strategy-making and environment: The third link. *Strategic Management Journal,* 4: 221-235.

Mills, P. K. 1986. *Managing service industries.* Cambridge, MA: Ballinger.

Mills, P. K., Chase, R. B., & Marguiles, N. 1983. Motivating the client/employee system as a service production strategy. *Academy of Management Review,* 8: 301-310.

Mills, P. K., & Morris, J. H. 1986. Clients as "partial employees" of service organizations: Role development in client participation. *Academy of Management Review,* 11: 726-735.

Nayyar, Y. R. 1990. Information asymmetries: A source of competitive advantage for diversified service firms. *Strategic Management Journal*, 11: 513-519.

Oliver, R. L. 1993. A conceptual model of service, quality and service satisfaction: Compatible goals, different concepts. In T. A. Swartz, D. E. Bowen, & S. W. Brown (Eds.), *Advances in services marketing and management*, vol. 2: 65-86. Greenwich, CT: JAI Press.

Parkhe, A. 1993. Strategic alliance structuring: A game theoretic and transaction cost examination of interfirm cooperation. *Academy of Management Journal*, 36: 794-829.

Pasmore, W., Frances, C., Haldeman, J., & Shani, A. 1982. Socio-technical systems: A North American reflection on empirical studies of the 70s. *Human Relations*, 35: 1179-1209.

Pelz, D. C. 1978. Some expanded perspectives on the use of social science in public policy. In J. M. Yinger & S. J. Cutler (Eds.), *Major social issues: A multidisciplinary view:* 346-357. New York: Free Press.

Peters, T. J., & Waterman, R. H. 1982. *In search of excellence*. New York: Harper & Row.

Pettigrew, A. 1973. *The politics of organizational decision making*. London: Tavistock.

Pfeffer, J. 1977. The ambiguity of leadership. *Academy of Management Review*, 2: 104-112.

Pfeffer, J. 1981. *Power in organizations*. Marshfield, MA: Pitman.

Pfeffer, J., & Salancik, G. R. 1978. *The external control of organizations: A resource dependence perspective*. New York: Harper & Row.

Phillips, L. W., Chang, D. R., & Buzzell, R. D. 1983. Product quality, cost position, and business performance: A test of some key hypotheses. *Journal of Marketing*, 47(2): 26-43.

Podsakoff, P. M., Todor, W. D., & Skov, R. 1982. Effects of leader contingent satisfaction. *Academy of Management Journal*, 25: 810-821.

Porter, M. E. 1985. *Competitive advantage: Creating and sustaining superior performance*. New York: Free Press.

Prahalad, C. K., & Hamel, G. 1990. The core competence of the corporation. *Harvard Business Review*, 68(3): 79-89.

Rafaeli, A. 1989a. When clerks meet customers: A test of variables related to emotional expressions on the job. *Journal of Applied Psychology*, 74: 385-393.

Rafaeli, A. 1989b. When cashiers meet customers: An analysis of the role of supermarket cashiers. *Academy of Management Journal*, 32: 245-273.

Rafaeli, A., & Sutton, R. I. 1990. Busy stores and demanding customers: How do they affect the display of positive emotions? *Academy of Management Journal*, 33: 623-637.

Rice, R. E., & Aydin, C. 1991. Attitudes toward new organizational technology: Network proximity as a mechanism for social information processing. *Administrative Science Quarterly*, 36: 219-244.

Ring, D. S., & Van de Ven, A. H. 1992. Structuring cooperative relationships between organizations. *Strategic Management Journal*, 13: 483-498.

Robinson, J. D. III, Akers, J. F., Artzt, E. L., Poling, H. A., Galvin, R. W., & Allaire, P. A. 1991. An open letter: TQM on the campus. *Harvard Business Review*, 69(6): 94-95.

Rynes, S., & Gerhart, B. 1990. Interviewer assessments of applicant "fit": An exploratory investigation. *Personnel Psychology*, 43: 13-34.

Salancik, G. R., & Pfeffer, J. 1978. A social information processing approach to job attitudes and task design. *Administration Science Quarterly*, 23: 224-253.

Schlesinger, L. A., & Zornitsky, J. 1991. Job satisfaction, service capability, and customer satisfaction: An examination of linkages and management implications. *Human Resource Planning*, 14: 141-150.

Schneider, B., & Bowen, D. E. 1985. Employee and customer perceptions of service in banks: Replication and extension. *Journal of Applied Psychology*, 70: 423-433.

Schneider, B., & Bowen, D. E. 1992. Personnel/human resources management in the service sector. In G. R. Ferris & K. M. Rowland (Eds.), *Research in personnel and human resources management:* 1-30. Greenwich, CT: JAI Press.

Schneider, B., Parkington, J. J., & Buxton, V. M. 1980. Employee and customer perceptions of service in banks. *Administrative Science Quarterly*, 25: 252-267.

Schoemaker, P. J. H. 1992. How to link strategic vision to core capabilities. *Sloan Management Review*, 34(1): 67-81.

Schonberger, R. J. 1992a. Is strategy strategic? Impact of total quality management on strategy. *Academy of Management Executive*, 6(3): 80-87.

Schonberger, R. I. 1992b. Total quality management cuts a broad swath—through manufacturing and beyond. *Organizational Dynamics*, Spring: 16-28.

Schuler, R. S., & Harris, D. L. 1991. Deming quality improvement: Implications for human resource management as illustrated in a small company. *Human Resource Planning*, 14: 191-208.

Schweiger, D. M., Sandberg, W. R., & Rechner, P. L. 1989. Experiential effects of dialectical inquiry, devil's advocacy, and consensus approaches to strategic decision making. *Academy of Management Journal*, 32: 745-772.

Scott, W. R. 1987. The adolescence of institutional theory. *Administrative Science Quarterly*, 32: 493-511.

Skivington, J. E., & Daft, R. L. 1991. A study of organizational "framework" and "process" modalities for the implementation of business-level strategic decisions. *Journal of Management Studies*, 28: 45-68.

Smith, K. G., Grimm, C. M., Gannon, M. J., & Chen, M. 1991. Organizational information processing, competitive responses, and performance in the U.S. domestic airline industry. *Academy of Management Journal*, 34: 60-85.

Snell, S. A., & Dean, J. W., Jr. 1992. Integrated manufacturing and human resource management: A human capital perspective. *Academy of Management Journal,* 35: 467-504.

Snell, S. A., & Dean, J. W., Jr. In press. Strategic compensation for integrated manufacturing: The moderating effects of jobs and inertia. *Academy of Management Journal,* 37.

Stalk, G., Jr., & Hout, T. M. 1990. *Competing against time: How time-based competition is reshaping global markets.* New York: Free Press.

Stewart, T. A. 1993. Reengineering: The hot new managing tool. *Fortune,* August 23: 41-48.

Taylor, F. W. 1911. *The principles of scientific management.* New York: Harper & Brothers.

Thomas, J. B., Clark, S. M., & Gioia, D. A. 1993. Strategic sensemaking and organizational performance: Linkages among scanning, interpretation, action, and outcomes. *Academy of Management Journal,* 36: 239-270.

Thomas, K. W., & Velthouse, B. A. 1990. Cognitive elements of empowerment: An interpretative model of intrinsic task motivation. *Academy of Management Review,* 15: 666-681.

Tichy, N. M., & Devanna, M. A. 1986. *The transformational leader.* New York: Wiley,

Tornow, W. W., & Wiley, J. W. 1991. Service quality and management practices: A look at employee attitudes, customer satisfaction, and bottom-line consequences. *Human Resource Planning,* 14: 105-116.

Trist, E., & Bamforth, K. W. 1952. Some social and psychological consequences of the long wall method of coal-getting. *Human Relations,* 4: 3-38.

Ulrich, D. 1989. Tie the corporate knot: Gaining complete customer commitment. *Sloan Management Review,* 30(4): 19-27.

Williamson, O. E. 1985. *The economic institutions of capitalism.* New York: Free Press.

Wright, P. M., & McMahan, G. C. 1992. Theoretical perspective for strategic human resource management. *Journal of Management,* 18: 295-320.

Zalesny, M. D., & Ford, J. K. 1990. Extending the social information processing perspective: New links to attitudes, behaviors and perceptions. *Organizational Behavior and Human Decision Processes,* 47: 205-246.

Chapter 2

Total Quality Management

Empirical, Conceptual, and Practical Issues

J. RICHARD HACKMAN
RUTH WAGEMAN

It has now been a decade since the core ideas of total quality management (TQM) set forth by W. Edwards Deming, Joseph Juran, and Kaoru Ishikawa gained significant acceptance in the U.S. management community. In that decade, TQM has become something of a social movement. It has spread from its industrial origins to health care organizations, public bureaucracies, nonprofit organizations, and educational institutions. It has become increasingly prominent in the popular press, in the portfolios of trainers and consultants, and, more recently, in the scholarly literature.[1] Institutions specifically chartered to promote TQM have been established, and a discernible TQM ideology has developed and diffused throughout the managerial community. And, in its maturity, TQM has become controversial—something whose worth and impact people argue about.

Some writers have asserted that TQM provides a historically unique approach to improving organizational effectiveness, one that has a solid conceptual foundation and, at the same time, offers a strategy for improving performance that takes account of how people and organizations actually operate (Wruck and Jensen, 1994). A more skeptical view is that TQM is but one in a long line of programs—in the tradition of T-groups, job enrichment, management by objectives, and a host of others—that have burst upon the managerial scene rich with promise, only to give way in a few years to yet another new management fashion.

In this commentary, we provide a conceptual analysis of TQM that places these competing claims in perspective. We ask whether there really is such a thing as TQM, or whether it has become mainly a banner under which a potpourri of essentially unrelated organizational changes are undertaken. We document how TQM activities and outcomes have been measured and evaluated by researchers and note some significant gaps in what has been learned. We explore the uneasy relation between behavioral processes that are central to TQM practice and mainline organizational scholarship about those same processes. And we conclude with an overall assessment of the current state of TQM theory and practice, including some speculations about what may be required if this potentially powerful approach is to take root and prosper in the years to come.

AUTHORS'NOTE: Reprinted with permission of *Administrative Science Quarterly,* Johnson Graduate School of Management, Cornell University, 20 Thornwood Drive, Ithaca, NY 14850-1265, from *Administrative Science Quarterly,* 40 (1995) pp. 309-342. Copyright © 1995 by Cornell University.

IS THERE SUCH A THING AS TQM?

As is inevitable for any idea that enjoys wide popularity in managerial and scholarly circles, total quality management has come to mean different things to different people. There is now such a diversity of things done under the name "total quality" that it has become unclear whether TQM still has an identifiable conceptual core, if it ever did. We begin with a close examination of what the movement's founders had to say about what TQM was supposed to be, and then we assess how TQM, as currently practiced, stacks up against the founders' values and prescriptions.

Virtually everything that has been written about TQM explicitly draws on the works of W. Edwards Deming, Joseph Juran, and Kaoru Ishikawa, the primary authorities of the TQM movement (for a review, see Crosby, 1989). Rather than providing here a precis of their writings, we draw on them to determine whether there exists among them (1) a coherent philosophical position that specifies the core values to be sought in TQM programs, and (2) a distinctive set of interventions (structures, systems, and/or work practices) that are intended specifically to promote those values.

TQM Philosophy

Deming, Ishikawa, and Juran share the view that an organization's primary purpose is to stay in business, so that it can promote the stability of the community, generate products and services that are useful to customers, and provide a setting for the satisfaction and growth of organization members (Juran, 1969: 1-5; Ishikawa, 1985: 1; Deming, 1986: preface). The focus is on the preservation and health of the organization, but there also are explicitly stated values about the organization's context (the community and customers) and about the well-being of individual organization members: As Ishikawa (1985: 27) said, "An organization whose members are not happy and cannot be happy does not deserve to exist." The TQM strategy for achieving its normative outcomes is rooted in four interlocked assumptions—about quality, people, organizations, and the role of senior management.

Assumptions. The first assumption is about quality, which is assumed to be less costly to an organization than is poor workmanship. A fundamental premise of TQM is that the costs of poor quality (such as inspection, rework, lost customers, and so on) are far greater than the costs of developing processes that produce high-quality products and services. Although the organizational purposes espoused by the TQM authorities do not explicitly address traditional economic and accounting criteria of organizational effectiveness, their view is that organizations that produce quality goods will eventually do better even on traditional measures such as profitability than will organizations that attempt to keep costs low by compromising quality (Juran, 1974: 5.1-5.15; Ishikawa, 1985: 104-105; Deming, 1986: 11-12). The strong version of this assumption, implicit in Juran and Ishikawa but explicit and prominent in Deming's writing, is that producing quality products and services is not merely less costly but, in fact, is absolutely essential to long-term organizational survival (Deming, 1993: xi-xii).

The second assumption is about people. Employees naturally care about the quality of work they do and will take initiatives to improve it—so long as they are provided with the tools and training that are needed for quality improvement, and management pays attention to their ideas. As stated by Juran (1974: 4.54), "The human being exhibits an instinctive drive for precision, beauty and perfection. When unrestrained by economics, this drive has created the art treasures of the ages." Deming and Ishikawa add that an organization must remove all organizational systems that create fear—such as punishment for poor performance, appraisal systems that involve the comparative evaluation of employees, and merit pay (Ishikawa, 1985: 26; Deming, 1986: 101-109).

The third assumption is that organizations are systems of highly interdependent parts, and the central problems they face invariably cross traditional functional lines. To produce high-quality products efficiently, for example, product designers must address manufacturing challenges and trade-offs as part of the design process. Deming and Juran are insistent that cross-functional problems must be addressed collectively by representatives of all relevant functions (Juran, 1969: 80-85; Deming, 1993: 50-93). Ishikawa, by contrast, is much less system-oriented: He states that cross-functional teams should not set overall directions; rather, each line division should set its own goals using local objective-setting procedures (Ishikawa, 1985: 116-117).

The final assumption concerns senior management. Quality is viewed as ultimately and inescapably the responsibility of top management. Because senior managers create the organizational systems that determine how products and services are designed and produced, the quality-improvement process must begin with management's own commitment to total quality. Employees' work effectiveness is viewed as a direct function of the quality of the systems that managers create (Juran, 1974: 21.1-21.4; Ishikawa, 1985: 122-128; Deming, 1986: 248-249).

Change principles. TQM authorities specify four principles that should guide any organizational interventions intended to improve quality. The first is to focus on work processes. The quality of products and services depends most of all on the processes by which they are designed and produced. It is not sufficient to provide clear direction about hoped-for outcomes; in addition, management must train and coach employees to assess, analyze, and improve work processes (Juran, 1974: 2.11-2.17; Ishikawa, 1985: 60; Deming, 1986: 52).

The second principle is analysis of variability. Uncontrolled variance in processes or outcomes is the primary cause of quality problems and must be analyzed and controlled by those who perform an organization's front-line work. Only when the root causes of variability have been identified are employees in a position to take appropriate steps to improve work processes. According to Deming (1986: 20), "The central problem of management . . . is to understand better the meaning of variation, and to ex-

tract the information contained in variation" (see also Juran, 1974: 2.10-2.17; Ishikawa, 1985: chap. 12).

The third principle is management by fact. TQM calls for the use of systematically collected data at every point in a problem-solving cycle—from determining high-priority problems, through analyzing their causes, to selecting and testing solutions (Juran, 1974: 22.1-28.1; Ishikawa, 1985: 104-105; Deming, 1986: chap. 8). Although Deming, Ishikawa, and Juran differ in their preferred analytical tools, each bases his quality-improvement program on collecting data, using statistics, and testing solutions by experiment.

The fourth principle is learning and continuous improvement. The long-term health of an enterprise depends on treating quality improvement as a never-ending quest. Opportunities to develop better methods for carrying out work always exist, and a commitment to continuous improvement ensures that people will never stop learning about the work they do (Juran, 1969: 2-3; Ishikawa, 1985: 55-56; Deming, 1986: 49-52).

TQM Interventions

Despite some differences in emphasis, the three TQM authorities have a common philosophical orientation and share a set of core values about people, organizations, and change processes. They prescribe five interventions to realize those values.

Explicit identification and measurement of customer requirements. To achieve quality, it is essential to know what customers want and to provide products or services that meet their requirements (Ishikawa, 1985: 43). It is necessary, therefore, for organization members to assess directly customer requirements such as durability, reliability, and speed of service (Juran, 1974: 2.2; Deming, 1986: 177-182). Some customers are external to the organization, others are internal, as when the output of some organization members is passed on to others. TQM defines the next process down the line as the "customer" for each process. Within the organization, then, the assessment of customer requirements serves as a tool to foster cross-functional cooperation (Ishikawa, 1985: 107-108).

With data about customer requirements in hand, quality improvement can focus specifically on those aspects of work processes that are most consequential for customer satisfaction. Even so, high quality is not assured. Some organizations actively manipulate customer preferences (for example, through advertising) to bring them into line with what the organization already is able to provide. And customers may define their own requirements in terms of existing products and services that may be low in quality (Hayes and Abernathy, 1980). Deming (1993: 7-9) suggests that this may be especially characteristic of customers in the United States, because they have grown accustomed to poor-quality products and services; U.S. organizations that rely too heavily on what customers say they want risk setting quality standards far below what employees actually are capable of achieving.

Creation of supplier partnerships. TQM authorities suggest that organizations should choose vendors on the basis of quality, rather than solely on price. Moreover, they recommend that organizations work directly with raw material suppliers to ensure that their materials are of the highest quality possible (Juran, 1974: 10.1-10.35; Ishikawa, 1985, chap. 9; Deming, 1986: 31-43).

Use of cross-functional teams to identify and solve quality problems. Although cross-functional teams can be used in multiple ways in TQM programs, their main purpose is to identify and analyze the "vital few" problems of the organization (Ishikawa, 1985: 113-119; Deming, 1993: 85-89). Juran (1969) refers to such teams as the "steering arm" of a quality effort. Other teams, also cross-functional, are created to diagnose the causes of problems that have been identified by the steering arm and to develop and test possible solutions to them. Diagnostic teams can be either temporary task forces or continuing organizational entities. In both cases, department heads are included as team members to ensure that stakeholder de-

partments will cooperate when the time comes to implement the team's recommendations. Juran, far more than Deming, advocates the use of quality-improvement teams within functions. But the team composition principle is the same: Choose people who can provide access to the data necessary for testing potential solutions and who are critical to implementing the solutions developed (Juran, 1969: 78-89).

Use of scientific methods to monitor performance and to identify points of high leverage for performance improvement. The three TQM authorities are of one voice in advocating the use of statistical tools to monitor and analyze work processes (Juran, 1974: chaps. 22-27; Ishikawa, 1985: 109-120; Deming, 1986: chaps. 8-9). A wide variety of statistical tools are available to identify the points of highest leverage for quality improvement, to evaluate alternative solutions to identified problems, and to document the results of process changes. Many of the tools involve applications of probability theory to generate findings that then can be summarized pictorially. Literally dozens of "quality tools" have been described in the literature (for a review, see Sashkin and Kiser, 1993). Three of the most commonly used tools are control charts, Pareto analysis, and cost-of-quality analysis.

A *control chart* provides a pictorial representation of the outputs of an ongoing process. Control charts are used to monitor the performance of a process and to determine whether that process is "in control"—whether the variance produced by the process is random or attributable to specific causes. It is assumed that all processes produce variance, but a stable process fluctuates randomly. Therefore, data from a stable process will tend to fall within predictable bounds. Scrutiny of a control chart allows the user to (1) determine whether a given process is in need of improvement, (2) identify points outside the control range so that the causes of uncontrolled variance can be sought, and (3) reassess the process after experimental attempts to improve it are completed (Deming, 1986: 323-346).

Pareto analysis is used to identify the major factors th]ributor to a problem can be quantified. For example, a group attempting to identify the vital few causes of high inventory costs would list each inventory item in order of total dollar value of materials kept in stock. Those materials that turn out to be major contributors to inventory costs are then addressed first (Juran, 1969: 43-54).

Cost-of-quality analysis is used to highlight the cost savings that can be achieved by doing the work right the first time. The analysis involves quantifying all costs associated with maintaining acceptable quality levels, such as the costs of preventing errors, and then comparing these with the costs incurred by failures to achieve acceptable quality, such as the cost of rework. Cost-of-quality analysis thus helps to identify those opportunities for improvement that offer the largest cost savings (Juran, 1974: chap. 5; Ishikawa, 1985: 54-55).

Use of process-management heuristics to enhance team effectiveness. The TQM authorities suggest several techniques to help quality teams use their collective knowledge effectively in identifying and analyzing opportunities to improve quality. Three of the most commonly used devices are flowcharts, brainstorming, and cause-and-effect diagrams.

A *flowchart* is a pictorial representation of the steps in a work process. Flowcharts, which use standardized symbols to represent types of activities in a process, help members identify activities that are repetitive, that add no value, or that excessively delay completion of the work (Deming, 1993: 58-61).

Brainstorming is used by groups to generate lists of ideas about matters such as the potential causes of a problem, possible solutions, and issues likely to be encountered in implementing those solutions. Its purpose is to tap the creativity of group members by explicitly ruling out the evaluation of member contributions to the list and actively encouraging building on others' ideas. Brainstorming often is followed by the Nominal Group Technique or multivoting to reduce and prioritize the list that has been generated (Ishikawa, 1985: 64-65).

A *cause-and-effect diagram* or "fishbone" was developed by Ishikawa to graphically represent the relationship between a problem and its potential causes. Fishbone diagrams can help

a group examine thoroughly all possible causes of a quality problem and discern the relationships among them. Group members place the problem at the right-hand side of the page (the head of the fish). The "bones" of the fish are lines on which members list the potential causes by category; the generic categories are causes related to people, tools, materials, and methods. Members then collect data to assess the potency of each of these potential causes (Ishikawa, 1985: 63-65).

According to the founders of TQM, the five interventions summarized above define the core of total quality management. Knowledge of customer requirements provides a test for considering and evaluating process changes. Supplier partnerships ensure that materials entering the organization are of acceptable quality. Cross-functional teams bring the full spectrum of relevant information and expertise to bear on decisions about systemwide problems. Scientific methods and statistical analyses provide teams with trustworthy data to use in their decision making. And process management heuristics can improve the quality of the decision-making process itself.

TQM in Practice

To assess how TQM actually is practiced in U.S. work organizations, we address two questions. First, in what ways are contemporary implementations of TQM consistent with the founders' tenets? Second, in what ways do current practices differ from their prescriptions, and do those differences enrich the core ideas of quality management or diverge from them?[2]

Continuities. Organizations that implement TQM are consistent with the founders' ideas in developing means for assessing their customers' preferences, altering relationships with suppliers, using teams (both cross-functional and within-function) to solve problems, investing in training in problem-solving tools and, to a lesser degree,] assumption that quality is ultimately a management responsibility and that attempts to improve quality must begin at the top. The five TQM practices described below, presented in order of their prevalence, are generally consistent with the ideas and techniques originally articulated by Deming, Ishikawa, and Juran.

A recent survey reports that the single most commonly used TQM technique is formation of short-term problem-solving teams with the overall objective of simplifying and streamlining work practices (Conference Board, 1991). Nearly all manufacturing firms using TQM use such teams, and 90 percent of service firms do so. Problem-solving teams work on a wide variety of tasks, ranging from cross-functional involvement in product design to solving within-unit workflow problems.

The second most commonly used practice is training. Organizations that implement TQM invest heavily in formal training for a large proportion of their employees. According to the Conference Board (1991), 92 percent of manufacturing companies and 75 percent of service companies implementing TQM use some form of training as part of their change effort. Typically, nearly all senior and middle managers are trained in quality practices, with a median of 16 hours of training. About 80 percent of first-line supervisors and 50 percent of nonmanagement employees receive a median of eight hours of training. Olian and Rynes (1991) found the most common training content to be, in order of frequency, interpersonal skills, quality-improvement processes and problem solving, team leading and building, running meetings, statistical analysis, supplier qualification training, and benchmarking.

The third practice is top-down implementation. In keeping with the TQM authorities' view that quality is ultimately the responsibility of top management, most TQM programs begin with the training of top managers in the quality philosophy, followed by the articulation of an organization-wide quality vision and communication of that vision throughout the organization (Conference Board, 1991: 18). Both education about TQM and implementation of TQM practices typically take place in cascading fashion, with each layer carrying the message to the next lower level of the organization.

The fourth practice is developing relationships with suppliers. At least 50 percent of

TQM organizations collaborate with their suppliers in some way to increase the quality of component parts (Lawler, Mohrman, and Ledford, 1992), often by sending "quality action teams" to consult with their major suppliers. The objective is to help suppliers use TQM to analyze and improve their *own* work processes (Sashkin and Kiser, 1993).

The fifth practice is obtaining data about customers. Although systematic data are not available on the proportion of TQM organizations that directly assess customer preferences and customer satisfaction, nearly all case studies of TQM companies include descriptions of the means such organizations use to obtain customer data. Commonly used devices for obtaining these data include toll-free complaint lines, marketing research firms, and customer focus groups (Olian and Rynes, 1991).

Enrichments. Two additional interventions—competitive benchmarking and employee involvement—have become strongly associated with TQM in the United States. Although not explicitly advocated by the TQM founders, these activities are generally consistent with their ideas. Benchmarking involves gathering information about "best practices" from other organizations. Thus, a company that wishes to improve its customer service might observe service practices in firms renowned for their service quality, regardless of their industry. The prevalence of benchmarking in contemporary TQM programs appears to derive primarily from its inclusion as a Baldrige Quality Award criterion (Malcolm Baldrige National Quality Award Consortium, 1990).

Benchmarking serves multiple functions consistent with TQM philosophy: (1) determining what customers can expect to get from the competition, as part of assessing customer requirements, (2) learning alternative work processes, and (3) in some cases, guiding the establishment of quality-improvement goals. The ambitious quality goals of many TQM programs, such as zero "defections," cutting defects by 90 percent in two years, or reducing cycle time by 50 percent may be more likely to be accepted by organization members once competitive benchmarking demonstrates that other organizations achieve them (Olian and Rynes, 1991). Just because a new idea has been discovered, however, does not mean it will be used. Ulrich, Von Glinow, and Jick (1993) noted that organizations that rely heavily on external benchmarking to identify superior work processes tend to have the most difficulty getting those processes adopted internally.

TQM organizations in the U.S. invariably introduce mechanisms for employee involvement in quality that extend beyond those that are integral to the TQM program itself (Lawler, 1994). According to the Conference Board (1991), 65 percent of TQM organizations create employee suggestion systems, and 70 percent have quality meetings between managers and employees and/or focus groups to solicit ideas about quality. The widespread use of "quality days" and other celebrations of quality-related events and achievements further reinforce the aspiration, in many organizations, to involve every member in quality-improvement processes. Such celebrations, moreover, are consistent with Deming's view that social approval and public recognition are important sources of human motivation (Deming, 1986: 85). Finally, some TQM organizations create self-managing teams to perform the regular work of the enterprise, thereby further expanding the involvement of organization members. KPMG Peat Marwick (1991) found that 15 percent of the TQM organizations studied used such teams, and among organizations with more than five years of TQM experience, almost 50 percent did so.

Divergencies. Some aspects of contemporary TQM practice dilute or redirect the core ideas of the movement's founders. Noteworthy are the attenuated role of scientific methods in TQM programs and an increasing reliance on performance measurement and performance-contingent rewards to motivate and control employees.

The use of scientific methods is among the most distinctive features of TQM. In contemporary practice, however, there is much greater emphasis on group-process techniques and interpersonal skills than on scientific methods. Nor is there evidence that organization mem-

bers actually use even those statistics they have been taught. In many organizations, the emphasis on statistics and experimentation is stripped away very early in the process of implementing TQM, leaving only the rhetoric of "management by fact" (Zbaracki, 1994).

A large majority of organizations using TQM modify their performance measurement and reward systems so that achievement of specific quality goals can be assessed and rewarded, even though Deming (1993) explicitly argues that such practices are counterproductive. According to the 1991 Conference Board survey, 85 percent of TQM organizations have developed programs to reward individuals and teams for quality achievements. In addition, 75 percent tie performance appraisals to quality, although principally for managers (only 46 percent of front-line employees are assessed on their use of quality tools). Such practices may derive from Juran's eclectic philosophy for managing individual performance. Unlike Deming and Ishikawa, Juran subscribes to no particular motivation theory. Rather, he calls for the use of a range of motivational techniques, from job enrichment to quality audits: "All available tools must be used, each directed at the specific problem it is able to solve. None are panaceas" (Juran, 1969: 18-19).

The longer an organization has been involved with TQM, the greater its reliance on incentives to motivate work toward quality improvement goals. The 1991 KPMG Peat Marwick survey found that 60 percent of organizations with five or more years of TQM experience explicitly rewarded the achievement of quality goals. The survey also showed, however, that organizations with greater experience with TQM tended to place greater emphasis on group, departmental, or organization-wide, rather than individual, rewards. This is consistent with the TQM authorities' emphasis on teamwork and between-unit interdependence and with their view that it is the system, not individual efforts, that ultimately determines quality. Such rewards, however, almost always are linked to quantitative performance measures, which Deming believed to be "limiting" (Deming, 1993: 47).

Conclusion

We have approached the question, "Is there such a thing as TQM?" in the same way that we would approach analysis of any construct: by assembling data relevant to its convergent and discriminant validity. Convergent validity, as adapted from Campbell and Fiske (1959) for present purposes, reflects the degree to which the versions of TQM promulgated by its founders and observed in organizational practice share a common set of assumptions and prescriptions. Discriminant validity refers to the degree to which TQM philosophy and practice can be reliably distinguished from other strategies for organizational improvement, such as participative management, management by objectives, and so on. Only if TQM passes these two validity tests does it make sense to dig more deeply into the conceptual, empirical, and practical issues that can inform its overall assessment.[3]

Convergent validity. We conclude that TQM passes the convergent validity test. As we have seen, there is substantial agreement among the movement's founders about the key assumptions and practices of total quality management. Moreover, contemporary TQM practice is generally consistent with the founders' ideas. The record is not perfect, however. Some of the sharpest and most distinctive ideas of the TQM founders have been sanded down a bit over the last decade. And there is, these days, greater adherence to TQM philosophy at the espoused than at the operational level, as seen, for example, by the diminished role of scientific methods and statistical tools in many TQM programs. Still, we find that there is impressive convergence across theorists, across practitioners, and across time—of the basic ideas of total quality management.

Discriminant validity. In assessing the distinctiveness of TQM, we consider three comparison groups: programs that are subsumed by a full-fledged TQM program, those that are clearly different from TQM, and those that are, like TQM, broad and multifaceted organizational improvement programs. As articulated by its founders, TQM clearly subsumes a number of smaller and more focused initiatives, such as quality circles, cross-functional project teams, and zero-defects programs. It also is distinct from interventions such as job enrichment, performance-contingent rewards, and goal setting, some of which are explicitly disavowed by one or more of the three TQM founders—for example, the emphasis of some job-design models on employee autonomy about methods, pay-for-performance programs that tie financial rewards to bottom-line outcomes, and goal-setting programs that specify explicit performance objectives within a department or function. We will have more to say about these discrepancies later; for now, we simply note that TQM is clearly different, both conceptually and operationally, from at least this sample of other change programs.

Finally, TQM as described by its founders is readily distinguishable from other broad, multifaceted initiatives, such as participative management and quality of worklife programs. As a concept, participative management would itself fail the convergent and discriminant validity tests. So many different interventions are mounted under this label that they appear to have only the most general kind of management philosophy in common. Moreover, participative management has no generally accepted set of "must do" management practices; the way participation is implemented in one organization often bears little resemblance to its use in another. Participative management, then, is the same kind of thing as TQM but is not as clean or distinctive conceptually.

The quality of worklife (QWL) movement, which peaked in prominence in the U.S. in the early 1980s, has many similarities to TQM (Lawler, 1986: 119-143). Both initiatives are rooted in identifiable philosophical positions and both have associated with them a specific set of interventions. The values of the QWL movement center on fostering labor-management cooperation to improve simultaneously productivity and the quality of employees' worklives. Key organizational devices in QWL include labor-management committees, surveys of employee satisfaction, and so on. QWL, like TQM, is a broad and multifaceted change effort that also passes the convergent validity test. But it clearly differs from TQM both in philosophy and in practice.

Our conclusion is that TQM does pass the discriminant validity test with reference to the writings of the TQM founders. But it is close to failing that test when one focuses on contemporary organizational practice. Many devices that are specifically eschewed by the founders are now commonly implemented in the name of TQM. And many practitioners now talk about "involvement" and "empowerment" as if they were synonymous with TQM and implement various employee involvement or empowerment interventions as part of a TQM package (Lawler, Mohrman, and Ledford, 1992). Thus, one can in 1995 still point with some confidence to the constellation of ideas and interventions that form the core of TQM, and one can, with less confidence, show how that constellation differs from others. At least for now, there is indeed a "there" there for TQM.

Measuring and Assessing TQM Activities and Outcomes

A full-fledged evaluation of a TQM program would include three distinct types of assessment. First is empirical demonstration that TQM has, in fact, been implemented, to confirm that it is TQM that is being assessed rather than, for example, some subset of the integrated TQM package, some related intervention, or some wholly different program that has been carried out using TQM rhetoric.

Second is determination of whether TQM alters how people work together to meet customer requirements. This analysis assesses *process criteria* of effectiveness—the degree to which the improvements in organizational functioning that are expected actually are observed. Finally comes assessment of *outcome criteria*—the degree to which improvements in bottom-line organizational effectiveness are found. It is important to examine both process and outcome criteria because, as scholars who study decision making know all too well, a capricious environment sometimes can intervene between process

and outcome in a way that turns behaviors that could not have been better into results that could hardly have been worse. As will be seen, empirical evaluation of TQM programs presents a significant challenge to researchers because what must be done to accomplish the three different assessments involves very different methods and analytic strategies.

Is It Really TQM?

To address substantive questions about the effects of TQM on organizations and their members, one must first establish that TQM actually has been installed. This is the organizational change equivalent of conducting a manipulation check in the research laboratory to ensure that the experimental intervention actually was implemented as intended. To accomplish this task in research on TQM, one would collect behavioral data to document that the five core features of TQM are in place. Specifically, (1) Are organization members assessing customer requirements and measuring performance against those requirements continuously? (2) Are suppliers chosen on the basis of quality, rather than solely on the basis of cost, and are organization members working with suppliers to improve suppliers' quality practices? (3) Are members operating interdependently, as teams, across traditional organizational functions, rather than independently or in ways that maintain functional separateness? (4) Are members using statistics and scientific reasoning to formulate and test hypotheses about work processes and strategies for performance improvement? and (5) Are members using process-management heuristics to enhance team problem solving and decision making? Research on TQM rarely addresses these questions, except for studies that focus on Baldrige Award-winning companies. Because application for that award involves careful inspection of actual quality practices, it is safe to assume that award winners actually have implemented the full TQM package (see Malcolm Baldrige National Quality Award Consortium, 1990).

More common is research that involves no attempt at all to assess the degree to which has been implemented: Of 99 papers about the effects of TQM published in academic and practitioner journals between 1989 and 1993, only 4 percent assessed the degree to which TQM interventions actually were in place. And even when "manipulation checks" were performed, they often involved inferences based on qualitative accounts of the evolution of a TQM program rather than on direct measurements of behavior (e.g., Fisher, 1992). Existing research findings about the effects of TQM on organizational performance, therefore, may be about programs that—although perhaps well-tailored to a given organization's needs— are not full-fledged implementations of TQM.[4]

What Are Its Effects on Work Processes?

The second challenge in research on TQM is to specify and collect data about those processes that would be expected to result from TQM and that should, all else being equal, contribute to organizational effectiveness. Considering group and organizational performance generally, without specific reference to TQM, Hackman (1987) has suggested three process criteria of unit effectiveness: (1) the level of *task-oriented effort* exhibited by unit members, (2) the amount of *knowledge and skill* members apply to their work, and (3) the appropriateness of the *task performance strategies* members use in carrying out the work. To the extent that a work unit has a high standing on these process criteria, the likelihood increases that its final product, service, or decision also will turn out well. To the extent that members exhibit insufficient effort, bring insufficient talent to bear on the work, or use task-inappropriate performance strategies, overall unit effectiveness is likely to suffer. Although these three process criteria are quite general and have been neither explicated nor endorsed by TQM scholars or practitioners, they might nonetheless be useful in assessing the impact of TQM interventions on work processes. We consider below the ways that a quality team's standing on each of the three criteria might be enhanced by TQM interventions.

Effort. Quality teams have challenging and significant work—specifically, collaborating to generate continuous improvement in meeting explicitly stated customer requirements—which motivation theory suggests should enhance collective effort. Moreover, use of the process-management techniques that are integral to TQM programs should decrease the degree to which effort is wasted through coordination losses and misdirection.

Knowledge and skill. TQM quality teams are composed of members from different functions, ensuring that there is more talent available for work on the collective task than would be the case for individuals operating on their own or in homogeneous teams whose members come exclusively from a single function or unit. Moreover, the use of statistical analyses and data-representation techniques should lessen the degree to which teams make decisions based on misapprehensions about the state of the work system. Finally, use of group process-management heuristics should enhance members' learning from one another, thereby increasing the total pool of talent available for the work. They also should decrease the likelihood that existing talent will be wasted, for example, by overlooking or inappropriately weighting the contributions of members who have special talent or insight.

Performance strategy. Task-performing teams sometimes head off in the wrong direction or go about their work in inefficient or inappropriate ways, merely because members are not entirely clear about what they are supposed to do or whom they are supposed to satisfy. Under TQM, these risks are minimized: Customers are specifically identified and their requirements are clearly explicated. Customer requirements provide an available and appropriate test for team members to use in inventing and choosing among alternative ways of proceeding with their work. Moreover, changes in those requirements can provide a clear signal that it is time to abandon or revise existing performance routines. The use of the process-management and problem-solving heuristics that are integral to the TQM package should increase the chances that members' deliberations about such matters will generate ways of generate ways of working together that are especially well-aligned with what customers want.

It appears, then, that these three process criteria—effort expended, knowledge and skill applied, and strategies used—may be of use in assessing the impact of TQM on how, and how well, organization members work together. If TQM is working as intended, organizational units should exhibit a high standing on all three of them.

Process criteria have the important advantage of being more accessible to reliable measurement than are outcome criteria. Moreover, assessing the process criteria allows researchers to check empirically the validity of TQM predictions about unit processes, for example, that TQM techniques help people work together more efficiently and productively. Yet process criteria—whether the three that we have mentioned or others—are almost never addressed in TQM research. Less than 15 percent of the studies of TQM programs that we examined document actual behavioral changes that occur after TQM has been adopted. And those that do address work behaviors rely on anecdotal descriptions of particular quality teams and their problem-solving processes. This oversight in TQM research has left a significant gap in knowledge about both the effects of TQM interventions and the means by which those effects are generated.

What Outcomes Are Obtained?

It is tempting to go for broke in research on the impact of interventions such as TQM, testing directly the relationship between the entire intervention package and global organizational outcomes. The logic is straightforward: Since TQM is supposed to enhance organizational effectiveness, then it should be a simple matter to determine whether organizations that use it improve on generally accepted performance measures. In fact, it is maddeningly difficult to do such research well, for several reasons.

First, there are serious measurement problems associated with even standard indices of firm performance such as market share, profitability, or stock price (Brief, 1984; Pennings, 1984; Kaplan and Norton, 1992); these prob-

lems are compounded for public and nonprofit organizations (Hage, 1984). One strategy for circumventing this difficulty is to obtain productivity measures at the individual or unit level and then to aggregate them across units. Such measures generally have psychometric problems of their own, however, and the link between individual and organizational productivity is far from straightforward (Goodman, Lerch, and Mukhopadhyay, 1994).

Second, as mentioned earlier, exogenous disturbances can significantly obscure the link between work processes and organizational outcomes. And even when a relationship does exist between intervention-induced process improvements and organizational outcomes, it may be so weak relative to other influences that it can be nearly impossible to confirm statistically unless one has a very large sample of organizations, which is unlikely in intervention research. Wruck and Jensen's (1994) study of the effects of TQM at Sterling Chemical provides a good case in point: Despite a TQM program that by all accounts was highly successful, measures of firm performance still exhibited a monotonic decline because of industry and market factors.

Third, temporal issues can obscure intervention-outcome relationships (Whetton and Cameron, 1994). There often is a discrepancy between short-term and long-term organizational results, and it is by no means straightforward to decide how long after an intervention one should wait before analyzing outcome measures. The longer one waits, the more opportunity TQM has to realize its effects on organization-wide results, but the more those results are open to confounding by other factors. Even longitudinal research that documents changes in outcome measures over time is of limited use in disentangling the effects of a focused intervention from those of other endogenous and exogenous changes.

Taken together, these three difficulties can make it nearly impossible to detect statistically the direct effects of TQM on global measures of organizational outcomes. As serious as these problems are, they are compounded by another, namely, the process by which attributions are made about the *reasons* for any observed performance changes. Every researcher knows that one cannot simply make an intervention, observe subsequent outcomes, and then conclude that any changes in the outcome measures were caused by the intervention. Many reports about TQM effects, however, do precisely that: TQM is implemented, unit productivity or organizational profitability improves, and it is concluded that TQM caused the improvement (e.g., Littman, 1991; Gilbert, 1992; Raffio, 1992). In fact, the observed gain could have been the result of other events that coincided temporally with the intervention, or by the phenomenon, sometimes referred to as the Hawthorne effect, of people working harder when they are being studied. But there is an even more prosaic explanation for performance improvements that are observed after introducing an organizational intervention such as TQM.

In a work unit that has been operating in business-as-usual mode for some time, inefficiencies and redundancies are likely to have gradually made that unit far less tight, lean, and efficient than it could be. Managers may select that unit as the target of an organizational change program—perhaps a quality intervention, perhaps something else. As managers and change agents begin to plan for implementation, they scrutinize the staffing, workflow, and internal organization of the unit in great detail, the first close look the unit has received in a long time. Any accumulated inefficiencies are likely to be noticed and, coincident with the intervention, corrected. If productivity improvements subsequently occur, it may seem obvious to those responsible for the change program that the favorable outcomes stemmed directly from the intervention. Although that may be true, the improvements may have resulted solely from the fat-trimming that accompanied, but was not integral to the intervention. Without appropriate control units and data on work processes as well as outcomes, there is no way to choose between the two explanations.

The research literature on TQM effects includes few studies whose designs permit definitive statements to be made about causes and effects. More than 80 percent of the published assessments of TQM describe what happened when the program was installed in one particu-

lar organization. The outcomes most frequently reported are (1) improvements in error rates, for example, "more accurate invoices" (Teresko, 1991), (2) decreased time needed to complete a process, for example, "assembly-line time decreased by 67 days" (McDonnell, 1992), and (3) dollar savings from process efficiencies, for example, "reduced laboratory turnaround time resulting in a $10,000 savings" (Koska, 1990). Such findings are consistent with the aims of TQM interventions, but the absence of appropriate research designs makes it impossible to attribute them directly to TQM.

Straightforward evaluation research that attempts to assess the effects of TQM on global measures of organizational effectiveness is fraught with both methodological difficulties and interpretative dangers. Although well-instrumented quasi-experimental studies can help with the design and measurement problems inherent in this type of research, not all of the problems can be solved. Still, the question that outcome-focused evaluation research studies seek to answer cannot be finessed: It *is* important to know whether TQM generates real organizational improvements. One way to gain purchase on this question is to return to the writings of the primary TQM authorities to extract their assertions about what is sought and expected from TQM programs and use those assertions as the primary criteria for assessing TQM outcomes. Deming, Ishikawa, and Juran are clear about what they expect TQM to achieve: (1) better performance in meeting customer requirements, (2) improved organizational performance capability, and (3) greater knowledge and work satisfaction on the part of organization members. Because these three outcomes are less vulnerable to the measurement and interpretive problems that plague global indices of firm-wide economic performance, they offer attractive options for research on TQM outcomes.

If TQM programs do increase the degree to which customer requirements are met and, in the process, improve the performance capability of the organization and the well-being of individual members, then global and economic measures of organizational effectiveness surely should improve over the long term as well. This prediction is stated explicitly by the TQM theorists whose work we have been reviewing, and it strikes us as entirely reasonable. Yet, for all the reasons discussed above, it may also be a prediction that can never be definitively confirmed in empirical research.

Conclusion

Research on the effects of TQM has focused largely on global outcomes. The results have been strongly positive, but they are almost all based on case reports. In part, this problem exists because TQM has captured more attention from practitioners than from researchers: Many assessments of TQM are descriptions written by a member of the focal organization. But if knowledge of the effects of TQM on organizational effectiveness is to cumulate, researchers must focus less on evaluation studies of the 30-percent-gain-in-productivity variety and more on research that includes both explicit manipulation checks and measurements of process criteria.

TQM practitioners are expected to focus their attention on work processes rather than on outcome measures and to use scientific methods to improve those processes continuously. These prescriptions rarely are applied to the study of TQM itself. It is ironic that the designs and methodologies used in research on TQM fall far short of the standards of research design, measurement, and analysis that would be required of organization members studying their own work processes under TQM.

Behavioral Processes Under TQM

To accomplish its purposes, TQM must alter how people actually behave at work. As suggested in the previous section, people should be working harder (i.e., with more effort), smarter (i.e., with greater knowledge and skill), and more responsively (i.e., with task performance strategies better attuned to customer requirements) under TQM than otherwise would be the case. Three behavioral processes are key to

achieving these aspirations: motivation, learning, and change.

Motivation

Deming and Ishikawa identify three different sources of human motivation at work. First is intrinsic motivation, the "joy of climbing a mountain just because it is there" (Ishikawa, 1985: 27) and, more generally, growing, learning, and developing one's self (Deming, 1986: 72-86). Second is task motivation, the good feeling that comes from accomplishing things and seeing them actually work (Ishikawa, 1985: 28; Deming, 1986: 72). Third is social motivation, the energy that comes from cooperating with others on a shared task and the incentive provided by recognition from others (Ishikawa, 1985: 28; Deming, 1986: 107).

How congruent are TQM interventions with its founders' propositions about motivation? In general, the fit is good. TQM provides people with opportunities to learn and to develop themselves through joint problem-solving efforts. Meeting clear and often challenging customer requirements and working to improve work processes continuously provide task challenges that should both test and stretch members' skills. And the insistent emphasis on teamwork and cross-functional relationships provides many opportunities for social interaction and social reinforcement. The fit between TQM practices and other motivational theories prominent in the organizational literature, however, is uneasy. Among the evidence we reviewed for the discriminant validity of TQM was the fact that TQM explicitly eschews a number of popular motivational devices, including work redesign (e.g., job enrichment), goal setting (e.g., management by objectives), and performance-contingent rewards (e.g., pay for performance). Although each of these interventions has been shown, in some circumstances, to enhance organization members' work motivation (Locke et al., 1980), all of them are in some significant way inconsistent with TQM theory and practice.

Work redesign. Work-redesign theory specifies that motivation is strengthened when the work itself is meaningful, when performers have considerable autonomy in determining the means by which it is accomplished, and when they receive regular, trustworthy knowledge about work outcomes (Hackman and Oldham, 1976). The first and third of these design specifications—meaningful work and knowledge of results—should be routinely present in TQM organizations. The tasks of meeting customer requirements and continuously improving processes are meaningful, and the emphasis on analyzing data about performance processes ensures that performers will be almost continuously aware of how they are doing.

The problem comes with the second design specification, autonomy about work methods. Under TQM, much energy is spent identifying the "best" work practices, those that bring work processes under the greatest possible control. Cross-functional teams undertake research projects to develop or identify such practices, managers do benchmarking visits to other organizations to learn about alternative ways of performing the work, and front-line employees are themselves expected to search continuously for improved and simplified work practices (Juran, 1969: 9-45; Ishikawa, 1985: 55-56; Deming, 1986: 49-52).

Once such practices are identified and documented, they are diffused throughout the organization and standardized, with the result that work-unit members may wind up with very little discretion about how they perform their tasks. The potential for overspecification of work procedures is so great that one is reminded of industrial engineering during the heyday of scientific management, when it was the job of process designers to identify the "one best way" to perform the work and the job of front-line producers to do the work precisely that way. The motivational costs of this approach are well documented (O'Toole, 1977; Hackman and Oldham, 1980).

Under TQM, standardized procedures are more likely to come from peers working on cross-functional quality teams than from industrial engineers. But it is not the source of the procedures that matters, nor is it the philosophy that lies behind their development and diffusion. What matters is the design of the work itself. TQM, along with other currently popular

reengineering initiatives, runs a risk of spawning a new version of old-time scientific management, complete with the human and organizational dysfunctions that prompted the job-enrichment corrective over two decades ago (Pallas and Neumann, 1993; Anderson, Rungtusanatham, and Schroeder, 1994; Spencer, 1994).

Some commentators dispute this view. Adler (1993), for example, interpreted findings from the NUMMI plant of General Motors-Toyota as showing that the motivational dysfunctions of standardized, routine, and repetitive tasks can be mitigated when workers are treated fairly and respectfully, provided with proper tools and training, and share in decision making about performance policies and standards. And Klein (1991, 1994) described how the loss of employee autonomy that accompanies standardization and process controls can be compensated for, to some extent, by greater collective autonomy about how tasks are designed in the first place.

The problem is that only a subset of the members of TQM organizations (often a small subset) have the opportunity to participate in the cross-functional quality teams that redesign tasks and develop improved work methods. Such teams typically do have ample autonomy in their work, sometimes even including the authority to implement the solutions they develop. Moreover, case reports document the energy, enthusiasm, and commitment exhibited by members of these teams. There remains, however, a pervasive and worrisome discrepancy between the motivationally engaging work of special TQM teams and the standardized work practices of those who perform the routine productive work of the organization.

Goal setting. Goal-setting theory predicts that motivation is greatest when performers focus their attention on achieving clear, specific, and challenging goals (Locke and Latham, 1990). Although research evidence generally supports these predictions, TQM authorities are ambivalent about both the appropriateness and the efficacy of setting specific goals in TQM programs. Deming is opposed: "The only number that is permissible for a manager to dangle in front of his people is a plain statement of fact with respect to survival . . . [such as] 'Unless our sales improve 10 per cent next year, we shall be out of business' " (Deming, 1986: 76). Explicit goals, he says, narrow performers' vision and implicitly invite them to slack off once a goal is achieved. Ishikawa, by contrast, views challenging goals as appropriate so long as they are about solving particular problems and are established in such a way as to allow cooperation among functions (Ishikawa, 1985: 60-61).

It is not surprising that there is disagreement among the TQM authorities about goal setting, because the nature of the work done by quality teams raises some complex issues about how goals and objectives are properly framed. Under TQM, the analysis of work processes focuses attention on deviant cases, the ones indicating that a work process is, to some extent, out of control. This emphasis on failures rather than successes also is evident in the language of TQM: One talks about the 1 percent of the cases for which existing processes did not work rather than the 99 percent of the cases for which they did (Ishikawa, 1985: 61-62; Juran, 1988: 130-132). Moreover, TQM methods help team members identify that subset of the 1 percent that represents the most pernicious or frequent problems so that they can be taken care of first, before moving on to the next most consequential problems. Both the work and the talk are more about problems than about successes.

Some commentators, such as Wruck and Jensen (1994: 271-272), have found value in this problem-focused approach. They noted that both managers and front-line employees exhibit a remarkable tendency to ignore or dismiss problems and mistakes, which usually results in a gradual erosion of organizational performance. Because TQM insistently focuses attention on the things that must be fixed, it can partially reverse the natural human tendency turn away from signs of trouble. But we also know that and challenging goals can engender levels of work motivation that rarely are observed when people are occupied mainly with things that are not going right (Conger and Kanungo, 1988; Locke and Latham, 1990). How might these two positions be reconciled? Clearly, there is a balance to be achieved between look-

ing at the dark and the bright sides of work processes. We need to know considerably more than we do at present about how that balance can best be managed in the context of TQM philosophy and practice.

Pay for performance. There is abundant research evidence about both the motivational benefits and the risks of basing compensation and other extrinsic rewards on measured performance. In contrast to their ambivalent views about the value of goal setting, TQM authorities are clear and decisive about basing pay on performance: Do not do it. The arguments they marshal to support their position are, in general, the same ones that have been well documented in the organizational and economic research literatures. One, organizations do get what they pay for, but sometimes they get only that (Kerr, 1975). Two, specific outcomes that are rewarded can become so salient that performers risk losing sight of the larger picture, for example, whom the organization exists to serve or what principles are supposed to guide provision of that service. Three, performance-contingent extrinsic rewards can undermine performers' intrinsic motivation (Deci, 1971). Four, reward systems that place people in competition for rewards that are distributed from a fixed pool not only divert performers' attention from customers' needs but also undermine relationships among members and make it difficult for them to work together on the collective tasks that are the organization's real work. Five, rewards necessarily are based on some measure, but few measures approximate the full dimensionality of the contributions that really are needed from organization members (Ishikawa, 1985: 25-28; Deming, 1986: 102).

Many TQM organizations avoid all of these problems in a single stroke. They avoid performance-contingent extrinsic rewards entirely and rely on intrinsic motivation. This solution, however, has significant opportunity costs. The best motivational state of affairs is obtained when an organization does not rely exclusively on either intrinsic or extrinsic rewards but, instead, structures the work in a way that fosters intrinsic motivation (for example, by providing challenge, autonomy, and direct feedback from customers) and then supports that positive motivation with performance-contingent extrinsic rewards. As recent findings of Amabile (1993) show, the supposed trade-off between intrinsic and extrinsic motivation is neither as straightforward nor as general as sometimes has been claimed. It is, in fact, possible to structure work and reward systems to promote both types of motivation simultaneously (Wageman, 1995). In TQM organizations, however, it is much easier to accomplish that for managerial staff, who have considerable autonomy, than for rank-and-file employees who, in their regular work, have little (Waldman, 1994).

TQM authorities acknowledge that social reinforcement, which is extrinsic, can enhance the motivation of organization members, and they do suggest that organization-wide gain-sharing or profit-sharing programs can appropriately be used to recognize and reward collective excellence (Juran, 1974: 18.19; Ishikawa, 1985: 26-27). If this can be done at the organizational level, then there would seem to be no conceptual reason to conclude that it could not also be done at the group level. A system in which rewards were contingent on gains in performance (such as bringing work processes increasingly under control), for example, would seem to fit rather nicely with the TQM philosophy of continuous improvement. The no-extrinsic-rewards principle, then, may be more an ideological stance of the TQM authorities than the result of reasoned conceptual judgment. Clearly, further thought and research is warranted on how, in TQM programs, one can capture simultaneously the benefits of both intrinsic and extrinsic rewards.

The motivational basis of TQM practices is generally sound. It is true that a number of positive sources of motivation are overlooked or forgone and that, by diffusing standardized "best practices" throughout the organization, members' regular work may be less well designed motivationally than it could be. Still, organizations that follow TQM practices should not fall victim to the known dysfunctions of poorly conceived or poorly implemented motivational programs. An interesting possibility is to find ways that TQM organizations can do a better job of having their motivational cake and eating it too—that is, of retaining the consider-

able motivational benefits that are built into orthodox TQM while also harvesting the motivational gains that can derive from well-designed work, from specific, challenging performance objectives, and from the use of extrinsic rewards to recognize and reinforce extraordinary accomplishment.

Learning

TQM is pro-learning, with a vengeance. The movement's founders note, correctly, that people inherently want to learn and develop. They also point out that this inclination is fragile, that it can be undermined by social systems that create fear and defensiveness. And even though the inclination to learn is built in, people also require tools and coaching if they are to express that inclination in their work behavior.

TQM practices create good learning environments both by minimizing fear in the organizational culture and by providing members with a rich and diverse set of learning tools. Moreover, TQM exposes workers to data about their work processes more or less continuously and encourages them to use scientific methods to analyze and improve those processes. Finally, members of TQM organizations are asked to reexamine their work processes repeatedly, and do so with no holds barred: "Ask not just why we do it that way and can we do it better, but also ask why we do that at *all*" (Juran, 1969: 118). In Argyris and Schon's (1978) terms, people in TQM organizations are expected to do double-loop as well as single-loop learning.

There are two quite different varieties of human learning. One variety, that on which TQM philosophy is based, is the wired-in human inclination to grow and develop in competence. This inclination is well known to anyone who has observed the joy experienced by very young children as they learn to pull themselves to a standing position in their cribs, take their first unsupported steps, or use language to express their wishes and feelings. The other variety is the robust but often-overlooked capacity of human organisms to adapt to the many problems that life inevitably brings. The human organism is capable of learning to make do even under conditions of profound disappointment and adversity, such as losing a spouse, a limb, or a means of livelihood.

These two opposing inclinations—to stretch and grow, and to adapt and make do—are present in all of us. Schools and work organizations are among the most important settings in which these opposing varieties of learning are engaged and played out. Experiences in these organizations have large and enduring effects on one's personality, intellectual style, and orientation toward future learning (Kohn and Schooler, 1978; Schooler, 1984). Sometimes the result is a life of continuous and ever-escalating growth and learning; other times it is a life characterized mainly by adaptation and acceptance of one's lot.

An excessive emphasis on either type of learning can be dysfunctional. Too strong an orientation toward adaptation can result in what commonly has been found in survey studies of job satisfaction at highly controlling organizations. People report on the surveys that they are satisfied, but closer analysis reveals that such "satisfaction" mainly expresses their acceptance of a life bereft of opportunities for career and personal growth. Growth-oriented learning has atrophied for such people, and their organizations are obtaining but a small portion of what they actually have to offer. Too strong an orientation toward personal growth and development also is sometimes observed in work organizations, especially those that are driven by humanistic, democratic, or spiritual ideologies. Members of such organizations may be encouraged to pursue their personal aspirations to such an extent that the capability of the organization to mount efficient collective action is compromised, eventually threatening its very survival.

How well do TQM organizations succeed in providing a balance between these two varieties of learning—at promoting continuous personal learning, but of a type and in a way that also generates efficient and effective collective performance? To address this question, we examine TQM learning processes in three arenas: (1) learning from one another in cross-functional quality and problem-solving teams, (2) learning about ways to improve work processes and performance, and (3) learning about what the collectivity *should* be doing—the double-loop learning espoused by Argyris and Schon (1978).

Learning from one another. The cross-functional quality teams that are among the hallmarks of TQM organizations stack the cards in favor of learning by the simple fact that they *are* cross-functional; individual members are exposed to more, and more diverse, points of view than would be the case if they worked mostly by themselves or in within-function units. Moreover, the group-process heuristics that teams are taught increase the chances that this built-in talent will be used well. Members are likely to learn, for example, how to solicit the contributions of quiet or recalcitrant members and how to weight the contributions of members in accord with their actual knowledge and expertise rather than on the basis of task-irrelevant factors such as demographic attributes or interpersonal style. Moreover, the group-process techniques teams use increase the chances that, over time, members will actively teach and learn from one another, thereby increasing the total pool of knowledge and skill available for the team's work. In all, TQM receives excellent marks for the ways and the extent to which it fosters interpersonal learning.

Learning about work processes. TQM strategies for learning about work processes rely heavily on numerical data (which are to be viewed as friendly even when they point to disconcerting trends), analyzed and interpreted using scientific and statistical tools (which are viewed as providing protection against human distortions and biases). There is reason for concern about both the sufficiency of the tools and the readiness of the people who use them to accept what the data show. Even in the institution of science, where scientific norms and tools are far more robust than the learning devices used in work organizations, scientists sometimes exhibit behaviors that are oriented more toward succeeding than toward learning. Data sometimes are collected in ways that virtually ensure that the scientist's hypothesis will be supported. Scientists sometimes continue to advocate favored theories despite the ready availability of disconfirming data. And some scientists even have been known to falsify data to make things come out the way they want them to. Merely focusing on data, and analyzing them using scientific and statistical tools, is insufficient to ensure the validity of the conclusions reached—even in science itself.

That more than just science is needed is shown by Edmondson's (1995) findings about quality-improvement efforts at a large teaching hospital. Among the data collected in hospital patient-care units were instances of drug-related errors—occasions when patients received the wrong drug, the wrong dose, or the right drug at the wrong time. Although unfortunate for the patient, such events provided friendly data for use by unit members in analyzing what went wrong and developing strategies to keep it from happening again. Edmondson found, however, that the degree to which those data were used—or errors were even *recorded*—depended on the kind of leadership provided by the unit's nurse manager. Units whose manager had a hands-on, supportive style reported far more errors than did units with more distant and stringent managers. Close analysis of this disconcerting finding showed that it derived not from any laxity on the part of the hands-on managers but, instead, from the fact that staff in those managers' units were far more willing to treat error data as friendly, and therefore to record them, than were staff in units led by more evaluative nurse managers.

Even in TQM organizations, data and scientific tools can be rendered impotent if systems, or leaders, put winning or succeeding ahead of learning. For this reason, the movement we have seen toward increasing use of performance-contingent financial incentives in TQM organizations is worrisome. The more potent those incentives are (and, to be effective, they should be as potent as managers can make them), the more likely it is that organization members will abandon the appropriate use of data and scientific methods in order to obtain them. Also troubling is the fact that implementations of TQM increasingly are giving only lip service to the use of scientific and statistical tools. Together, these developments raise concerns about the future role of scientific methods—which unquestionably are among the most distinctive features of TQM philosophy—in actual TQM practice.

Learning about collective goals. To learn how to improve work processes is single-loop learning: The means by which organizational purposes are accomplished are open to analysis and improvement but the purposes themselves are not. To inquire about collective purposes, however, involves double-loop learning: The focus is on what is being done as well as how it is being done. Neither the philosophy nor the practice of total quality management draws significantly on members' ideas or experiences about collective purposes. TQM is a single-loop, top-down undertaking that seeks to provide those on the front line with the direction, the tools, and the coaching that they require to serve the enterprise well. It is noteworthy that the quotation given earlier from Juran (that one should ask not just about doing it better, but also "why we do that at *all*") was directed specifically to managers, not to rank-and-file workers.

Some commentators suggest that TQM achieves an appropriate balance between managerial control and employee participation, between single- and double-loop learning. In contrast to devices such as quality circles, it is argued, TQM institutionalizes meaningful employee participation even as it retains top-down managerial control of the enterprise (Hill, 1991). Still, some organization members are likely to chafe at the uncompromising top-down orientation of TQM. In response, managers may find themselves tempted to engage in pseudo-participation: Members are invited to join in discussions about decisions that already have been made or that will be made by someone else. Pseudo-participation is ill-advised, because people almost always are able to tell when they are being manipulated. A far preferable stance, in our view, is for managers to be unapologetic about the fact that TQM neither espouses nor practices the engagement of all organization members in reflective learning about collective purposes.

Overall, TQM is about as learning-oriented as it is possible for a management program to be. Even so, there are many reports in the case literature on TQM of learning failures and of antilearning group norms developing. It may be that such reports come mainly from organizations in which TQM has been implemented incompletely or incompetently. It may be that the previous organizational experiences of members have left a residue of antilearning habits and attitudes so strong that it cannot be penetrated even by all of the pro-learning tools and supports that well-implemented TQM provides. Perhaps enduring systemic forces—such as an organization's top-down orientation, emphasis on control, or focus on success above all else—overwhelms learning-oriented TQM tools and practices. Or it may be that general cultural norms about learning (for example, that it is done in school but not at work) are sometimes too strong for TQM to counter.

All these possibilities, and others, merit consideration as explanations for those instances in which a learning orientation does not blossom even in TQM organizations. Yet we should not be too hard on TQM practitioners for not fully succeeding in realizing this part of the movement's philosophy. As Argyris (1993), Senge (1990), and others have noted, it is extremely difficult to create and sustain a thorough-going learning orientation in purposive enterprises. Clearly, there is both opportunity and need for research on how to create social systems in which learning and production go hand in hand (Sitkin, Sutcliffe, and Schroeder, 1994). Organizations in which TQM has been well and fully implemented provide a high platform for continuing the process of learning about learning in social systems.

Change

Under TQM, organization members are expected to improve work processes continuously so that their customers are served as well as possible. This can result in performance strategies uniquely well tailored to environmental constraints and resources, especially those emanating from customers. It is one of the great strengths of the TQM approach. But what happens when the environment changes? Ideally, organizational units would be so closely in touch with the environment—including process innovations introduced by other organizations as well as changes in customers' needs—that they could adapt their performance strategies with little lag and, perhaps, even stay a step or two ahead of customers' wishes. This level of responsiveness, however, is unusual even in TQM organizations where continuous improvement is a core value and organizational policies and practices are specifically tailored to foster responsiveness to environmental changes.

The difficulties encountered by TQM units in responding to exogenous changes are of two types—one rooted in how people process information, the other in their tendency to develop emotional commitment to locally invented ways of operating.

Information processing. Once an individual, a group, or an organization develops a strategy for handling a certain kind of problem, that strategy is likely to become a standard routine, what we call, at the individual level, a habit (March and Simon, 1958; Gersick and Hackman, 1990; Louis and Sutton, 1991). Routines contribute enormously to the efficiency of daily life. Over time, however, they can become so integral to social systems that members continue to rely on them even when the situation changes markedly. In Langer's (1989) terms, individuals and groups tend to go about their work mindlessly, which can result in nificant performance decrements when environmental opportunities and constraints change.

Moreover, when members do discover that things are not working as well as they did formerly, they commonly respond by executing their existing behavioral routines more vigorously than ever, rather than using the early signs of trouble as an occasion for reflection on the adequacy of those routines. The individual-level dynamics of this phenomenon are well known. A state of arousal increases the likelihood that one's dominant response (the one highest in the hierarchy of possible responses) will be exhibited with minimal cognitive mediation. Similar dynamics are observed at the group and organizational levels of analysis: Under arousing conditions (of which learning that standard routines are no longer generating hoped-for results is an instance), performers are as likely to exhibit those routines with even greater vigor as they are to inspect, reflect upon, and reconsider them (Staw, Sandelands, and Dutton, 1981; Ocasio, 1995).

Emotional commitment. The second impediment to responsiveness is rooted more in emotionality than in efficiency. When a work unit has invented its own performance strategy—which certainly is more characteristic of TQM organizations than of those with traditional management hierarchies—members can become quite reluctant to change it. The research literature is filled with cases in which a group or organization had ample data showing that strategic change was called for, but performers either ignored those data, dismissed them as irrelevant, or engaged in manifestly irrational behaviors to avoid having to deal with them (Janis, 1982; Argyris, 1993). Only when the situation gets so bad that it threatens the unit's very survival (at which time it may be too late to recover) can one count on a social system taking seriously the need to make significant change (Miller and Friesen, 1980; Jensen, 1993).

Both processes sketched above contribute to the difficulties work units have in altering their performance strategies in response to environmental change. Moreover, the likelihood of responsive change may be lessened under precisely those circumstances in which change is needed most (Miller, 1993). There are exceptions, of course. Some groups and organizations do manage to stay even with, or even ahead of, changes in their environments. Some even welcome signs of trouble and use them as occasions for innovation rather than as a time to dig in their heels and do more of what has always been done. Still, the tendency to hold onto familiar, locally invented performance strategies appears to be nearly as pervasive as it is pernicious.

TQM organizations should be more likely than most to transcend the limitations of human information processing and emotionality in responding to environmental change. The learning orientation of TQM organizations, their commitment to management by fact, and their close links with customers should increase the likelihood that members will attend to unsettling data before they become too threatening to deal with. Moreover, TQM units are especially likely to encounter the conditions that Gersick and Hackman (1990) have identified as those that prompt inspection and reconsideration of habitual routines, such as having to deal with novelty, receiving an external intervention, or coming to terms with structural alterations of the performing unit. Even so, the challenge of altering performance strategies—especially those that have been locally invented—is a significant one for TQM organizations. Precisely because of their orientation to learning, data, and customers, such organizations should be a fruitful site for research that identifies and explores alternative ways of meeting that challenge.

Prospects for TQM

Although dinner may seem assured to a snake who notices a rabbit strolling nearby, there is no guarantee of nourishment. If the rabbit is extraordinarily large, it may get stuck in the snake's throat; snakes have, on occasion, died when their eyes were too large for their throat. And if the rabbit is just a baby, consumption and digestion are easy, but there is little real nourishment. Eating a baby rabbit is hardly worth the trouble it takes to catch it.

Organizational change programs, including TQM, can go wrong for the same two reasons that snakes sometimes have trouble with their dinners. One, the changes may be so ambitious and involve such fundamental alterations of the social system that, for all their potential merit, the organization cannot accommodate to them. Espoused changes may appear to fail when in fact they never got implemented. Two, the changes may be more window-dressing than real, as in a program that exhorts people to alter their behavior but that requires managers to do little other than issue the exhortation. In this case, implementation is easy, but the old organizational structures and systems remain untouched and continue to generate the same behavioral dynamics as before.

When implemented fully and well, TQM can thread its way between these two extremes (Reger et al., 1994). TQM changes are real rather than ephemeral, and they are generally consistent with research evidence about the factors that promote performance effectiveness. When TQM does tilt toward one or the other extreme, it invariably is toward interventions that are too modest. The reason is that TQM, by philosophy and design, skirts four features of work systems that are fundamental to organizational behavior and performance: (1) how front-line work is structured, (2) how gains are allocated, (3) how opportunities for learning are apportioned, and (4) how authority is distributed. For TQM, the aspiration is to implement changes that are substantial enough to make a real difference without altering the core premises of the enterprise—in effect, to achieve fundamental change without changing the fundamentals.[5] This aspiration presents practitioners with a series of troublesome dilemmas, the resolution of which often results in changes that are less risky, but also far less impactful, than would have been the case had the fundamentals been addressed frontally.

Design of work. Cross-functional quality teams and task forces are among the most common features of TQM organizations, and the work of such teams is usually quite well designed motivationally. By contrast, much less attention is given to the design of the work of front-line producers. Aside from the opportunity some employees have to work on quality teams or to perform support activities of the type formerly done by organization staff, the motivational structure of front-line jobs is unaltered in many, perhaps most, TQM implementations:

> *Dilemma 1:* Motivating front-line organization members toward continuous improvement and the highest quality of output—but doing so without fundamentally changing the motivational structure of their work.

Allocation of gains. TQM philosophy is explicit that extrinsic rewards, including pay, should not be contingent on measured individual or team performance. This stance leaves some

powerful motivational cards on the table. It is, moreover, unstable over the longer term. When workers perceive that they are contributing more to the organization than they did previously, their initial response may be pride and pleasure. That may suffice for a while. Eventually, however, members of profit-making firms will realize that *somebody* is making more money as a result of their greater contributions, and it is not them. At that point, they may begin to withdraw their commitment to the enterprise, and signs of a motivational backlash may even be seen:

> *Dilemma 2:* Creating the kind of alignment with, and commitment to, organizational purposes that can come from sharing in collective gains—but doing so without actually altering how organizational rewards are apportioned.

Opportunities for learning. The TQM aspiration of continuous improvement in meeting customer requirements is supported by a thorough-going learning orientation, including substantial investments in training and the widespread use of statistical and interpersonal techniques designed to promote individual and team learning. This orientation extends even beyond the organization's boundaries, as is seen in programs to teach quality practices to suppliers and in benchmarking visits to capture the best of other organizations' ideas and innovations.

Although front-line employees are encouraged to find ever-better ways to accomplish their assigned tasks, they are not invited to reflect on the purposes their work serves. Moreover, once something has been discovered that improves work practices—whether from the deliberations of a quality team, from benchmarking, or from a front-line work unit—then that improvement is likely to be identified as a best practice that everyone is expected to follow. Learning is indeed a core value in TQM organizations, but there are nontrivial constraints on what is to be learned about, who is to do the learning, and when learning should be set aside in favor of performing:

> *Dilemma 3:* Achieving continuous learning by front-line organization members—while also requiring them to adhere closely to standard-

ized best practices that have been developed by quality teams or imported from other organizations.

Distribution of authority. Consistent with Deming's position that it is *management's* job to create the systems within which employees do their work, the distribution of authority in organizations typically does not change much when TQM is implemented. Senior managers make the initial decision to adopt TQM and then manage its diffusion throughout the organization. They legitimize in advance the creation of all cross-functional quality teams and task forces. And they decide which of the ideas generated by those teams will actually be adopted. Keeping authority centralized reduces the risk that chaos will develop as various teams and task forces simultaneously come up with potentially incompatible work processes. And a clear, top-down chain of command surely makes it easier to secure the cooperation of middle managers when TQM itself is implemented, since they need not worry about their own authority being eroded.

The TQM founders also note, however, that those who will have to implement solutions to problems should be actively involved in analyzing and solving those problems. This principle is most evident in the widespread use of cross-functional teams to generate improved work methods, but sometimes it also is seen in widespread consultations with front-line workers about other organizational practices. As shown by Graham (1993), there is in many TQM organizations a chasm between front-line workers' involvement and accountability, on the one hand, and their actual decision-making authority, on the other:

> *Dilemma 4:* Empowering organization members to be full participants in achieving collective purposes—but doing so without threatening top-down managerial control of the enterprise.

If radical changes in the design of work, the allocation of rewards, the structure of learning opportunities, and the distribution of authority were included as part of the basic TQM imple-

mentation package, then the chances of successful installation certainly would diminish. There are powerful people in virtually every organization who have strong personal or political stakes in keeping those four fundamentals intact. Moreover, radical changes can challenge employees' beliefs about organizational premises to such an extent that they may be unable to comprehend and accommodate to them (Reger et al., 1994). Prospects for the long-term success of those programs that *did* get implemented, however, might well be higher.

We suspect that the TQM authorities to whom we have been referring throughout this commentary would disagree that more radical changes would bring greater success. The strength of TQM, they might counter, is precisely that its prescriptions, as demanding and substantial as they are, are not too radical to be installed in everyday organizations. And when they are installed, the chances are excellent that significant improvements will develop in the organization's viability as a work system, in its contributions to the broader community, and in the learning and well-being of individual members.

These are significant outcomes, and we concur that they are well worth the expenditure of time and energy to achieve. It is with regret, therefore, that we conclude our commentary with a relatively gloomy projection about the future of total quality management. TQM, in our view, is far more likely gradually to lose the prominence and popularity it now enjoys than it is to revolutionize organizational practice. We see three worrisome trends, none of which, ironically, has anything to do with the quality of the ideas that were set forth by the TQM founders.

Trend one. Rhetoric is winning out over substance. The rhetoric of TQM is engaging, attractive, and consistent with both the managerial *Zeitgeist* in the United States and this country's preference for organizational solutions that smack of rationality. These features surely have aided TQM implementations and helped fuel its rapid contagion across organizations (March, 1981: 565). The problem is that what many organizations are actually implementing is a pale or highly distorted version of what Deming, Ishikawa, and Juran laid out. This problem is so serious that it shaped the organization of this commentary: Had we attempted to organize our thoughts exclusively around contemporary TQM practice rather than use the philosophy and prescriptions of the TQM founders as our point of departure, it would have been impossible to write. In too many TQM programs, moreover, it is the difficult-to-implement portions of the program that are being finessed or ignored and the rhetoric that is being retained. Science is fading, the slogans are staying, and the implications are worrisome.

Trend two. An astonishing number of other interventions, some related to TQM and some not, are increasingly being herded under the TQM banner. In one or another book or article, virtually every intervention ever tried by an organization development consultant has been specified as something that is supposed to be done as part of TQM. The most frequently chosen add-on interventions (such as group-level performance-contingent rewards, work redesign, and empowerment programs) may reflect, in part, practitioners' struggles to deal with the four dilemmas discussed above. That the sharp and defining edges of a management program become blurred as more and more initiatives are launched in its name is, if not inevitable, at least a sign of that program's popularity and acceptance. But by destroying the distinctiveness of orthodox TQM, the entire approach is put at risk. For TQM, this is occurring at the hands of the very people who view themselves as the movement's best friends and most committed advocates.

Trend three. Research is not providing the corrective function for TQM that it could and should. There is plenty of room for additional learning, driven by research, on how TQM theory and practice could be improved. As we pointed out earlier, the conduct of such research is entirely consistent with the continuous-improvement idea prominent in TQM philosophy. But we researchers have not been carrying our

share of the load: Too much of the TQM literature consists of anecdotal case reports or simplistic before-and-after evaluation studies that may be of more use politically in promoting TQM (or, for skeptics, in debunking it) than they are in building knowledge about TQM processes and practices.

Total quality management as articulated by Deming, Ishikawa, and Juran is a set of powerful interventions wrapped in a highly attractive package. When implemented well, TQM can help an organization improve itself and, in the process, better serve its community and its own members. If TQM is to prosper, however, rhetorical excesses will have to be kept in better check than they are at present, and researchers will have to do a better job of illuminating the mechanisms through which TQM practices realize their effects. For only if the continuous improvement idea comes to apply to TQM itself will this provocative philosophy have a chance of sustaining itself over time.

Notes

1. We do not provide here a comprehensive review of the large and rapidly growing literature on TQM. For a sampling, see Jablonski (1992), Krishnan et al. (1993), Sashkin and Kiser (1993), and the July 1994 special issue of the *Academy of Management Review* (vol. 19, no. 3) on "total quality."

2. For findings from surveys of U.S. organizations about their TQM practices, see Conference Board (1991), Delta Consulting Group (1993), KPMG Peat Marwick (1991), and Lawler, Mohrman, and Ledford (1992). Neither these surveys nor this commentary address differences between TQM practices in the U.S. and other countries.

3. This is a characteristically psychological approach, which is consistent with our own backgrounds. For an excellent analysis from the perspective of economics, see Wruck and Jensen (1994); for one from the perspective of sociology, see Zbaracki (1994); and for one from the perspective of management theory, see Anderson, Rungtusanatham, and Schroeder (1994).

4. This problem is not unique to TQM. Frank and Hackman (1975) empirically documented the same difficulty in evaluations of the impact of job-enrichment programs.

5. Grant, Shani, and Krishnan (1994) provide an alternative view: that TQM is a revolutionary philosophy that does require fundamental changes in the very premises of an organization.

References

Adler, Paul S.
1993 "Time and motion regained." Harvard Business Review, 71(1): 97-108.

Amabile, Teresa M.
1993 "Motivational synergy: Toward new conceptualizations of intrinsic and extrinsic motivation in the workplace." Human Resource Management Review, 3: 185-201.

Anderson, John C., Manus Rungtusanatham, and Roger G. Schroeder
1994 "A theory of quality management underlying the Deming management method." Academy of Management Review, 19: 472-509.

Argyris, Chris
1993 Knowledge for Action. San Francisco: Jossey-Bass.

Argyris, Chris, and Donald A. Schon
1978 Organizational Learning. Reading, MA: Addison-Wesley.

Brief, Arthur P. (ed.)
1984 Productivity Research in the Behavioral and Social Sciences. New York: Praeger.

Campbell, Donald T., and Donald W. Fiske
1959 "Convergent and discriminant validation by the multitrait-multimethod matrix." Psychological Bulletin, 56: 81-105.

Conference Board
1991 Employee Buy-in to Total Quality. New York: Conference Board.

Conger, Jay A., and Rabindra N. Kanungo (eds.)
1988 Charismatic Leadership: The Elusive Factor in Organizational Effectiveness. San Francisco: Jossey-Bass.

Crosby, Philip B.
1989 Let's Talk Quality. New York: McGraw-Hill.

Deci, Edward L.
1971 "Effects of externally-mediated rewards on intrinsic motivation." Journal of Personality and Social Psychology, 18: 105-115.

Delta Consulting Group
1993 Ten Years After: Learning about Total Quality Management. New York: Delta Consulting Group.

Deming, W. Edwards
1986 Out of the Crisis. Cambridge, MA: MIT Center for Advanced Engineering Study.

Deming, W. Edwards
1993 The New Economics for Industry, Government, Education. Cambridge, MA: MIT Center for Advanced Engineering Study.

Edmondson, Amy C.
1995 "Learning from mistakes is easier said than done: Group and organizational influences on detection and correction of human error." Unpublished manuscript, Dept. of Psychology, Harvard University.

Fisher, Thomas J.
1992 "The impact of quality management on productivity." International Journal of Quality and Reliability Management, 9: 44-52.

Frank, Linda L., and J. Richard Hackman
1975 "A failure of job enrichment: The case of the change that wasn't." Journal of Applied Behavioral Science. 11: 413-436.

Gersick, Connie J. G., and J. Richard Hackman
1990 "Habitual routines in task-performing groups." Organizational behavior and Human Decision Processes, 47: 65-97.

Gilbert, James D.
1992 "TQM flops: A chance to learn from the mistakes of others." National Productivity Review, 11: 491-499.

Goodman, Paul S., F. Javier Lerch, and Tridas Mukhopadhyay
1994 "Individual and organizational productivity: Linkages and processes." In Douglas H. Harris (ed.), Organizational Linkages: Understanding the Productivity Paradox: 54-80. Washington, DC: National Academy Press.

Graham, Laurie
1993 "Inside a Japanese transplant: A critical perspective." Work and Occupations, 20: 147-193.

Grant, Robert M., Rami Shani, and R. Krishnan
1994 "TQM's challenge to management theory and practice." Sloan Management Review, 36(Winter): 25-35.

Hackman, J. Richard
1987 "The design of work teams." In Jay W. Lorsch (ed.), Handbook of Organizational Behavior: 315-342. Englewood Cliffs, NJ: Prentice Hall.

Hackman, J. Richard, and Greg R. Oldham
1976 "Motivation through the design of work: Test of a theory." Organizational Behavior and Human Performance, 60: 159-170.

Hackman, J. Richard, and Greg R. Oldham
1980 Work Redesign. Reading, MA: Addison-Wesley.

Hage, Jerald
1984 "Organizational theory and the concept of productivity." In Arthur P. Brief (ed.), Productivity Research in the Behavioral and Social Sciences: 91-126. New York: Praeger.

Hayes, Robert H., and William J. Abernathy
1980 "Managing our way to economic decline." Harvard Business Review, 58(4): 67-77.

Hill, Stephen
1991 "Why quality circles failed but Total Quality Management might succeed." British Journal of Industrial Relations, 29: 541-568.

Ishikawa, Kaoru
1985 What is Total Quality Control? The Japanese Way. Englewood Cliffs, NJ: Prentice Hall.

Jablonski, Joseph R.
1992 Implementing TQM: Competing in the Nineties through Total Quality Management, 2nd ed. San Diego: Pfeiffer.

Janis, Irving L.
1982 Victims of Groupthink, 2nd ed. Boston: Houghton Mifflin.

Jensen, Michael C.
1993 "The modern industrial revolution, exit, and the

failure of internal control systems." Journal of Finance, 48: 831-880.

Juran, Joseph M.
1969 Managerial Breakthrough: A New Concept of the Manager's Job. New York: McGraw-Hill.

Juran, Joseph M.
1974 The Quality Control Handbook, 3rd ed. New York: McGraw-Hill.

Juran, Joseph M.
1988 Juran on Planning for Quality. New York: Free Press.

Kaplan, Robert S., and David P. Norton
1992 "The balanced scorecard: Measures that drive performance." Harvard Business Review, 70(1): 71-79.

Kerr, Steven
1975 "On the folly of rewarding A while hoping for B." Academy of Management Journal, 18: 769-783.

Klein, Janice A.
1991 "A reexamination of autonomy in light of new manufacturing practices." Human Relations, 44: 21-38.

Klein, Janice A.
1994 "The paradox of quality management: Commitment, ownership, and control." In Charles Heckscher and Anne Donnellon (eds.), The Post-Bureaucratic Organization: New Perspectives on Organizational Change: 178-194. Thousand Oaks, CA: Sage.

Kohn, Marvin L., and Carmi Schooler
1978 "The reciprocal effects of the substantive complexity of work and intellectual flexibility: A longitudinal assessment." American Journal of Sociology, 84: 24-52.

Koska, Mary T.
1990 "Case study: Quality improvement in a diversified health center." Hospitals, 64: 38-39.

KPMG Peat Marwick
1991 Quality Improvement Initiatives through the Management of Human Resources. Short Hills, NJ: KPMG Peat Marwick.

Krishnan, R., A. B. (Rami) Shani, R. M. Grant and R. Baer
1993 "In search of quality improvement: Problems of design and implementation." Academy of Management Executive, 7(4): 7-20.

Langer, Ellen J.
1989 "Minding matters: The mindlessness/mindfulness theory of cognitive activity." In Leonard Berkowitz (ed.), Advances in Experimental Social Psychology: 137-173. New York: Academic Press.

Lawler, Edward E., III
1986 High-Involvement Management. San Francisco: Jossey-Bass.

Lawler, Edward E., III
1994 "Total Quality Management and employee involvement: Are they compatible?" Academy of Management Executive, 8(1): 68-76.

Lawler, Edward E., III, Susan Albers Mohrman, and Gerald E. Ledford, Jr.
1992 Employee Involvement and Total Quality Management: Practices and Results in Fortune 1000 Companies. San Francisco: Jossey-Bass.

Littman, Ian D.
1991 "A partner in excellence." Quality, 31: Q11-Q12.

Locke, E. A., D. B. Feren, V. M. McCaleb, K. N. Shaw, and A. T. Denny
1980 "The relative effectiveness of four methods of motivating employee performance." In K. D. Duncan, M. M. Gruneberg, and D. Wallis (eds.), Changes in Working Life: 363-385. Chichester, UK: Wiley.

Locke, Edwin A., and Gary P. Latham
1990 A Theory of Goal Setting and Task Performance. Englewood Cliffs, NJ: Prentice Hall.

Louis, Meryl Reis, and Robert I. Sutton
1991 "Switching cognitive gears: From habits of mind to active thinking." Human Relations, 44: 55-76.

Malcolm Baldrige National Quality Award Consortium
1990 Malcolm Baldrige National Quality Award Application Guidelines. Milwaukee: Malcolm Baldrige National Quality Award Consortium.

March, James G.
1981 "Footnotes to organizational change." Administrative Science Quarterly, 26: 563-577.

March, James G., and Herbert A. Simon
1958 Organizations. New York: Wiley.

McDonnell, John F.
1992 "Three years of Total Quality Management." Journal for Quality and Participation, 15: 6-12.

Miller, Danny
1993 "The architecture of simplicity." Academy of Management Review, 18: 116-138.

Miller, Danny, and Peter H. Friesen
1980 "Momentum and revolution in organizational adaptation." Academy of Management Journal, 23: 591-614.

Ocasio, William
1995 "The enactment of economic adversity: A reconciliation of theories of failure-induced change and threat-rigidity." In L. L. Cummings and Barry M. Staw (eds.), Research in Organizational Behavior, 17: 287-331. Greenwich, CT: JAI Press.

Olian, Judy D., and Sara L. Rynes
1991 "Making Total Quality work: Aligning organizational processes, performance measures, and stakeholders." Human Resource Management, 30: 303-333.

O'Toole, James
1977 Work, Learning, and the American Future. San Francisco: Jossey-Bass.

Pallas, Aaron M., and Anna Neumann
1993 "Blinded by the light: The applicability of Total Quality Management to educational organizations." Paper presented at the Annual Meeting of the American Educational Research Association, Atlanta.

Pennings, Johannes M.
1984 "Productivity: Some old and new issues." In Arthur P. Brief (ed.), Productivity Research in the Behavioral and Social Sciences: 127-140. New York: Praeger.

Raffio, Thomas
1992 "Delta Dental Plan of Massachusetts." Sloan Management Review, 34(Fall): 101-110.

Reger, Rhonda K., Loren T. Gustafson, Samuel M. DeMarie, and John V. Mullane

1994 "Reframing the organization: Why implementing total quality is easier said than done." Academy of Management Review, 19: 565-584.

Sashkin, Marshall, and Kenneth J. Kiser
1993 Putting Total Quality Management to Work. San Francisco: Berrett-Koehler.

Schooler, Carmi
1984 "Psychological effects of complex environments during the life span: A review and theory." Intelligence, 8: 259-281.

Senge, Peter M.
1990 The Fifth Discipline: The Art and Practice of the Learning Organization. New York: Doubleday.

Sitkin, Sim B., Kathleen M. Sutcliffe, and Roger G. Schroeder
1994 "Distinguishing control from learning in Total Quality Management: A contingency perspective." Academy of Management Review, 19: 537-564.

Spencer, Barbara A.
1994 "Models of organization and Total Quality Management: A comparison and critical evaluation." Academy of Management Review, 19: 446-471.

Staw, Barry M., Lance E. Sandelands, and Jane E. Dutton
1981 "Threat-rigidity effects in organizational behavior: A multilevel analysis." Administrative Science Quarterly, 26: 501-524.

Teresko, John
1991 "Hewlett Packard keeps reinventing itself." Industry Week, 240: 44-52.

Ulrich, Dave, Mary Ann Von Glinow, and Todd Jick
1993 "High-impact learning: Building and diffusing learning capability." Organizational Dynamics, Autumn: 52-66.

Wageman, Ruth
1995 "Interdependence and group effectiveness." Administrative Science Quarterly, 40: 145-180.

Waldman, David A.
1994 "The contributions of Total Quality Management to a theory of work performance." Academy of Management Review, 19: 510-536.

Whetton, David A., and Kim S. Cameron
1994 "Organizational effectiveness: Old models and new constructs." In Jerald Greenberg (ed.), Organizational Behavior: The State of the Science: 135-153. Hillsdale, NJ: Erlbaum.

Wruck, Karen H., and Michael C. Jensen
1994 "Science, specific knowledge, and Total Quality Management." Journal of Accounting and Economics, 18: 247-287.

Zbaracki, Mark J.
1994 "The rhetoric and reality of Total Quality Management." Paper presented at the Society of Industrial and Organizational Psychology Annual Meeting, Nashville.

Chapter 3

Organizing for Continuous Improvement

Evolutionary Theory Meets the Quality Revolution

SIDNEY G. WINTER

The producers of management advice operate in an economic environment where the tides of fad and fashion run strong. Frameworks, slogans, and buzzwords are brought forth in great profusion with attendant fanfare and claims of novelty. Although large rewards often accrue to successful fashion leaders, it is open to question whether organizations actually perform much better as a result of this activity. To the jaded eye, the latest widely acclaimed insight often looks suspiciously like a fancy repackaging of some familiar platitude or truism. Alternatively, it may be that this year's fashionable ideas are genuinely valuable—but largely because they help to correct a misallocation of attention that was itself produced by an excess of enthusiasm for ideas fashionable in the recent past.

Quality is now a very fashionable word in the management vocabulary. Not too long ago, *Business Week* devoted a special issue to "The Quality Imperative," declaring in its introduction that a focus on quality is producing a "global revolution, affecting every facet of business" (1991:7). Skeptics are not hard to find, however.

If the quality revolution is as significant as its proponents claim, it may well be the most important management innovation of the 20th (and early 21st) century. If its significance is only a fraction of what is claimed, it could still be quite important. In either of these cases, its importance would relate not merely to the theory and practice of management, but also to the assessment of the long-term economic outlook. For example, a major part of the "competitiveness" problem of the U.S. economy might be attributable to the follower status of the United States in the diffusion of quality management innovations. On the other hand, if quality management is merely a collection of buzzwords, it is safe to tune out—unless one has a stake in being in touch with current fashion.

That quality management should be taken seriously is the major conclusion of this chapter, but also, in a sense, its major premise: the chapter would not exist if I had reached the opposite conclusion. Quality management ideas provide an interesting perspective on the nature of productive knowledge and the processes by which it is maintained and improved in organi-

AUTHOR'S NOTE: From *Evolutionary Dynamics of Organization,* edited by Joel Baum and Jitendra Singh. Copyright © 1994 by Oxford University Press, Inc. Used by permission of Oxford University Press, Inc.

zations. It seems clear that their importance as a source of improvement in organizational performance is substantial; how far the revolution may go and what its consequences may be are important and interesting questions. I seek to explain and assess the quality revolution in terms that link its principal ideas to the characterization of firm behavior in evolutionary economic theory (Nelson and Winter, 1982). Many of the perspective offered here are specifically and obviously *economic* perspectives—but the evolutionary, ecological, and organization-theoretic aspects of evolutionary economic theory also inform this appraisal in significant ways. In particular, the final major section of the chapter sketches some general hypotheses about the ecology of quality management—the characteristics of the organizational and economic niches in which this management innovation is likely to grow and prosper. The chapter may thus serve, indirectly, to link quality management ideas to economics, evolutionary theory, and organization theory generally.

In discussing these ideas, I attempt to minimize the use of quality management jargon and acronyms. Quality management maxims and statements of the recognized "gurus" of the subject are sprinkled in occasionally for clarification and seasoning. One has to concede that "Seek out the low-hanging fruit first!" has a certain appeal relative to its proximate equivalent in economic theory, "Allocate effort to where its marginal product is the highest!"[1]

The ideas and literature of the quality revolution derive from a number of different sources and involve a number of major themes. Most current accounts of the history of thought in the area emphasize the influence of two Americans, W. Edwards Deming and J. M. Juran. There are numerous parallels between the careers of these two men, including their becoming influential in the United States after first being so in Japan, and the fact that both remain vigorous and active in the quality movement at advanced ages. It is clear, however, that the Japanese themselves have not only led the way in making the quality revolution a reality, but have also contributed fundamentally to its intellectual foundations.[2] Further, not only have there been many "follow-on inventions" in the quality field, but

there have been numerous precursors, foreshadowers, and independent coinventors of major themes. As a result, attributions of ideas involve more than the usual hazards.

I make only occasional attributions; the principal focus is on the ideas themselves, not on their sources. As a corollary, the account of quality management here is more my own synthesis of what seems particularly interesting than an attempt to reproduce accurately a particular school of thought.[3]

Evidence and Interpretation

The available evidence that supports the effectiveness of quality management methods is of several kinds. Some of the world's most successful competitors are acknowledged leaders in the practice of quality management and emphatically state their full allegiance to quality management principles—Toyota is perhaps the leading example. Also, there are strong adherents of quality management among executives of struggling or moderately successful companies as well as of highly successful companies. These adherents from less successful companies do not typically blame the quality management tools for their problems; they blame themselves and their fellows for making a late start.

The time required for quality management methods to produce results is, in fact, a key issue. For external observers interested in checking the claims made for quality management, it would be convenient if these tools were touted as the functional equivalent of a magic wand that produces instant, companywide performance improvements. Assuming that the waving of the wand were itself an observable event, it would then be relatively easy to check the validity of the claims. Inconveniently for external observers, the magic wand claim is rarely if ever made. Instead, the usual account is that the introduction of quality management is an incremental, time-consuming (even never-ending) process.

It is not surprising, therefore, that some of the most interesting evidence about quality management methods comes from a very microscopic level, relating to improvements achieved in particular processes. Much of this evidence consists of quantitative anecdotes—accounts of improvements by large factors that were made in particular performance indicators. Among the type of indicators often featured in these stories are defect rates and cycle times. For example, the *Business Week* special issue contains the following story from Hewlett-Packard: "At one HP factory a decade ago, four of every 1,000 soldered connections were defective, not bad for those days. Engineers were called in, and they cut the defect rate in half by modifying the process. Then, HP turned to its workers. They practically rebuilt the operation—and slashed defects a thousandfold, to under two per million" (1991:16).

As illustrated by the examples of defect rates and cycle times, the performance indicators that typically appear in quality management success stories are not direct measures of profitability.[4] Neither do they relate directly to variables like unit cost or market share, whose links to profitability are familiar themes in economic discussion. In some cases, the indicators may be regarded as proxies for what economists call technical efficiency (at the process level). They are imperfect proxies, however, because the improvements reported in "output" measures typically occur at the expense of increases in some inputs. Further, some investment of resources is always required to bring about the improvement in the first place. Regardless of whether this investment is treated as R&D expenditure for accounting purposes, in economic substance it is process R&D expenditure.

To any individual success story, therefore, a skeptical economist might reasonably respond with "So what?" Not enough information is presented about the bottom-line value of the improvement reported, or about the investment costs and continuing costs of the improvement, to permit an assessment of its economic merit. Further, an economic assessment of the general methods whose power is supposedly illustrated in the success stories would have to address the obvious sampling problem: there are failure stories as well as success stories, and those must be given appropriate weight in an overall assessment. That quality management methods have produced positive results in some organizations is beyond dispute; that these methods are generally economically effective by conventional standards has not been demonstrated.

The phrase "by conventional standards" implicitly invokes an important assumption. Although there is continuing debate about the appropriate goals of the large corporation, economists generally take a narrow view of the matter: they think that private sector managers should concern themselves with profit or present value or perhaps the market value of the firm. Efforts to lower defect rates (for example) may or may not contribute to success in this sense. If they do, fine. If not, the costly pursuit of such technical goals is ill-advised.

Two aspects of this assessment need to be considered, one relating to the actual preeminence of the profit goal and the other to its explicitness. The first involves basic questions about the role of the corporate form in economic organization. If the fundamental social rationale of the corporation is strictly to help investors make money, there may be correspondingly fundamental limits to the efficiency gains achievable by imbuing managers and workers with a culture of mutual trust and cooperation. This issue is discussed further, though of course far from comprehensively, later in this chapter.

The explicitness aspect can again be divided into two parts. First, there is a further perspective on the profit goal. If long-run profit maximization is the goal of the investors who are ultimately in control, it is conceivable that their interests are served by keeping that fact as secret as possible. Perhaps such a deceit is the most effective way to approach the fundamental efficiency limits referred to earlier. There is a school of thought regarding quality management that interprets it as the latest manifestation of a recurring pattern in which owners and/or managers pursue their own interests by attempting to deceive workers—talk of efficiency and cooperation masks an attempt to induce workers to work harder while conceding as little as possible of the resulting product.[5]

There is also the question of whether explicit attention to ultimate goals is otherwise desirable, apart from the fact that it may involve the sacrifice of gains attainable through obfuscation or deceit. In its emphasis on the pursuit of a large number of narrow technical goals, quality management doctrine often appears indifferent to the economic logic of resource allocation. Such indifference may lead to overinvestment in the pursuit of technical achievements that do not actually matter very much. Although this observation has some force, it is simplistic to assume that explicit attention to ultimate goals is always instrumental in achieving those goals. Should the receiver, leaping to catch the pass from the quarterback, be thinking about advancing the ball and winning the game—or should he focus on *catching* the ball? Common wisdom on the subject advises the latter. Similarly, quality management's emphasis on proximate goals and measurable achievements may be sound advice in a world where the effective allocation of scarce attention is a real issue.

Quality Management as Heuristic Problem Solving

In the following section, I characterize quality management methods in terms of specific attributes. For present purposes, I require only the following broad characterization of what "quality management" refers to: Quality management is the quest for improvement in organizational routines through the application of a particular collection of problem-solving heuristics and techniques. An important premise underlying most of these heuristics and techniques is that key information required for the improvement of a routine can be obtained only with the active cooperation of those involved in its performance.

A problem-solving heuristic is an approach to problem solving that is useful in spite of limitations deriving in part from vagueness and in part from uncertainty regarding its domain of application. Because of these limitations, shared with all heuristic methods, quality management cannot be expected to *optimize* routines in the sense that optimization is understood in formal economic theory.

At an abstract level, "optimization" means getting the right answer to the problem, and no other approach can logically surpass it. Realistically, however, no approach guarantees getting the right answer, even supposing the formulation of the right question. When real world problems are attacked with optimization methods, it is not the theoretical kind of optimization but optimization-as-heuristic that is at work (Nelson and Winter, 1982:133, 381).

The optimization heuristic advises that the real problem be described and represented in a way that maps it into the known domain of some well-defined optimization method-an optimization algorithm-and that the algorithm then be applied. The processes of identifying the criterion and the constraints gathering relevant data, and achieving the required representation are part of the optimization heuristic, but they are not part of any algorithm. The cost-benefit analysis of the selection of a particular algorithm, with its associated implementation requirements and costs, is also not within the scope of any algorithm. The optimization heuristic is vague about these matters and offers little guidance regarding the limits of its own applicability.

Assessing the practical merits of any body of heuristic methods is inevitably a chancy business. If there is a leap of faith involved in the adoption of quality management as a problem-solving approach, some such leap is also involved in the practical application of linear programming, capital asset pricing, or computable general equilibrium models.

One difference, important to economists if not otherwise, is that the latter methods carry the cachet of economic theory, whereas quality management in its present form is largely a body of methods that have emerged from practice. A corollary observation is that quality management is more explicit in its guidance regarding practical implementation than are problem-solving techniques whose intellectual roots are in economics or operations research.

Key Features of Quality Management

The quality revolution may constitute a major peak in understanding of organization and management, but it is a peak that is often shrouded in a fog of confusion and misunderstanding. A number of conditions contribute to the formation of this fog. The quasi-religious fervor of some advocates is by itself enough to put a reasonable person on guard, and the more so if the advocate is also a seller who stands to profit from a successful pitch. The "empowerment" of employees is a major theme in quality management discussion, and for the casual listener such discussion may be reminiscent of all-too-familiar ideological controversies (just when we thought that chapter of history was safely closed). There is proliferation of jargon, there is aggressive product differentiation effort by purveyors, and there is sectarian controversy—reminiscent, again, of ideological ferment of a political or religious nature. (*Business Week*, 1991:53).

Above all, the word *quality* itself invites misunderstanding. Quality in the sense of reliability, durability, product features, and so forth, is clearly important, but does it deserve attention to the utter exclusion of other economically significant measures, such as cost, price, and productivity? The answer is that no such exclusion is involved. Indeed, it is quite possible that the most important contributions of quality management might fall under the familiar heading that economists label "cost reduction" rather than "quality improvement" in the conventional sense.

Process Orientation

This potential for misunderstanding of "quality" derives directly from the most important feature of modern quality management: it directs attention to the improvement of production processes, and not simply to the characteristics of the products. To a degree, it involves a rejection of the original formulation of quality control, which sought assurance that the characteristics of the end-product fell within preassigned tolerance limits. The critical shortcoming of that approach is that is offers a very limited range of responses when instances of inadequate quality are discovered. Defective products can be discarded, but this implies the waste of the labor and capital services that went into their production, and in most cases of materials and components as well. Or additional costs can be incurred to bring the defective units up to standard—repair and rework costs. Deliberately or otherwise, some below-standard products may be delivered to market, where they will ultimately inflict warranty costs, damage to the producer's reputation, or both. Quality management experts and practitioners assert that these various costs associated with poor quality—not just in final products but at any point in the organization's functioning— are, in combination, very large.[6]

By contrast, a quality control approach that treats the entire production process as within its purview can incorporate quality checks and generate diagnostic information at every stage. The intermediate quality checks serve to limit the amount of faulty production generated when individual processes go out of tolerance, prompting corrective action before the units affected encounter the final quality check. More importantly, intermediate checks are directly useful in locating the source of the difficulty and can be supplemented with additional aids to diagnosis. This information can guide not only immediate short-term corrective action, but long-term efforts at improvement. In both the short and long term, the result is not merely the enhancement of the quality of the final product in conventional terms, but also the reduction of production costs by saving resources formerly devoted to producing discards, or to repair and rework.

Customer Focus

Complementing the concern with the production process "upstream" from its nominal end-point is an enhanced sensitivity to what happens "downstream" from that point—to how well the product or service meets customer needs. This involves a rejection of a narrowly technocratic and inward-looking definition of quality in favor of a more comprehensive and outward-looking definition, a switch from "quality is what our engineers say it is" to "quality is what our customers say it is." In this respect the quality management literature follows a long tradition in economic thought, which insists that the truest indicator of quality is provided by the buyer's utility function.

To implement this approach, information on customer needs and reactions must be gathered. A variety of methods are employed to this end, with the mix depending to some extent on the context. In markets where firms supply innovative products produced to order for other firms, design teams may be expanded to include customer technical representatives. In other markets, the channels of communication to customers may be opened by surveys and focus group discussions, or by 800 numbers to facilitate complaints and comments. It is often recommended that management, at all levels, devote some time to receiving customer feedback directly rather than relying entirely on summary information that has been filtered through the system.

There are limitations, ambiguities, and pitfalls in the notion of customer-defined quality. These derive primarily from the limitations of the customer's information and, relatedly, from the distinction between the customer's satisfaction in the short run and in the long. Some attributes that are actually quite important to the customer—such as safety features—may be difficult for the customer to assess. The most obvious candidate for the role of customer—for example, a purchasing agent—may not fully reflect the long-run interests of the more remote customers who are importantly affected by the product. Customers may be overly conservative, perhaps because they have little idea of what options are actually on the menu, or because they are wary of the risks and inconvenience associated with being early users of innovative products.

Finally, from a social point of view, the notion of customer-defined quality is subject to the same critiques applicable to the closely related idea of consumer sovereignty. Warning labels on cigarettes and alcohol, or motorcycle helmet laws, illustrate the expression in the public policy realm of skepticism about the social merits of choices that individual consumers often make.

These concerns are important qualifications to the simple formulation that "the customer is the final arbiter of quality." There is not, however, much sign that the progress of quality management has been seriously impeded by simplistic notions of customer satisfaction. On the contrary, many companies seem quite flexible and creative in their willingness to expand the concept of "the customer" and seek useful information from behind the facade that they directly encounter in the marketplace.

An important link between the process orientation and customer focus of quality management is the concept of the internal customer. This concept emphasizes that relationships within the producing organization—particularly among successive stages in the production process or in new product development—are akin to relationships at the "market interface" between the organization and its customers. The same techniques that are used to enhance the responsiveness of the organization to its customers are applicable to the internal relationships—particularly, the attempt to meet the needs of internal customers better through improved communication between them and their internal suppliers.

The "internal customer" may be viewed as quality management's counterpart to the financial management device of establishing "profit centers." Like the profit center approach, it seeks to infuse the internal relations of a large organization with an element of market discipline, at the same time heightening appreciation of the fact that the success achieved by the organization as a whole is the sum of many smaller successes or failures. In contrast to the profit center approach, it emphasizes measurement and communication to facilitate horizontal relationships among sub-units, rather than to establish marketlike incentives for subunits and to facilitate performance evaluation from the top.

Analytical and Factual Basis

Quality management techniques facilitate a *disciplined* quest for process involvement. Random tinkering is not advised; neither is the impulsive implementation of a bright idea, whether from top management or from the shop floor. (Suggestions are strongly encouraged, but for study, not immediate implementation.) These familiar methods of seeking improvement are considered inadequate because of their failure to probe the causes of process shortcomings in sufficient depth or to take adequate account of contextual factors. The consequences of such attempts are expected to be small, temporary, and possibly adverse. "Think of the chaos that would come if everyone did his best, not knowing what to do" (Deming, 1986:19).

The techniques employed to guide and structure the quest for improvements constitute the heart of quality management, and they are too numerous for a detailed survey here.[7] Quality consultants and quality management literature offer a wide selection of quite detailed recipes for implementing quality management—or at least attempting to do so. These recipes describe roles, required actions, and rough time-tables for action at all levels of the organization. Whether the effort ultimately succeeds or fails depends, however, on the cumulative effect of a large number of individual quality improvement projects. Such projects address particular problems or "opportunities for improvement"; they are typically conducted by project teams composed at least in part of individuals regularly involved with the subprocess in which the problem arises.

In a variety of formulations, quality management authorities and practitioners urge that the first step toward improvement is to achieve understanding of the process as it currently exists. ("If you want to improve a system or process, you must first understand how it works now.") Flowcharting of the current process is a conceptually simple but powerful tool that often produces surprising insights. ("We cannot improve any process until we can flowchart it.") To encounter difficulty in describing and measuring the current "process" is more ominous than to describe successfully an obviously flawed process. It suggests that there *is* no current process; a portion of the organization is simply adrift. ("Adherence precedes improvement.") Identification of the sources of defects or delays and measurement of their frequency and magnitude serve to focus attention on areas where the payoff to improvement may be greatest. Consultation with internal customers and suppliers of the process under examination may permit identification of parts of the process that serve no significant purpose and provide a context for review of proposed changes. Measurement and analysis must continue beyond the identification and attempted implementation of a recommended process change, to determine both whether anticipated favorable results have actually occurred and whether *un*anticipated *unfavorable* results have occurred. If the answers are no, yes, or both no and yes, the quest for improvement must be renewed. The refusal to accept "implementation gaps" is built in.

Leadership and Participation Issues

Much of the intensity and fervor associated with quality management derive from its implications for the roles of managers at various levels, as distinguished from the roles of "hands-on" employees. A distinctive feature of quality management doctrine—especially in the Deming formulation—is that it places responsibility for malfunctioning organizations squarely at the door of top management. ("Export anything to a friendly country except American management" [Deming, as quoted in Walton, 1990:13]). Of the many nostrums profitably peddled to American management over the years, few indeed have so clearly identified the clients themselves as the principal culprits in the difficulties their organizations were suffering.

Management is responsible for the problems because management is responsible for the systems, and it is the systems above all that generate the problems. Deming's "85-15 Rule" holds that 85 percent of what goes wrong is with the system, and only 15 percent with the individual person or thing (Walton, 1990:20). A related idea is that "the people who know the work best are those who perform it" (Walton, 1990:22). Finally, the general assumption about worker motivation is that pride of workmanship is a powerful motivator: "Give the work force a chance to work with pride, and the 3 per cent that apparently don't care will erode itself by per pressure" (Deming, 1986:85).[8] On the other hand, people may not know how to do a good job, much less how to do a better job in the face of the numerous constraints the organization imposes on them.

These three propositions—that process problems are predominantly attributable to system flaws, that the experts on the work are the people who do it, and that people are fundamentally motivated to do a good job—together imply a need for major recasting of managerial roles in the interests of organizational effectiveness. Although there may be other significant grounds for favoring such a change, they are redundant once the need for improved organized performance is acknowledged. Management must behave so as to provide a supportive structure within which people at lower levels can act effectively to improve performance. It cannot achieve significant performance improvements by its own unilateral action, for it lacks the detailed knowledge required to do so. It might attempt to force the required knowledge to the surface by fiat, but what is likely to surface instead is an account that is brief, abstract, and simple enough for management to understand, and bowdlerized to conform to perceptions of what management is believed to think should be going on. If the real thing were somehow made to surface, management would immediately collapse from information overload—or perhaps from despair.

From this assessment, the need to involve and empower employees becomes apparent, granting only the premise that the need to improve performance exists. The involvement and empowerment of employees are not, of course, objectives that can be accomplished by announcing them one morning as the new corporate policy. Managers must behave in new ways that neither they nor their subordinates fully understand, and they must overcome a long heritage of distrust and justifiable cynicism about change.[9]

Routines, Quality Management, and Evolutionary Theory

Quality management ideas provide an interesting perspective on what organizational capabilities are like in the first place, quite apart from any attempt to improve them. This perspective is similar in many ways to the view of the same issues taken in evolutionary economic theory.

A basic point of contention between the evolutionary theory and orthodox economics is the degree of reality that should be imputed to the orthodox concepts of production sets and production functions—especially long run production functions. As discussed by Nelson and Winter (1982, chapter 3), there are three challenging questions to be raised about the orthodox approach: (1) Where does the knowledge reside? (2) What real considerations could produce a sharp distinction between "technically possible" and "technically impossible" production activities? (3) How does the knowledge possessed by one firm relate to that of others, and to the knowledge environment generally?

On the first point, the orthodox commitment is vague in its details but clearly carries the implication that knowledge is represented in the firm in a form that makes alternative ways of doing things accessible to an effective survey, leading to a choice founded on economic criteria. There is no status quo way of doing things that has special prominence so far as knowledge is concerned; only a costless act of optimizing choice distinguishes the production technique actually used from an alternative that would have been used if prices were different. By contrast, evolutionary theory sees organizational capabilities as fragmented, distributed, and embedded in organizational routines. No individual knows how the organization accomplishes what it actually does, much less what alternatives are available. Although elements of economic choice are built into some routines, the routines themselves are not the consequence of an antecedent choice from a large menu, but of organizational learning.

The quality management perspective is entirely congenial to the evolutionary view but virtually incomprehensible to the orthodox view. Quality management stresses the importance of first *finding out* what process (routine, technique of production) the organization is currently using. Further, this task cannot be approached in a comprehensive way, but only in a fragmented and incremental way that corresponds to the actual distribution of capabilities in the organization. As subprocesses are flowcharted and analyzed, unexpected discoveries are made about how the organization works.

On the second point, the orthodox view sees business firms as operating in a technically efficient manner—right on the cliff edge where the known leaves off and the abyss of the unknown begins. It may be possible to move the cliff edge by investment in research and development, but it is still a cliff edge. Once the engineers have defined the cliff edge, economic choice determines where on that edge the firm operates. On the evolutionary view, there is no cliff edge, and also no sharp distinction between the economics of technical change and the economics of everyday performance. The prevailing organizational routines do not mark the edge of the feasible, but the point where learning stopped—or, more optimistically, the point that learning has now reached.

On the evolutionary view, therefore, it is not particularly surprising that systematic critical scrutiny directed to prevailing routines might turn up major opportunities for improvement in both "technical" methods and "organizational" arrangements. (Evolutionary theory and quality management concur again on the point that the line between the technical and the organizational is not sharply drawn.) There is no general presumption that the prevailing routines ever had such scrutiny in the past. And while "critical scrutiny" may sound simple in principle, quality management teaches that it is anything but simple in practice. Evolutionary theory and quality management doctrine concur again on many specific observations regarding resistance to change—including the important point that such resistance is often functional.

On the third point, evolutionary theory emphasizes that the capabilities of individual firms are not selections from a common technical handbook, but idiosyncratic outcomes of unique firm histories. While imitation across organizational boundaries is a powerful mechanism spreading change through the economy, it is hampered by the general factors tending to stabilize prevailing routines of the imitator and sometimes by attempts at secrecy by the imitatee. The result is something far short of homogenization of method, even within narrowly defined industry categories. The quality management literature takes it for granted that a firm can understand its own methods only by systematic (though fragmented and decentralized) self-study. Methods used by other firms are an important source of ideas for improvement; indeed "competitive benchmarking" is an important branch of quality improvement technique. Effective imitation of the routines of another organization requires, however, at least as much careful analysis and planning as are needed for "home grown" improvement ideas.

In short, there is much common ground between quality management doctrine and evolutionary economic theory with regard to the characterization of organizational capabilities. The improvement program offered by quality management raises somewhat different issues and there is less overlap as a result. (Since evolutionary theory is not a normative approach to management, it is silent on many of the issues that quality management forcefully addresses.) There are, however, some interesting points of contact.

Tacit Knowledge

Evolutionary theory emphasizes that much of the knowledge that underlies organizational capabilities is tacit knowledge; it is not understood or communicable in symbolic form. Two different senses in which this is true have been identified. First, individual skills have large tacit components, and organizational routines involve tacit knowledge to the extent that they involve the exercise of such skills. The second sense relates to the point that organizational knowledge is fragmented. Knowledge that is articulable by some individuals may be inaccessible to others, and to top management in particular. The fact that the organization functions reasonably effectively and is more or less responsive to direction from the top is somewhat mysterious when contemplated from the top—in a sense akin to the CEO's mysterious ability to control his or her car or golf swing, without conscious awareness of how it happens.

The quality management approach to understanding the process as it exists suggests a third, somewhat different perspective on the tacitness of routines. Aspects of a routine that are unknown to any participant may become both known and articulable if the participants get together and talk it over (something they have no occasion to do under routine operation). Together, comparing notes and piecing things together, the team may create an account of how the routine works that simply did not exist before. Such an account provides a framework for predicting the consequences of alterations of the routine and hence an opportunity to plan a successful intervention. Viewed in this light, the injunction "first understand how it works now" calls for an attack on the obstacles to improvement that derive from the tacitness of routines.

This appraisal helps to explain the promise of the method but also suggests some vulnerabilities. There is no chance of articulating all the knowledge that underlies the routine; important areas of tacitness will inevitably remain and can be the source of unintended consequences from improvement efforts. Also, by casting top management in a supporting role in the improvement process, quality management offers relatively little to mitigate the tacitness problem at the top of the organization. It would presumably be helpful for top management to have a better idea of what the organization as a whole can and cannot do; quality management largely defers that problem to some future date—perhaps wisely, perhaps not.

The Ecology of Quality Management

The preceding discussion suggests that quality management is a promising innovation. More accurately, it is meta-innovation, a loose collection of heuristic methods for producing improvements in organizational routines. In a world of imperfect information and understanding, latent opportunities for performance improvement are always abundant. Quality management methods provide some novel ways of converting a portion of these latent opportunities into recognized opportunities, and recognized opportunities into actual improvements. An attempt to assess the likely future influence of these methods, and to identify their most promising niche in the managerial environment, is in order.

In this connection, the general understanding that has been achieved of the processes of diffusion of innovation is clearly relevant. More specifically relevant—and perhaps discouraging for the prospects for successful prognostication and systematic hypothesis testing—is the literature on the diffusion of relatively "soft" innovations that are characterized by substantial ambiguity of definition. Such innovations mutate as they infiltrate differentiated environments, leaving a puzzling trail of definitional issues for the analyst (Walker, 1969; Downs and Mohr, 1976). Given the diversity and complexity of quality management ideas, this problem looms as a serious one.

Leaving this difficulty to one side, the following discussion explores some of the factors that may shape the application and development of quality management.

The "Buy-In" Problem

It has been argued that the need for a major transformation of managerial roles is an implication of quality management insights regarding the locus of productive knowledge in organizations. While this observation provides sufficient justification for the transformation at the theoretical level, it certainly does not sufficiently motivate it at the practical level. Proponents and practitioners of quality management agree that this transformation is unlikely to occur in the absence of a strong commitment at the top of the organization.[10] The innumerable instances of resistance to change in the organization as a whole can be overcome only if the transformation is fully embraced, supported, and enacted at the top.

In principle, such a commitment might arise from a purely intellectual recognition of the possibility of improved performance and the necessity of organizational change to achieve the improvement. Perhaps the early adopters in Japan were motivated in this way. At the present time and in the American context, however, it seems that the commitment is more likely to arise when it is the necessity of improved performance that is clear and quality management doctrine offers one of the few promising paths available. For example, the willingness of Motorola's management to "buy in" to quality management was stimulated by the discovery that its Japanese competitors had vastly superior quality: "Basically, you had better demonstrate the need or the fear or something that's emotional up front . . . we put on something we called 'Rise to the Challenge.' The intention of 'Rise to the Challenge' was to make it evident to everybody that there was a need: in fact, this scared the heck out of everybody"—George Fisher, Motorola CEO (Dobyns and Crawford-Mason, 1991:130).

If fear is indeed the most reliable motivator for the adoption of quality management, some significant implications follow. First, an answer is suggested for the economist's perennial question of whether the favored management nostrum of the moment is an offer of free lunch, and if not, who is paying for it. The answer is that quality management is not a free lunch. It requires costly and risky investments in the effort to improve existing routines. Some of these costs may be reflected in a temporary decline in the measured profitability of the organization as resources are diverted to the quality management effort, but much of the finance comes "out of the hides" of organization members, particularly managers.

The desire to assure organizational survival probably looms large among the several motivating factors that lead people to contribute extraordinary effort to quality management.[11] The willingness of individuals to contribute such efforts may depend on assurance that the gains from any improvement in organizational performance will be shared with the contributors. When specialized knowledge that defines a worker's role relates to routines that need dramatic change, or when the quality management task group confronts the possibility of eliminating some of the roles occupied by its own members, the quality management effort may lose its motivational traction and stall.

The Ecology of Inefficiency

Inefficiency in prevailing routines is like high-quality ore for quality management to mine. The more of it there is, the higher the returns to digging it out. Other factors equal (including particularly the commitment to improvement), quality management methods are most likely to deliver good results in organizations where the existing situation is the worst.

Where are the most ample funds of waste likely to be found? To address this question it is helpful to consider the origins of routines in more detail. Under the general interpretation offered here, routines emerge in an organization through a protracted process of organizational learning (Levitt and March, 1988). Although this process may be initiated and partially guided by plans and overt deliberation, a functioning routine involves more details than it is possible to settle at the symbolic level. The initial learning phase ends or fades away when performance that is deemed satisfactory is achieved. Or, to put the point somewhat differently, learning stops when the improvement of the routine is an issue that no longer successfully competes for attention of the kind that is actually needed to produce improvement.[12] The pressure for improvement falls because performance reaches a level that satisfies criteria deriving from general considerations that are remote from the costs and benefits of further improvement in the particular routine—the satisfactory profitability of the organization as a whole, or market acceptance of the final product. It is entirely possible that attractive opportunities for further improvement lie just around the corner when the search for them is abandoned.[13]

The nature of the processes that end an initial learning phase would be of little significance if the timely renewal of improvement efforts could be taken for granted. Attractive opportunities that were missed in the first learning phase would likely be recognized and developed in the second or third. The importance of renewing the search—or maintaining it continuously—is the key admonition of modern quality management. This admonition is far from redundant in the context of typical organizational practice; on the contrary, one of the stronger generalizations about typical patterns in organizations is to just the opposite effect. As Cyert and March (1963) observed, organizational search is "problemistic"—initiated in response to perceived problems, including shortfalls relative to familiar performance standards, and, focused (at least initially) in the vicinity of the problem and its symptoms.[14]

If the environment changes over time in ways that enrich the field of search for improvements, large and widening gaps may develop between actual performance and what could be accomplished if learning were renewed. While the shelf of potential improvements in a given routine becomes increasingly laden with contributions from new technology, new modes of organization, and observable innovations adopted elsewhere, an organization that searches only "problemistically" does not look at the shelf until it suffers a breakdown in that particular routine, or overall performance deteriorates to the point where threats to long-term survival are finally acknowledged and *all* routines are open to question.

The foregoing considerations suggest the following hypothesis about quality management: its potential contribution is the greatest in organizations that have survived longest without being required to reinitiate learning but are now challenged to do so. In such organizations, many routines remain in much the same form they were in when they first stabilized. Few occasions for change have occurred, and a large backlog of opportunities for improvement has accumulated.

More specifically, quality management methods are likely to find their most fruitful application in large organizations marked by long histories of consistent but gradually waning success. An industry founder that went virtually unchallenged for a long period because of its strong position in basic patents, and has encountered serious competition only recently,

would be an illustrative candidate. A company that was a vigorous competitor and strong survivor in some now-remote shakeout phase in its principal industry, and has had only gradually mounting challenges since, would be an alternative prototypical example of fertile ground for quality management. Both of these prototypes portray companies that were excellent by the standards of an earlier era, but whose more recent history has been an accumulation of minor disappointments—portending more significant disappointments in the future. Never having received a "wake-up call," these companies have had the maximum opportunity to continue on as living museums for managerial choices that were made long ago—choices that have long hindered rather than guided any quest for improvement.

Although the profile just sketched could fit companies over a wide size range, it is the larger companies that seem most likely to offer the best targets for quality management. Size and complexity make the organization's problems less transparent to top management (there is greater tacitness in the second of the senses identified previously). A larger fraction of the organization's productive knowledge involves routinized relationships, as opposed to personal knowledge held in the heads of a few key individuals. But the stability of relationships and expectations that permits the large organization to function may itself be the most formidable barrier to change. As J. M. Juran remarks,

> Some . . . deficiencies are of an *intra*departmental nature; the symptoms, causes and remedies are all within the scope of one departmental manager. However, the major wastes are *inter*departmental in nature. The symptoms show up in department X, but there is no agreement on what are the causes, and hence no agreement on what remedial action should be taken. Neither does there exist any organizational mechanism that can help the department managers deal with those interdepartmental problems. (1989:34)

Finally, large size may provide buffers against adversity that postpone the day when a general alarm sounds for the organization as a whole. Selling off a business unit now and then can provide the resources to sustain "business as usual" satisficing behavior in the remainder of the organization.[15]

Organizational Versus Individual Goals

It has been suggested that the most reliable source of fundamental commitment to quality management is a perceived long-term threat to the survival of the organization. At the level of narrow economic motivation, investment in quality management initiatives can be "financed" by extraordinary efforts that are put forward because participants at all levels are prepared to sacrifice a portion of their current well-being to protect their long-term well-being—when the latter is intimately tied to the survival of the organization. This logic does not track unless the "investors" have reasonable assurance that they will in fact be among the beneficiaries of their investments.

This observation connects the ecology of quality management to a broader set of institutional questions concerning corporate goals and corporate governance. In the 1980s, a surge of activity in the market for corporate control, and of hostile take-overs in particular, was accompanied by a surge of academic commentary endorsing this activity as one of capitalism's most fundamental defenses against managerial sloth and malfeasance (Jensen, 1988). Other commentators, however, took quite a different view. They argued that much of the gain ascribed to the efficiency-demanding discipline of the capital market could equally well be characterized in terms of breach of (implicit) contracts (Shleifer and Summers, 1988). Incumbent—or formerly incumbent—top management was a party to an implicit contract that declared the jobs of middle managers and of key employees at lower levels secure so long as the survival of the corporation itself was not threatened.

Since I have discussed the interpretation of this episode elsewhere (Winter, 1993), I will not address it fully here. Two *Business Week* covers provide a concise metaphor for the issue raised. Five years before the special issue "The Quality Imperative," *Business Week's* cover story was

"The End of Corporate Loyalty?" The story noted the possible threats to morale and productivity resulting from the breakdown of long-standing implicit contracts between middle managers and large corporations. Indeed, nothing that is understood about the requirements for successful response to "The Quality Imperative" suggests that it is compatible with the end of loyalty.

Technical Perfectionism Versus Economizing

The pursuit of improvement relative to measurable, analyzable proximate goals is the heart and soul of quality management. It is this conceptualization of the improvement task that provides the crucial impetus for decentralization and employee empowerment, driving the quest for improvement down the hierarchy to where the relevant resources of knowledge and imagination actually reside. And it is this same conceptualization that makes it possible to prescribe and elaborate a quality management tool kit—teachable methods that actually yield results in pursuit of those proximate goals. It is a view that correctly challenges the comfortable but crippling assessment, shared by corporate bureaucrats and most academic economists, that anything that has been done the same way for a long time is presumptively being done about right. Finally, this conceptualization supports a managerial rhetoric that urges the productive forces ever onward in the quest for improvement, and in so doing provides valid and emphatic warning against the dangers of smugness in an environment that is increasingly competitive in increasingly unpredictable ways. These are potent virtues.

Still, there are some inherent problems in quality management ideas that may limit their influence in the long term. As was noted previously, quality management is at least superficially indifferent to the economic logic of resource allocation. For example, many proponents emphatically reject as a fallacy the proposition that improving quality raises unit costs. On the contrary, they say, effectively addressing quality issues generally lower costs.

The preceding discussion gives the reasons why (and the sense in which) they may be right about this. It seems reasonable to assume, however, that sustained attack on the waste in existing routines will ultimately deplete the "ore body"—the fund of chronic waste. At that point, further quests for improvement may resemble, more and more closely, tentative probes in one direction or another along a transformation frontier relating unit cost to quality of the final product or service. Whether a particular probe promises improvement may seem clearer to the project team that proposed it than to the rest of the organization. While the quest for improvement could continue, the effectiveness of the effort might dwindle and its costs rise in subtle as well as obvious ways. In particular, the problem of "interdepartmental" sources of waste, described by Juran, is as much a hazard for quality management as for any activity. While a project team attempts a coordinated solution to a problem involving the relationship between departments A and B, the quality management effort itself may be generating new costs diffused through departments H, I, J, and K. Indeed, the doctrine that quality can be improved costlessly may actually encourage team members to focus on solutions that generate relatively diffuse and invisible cost increases. For example, the costs may be covered "out of the hides" of numerous participants not represented on the team, who did not volunteer their hides for that purpose. As the quest for improvements demands more trade-off choices an broader participation, effective quality management will itself become more costly and challenging.

While the enthusiasm for quality management is partly a fad and partly the fruit borne by aggressive promotion, the idea of a quality revolution is not merely a media event hyped by the business press. The organizational ailments and dysfunctions that quality management addresses are real phenomena, with sources that lie in the fundamentals of what productive competence is, how it is created, and how it is maintained and improved. Many other observers had noted the existence of these phenomena before the term "quality management" gained currency.

The prescriptions offered by quality management involve more novelty, and also more uncertainty regarding their validity, than the diagnoses. They derive credibility, first, from the fact that they do not directly offer solutions, but a collection of methods for pursuing answers. Also, they are not directed simply to the corporate boardroom or to the offices of top management, but to the entire organization. Finally, they strongly encourage maintaining focus on the quest for problem solutions and attempt to discourage investment in figuring out whom to blame. For these reasons, quality management methods have a much stronger claim to being applicable methods for producing real change in real organizations than the typical management consultant's nostrums of years past.

Substantial investments are being made in the implementation of quality management methods, both in the companies that have adopted programs and in the new service industry that supplies quality management programs and consultation. These investments are being made in full recognition of the fact that quality management does not promise near-term results and that its greatest benefits are achievable only through profound cultural transformation of business organizations.

In this chapter, I have offered some predictions—or theoretically grounded speculations—as to where the principal successes of quality management methods are likely to occur. To assess the likely overall impact of this management innovation is a more hazardous undertaking. It is obvious that there are many identifiable complexities and pitfalls; much winnowing will have to occur to identify the most valuable parts of the contribution, and it is conceivable that the valid core of quality management might be discredited by the bursting of some speculative bubble of extravagant claims. In my view, powerful forces in the global economic situation favor the wide diffusion of quality management methods. With increasing globalization, expanding technical possibilities, and rising sophistication concerning organizational options, few companies will find it possible to compete successfully without committing themselves to continuous improvement. While labels may change and fine points of doctrine remain in dispute, much of what has been identified here as central to quality management will prove indispensable in the struggle for competitive survival.

Notes

1. The "low-hanging fruit" maxim is the first of several quality management slogans and aphorisms that are quoted in this chapter without attribution. I encountered these phrases in one or more discussions, briefings, or speeches on quality management but cannot at this point provide a citation to a written source.

2. Deming (1986:486-492) provides a brief account of the origins of the quality movement in Japan after World War II.

3. A GAO report on quality management (U.S. General Accounting Office, 1991) was issued on May 2, 1991. By September 25, 1991, more copies of that report had been distributed than of any other report in the GAO's history, and requests for copies were then coming in at a rate of 1,000 per week. The overview of quality management given here draws on that report as well as other sources.

4. For other examples of success stories, see the "quality stories" sections in several chapters of Walton (1990).

5. See Adler (1993, especially pp. 80-93) for an excellent discussion of this issue set in the context of extensive interview data from the NUMMI plant (the GM-Toyota joint venture in Fremont, California).

6. For example: "In the United States, probably about a third of what is done consists of redoing what was done previously, because of quality deficiencies" (Juran, 1989:78).

7. For discussion of many of these techniques, see Deming (1986), Feigenbaum (1991), Juran (1989).

8. On this point, quality management is aligned with the human relations approach to management, generally, and with "Theory Y" in particular (McGregor, 1960). For a review and critique of the human relations model, see Perrow (1986). The interventions that quality management proposes in order to unleash presumptively constructive worker motivations are quite different from those proposed by the human relations school, although there is significant overlap.

9. See Juran (1989:77) on the "Here-comes-another-one" syndrome as an obstacle to change.

10. The meaning of "top" in this connection is somewhat ambiguous. In a large organization, quality management may succeed at the division, business unit, or plant level without necessarily being embraced at the peak of the full organization. But there is at least a requirement for tolerance at the peak and commitment at a level that has substantial authority and autonomy in day-to-day operations.

11. Adler (1993) discusses the role of the survival motivation (i.e., fear of unemployment) at NUMMI (pp. 25-26).

12. That is, the end of initial learning may be the result of a satisficing decision (Simon, 1955, 1956, 1987) or something more akin to a lapse of attention. In either case, it reflects the bounded rationality of those whose attention is needed to push learning forward.

13. Of course, even greater benefits might be attainable if commitments made early in the learning process could somehow be reversed and the resources devoted to elaborating those commitments recovered. Chance events early in the process may commit the organization to a learning path that in the long term is markedly inferior to some alternative. Learning itself then reinforces the commitment and makes escape improbable—a "competency trap" (Arthur, 1984; Levitt and March, 1988; Levinthal, 1992).

14. To say that search is "initiated in response to perceived problems" is to say that the satisficing principle applies to the initiation or renewal of search as well as to its termination (Winter, 1971).

15. Some of the points made in the foregoing discussion have been addressed in a large and diverse literature dealing with organizational slack (or "X-inefficiency") and its relationship to risk-taking behavior, performance, and organizational change. See, among others, Cyert and March, 1963; Leibenstein, 1966; Bowman, 1982; Singh, 1986; Meyer and Zucker, 1989; Bromiley, 1991.

References

Adler, P. S. 1993. "The 'learning bureaucracy': New United Motor Manufacturing, Inc." *Research in Organizational Behavior.*

Arthur, B. 1984. "Competing technologies." In G. Dosi et al. (eds.), *Technical Change and Economic Theory.* London: Pinter.

Bowman, E. H. 1982. "Risk-taking by troubled firms." *Sloan Management Review* 23:33-42.

Bromiley, Phillip. 1991. "Testing a causal model of corporate risk-taking and performance." *Academy of Management Journal* 34:37-59.

Business Week, October 25, 1991. *The Quality Imperative* (special issue).

Cyert, R. M., and J. G. March. 1963. *A Behavioral Theory of the Firm.* Englewood Cliffs, NJ: Prentice-Hall.

Deming, W. E. 1986. *Out of the Crisis.* Cambridge, MA: MIT Center for Advanced Engineering Study.

Dobyns, L., and C. Crawford-Mason. 1991. *Quality of Else: The Revolution in World Business.* Boston: Houghton Mifflin.

Downs, G., and L. B. Mohr. 1976. "Conceptual issues in the study of innovation." *Administrative Science Quarterly* 21:700-14.

Feigenbaum, A. V. 1991. *Total Quality Control.* 3d ed. New York: McGraw-Hill.

Jensen, M. C. 1988. "Takeovers: Their causes and consequences." *Journal of Economic Perspectives* 2:21-48.

Juran, J. M. 1989. *Juran on Leadership for Quality: An Executive Handbook.* New York: The Free Press.

Leibenstein, H. 1966. "Allocative efficiency vs. X-efficiency." *American Economic Review* 56:392-415.

Levinthal, Daniel. 1992. "Surviving Schumpeterian environments: an evolutionary perspective." *Industrial and Corporate Change* 1:427-43.

Levitt, B., and J. G. March. 1988. "Organizational learning." *Annual Review of Sociology* 14:319-40.

Meyer, M., and L. G. Zucker. 1989. *Permanently Failing Organizations.* Newbury Park, CA: Sage.

Nelson, R. R., and S. G. Winter. 1982. *An Evolutionary Theory of Economic Change.* Cambridge, MA: Harvard University Press.

Perrow, Charles. 1986. *Complex Organizations: A Critical Essay.* 3d ed. New York: Random House.

Shleifer, A., and L. H. Summers. 1988. "Breach of trust in hostile takeovers." In A. J. Auerbach (ed.), *Corporate Takeovers: Causes and Consequences.* Chicago: University of Chicago Press.

Simon, H. A. 1955. "A behavioral model of rational choice." *Quarterly Journal of Economics* 69:99-118.

Simon, H. A. 1956. "Rational choice and the structure of the environment." *Psychological Review* 63:129-38.

Simon, H. A. 1987. "Satisficing." In J. Eatwell, M. Millgate, and P. Newman (eds.), *The New Palgrave: A Dictionary of Economics* 4:243-45.

Singh, J. V. 1986. "Performance, slack, and risk taking in organizational decision making." *Academy of Management Journal* 29:562-85.

U.S. General Accounting Office. 1991. *Management Practices: U.S. Companies Improve Performance Through Quality Efforts* (GAO/NSIAD 91-190). Washington, DC: U.S. General Accounting Office.

Walker, J. L. 1969. "The diffusion of innovations among American states." *American Political Science Review* 63:880-99.

Walton, M. 1990. *Deming Management at Work.* New York: Putnam.

Winter, S. G. 1971. "Satisficing, selection and the innovating remnant." *Quarterly Journal of Economics* 85:237-61.

Winter, Sidney G. 1993. "Routines, Cash Flows and Unconventional Assets: Corporate Change in the 1980s." In M. Blair (ed.), *The Deal Decade: What Takeovers and Leveraged Buyouts Mean for Corporate Governance.* Washington, DC: The Brookings Institution. Forthcoming.

PART II

The Quality Movement in America

Chapter 4

Market Pressures and Institutional Forces

The Early Years of the Quality Movement

ROBERT E. COLE

This is a story about quality as a competitive factor rather than one about total quality management (TQM), although TQM is a label given to a variety of approaches designed to improve quality performance. It is a story designed to assess how effectively American managers responded to the Japanese quality challenge of the early 1980s and the theoretical implications of this response. Indisputably, quality as a competitive factor in the manufacturing sector has been greatly enhanced over the past 15 years, paralleled by growing investment in quality improvement and improved quality performance itself. The bar—as measured on a variety of dimensions, such as product reliability and yield—is constantly being raised as to what constitutes superior quality performance, particularly in internationally competitive industries. The data on which I draw are largely from the auto and the semiconductor industries.

First, a definition of quality is in order. We do not adopt a transcendental view of quality as being synonymous with innate excellence—an innate excellence that is both absolute and universally recognizable. Instead, our focus is on organizational behavior that enhances customer satisfaction through continuous improvement of all business operations using various forms of teamwork to eliminate waste, rework, and inefficiency. Thus, we follow a process improvement and market-based approach to quality. Following Garvin (1988), the eight dimensions of quality on which manufacturing firms can compete are as follows: performance, features, reliability, conformance, durability, serviceability, aesthetics, and perceived quality. The Japanese chose particularly to compete on the reliability dimension in the early 1980s and effectively used it to gain entry in many U.S. manufacturing markets.

AUTHOR'S NOTE: This chapter draws heavily from the first five chapters of my book *Managing Quality Fads: How American Business Learned to Play the Quality Game*, Oxford University Press, 1999. I am indebted to a fellowship at the Center for Advanced Studies in the Behavioral Sciences (made possible by a grant from the National Science Foundation #SES-9022192) and a grant from the Air Force Office of Scientific Research Grant #F49620-95-I-0042 for providing me with the time to conduct this research. In addition to fellow conference participants represented in this volume, I want to thank Richard Woods for careful reading and commentary on an earlier draft.

The time frame covered in this analysis is the early years of the quality movement, roughly 1980 to 1985. The perspective underlying this analysis is that we can understand what happened and did not happen only in terms of the interaction between market forces and institutional practices and pressures. We will argue that during the early 1980s, entrenched institutional forces operated to slow down the response of American manufacturers to market pressures. Over time, and becoming more apparent in the late 1980s, firms began to develop new institutional arrangements that served to facilitate the spread of the new quality practices. Indeed, U.S. firms succeeded in greatly closing the quality performance gap with the Japanese across a broad range of key manufacturing industries by the mid 1990s (e.g., Angel, 1994; MacDuffie & Pil, 1997). In this chapter, the focus is on the first half of that story. For those believers in the efficiency of the market, the second half of the story is more attractive, which is why we need to understand the first half of the story as well.

A new quality model developed in Japan in the period between 1955 and 1980. It arose out of a sense of crisis after the devastation left in the wake of World War II. Managers came to believe that quality improvement was imperative to make Japanese goods more competitive on world markets. They were successful beyond their wildest dreams. Not only did the Japanese find that they were able to eliminate poor quality as a disadvantage, but they had turned high quality into a strong competitive weapon in international markets. The large, export-oriented manufacturing firms did this in part through evolving a disciplined approach to quality improvement.

In the period around 1980, a series of widely publicized events highlighted the poor-quality performance of American producers relative to the Japanese. Notable among them were a Hewlett-Packard manager's public announcement of the poor quality of domestically supplied chips relative to those delivered by Japanese suppliers; the highly influential NBC documentary "If Japan Can, Why Can't We" which introduced Dr. Deming to the American public; and the ensuing media blitz on the poor quality of American manufactured products, with autos being singled out for particular attention. How did American manufacturing firms respond to this seemingly new competitive reality? When did firms make the decision to respond? Moreover, once firms made the decision to adopt new practices, what did they choose to adopt, and how did managers choose their strategies and tactics for implementation? What determined their decisions? Above all, what institutional arrangements shaped, mediated, and channeled those changes?

Table 4.1 shows the new quality model circa 1990, contrasting it to the old quality model. Since 1990, firms have moved to further integrate quality with other key business objectives, thereby de-emphasizing quality's stand-alone chraracter.

No one company fully manifests the old or the new quality model. If you looked, however, at the leading manufacturers in the United States in 1980—Boeing, General Motors, Intel, Xerox, GE, and Whirlpool—and compared them to the leading manufacturers in Japan at the same time—Toyota, Komatsu, Matsushita, Ishikawajima Harima, and NEC—then it is clear that the American firms were characterized much more by the approaches represented in the old quality model, and the Japanese more by approaches reflected in the new quality model.

Because the categories of each type shown in Table 4.1 are reasonably self-explaining, I will not discuss each of them. Two overview observations, however, are in order. First, an overriding difference between the two models is captured in the inward orientation of the old model as reflected in its emphasis on conformance to requirements; in contrast, the new model is outward oriented—user oriented—as reflected in its customer orientation and the effort to build the study and internalization of customer needs into all parts and levels of the firm. Yet the control element present in the emphasis on conformance to requirements in the old model continues to be important in the new model, but only in balance with a strong thrust for innovation and improvement based on a customer orientation.

The second observation about the two models is the inference of discontinuity between the

TABLE 4.1   Characteristics of Old and New Quality Models

Old Quality Model	New Quality Model
1. Internal orientation stressing conformance to requirements (fitness to standard); reduction of internal costs is filter used to evaluate quality improvement proposals	1. "Market-in" approach provides strong customer orientation; customer acceptability is initial filter used to evaluate quality improvement proposals
2. Quality just one of many functional specialties	2. Quality as umbrella theme for organizing work; used as common language throughout the firm
3. Quality not seen as competitive element as long as you match your competitors	3. Improved quality as strong competitive strategy
4. Quality as specialized function carried out by small number of experts in quality department reporting to manufacturing	4. All-employee, all-departmental involvement pivotal strategy for improving quality of strategic business processes; attention to incentives for all employees
5. Downstream focus on inspection, defect detection, and Band-Aid™ solutions	5. Upstream prevention activities key to quality improvement; build in quality
6. Quality improvement activities involve limited repetitive cycle of detect and repair leading at best to stable equilibrium	6. Well-defined problem-solving methodology and training activities tied to continuous quality improvement; aimed at improving key processes pivotal for business success
7. Quality as stand-alone effort promoted by quality department, not well integrated into rest of organizational activities	7. Integration of quality into control system of goals, plans, and actions
8. Each functional specialty operating as independently as possible and maximizing its own functional goals, sometimes at expense of the firm	8. Focus on cross-functional cooperation to achieve firm-level objectives
9. See number 1	9. Anticipation of customer need before customers are aware of these needs (fitness to latent requirements)

NOTE: These characteristics are drawn from the literature (Ishikawa, 1985; Mizuno, 1988; Scherkenbach, 1986; Shiba, Graham, & Walden, 1993) as well as my own research on the subject in 1989. This research involved interviewing officials at 20 leading Japanese manufacturing firms noted for their quality achievements across a broad range of industries.

old and new quality models. This is critical to subsequent arguments. David Garvin (1988, pp. 3-20) sees the transition from the old to new quality models as an evolutionary one. That may be true at an analytic level, as reflected in the thinking of leading gurus in the field. To emphasize that, however, is to lose the shock, confusion, and paralysis that characterized the initial management response to the Japanese quality challenge in the early 1980s.

One way to bring evidence to bear on that argument is to look at who became the new quality leaders in the major manufacturing corporations in the 1980s and 1990s. If the evolutionary principle holds sway, we would expect that many of the leaders of the new quality initiatives would be those trained in traditional qual-

ity control. This would suggest a competence-enhancing technological advance, to use the distinction made by Tushman and Anderson (1986). But if there is a more radical break, we would expect a new cadre of leaders to emerge that did not have its roots in traditional quality control. In other words, we would have a "competence-destroying" technical advance.

We have some data that speak to this issue. The Conference Board did a survey in 1992 of the highest ranking quality officers in the *Fortune* 500 manufacturing firms. They report the prior jobs of these leading quality executives. Only 26% had their previous job in the quality area, 15% had their second previous job in the quality area, and 9% had their third previous job in the quality area. In other words, we don't see any great continuity in skills or careers. In short, the message is one of discontinuity, not continuity.[1]

How Broad the Quality Challenge?

For a great number of large- and medium-size American manufacturing firms, especially those subject to international competition, the pressures to find a competitive response to the Japanese came to be incredibly intense across a broad array of manufacturing industries—from air conditioning to autos, from consumer electronics to computers, from copiers to color TVs, from steel to semiconductor equipment, and from metal fabrication to machine tools. In almost all of these cases, we can document a major quality gap between U.S. and Japanese companies in the early 1980s.[2] Nor was it typically a trivial gap. On measures of reliability in auto and certain semiconductor products, the Japanese were orders of magnitude better—often 5 to 10 times better!

Responses to the Quality Challenge

The ability of U.S. manufacturing firms to generate profits, hold market share, and, indeed, to survive in some cases, was challenged by shifting customer preferences. In autos, for example, quality went from a low ranking factor in consumer purchase decisions in the mid 1970s to one of the highest ranking factors in the early 1980s. Yet the process by which firms came to acknowledge the quality threat was quite slow given the market pressures; when executives were faced with evidence, their initial inclination was denial (not only publicly), and even when denial was no longer possible, confusion reigned. Learning how to respond effectively was a very slow process. For those firms and industries facing the strongest pressures as a result of their inferior quality performance, the interesting question is, Why did the development of an effective adaptive response take so long?

From a rational actor perspective, it is hard to make sense of these events. Rapid imitation of the Japanese quality approaches would have stemmed market share losses and, hence, profit losses across a broad range of industries. That did not happen, and, in the process, hundreds of thousands of jobs were lost and wealth transferred overseas. Firms, technologies (DRAMs), and even whole industries (color TV) were lost to the Japanese. To be sure, quality performance was by no means the only factor in the weakened competitive stance of firms, but it was a factor of some importance.

Why should we regard the 10 to 15 years it took to at least partially absorb the new Japanese quality model as excessively long? After all, from a historical perspective, this is a short period of time. Nevertheless, it was slow given the intense market pressures in the United States in the early 1980s across a broad range of manufacturing industries (not nearly as strong in comparable European industries at this time). The slow response led to the loss of jobs, market share, and profits just mentioned. The slowness to emulate the Japanese did have real competitive consequences that could have been mitigated if action had come about earlier. Moreover, some firms (e.g., Ford, Motorola) did respond more rapidly and effectively than others, showing that it was indeed possible.

Rational Actors, Markets, and Learning

Why weren't more firms more adaptive? This question rests on the assumption that economic outcomes can be explained as a result of rational actors making choices that maximize their utility given the constraints that they face, and making no systematic errors in these choices. Certainly, a major problem for U.S. managers in adopting the new quality model was incomplete information, but this is a constraint that neoclassical theory recognizes and can deal with.

Yet a variety of systematic errors suggests that firms were not maximizing their utility. These errors flowed from "belief perseverance" in the face of contrary evidence, cognitive leaps that proved difficult for managers, lack of management norms legitimating learning from the Japanese, framing of the solutions in ways that inhibited learning, and errors of judgment that led to intensification of existing approaches. I will describe each of these in more detail. These responses, in turn, were often mixed with heavy doses of hubris and arrogance, reflecting the incredulity of American managers toward the new information to which they were being exposed. Yet I suggest that the requisite information for identifying the problem and the ways to resolve it were available to the actors if they had only pursued some obvious avenues of search and understanding. Of course, rational choice advocates might argue that if managers did not perceive the obvious choices, then they were not so obvious. To argue in this fashion, however, runs the risk of tautology. One can build more and more "ignorance" into the actor, thereby ensuring that *whatever the circumstances,* he or she was acting rationally. The weakness, of course, with this kind of logic is that it does not allow one to refute the hypothesis that actors are behaving rationally (cf. Tetlock, 1991, pp. 26, 44). I will show that by reasonable standards, information and cues were available for managers had they chosen to see, listen, and look in reasonably obvious places. In the end, however, this misses the point. Ultimately, managers did not pick up on many of these cues because of entrenched institutional factors that conditioned them to look in different places and because of the overall difficulty that managers had in extracting quality competitiveness and its causes from a complex historical flow of events and explanations.

Nelson argues that rational choice theory does not do well in situations where the actors cannot be presumed to have much applicable experience and where there is a great deal of trial-and-error learning. Neoclassical theory would predict that efficient markets would price and allocate resources to rapidly eliminate the quality performance gap; barring that, efficient markets would eliminate slow-moving firms. Yet the former seems not to have happened, and there are many exceptions to the latter effects as well. The fallback response by some is to argue

that actors will learn to make correct decisions and that learning plus competitive selection will eliminate firms that are not efficient.

Yet as Tversky and Kahneman (1986) and Tetlock (1991, pp. 35-36) remind us, learning does not occur by magic. Effective learning occurs only under certain conditions. It requires accurate and immediate feedback about the relationship between the existing situation and the appropriate response. This is particularly the case when we are interested in learning that involves matching up means-and-end relationships in more efficient or effective ways. This kind of feedback is often absent for managers because of four factors:

1. Outcomes are commonly delayed and not easily attributable to a particular action.
2. Variability in the environment degrades the reliability of the feedback.
3. There is often no information about what the outcome would have been if another decision had been taken.
4. Important decisions are often unique and therefore provide little opportunity for learning.

If this is true in general, it was true in extremis for learning about how to improve quality in the early 1980s. Let us consider the applicability of Tversky and Kahneman's (1986) observations to management's experiences with the new quality model.

1. A consistent refrain among promoters of the new quality model was that it would take from 3 to 5 years before significant corporatewide results would appear. Dr. Deming stressed management's need for "constancy of purpose" precisely to deal with this problem. In short, there is an enormous delay in feedback time at the level of firm or even factory performance, and as a result of the long time frame, there was ample opportunity to attribute positive results to a variety of other changes that coincided with adoption of new quality practices. Alternatively, if the adoption resulted in failure, one could attribute it to the presence of a variety of other possible causal factors. Consistent with Tversky and Kahneman, this made effective

learning very difficult. Without being able to show clear results attached to specific initiatives, management was reluctant to move forward. Only gradually were practices developed and institutional arrangements put in place that dealt effectively with these problems.

2. There was great variability in the environment in which the initial experiments with quality improvement in American firms were undertaken. Industry- and firm-level conditions varied enormously, and this compounded the problem of learning from individual experiences and applying that information more broadly. If an event does not happen frequently enough under similar conditions, it is difficult to know reliably what the central tendency of outcomes (the on-average performance) is. This sharply increases the probability of misjudging results and making inappropriate policy responses.

3. Consistent with Tversky, there was very little information about what the outcome would have been if firms had either taken a different approach to quality improvement or had bet on another set of competitive strategies. Selection is a stochastic process, and the winnowing-out process involves large numbers of firms and takes a long time to illuminate winning and losing strategies (Carroll & Harrison, 1994, p. 746). Firms adopted a broad range of policies in their initial attempts to respond to the Japanese quality challenge.

4. Because of the discontinuity between knowledge required for the old and new quality model and the largely exogenous nature of the quality challenge, there was little evolutionary learning that prepared management for responding to the quality competition that burst on the scene in the early 1980s. That is to say, the quality challenge appeared to U.S. companies, for all practical purposes, to be a one-time, "never having been seen before" event.

As if this was not enough, managers were also uncertain about what "quality" was (the goal) and about how efficient particular technologies (quality improvement methodologies) were in reaching those goals. Yet the rational actor model is premised on the assumption of certainty of goals and the means to achieve them. It fails us here because, as Philip Tetlock (1991) put it, "it fails to address how decision makers cope with the causal ambiguity inherent in a complex historical flow of events" (p. 26). A great deal of learning had to take place before effective responses could be developed. We are not talking about a simple additive learning process in which managers had to acknowledge only that more quality was better than less quality. Rather, we will see that the new model of quality challenged the cognitive assumptions of management. It claimed that black was white! Moreover, beyond the cognitive barriers, one had to actually figure out what to do to put the new model into effect. Indeed, sometimes, the new practices preceded rather than followed the shift in cognitive understanding. In summary, the conditions for effective learning about the new quality model were not met, and information on how to implement was not immediately available. Thus, much time elapsed before an effective response to the Japanese quality challenge could be mounted.

Belief Perseverance

The starting point of American management in the late 1970s dramatically affected the choices that managers made on both strategies and tactics for confronting the Japanese quality challenge. To assert this is to say that the learning process of management was path dependent. The norms, values, beliefs, and prevailing practices that pervaded and reflected managerial thinking had a powerful effect on the response that American firms made to the Japanese quality challenge.

What were some of these norms, values, and practices? It was not until the late 1970s and early 1980s that a general understanding grew among managers that a quality deficit was a major factor in their competitive problems. That top management did not recognize this earlier, despite ample signs, was the result of a mind-set that simply did not take quality seriously as a major competitive factor in mass markets. These were men (by and large) who were accustomed to thinking in terms of competing over lower unit costs, new products, expanding markets, building better sales networks, achieving economies of scale and scope, increased output per worker, technology, brand names, and product differentiation. They had made their careers in functional departments such as marketing and finance, and they were dedicated to realizing corporate objectives through applying the principles learned in these departments. The upshot is that they consistently underestimated the scope of the quality challenge in these early years.

Starbuck and Milliken (1988), among others, observe that those at the top of organizational hierarchies tend to have expertise related to older and more stable job routines; therefore, they are prone to interpret events in terms of these tasks. They also favor strategies that will keep these tasks central. The leaders of many U.S. manufacturing firms in the 1980s had, in effect, what Thorstein Veblen called "trained incapacity." These managers found themselves in a historical situation in which their abilities came to function as inadequacies or blind spots. Actions based on training and skills that have been successfully applied in the past resulted in inappropriate responses under the changed conditions. The new conditions were not recognized as sufficiently different, and so the very soundness of past experience and training, and the rewards associated with them, led managers to adopt familiar, but wrong, solutions.

Denial took two forms in the late 1970s and early 1980s. First, managers denied quality as a major competitive factor and/or they denied Japanese superiority. To deny strong evidence, typically, individuals require a cognitive mechanism that can provide a plausible account that would explain events in a different fashion. In this case, it involved blaming their competitive problems with the Japanese on a variety of other factors. Cost competition based on low wages, their access to cheap capital, government support, and manipulation of currency rates were all prominent parts of this alternative explanation loudly voiced in the late 1970s and early 1980s. Singly or in combination, these accounts provided the cognitive grounds that protected existing beliefs from the impact of logical and empirical attacks asserting the primacy of Japanese quality. These accounts allowed managers to resist what otherwise might have seemed irresistible—at least for awhile. Because there are limits on management's attention, information about these alleged sources of Japanese superiority tended to crowd out alternative explanations, resulting in a constriction of information flow regarding these alternative explanations. Staw, Sandelands, and Dutton (1982, pp. 515-516) described these general processes, showing how they produce rigidity in organizations as they seek to respond to threat.

Viewed in this broad perspective, it is plausible that managers would not even notice some of the early cues that pointed in the direction of quality becoming a major competitive issue. Yet as various scholars have noted, if you do not notice important cues, they are not available for "sensemaking" (Starbuck & Milliken, 1988, p. 45; Weick, 1995). Instead of learning from the experience of industries such as sewing machines, cameras, watches, and color TVs throughout the 1970s and the early inroads on their own markets, managers found it much easier to attribute the failure of these industries to unique industry factors, normal product cycle developments, and unfair competition from the Japanese. In particular, many managers in the early 1980s, in dismissing Japanese quality competition, displayed an enormous capacity to argue that their industry or division or plant or technology was different and, therefore, the lessons learned elsewhere did not apply. The ability to hide from an emergent reality in this fashion should not be underestimated.

The claim of a quality advantage for the Japanese called into question the very competence of America's senior manufacturing managers as managers. After all, if they were competent, people would expect that they would have known about the problem much earlier, the gap would not now be so large, they would know what to do about it, and they would have done it. Faced with these kinds of evaluations, both manifest and latent, it is easy to understand how managers tended to avoid facing up to the problem. It is also easy to see how networks of managers unconsciously "conspired" to reinforce these denials.

The language above makes it sound like management failures were the result of some combination of stupidity, deviousness, and defensiveness. But ultimately, the problem was that there were many seemingly compelling explanations floating around as to the causes of Japanese competitive success. U.S. managers faced enormous problems in extracting explanations that isolated quality competitiveness and its causes as a key success variable. One could make a credible argument at the time, for example, that cost disadvantages were the real culprit, and these had to be rooted out through traditional cost reduction techniques or else production would have to be moved abroad. Indeed, there were many examples of firms acting on just these assumptions. Thus, to say that managers did not operate as rational actors by immediately recognizing quality as the problem and identifying its sources is hardly surprising.

Cognitive Challenges

We now turn to the second item on our list of systematic errors. There were a number of cognitive challenges that American manufacturing managers found particularly hard to overcome in the early 1980s. David Nadler (Nadler, Gerstein, Shaw, & Associates, 1992) has characterized quality-hostile assumptions that have limited the success of American corporate initiatives in quality improvement. An adapted version is shown in Table 4.2. Together, these assumptions capture a broad set of problems that underlies many of the barriers to adoption.

We know that institutionalized behavior is behavior that has a large taken-for-granted character. It is hard to change what we take for granted because we do not even recognize the way that our taken-for-granted assumptions underlie our existing behavior. We can think of these assembled assumptions as providing an integrated cognitive structure for many managers that operated to structure social interaction.

Each element in this cognitive map is consistent with the old quality model and the low status of quality in the organizations that practiced

the old model. These elements also flow from the dominance of finance and marketing personnel and their trained incapacity described above. With these earlier discussions in mind, my discussion of Table 4.2 deals only with the first two performance assumptions: It costs more to provide a quality product or service and we will not recover the added cost; and the law of diminishing returns makes continuous improvement unworkable.

These contrary assumptions—that higher quality can bring about lower cost and that continuous improvement should be the centerpiece of corporate improvement efforts—are both counterintuitive to those wedded to the old model. Together, they constituted perhaps the primary cognitive roadblocks to the implementation of the new model in the early and mid 1980s. Many top-management leaders jumped aboard the quality bandwagon in the early 1980s without a very deep understanding of what was involved. The critical layers of management below them, which were responsible for actually doing something, however, often voiced strong reservations that were reflected in these first two performance assumptions. Both had to do with the relationship between costs and quality improvement and therefore touched some of the core beliefs concerning the centrality of financial management of the firm.

The first, the idea that high quality and low cost could go together, was simply not on the mental horizons of top American managers in the early 1980s (Robinson, 1980, p. 585). There was literally a cognitive gap that did not allow U.S. managers to conceive of the possibility of a unity between low cost and high quality. In the traditional model, higher quality was thought of in terms of more product attributes, and that logically meant that if you added new or better attributes, it would result in higher costs. It was a model that was intuitively appealing to managers based on their experiences. Quality was thus seen in a trade-off relationship with higher costs. You could only add so much in the way of costs associated with additional attributes before consumer demand would fall off.

The idea that high quality and low costs went together, however, was not a foreign concept to a number of American experts. Armand Feigen-

TABLE 4.2 Quality-Hostile Assumptions

Cluster	Illustrative Assumptions
Corporate purpose	Our primary and overriding purpose is to make money—to produce near-term shareholder return.
	Our key audience is the financial markets and, in particular, the analysts.
Customers	We are smarter than our customers; we know what they really need.
	Quality is not a major factor in the customers' decisions; they cannot tell the difference.
Performance	It costs more to provide a quality product or service, and we will not recover the added cost.
	The law of diminishing returns makes continuous improvement unworkable.
	Strategic success comes from large, one-time innovative leaps rather than from continuous improvement.
	The way to influence corporate performance is portfolio management and creative accounting.
	We will never be able to manufacture competitively at the low end.
People	Managers are paid to make decisions; workers are paid to do, not to think.
	We do not trust our people.
	The job of senior management is strategy, not operations or implementation.
	The key disciplines from which to draw senior management are finance and marketing.
Problem solving and improvement	To err is human; perfection is an unattainable and unrealistic goal.
	Quality improvement can be delegated; it is something the top can tell the middle to do to the bottom.
	Celebrate success and shun failure; there is not much to learn by dwelling on our mistakes.
	If it ain't broke, don't fix it.
Organization	Functional loyalties take precedence over other loyalties.
	An emphasis on system inevitably leads to deadly bureaucracy.

SOURCE: Adapted from Nadler et al. (1992, p. 151).

baum and Joseph Juran had long preached this message. These principles grew out of prewar and early postwar thinking in industrial engineering that if one concentrated on basic work elements and tasks, one could reduce costs by identifying which tasks could be reduced or eliminated if things were done right the first time. While such conceptualizations were part of the thinking of selected American scholars and practitioners, the advocates' voices were clearly whispers in the wind to which few companies paid attention. Again, we see available cues going unnoticed.

I attended a number of management seminars in the early 1980s in which managers challenged the logical possibilities that low cost and high quality could go together based on their understanding of the traditional model. Yet this unity was at the heart of corporate Japan's approach; by eliminating waste and rework in business processes, one could achieve both higher quality and lower costs. The Japanese were using a process rather than product definition to quality improvement. In short, the prevailing narrowly constrained definition of quality among American managers blocked conceptual clarification.

By the mid and late 1980s, we start to see many American managers begin to publicly accept the counterintuitive claims that high quality and low cost go together and that continuous improvement can be financially rewarding. Yet the new slogans were initially often recited as mantra and used as litmus tests by lower level employees to test management's newfound commitment to quality. Many managers and lower level employees still did not understand the mechanics that produced the desired results. Predictably, we could expect that this lack of understanding would delay the production of the desired outcome: improved quality.

The second counterintuitive assumption of the new quality model was that continual improvement was cost-effective. The old model stressed that the law of diminishing returns would set in, and thus the cost of additional quality increments would eventually exceed the benefits. The "costing out" of the benefits of improvement and the setting of minimum thresholds for instituting improvements was deeply ingrained in the culture of American manufacturing firms and reflected a primary means by which the finance department exerted control over manufacturing.

Skeptics of continuous improvement confused the real dangers of perfectionism with the careful targeting of improvement targets. First, under the new quality model, not any quality improvement path is acceptable. In my investigation of quality practices among 20 leading Japanese companies in 1989, it became clear that costly quality improvement paths were rejected on the shopfloor, with strong organizational pressure being exerted on behalf of a search for least-cost improvement measures. In short, the costs of improvement can be minimized. Put more strongly, optimum quality costs (a sum of prevention, appraisal, and failure costs) can lie very near or at zero defects if the incremental costs of approaching zero defects are less than the incremental return from the resulting improvement. Schneiderman (1986) demonstrates a variety of circumstances under which this could be true. Fine (1986) observes that learning benefits accrue to high-quality performers with a reduction in cost for increased conformance.

Second, skeptics ignored the possibility of disrupting the quality-cost trade-off through breakthrough practices (Kondo, 1979). For ex-

ample, if a manager could not justify the cost of the improved quality that would result from buying a new machine for a given process, one might instead thoroughly reinvent the process, thereby improving quality. Third, the benefits of improved quality and the costs of poor quality are often insufficiently measured. In 1989, I interviewed the head of the quality department at Toyota Motor Co. and specifically asked if there was merit in continuous improvement. He responded,

> This has always been a problem, because to research a 20-yen problem, you may have to spend 100 yen. However, we have stopped arguing about whether the research compensates for the loss in money. We stopped it 20 years ago. This is because failure cost is really only a small part of the total cost. For example, with our warranty system, a customer will bring a faulty automobile, which we fix for free. So, it takes a certain amount of money on our side for repairs. But the customer must pay for gasoline to bring the car to the shop, and he must find a way to get home, plus he will not be able to use the car for a certain period. And since the car is not being used, this is a minus for the national economy. Therefore, we are not covering all of these losses with the money we use at the factory to repair the car. In short, the losses far exceed the costs we incurred fixing the problem.

Critical here is the implicit assumption that the unmeasured customer- and society-incurred costs will become company costs (through negative reputational effects) if not addressed, and that reducing these costs, even if we cannot measure them in a precise fashion, is well worth the investment. Moreover, by adopting the approach it did, Toyota reduced decision costs as well. No top management team at the American auto manufacturers was even remotely thinking in these terms in the early and mid 1980s.

Where's the Evidence?

With regard to both of these assumptions, management demanded hard evidence to support these counterintuitive claims. It is a social psychology truism that individuals are willing to make inferences and take action without evidence when the inferences are consistent with their prior beliefs. However, when the inferences challenge existing beliefs, individuals want evidence before taking action (see Ross & Lepper, 1980). The more problematic the nature of a claim, the more social actors want standard scientific evidence to support that claim before they invest in its purported solution (Stinchcombe, 1990, pp. 176-179). Faced with great uncertainty as to the nature of the new quality model and how to go about implementing it, management responded in just this fashion.

The evidence that managers wanted, however, was hard to get. Even in those cases where it existed, they did not know the right questions to ask or where to look for it. Moreover, they often rejected what evidence there was. Experience with applying the new quality model was still modest in the United States, and it took time for sufficient experience to accumulate that would yield credible data. Nor was this a subject in which American academics were yet interested, and thus they were of no help on this matter. Garvin (1988, pp. 69-92) published one of the first serious efforts to look at the correlates of quality in 1988, and his results were "tentative and inconsistent."

The Japanese experience presumably offered a stock of experience, but this was often seen as inaccessible. Moreover, the Japanese seemed to have a much more relaxed approach to measurement in many areas than did the Americans. This made the Americans, steeped in measurable cost-benefit calculus, reluctant to take their explanations seriously. Compounding the problem were the American quality zealots, who made many extravagant claims for the benefits of quality improvement, thereby alienating many intelligent and experienced managers. This muddied the water regarding the benefits of a strong quality improvement focus and made many managers reluctant to proceed.

Finally, not all evidence is equal. Even when an empirically based and logically sound presentation could be made, it was likely to be rejected if it attacked strongly held predispositions. This is entirely consistent with social psychological research; indeed, such attacks sometimes have the effect of strengthening existing predispositions (Ross & Lepper, 1980).

Rejection took the form of managers questioning whether the results really held or applied to their situation, or whether there was some other possible explanation for the findings. Information that is concrete, directly comparable, and based on firsthand experience is more likely to overcome prior beliefs (Ross & Lepper, 1980, p. 30). Alex Mair, vice president of General Motors, was well known within GM for his convincing demonstrations in 1986 in which he would hold up and compare two connecting rods from GM and Honda engines. Point by point, he would show how much poorer in every respect was GM's mode of production and technology and how it translated into poorer quality and higher costs from a customer perspective (Ingrassia & White, 1994, pp. 88-93). Parenthetically, we note here that in 1986, GM was still struggling to generate awareness among employees that the company had a serious quality problem. In any case, if it took that long to make the case for hard, concrete technologies, it is not surprising that Flynn and Andrea (1994) found that American auto firms found it harder to accept the superiority of Japanese soft/linking technologies (organizational practices that cross departments and functions); predictably, they also were less likely to adopt these soft/linking technologies in their operations.

The thrust of this discussion is that evidence as a factor in changing management's working assumptions is much overrated. It takes an awful lot to overcome deeply held core beliefs. Yet a strong belief in the power of evidence is exactly what generates expectations that individual actors will act rationally to embrace needed changes.

Given the accumulated weight of all of these quality-hostile assumptions, it is not surprising that managerial response to pressures for change was slow to develop. These assumptions represented, on balance, a strong reinforcing system for regulating behavior. Paraphrasing the language of Bourdieu (1981), members of the top management group share common histories and a similar "habitus," creating regularities in thought, aspirations, dispositions, patterns of appreciation, and strategies of action linked to their particular positions in the organizational structure. The instincts and interac-

tions of people in such a system serve to reproduce, not to change, behavior.

The Legitimacy of Learning From the Japanese

Many U.S. managers had a problem with learning from the Japanese. If the Japanese were the
best practitioners of the new quality model,
however, one might expect that American managers would go and learn from them. In fact, the
Japanese were remarkably open to such efforts
at this time. The information was there, and Japan was an obvious place to look. But it was
simply not seen as legitimate to be learning
from the Japanese by many of the older senior
executives at leading American corporations.
There was no norm that legitimated learning
from the Japanese. "We were the leaders, they
were the backward upstarts." Such views were
particularly strong in the old-line industries,
such as steel.

If you start with an assumption that you
could not possibly have anything to learn from a
set of people, you never get to the content of the
ideas they embody. I came to understand the full
significance of this statement in 1990 when I
was visiting the European plants of a large multinational company to help assess their standing
on quality. When I visited the German plant
near Stuttgart, I said to the managers, "You
could learn a lot from the Italian plant on how to
cooperate across functions in your product development process." I cannot begin to capture in
words the look of astonishment and incredulity
on the face of the German managers. That
someone would suggest that we Germans,
known for our quality, would have something to
learn from the Italians in product development
practices could only mean that this individual
was either incredibly stupid or, at best, incredibly naive. There was no way these managers
could get past the idea of learning from the Italians to ever get around to examining the content
of my suggestion. Many American managers
displayed just this reaction to learning basic
management principles from thc Japanese in
the 1970s and early 1980s.

What is the mechanism by which the Americans were able to dismiss the Japanese results?
The framing concept of Tversky and Kahneman
(1986) provides a useful guide. By labeling what
the Japanese were doing as Japanese rather than
seeing it as universally applicable manufacturing practice, American managers put Japanese
practices off limits for serious learning. This
made it an unattractive object for borrowing to
solve their quality problems by weighing it
down with potentially negative cultural content.
Yet they would later try to adopt these very same
ideas once they were "unpacked" and became
available in an American environment.

By waiting until these models became available in the United States, however, valuable time
was lost. Most major U.S. manufacturing companies, to be sure, did the obligatory 1- or
2-week tour of Japanese manufacturing plants
in the early 1980s, but very few went on to establish systematic learning relationships. By
waiting and learning from U.S. companies,
many potential adopters reduced the transaction
costs that would have resulted from efforts to
learn directly from the Japanese. These costs
flowed from language and cultural barriers, the
logistics of long-distance learning, the efforts
necessary to unearth tacit knowledge, and the
costs of separating out universal from pecu-
liarly Japanese features. There is no doubt that
great effort and expense were required to overcome these problems. Instead of incurring these
costs, most U.S. companies chose to be late
adopters, taking advantage of the efforts of
those few companies that did choose to learn directly from the Japanese. In so doing, however,
they lost much time and thereby added costs associated with their slow response time. These
costs included declining market share, continued negative reputational effects for their poor
quality, and lost jobs and profits. For those companies not under great competitive pressures
from their quality disadvantage, it made some
sense to wait. For those who were under great
pressure, such as the automobile and semiconductor companies, however, it seems hard to
justify. They and their employees bore the
heavy costs of not systematically studying at the
social location of the earliest available information (cf. Stinchcombe, 1990).

Seeming to work against the reluctance to learn directly from the Japanese was the popular myth that the Japanese were only doing what Dr. W. Edwards Deming taught them, and therefore, one would really be borrowing American ideas if one was to learn from the Japanese. But, then, why go to Japan? Just study Dr. Deming's ideas here. Unfortunately, Dr. Deming did not have a unified, coherent management theory, much less detailed guidelines on how to implement quality improvement. Evidence for this statement can be found in George Easton's finding in Chapter 5 of this book that Dr. Deming was much less of a starting point for companies than one might have thought, given the attention he received from the American media. Observing, studying, imitating, and adapting practice in Japan would have been a much better guide for them than studying Dr. Deming's quality principles.

There were a few exceptions to this reluctance to learn directly from the Japanese. Some companies with equity shares in Japanese companies or joint ventures did, indeed, choose to learn quality improvement directly from the Japanese. Prominent among them were Ford Motor Company from Mazda, Xerox (to a much lesser extent) from Fuji-Xerox, and Hewlett Packard from Yokogawa Hewlett-Packard. Indeed, these companies are generally recognized for their leadership role in adopting the new quality model.

A notable case is Florida Power and Light, which had no history of Japanese business ties but nevertheless became the most enthusiastic and visible student of Japanese quality practices. FPL adopted Japanese practices wholesale starting in 1985 and engaged in a formal technology transfer agreement with a Japanese utility company. It was not until the mid and late 1980s that it had a strong body of experience to show. FPL then became the mecca for quality studies in the United States. American managers trooped to Miami to attend its monthly seminars. They estimate that 90% of *Fortune* 1000 companies visited by the end of the 1980s. So popular were they that FPL set up a consulting subsidiary, Qualtec, that worked regularly with a large number of major companies. Procter & Gamble and AT&T were just two of the larger companies heavily influenced by FPL.

American firms were willing to learn from FPL because its quality practices could be labeled "American." These same firms were unwilling to learn from the Japanese because their quality was labeled "Japanese." Yet FPL consciously and publicly chose to mimic Japanese practices as much as possible. There was little substantive difference in what American companies learned from FPL compared to what they would have learned several years earlier directly from the Japanese. This is a classic framing issue of the kind noted by Tversky. By waiting to learn from FPL, firms saved a lot in transaction costs, to be sure. But they lost several years in the learning process, years in which market share, profits, and jobs were often eroding. It does not appear to have been a rational choice, at least for those firms under strong competitive pressure from the Japanese.[3]

Doing What We Know Best

Although no single element of the new quality model required rocket science expertise, the required integration of all of the key elements involved a degree of organizational transformation for which few companies were prepared. The Japanese quality challenge was largely exogenous. There were typically no strong internal contradictions that gave rise to the pressure for change among managers.

Under these circumstances, the process is similar to Neil Fligstein's (1991) description of the growth of diversification among American businesses in response to the exogenous shock of the Great Depression. Initially, people are confused, response is slow, and management relies on tools in their existing repertoire. Although reliance on existing expertise might at first seem odd, on closer examination, it seems quite reasonable. When hit with an unforeseen crisis, the magnitude and character of which was not well understood, it is natural that individual actors would choose behaviors and policies with which they are most familiar. One can understand their initial reasoning: "We are in this problem because we are not performing our existing work routines very efficiently." In other words, we need to execute much better what we are already doing.

These observations are quite consistent with research findings at the individual level that psychological stress, anxiety, and arousal tend to lead individuals to persevere in well-learned courses of action. Individuals seek out familiar explanations. Attention gets narrowed to include dominant familiar cues and exclude peripheral, less familiar ones. Adoption of prior well-learned responses in the face of threat reflects a rigidity based on a constriction in the flow of information and a shift in control to higher levels in the organization (Staw et al., 1982, pp. 506-507). In parallel fashion at the organizational level, the entity focuses attention on the sources of danger, economizing on nonrelevant input and processing functions and responding with well-learned habitual responses. Such responses often work well for familiar threats; they work less well with threats of unknown dimensions, such as was the case with the quality challenge. The early responses of American automakers and semiconductor manufacturers in the early 1980s to the Japanese quality challenge were characterized by paralysis as top leaders struggled to understand the nature of the threat, cope with reduced market share, and create a unified corporate response (Cole, 1999). Yet survival in the face of unfamiliar threats is enhanced by a diversity of inputs, and variety in experimental responses is required (Staw et al., 1982, p. 517). It took considerable time for these kinds of responses to develop.

Phil Tetlock (1991, pp. 28-32) approaches the matter from a slightly different angle in his analysis of learning in U.S. and Soviet foreign policy. Applying his model to our analysis, we see management belief systems as being organized hierarchically, with fundamental assumptions and policy objectives at the apex of a system; strategic policy beliefs and preferences at an intermediate level; and tactical beliefs, preferences, and practices at the base of the system. The initial response of actors to new evidence and arguments is to accommodate them by minimizing the number of related cognitions, preferences, and practices that must be changed in the process of incorporating the new evidence into the belief system. Thus, a typical response would be to try new tactics before considering any changes in strategic policy beliefs, preferences, or practices that derive from them. Only when there is repeated failure to come up with a tactical solution does management begin to question its strategy. Similarly, only after repeated failure to come up with a strategic solution do managers question their fundamental goal. This model fits surprisingly well with the actions that management initially took in response to the quality challenge. That response was dominated by tactics. This included quality by exhortation, the receptivity to the model proposed by Philip Crosby, and the popularity of the quality circle movement.

It is perhaps not surprising that the most common early response of top management to the quality challenge in the early 1980s was "quality by exhortation" (cf., Juran, 1995, pp. 584-585). Many managers thought that by raising employee quality awareness through speeches to employees, they could motivate employees to improve quality. At a time when quality problems were thought to be located at the individual level, this seemed quite reasonable. It also gave managers a sense that they were addressing the problem. Such exhortations are in the great American tradition of positive thinking, in which individual effort is seen as overcoming institutional barriers. Not surprisingly, there is little evidence that such exhortations had much effect.

A major figure in the early 1980s was Philip Crosby, a former corporate vice president for quality at ITT. His appeal to American managers in this early period confirms the strong tendency of managers to turn to their existing toolkit in order to find an effective response to a crisis they did not anticipate or understand. In 1979, Philip Crosby published *Quality Is Free*, widely acknowledged as the first and probably only book on quality that American top management read, at least through the first half of the 1980s (Groocock, 1986, p. 22). It is said to have sold 2 million copies in several languages. Many companies purchased the book in bulk and distributed it to all of their managers. Unlike Juran and Deming, Crosby was "untainted" by any Japanese influence. Japanese company practices were notable by their absence in his books and training materials; for those looking for an American solution to our quality problems, Crosby seemed to offer a new direction.

Quality Is Free probably did more to raise top managers' awareness of quality as a major issue linked to the financial performance of the firm than any other event or publication during the early 1980s. The title *Quality Is Free* was a marketing stroke of genius. Moreover, Crosby was clear about management's responsibility for improving quality. Above all, the book contributed greatly to managerial awareness of the cost of quality (costs of poor quality) and its impact on the bottom line. It did this through encouraging firms to measure "the price of nonconformance."

Crosby stressed what he called the four basic absolutes of quality management: the definition of quality as conformance to requirements, the system of causing quality is prevention, the performance standard for quality is zero defects, and the measurement of quality is the price of nonconformance. He described a 14-point program for implementing his approach. The 14 steps are as follows:

1. Management Commitment
2. Quality Improvement Team
3. Measurement
4. Cost of Quality
5. Awareness
6. Corrective Action
7. Zero Defects Planting
8. Employee Education
9. Zero Defects Day
10. Goal Setting
11. Error Cause Removal
12. Recognition
13. Quality Councils
14. Do It All Again

One way to see how Crosby's program reinforced a "more of the same but do it better" mentality is to compare its core elements to the characteristics of the old and new quality models reported in Table 4.1. Looking at the characteristics of the new quality model, we can see Crosby's teachings in the early 1980s as consistent with the use of quality as a strong competitive strategy; a prevention focus; the integration of quality into the control system of goals, plans, and actions; and a focus on cross-functional cooperation to achieve firm-level objectives. It was most at variance with the new quality model in terms of its almost total absence of focus on customers (final users), which is the central organizing element of the new quality model, and in its neglect of a concrete strategy of all employee involvement involving a well-defined problem-solving methodology. Crosby eschewed the use of statistical methods. He did not see the significance of statistics in characterizing a process, nor in prevention. Although there were some cosmetic references to employee involvement and problem solving, they were clearly tertiary themes with no operational implications. To be sure, the training materials were rich in the vocabulary of customers, but the focus was overwhelmingly on describing each employee as a consumer and customer of internal services.

Even some of the seeming similarities between Crosby's ideas and the new quality model are deceptive. Although Crosby did stress the importance of prevention, he focused on individual attitude change rather than on upstream prevention devoted to developing tools and systems for defect-free processes in the design stage. Similarly, although Crosby talked about cross-functional cooperation and integration of quality into the corporate control system, it was more a matter of labeling an area rather than doing the hard work of developing a structured approach to achieving these ends. As one CEO who relied heavily on Crosby said to me, "Crosby was no help in navigating the corporate hierarchy to make quality happen."

A different story emerges when we compare the old quality model and its fit with the Crosby model. To be sure, Crosby would reject many of its elements, such as quality as a stand-alone effort and quality as a specialized function carried out by quality experts. His model is quite in agreement, however, with the old model's defining theme, which is its inward-looking orientation with an overriding emphasis on conformance to requirements. Moreover, in keeping with the old quality model, Crosby kept the emphasis on the quality manager as cop, whose role was to monitor the operations personnel to ensure that they were producing quality products and services. In summary, Crosby's ideas in the early 1980s fit much better with the old than the new quality model.

The appeal of Crosby in the early 1980s was based on his personal skills at motivating top management and the sense among managers that, unlike others, he had a method. The CEO of a medium-size integrated circuit maker explained his adoption of the Crosby package in the early 1980s as follows: "No one else at the time seemed to have a method. We hadn't yet heard of Deming, and Juran was a guy whose lectures seemed to put people to sleep. Crosby talked the language of management." Note that this statement implicitly assumes that the Japanese are not available as a reliable source of information on how to do quality. In a similar vein, a high-level official at Arco Product Co. explained the appeal of Crosby at his company in the 1980s, noting that Crosby had an especially strong appeal to engineers, who liked that he had a "formula" and "deliverables."

All of these observations are consistent with the findings of Easton (see Chapter 5 in this volume) that Crosby was the most influential of the quality gurus in giving companies a new start with quality, even if these efforts stalled out after a few years. By providing a coherent managerial system, as deficient as it turned out to be, it proved to be the "only game in town" at the time. The Japanese experience was in another town and judged to be irrelevant.

In 1979, Crosby left ITT and set up Philip Crosby Associates in Winter Park, Florida as a residential training center. By 1985, the firm was grossing $20 million per year in revenues, and by 1990, 20,000 managers were passing through its classrooms paying a total of $84 million for the company's services (Byrne, 1991, pp. 52, 56). Crosby developed a 2½-day seminar for senior managers and a weeklong one for middle managers at his "executive college" to teach his program. The firm also did in-house training and set up other training centers. He went on from his initial training for IBM to teach managers from an estimated 1,500 companies by 1990 (Dobyns & Crawford-Ma-

son, 1991, p. 68). Signetics, the sixth largest integrated circuit maker at the time, was one of the early adopters of the Crosby program. General Motors and Chrysler were also major customers of the firm in the early and mid 1980s; General Motors went so far as to buy 10% of the firm for $4 million. In 1985, the firm went public, and in 1989, Crosby sold off his interest in the firm (he bought it back in 1997). As of December 1986, General Motors had sent 4,000 employees, mostly executives, to the GM Quality Institute, which was licensed to teach Crosby materials (Cole, 1989, p. 253). Numerous other GM executives attended the Crosby program at his Winter Park facility. General Motors stayed committed to Crosby's approaches until the late 1980s, long after many others had moved on.

Given the enormous quality challenge facing many manufacturing firms during the early 1980s and the sense of crisis, it is of no small interest to understand how it was that managers looking for radical solutions to their problems would end up implementing very conservative ones. Crosby's training stressed that managers experiencing it would be transformed as managers. They will see and be able to act with fresh insight. Yet once managers returned to the workplace, they often ended up reinforcing the old approaches (doing more of the same). How can we reconcile these two seemingly contradictory observations, given the assumption that these managers were intelligent individuals selected for their talent, capabilities, and analytic skills?[4]

The understandings arrived at by middle managers at a weeklong training in a isolated residential facility are one thing. Returning to apply these ideas in the workplace is another. We know enough about the ability of leaders to construct new realities among participants in isolated settings to believe that managers could undergo a kind of transformation that would make them true believers. Crosby's approach contains some central characteristics that are strikingly similar to those that Ernest Gellner (1979, pp. 118-121), the philosopher, identifies with ideology. In Gellner's terminology, Crosby's package contains bait, a unifying idea, and an organizing concept with explanatory power; it illustrates what was previously seen as obscure; and it contains both promise to the believer and fear to those who do not believe, thereby separating believers from skeptics.

The bait is zero defects—a promise of perfection. The unifying idea is conformance to requirements, which is a concept with putative explanatory power. Its absence explains why we are doing so badly, and its presence is the precondition for success. Conformance to requirements illuminates what has previously been obscure, and it does so in exquisitely simple terms. Above all, it promises salvation—zero defects leading to competitive success. In so doing, it raises the stakes, suggesting hope for those who believe and fear for those who do not. Taken in its entirety, it provides a way of looking at the world that separates the believer from the skeptic. What comes through here is the power of Crosby's ideas as a logically consistent marketable package presented in an isolated setting conducive to its acceptance.

The inability of participants to verify empirically the assertions being made in isolated settings lends great power to the leaders seeking such a transformation. Crosby and his teachers' lecture style reinforced this outcome. Students were not encouraged to think and work through problems and arrive at solutions themselves. There were no cases. Rather, students were receptacles for the new understandings that were imparted through lectures by the teachers. Not surprisingly, this put participants in a weak position to evaluate critically what they were experiencing.

Once back in the workplace, however, the seminar participants were surrounded by peers, subordinates, and even superiors who did not share their assumptions. Paradoxically, in the short term, this often had the effect of strengthening their beliefs by letting those managers who had been through the Crosby training realize just how far they had come relative to their coworkers. The presence of uninformed coworkers highlights the shining virtue of those who have attained truth (Gellner, 1979, p. 138). In the long run, however, they were forced to trim their radical initiatives in ways that, in the end, were profoundly conservative.

At the training sessions and in written publications, the language used was clear and straightforward; trainers talked about how simple quality improvement is if you just understand the aforementioned four basic principles. The stress was on implementing Crosby's clear 14-point program in ways that would yield change. Because it was easy to show managers that the costs of quality (cost of nonconformance) at major manufacturing firms typically was 20% or more of their total costs, it seemed only logical to conclude that conformance to requirements was the right direction to pursue solutions. Saving that 20-odd percent would go right to the bottom line, and you would get high quality to boot. This was a heady brew that was hard for managers to resist. This logic, however, ignored the fundamental problem that you could have a perfectly conforming product in which customers had little interest because it was the wrong product, it had the wrong price or the wrong features, or it performed poorly on some other quality dimension important to customers.

The rhetoric of the training was about making business processes transparent so that proper requirements could be set. This, in turn, would lead to new requirements and, hence, change. Participants were told that failure to follow agreed-upon requirements had been a persistent source of quality problems, something upon which they could all agree and recognize. In this context, getting employees to follow the agreed-upon requirements in itself could be seen as a revolutionary act.

Despite attempts to disavow that his was a motivational program (a matter about which some leading quality professionals had roundly criticized Crosby over the years), there was a great stress put on the importance of getting every individual employee to adopt a zero-defect mentality. Employees were asked to sign declarations promising not to make any errors on a given day or for the next 30 days. Recall management's tendency in those days to see quality improvement as simply the aggregate of individual commitments to a high-quality standard. At the same time, instead of providing any real engine for change, managers were taught to strengthen the motivational focus through a reliance on "trinket awards," such as zero-defect hats and T-shirts, Zero Defect Day, and so on.

Crosby was strongly opposed to financial rewards for quality improvement.

What happens when these initiates returned to the workplace? They are supposed to be leaders. Crosby typically gave all graduates a baton to symbolize their role as transformational leaders. Yet the methodologies for how to set the new requirements were abstract. This often led to boilerplate specification of which requirements were necessary to make the process work, as seen from the point of view of the person in charge (e.g., number of employees required, who had to be where at what time, etc.).

The pronoun used in many of the training materials was "you," as if there were a universal "you." Thus, there was no specification of a social process in which individuals collectively identified these requirements. Nor was there a collective problem-solving methodology that provided an engine for change. The image is of an organization in which all employees need to be programmed with the same imperatives to identify the requirements of the process for which they are responsible and to aim for zero defects. There is little social structure in this abstracted firm. The simplicity that this allows for in one-size-fits-all training materials is appealing to managers going through the courses, in that the lessons taught seem to apply to everyone. From the consultant's point of view, it is ideal because it enables the delivery of a standard product without the extra cost of customizing it to a given firm, industry, or type of employee. Employees in the workplace, however, when subjected to the new regime, tended to perceive it as so abstract as not to provide them much guidance in their daily work.

Employees ultimately tire of the hoopla of zero-defect day and the plastering of the workplace with quality slogans. In the face of disaffection and the lack of concrete courses of action, managers fall back on the idea that change is about getting employees to follow agreed-upon requirements—executing better what we are already doing. Because there is no operational mechanism for getting those operating processes to be involved in creating new and improved processes, it is managers who end up setting the rules for the agreed-upon requirements. They tended to do this using traditional criteria and without strong efforts to meet external customer needs.

All that is left in the end is the managerial admonition to employees that "your job is to follow the existing rules." This meshes nicely with the control-oriented large bureaucracies of the 1980s. Ross Perot, a General Motors board of directors member in the mid 1980s, and an individual whose judgment on business seems more finely honed than his judgments on politics, captured the problem nicely. He wrote,

> In a lot of these big companies, what it takes to be successful has nothing to do with making better products or serving the customer or what I call the rules of the marketplace. It has to do with following procedures. (*Detroit Free Press* Staff, 1986, p. 4C).

In short, stressing conformance to requirements, as Crosby did, was not the revolutionary act he claimed it to be. Rather, in the bureaucratic world of many large corporations, it often ended up perpetuating existing rule-oriented thinking. It tended to be interpreted by employees as just another set of arbitrary rules, and these employees had a wealth of experience in how to subvert what they saw as arbitrary management rules. In the end, what was seen by its proponents as a program of radical transformation often got translated into profoundly conservative acts.[5]

One last element of Crosby's appeal requires discussion. There is no doubt that in many companies the application of Crosby's ideas initially did produce quality improvement. Without that being the case, his ideas would not have endured as long as they did. How do we explain this in light of our discussion? Forceful application of the old quality model could produce quality improvement for awhile by virtue of concentrating management and employee attention on quality and the need to avoid error. Just putting quality in the corporate spotlight could give rise to improvements. What these efforts could not produce, however, was sustained quality improvement with the customer as the driver.

The following two examples show how the Crosby program could generate improvements. Some management teams succeeded with

Crosby for a longer time by virtue of the fact that they were very good managers who knew how to motivate their employees; often, they overlaid Crosby with progressive ideas. At Arco Products, a strong, Crosby-inspired, corporate-wide initiative in the early 1980s was sustained until the late 1980s only at their Cherrypoint facility. When asked to explain why it was sustained for so long at this facility, an Arco manager explained that the management at that facility had been "kind of socialistic." By that, he meant that they already had a very strong employee involvement culture with a decentralized approach to problem solving. They were able to use this culture to drive quality improvement. As I noted earlier, employee involvement was a feature that was all but absent from Crosby's ideas. At Cherrypoint, they also absorbed a variety of quality tools independent of Crosby's program. In short, it is possible to argue that Cherrypoint succeeded for a time with Crosby only when it was overlaid with some critical missing ingredients.

A related experience occurred at Signetics, which adopted Crosby's program in the early 1980s.[6] In the course of adopting these ideas, they modified them in some important ways. Above all, they introduced using quality performance as an important element in all of Signetic's managers' semiannual performance reviews and acted on that information in the distribution of pay increases and promotions. That alone was likely to lead managers to search for effective means of improving quality and to encourage subordinates to do likewise. The firm also became involved with a major customer in a "parts per million" contract for supplying integrated circuits for automotive engine controls. This experience led to a great deal of new learning, including, for the first time, a focus on measuring quality performance as a key element in a contractual relationship. It also led to pressure to push problem solving back to fundamental design issues. Although Crosby talked about prevention, he did not give any significant guidance for how it was to occur. The new contract provided the structure for such action to take place. The contract became a flagship program for the rest of the corporation. In other words, companies sometimes made progress while us-

ing Crosby's program because they were doing other positive things as well, and this kept them committed to Crosby for longer than one might have expected.

Conclusion

It is hard to exaggerate the impact of the Japanese quality challenge upon American management. The Americans were truly blindsided by the strong Japanese attack on their prevailing understanding as to the very basis of competitive activity. An indicator of how slow the American response was is that in autos and semiconductors, the quality gap seems to have actually grown between 1980 and 1985 (for semiconductors, see U.S. General Accounting Office, 1992, p. 10; for autos, see Juran, 1995, p. 582).

We are dealing literally with how managers over the course of a decade and more constructed new social meanings and made sense of their new competitive environment as they slowly came to grips with the content of the new quality model. For the first several years of the new quality challenge, however, the conditions for effective learning were not met. Many entrenched institutional factors worked against the recognition of quality as a competitive factor and against learning effective responses to this challenge. We have seen how a variety of systematic errors slowed the progress of absorbing the new quality model. Not only did they have incomplete information, but managers were prisoners of their existing values, norms, and practices. This strongly conditioned the nature of their search for understanding the quality problem and what they saw during that search. As a consequence, a great deal of resources invested in quality improvement were wasted in the pursuit of failed initiatives. In response to a threat of unknown proportions, the initial response, not surprisingly, reflected a rigidity that manifested itself in paralysis and doing more of the same.

Management's initial efforts were mostly at the level of tactics using management by exhortation, as well as giving a strong reception to the

Crosby model, which led them, in the end, to engage in relatively conservative tactical actions. Although I have not discussed it here for lack of space, the other major response was the extensive experimentation with quality circles. At the height of the movement in the early 1980s, it became de rigeur for *Fortune* 500 companies to initiate such programs. Typically, however, they were totally divorced from any strategic initiatives by the company and certainly did not challenge fundamental beliefs and objectives. By the mid 1980s, quality circles were no longer in vogue, and many of the initial efforts to apply Crosby were stalled. As a consequence, management was forced to think more deeply about the appropriate corporate strategies. In summary, throughout much of the early and mid 1980s, management actions were at the tactical level and as such were quite consistent with the Tetlock model described earlier.

Yet out of the debris left by the trial-and-error learning of the early 1980s, valuable experience was gained. Motivational programs based on individual improvement came to be understood as insufficient. Quality improvement by management exhortation and directive was shown to be ineffective. System approaches to prevention and process improvement came to be recognized as positive, as did setting high goals for improvement (zero defects). In retrospect, Crosby's approach appears primitive and counterproductive in many respects; clearly, it was grossly inadequate for solving "the quality problem." Yet it got top executives thinking more seriously about quality and the cost of quality failures. It got companies started doing something, and something is often better than nothing, however inadequate it may be. Managers reached out to the Crosby formulations, as the scholar Sidney Winter put it in our initial conference, as a "yellow page heuristic"; it was the first approach they could find that seemed to make sense to them. As such, Crosby's model did get many companies started and, in that sense, laid some groundwork for future efforts viewed over the longer term (see Easton, Chapter 5 in this volume). The early failures provided the foundation for questioning the strategic policy beliefs, preferences, and, ultimately, practices that stood in the way of implementing

more thoroughgoing responses to the Japanese quality challenge.

Alongside the weak approaches discussed here, promising alternative routes were pursued as well, such as OEM's reducing its number of suppliers so that it could work more closely with the suppliers to improve quality. These and other understandings became the basis for the more productive efforts of the late 1980s and early 1990s. All of this, however, took time—lots of time! For those firms under strong competitive pressure from a quality deficit, these were costly delays indeed.

Notes

1. Additional analyses of this data set, as well as another, all point in the direction of discontinuity, as do the case study data (see Cole, 1999).

2. For sheet steel, see American Iron and Steel Institute (1985, p. 57); for copiers, see Kearns and Nadler (1992); for automobiles, see Abernathy (1982); for semiconductors, see Okimoto, Sugano, and Weinstein (1984, pp. 51-62); for color TVs, see Juran (1978, pp. 10-18); and for air conditioners, see Garvin (1983).

3. In the early 1990s, FPL was to become a negative role model as the company that learned too much from the Japanese and did not sufficiently adapt what it learned to U.S. conditions. Nevertheless, there is no denying its strong influence on other U.S. companies. Indeed, some managers from visiting companies such as Alcoa specifically complained about this feature of FPL, while also making it clear that they had much to learn. I am indebted to conversations with Pete Kolesar for this last observation; he served as a quality advisor to Alcoa during this period (interview in January 1996).

4. I am indebted to my eminent colleague at the Center for Advanced Study in the Behavioral Sciences in 1996, Pascal Boyer, an anthropologist at the Centre National de la Recherche Scientifique in Lyons, France, for his insights on this matter. Dr. Boyer worked for the Paris office of Philip Crosby Associates in the mid 1980s. The firm prides itself on teaching its materials in exactly the same way so that everyone learns exactly the same thing no matter where they are learning it (Byrne, 1991, p. 56).

5. These observations are not intended as a statement on the current activities of Philip Crosby Associates. Its approach evolved over time. It now teaches business process reengineering, applied statistical quality control, and so on. Our analysis here is intended only to capture the dynamics of the early and mid 1980s.

6. Interview with Charles Harwood, who was the CEO at Signetics at this time (Palo Alto, CA, July 15, 1996).

References

Abernathy, W. (1982). *The competitive status of the U.S. auto industry.* Washington, DC: National Academy Press.

Angel, D. (1994). *Restructuring for innovation: The remaking of the U.S. semiconductor industry.* New York: Guilford.

American Iron and Steel Institute. (1985). Domestic steel producers respond to automakers' demand: "quality or else." *Quality Progress, 18,* 57-59.

Bourdieu, P. (1981). Men and machines. In K. Knorr-Cetina & A. Cicourel (Eds.), *Advances in social theory and methodology* (pp. 304-318). Boston: Routledge & Kegan Paul.

Byrne, J. (1986, January 20). Business fads: What's in and what's out. *Business Week,* pp. 40-47.

Byrne, J. (1991, October 25). Managing for quality: High priests and hucksters. *Business Week,* pp. 52-57.

Carroll, G., & Harrison, J. R. (1994). On the historical efficiency of competition between organizational populations. *American Journal of Sociology, 100,* 720-749.

Cole, R. (1989). Large-scale change and the quality revolution. In A. Mohrman, Jr., S. Mohrman, G. Ledford, Jr., T. Cumming, & E. Lawler (Eds.), *Large-scale organizational change* (pp. 229-254). San Francisco: Jossey-Bass.

Cole, R. (1999). *Managing quality fads: How American business learned to play the quality game.* New York: Oxford University Press.

Crosby, P. (1979). *Quality is free.* New York: McGraw-Hill.

Detroit Free Press Staff. (1986, November 25). Ross Perot: The man who speaks his mind on GM. *Detroit Free Press,* p. 4C.

Dobyns, L., & Crawford-Mason, C. (1991). *Quality or else.* Boston: Houghton Mifflin.

Fine, C. (1986). Quality improvement and learning in productive systems. *Management Science, 32,* 1301-1315.

Fligstein, N. (1991). The structural transformation of American industry: An institutional account of the causes of diversification in the largest firms, 1919-1979. In W. Powell & P. DiMaggio (Eds.), *The new institutionalism in organizational analysis* (pp. 311-336). Chicago: University of Chicago Press.

Flynn, M., & Andrea, D. (1994). *Corporate learning from Japan: The automotive industry* (Report no. 94-14). Ann Arbor: University of Michigan, Office for the Study of Automotive Transportation.

Garvin, D. (1983, September-October). Quality on the line. *Harvard Business Review,* pp. 64-75.

Garvin, D. (1988). *Managing quality.* New York: Free Press.

Gellner, E. (1979). *Spectacles and predicaments.* Cambridge, UK: Cambridge University Press.

Groocock, J. (1986). *The chain of quality.* New York: Wiley.

Ingrassia, P., & White, J. (1994). *Comeback.* New York: Simon & Schuster.

Ishikawa, K. (1985). *What is total quality control?* Englewood Cliffs, NJ: Prentice Hall.

Juran, J. (1978, December). Japanese and Western quality: A contrast. *Quality Progress, 11,* 10-18.

Juran, J. (1995). *A history of managing for quality.* Milwaukee, WI: ASQC Quality Press.

Kearns, D., & Nadler, D. (1992). *Prophets in the dark.* New York: Harper Business.

Kondo, Y. (1979). Ningensei to QC (II) [Humanity and QC (II)]. *Hinshitsu, 9,* 5-10.

MacDuffie, J. P., & Pil, F. (1997, May). *High involvement work systems and quality/productivity performance in the world auto industry 1989-1994: Contingency vs. one best way perspectives.* Paper presented at a National Science Foundation workshop, "Integrating Social Science Theory and Research in Quality Improvement," Berkeley, CA.

Mizuno, S. (1988). *Company-wide total quality control.* Tokyo: Asian Productivity Organization.

Nadler, D., Gerstein, M., Shaw, R., & Associates. (1992). *Organizational architecture.* San Francisco: Jossey-Bass.

Okimoto, D., Sugano, T., & Weinstein, F. (1984). *Competitive edge: The semiconductor industry in the U.S. and Japan.* Palo Alto, CA: Stanford University Press.

Robinson, A. (1980). Perilous times for U.S. microcircuit makers. *Science, 208,* 582-584.

Ross, L., & Lepper, M. (1980). The perseverance of beliefs: Empirical and normative considerations. In R. Shweder (Ed.), *Fallible judgment in behavioral research.* San Francisco: Jossey-Bass.

Scherkenbach, W. (1986). *The Deming route to quality and productivity.* Washington, DC: CeePress.

Schneiderman, A. (1986, November). Optimum quality costs and zero defects: Are they contradictory concepts? *Quality Progress, 19,* 28-31.

Shiba, S., Graham, A., & Walden, D. (1993). *A new American TQM.* Portland, OR: Productivity Press.

Starbuck, W., & Milliken, F. J. (1988). Executives' perceptual filters: What they notice and how they make sense. In D. C. Hambrick (Ed.), *The executive effect: Concepts and methods for studying top managers* (pp. 35-65). Greenwich, CT: JAI.

Staw, B., Sandelands, L., & Dutton, J. (1982). Threat-rigidity effects in organizational behavior: A multilevel analysis. *Administrative Science Quarterly, 26,* 501-524.

Stinchcombe, A. (1990). *Information and organizations.* Berkeley: University of California Press.

Tetlock, P. E. (1991). Learning in U.S. and Soviet foreign policy: In search of an elusive concept. In G. Breslauer & P. E. Tetlock (Eds.), *Learning in U.S. and Soviet foreign policy* (pp. 20-61). Boulder, CO: Westview.

Tushman, M., & Anderson, P. (1986). Technological discontinuities and organizational environments. *Administrative Science Quarterly, 31,* 439-465.

Tversky, A., & Kahneman, D. (1986). Rational choice and the framing of decisions. *Journal of Business, 59*(4), S251-S278.

U.S. General Accounting Office. (1992). *SEMATECH's technological progress and proposed R&D program* (GAO/RCED-92-223BR, pp. 1-44.) Washington, DC: Government Printing Office.

Weick, K. (1995). *Sensemaking in organizations.* Thousand Oaks, CA: Sage.

Chapter 5

Patterns in the Deployment of Total Quality Management

An Analysis of 44 Leading Companies

GEORGE S. EASTON
SHERRY L. JARRELL

Total quality management (TQM) represents probably the most significant management phenomenon of the past 20 years in the United States. Although the specific term "TQM" has lost favor over the past few years (even generating significant backlash), virtually all of the key themes of the TQM movement of the 1980s and early 1990s persist today. These themes underlie much of the current genuine management innovation, as well as many of the current management fads. Examples of such themes include process concepts, systematic improvement, employee involvement, empowerment, teamwork, customer focus, supplier integration, emphasis on metrics, and cycle time reduction, among others. These themes are fundamental components of subsequent "named" management trends, such as reengineering (TQM-related themes: process focus, improvement, metrics, cycle time reduction); supply chain management (process focus, cycle time reduction, supplier integration); and high-performance work systems (employee involvement, empowerment, teamwork).[1]

All of the themes mentioned above, of course, existed prior to the onset of the U.S. TQM movement in the early 1980s. It is not difficult to credibly argue, however, that TQM was key in legitimizing many of them in corporate America, and it was thus a key enabler of the subsequent named management phenomena. For example, employee participation and team concepts had been around for many years prior to the beginning of the TQM movement. TQM, however, was instrumental in legitimizing team-based management approaches, and, in

AUTHORS' NOTE: The authors would like to thank the companies that participated in this research. This research was supported by National Science Foundation grants SBR-9523962 and SBR-9523003; by a grant from the conference "Field Studies in Quality Management" at the Simon Graduate School of Business Administration, University of Rochester; and by summer research grants from the University of Chicago Graduate School of Business, the Goizueta Business School at Emory University, Indiana University School of Business, and the Babcock Graduate School of Management at Wake Forest University.

fact, the maturing of teamwork in TQM companies, combined with the ideas of process management and a general orientation toward empowerment, was largely responsible for self-managed work teams (which generally are organized around a specific process) becoming more than an isolated and sporadic occurrence (they are still not common). Because of these kinds of influence, there is no question that TQM has had an important and sustained impact on both U.S. management practice and academic theory, reaching far beyond the companies that were specifically committed to implementing TQM.

Because most of the themes and approaches that make up TQM were not originated as a part of TQM, but, rather, adopted by TQM, much of the contribution of TQM has to do with the integration of the various themes into a coherent management system. More than any of TQM's specific aspects, it is this integration of technical, cultural, behavioral, and organizational facets that makes TQM a distinct phenomenon.[2] Part of such a successful integration includes understanding how to make various specific methods effective in the complex context of real organizations. In retrospect, it is probably not surprising that TQM has, over time, fragmented into a variety of related submovements, and that efforts to distinguish these submovements has contributed to mischaracterization of TQM (e.g., TQM is only about incremental improvement) and subsequent TQM backlash. Thus, we argue that in spite of the current rhetoric of some, TQM is an important phenomenon and a valid subject of study.

The objective of this study is to examine some of the patterns in the implementation of TQM experienced by a sample of companies that achieved relatively advanced TQM systems. The companies we study began serious efforts to implement TQM between 1982 and 1990. We examine these companies in order to understand if there are common themes concerning how their TQM approaches began, which strategies were used for deployment, what were the key influences, and what made these companies successful. Part of this is retrospective "sensemaking," but in doing so, we hope to learn not only what happened and what

factors appear to have made TQM successful but also, more broadly, about successful organizational change.

Before turning to a detailed description of the research methodology, it is perhaps useful to characterize TQM in more detail than is provided in the introductory discussion above. Although a complete definition of TQM is beyond the scope of this chapter,[3] some of TQM's key characteristics include the following:

- Emphasis on the concept of "process" as a fundamental building block of the organization with a resulting emphasis on process definition, process management, and process improvement

- Widespread organizational focus on quality improvement, cycle time reduction, and waste (cost) reduction; adoption of a "prevention" focus

- Efforts to apply the process concept and focus on improvement (quality improvement, cycle time reduction, and waste reduction) throughout the company, including areas outside of production, such as product development and business support processes

- Emphasis on customer focus; "customer focus" is a complex concept in the context of quality management and includes (a) emphasis on customer requirements and customer satisfaction to define product and service quality ("customer-defined quality"); (b) emphasis on customer service (lead-time reduction, on-time delivery, field support, technical support, etc.); (c) integration of customer information into the management and improvement systems, particularly into the new product development process and the production and service quality control and improvement processes; and (d) efforts to become integrated with customers as appropriate (often called "partnering"), such as joint improvement teams; participation in the customer's new product development processes; or involving customers in the company's own internal processes, such as planning, new product development, R&D, or technology forecasting

- Emphasis on the deployment of systematic, fact-based decision making driven by objective data and information ("management by fact")

- Widespread employee involvement in improvement (quality, cycle time, and waste), usually through teams; strong emphasis on employee development through training, leading to increased empowerment and a general tendency to drive decision making closer to the actual processes. In advanced implementations, these characteristics usually lead to implementation of self-managed teams.

- Explicit emphasis on cross-functional management, including cross-functional improvement as well as cross-functional involvement in key processes, such as new product development. Part of the cross-functional emphasis stems from the focus on processes (which typically cross multiple functions). However, the overall cross-functional emphasis is much stronger and recognizes that cross-functional issues and involvement require specific leadership and organizational focus in order to achieve highly effective management systems.

- Emphasis on supplier quality and service, supplier improvement, and supplier involvement and integration (supplier partnerships), such as joint quality improvement and participation in new product development, technology development and planning, and even strategic planning

- Recognition that implementation and aggressive refinement of the above management model is a critical competitive strategy and, thus, a primary concern of all levels of management, including senior management. The role of senior management in providing leadership for the development and deployment of quality management is a natural consequence of recognition of quality management as a (perhaps the) critical competitive strategy.

Many specific processes (e.g., Quality Function Deployment), tools (e.g., Pareto diagram), and other specific methods support the TQM characteristics described above. In fact, TQM is sometimes mistakenly defined in terms of the specific tools. The use of specific methods and tools *is* a key part of TQM, and their necessity follows from the focus on processes (which requires well-defined approaches) and the emphasis on systematic analysis that is a part of management-by-fact. However, in the enumeration of the characteristics of TQM above, we have chosen to focus on what we believe are the fundamental themes that characterize TQM and underlie the specific processes and tools that might be used in implementing TQM.

In this chapter, we examine how TQM was deployed in a sample of 44 companies that achieved relatively advanced systems. We specifically focus on how these companies' TQM systems began, how they were influenced by the various TQM gurus, and what the subsequent major phases were in their development toward mature systems. We examine these questions by analyzing interviews conducted with senior quality executives at each of the companies. The interviews analyzed here were part of 176 interviews conducted in conjunction with a prior study on the impact of TQM on corporate performance (Easton & Jarrell, 1998; Jarrell & Easton, 1997). These interviews were conducted because reliable public information concerning the state of development of these firms' TQM systems and when their development began is not generally available. The research issues involved in assessing the impact of TQM on firm performance are discussed further in Easton and Jarrell (1999).

Of the 176 firms interviewed, 108 were identified (based on the interviews) as having made serious efforts to deploy TQM in the majority of their business(es). Of these, 44 were identified as having developed more advanced TQM systems. These 44 advanced firms are analyzed in this chapter. Analysis of the remainder of the 176 interviews is the focus of ongoing research.

The remainder of this chapter is organized as follows. The next section discusses the sample selection method, followed by a description of the interviewing technique and how the interview notes were analyzed. Next are the results of the analysis organized around the key questions examined in this chapter, together with some discussion. The chapter concludes with a summary and brief discussion of some additional implications of the findings of this research.

Sample Selection

Candidate firms for the sample of TQM firms whose financial performance was analyzed in

Easton and Jarrell (1998, and reported in Chapter 10, this volume) were initially identified through publicly available information sources. Although the search for firms was very comprehensive, it was not intended to be exhaustive. The primary sources used were the ARS full-text database of on-line annual reports from Nexus/Lexus (since 1987), the Businesswire full-text database of press releases (since 1986), Standard and Poor's Corporate Register of Directors (1993), and the U.S. General Accounting Office (GAO) (1991) Report's list of Baldrige Award site-visited companies.

The identification of the sample of firms for the study and the interviews occurred in two phases. The first (pilot) phase was based on companies initially identified through annual report searches. The searches were for the key words "total quality management," "just-in-time" or "JIT," "Baldrige," "Deming," "Juran," and "Crosby," and 274 firms were identified. Relevant excerpts from the annual reports were reviewed to select only firms whose annual reports clearly indicated implementation of at least one specific quality management approach (e.g., statistical process control, just-in-time manufacturing, quality training, etc.).

Review of the annual report searches resulted in a list of 78 firms. These firms were contacted to set up an interview with a senior manager familiar with the development of the firm's quality management systems, generally a vice president or director of quality. Of the 78 firms, 59 were interviewed. Firms were not interviewed for several reasons. In 11 cases, interviews were not conducted because it became clear in conversations that the firm was not actually implementing TQM. In the remaining 8 cases, the request was refused. Of the 59 firms interviewed, 15 were eliminated because the interviews did not indicate serious efforts to implement TQM in a majority of their business. An additional 5 firms were eliminated because the required performance data were not available. The remaining 39 firms formed the sample of event firms in the pilot phase of the study. The interviews for the pilot sample were conducted between January and March 1993.

In the second phase of the study, additional candidate firms were identified using a variety of sources. First, an additional 54 firms were selected after a second review of the original 274 firms identified by the pilot sample annual report searches. Second, new candidate firms were sought through additional database searches, as well as from some additional lists. The Businesswire database was searched for references to quality awards. Searches were also made for quality-related titles. The annual report database was searched for "quality" within five words of "vice president" or "director," and the Businesswire database was searched for "total" or "continuous" within three words, and "focus" and "satisfaction" within five words, of "vice president" or "director." These searches resulted in 89 candidate firms. The 1993 Standard and Poor's Register of Directors and Executives was searched for quality-related executive titles by searching for "quality" within five words of "vice president" or "director," resulting in 71 candidate firms. Finally, lists of site-visited firms from the GAO study and lists of the institutional affiliations of Baldrige Award Examiners for the years 1989 to 1993 (available from the Baldrige Award Office, National Institute of Standards and Technology [NIST]) were reviewed, resulting in 67 candidate firms. Thus, 281 new candidate firms were identified in the second phase of the study.

As in the pilot phase of the study, the information on the new candidate firms obtained through the searches was reviewed for evidence of deployment of quality management approaches. This resulted in a list of 129 firms that were contacted for interviews. Of these, 117 agreed to be interviewed. Of the 12 firms that were not interviewed, 6 declined to participate and 6 obviously did not have TQM programs. Of the firms that were interviewed, 38 were eliminated because the interviews did not confirm serious efforts to implement TQM in a majority of their business, and 10 were eliminated because the required performance data were not available. This resulted in 69 additional event firms. These interviews were conducted between August 1993 and January 1994.

In summary, information on more than 500 firms was reviewed to identify potential sample firms. Of these, 207 were approached for interviews. Fourteen firms declined to participate, giving an overall response rate of 93%. In trying to set up the interviews, 17 firms were found not to have a TQM system. Thus 176 firms were actually interviewed. As a result of the interviews, 53 firms (30% of those interviewed) were eliminated because their efforts to implement TQM did not appear to be adequate. An additional 15 firms were eliminated because the required performance data were unavailable. This process resulted in 108 TQM firms. Appendix 5.1 lists the TQM firms together with the year their corporatewide TQM implementation was determined to have begun.

Based on the interviews, a subsample of 44 firms was selected, the members of which were judged to have more mature quality management systems. The interview methodology and the basis for selection of these firms are discussed in the next section. These 44 advanced firms constitute the sample of firms analyzed in this chapter. For confidentiality reasons (also discussed further in the next section), the subsample of 44 more advanced firms cannot be specifically identified here.

Interview Methodology

Each of the candidate firms was contacted to set up an interview with a senior manager who was familiar with the development of the company's quality management systems. Once identified, the senior manager, generally a vice president or director of quality, was contacted first with a letter describing the research project and purpose of the interview and then by telephone to set up the interview. The interviews were conducted by telephone by George S. Easton, a former Examiner and Senior Examiner for the Malcolm Baldrige National Quality Award for 4 years. The interviews generally lasted about 45 minutes. The objective of the interview process was to construct a time line of the development of the company's TQM systems; determine which key approaches were used; and, through in-depth probing in a few areas, determine the actual extent of deployment of the company's approaches. The interviews were conducted using a semistructured approach that allowed flex-

ibility in the specific topics discussed. The managers were promised complete confidentiality concerning the content of the interviews.

The interviews were conducted in two phases. The objective of the first phase was to elicit from the manager, with minimal prompting, the major milestones in the development of the company's TQM approaches as they came to the manager's mind. After a brief introduction, the interview began with questions such as "How did your company begin TQM?" or "How did your company become interested in TQM?" Questions were asked as necessary to establish the level of detail required. Questions were also asked to make vague, philosophical, or broad discussions more concrete and to determine if changes in philosophy or perspective resulted in specific events, organizational structures (such as teams), or documents. Such questions might include the following: "How and when was this communicated to the workforce?" "Was this change in thinking (or values or beliefs) summarized in a document?" "How was this deployed?" or "How did this change what the workforce (or management) did on a day-to-day basis?" Questions were asked to determine as specifically as possible the dates of the events described (especially those surrounding the beginning of the TQM approaches) and who was involved. Questions about approaches or methods not mentioned by the manager, however, were avoided in order to not influence the initial description.

Once a phase of the company's TQM approach was described, if the executive did not automatically continue with the time line of the deployment of the TQM system, the interview was continued with questions such as "What was the next major milestone?" "What was the next critical event?" or "What was the next phase?" Such questions were also used to move an interview forward in the event that an executive was providing too much detail or pursuing unrelated discussion.

The managers' impromptu descriptions are very revealing concerning which aspects of the development of the TQM system the manager believes are important and what the key drivers of the system actually are. Thus, these descriptions tend to reveal how management thinks about its TQM systems. This approach to conducting the interviews was selected based on considerable experience conducting interviews as a part of the Baldrige Award process and in a consulting context. When combined with specific questioning as described below in Phase 2 of the interviews, it is a highly effective way to elicit a description of the key aspects of the management system and to understand the themes that drive the system's development. It should be noted that the executives interviewed were selected because they (should) have a coherent, overall view of the company's management system.

In contrast, interview approaches based on listing techniques have a tendency to degenerate into "checklist" responses of "Yes, we do (or have) that." This is particularly true in large companies because most quality-related techniques or approaches will virtually all have been tried somewhere in the organization at some time. In large organizations, there are even likely to be "pockets of excellence" in the use or deployment of an approach, even when it is not an important component of the overall management system and is not widely deployed in the company as a whole.

The second phase of the interview process was intended to fill in any important gaps in the description of the management system given in Phase 1 and to probe in depth some key areas in order to assess actual levels of deployment. The list of interview topics given in Appendix 5.2 was used as a prompt for the interviewer. The objective was not to try to discuss every topic in each interview but, rather, to discuss in detail a few areas as appropriate for the company's particular approaches and the expertise and experience of the manager. In most cases, the areas probed were related to approaches or events described during Phase 1. Phase 1 of the interview process not only helped provide the information necessary to ask relevant specific questions, but also provided context for interpreting the responses.

If not adequately addressed by the manager's initial description of the time line, four areas in the list of interview topics were always covered: production, customer satisfaction measurement, supplier management, and new product development and design. In general, the extent of deployment of the approaches mentioned was assessed by asking specific questions concerning the number of employees involved, the training they have received, and the dates of the various events mentioned. Other questions used to determine the actual extent of deployment include the following: "What were the lessons learned in the first round of deployment?" "What was done particularly well the first time?" "How was the approach changed for the second or third rounds of deployment and why?" "What groups or types of employees had particular difficulty with the approach?" "What would you do differently if you were to begin implementing this approach again?" When the approaches described have actually been deployed, there is generally a rich story surrounding them, and it is fairly easy for a knowledgeable interviewer to determine if significant deployment has actually occurred.

Analysis Methods

The notes from each company's interview (which were not sequential, in part because of the two-phased approach) were rewritten into a time line summarizing the company's major approaches. An example of such a time line is given in Appendix 5.3. Companies were included in the sample of 108 firms used in Easton and Jarrell (1998) to assess the impact of TQM on corporate performance if, based on the interviews, they appeared to have made serious efforts to implement TQM approaches in the majority of their business(es). The TQM efforts must have been deployed in a majority of the company (as measured by sales) for there to be any reasonable expectation that the results could be observable in the company's overall financial statements. The standard of "serious efforts" for inclusion in the sample is quite low; it is not a requirement that the company's efforts resulted in a comprehensive and well-integrated approach.

Based on the interviews, companies were eliminated from the sample for a variety of reasons. In many cases, companies were eliminated because their TQM efforts were deployed in only a small fraction of the company. Other reasons range from a lack of evidence of any significant deployment efforts to confusion of TQM with other approaches (such as quality improvements due solely to automation).

For the companies that were included in the sample, the start date was selected based on the time line developed from the interview notes. In this chapter, the start date for most of the companies was selected to be the initial deployment of the first major companywide initiative. This major initiative was usually the deployment of widespread quality training. In some companies, however, other major initiatives marked the beginning of the development of their TQM systems, such as major changes in customer satisfaction measurement, major changes in product development, or deployment of a quality management systems assessment process. In some companies, there was no clear companywide initiative that marked the beginning of the company's deployment. In these cases, there was generally a fairly specific period during which approaches in multiple divisions or departments coalesced into a reasonably well-identified companywide system. In these cases, this period was selected to be the start date.

Note that the start dates used in the analysis in this chapter are slightly different from those used in Easton and Jarrell (1998). In that study, the start date was chosen to be 6 months after the first companywide initiative (or the period during which the company's efforts coalesced). The selection of the start date in Easton and Jarrell (1998) took into consideration the methodology used to measure financial performance and sought to balance a number of factors as discussed in that paper. In particular, when financial performance was the focus, it was reasonable to believe that the financial impact of initiatives would be delayed considerably after the initial deployment because most of the initiatives take a substantial period of time to roll out. For example, it is not uncommon for widespread training initiatives to take more than a year, and sometimes 3 or 4 years, to complete. Furthermore, there is usually a lag between the initiative and the beginning of any substantive

organizational or operational changes. In particular, there is generally a lag between quality improvement training, deployment of improvement teams, and completion of the improvement projects that actually generate improvements. In contrast, in this chapter, we are interested in the specific approaches used and their timing rather than the impact on financial performance. Note that the "Year of Implementation" listed in Appendix 5.1 is the same as used in Easton and Jarrell (1998) and thus is different (based on approximately a 6-month delay) from the start dates in the interview notes that are the basis for the analysis in this study.

The companies that were retained for the sample of firms in Easton and Jarrell (1998) were divided into a group of 44 firms with more advanced TQM systems and 64 firms with less advanced TQM systems. The 44 advanced firms form the sample in this chapter. The separation between the more advanced and less advanced firms was made by making a rough estimate, based solely on the interviews, of what the firm's score would be in terms of the approach and deployment aspects of the Baldrige criteria. It should be noted that the interviews focused only on the approaches taken and the extent of their deployment and not on the operational or financial results that were achieved. The firms selected for the more advanced TQM subsample had estimated scores above 450 out of the 1,000 possible points. The median score of companies that actually apply for the Baldrige Award is generally below 500 (e.g., see Easton, 1993a). A Baldrige score above 450 represents considerable success in developing and deploying a TQM system.

The key differences between the companies selected as more advanced and less advanced were in the scope of the (Baldrige criteria) issues that were addressed by their TQM systems and the extent of deployment of their approaches. Some of the firms in the less advanced group had successfully deployed basic approaches, such as quality training and improvement teams, but then had not further developed their quality management systems. Others had deployed approaches that address a broader scope of the Baldrige criteria but had only limited deployment. The firms in the more advanced group have better deployment of the basic approaches together with the deployment of systems that address a broader scope of the Baldrige criteria. These companies typically have had multiple phases in the development of their TQM systems, as was discussed in the previous section.

For the analysis in this chapter, the statements in the companies' time lines were recorded as individual records in a relational database program. The following is an example of a typical record in the database:

Record Number: ####
Date (text, from notes): Late 84-85
Date (numeric): 12/1/84
Record: Realized the need for tools—designed three new 2-day courses: communications and group dynamics, problem solving, data collection and display
Keys: Basic training, advanced training, tools, problem solving, teamwork

---

Each record was then coded with keywords that capture the key topics that relate to the statement in the record. The keyword coding is the result of multiple iterations of refinement that included consolidation of multiple keys and several independent reviews of the keywords associated with each record by both authors. These keywords were then used as the basis for a content analysis of the interview notes via automated database queries. For the 44 companies comprising the sample of more advanced TQM firms, the database consists of 972 records. The database approach was used because manual content analysis was attempted and proved intractable.

The keywords used in the database are listed in Appendix 5.4. The keyword list is comprehensive, containing approximately 200 entries. Its scope is far beyond the topics analyzed in this chapter. The keys were developed with the specific intent to not limit future research. They are intended to both capture general topics (e.g., training), as well as to capture specific topics relevant to TQM that were mentioned by only a few companies. We feel that the fact that some

topics were not mentioned or seldom mentioned is also of potential interest in the analysis of the database. The individual queries used in the analysis are described in the next section.

Because of the promise of confidentiality made to the executives interviewed, the firms in the more advanced sample cannot be identified in this chapter. To identify this subsample automatically identifies the subsample of less advanced firms. The potential sensitivities associated with being identified as "less advanced" are obvious. Company identifiers have been removed from the content analyses presented. Finally, the statements from the notes presented have been "sanitized" to remove program or approach names that are likely to identify specific companies. The authors believe that the confidentiality of the companies has been preserved while at the same time key features of the interviews and analysis have been presented accurately.

Results and Discussion

In this section, we examine, using the interview time lines, the three main issues that are the focus of this study:

1. How did these more advanced companies begin deploying TQM?
2. What were the influences of the TQM gurus: Deming, Juran, Crosby, and the Japanese?
3. What were the patterns in the major phases of deployment of TQM by these companies?

For each of these questions, we discuss the implications of the analysis of the interviews.

The content analyses are presented in the appendixes organized by topic. They include the records from the interviews together with either the year to which the record refers or the number of years into the deployment of the company's TQM system. In interpreting these results, it is important to keep in mind that because the interviews were designed to elicit the important features of the deployment of the companies' quality management approaches, absence of mention of a particular technique in a company's time line does not necessarily imply that the approach was not used. Rather, absence should be interpreted as suggesting that the approach is not considered to be one of the most important or critical aspects of the company's overall TQM system at the corporate level. The nature of the approaches reported in the interviews appears to vary somewhat with the size and organization of the companies. In particular, in large companies with many relatively autonomous divisions or business units, the specificity of the descriptions of the quality management systems tended to, in a sense, parallel the level of the corporate structure. In these companies, fewer specific details were given about approaches within the business units or divisions, and there was a corresponding higher emphasis on more general programs or more global strategies and approaches. Taken together, however, the interviews give a very clear picture of how the TQM movement developed and when various approaches came on the scene.

Also note in interpreting the results that the company identifiers are artificial and are not the same between appendixes. Thus, for example, Company 1 in Appendix 5.5 is not the same as Company 1 in Appendix 5.6. Within an appendix, and thus a topic, the identifiers do refer to the same company; for example, the two comments identified as Company 1 in Appendix 5.5 do refer to the same company. This was done so that, within a topic, multiple comments by each company can be grouped while also protecting the confidentiality of the companies by preventing reconstruction of their time lines across topics.

Initial Deployment

We begin by examining how the companies' TQM programs were initiated. What constituted the real beginning of a company's TQM approach depends on how the beginning is defined by the researchers. The way that we have defined the beginning of a company's TQM deployment in this chapter was directly influenced by the fact that these interviews were originally conducted with the specific intent of assessing the impact of TQM on corporate financial per-

formance. Because overall corporate financial performance can only plausibly be affected by significant and widespread system changes, this leads to a definition of "start" that focuses on an event (or collection of events during a relatively short period) that is widespread and has some potential for tangible impact. In keeping with this, as discussed above, we define the start of the TQM system to be the first significant corporatewide, TQM-related initiative. Obviously, some judgment is required, if there is no clear corporatewide starting event, as to when the predeployment activities organize or coalesce into the critical mass required to mark the beginning of the corporatewide TQM system. What is perhaps surprising is how frequently there is a relatively well-defined corporatewide starting event.

Partially because of this focus on the potential for tangible impact in the definition of the starting date, it became very clear that many companies go through a multiyear predeployment phase of discussion, exploration, experimentation, and limited deployment (e.g., pilot projects or emphasis on only one group of employees, such as quality technicians) before executive management (and, to some extent, the rest of the organization) decides to implement TQM in earnest. We believe that this is one of the significant findings of the study, as is discussed further below, and it has some interesting relationships with several of the other chapters in this book.

The interview records associated with the beginning of the companies' actual TQM deployment were coded with the keyword "start." Appendix 5.5 shows the results of the search for this keyword. For these companies, initial deployment of their TQM systems occurred between 1982 and 1990, with a median of 1984. Figure 5.1 shows a histogram of the initial deployment years. For comparison, Figure 5.2 also shows the initial deployment dates for the full sample of 108 firms from Easton and Jarrell (1998). Comparison of Figures 5.1 and 5.2 shows that the 44 companies analyzed in this chapter overall represent early TQM adopters.

Table 5.1 summarizes some of the key approaches mentioned in conjunction with the start of widespread deployment of the compa-

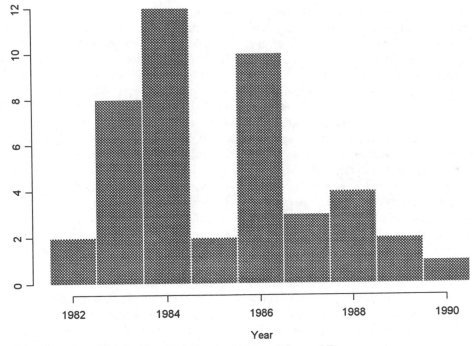

Figure 5.1. Histogram of the Starting Years for the 44 More Advanced Firms

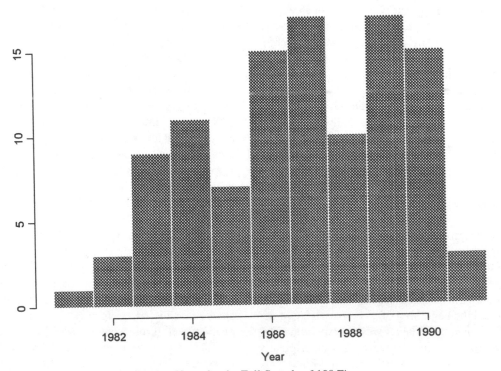

Figure 5.2. Histogram of the Starting Years for the Full Sample of 108 Firms

TABLE 5.1 Key Topics Associated With the Start of the More Advanced Companies' TQM Systems ($n = 44$)

Topic	Number of Companies	Number of Mentions
Training	32	46
Senior executive involvement	17	22
Quality councils	14	14
Teams	13	16
Crosby	12	25
SPC	12	14
Customer	8	11
Suppliers	8	9
Mission statement	7	7
Assessments	6	6
JIT/cycle time reduction/cells	6	6
Baldrige	4	4
New product development	4	6
Ford Q1	3	4
Juran	3	4
Deming	2	2
Japanese influence	2	2

nies' TQM systems. The theme of training in TQM is clear from the comments in Appendix 5.5. As shown in Table 5.1, training is specifically associated with the beginning of widespread deployment of the TQM system for 32 of the 44 companies. Of these, 22 specifically described widespread training initiatives, and these initiatives generally provide a well-defined event indicating the start of the corporatewide TQM system. In addition, two companies describe training for which the extent of deployment was unclear (e.g., "JIT training rolled out"), and two companies describe training limited to the top managers. Widespread training initiatives are implied (e.g., adoption of a Crosby approach implies widespread training) for five additional companies, so that training either specifically marks the beginning of the TQM system or is implied for a total of 37 of the 44 companies. The initial training is generally of three types—quality aware-

ness training (including company mission, values, etc.); team problem-solving training; or specific methodology training, such as SPC or setup time reduction. Quality awareness and team problem-solving training are the most common.

For the 8 companies (out of 44) for which training was not either specifically described or implied, a variety of approaches marked the beginning of the TQM systems. These include a major change in the new product development process together with changes in customer measurement and supplier audits; deployment of work cells together with a self-assessment tool that was also used for suppliers; a Baldrige Award application; formal Baldrige audits together with formation of a Crosby-type QIT; and creation of a new VP of Quality position together with creation of mission and vision statements and the beginning of self-assessments.

Table 5.1 also shows the number of companies mentioning (in conjunction with the beginning of their TQM systems) other approaches and the number of mentions (because more than one mention per company is possible). After training, companies most frequently mention some type of senior executive activity or involvement (e.g., the involvement of senior executives in training or in creating a mission statement), the formation of quality councils or steering committees, and the creation of teams. Twelve companies also specifically mentioned using Crosby's approach to quality management (Crosby, 1979) in comparison to two that specifically mentioned using Deming's.

Appendix 5.6 shows the interview records corresponding to the companies' activities prior to the corporatewide deployment date. Figure 5.3 shows a histogram of the pre-start-date activities (multiple activities per company are common). The median pre-start-date activity occurred 2 years before (t = min2) the corporatewide deployment. Figure 5.4 shows the histogram of the *earliest* quality-related pre-start-date activity mentioned by each company, eliminating multiple activities per company. Overall, this histogram is similar to Figure 5.3, but with a median of min2.5 years.

Some of the corporatewide pre-start-date activities mentioned by the interview subjects

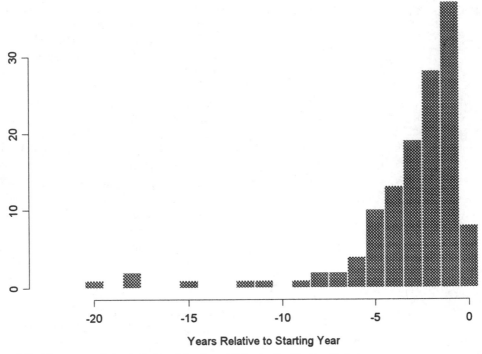

Figure 5.3. Histogram of the Activities Mentioned Prior to the Starting Dates

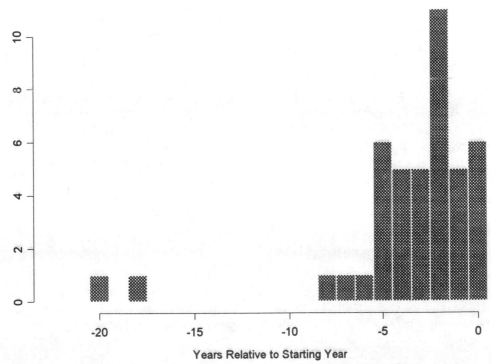

Figure 5.4. Histogram of the Earliest Quality-Related Activities Prior to the Starting Dates

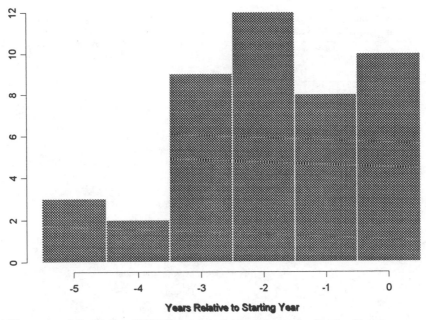

Figure 5.5. Histogram of the Earliest TQM-Related Activities Prior to the Starting Dates

were judged not to be directly related to the companies' subsequent deployment of TQM. For example, seven of the companies specifically mentioned "Quality Circles" initiatives during the period from 1978 to 1982, prior to the deployment of their TQM systems. The Quality Circles were generally mentioned to distinguish these activities from subsequent team-based employee involvement activities that occurred as a part of the deployment of TQM. The Quality Circles movement in the late 1970s and early 1980s appears to have been an employee participation movement (apparently largely for the sake of participation) that was primarily focused on quality-of-worklife issues. This is in contrast to team-based employee involvement as a part of TQM, where the teams are specifically focused on quality improvement, are generally trained in a problem-solving methodology and in supporting analysis tools (e.g., the seven QC tools), and are more actively managed as a part of a team management (and review) system (e.g., quality councils, site QITs). Thus, in spite of the fact that their name was borrowed from the Japanese Quality Control Circles, the U.S. Quality Circle movement of the late 1970s had virtually nothing to do with the subsequent TQM movement (Lillrank & Kano, 1989). Only one of the companies in the sample appears to have redeployed Quality Circle teams into the subsequent TQM system.

Figure 5.5 shows a histogram of the earliest predeployment activities, with those judged not directly related to the subsequent TQM deployment omitted. This histogram shows that the earliest pre-TQM-deployment activity mentioned was 5 years prior to the actual corporatewide deployment. The median is 2 years prior to corporatewide deployment. Thus, it appears quite typical for a company to go through a period of about 2 or 3 years of disorganized and uncoordinated discussion, exploration, experimentation, and limited deployment prior to the coalescence of the initiative into a coordinated, corporatewide deployment of TQM.

Table 5.2 shows the key topics mentioned that were prior to the companies' start dates together with their frequency of mention. The kinds of activities are consistent with the idea that companies usually go through about a 3-year period of coming to terms with TQM prior to corporatewide deployment. These activities include the following:

TABLE 5.2 Key Topics Prior to the Start of the Companies' TQM Systems

Topic	Number of Companies	Number of Mentions
Senior executive involvement	24	39
Training	18	23
Teams	11	12
Crosby	10	15
Suppliers	9	10
Customer	8	11
SPC	8	8
Deming	7	8
Ford Q1	4	6
Mission statement	4	4
New product development	4	4
Assessments	3	3
Juran	3	3
Quality councils	3	3
Baldrige	2	2
Japanese influence	2	7

- Meetings, task forces, and so on to determine strategy and to set goals
- Studies of competitive position, customer satisfaction, product performance, and so on, often conducted by third parties
- Study trips to other companies (most notably, Japanese companies)
- Training of a limited number of executives (e.g., Crosby's Quality College or Deming's four-day training)
- Development of a quality department, quality institute, and/or appointment of a senior quality office (a Corporate VP of Quality, Customer Satisfaction, etc.)
- Meetings with consultants or gurus
- Development of mission, values, beliefs, policy, or similar statements
- Responding to customer audits or customer pressure
- Supplier tracking, certification, and audits, and some supplier base reduction (It is often more palatable to start with somebody else.)
- Limited training and deployment, such as deployment in one division or plant, or efforts

TABLE 5.3 Key Topics Prior to or Associated With the Start of Widespread Deployment of the Companies' TQM Systems

Topic	Number of Companies	Number of Mentions
Training	36	70
Senior executive involvement	31	58
Teams	20	28
SPC	19	22
Crosby	16	39
Quality councils	16	17
Suppliers	14	19
Customer	13	22
Mission statement	10	11
Deming	8	10
New product development	8	10
Assessments	7	9
Baldrige	6	6
Ford Q1	6	10
JIT/cycle time reduction/cells	6	6
Juran	5	7

with limited focus, such as training of quality technicians
- Use of traditional quality approaches, such as inspection and SPC

Table 5.3 shows the frequencies for topics mentioned both prior to and associated with the start of widespread deployment of the companies' TQM systems (essentially, a combination of Tables 5.1 and 5.2).

The evidence of this period of coming to terms with TQM prior to companywide deployment is potentially interesting for two reasons. First, it would appear that this period represents sensemaking (Weick, 1995) and consensus generation among the senior managers of the firms, the senior managers whose commitment to TQM is later necessary for driving deployment. It is a period of retrospectively understanding and agreeing upon the causes of competitive disadvantage, of understanding and making sense of TQM, and of determining and agreeing upon a course of action. In Chapter 7 of this book, Weick explores in detail the theme of sensemaking and TQM.

The prevalence of this predeployment period of coming to terms with TQM among this sample of firms that went on to be successful in implementing TQM has implications for the management of any significant discontinuous and fundamental change within an organization. In particular, such a period may be either unavoidable or very difficult to avoid. The existence of this period supports Cole's hypothesis in Chapter 4 that U.S. firms were slow to adopt TQM. For many of the firms in this sample—and these firms represent the early adopters, the relatively fast ones—this predeployment period represented a period of continued competitive decline during which not much was done. In terms of the competitiveness of these firms, it is a 3-year period in addition to the 3 to 5 years that are typically required before TQM provides financial impact once implementation has really begun.

It is not clear, as indicated above, that this predeployment period of sensemaking and consensus generation can be avoided. In Chapter 4, Cole discusses many of the reasons: belief perseverance; cognitive challenges, such as abandoning the idea of a trade-off between cost and quality; the lack of hard evidence, especially in the face of the strong belief held by many managers that their circumstances are unique; the resistance to learning from the Japanese; and the tendency to rely on familiar tactics. Reger, Gustafson, Demarie, and Mullane (1994) comment that managers tend to understand their organizations and the practice of management itself in terms of schema consisting of bipolar constructs (cost vs. quality, control vs. continuous change, low cost vs. differentiated, low inventory vs. customer responsiveness, etc.), and that it is generally much more difficult to abandon these bipolar constructs than it is to reposition interpretation of reality along them. One reason why TQM may have been (and remains) so difficult for managers to fully understand and operationalize is that it requires abandonment of an unusually large number of traditional management's bipolar beliefs.

In addition, much of what happens during the predeployment period legitimately requires time. Making sense of the environment takes time; understanding the operational characteristics of their organizations requires time; and it takes time for opinions to be expressed and explored, for perspectives to be aligned, and for a critical mass of consensus (or at least acceptance) to form that allows successful companywide TQM deployment. Recognition that this kind of predeployment period is typical prior to major organizational change should provide both managers and researchers with useful perspective. This perspective has some very practical implications for managers in terms of assessing the state of development of a company's TQM system and the adequacy of the results that have been achieved. In several cases, managers have expressed to us dissatisfaction with the level of development of their TQM systems and the results achieved, remarking, "We have been at this for 5 years. We should have gotten more results by now." These managers had been thinking about TQM for 5 or 6 years, but the actual duration of serious deployment in their organizations was on the order of 2 or 3 years. Recognition of the actual phase of the company's development has important practical implications for assessment of the results and for anticipation of future phases.

It should be noted that the companies that make up this sample are not the focus of Cole's discussion in Chapter 4. Our sample represents companies that were early and fast adopters and achieved considerable success in deploying TQM. Cole's discussion focuses on more typical companies. For typical companies, the predeployment period is a period of risk. In many companies, the TQM initiatives do not survive this predeployment period, and the TQM program fails before it has even begun. This phenomenon is likely to explain many of the TQM "failures" that have been reported in the popular press.

Influence of the Gurus

The comments in Appendixes 5.5 and 5.6 associated with the initial TQM deployment and

TABLE 5.4 Mentions of Crosby, Juran, Deming, and Japanese Influence

Influence	Number of Companies	Number of Mentions
Crosby	17	60
Japanese influence	9	23
Juran	9	11
Deming	8	13

predeployment activities clearly indicate the influence of the gurus, specifically Deming, Juran, and Crosby. In Appendix 5.7, we explore the influence of these gurus, as well as direct Japanese influence—for example, direct influence by Japanese Total Quality Control (TQC) and the Deming prize. The number of mentions of each of these sources of influence in the interviews is summarized in Table 5.4. The most surprising result of this analysis is the obvious enormous direct impact of Crosby, particularly on the initial deployment of these companies' quality management systems. Crosby's influence and the adoption of Crosby's quality management system (Crosby, 1979) were mentioned by approximately twice as many companies as each of the other sources.

It is also interesting to note that the number of companies specifically mentioning Juran, Deming, or direct Japanese influence were similar. The number of specific mentions of Japanese influence, however, was much higher than the number of specific mentions of Deming or Juran. Note that "Japanese influence" is defined here to be direct influence; for example, learning from a Japanese supplier, Japanese joint venture or consultant (such as a JUSE counselor), or a study trip to visit Japanese companies. It does not include indirect influence, such as the implementation of a Japanese method like Quality Function Deployment (QFD). In the context of Cole's discussion in Chapter 4 linking the unwillingness of U.S. managers to learn from the Japanese to the slow response of U.S. companies to the Japanese threat, the fact that the number of companies mentioning direct Japanese influence is similar to the number of companies mentioning Deming and Juran is in-

teresting. Perhaps one factor that explains the success of these companies in developing more advanced TQM systems is that, as a group, they were more willing to learn directly from the Japanese.

The character of the comments also differs between Crosby and the other sources of influence. For Crosby's approach, companies were attempting to implement entire Crosby-based management systems. The comments referring to Juran and Deming tended to be much more limited in scope, referring to specific principles (e.g., constancy of purpose), team structures (e.g., the Juran team format), training (e.g., Deming 4-day seminars or Juran team training), or specific approaches (e.g., PDCA). As defined here, mentions of Japanese influence tended to refer to specific companies or consultants or to Japanese TQC.

The results in Appendix 5.7 and Table 5.4 provide clear support for Cole's discussion of the influence of Crosby in Chapter 4. Seventeen of the 44 companies in this sample (39%) were influenced by Crosby. Review of the interview records shows that of these, 13 (30% of the sample) were trying to implement a complete Crosby approach. We believe that this is clear empirical evidence of the major impact of Crosby, especially in the early phases of the quality management movement in the 1980s. Building on Cole's discussion in Chapter 4 (which describes many characteristics of Crosby's approach), one key advantage of Crosby's approach is that it fit well with U.S. management culture. As a result, Crosby's approach felt relatively natural to U.S. executives and thus was easy for them to adopt. We concur with Cole that Crosby's approach is fundamentally flawed. In fact, the data from this sample of companies suggest that a Crosby approach is virtually certain to stall after about 3 years. This, however, appears to also be true of all of the guru-based approaches, as is discussed further below.

Although Crosby's approach is fundamentally flawed, we view his contribution somewhat more positively than does Cole. For these companies, Crosby's approach represented a beginning—a relatively natural transition into the difficult issues and cognitive challenges of quality management. Crosby's approach provided a starting point for the development of these companies' quality management systems, which ultimately became well-developed. Although all of the companies implementing a Crosby-based approach experienced stalling after a few years, they were able to integrate methods and approaches from other sources, including the other gurus and the Japanese, and move the development of their TQM systems to a new phase. This provides strong evidence that a Crosby-based approach can be evolved into an advanced quality management system, and that Crosby's approach does not somehow prevent eventual success. Furthermore, our field research experience indicates that in many of these companies, the basic structure of the Crosby system can still be observed, even when the company reaches an advanced level of development of their quality management system.

Even though Crosby's approach is flawed, the system has both a logic and a coherence that results in effective improvement over the short term. Crosby's system is basically a suggestion-based system. As discussed by Cole in Chapter 4, Crosby defines quality as conformance to requirements and insists on a drive to "zero defects." In many companies, this zero-defects focus caused clarification by senior management of what the actual requirements were. In many organizations (even today), because the written requirements were not up-to-date, and because the requirements that replaced them through the informal organization were muddled and poorly aligned with actual customer requirements, this clarification alone resulted in significant quality improvement.

In a Crosby-based system, management's focus on zero defects drives the improvement. In a sense, it is the energy input into the system. In response to this pressure, front-line employees are supposed to identify the things that are preventing them from achieving defect-free work. They do this by documenting the causes of the defects on a suggestion form, which is usually called an error-cause removal form (ECR). The ECR does not necessarily have to include a solution to the problem—the focus is on identifying the cause of the defect. This ECR form is given to the supervisor. The supervisor is re-

sponsible for immediately resolving as many of the ECRs as possible (given his or her level of power and resources). The expectation is that the supervisor will be able to resolve the majority of the ECRs. Any ECR that cannot be resolved by the supervisor is passed on to the location's QIT (Quality Improvement Team). There is supposed to be a QIT at each location that serves as a steering committee to oversee the implementation of Crosby's 14 steps.

With respect to the ECRs, the QIT is supposed to resolve the ones that are not immediately resolved by the supervisors. In many cases, the QIT has the authority and resources for immediate resolution: immediate rejection (the suggestor should be given the reason) or implementation. For difficult problems, the QIT spawns a problem-solving or study team that is generally called a corrective action team (CAT). The CATs are temporary problem-focused teams that work to resolve the assigned problem.

In addition to the basic structure described above, two other key features of Crosby's approach are Cost of Quality and Quality Measurement, both formalized as "steps." Cost of Quality is important because it represents the quality performance tracking system for senior management. The Quality Measurement step is important, not so much because of the manner in which it is usually formally implemented, but because, in conjunction with the pressure for zero defects, it generally causes measurement systems to be put in place that provide rapid feedback about defects to process operators. With the emphasis on quality as conformance to requirements and the pressure for zero defects, the need to provide the operators with feedback concerning defects quickly became obvious to senior managers implementing Crosby-based approaches. Like the clarification of the requirements, the implementation of measurement systems allowed the operators to "see" the defects that were occurring, often for the first time. This frequently resulted in substantial improvement.

Although the development of systems to provide operators with feedback concerning defects may be the most important aspect of measurement in the Crosby system, the measurement step is generally interpreted to be the display by each workgroup of the performance trend for a metric that they choose. This aspect of the measurement step has little effect in most of the companies that implemented a Crosby approach—the measures chosen by the workgroups often were not the critical ones, contained sources of variation outside the group's control, and did not align between groups or with overall strategy.

In many companies that implemented Crosby's approach, the "measure and display" step was more like a motivational activity than like the metrics-driven problem solving and quality improvement that is, for example, a part of Japanese TQC. Overall, Crosby's system relies heavily on promotional and motivational approaches. The Zero-Defects (ZD) days are the most obvious example. Crosby's approach—particularly as generally implemented by companies, and like the approaches of the other gurus and the Japanese—also heavily emphasized widespread basic training. As a part of Crosby's approach, the basic training was called Quality Education Systems (QES).

The key conclusion, then, supported by this sample of 44 companies as well as our other field and consulting experience, is that, in the beginning, Crosby's system works. Furthermore, there is a clean logic in the approach that is often missing from the other approaches (e.g., Deming's). The management pressure for zero defects is the driver of the system, and the ECR system is the outlet for the pressure exerted on the workforce. The ECR system clearly assigned responsibility for response to suggestions: The role of supervisor was specifically defined to include elimination of causes of defects, and supervisors were thus empowered to resolve problems. Supervisors were also usually given specific resources for this purpose and were supported by the QITs, which would take ownership of problems that the supervisors could not resolve. The QITs formed CATs to address more difficult problems and could, at least in theory, obtain the necessary expertise.

In summary, the initial improvements that resulted from implementing Crosby's approach usually came through clarification of the actual requirements, implementation of the metric

systems, and because there are always, in organizations that are beginning to implement a quality management system, a multitude of obvious problems with readily available solutions. Until one has actually looked at the state of operations in companies where senior management has been inattentive to quality and operational excellence for a long period, it is hard to imagine the actual state that frequently exists. This state is due to a multitude of "disconnects," such as lack of the measurement systems necessary to provide quality performance feedback (especially from the customer's perspective) to the operators, lack of clarity about performance requirements, misalignment between departments, disconnects between the level of authority required to solve problems and information that the problems actually exist, and overtly conflicting objectives. Thus, implementation of Crosby's approach frequently resulted in dramatic improvement as many problems are identified and resolved.

Crosby's approach is also not in conflict with traditional U.S. management thinking. In particular, the role for senior management in the Crosby system is quite a comfortable one. It does not require a fundamental rethinking of the role of leadership, rather only a readjustment in emphasis. In Crosby's system, the role of senior management primarily involves motivation; goal setting; and review of the key performance metric, the cost of quality. Direct responsibility for the systems that drive improvement is delegated. Crosby's system, based on ECRs, QITs, CATs, and the QES, is well defined, especially initially, and the employees involved were reasonably comfortable with their roles.

As a result, Crosby's approach was very attractive to many companies and many of the companies that adopted it experienced initial success. In addition, as discussed by Cole in Chapter 4, Crosby himself was a superlative motivational speaker, so that executives who attended the Quality College tended to return to their companies with true enthusiasm for Crosby's approach.

We now turn to a discussion of why Crosby's approach is fundamentally flawed. In Chapter 4, Cole discussed a number of the reasons, including the lack of customer focus, the absence of a well-defined problem-solving methodology, and the lack of use of statistical methods. From our point of view, there are two fundamental, although unstated, premises in Crosby's approach that are false, and these lead to the failure of a pure Crosby-based approach after a few years. Both are related to the problems with Crosby's approach that are discussed by Cole. These flawed premises in Crosby's approach stem from the basic assumption that the process operators will be able to identify the causes (not necessarily the solutions) of defects. The first is the tacit presumption that the systems that are in place are fundamentally capable (able to reliably produce defect-free product), and that defects that occur are caused by special causes (disruptions of the system). In reality, much of the reason for defects almost always is that the systems are fundamentally not capable. Improvement of the capability of the process generally cannot be driven by the front-line workforce (although the workforce has a clear and important role; see Easton, 1993b). Rather, it must be directly driven by management and technical staff. The second tacit premise is that the front-line workforce, without any significant changes in either its problem-solving ability or its empowerment, will be able to identify the special causes that are generating the defects. Whereas a trained and empowered workforce, especially when effectively managed as a part of a well-developed team management system, is highly effective at identifying and eliminating special causes, under what was then the status quo, a workforce that has not been trained in problem solving is, at best, only partially effective at identifying special causes. The net result is that Crosby-based systems experience an initial period of success, lasting no more than 3 to 5 years, during which the many special causes that are obvious to the front-line workforce are identified and resolved. But once this initial pool of problems dwindles, identification of special causes becomes more difficult, and a Crosby-based system will stall.

It should also be noted that Crosby's approach is very production focused. Crosby is essentially silent on key upstream issues such as product design or external customer focus. Crosby has virtually no discussion of planning or integration. Because Crosby does not emphasize problem-solving methodology or analysis tools, there is no emphasis on team-based problem solving or employee involvement. It follows that Crosby's approach does not address advanced tools or methods—tools on the order of QFD, DOE, DFM, and so on. In Chapter 4, Cole specifically points out Crosby's lack of emphasis on statistical methods and employee participation. Finally, Cost of Quality by itself does not represent a comprehensive quality management tracking or reporting system. Although Cost of Quality is useful, it is also a somewhat problematic measure because it is very difficult to define accurately and is difficult to use for root-cause diagnosis.

In interpreting the above criticism of Crosby's approach, it is important to note that many of the same criticisms apply to approaches based on Deming or Juran. In particular, one of the findings of this study is that approaches based on any of the three key gurus—Deming, Juran, and Crosby—all stall after a period of a few years. In order to develop mature quality management systems, it is necessary for companies that start with any of these approaches to reassess after a few years and to bring in new methods and additional influences. Deming, for example, does not develop in his writings anything like a complete and coherent quality management system (Deming, 1982, 1986; Kolesar, 1994); we agree with Cole's assessment of Deming's approach in Chapter 4. This is not to minimize the importance of ideas in Deming's writings such as "constancy of purpose," or the importance of operational definitions.

The companies that actually claimed to be following Deming's teachings generally implemented an approach that heavily emphasized SPC—usually the responsibility of technicians—and front-line workforce teams trained in a basic problem-solving framework (Plan-Do-Check-Act, the Shewart Cycle) and the seven basic QC tools. As discussed in Easton (1993b), generally, there appeared to be an attitude that these workforce teams would be the drivers of improvement in the company and that the role of senior management was to empower them by staying out of their way. In these

Deming companies, the approach also generally stalled after a few years because the workforce was not capable of sustaining or aligning improvement, and, although a very important tool, traditional SPC was not a solution to many of the structural problems. Deming's writings emphasize statistical methods, but they have little direct emphasis on issues such as new product development, planning, business processes, and customer focus, which are necessary to develop an advanced TQM system.

Juran provides the most comprehensive, complete, and insightful discussion of quality control and improvement of the three gurus (Juran, 1981, 1988, 1989, 1995; Juran & Gryna, 1988). His approach is unique in that, in addition to the technical tools, he discusses many of the organizational and behavioral aspects of quality improvement. Juran makes many important and insightful observations. For example, he points out that one reason why quality improvement often does not happen in real organizations is that there is no clear organizational responsibility for diagnosis. He also discusses the requirements for defects to be truly operator controllable, an assumption that management often tends to make and the assumption underlying Crosby's approach as described above. Juran discusses how untested hypotheses become, over time, beliefs in which employees develop a stake that can ultimately lead to resistance against testing the beliefs.

In spite of such insights, Juran's writings nevertheless have a middle management and front-line flavor. Very few of the companies in this sample appeared to be initially trying to implement a Juran-based quality system, although quite a few integrated Juran's approaches later in the development of their TQM systems. Given the comprehensiveness of Juran's discussion of quality improvement and the behavioral and organizational insights he provides, the reasons why so few companies chose to start with a Juran-based approach during the period we are examining are not entirely clear to us. Juran-based approaches, however, also appear to need an infusion of new perspectives and additional tools after a few years, especially to address issues such as new product development, planning, and customer focus.

In conclusion, we believe that analysis of these interviews provides evidence of the major impact of Crosby in the early phases of the quality management movement. We believe that this impact was a net positive because Crosby's approach fit reasonably well with traditional U.S. management culture and beliefs, implementation of a Crosby-based system was not too unnatural, and the use of Croby's system got many companies started on quality management. Furthermore, as the sample examined here demonstrates, Crosby-based systems can be revitalized and can evolve, through inclusion of additional perspectives and approaches, into advanced TQM systems. We have examined this issue in some depth here because both the practitioner and academic literatures appear to us to underrate the impact of Crosby's ideas on the quality movement and have failed to fully appreciate the nature of their contribution.

Although our assessment of Crosby's impact as a part of the development of quality management in the United States is reasonably positive, lest we be misinterpreted, we would like to reiterate that the Crosby-based approach is fundamentally flawed on several dimensions. We should also point out that although our sample demonstrates the influence of Crosby among companies that developed mature TQM approaches it does not indicate the relative success rate for companies that began with a Crosby-based approach in comparison to companies that began with other approaches. It is possible that we see such a high percentage of companies that started with a Crosby-based approach in our sample of advanced firms merely because many more companies started with a Crosby-based approach.

Phases in the Deployment of TQM

Our preliminary analysis of these interviews indicates that one of the key characteristics of companies that achieve relatively advanced TQM systems is that they go through multiple phases of development. Although there are many different specific paths taken in deploying TQM among the companies in this sample, there are also common overall themes. Table 5.5

summarizes a model of the most common pattern of TQM deployment. The model consists of a predeployment phase and three phases of deployment: an internally focused initial deployment phase, a phase of refinement and expansion of the core approaches, and an advanced phase of integration and a focus on high-level processes such as new product development and advanced methods.

We have already discussed the predeployment phase in the section on initial deployment. This is a period, generally lasting 2 to 5 years, of coming to terms with the need for quality management and of generating consensus as to the specific approach to be taken. The typical activities include planning meetings; creation of task forces to study the competitive situation; study trips to other companies; training of a limited number of executives; development of mission, vision, and/or values statements; meetings with gurus or consultants; and internal announcements of the new program. In some cases, this period also involves understanding customer dissatisfaction either through customer contact by senior executives or through surveys.

For almost all of the companies in the sample, the first phase of deployment involved an internal focus, primarily on production processes. As discussed in the section on initial deployment, in the majority of the cases, this phase began with widespread training. At a minimum, this training was quality awareness training. Typically, however, the training went beyond awareness to include training in a team-based, problem-solving methodology (e.g., Plan-Do-Check-Act) together with some basic analysis tools, such as the Pareto diagram. Following the training, teams were formed in production areas to work on improvement. The focus of the team-based improvement tended to be narrow in scope. In most cases, the focus was on elimination of defects (special causes), although some companies began with an explicit focus on cycle time reduction. During this period, there was also frequently the formation of a parallel management structure of quality councils or steering committees to manage the teams and the deployment of TQM. During this phase in a Crosby-based approach, training occurred as a part of the Quality Education System

(QES), the Error Cause Removal (ECR) suggestion system was deployed, and steering committees (QITs) were formed at each location.

Although the training and deployment of teams was the core activity during this period, most companies' approaches included a number of other efforts. In many cases, supplier performance tracking efforts began, and specific attention was given to major problem suppliers. Often, there were also efforts with customers. However, these efforts tended to be more like damage control (possibly team-based) than true customer focus. Some type of customer survey was also frequently performed during this period. In many cases, there were also efforts made to develop and deploy quality metrics (the beginnings of a quality reporting system) and to set goals. A key characteristic of these efforts was that they were tacitly framed as one-time, ad hoc activities, and not as part of the development of systematic approaches (which occurred later). This phase generally lasted from 1 to 3 years.

In the second phase of deployment, one of the key characteristics was a revisiting of the efforts begun in Phase 1. For example, although the initial deployment of teams generally resulted in a great deal of improvement as many of the obvious and easy problems were solved, process management concepts were often not fully understood, much less deployed, even in manufacturing. Specifically, process documentation was frequently out-of-date and bureaucratic. The critical issues in the control of the processes had not been identified, and existing control plans were frequently incomplete or lacking, or else they emphasized noncritical issues. In companies where issues such as process documentation or control plans had been addressed, it had often been without the involvement of the process operators and thus did not have their buy-in. In short, concepts of process standardization and control, and their relationship to employee involvement, were either misunderstood by management or not effectively implemented.

The improvements that occurred during Phase 1 were generated by a team-based best-efforts approach that made improvements to existing processes within the same overall context that had existed prior to the TQM initiative. Fundamental redesign of the existing processes, such as reorganization of the production facilities into cells or deployment of self-managed work teams, usually did not occur until at least midway into Phase 2 or later.

Partially as a result of the initial efforts to improve the existing processes, many companies began to understand what was required to standardize processes and achieve a state of control. This transition sometimes began to occur during Phase 1, but achieving this change in process management and the improvement efforts is a characteristic of Phase 2. Many companies also revisited the effectiveness of team problem solving, which frequently relied only on brainstorming during Phase 1 and lacked rigor and effective use of the quality tools. In conjunction with transition to Phase 2, companies began to realize the extent of the role of managers, supervisors, and technical staff in process management, improvement, and teamwork. Training specifically focused on management and supervision often occurred.

A second key characteristic of Phase 2 is a filling in of the gaps in the basic quality management system. In Phase 1, the primary focus was generally quite narrow, and the need for additional scope was becoming apparent by the end of Phase 1. For example, companies that had begun with a focus on defect reduction often began to add cycle time reduction efforts and (if appropriate) implementation of JIT. Companies that had begun with an emphasis on cycle time began to realize the need for process control and defect reduction in conjunction with their cycle time efforts. It is during Phase 2 that single-guru focus is typically abandoned in favor of multiple influences and use of methods from a variety of sources.

Efforts in four additional major areas are also characteristic of Phase 2:

- Efforts to address new product development began. This frequently took the form of training in specific tools or methodologies, such as quality function deployment (QFD), design-of-experiments (DOE), Taguchi methods, design-for-manufacturability (DFM), failure mode and effects analysis (FMEA),

and so on. Formalization of the design process is also typically begun during this phase, although this is generally very difficult, and the degree of success achieved during Phase 2 varied widely. Another key change in new product development that occurred during this phase (if not earlier) was the creation of cross-functional design teams that included members representing production, field service, sales, marketing, and perhaps others.

- During this phase, customer satisfaction measurement approaches became systematic and routine, and the results began to be effectively mapped back into the organization to drive process improvement and new product development. The development of a customer satisfaction measurement system often evolved out of customer surveys or other efforts made during Phase 1. There are two key differences that delineate Phase 1 and Phase 2 on this dimension. First, the customer satisfaction measurement efforts tended to be preliminary and ad hoc in Phase 1. It is the development of a customer satisfaction measurement system that characterizes Phase 2. Second, in Phase 2, the customer information begins to be effectively mapped back into the organization to drive process control and improvement, new product development, and customer service.

- The supplier management system became formalized during this phase. Specifically, well-developed systems for tracking supplier performance and providing feedback were deployed. Furthermore, suppliers were expected to demonstrate the capability of their processes by providing statistical evidence of process control and capability. In conjunction with this, traditional supplier management approaches, such as incoming inspection, typically were reduced dramatically. Furthermore, dramatic supplier-base reduction typically would have occurred by the end of this phase. Supplier audits would be performed for key suppliers, with the scope of these audits expanding from traditional quality assurance audits to quality management systems assessments. Some joint supplier improvement or limited supplier involvement in new product development is also likely to have occurred.

- Process management and improvement for business processes and customer service processes outside of the key production processes began in earnest during Phase 2. In many companies, some efforts in these areas would have occurred during Phase 1, but these generally are sporadic.

Many other specific activities also usually occurred during Phase 2. Examples include development of reward and recognition programs; changes in performance evaluation; deployment or refinement of stretch goals; and development of the quality reporting system, including implementation of databases, some benchmarking, and so on.

It should be noted that making significant progress on the major areas listed above is an enormous task. To reach the end of Phase 2, companies typically would have made major progress in at least two of these areas and would have significant activity in all four. The length of Phase 2 is a minimum of about 3 years, and many companies never complete the phase. The criterion for inclusion in the sample of companies examined in this chapter is a Baldrige score above 450, which is roughly equivalent to the requirement that the companies are reaching the end of Phase 2 of their development. In summary, then, Phase 2 is a period of refinement of the basic approaches begun in Phase 1 and of expansion of efforts into difficult but critical areas such as new product development.

Phase 3 is a period of maturity for the advanced approaches begun in Phase 2, of achievement of integration and an overall level of coherence of the various parts of the TQM system, of integration of the key TQM concepts with senior management thinking at both strategic and tactical levels, and of achieving true innovation in some areas. Specifically, new product development efforts are maturing during this phase in the sense that new product development becomes formalized as a well-defined process and the use of related analysis tools and design strategies becomes effective. Cross-functional involvement in key processes such as new product development becomes the natural way of managing. True customer focus is becoming the reality in the sense that the customer measurement system integrates customer information from multiple sources. Specific approaches are developed for anticipating future customer requirements. This information is integrated into key processes such as new product

development. True customer partnerships are developing with some customers.

By this phase, the basic production processes have been through many cycles of refinement that have improved quality, cost (waste), and cycle time. The TQM approaches have extended to maintenance, and there have been major successes in improvement of business processes. The customer service processes will be well developed and have been through several cycles of refinement. Problem solving and the use of advanced analysis methods start to become very effective. Some leading-edge approaches, such as self-managed work teams, will be under way, and in many companies at this level, these approaches will be very effective in some areas. The supplier management system is highly refined, and true partnerships will be developing with key suppliers.

One of the distinguishing features of companies that achieve an advanced stage of development is the integration of TQM into both tactical and strategic decision making. Some of the characteristics include development of an effective planning system (e.g., based on Japanese Hoshin planning) that achieves organizational alignment and focus, clear and demanding goals, and use of a management system assessment process (e.g., Baldrige) to drive improvement of the management system. Benchmarking also tends to become a key driver because it is necessary in order to define operational excellence.

Although the above four-phase model describes the characteristics of a typical path of TQM development, many variations in specific approaches occur, and the phases are not necessarily as distinct as described above. Nevertheless, this model captures the general character of the vast majority of the TQM implementations. There were, however, several significant variations, particularly in how the TQM systems were initiated. Specifically, in three companies, the TQM efforts began with significant changes in new product development rather than the internal focus on production processes that was the case for most companies. In three companies that began in the late 1980s, Baldrige-based assessment was used to drive development of the TQM system. Finally, in three companies, the initial deployment of

TQM was driven by changes in customer satisfaction measurement rather than the usual internal focus on process improvement.

Conclusion

In this chapter, we have examined patterns in how TQM was deployed in a sample of 44 firms that developed relatively advanced quality management systems. We have also examined the apparent direct influence of the gurus and the Japanese on these companies. Among our key findings is that most companies go through multiple phases in the deployment of their systems and that these phases are quite distinct in character. One finding that has real implications for the management of change is that most companies go through a phase of several years before actual deployment of companywide initiatives begins in earnest. One implication of this is that major change efforts may *require* this period of sensemaking and consensus generation and that such a period must be factored into the planning of change initiatives. Another implication—one that affects senior management's assessment of the success of the TQM initiative—is that this predeployment makes it appear to senior management that the TQM efforts have been under way longer than they actually have been (in terms of changes that could directly affect performance). It is important for managers to understand how such initiatives tend to roll out so that they have the patience to persist and do not declare failure before it has actually occurred.

Another key finding of this study is the surprising influence of Crosby on the beginning of these companies' TQM systems. This finding is interesting in terms of historical perspective, but it also suggests management implications. In particular, the success of Crosby's approach in becoming the basis for the initial TQM deployment of so many companies suggests that fundamental cultural change may require an intermediate approach that is reasonably culturally compatible with the current state. As discussed by Cole in Chapter 4, TQM challenged many traditional management norms and beliefs, and we suspect that in many companies TQM was so foreign that the "cultural antibodies" rejected it before it had any real chance of successful invasion. Crosby's approach may have been able to serve as a successful transition state.

Examining the overall patterns of deployment indicate some additional factors that may be necessary for success. Probably the most obvious is the level of persistence required to achieve success. This kind of persistence requires a committed senior executive leadership and a high degree of constancy of purpose. This constancy of purpose does not mean unyielding commitment to one particular approach (e.g., a Crosby-based system) but, rather, commitment to the overarching values of customer focus, quality improvement, responsiveness, and total involvement. In fact, a characteristic of these companies is that they continue to revisit and refine their approaches, and when an approach or technique fails, they adjust and seek alternative approaches. Thus, we believe that one of the findings from this analysis is that organizations are quite tolerant of significant adjustment to the approaches taken, and even of false starts, provided there is no change in the commitment of leadership to the overarching values.

So, what is required for TQM to become self-sustaining and TQM practices to become embedded? The answers to these questions depend on what one means by "self-sustaining" and "embedded." If self-sustaining means, as generally seems to be the case, that a company's leadership can turn its attention away from driving aggressive improvement and the quest of achieving world-class processes, then we would argue that TQM virtually never becomes self-sustaining. The experience of the Japanese would support this. After more than 30 years of effort, "TQC promotion committees" led by senior managers still appear to be required. Achieving and maintaining world-class systems is not easy and, frankly, not natural. To do so requires enormous energy input into the system, which is one of the key roles of leadership. This need probably never goes away.

The answer to the embedded practice part of the above question is similar. In many ways, the concept of "process" in the context of TQM is about forcing the embedding of practices through the formalization of process, measurement, audit, goal setting, and reward and recognition. Some practices do not require formal processes to embed because they are natural and driven by the culture. For practices that occur naturally, developing formal processes is a poor idea because the development and management of processes requires a great deal of effort. Wasting process efforts on practices that occur naturally makes little sense. Thus, the concept of process is really about practices that are not embedded.

Some practices that are formalized in processes will embed over time as habits change, and the results of the practice, when consistently implemented, will become apparent. As a result, the emphasis of the formal process will change to address other issues that are not yet embedded. This kind of evolution of the formal process is one of the results of continuous improvement efforts. Some practices, however, will never embed because they are not natural, they require high levels of discipline, or their effects are obscured either by other sources of variation or by long periods of time before the results become apparent. These are some of the same cognitive issues discussed by Cole in Chapter 4. The existence of practices that are difficult or impossible to embed in the organization is well known in the quality literature. For example, Juran defines reversible improvements as those that depend on changes in operator behavior, and he indicates that such improvements must be audited to ensure that they are permanent. In addition, there will always be a new set of practices that is not yet embedded as the process is changed by new technology or as customer requirements change.[4]

Exactly which practices are already naturally embedded, which practices will embed over time if formalized in the process, and which practices will never embed and thus will always require formalization in the process depends on the culture of the organization as well as the culture of the country. Emphasis on consensus is a part of Japanese culture and, as a result, requires little formal reinforcement by Japanese processes. This is far less the case in the United States, and consensus generation frequently requires more formal treatment in the United States. However, no matter what the company or national culture, there will be sets of practices that do and do not embed, and the formal processes should emphasize the practices that require reinforcement. This explains many of the differences between the implementation of TQM in the United States and TQC in Japan.[5] To us, what is surprising is not the extent to which differences are encountered but, rather, the remarkable overall level of similarity.

Appendix 5.1 Sample of Firms

TQM Firm	Year of Implementation	TQM Firm	Year of Implementation
ADC Communications	1987	Hillenbrand Inds Inc.	1987
Advanced Micro Devices	1988	George A. Hormel & Co.	1986
Air Products	1987	IBM	1989
Albany International Corporation	1987	Integrated Device Technology	1989
Alcoa	1990	Intel	1985
Allied Signal Inc.	1991	International Paper	1985
Amdahl Corporation	1984	James River	1986
American Express[a]	1989	Johnson Controls	1986
Analog Devices	1987	Kulicke and Soffa	1988
Applied Materials	1985	Lubrizol Corporation	1988
Ark Best Corporation[a]	1984	Lyondell Petroleum	1989
Armstrong World Industries	1983	Micron Technology	1988
Arvin Industries	1986	Millipore Corporation	1986
AT&T	1988	Minnesota Mining & Manufacturing (3M)	1984
Baldor Electric Co.	1987	Molex Inc.	1986
Banc One Corporation[a]	1986	Moog Inc.	1989
Bausch & Lomb	1989	Morton International	1991
Baxter International	1985	Motorola Inc.	1983
Black & Decker	1990	Nashua Corporation	1981
Boise Cascade	1990	National Semiconductor	1990
Cameron Iron Works Inc.	1984	Pacific Telesis[a]	1989
Carolina Freight Corporation[a]	1984	Perkin Elmer Corporation	1984
Carpenter Technology Corporation	1987	PPG Industries	1986
Caterpillar	1983	Procter & Gamble	1987
Ceridian	1984	Raychem Corporation	1987
Chevron	1987	Roadway Services[a]	1989
Chrysler	1985	Rockwell International Corporation	1986
Conner Peripherals	1989	Rogers Corporation	1983
Consolidated Freight[a]	1990	Rohr Industries	1989
Corning Glass	1984	Scotsman Industries	1990
Cummins Engine	1983	Sealed Air Corporation	1989
Dana Corporation	1984	Snap-on Tools	1986
Diebold Inc.	1990	Square D	1987
Digital Equipment	1989	Standard Register	1989
Dun & Bradstreet[a]	1991	Sterling Chemical	1990
DuPont	1987	Storage Technology	1988
Eastman Kodak Co.	1983	Sun Microsystems	1988
Ethyl Corporation	1986	Tektronix Inc.	1989
Federal Express[a]	1986	Teradyne	1990
Firestone Tire	1982	Texas Instruments Inc.	1982
First Chicago[a]	1985	Thomas & Betts	1987
Fluke (John) Mfg. Co. Inc.	1990	Timken Company	1983
Ford Motor	1984	Union Camp Corporation	1987
FPL Groups	1986	Union Carbide	1988
Gaylord Container Corporation	1990	Unisys	1988
General Datacomm	1987	United Technologies	1984
General Motors	1985	Varian Associates Inc.	1987
Goodyear Tire	1990	VLSI Technology	1989
Goulds Pumps	1989	Westinghouse Electric Corporation	1982
Grumman	1988	Weyerhaeuser Co.	1989
GTE Corporations	1986	Whirlpool Corporation	1990
Hanna (M.A.) Co.	1990	WPL Holdings Inc.[a]	1987
Harris Corporation	1986	Xerox Corporation	1983
Hewlett Packard Company	1983	Yellow Corporation	1990

a. A predominantly service firm.

Appendix 5.2 Interview Topics

General Category	Specific Approach	General Category	Specific Approach
Training	Senior management training Awareness training Training of other management levels Workforce basic training Technical training Training for engineering	Team processes and tools	Problem-solving process Flowcharting Plan-Do-Check-Act Seven basic QC tools Seven management tools Root-cause analysis
Teams	Workforce improvement teams Natural workgroup teams Cross-functional teams Vertical teams Work cell teams Self-managed teams Project-oriented teams Management teams	Involvement and morale	Suggestion systems Employee quality recognition Employee morale survey
		Design and engineering	Design-for-manufacturability Concurrent/simultaneous engineering Design of experiments Taguchi methods Quality function deployment
Customers	Customer satisfaction surveys Customer complaint tracking Customer audits	Production	SPC JIT/cycle time reduction/SMED Activity-based costing Work cells

Organizational
structures
	Senior management quality
	   council
	Departmental quality councils
	Specific location quality
	   councils
	Internal quality consultants
		Suppliers	Supplier tracking
			Supplier certification
			Supplier quality audits
			Supplier training
			Joint supplier teams

Planning/values	Written quality values and/or
	   mission statement
	Hoshin planning/policy
	   deployment
	Formal benchmarking
	Quality/customer satisfaction
	   measures reported to senior
	   management
			Ship-to-stock/production
			   relationships
			Supplier integration into
			   product development

		Crosby	Quality Improvement Teams Error Cause Removal system Corrective Action Teams Cost of Quality/price of nonconformance
Audits	Quality assurance audits ISO 9000 Baldrige self-assessments Other management systems audits		Measure and display QES training Zero Defects days

Appendix 5.3 Sample Time Line From an Interview

1984	Senior management adopts Crosby approach. Senior managers attend Crosby Quality College. Adopt four absolutes: Begin QES training. Councils formed.	1990	Customer survey by third party begins. Based on survey of eight key people in customer's organization. Also, ongoing satisfaction survey. (Previously, report card was filled out by sales.)
1985	Supplier tracking begins.	1991	Rigorous supplier certification. On-site audits. Only certified four suppliers.
1986	Additional training developed: SPC, quality toolkit, based on Juran.		
1986	President's Award created for groups.	1991	Reliability training.
1988-1989	Three major programs: cycle time, continuous improvement, employee involvement. Mechanisms are weak.	1992	DFM. Two days of training from Motorola.
		1992	SPC.
1988	Supplier symposium and awards.	1992	Structured product development process developed.
1990	Reestablished criteria for President's Award based on Baldrige criteria.		
1990	Design process management approach based on IBM. Five levels of process certification. More than 200 certified processes.	Mid 1992	Train 60 people in AT&T benchmarking process.
		1993	By 1993, had developed specialists (facilitators) in SPC, reliability, business process management.
1990	Develop six-sigma-type training. Merged QES and six sigma.	1993	Small teams award.
1990	All employees get 40 hours of training per year (all types).	1993	Working on measures to predict customer satisfaction.

Appendix 5.4 Classification Topics (database keywords)

ABC	downsizing	JUSE	service
absolutes	driver	Kano	set up time
advanced methods	ECR	leadership	site visit
advanced training	EDI	learning organization	six sigma
agenda	employee focus groups	life cycle	software
alignment	employee involvement	literacy	SPC
analysis	employee satisfaction	maintenance	start
autonomy	employee surveys	manager involvement	statistics
awards	empowerment	marketing	strategy
awareness training	environment	MBO	stretch goals
Baldrige	event	metrics	study trip
Baldrige application	external leadership	mission	suggestion systems
Baldrige assessment	facilitation	NPD	supplier audits
basic training	failure	partnerships	supplier certification
benchmarking	Feigenbaum	performance appraisal	supplier event
best practices	field failure	Peters	supplier goals
business processes	finance	planning	supplier improvement
CAR	financial measures—	prediction	supplier involvement
cascaded training	asked	president's audit	supplier management
CATs	flexibility	prevention	supplier partnerships
celebration	FMEA	preventive maintenance	supplier recognition
cells	focus	prior	supplier reduction
communication	focus groups	problem solving	supplier tracking
competitive comparison	Ford Q1	process capability	supplier training
complaints	gainsharing	process certification	Taguchi
concurrent engineering	Garvin	process characterization	teams
conference	goals	process control	teamwork
consultants	greenfield site	process management	technology
continuous improvement	gurus	project management	themes
core competencies	hiring	project teams	third party audit
cost	hoshin planning	public responsibility	tools
cost of quality	improvement projects	quality councils	Toyota production system
councils	improvement teams	quality executive	TPM
crisis	incentives	QC circles	TQC
Crosby	information systems	QES	TQM systems
cross functional	innovation	QFD	traceability
management	inspection	QITs	tracking
cross training	integration	quality awards	training organization
customer audits	internal assessment	quality of work life	turnover
customer focus	internal audit	quality organization	union
customer focus groups	internal customers	quality policy	uptime
customer partnerships	internal focus	quality principles	values
customer satisfaction	inventory	quality strategy	VE
customer surveys	Ishikawa	R&D	vision
cycle time	ISO	recognition	waste reduction
defects	Item 4.1	reengineering	work group teams
Deming	Japanese influence	reliability	
Deming prize	JIT	reorganization	
design reviews	joint customer	reviews	
DFA	improvement	safety	
DFM	joint customer teams	sales	
DFR	joint supplier	SEI	
documentation	improvement	self-managed teams	
DOE	Juran	senior	

Appendix 5.5 Initial Companywide Deployment

Start Year	ID	Record Year	Record
1982	1	1982	Training in problem solving, SPC, Pareto analysis. Did not link well to use in work. Not that successful. Wasted a lot of money.
1982	1	1983	Started internal audits. Team would go on-site for a week. A report would be written indicating findings. Gave a basis for quantitative comparison. Expected 35% improvement every 5 years. Results reported to senior management.
1982	1	1983	Quality council: Information sharing once per quarter. Fifty people around the world.
1982	2	1982	Two hundred to 300 managers to Crosby training. Bought Juran videos. Cascaded training. Appointed Corp. Director of Quality. Formed departmental QITs.
1982	2	1982	MIR (Method Improvement Report) Suggestion system.
1983	3	1983	Started as a result of unreliable new product. Top down. CEO turned on to Crosby. Sixty executives trained early in 1983.
1983	3	1983	Sent several hundred to Crosby's train the trainer.
1983	3	1984	Trained all employees in 30 hours of basic training.
1983	4	1983	Used Juran team format (steering committee, etc.). Primarily focused on management and technical teams. Fifty percent participation.
1983	4	1983	SPC training for production.
1983	4	1983	Roll-out of training for management. One day with Juran. Then used Juran tapes—16 hours. Followed by one or two interactive sessions.
1983	5	1983	Off-site senior management conference to define TQC. Redefined job of quality from inspection to prevention.
1983	5	1983	Problem-solving training.
1983	6	1982	Refocusing on cross-functional teams focused on strategically identified projects. Two years to roll out.
1983	6	1983	Developed cost/time profiling analysis method. Find critical variable is time—focuses on cycle time reduction.
1983	6	1983	SPC quite widespread.
1983	7	1983	Phase 1, Crosby phase. Begin Crosby approach. Had 158 QITs. Cascaded training. Used 14 steps with a champion for each step. CATs.
1983	8	1984	Finish training in 1984 (U.S. employees).
1983	8	1983	Kicked off pure Crosby approach.Formed corporate QIT. Error Cause Removal System. Fifteen weeks training, 2 hours per week.
1983	8	1984	Began SPC and JIT in one plant.
1983	8	1984	First ZD day.
1983	8	1983	First Crosby Supplier Day.
1983	9	1983	Completed training cascade.
1983	9	1983	Senior management steering committee.
1983	9	1983	Supplier training begins.
1983	9	1983	Quality values made explicit.
1983	10	1983	Use of process capability. Currently report process capabilities to 39 customers.
1983	10	1983	Roll-out of SPC worldwide. Increases in yield 93% to 97%.
1983	10	1982	First Q1 recognition.
1984	13	1984	Management teams created to manage 10 actions (based on Crosby's 14 steps).
1983	10	1983	Began to deploy SPC.
1984	11	1984	Senior management adopts Crosby approach. Senior managers attend Crosby Quality College. Adopt four absolutes: Begin QES training. Councils formed.
1984	12	1985	Roll out Crosby QES and Quality Awareness training. QES = 15 modules of 2 hours. Quality Awareness for Workforce, five 1-hour meetings.

Start Year	ID	Record Year	Record
1984	13	1984	Quality council formed. Consisted of quality leaders from each unit.
1984	13	1984	Quality Institute began. Roll out 2-day course (3 days for QITs). Based on Crosby approach.
1984	13	1984	Basic training rolled out to 18,000 employees worldwide.
1984	13	1984	Management teams created to manage 10 actions (based on Crosby's 14 steps).
1984	13	1984	QITs formed at each location. Started with plant management and staff—quickly included all levels.
1984	14	1984	Trained 100 top managers. Used Komatsu's corporate trainers and Ishikawa (1983).
1984	14	1984	Lowered prices 30%. Forced intense focus on cost and quality.
1984	14	1984	Three years installing basic system. Developed New Product Planning System. Parallel flow, cross-functional, focus on capabilities. (Did not use QFD.)
1984	15	1984	Major initiative Excellence in Manufacturing begins. Focus on inventory reduction. Massive training. One hundred and five trainers trained 13 weeks. Five hundred went to Japan, including all trainers. Large number of workforce teams.
1984	16	1981	Overall quality goal: quality products and services.
			Themes:
			Meeting minimum performance
			Quality, innovation, profitability
			Teamwork
			Measures
			Linking measures and satisfaction
			Publish performance
			External customer
			Reward and recognition
1984	16	1985	Goal: Meet customer expectations
			Themes:
			Sales excellence
			Think like customers
			Help customers succeed
			Perfect sales and service
			Market research and stratification
			Award for excellence
			Dedicated division education unit created
			Team orientation
			Benchmarking
			Bundled products
1984	16	1982	Training in process improvement. Area managers formed teams as they decided. Some were workforce or workgroup teams, others were project oriented and made up of managers.
1984	17	1983	Mission values and guiding principles developed.
1984	17	1982	Team development begins for new product using 10-stage development process.
1984	17	1984	Major revision in supplier and internal audit.
1984	17	1984	Major changes in customer measurement: Focus groups. Developed proprietary system for predicting future customer requirements—based on leading-edge customer groups.
1984	18	1984	Begin to develop some clarity about managing total quality.
1984	18	1983	Managing total quality begins. Deploy values statement—five key values. Create quality management services.
1984	19	1983	Senior management conference. Created quality policy and initiated training cascade. Training includes nine-step QI process + behavioral training. Training by Natural Work Group.
1984	20	1984	Q-net computer network for suggestions (ECRs). Does not appear to be a main focus.
1984	20	1984	First internal class. First focused on branch managers, then managers. Three thousand trained.

(Continued)

Start Year	ID	Record Year	Record
1984	21	1984	Quality policy and mission created employee training; 7 hours in fourteen 30-minute sessions.
1984	21	1984	Crosby-type executive steering committee formed.
1984	21	1984	Trainers trained all managers.
1984	21	1984	Finished training directors and above. Trained 21 trainers.
1984	22	1984	Developed quality business plan. Developed a list of things that must exist in all areas: quality policy, quality steering committee, quality training, problem-solving teams.
1985	23	1985	QIP process begins based on Crosby. Companywide, everyone trained. QIT in every location. Took 3 or 4 years to train everyone, but most (70%) trained in first 2 years.
1985	23	1985	Worked hard to reintroduce SPC, FMEA, reliability engineering, DOE in both plants and purchasing activities. Toughened up supplier requirements. Numerical literacy programs implemented.
1985	24	1985	Heavy focus on SPC. Much SPC training. Hired 20 to 25 statisticians. One in every factor. Statisticians were effective within 1 year.
1985	24	1985	Work with packaging suppliers.
1985	24	1985	Recession. Pressure by customers (Ford, IBM). Change of focus.
1985	24	1984	Reduction of key suppliers: 500 down to 200.
1985	24	1985	QIP training. Problem-solving process. Lots of teams all over company. Teams tracked and success stories written up and given visibility.
1985	24	1985	First Ford Q1.
1986	25	1986	Focus on set-up time reduction, quick change, cells, uptime.
1986	26	1986	Internal television system for all locations.
1986	27	1986	Three-day training by XXXX: Day 1: What is quality?; Day 2: How to implement; Day 3: What is senior management's role? Format: 1/2-day lecture, then workshops. 1st class CEO, CFO, and senior executives. All left with a plan.
1986	27	1986	Started new outside customer survey approaches (survey other companies' customers, too, for comparison).
1986	27	1986	Quality was on agenda for reports to corporate management. Every business unit must have a senior management communications plan and must report status. Must also competitively compare customer satisfaction.
1986	27	1986	Process management courses began. Trained 10,000. Billing process was the first worked on.
1986	28	1987	Training (awareness) begins.
1986	28	1986	Senior executives become knowledgeable. Several courses developed: 2-day awareness, tools, philosophy. Also QFD.
1986	29	1985	Start work with JUSE counselors.
1986	29	1985	Policy deployment.Train all employees 3 days.Train team leaders 3 days. Executive visits conducted (president's audit).
1986	30	1985	Transfer of approaches to second major division.
1986	30	1985	SPC and SPM in one major division.
1986	30	1986	Began drastic reduction of number of suppliers.
1986	30	1984	Deployment of steering committees in electronics sector. Creation of teams, EITs (natural workgroup teams—employee involvement team?) and SIPs (project teams—system improvement projects).
1986	31	1986	Roll out QES training. Trained 5,000 employees.
1986	31	1986	Begin cost-of-quality development.
1986	31	1986	Formed 34 QITs in all locations.

Start Year	ID	Record Year	Record
1986	31	1986	Top executive decided to implement Crosby companywide. Motivated by informal feedback from distributors about both product and service quality.
1986	31	1986	Started Crosby training.
1986	32	1986	SPC group used (formed?) to train and do internal consulting.
1986	32	1986	Basic quality course rolled out. Made case for quality. Taught Deming's 14 points. Employees tested on 14 points.
1986	32	1986	Quality council restructured a little. Position for VP of Quality created.
1986	33	1985	Began implementing SPC in some areas lead by management and engineering teams.
1986	33	1986	Work cells.
1986	33	1986	First self-assessment tool. Also used to audit suppliers.
1986	34	1986	Supplier process certification.
1986	34	1986	Focus on SPC, JIT, QFD, cycle time, core competencies, and metrics. XXX uses this forum to track state of development in each division.
1987	35	1988	Looked at MBNQA. Applied in 1988, did not win.
1987	35	1987	Engineering strategies develop front-end loading of work (front-end planning?).
1987	36	1986	Developed mission statement.
1987	36	1987	Developed "Managing the [company name] Way" statement. Had 16 points—later trimmed to 10: low-cost producer, quality, entrepreneurship/innovation, action orientation, people focus, responsibility/accountability, teamwork, communication, safety, social responsibility (environment)/ethics.
1987	36	1987	Began QC circle training for all employees. Teams are voluntary. Problem-solving training. Called TAPS teams. TAPS = Team Approach to Problem Solving.
1987	36	1987	Began to add Juran's approaches. Created project teams called Quality Breakthrough Teams.
1987	36	1987	Won Association for Quality and Participation Award for QC circles in XXXX area.
1987	37	1987	Employee attitude survey.
1987	37	1987	Crosby QIT formed.
1987	37	1987	Formal Baldrige audits.
1987	37	1987	SPC training. One hundred and fifty people trained in California as a result of training grant.
1988	38	1987	Developed 10 key courses in quality curriculum.
1988	38	1988	Quality Steering Committee formed from quality manager in each division.
1988	38	1987	JIT training rolled out.
1988	38	1988	Corporate Quality office gets a VP. Coincided with new CEO.
1988	39	1988	Two years of intense training. Created institute. Critical problem committees formed. QATs, process management training, recognition. XXX was an outstanding consultant.
1988	39	1988	Training in quality begins for chairman and unit presidents. Two days.
1988	40	1988	Started Vision College. 2-day off-site training. Everyone trained 20,000 people. Took 3 years. Course created culture by which to operate. Three themes: customer service, quality as a way of life, personal accountability. Tried to create a culture shift, don't hang up brain on way in. Employee involvement—3P process: permission, power, protection. Tried to put everyone on a level playing field. Mixed levels of employees in training created one problem: employees sometimes trained before their manager.
1988	41	1989	Focus on rigorous inspection methodology to protect customers.
1988	41	1988	Corporate quality manual was out of date and also poor. Implemented rigorous rules for release.

(Continued)

Start Year	ID	Record Year	Record
1988	41	1988	Started to understand Deming approach. Organization already had very strong statistical and analytical capabilities.
1988	41	1988	Manufacturing model-layers: Core: Design rules for semiconductor physics (density, etc.); Layer 1: Circuit design; Layer 2: Semiconductor build process; Layer 3: Package design; Layer 4: Test.
1989	42	1989	Began overview of quality training called Under New Management. Two days of training including problem-solving process, etc. Cascaded to top 700 managers. Quality department continued to teach the course. Five thousand trained.
1989	43	1989	Second employee opinion survey.
1989	43	1989	Created VP of Quality position. Started assessment efforts. Created mission and vision.
1990	44	1990	VP quality position created.
1990	44	1990	First Baldrige-based assessment. Score 289.
1990	44	1990	Hired Director of Quality.
1990	44	1990	Second meeting with consultants. Tried to bring the right people.
1990	44	1990	Eighteen months of leadership training. Had numerous speakers.
1990	44	1990	When approaches were starting, performance was somewhat flat, but company not under serious pressure—was not losing market share, etc.

Appendix 5.6 Activities Prior to Major Corporate TQM Initiatives

Years Prior	Record Year	ID	Record
27	1956	1	One of the founders noticed that warranty costs were rising faster than profits. Big focus on reliability and warranty costs were driven down. Company believed in Theory Y before Theory Y was invented.
22	1962	2	Japanese joint venture.
20	1964	3	Supplier audit developed. Seen seven major revisions.
18	1968	4	High-performance work systems (appears to be a type of self-managed teams).
18	1968	5	Started SPC on weight and packaging dimensions by quality assurance.
12	1974	6	Company founded on employee satisfaction principle.
11	1973	3	Internal supplier subject to audit as well.
11	1978	7	Implemented companywide suggestion system with monetary award. Could not handle volume. Never worked well. Backed away.
9	1975	2	Japanese joint venture began to lose market share and face stiff competition. Started TQC program.
8	1979	8	Phase 1: Training for formal quality initiative begins. Two to 4 days of formal training. Focus on product quality. Statistical Process Control. Focus on technicians and professional engineering. Corporate program. Called PQM = Product Quality Management. Initiated formal PQM audits. Had to identify critical properties for customer's standpoint. Twelve areas of monitoring. CQMS computer system developed.
7	1979	16	Began survey/feedback/action.
7	1976	1	Japanese joint venture began TQC.
6	1978	9	Created XXXX University.
6	1978	3	Chairman gave a speech saying that quality was #1 focus.
6	1978	10	CEO decided quality is important. Partially motivated by a lawsuit concerning labeling of a sponge—not important in terms of $.
6	1983	11	Began hearing from customers that they should have quality process.
5	1979	12	Team-based management. Semi-self-management. Cross-training. Driven by belief in people.
5	1981	6	Developed Guaranteed Fair Treatment policy (grievance policy).
5	1981	13	Chairman launched best program because of very negative press. The best program required that competitive comparison be performed by each business unit from the customer's perspective on quality. Many consultants were hired.
5	1980	14	Company 25 years old. Things always done well—discipline, results, risk taking. Always very profitable (except one year). Tightly managed: Tight budget controls updated monthly. Intel Management by Objectives (IMBO) a way of life—still is. IMBOs updated quarterly. Quality systems included thorough tracking. Entrepreneurial culture—get it done—good at solving crises. Around 1980: QC circles (focused on quality-of-worklife?). Petered out.
5	1979	10	Turn division heads loose on quality. Had Juran, Deming, Crosby, etc. Visit various divisions.
5	1981	15	QC circles started. QWC focused.
5	1981	16	QC circles. Did not work.
5	1981	17	Significant thrust toward reengineering the organization. Emphasis on strategy: Blocking-and-tackling. Expert assigned to each organization through the 1980s—moderate success in pockets, asset management improvement as a result of process improvement has been important.
5	1983	18	Crisis: Companies moved to sole suppliers, which cut XXXXXXX out. Also had focused on bipolar technology while industry turned to CMOS.
5	1983	18	Also, scandal hit competitor—had sold uninspected product to military while charging inspected prices. This was occurring because of process capability gains—none of product failed military standards. Once focus [of the DOD] on competitor declined, XXXX was next target [for DOD audit].
4	1984	19	Reorganization: Recognized quality even more of a strategic issue. Realized had been high quality at high cost—overdesigned, overengineered, overinspected.
4	1979	20	Began formal supplier certification. Based on performance and audits by a certification team. Annual quality improvement plan required.

(Continued)

Years Prior	Record Year	ID	Record
4	1981	21	Partnerships with UAW. Negotiate joint structure-jointly managed quality councils.
4	1980	3	NBC White Paper on quality-influenced management.
4	1982	13	Information started to come in. Confirmed problems. Much denial. Many consultants fired. Note: Financial performance was still very good.
4	1979	1	CEO declares 10x improvement goal for the decade of the 1980s for warranty costs. Saved $800 million in warranty costs and achieved 5-to-1 improvement in productivity.
4	1979	1	Much pressure from Japanese joint venture to improve designs, most of which were done in the United States.
4	1979	1	Discovered QC circles.
4	1979	1	Cost-of-quality study for hardware.
4	1979	22	President formed a task force to investigate competitiveness issues. Motivated by competitive pressure in overseas markets, especially because of Japan. Focus on productivity.
4	1980	2	Japanese joint venture won Deming prize and began to have great success winning back market share—CEO observed this.
4	1985	11	Kicked off quality teams. Got all management together. Told all areas they must have a team by March. Would come back in May and see how they were doing. Focus on nonunion employees. Team approach was intended to empower. Somewhat successful. Recognition.
4	1984	18	Only 15% of sales was military, but military systems were the basis for quality until 1984.
3	1985	19	Sponsor of Quality Month.
3	1985	19	Corporate Quality Office formed. One supervisor and two people.
3	1985	19	Quality policy—first companywide quality act.
3	1982	21	Supplier quality programs began. Similar to Q1.Buy 70% of parts.
3	1982	21	Quality circle activities. Mostly salaried. Supported by training, but not focused. Often worked on things like parking spaces.
3	1981	12	Licensed Japanese company to build product. Saw what they could achieve. Also pressure from another Japanese company.
3	1981	23	Product problem in one division with new product. Problems started with a computer conversion that was buggy. Decided needed [quality].
3	1981	23	Senior management interviews customers to determine which measures are appropriate.
3	1981	3	Deming met with new CEO and senior management. Senior management came away with constancy of purpose message. Took 3 years to figure out what that purpose was.
3	1979	24	Need for quality improvement identified at officers' meeting. People involved with distribution were complaining about failure rates.
3	1983	4	Many divisions became aware of Deming. Lots of activity, SPC, some joint supplier teams. Twenty-five percent of workforce involved.
3	1981	10	One hundred formal teams (QWL-type QC circles).
3	1980	22	First VP of Productivity appointed. First in *Fortune* 500.
3	1981	2	Team of 11 created to find solution. CEO made 23 trips to Japan. Extensive benchmarking.
3	1980	24	Management training—using cascade approach.
3	1980	24	First SPC teams—not TQM.
3	1986	11	Began to involve union employees.
3	1986	11	First employee opinion survey.
2	1984	25	Initial efforts as a result of Ford Q1. Initial focus to staff up with the appropriate technical people.
2	1986	19	Award in one division. Was almost a pilot for later Baldrige assessment process.
2	1982	26	Senior executives begin to become interested. Some went to Crosby College.
2	1982	27	Some quality circles.
2	1985	8	Phase 2: Decentralized and autonomous. Traditional TQM approach—many gurus. Formed QAT (quality action teams). QIT (sounded like QIT in Crosby sense). Task teams. This initiative was spearheaded by quality professionals.
2	1984	13	Policy committee met for 3 days to address quality and develop plans. Three components were developed: (a) define quality as customer requirements and satisfaction—from customer's point of view; (b) develop quality policy—to be quality leader; (c) Corporate VP of Quality position created.
2	1983	14	Begin supplier partnerships.
2	1980	24	First Quality Officer at end of 1979. Quality became a regular agenda item at senior management meetings.

Years Prior	Record Year	ID	Record
2	1980	24	Had started to analyze sources of field failures. Found that areas where there were problems in the field were highly correlated to areas where there were problems in the factory. This ultimately drove the focus on defects.
2	1980	24	Developed 10x goal in 5 years. Stretch goals developed because of the way technology companies are managed. Do not wait for R&D to develop products (come to you). Instead, create product concepts and ask R&D to develop technology to implement them. Concepts developed even when technology not clear. Decided this would work for quality as well. Also had the benefit of some benchmarking knowledge.
2	1982	10	Management Quality Expo.
2	1982	10	Supplier activities.
2	1982	10	Morale survey of all employees. Survey 1/3 of employees ever since annually.
2	1981	22	Twenty-five hundred QC circles. Very successful until 1982. Stalled. Not cross-functional because ground rules prevented.
2	1981	22	Productivity Center formed. Pulled in existing expertise from around the company—industrial engineers, scientific management, small group interaction, QC, organizational design. Mission included authority and budget and responsibility to implement 200 people in the center.
2	1981	28	Began employee involvement using American Productivity Center approach. Formed QC-type circles working on quality of worklife issues.
2	1984	15	Twelve high-level managers study quality. Worked for 9 months. Motivated by VP reading book, gave to president.
2	1984	16	Second phase began. Developed training materials for teachers.
2	1985	29	First teams in business process areas.
2	1985	29	Began move toward Deming's philosophy.
2	1985	29	Supplier partnership approaches begin.
2	1985	29	Company formed from 3 divisions of XXX. Two of these facilities had Crosby-based initiatives under way. Crosby training was done in early 1980s.
2	1985	29	After company formed, reorganized and trimmed 25% of the people.
2	1984	30	One VP discovered Deming's book *Quality, Productivity, and Competitive Position*. He issued a copy to each of the 700 employees.
2	1987	11	Focus on supervisor training.
2	1986	31	SPC efforts begin.
2	1985	32	Began to focus—passed out *Quality Is Free* to all executives.
1	1985	25	SPC deployed.
1	1987	19	Corporate Quality Office gets a manager in 1987.
1	1983	26	Twenty-five hundred executives were trained, including Chairman, CEO, and all direct reports.
1	1983	26	Formed executive committee—now disbanded.
1	1983	26	Trained hundreds of trainers.
1	1982	20	Contracted several consultants, including Juran. Primarily used Juran's approach. Created eight-point plan. Included Ladder of Excellence road map. Asked each unit to create plan. Tracked units against the plan.
1	1983	27	Announced major quality program because of (a) new chairman, (b) poor profits, (c) low employee participation, (d) stiff competition. In 1983, were closing plants.
1	1983	27	VP of quality appointed (respected senior executive).
1	1983	9	Focus on SPC begins—gauge control.
1	1986	8	Auto industry audits appear on the scene heavily. Are a large supplier to automotive industry. Ford especially influential. Force documentation of processes and quality management systems. Raised awareness.
1	1986	8	TQM efforts began to flounder. Auto industry still pushing.
1	1985	6	Had rapid growth and high turnover in management. Developed LEAP program to put right managers in right positions.
1	1987	33	Consultants report results in shock. Denial. Commission McKenzie. Confirmed. Then commissioned a third group. All confirmed. Technical arrogance a big problem.
1	1987	33	Interest in quality began for survival reasons. Had begun to mirror major customer—government. Commission survey by a consultant.
1	1985	13	Corporate VP of Quality visited every location.
1	1985	13	Plan training for senior management. Took 7 months. Pilot-tested on group of managers prior to training senior management.

(Continued)

Years Prior	Record Year	ID	Record
1	1982	1	Japanese joint venture. Won Deming prize. First not all-Japanese company to win.
1	1981	24	Announced stretch goals. 10x in 5 years. Could not achieve this with usual way of doing business. A lot of people did not buy in. Everyone made the goal. Those who bought in made the goal in 2 years, those who didn't made it in 5 years.
1	1983	10	Brainstorm and agree on key values.
1	1983	10	Six hundred to 700 formal QWL-type QC circles.
1	1982	28	Upper management went to Crosby.
1	1983	34	Search for approach. Five executives went to Crosby College. Settle on leads. Begin training all directors and above.
1	1985	30	Purchased Deming tapes. Used to train everyone. Includes introduction to SPC (SPC philosophy).
1	1985	30	Training council formed. Basic quality course developed.
1	1985	35	Had senior management meeting—chose consultant.
1	1985	35	Hired two quality directors in different divisions. Researched consultants.
1	1988	7	At this time, there were some efforts under way, most notably in the supplier area. Some purchasing people had been to Crosby Quality College.
1	1988	7	CEO became interested in TQM because of forums with peers, creation of the Baldrige Award, etc. Began Corporate Quality Center.
1	1983	36	Quality circles. Work on departmental issues. People building. Monthly direct labor. Eight percent to 10% of workforce participated.
1	1988	11	Started corporate advisory council consisting of customers.
1	1988	11	Made a review of the quality process and realized it needed to be elevated.
1	1985	17	Beginning of external pressure for change. Lost major account. Beginning of decline in industry.
1	1986	32	Resources devoted to quality. Three hundred trained by Crosby and Juran.
1	1986	32	Cost of quality developed—still a major measure.
1	1989	37	Took a busload of managers to session on TQM at a major university. Realized had brought the wrong people.
1	1989	37	Senior executive of largest sector began to think that TQM was important.
1	1987	18	Took over another company to try to solve problems.
0	1983	38	Started as a result of unreliable new product. Top down. CEO turned on to Crosby. Sixty executives trained early in 1983.
0	1988	33	Survey process ends. Finally persuaded.
0	1984	39	Crosby College-trained instructors.
0	1984	39	Senior VP and president went to Crosby Quality College. Interest because of 3M and Johnson & Johnson.
0	1984	34	Finished training directors and above. Trained 21 trainers.
0	1986	31	Simultaneous engineering in semiconductors.
0	1986	31	Some quality-related activity, but not well developed and organized.
0	1990	37	VP of Quality position created.
		26	Always had technical quality: since mid 1960s for medical devices, since mid 1970s for pharmaceuticals.
		20	Quality creed is more than 25 years old.
		6	Always done extensive market research.
		4	Since the beginning: Focus on consumer. Set up 800 number. Complaint reporting. Focus on employees and employee morale.
		2	QWL-focused QC circles. Low participation—5%.
		17	Emphasis on decentralization. Approach based on 25 areas business unit managers must know, understand, and select among.
		37	Eighty-year focus on product quality.
		18	[Company name] has had consistent leadership since inception.
		18	Strategy was based on companies' requirements of multiple sources. Manufactured under license generally. Also focus on military. Produced to military spec 883 for free.
		18	Traditional inspection orientation. Large quality assurance organization.

Appendix 5.7 Influences of the Gurus

Record Year	Years Into	ID	Record
Crosby		1	Approach based on Crosby's 14 points. Distilled 14 into 10.
1979	−5	2	Turn division heads loose on quality. Had Juran, Deming, Crosby, etc. Visit various divisions.
1982	−2	3	Senior executives begin to become interested. Some went to Crosby College.
1982	−1	4	Upper management went to Crosby.
1982	0	5	Two hundred to 300 managers to Crosby training. Bought Juran videos. Cascaded training. Appoint Corporate Director of Quality. Formed departmental QITs.
1982	0	5	MIR (Method Improvement Report) Suggestion system.
1983	0	6	Started as a result of unreliable new product. Top down. CEO turned on to Crosby. Sixty executives trained early in 1983.
1983	0	6	Sent several hundred to Crosby's train the trainer.
1983	−1	3	Twenty-five hundred executives were trained, including chairman, CEO, and all direct reports.
1983	−1	3	Trained hundreds of trainers.
1983	0	7	Phase 1, Crosby phase. Begin Crosby approach. Had 158 QITs. Cascaded training. Used 14 steps with a champion for each step. CATs.
1983	0	4	First Crosby Supplier Day.
1983	0	4	Kicked off pure Crosby approach. Formed corporate QIT. Error Cause Removal System. Fifteen weeks training, 2 hours per week.
1983	−1	8	Search for approach. Five executives went to Crosby College. Settle on leads. Begin training all directors and above.
1984	1	6	Trained all employees in 30 hours of basic training.
1984	0	9	Senior management adopts Crosby approach. Senior managers attend Crosby Quality College. Adopt four absolutes: Begin QES training. Councils formed.
1984	0	10	Quality Institute began. Roll out 2-day course (3 for QITs). Based on Crosby approach.
1984	0	10	Basic training rolled out to 18,000 employees worldwide.
1984	0	10	QITs formed at each location. Started with plant management and staff—quickly included all levels.
1984	0	10	First Quality Milestone meeting. QITs came to discuss quality. Two hundred people.
1984	0	10	Management teams created to manage 10 actions (based on Crosby's 14 steps).
1984	0	1	Q-net computer network for suggestions (ECRs). Does not appear to be a main focus.
1984	0	1	First internal class. First focused on branch managers, then managers. Three thousand trained.
1984	0	1	Crosby College-trained instructors.
1984	0	1	Senior VP and president went to Crosby Quality College. Interest because of 3M and Johnson & Johnson.
1984	1	7	Cost of quality.
1984	1	4	First ZD day.
1984	1	4	Finish training in 1984 (U.S. employees).
1984	0	8	Crosby-type executive steering committee formed.
1985	2	6	Textbook Crosby program for about 1 year. Very positive results. Picked low-hanging fruit. Management of quality was decentralized. Thirty-five hundred to 4,000 employees at this time. Functional organization.
1985	1	3	Roll out Crosby QES and Quality Awareness training. QES = 15 modules of 2 hours. Quality Awareness for Workforce, five 1-hour meetings.
1985	0	11	QIP process begins based on Crosby. Companywide, everyone trained. QIT in every location. Took 3 or 4 years to train everyone, but most (70%) trained in first 2 years.
1985	−2	12	Phase 2: Decentralized and autonomous. Traditional TQM approach—many gurus. Formed QAT (quality action teams). QIT (sounded like QIT in Crosby sense). Task teams. This initiative was spearheaded by quality professionals.
1985	1	1	QIT formed at each location.
1985	1	1	Begin training supervisors.
1985	1	8	An officer was assigned to each of the 10 Crosby-type steps.
1985	1	8	Quality Event Day (ZD day).
1985	−2	13	Company formed from three divisions of another company. Two of these facilities had Crosby-based initiatives under way. Crosby training was done in early 1980s.

(Continued)

Record Year	Years Into	ID	Record
1985	−2	14	Began to focus—passed out *Quality Is Free* to all executives.
1986	2	3	Redeveloped training to merge Crosby, Juran, Deming, etc.
1986	0	15	Started Crosby training.
1986	0	15	Begin cost-of-quality development.
1986	0	15	Roll out QES training. Trained 5,000 employees.
1986	0	15	Top executive decided to implement Crosby companywide. Motivated by informal feedback from distributors about both product and service quality.
1986	−1	14	Resources devoted to quality. Three hundred trained by Crosby and Juran.
1986	−1	14	ECR suggestion system. 2/3 business units still have it.
1986	−1	14	Cost of quality developed—still a major measure.
1987	4	16	Various units using a variety of consultants, including Feigenbaum, Crosby.
1987	1	15	CAT teams appear.
1987	1	15	PONC report routine.
1987	0	14	Crosby QIT formed.
1988	5	6	Corporate Quality Council looked beyond Crosby. Started uncoordinated cycle time reduction. SPC—did not stick.
1988	5	4	Crosby Quality Fanatics Award.
1988	2	15	ZD [zero defects] days through 1990.

1988	2	15	Modified Crosby's 14 steps to 10, including three new areas. They are
			    Customer Satisfaction
			    Problem Solving
			    Quality Planning and Measurement
			    Awareness and Recognition
			    Employee Enrichment
			    Quality Commitment
			    Quality Education
			    Supplier Quality
			    Quality Council
			    Quality Appreciation (ZD days)

1988	−1	18	At this time, there were some efforts under way, most notably in the supplier area. Some purchasing people had been to Crosby Quality College.
1991	8	6	Trained all employees in action methodology (based on Crosby with more root cause analysis).
1991	7	1	What is Quality 3 video? Revamp CAR—make new videos.
1991	7	1	PONC report created—focus on 12 categories.
1992	5	14	New survey (employee). Used in United States and Canada. Evolved from Crosby questionnaire (50 questions). Now has 200 questions.

Record Year	Years Into	ID	Record
Juran			
1979	−5	2	Turn division heads loose on quality. Had Juran, Deming, Crosby, etc. Visit various divisions.
1982	−1	16	Contracted several consultants, including Juran. Primarily used Juran's approach. Created 8-point plan. Included Ladder of Excellence road map. Asked each unit to create plan. Tracked units against the plan.
1982	0	5	Two hundred to 300 managers to Crosby training. Bought Juran videos. Cascaded training. Appoint Corporate Director of Quality. Formed departmental QITs.
1983	0	16	Used Juran team format (steering committee, etc.). Primarily focused on management and technical teams. 50% participation.
1983	0	16	Roll-out of training for management. One day with Juran. Then used Juran tapes—16 hours. Followed by one or two interactive sessions.
1986	2	9	Additional training developed: SPC, quality toolkit. Based on Juran.
1986	2	3	Redeveloped training to merge Crosby, Juran, Deming, etc.
1986	2	18	Juran training. Middle management taskforces. Seventy-five percent to 80% trained.
1986	−1	14	Resources devoted to quality. Three hundred trained by Crosby and Juran.
1987	0	13	Began to add Juran's approaches. Created project teams called Quality Breakthrough Teams.
1989	3	19	Program by Juran brought in by satellite. Every manager saw it.

Record Year	Years Into	ID	Record
Deming			
1979	−5	2	Turn division heads loose on quality. Had Juran, Deming, Crosby, etc. Visit various divisions.
1981	−3	20	Deming met with new CEO and senior management. Senior management came away with constancy of purpose message. Took 3 years to figure out what that purpose is.
1983	−3	21	Many divisions became aware of Deming. Lots of activity, SPC, some joint supplier teams. Twenty-five percent of workforce involved.
1983	0	4	Opened new plant based on EI. Added SPC, JIT in 1985-1986. Cells—semiautonomous teams, Deming.
1984	−2	19	One VP discovered Deming's book *Quality, Productivity, and Competitive Position*. He issued a copy to each of 700 employees.
1985	−2	13	Began move toward Deming's philosophy.
1985	−1	19	Purchased Deming tapes. Used to train everyone. Includes introduction to SPC (SPC philosophy).
1986	2	3	Redeveloped training to merge Crosby, Juran, Deming, etc.
1986	3	4	Went international—more focus on Deming-type stuff.
1986	0	19	Basic quality course rolled out. Made case for quality. Taught Deming's 14 points. Employees tested on 14 points.
1988	2	19	Mary Walton's Deming Management Method handed out to every employee with paycheck.
1988	0	22	Started to understand Deming approach. Organization already had very strong statistical and analytical capabilities.

Notes

1. Note that the proponents of these various other approaches, which we view as largely derivative, almost uniformly distance their approaches from TQM in order to enhance their uniqueness. Thus, they would be unlikely to concur that the themes underlying these other approaches have direct links to the TQM movement.

2. As is well known, the original TQM systems were developed by the Japanese under the name Total Quality Control (TQC). We focus here only on the development of TQM in the United States and do not intend to claim for U.S. TQM the credit for innovation that rightfully belongs to the development of Japanese TQC. The development of U.S. TQM, however, consisted of both adaptation of Japanese approaches into the United States as well as genuine U.S. innovations, including the adoption and refinement of existing U.S. approaches.

3. From the point of view of the research methodology used in this chapter, we define TQM to be a management system that substantially addresses the 1994 criteria of the Malcolm Baldrige National Quality Award (National Institute of Standards and Technology, 1994). That is, we use the Baldrige criteria to provide an operational definition of TQM.

4. It is generally incorrect to view processes as static. In reality, they are constantly changed by external forces such as new technologies or changes in customer requirements. These changes are in addition to internally driven changes made to improve the process, and in many cases, the external changes make obsolete the process improvement. The usual situation is one of always being on the steep part of the learning curve in response to the external changes. This is one reason why continuous improvement efforts generally do not suffer from diminishing returns.

5. For example, the interview data show that, with the exception of the ECR system in initial implementation of a Crosby-based approach, suggestion systems are almost never cited as an important part of a TQM system in the United States.

References

Crosby, P. (1979). *Quality is free.* New York: McGraw-Hill.

Deming, W. E. (1982). *Quality, productivity, and competitive position.* Cambridge: Massachusetts Institute of Technology, Center for Advanced Engineering Study.

Deming, W. E. (1986). *Out of the crisis.* Cambridge: Massachusetts Institute of Technology, Center for Advanced Engineering Study.

Easton, G. S. (1993a). The 1993 state of U.S. total quality management: A Baldrige examiner's perspective. *California Management Review, 35*(3), 33-54.

Easton, G. S. (1993b). *The role of employee involvement in total quality management.* Working paper, Goizueta Business School, Emory University, Atlanta, GA.

Easton, G. S., & Jarrell, S. L. (1998). The effects of total quality management on corporate performance: An empirical investigation. *Journal of Business, 71,* 253-307.

Easton, G. S., & Jarrell, S. L. (1999). The emerging academic research on the link between total quality management and corporate financial performance: A critical review. In M. J. Stahl (Ed.), *Perspectives in total quality* (pp. 27-70). Oxford, UK: Basil Blackwell.

Jarrell, S. L., & Easton, G. S. (1997). An exploratory empirical investigation of the effects of total quality management on corporate performance. In U. Karmarkar & P. Lederer (Eds.), *The practice of quality management.* Boston: Kluwer.

Juran, J. M. (1981). *Juran on quality improvement* [Videocassette series]. Wilton, CT: Juran Institute.

Juran, J. M. (1988). *Juran on planning for quality.* New York: Free Press.

Juran, J. M. (1989). *Juran on leadership for quality: An executive handbook.* New York: Free Press.

Juran, J. M. (1995). *Managerial breakthrough: The classic book on improving management performance.* New York: McGraw-Hill.

Juran, J. M., & Gryna, F. M. (1988). *Juran's quality control handbook.* New York: McGraw-Hill.

Kolesar, P. J. (1994). What Deming told the Japanese. *Quality Management Journal, 2*(1), 9-24.

Lillrank, P. M., & Kano, N. (1989). *Continuous improvement: Quality control circles in Japanese industry.* Ann Arbor: University of Michigan, Center for Japanese Studies.

National Institute of Standards and Technology. (1994). *Malcolm Baldrige National Quality Award 1994 award criteria.* Washington, DC: Author.

Reger, R. K., Gustafson, L. T., Demarie, S. M., & Mullane, J. V. (1994). Reframing the organization: Why implementing total quality is easier said than done. *Academy of Management Review, 19,* 565-584.

Weick, K. E. (1995). *Sensemaking in organizations.* Thousand Oaks, CA: Sage.

Chapter 6

Quality Comes
to the Public Sector

LINDA KABOOLIAN

The public sector has vigorously embraced the "new quality paradigm" to enhance the performance of government organizations.[1] The movement that began in the 1980s with the adoption of Total Quality Management (TQM) has grown to engage nearly every level and branch of government in conversations about more generic principles and practices such as "world class service" and "customer satisfaction."[2] The adoption of these methods has proceeded independent of systematic evidence of the power of these methods to improve the performance of public organizations.

This chapter describes the wide variety of conditions that exist in the public sector and questions the appropriateness of wholesale efforts to adopt quality techniques. Anecdotal evidence demonstrates that the basic tenets of quality improvement technologies are useful in a specific subset of public organizations and subunits of those organizations. Even where quality methods might be most appropriate and useful, public organizations have more constraints on their ability to act and thus capture less of the potential for organizational learning. This occurs because political constraints on public or-

ganizations trump managerial considerations. Hypotheses for a more systematic examination of usefulness are enumerated.

This chapter also describes why, despite the limitations of quality methods for improving the performance of public organizations, dissemination and adoption of quality methods are widespread in the public sector. Legitimacy needs that cause the migration of techniques developed in the private sector to the public sector will be examined, as will the effect of the enormous demands on public organizations to be efficient and reduce costs, even when organizational conditions do not favor efficiency. Finally, an analysis is presented that argues that quality methods represent important sense-making routines in public organizations, creating meaning and legitimacy.

The lessons of this examination for the public sector center around avoidance of wholesale adoption of managerial reforms. No one reform can possibly address the variety of conditions present in the public sector. Investments in time, technology, and attention to acquire and use methods that are inappropriate are wasteful at best and may possibly reduce the performance

AUTHOR'S NOTE: The author acknowledges the helpful comments of Robert Cole, John Dunlop, Barbara Dyer, Arn Howitt, Larry Lynn, Sue Michaelson, Beryl Radin, Don Kettl, Mark Moore, W. Richard Scott, Janet Weiss, Sidney Winter, and the participants in the Workshop on Integrating Social Science Theory and Research in Quality Improvement.

of public organizations. This latter occurrence may result from misapplication of a technique or from misdiagnosis of the source of performance problems. In either event, wastefulness and the diminishing of performance are contrary to the stated goals of reform efforts.

Similarly, lessons for the private sector from the experience of public sector organizations with quality techniques also center around the organizational conditions that enhance or limit the usefulness to organizational improvement. Public organizations demonstrate to private organizations that in situations where goals are ambiguous, technologies uncertain, and environments complex and dynamic, quality methods are unlikely to be very useful. In addition, where private sector organizations and their subunits engage in activities formerly reserved for the public sector, they may find themselves operating under conditions that limit their ability to learn from quality methods.

Quality Comes to the Public Sector

Evidence of the interest in and adoption by the public sector of the generic principles and techniques of the quality movement abounds. It is virtually impossible to pick up any publication reporting on management of government organizations in the United States from the late 1980s to the present day without reading about the principles of "quality management" and their application to the public sector. Recently published textbooks on public administration now include chapters on TQM along with more traditional topics, such as "Administrative Responsibility and Ethics" (e.g., see Starling, 1998). A new genre of manuals for public managers directly addresses quality techniques (Cohen & Brand, 1993; Hunt, 1993). More broadly aimed management publications on quality have chapters on the public sector (Milakovich, 1995; Oakland, 1989). Professional conferences to coach managers in quality techniques are organized by government agencies as well as private organizations.[3] Management consulting firms have expanded to provide

services to government organizations (Mickelthwaite & Woolridge, 1996). There are quality award programs for organizations at all levels of government; some programs are sponsored by trade associations, others by public agencies.[4] Information for public managers on quality techniques can be sought on the Internet from a variety of sites, including the Alliance for Reinventing Government and the Council for Excellence in Government.[5] General interest in the topic of quality in the public sector may be partially gauged by the appearance on the *New York Times* bestseller list of two books on the public sector (Gore, 1993; Osborne & Gaebler, 1992). Even political scientists feel compelled to address quality in their analyses of the public sector (DiIulio, Garvey, & Kettl, 1993).

The most well-known brand-name quality activity—TQM—was mandated for use by all federal agencies by an Executive Order in 1988.[6] The diffusion and utilization of TQM had important sponsorship from oversight organizations such as the Office of Management and Budget (OMB), the Office of Personnel Management (OPM), and the General Accounting Office (GAO). Primarily an oversight agency that monitors the performance of federal organizations, the GAO hosted a rare visit to its own offices by W. Edwards Deming to "assess the implications of adopting a quality management approach at GAO" (GAO, 1990). The interest of the GAO in TQM is an indicator of the depth of interest in quality in the federal sector. Because the GAO is usually shielded from currents of change, its flirtation with TQM represented a rare incursion of innovative practices into the staid organization. In other parts of the federal sector, adoption of TQM was rapid. Just 4 years after the issuance of the Executive Order establishing the program, a survey by the GAO found that 68% of all federal installations had initiated TQM programs (GAO, 1992, p. 53).

Similarly, states and municipalities have been affected by TQM. A survey of state practices (including those in Puerto Rico and Washington, D.C.) conducted in 1994 revealed widespread diffusion of TQM, although the pattern of adoption of associated quality practices showed some interesting incongruities (National Association of State Budget Officers

[NAoSBO], 1995). For example, 39 jurisdictions had implemented statewide "quality initiatives such as TQM," but only 28 have "established means or mechanisms to enable agencies to identify customer needs/preferences and feedback on services," and only 14 had "established formal boards, commissions, or oversight groups to enable community groups or citizens to have some say in the services being delivered" (NAoSBO, 1995, pp. 86, 107). Although 31 jurisdictions had statewide commissions or processes to examine productivity or quality issues, most of these processes did not involve public unions where unions were present (NAoSBO, 1995, p. 86).

To support their TQM efforts, 24 state-level jurisdictions offered all employees training in quality techniques (NAoSBO, 1995, p. 76). Although it may seem surprising that only two thirds of jurisdictions that implemented TQM offered training to employees, this must be juxtaposed against the relative scarcity of training in the public sector: Only 23 jurisdictions offered training to all employees on all other topics (NAoSBO, 1995, p. 76).

A similar story can be told about the experience of municipalities with TQM. A 1993 survey of municipalities with more than 25,000 residents found that nearly 30% were implementing TQM (Berman & West, 1995). Madison, Wisconsin, an early adopter of TQM, is also one of the leading examples of the program at the municipal level. After attending a lecture by W. Edwards Deming in 1983, the mayor of Madison, Joseph Sensenbrenner, brought TQM to the city's garage (Sensenbrenner, 1991). Reduction in turnaround times for vehicle maintenance and savings due to increased preventive maintenance stimulated expansion of the program to other city services. Among the six departments that embraced TQM was the police department, which surveyed every 50th person it encountered, "whether a victim of crime, a witness, a complainant, or a criminal," in order to "improve the quality of . . . service in the future" (Osborne & Gaebler, 1992, p. 173).

States and municipalities also have engaged in more generic quality practices. For example, the Ohio Quality Services through Partnership (QStP) program, begun in 1993, is a partnership between the Ohio Civil Service Employees Association and the administration of Governor George Voinovich.[7] Initiated by the union, QStP is formalized in the collective bargaining agreement between the parties.[8] The program includes the training of employees and managers in problem-solving methods, as well as the operation of labor-management teams "to streamline bureaucracy, analyze problems and improve [their] ability to respond to customer needs" (U.S. Department of Labor, 1996, p. 89).

The federal sector also has launched a generic movement to "reinvent government," beginning in 1993 with the National Performance Review (NPR). Influenced by David Osborne and Ted Gaebler's book *Reinventing Government,* as well as federal government reform efforts already occurring in the United Kingdom, Australia, and New Zealand, the NPR recommended adoption of a number of practices associated with quality techniques.[9] The NPR resulted in orders to all federal agencies to engage in partnerships with their unions and establish customer service standards, among other actions.[10]

Do Quality Practices Improve the Performance of Public Organizations?

The volume of quality-related activities in the public sector begs examination of the effects these activities have had on the performance of public organizations. As Winter (1994) points out, the adoption of quality techniques is not as important as the effects on organizational performance. Ample anecdotal evidence shows that some public organizations have had considerable success using quality techniques. Many public organizations have won recognition from trade associations and the media for improving service delivery. For example, the Social Security Administration's toll-free telephone number, long a problematic operation, won a national quality award for improving response time and the accuracy of answers (Kettl, 1997). Social Security clients calling the toll-free number reported high levels of satisfaction. Additionally, some organizations, such as the Ohio Department of Transportation, report reduced costs as a result of QStP (Kaboolian, 1996). Many similar reports come from all levels of government. However, Winter warns us not to generalize from anecdotal evidence. The success stories have not been studied systematically, and failures are likely to be unreported.

Many scholars of public administration have criticized the adoption of quality methods by the public sector. Because quality management is an import from the private sector, it would be simple to assign this criticism to the "not invented here" attitude of U.S. managers about Japanese quality practices, described by Cole (1996). However, the public sector has a long history of borrowing and adapting from the private sector, often to great acclaim by scholars.

The tenor of the criticism about their use in the public sector is that quality practices, particularly those represented by TQM, are "not suitable here" because of fundamental differences between public and private sector organizations. The focus of quality techniques on products rather than services, on inputs and processes rather than programmatic outcomes, and on customers limits their applicability in the public sector, argue these critics. For example,

> the use of TQM in government has several major problems: insufficient modification for services; insensitivity to the problems of defining governmental customers; inappropriate emphasis on inputs and processes; and demands for top-level intensity that can rarely be met by the governmental culture. (Swiss, 1992, p. 358)

Furthermore, the very purpose of government makes quality an inappropriate strategy. The public sector is not about "shoes" but about "government," Fredrickson (1993, p. 4) argues. Policy decisions, not operational concerns, drive the performance of public organizations, and policies are fundamentally political:

> The real problems of American government have little to do with management or administration. Public administration, in my view, is usually done rather well. The problems of government have mostly to do with the failure of political will, the power of interest groups and weakness in conduct of statecraft by elected leaders. (Fredrickson, 1993, p. 5)

Milakovich (1995), speaking to the politics around policies, provides a more technical explanation:

> There is basic conflict between the quality approach, which stresses the 85:15 Pareto rule for problem identification, and the political-distributive models, which tend to disregard the most difficult problems or spread resources among the many interests represented in the political process. Often the net result is that nothing gets done. (p. 159)

Locating public managers and their actions in this political scenario, Terry (1997) argues for circumspection. Political processes triumph over managerial considerations so that the sovereignty authority of citizens and their agents, elected leaders, and legislators can be maintained. As a result, Terry argues, the discretion of public managers should be limited, and their actions should be focused on preserving the legitimacy of the Constitution. Quality practices that encourage entrepreneurism and reward managers for performance improvements, particularly if the practices suggest the existence of motivations such as economic self-interest, may undermine the trust placed in public managers.

Some argue the case of "public sector exceptionalism"—that is, because public sector organizations are fundamentally unique in character, practices such as quality methods designed primarily for private sector organizations have no or limited use in the political environment of the public sector. (This argument is in direct contrast to the early studies of bureaucracy, production processes, and administrative behavior, which were relatively insensitive to the implications of the location of organizations in either the public or the private sector; Rainey, 1991, pp. 1, 4-6, 16-19). In these works, private sector status is considered normative, and theories of organization and management assume the conditions of the private sector (although the variance within those conditions, such as technology and size, is treated with great attention to detail). When public sector organizations have been recognized by organizational theorists, they are assumed to have more similarities to than differences from private organizations.[11]

Assumed similarities notwithstanding, empirical comparisons of public and private organizations in the same industries (e.g., hospitals, schools) demonstrate that the public status of an organization does have consequences for the behavior of the organization on many dimensions.[12] These findings beg the question raised by the critics of quality methods in the public sector: Are the critics correct in their assertion that the character of the public sector means that quality methods are ineffectual in public organizations?

Criteria for Assessing the Utility of Quality Improvement Techniques in the Public Sector

To begin an assessment of the worth of quality methods to public organizations, consider the designed purpose of quality improvement (QI) techniques: to improve the performance of organizations. Performance improvements, however, are instrumental efforts toward more fundamental goals. Hackman and Wageman (1995) cite the survival of the organization as the ultimate goal. Choi and Behling (1997) have a more contingent approach that offers a variety of goals, although survival underlies each. Quality methods can be used for defensive purposes to ensure survival in a hostile environment, for tactical purposes to satisfy immediate customers, or for developmental purposes that enable the organization to acquire new capacities better suited to the future. In the logic of quality management, the use of techniques such as process analysis to reduce costs, customer focus, and even organizational learning is important because they are part of a strategy to improve the competitive position of the organization relative to other organizations (Cole, 1996).

The public sector offers a challenge to the assessment of quality techniques based on survival or competitiveness criteria because of the very nature of the public sector. Consider the definition of "publicness" offered by Moore, Kaboolian, Howitt, and Augusto (1995). An organization can be said to be "public" because of its characteristics on these features: its purposes, the source of its resources, and the targets of accountability. Public organizations are established in order to achieve *public purposes defined collectively by political processes* (not economic ones), rather than to pursue private interests. To achieve these purposes, public organizations are given public resources, including tangible ones, such as tax dollars, and intangible ones, such as the right to license or prohibit behavior. Finally, but perhaps most important, public organizations are accountable to representatives of the polity for their use of public resources and accomplishment of public purposes. Organizations sharing these institutional conditions can be said to be in the public sector.

As the definition suggests, organizational competitiveness is not an overarching goal in the public sector. Rarely do public organizations compete against other organizations, public or private, for business or resources.[13] Public organizations may survive to address public purposes because of political decisions to ensure that survival, even if they are not successful or are less successful than alternative methods of achieving the same purposes. If survival is not the criterion for assessment, the usefulness of quality techniques must address the other characteristic of "publicness": accountability for the use of resources and progress toward defined goals. Political overseers demand optimal returns on resources gathered, in part, by coercion, for purposes collectively, though not consensually, defined. Practically, this means that public organizations are accountable for their performance, an intermediate but important target of quality methods. It is at this point that the characteristics of public organizations *as organizations,* rather than as a sector, become most salient.

Like all organizations, public organizations exist in environments and have internal characteristics that affect behavior and performance. Similar to that of private organizations, the behavior of public sector organizations is largely a response to the complex, authoritative, and uncertain environments in which the organizations reside (Lawrence & Lorsch, 1967).

It is also the case that public organizations have important internal attributes that vary independently of external conditions. Task environment, which includes the ambiguity of goals, the certainty of technologies, and accountability mechanisms, plays a role in determining the actions of public organizations (Perrow, 1970).

Proponents and critics of the use of quality methods in the public sector fail to recognize the great variety of organizational characteristics within the public sector, such as environment, form of governance, tasks, and production processes. As a result, they fail to consider the usefulness of quality methods in the context of that variance.[13] In describing the widespread adoption of quality methods by public organizations, this chapter also has treated the public sector as an undifferentiated whole up to this point. However, it would be a mistake to think of public sector organizations as homogeneous: Variation exists on both environmental and internal attributes.

The recognition of the importance of variance in the external environment suggests an organic view of public organizations in which variation in environmental conditions leads to adaptations in behavior (Burns & Stalker, 1961). On internal characteristics, the range of variance describes the complex continuum of types of products, technologies, and conditions in public organizations.

It is important to note that the variance on organizational characteristics among public organizations (i.e., within the public sector) may be greater than the variance between organizations in the public and private sectors. For example, the product line of the National Direct Student Loan Program (NDSL), a federal program that provides loans to college students, is identical to loan instruments provided by private sector banks. This similarity might argue for a consideration of the application of quality methods *within the financial sector,* including both the NDSL and private lenders, rather than a comparison *between the public program and private lenders* in their applications of quality

methods.[15] However, when the comparison is with the product line of another public financial agency, the Internal Revenue Service (IRS), the differences between the NDSL and the IRS are greater than those between the NDSL and the private lenders. These comparisons provide evidence for the claim that although "publicness" of the sector matters, organizational dimensions matter as well.

Assessing the usefulness of quality techniques in the public sector warrants an examination of the dimensions on which public organizations can be analyzed as organizations, the variance on those dimensions, and the consequences of those characteristics for the use of quality methods. Only in this way is it possible to more fully understand and assess the effect of quality methods on the performance of public organizations.

The External Environment of Public Organizations

Although all organizations, public and private, must respond to the economic and political forces in their environment, the relative importance of each of these forces for public organizations is the inverse of those for private organizations. More specifically, the market is relatively unimportant to public organizations, and political processes are extremely important (Bozeman, 1987). If the environment were conceptualized as a two-dimensional space with market forces on one axis and political forces on the second, in their purest forms, public and private sector organizations would be located on the far ends of the diagonal.

Of course, organizations in both sectors show variance on these dimensions. Some private sector organizations are relatively insulated from market forces by government regulation or intervention (e.g., many utilities and insurance carriers), and some public sector organizations must address market conditions or even compete with private sector firms (e.g., the National Direct Student Loan Program). Similarly, some public institutions are relatively insulated from political forces (e.g., the GAO), whereas some private sector organizations are targets of political processes (e.g., tobacco companies). Where variance occurs *across* public organizations, it is more typically occurring and widest on the market dimension. The consequences of the variance on each dimension for the adoption and usefulness of quality techniques are discussed below.

The Political Environment

The potency of the political environment for the definition of an organization's goals, management methods, and criteria for success cannot be overestimated for public organizations. The sovereignty of political entities, and politics more broadly, to determine the purposes, practices, and resources of public organizations is deeply embedded in our political culture and constitutional arrangements. Among public management theorists, the debate over the range of discretion permitted public managers (read "career civil servants") in opposition to the constraints of political oversight has raged for more than 100 years.[16] Although the strength or closeness of political oversight may vary for public organizations, it is generally the case that career managers are dominated by this authority, either bowing to the will of political overseers or strategizing to gain their authorization to act.[17]

Political oversight creates an environment for public organizations that is complex, dynamic, and authoritative (Moore, 1995). The determining feature of the environment is the nature of the stakeholders. Public organizations vary in the number, interests, and unification of their stakeholder groups. James Q. Wilson (1987), concerned about "capture" of public organizations by stakeholders, provides a useful typology of external environments in which public organizations exist based on the characteristics of stakeholders.

In the simplest case representing few public organizations, no stakeholders are continuously active. Wilson calls this a "majoritarian" environment. Agencies that affect few interests or affect them in a singular manner are more likely to experience this type of environment. Examples draw primarily from staff agencies, including centralized personnel and procurement agencies, as well as auditing divisions such as

the GAO. These organizations are likely to be extremely insulated from external standards, largely because no organized interests are very concerned about the agencies' performance. Quality initiatives, if introduced, are more likely to come from internal sources, as in the case of the GAO's experience with TQM, described above. The utility of these initiatives will be evaluated largely by the agency itself. It is important to reiterate that this condition exists for very few public organizations.

Where organizations have a single dominant stakeholder that benefits from the organization's activities, the environment is dominated by "client politics." In these circumstances, the stakeholders are supportive of the organization and organize to pressure political overseers to fund the organization's activities. An example of this type of organization is the Old Age and Retirement Insurance (OARI) division of the Social Security Administration (SSA). Here, the clients are well organized and often speak with a single voice. Servicing their needs in a timely fashion makes quality methods quite applicable to the processes and products of this division of the SSA. Not surprisingly, these processes reap the greatest improvements in organizational performance from quality efforts.

Many public organizations have multiple stakeholders in various roles, some with legally specified authority (such as legislatures that appropriate resources, courts that monitor behavior) and others attempting to seek authority to affect organizational decisions (such as interest groups, employee unions, and the media). Of course, the interests of these players rarely coalesce. Fragmentation of interests within groups of players occurs more often than consensus across groups. Wilson calls this the "interest group politics" environment and suggests that the opposed forces in the environment hold the organization erect. In expressing their interests, stakeholders of public organizations, in contrast to stakeholders of private organizations, are more likely to use "voice" than "exit" when they are dissatisfied with the organization.[18] The effect of "voice" strategy is that the losers in the negotiations over the purpose or management of the organization, rather than "exit," remain within the environment to criticize and continue to reassert their interests, often overturning negotiated settlements (Allison & Moe, 1988).

Opposition in the environment has enormous consequences for the operational definition of goals and performance measures, as well as organizational performance. A case in point is provided by the recent welfare reform law, which reversed the process for adjudicating claims on benefits by disabled children. Originally, the process presumed that the applicant was disabled until the assertion was disproved. In the early 1980s, the Reagan administration reversed the practice and presumed ineligibility. The parents of disabled children sued, and in the early 1990s, the U.S. Supreme Court ordered yet another reversal of the practice (to presumed eligibility pending review of applications). The effect of this decision was to require that the SSA reprocess 300,000 applications, some of which were 10 years old. This was a workload that brought the disability determination process to its knees ("Final Report," 1994).

In 1996, 3 years into the effort to reinvent government and improve customer service, the welfare reform act once again reversed the practice and required notification to many of the same recipients that their benefits would be cut off. The parents of disabled children sued, and the federal courts overturned the reversal, reinstating benefits. Public managers at the SSA have dealt with the reversal of practice and standards of quality by first the executive branch, then the courts, and finally legislative authorities—the additional work created by these overseers as well as by the inquiries from overseers about complaints of disgruntled client-constituents. Not surprisingly, the performance of the childhood disability determination process continues to be evaluated as problematic by the congressional and executive oversight agencies, having gained few improvements from efforts to use quality methods.

It is sometimes the case that stakeholders are interested in seeing an organization fail to meet its goals, if not fail entirely. Although this may happen in private organizations, the damage is usually limited to a product line or market niche rather than the survival of the organization.[19] In less obvious cases, public organizations, more often their programs, are designed to be minimally effective (Ban, 1996). James Wilson (1987, pp. 77-80) refers to this condition as an "entrepreneurial environment." Authorizers can use numerous devices to minimize effectiveness: Inadequate resources may be allotted, workload or reporting requirements may be overly burdensome, or missions may be defined in ways that make ineffectiveness or failure a foregone conclusion. Recent legislative debates over many of the federal enforcement agencies, such as the Environmental Protection Agency, the Food and Drug Administration, and the Departments of Labor and Commerce, represent examples of this type of politics. The consequences for managers working under these circumstances are enormous. Quality methods lose all meaning when the external environment prefers to see inaction, ineffectiveness, or failure.

The existence of multiple and fragmented stakeholder groups creates both complexity and dynamism in the environment of public organizations. Stakeholder groups are unstable in their membership and in the positions they assume. Circumstances such as periodic elections (every 2 years in the U.S. House of Representatives) can change the environment literally overnight (as anyone who negotiated legislation during the fall of 1994 can testify). Small amendments to big directives can radically change the position of interest groups, jeopardizing the larger package. Additionally, politically appointed managerial leadership turns over, on average, every 18 months. Thus, even if other features of the environment remain stable, the life expectancy of the principal operating managers may slightly exceed the amount of time it takes to reprint the agency's stationery.

The consequences of the complexity and dynamism of the political environment for the performance of public organizations are enormous, although perhaps desirable in light of the purpose of public organizations and the value placed on responsiveness to overseers. The result, however, is that the political environment makes it extremely difficult for many public organizations to learn from their experiences with quality methods (Sitkin, Sutcliffe, & Schroeder, 1994). The more complex and fractious the political environment and the more exposed the organization is to its environment, the less likely it will have stable measures of performance. The ability to act on the analysis of information collected on those measures will also be determined by the nature of the political environment. In most political environments, it is more likely that benefits from quality methods, if any, will be limited to what Sitkin et al. call "quality control" rather than "quality learning."

The Market Environment

As noted above, the nature of the market environment of public organizations also varies. Many public organizations are monopoly providers of goods and services that are not available in the private sector. However, at least some public organizations operate in marketlike conditions either by competing directly with private sector organizations or simply by having identifiable "customers," in the private sector sense of the word. The National Direct Student Loan Program, described earlier, is an example of a public program in a highly competitive market. Similarly, the Defense Logistics division of the Department of Defense competes with private contractors to provide manufactured goods and inventory services to the armed forces. Some agencies (e.g., state and municipal park and recreation departments, libraries, and museums) interact directly with the consumer public and need to attract users to satisfy their mission. Staff and oversight agencies, competing with privatized services to perform their functions, have internal customers in their own agencies or in other public organizations.

Public organizations in marketlike environments with identifiable customers appear to be among those organizations that have used quality methods most effectively. In these circumstances, standards for organizational performance may be benchmarked against the performance in private organizations, and performance may be measured through competition. Market forces appear to lend more stability to performance standards than the fractious and dynamic political environment can achieve. For example, the Defense Logistics division of the Department of Defense, with 19 honors, has

won more than its share of the 45 President's Quality Awards for organizational improvement by capturing new customers. Similarly, the National Direct Student Loan Program, in 2 short years, won nearly two thirds of the market by focusing on customer needs.

Internal Attributes

The Task Environment

The complexity and dynamism of the political environment contribute to the "ambiguity of intention" experienced by many public organizations (March & Olsen, 1978, p. 250). Like private sector organizations that are experiencing a fractured, contentious, and dynamic environment, public organizations also receive very mixed signals from the environment. For private sector organizations, these signals may force the organization to choose among various courses of action (e.g., profits vs. market share; new product line vs. "stick to knitting"). Questions of fundamental purpose (e.g., profits vs. no profits) are rarely at issue. Public sector managers face uncertainties about the very purpose of their organizations, and their actions are more constrained by the authoritative nature of the environment. Indeed, public management courses begin by asking, "Where do public managers find the mission of their organizations?" An obvious avenue to examine is authorizing legislation, although the point is often made that purposes are left deliberately ambiguous and undefined to accommodate the unresolved conflicts among the stakeholders (Levin, 1994). A thorough search for the true purpose of most public organizations reveals that, like the environment, the organization's goals are multiple, diverse, and often contradictory.[20]

In fairness to the stakeholders, goal uncertainty is a consequence of more than their unresolved conflicts; it is often the consequence of the nature of problems tackled by public organizations. Some, such as "fighting poverty," "providing national defense," and "protecting the environment," are in the public sector because the market has rejected them as "too big," "too hard," or otherwise unsuitable for more goal-oriented organizations (Hargrove & Glidewell,

1990). Additionally, the public sector is often charged with pursuing objectives that have symbolic rather than substantive value (Edelman, 1971).

It is important to remember that there is variance in the degree of goal ambiguity in public organizations. Some organizations, such as the Old Age and Retirement Insurance division of the SSA, have clear mandates ("the right check, to the right person, in the right amount, on time"). Other public organizations have a clear mandate but are misconstrued by observers as serving other purposes. For example, many people believe that the Immigration and Naturalization Service (INS) is a service provider to aliens seeking visas and citizenship, not realizing that it is an enforcement agency serving the interests of citizens by regulating the activities of noncitizens. This misconstrual led to the statement overheard in a local INS office: "You should take the word 'service' out of INS." Still other organizations, such as state "drug czar" offices, have poorly defined purposes; nevertheless, almost every state has such an office.

The importance of the clarity and certainty of purposes to management in general and quality techniques specifically is clear (Thompson, 1976). Goals represent a positive resource for organizations around which to organize activity, set priorities, and allocate resources (Perrow, 1970). They also broadly define the measures to be attained through quality techniques. Where goals are clearly identifiable—such as "paved roads"—quality techniques have been adopted more quickly, more widely, and more successfully (Berman & West, 1995).

Independent of the degree of goal ambiguity, the challenge of implementing quality techniques in the public sector is exacerbated by a competition for the attention between ambiguous and often-changing substantive goals and less obvious but more stable procedural goals: efficiency, economy, equity, transparency, and accountability (J. Wilson, 1987, pp. 315-317, 349-360). Although these goals are not often explicit, there is considerable evidence that when Americans express opinions about their government, they refer to procedural issues rather than substantive outcomes.[21] It is easy to see how, in combination with ambiguous or conflicting substantive goals, responsibility for process attributes focuses the attention of managers away from outcomes and toward defect detection. The consequence of this focus may be adherence to older quality techniques, more closely approximating the paradigm of quality control. Federal agencies are thick with Offices of Inspectors General and Program Integrity and Review, which measure and monitor how work is done, regardless of the effectiveness of the work.

These quality control mechanisms operate under the adage: "Government work is like toast: you burn, I'll scrape" (Sensenbrenner, 1991, p. 62). New quality practices that emphasize organizational effectiveness and outcomes through organizational learning will be overwhelmed by the history, competencies, and requirements of procedural goals (Cole, 1996).

Technologies

Public organizations face yet another difficulty in that ambiguity about their goals is compounded by "ambiguity of understanding" about the nature of the technology available to address the problems they are supposed to solve (March & Olsen, 1978, p. 250). For example, what is the best way to protect the environment—create a market for pollution or ensure compliance with regulations? How best can compliance be ensured—through strict oversight of potential polluters or by coaching firms about how best to comply? Very few public production processes approximate manufacturing with a clearly identifiable product and well-established technologies. Where these conditions occur, as in claims processing at any number of public agencies, water treatment plants, and Departments of Motor Vehicles, TQM took a very early hold and did help improve organizational performance. Where these conditions do not occur but methods such as TQM were adopted nonetheless, the mismatch between the task environment and the quality techniques led managers to "talk the talk" but distrust the techniques and keep them at arm's length.

The Interaction of Task and Technology

Considerations of the internal environment of organizations are greatly explained by Perrow's (1970) typology of organizations based on dimensions of task (routine or variable) and technology (routine or variable). Perrow's purpose was to propose a model of structural features of organizations based on the interaction of the characteristics of tasks with the nature of various technologies. Although not citing Perrow directly, James Wilson (1987) provides a similar typology for public organizations based on interactions between the nature of the task (observable: yes or no) with the nature of the outcomes (observable: yes or no). Wilson speaks directly to the concerns described above about the ambiguity and conflict in the goals of public organizations, as well as to concerns about the wider range of technologies used in the public sector and uncertainties about their effectiveness, also described above.

A 2 × 2 table of the observability of outcomes (yes/no) and the observability of the task (yes/no) creates four classes of public organizations (see Table 6.1).

Radin and Coffee (1993) use these categories to rate the utility of quality methods in public organizations. Public production organizations are most like private manufacturing plants when the processes are certain *and* when the products are measurable. In these circumstances, the implementation of quality methods is more likely to effect improvements in processes on dimensions such as cost and in products on dimensions such as error rates. This category is similar to the highly developed technical environment described by Scott and Meyer (1991). Not surprisingly, Scott and Meyer predict that in these circumstances, the characteristics of outcomes will be important. This—certain processes and measurable products—is the condition that is most conducive to quality methods as they are now designed.

Quality methods are less useful for the remaining three categories of organizations. In procedural organizations, where the outcomes are far in the future or loosely connected to the work performed, performance standards are

TABLE 6.1

Can Results Be Observed?	Can Operators Be Observed?	
	Yes	No
Yes	*Production Organization* e.g., SSA Old Age & Retirement Insurance	*Craft Organization* e.g., Army Corps of Engineers
No	*Procedural Organization* e.g., OSHA	*Coping Organization* e.g., schools, police force

likely to focus on compliance with procedures rather than on measurable outcomes. Craft organizations, in which the outcomes are measurable but the work is often nonroutine and requires craft knowledge or professional judgment, are also unlikely candidates for successful use of quality methods.

Finally, coping organizations, with neither measurable outcomes nor routine work, Radin and Coffee (1993) argue, are the least likely to use quality methods successfully. In all of these circumstances, public organizations are not likely to find quality methods and their focus on products and process improvements helpful.

Accountability: Four Tensions

Many unsophisticated observers believe that public sector managers are insulated from accountability because of the relatively weak role of market forces in their environment. Nothing could be further from reality. Like all organizations competing for resources and requiring resources for survival, public organizations attempt to identify the demands of their environment and the characteristics of their competitors, and to act strategically. Unlike private sector organizations, where the volatility is in the production end of the process, public managers experience volatility in the reporting end (Moore, 1997). They report that they spend most of their time managing the external environment and working with authorizers to operationalize the mission from vague cues. Because this is a multiple-stage transaction, accountability for past grants of resources and for contracts for future resources is extremely important. Public managers laboring under the burden of fragmented authority structures and ambiguous goals know that they are ideal examples of Perrow's "good goldfish," who know that they are always being scrutinized (Perrow, 1970, p. 99). Their organizations have protected status in society as long as their output is considered legitimate, and legitimacy is closely monitored.

Process Versus Outcomes

The investment that public managers make in satisfying their external environment may be of little use in changing operations for the purpose of achieving quality in outcomes (Wilson, 1987, p. 32). Focusing on visible processes rather than hard-to-operationalize substantive goals allows authorizers to micromanage and limit the discretion of managers about how to meet their (ambiguous) goals. Budgetary constraints, staffing limits, and accounting mechanisms are various methods that elected executives and legislators can use. The specter of litigation over rights violated by agency procedures further emphasizes the importance of process. Managers collude with this emphasis by managing adherence to constraints rather than by struggling toward vague substantive goals (Wilson, 1987, p. 126).

A case in point is provided by the disability determination process in the SSA. In the past decade, the disability program has grown enormously: The disability-prone population has grown by 17%, but the number of disability recipients grew by 49%. Program and administrative costs have increased 55% in constant dollars. Not surprisingly, these changes caught the attention of congressional overseers. Investigation into the causes of the growth in the program led to some startling findings.

The quality control system that measured the accuracy of the eligibility determination system sampled only cases that were awarded benefits. Why? Because these were the cases with fiscal impact. SSA managers could confidently report

to Congress extremely high accuracy rates for these samples. Almost no one received disability checks based on fraudulent claims; therefore, the agency was a good steward for the disability trust fund, and Congress was satisfied.

However, claimants had a right to multiple levels of appeals. The SSA, obligated to elaborate rules of procedural justice, provided legal advocates at its own expense to assist in those appeals and did not defend itself, attempting to avoid creating an adversarial proceeding. Not surprisingly, half of denied claims were appealed. Two thirds of the denied claims were awarded benefits at the second level of appeal, and nearly all claims that reached the final levels of appeal were awarded benefits. Appeals not only consumed resources in the rework process, they also signaled to advocates that the probability of being granted benefits was high on appeal, thereby generating escalating appeal rates. Because the fees to advocates were set at a fixed percentage of the retroactive award, advocates delayed settlement of cases for as long as possible, creating processing backlogs of up to 550 days.

It was not obvious to the Office of Program Integrity Review at the SSA that there was a dynamic consequence to a quality control system that sampled and corrected only for false positives and made no quality adjustments for false negatives because, theoretically, these had no impact on the trust fund (Repenning & Sterman, 1997). SSA was meeting its procedural and integrity obligations. If the trust fund had not approached insolvency, it is not clear when the accountability system would have been addressed. The idea that the appeal rate should be examined as a problem in and of itself was not addressed until all other definitions of the crisis had been examined.

Success Versus Satisfying Overseers

The fragmentation of the external environment presents difficulties for accountability. The definition of success may very well depend on where one sits. Advocates are clearly unhappy when enforcement agencies succeed against their clients. Even programs that meet some objective standards of success may run up against value preferences for less government, not more successful government. A case in point is provided by the National Direct Student Loan (NDSL) Program, which, in 1 year, captured 66% of the student loan market by increasing its responsiveness to customers (i.e., sponsoring colleges and universities). After surveying the largest disbursers of student loans and learning that fast, available cash would give them incentive to steer students their way, the NDSL overhauled its information technology link. As a result, students could apply via computer screen in their college financial aid office, and, within a week, their loan would be approved and their college would have the money deposited in its bank account.

The NDSL not only satisfied colleges and students, it resulted in lower default rates that were an artifact of the guarantee mechanism. Unfortunately, a newly elected Congress, displeased with the success of this program and the threat it posed to private lenders, capped the share of the market it could service in order to sustain the private lenders. In the second year of the program, Congress moved to reduce funding under the argument that the program contributed to the growing national debt.

Measurement

It is obvious that evaluating and reporting on performance is difficult for public sector processes with ambiguous goals. However, even processes with clearer goals or greater consensus about their goals may find these tasks difficult. For example, how do we measure prevention? Repenning and Sterman (1997) tell us that "no one gets credit for fixing problems that never happened" (p. 13). A vast majority of public sector processes are enforcement or compliance functions. Although it is possible to measure decreasing incidence over time and even deal with the false negative problem, once an output is no longer visible it is likely to be less legitimate. "Drunk drivers apprehended at roadside checks" reports well and garners support. No drunk drivers apprehended due to increased prevention leaves questions about what is being done and whether it requires resources.

Performance Versus Rewards

The final difficulty presented by the accountability structure of public organizations is caused by the disconnect between performance and environmental reaction (March & Olsen, 1978, p. 260). How can organizations learn if the signals appear confused? Private sector organizations have faced similar situations; award-winning quality efforts have been abandoned, seemingly high-performance organizations have expired. Although these examples may not have been predictable, they are analyzable for lessons that can guide future performance. Much research on quality management and organizational performance focuses on this. The public sector is more complex: Research may conclude that the complexity and dynamism of the context make prescription very difficult.

We have some evidence that the disconnect between performance and reaction can be problematic for managers. Managers report that they are "hard-working bureaucrats in non-working bureaucracies" (Gore, 1993). On the other hand, the relationship between public organizations and their environments is an interactive one. Public managers may try to wish away their overseers, but the overseers will remain. The application of quality techniques to learning about the environment may be useful. Interaction with the environment can teach organizations how to reduce uncertainty and learn about and satisfy overseers. Interaction with the organization can change political overseers both positively and negatively.

Hypotheses About the Usefulness of QI Techniques

Three dimensions of the nature of public sector organizations have been examined—the external environment, the internal task environment, and accountability mechanisms—to ascertain how variation in these dimensions may affect the usefulness of quality improvement techniques. Although some systematic studies have examined the adoption of quality improvement techniques by public organizations, no systematic study has examined the usefulness of the techniques.[22]

Winter (1994, p. 91) calls for the definition of the ecological niche that best supports the effective use of quality methods. The analysis of organizational conditions presented in this chapter leads to the hypotheses presented below.

Quality methods are most likely to be useful for improving the performance of public organizations where

H1: Stakeholders are united and support the organization's goals.
H2: Stakeholders are silent and management adopts the methods.
H3: The external environment more closely approximates a market with identifiable customers.
H4: Tasks are clearly defined.
H5: Goals are defined as outcomes rather than processes.
H6: Technologies are more certain to produce desired results.
H7: Definitions of organizational performance and success are clear and uncontested.
H8: Outcomes can be measured.
H9: Rewards are linked to performance.

In designing a study to examine the usefulness of quality methods to public sector organizations, careful consideration should be given to identifying the most useful level of organizational aggregation. Scott and Meyer (1991, p. 119) point out that many organizations are complex entities. The conditions that exist at the agency level may not exist at the establishment subunit level. This is particularly true for federal organizations, where even within an organization, different programs may have different stakeholders, tasks, technologies, and accountability mechanisms. For example, several programs of the SSA have been used in the preceding discussion of stakeholders to demonstrate the consequences of extremely different stakeholder environments.

Why Quality Methods Are Adopted in the Public Sector

There is little systematic evidence about the effectiveness of quality methods for the performance of public organizations. As the hypotheses suggest, quality methods are likely to be useful only in a subset of public organizations with specific characteristics. Yet these methods have been adopted widely at all levels of government. What contributes to the use, if not usefulness, of quality methods in the public sector?

The Tendency to Adopt Innovations From the Private Sector

Ciampa could have been describing public sector management innovations when he described the private sector quality movement as "another chapter in the ongoing search for a formula for organizational excellence" (Ciampa, quoted in Dean & Bowen, 1994, p. 397). The tome recording the administrative history of the public sector in the post-World War II era is thick with descriptions of efforts to improve the performance of public organizations (Ciampa, quoted in Dean & Bowen, 1994, p. 397). As with the new quality techniques, earlier systemwide efforts such as Management by Objective (MBO) and Zero-Base Budgeting (ZBB) were adopted from the private sector.[23] The tendency to bow to techniques developed in the private sector should not be surprising; in fact, it can be argued that it is a tendency that is somewhat overdetermined.

Temporal Order of Innovation

Migration of private sector practices into the public sector is due in part to the temporal order of innovation and adoption. In the private sector, the competitive pressures of the market stimulate design and diffusion of new practices. Increased managerial discretion, which allows the investment of resources in development, training, and dissemination, permits private sector organizations to move more quickly and take more risks than public organizations can. As a result, the private sector generally, though not always, is ahead of the public sector in innovating (DiMaggio & Powell, 1983).

The presence of new quality improvement techniques in the larger environment affects public institutions in several ways (Winter, 1994). The first is that a discourse develops that

1994). The first is that a discourse develops that identifies the problematic aspects of organizations' performance. In the present case, "quality" was identified as the problem in the private sector. Nevertheless, although there is evidence that international competitors were demonstrating to the domestic private sector the effectiveness of focusing on quality, one would be hard pressed to prove that quality should have grabbed the limited attention of public managers.

Second, inherent in that discourse are elements of the solution, in this case, the heuristic "quality management," specified through a series of techniques such as TQM and "customer focus," and also as a general approach (Weiss, 1989). Although many of the innovative solutions that were developed in the private sector remain secreted from view, once some emerge and become available for adoption, public organizations have a "garbage can" of developing, if not mature, solutions to adopt (March & Olsen, 1986).

Isomorphic Tendencies

More important than temporal order are the various isomorphic processes that encourage adoption of private sector practices. The most powerful impetus of public sector isomorphism is the need for legitimacy. Born in revolution, the political culture and structure of U.S. government that ensures checks and balances sets a tone of general distrust and distaste for government. In comparison with the citizens of other advanced industrialized countries, Americans trust their government less and are less satisfied with its performance (Orren, 1997). Over the past 20 years, this innate skepticism has led to alarmingly low levels of confidence, dipping to 15% in 1995.[24]

The basic skepticism about government has been augmented by dissatisfaction with public services and resistance to the level of taxes required to support these services. In a recent survey, 42% of Americans could not cite one success of the federal government in the past 30 years.[25] Satisfaction with services is very low: Only 8% of Americans say that they are "very satisfied" with the quality of government ser-

vices.[26] Levels of satisfaction with public services show some variance across levels of government, however. The services of the federal sector tend to be less satisfactory to citizens than do the services of the state and municipal sectors. In a survey about the federal government shutdown in 1995, only 6% of Americans said that the federal government "basically performs well."[27] However, in a recent poll, even the higher-rated local government services received a mediocre grade. On a scale from 1 to 10, where 1 was "very poor service" and 10 was "very high quality service," the mean score was 5.3.[28]

Further dissatisfaction is evidenced in attitudes regarding taxes. Tax revolts began in 1978 with Proposition 13 in California, which cut local property taxes in half. Four years later, the Reagan administration successfully cut 25% of federal aid to states and municipalities (Osborne & Gaebler, 1992, pp. 16-17, 23, 29, 76). Resistance to tax increases has remained steady, independent of economic conditions, until the present time. Many observers see this as a powerful message about dissatisfaction with the public sector. Charting trends over the past 30 years in confidence in government and concerns about wasteful spending by the public sector, Craig (1996, p. 50) demonstrates the correlations between these opinions.

The political rhetoric of the past three decades about the performance of public organizations relative to their private sector counterparts created something of a crisis for public managers. Sensitive to the sentiments of the public, public managers began to act. In the survey of TQM adoption in the municipal sector, Berman and West found that public complaints about certain city services, such as trash pickup, were cited by 75% of respondents who were asked about important external forces that motivated the adoption of quality improvement techniques. "Voter demands," which is a politically based response, also played an important role, cited by 59% of respondents (Berman & West, 1995, p. 62). The National Performance Review cites public dissatisfaction with tax levels and services, particularly in comparison with the private sector, as a motivator behind its reforms (Gore, 1997; Kamensky, 1996).

Adoption of quality improvement techniques fits the legitimization needs of public organizations. The embrace of successful quality techniques developed in the private sector is rational given the ambiguous nature of many of the goals and technologies in the public sector. In the pursuit of ambiguous goals, organizations tend to incorporate techniques thought to be rational and that demonstrate conformity to institutional practices (Meyer & Rowan, 1977). Proactive attempts to develop unique strategies are least likely under these conditions (Wechsler, Berry, Park, & Tao, 1997, p. 11). Quality improvement techniques, particularly TQM, fit this description. Adoption signals that efforts are under way to improve the performance of public organizations. Additionally, the selection of this particular approach signals that public organizations are taking the lead from the private sector, where operations are assumed to be functioning well.

The Power of the Private Sector Model

The private sector has traditionally provided the benchmark for the expected performance of public organizations, based on the assumption that market mechanisms discipline the private sector and therefore lead to greater economy, efficiency, and productivity. The assumption that waste, fraud, and abuse are exclusively public sector phenomena is bolstered by the antitax sentiment in the political culture. Out of this school of thought emerges the Golden Fleece Awards and media stories about $2,000 toilet seats and $500 hammers. These strains have support among the American people, in that 77% believe that the government could be more effective if better managed.[29]

Americans do not differentiate between the private and public sectors. More than one half of Americans believe that "the objectives of government organizations (civilian and military) are not really different from private sector organizations."[30] In thinking about solutions for government performance, they believe that the logic of the marketplace and the lessons of the private sector can be applied directly. Nearly three fourths of Americans believe that the performance of public organizations could be improved by "bringing private sector values and

practices into government."[31] Nearly one half of Americans say that "the federal government is inefficient, and needs to undergo the same kind of dramatic restructuring and downsizing that is taking place in the private sector."[32] One third of Americans think that government services should be provided by the private sector.[33] The analysis of these sentiments results in efforts to improve government services by pursuing techniques to "make government business less unbusinesslike," primarily by focusing on private sector techniques to lower costs (Light, 1997, p. 18).

Vehicles to Transfer Quality Methods to the Public Sector

DiMaggio and Powell (1983) describe the process of organizational adaptation as evolutionary, resulting from the interactions between organizations that share the same environment or field. Under many conditions, organizations choose structures and processes that are experienced as rational means to pursue collective purposes. When quality practices became embedded in private sector organizations, public sector organizations that had procurement transactions or contact through professional or industrial associations were introduced to influential models to mimic.

The vehicle that conveyed techniques developed in the private sector to the federal sector was extremely efficient. The Federal Quality Institute created an approved list of vendors of training and technical assistance in order to ease and speed up procurement of these services.[34] Some of the approved vendors were spin-offs of quality initiatives in private sector firms. In all cases, the vendors were organizations whose primary clients were in the private sector and who were adapting their packages for public clients. As a result of their prior private sector experience, the vendors carried information and techniques into the public sector.[35] Within 1 year of the Executive Order to adopt TQM, 88.5% of Department of Defense managers were familiar with the concepts.

In the state and municipal sectors, support for resources to pursue quality practices was solicited from the business sector directly. Many jurisdictions relied on donations from the private sector of staff time for training and technical assistance. For example, the statewide quality program in Ohio began with the assistance of Xerox (Kaboolian, 1996). Louisville called on General Electric for help in designing the participatory "workout process" to improve city services (Husock, 1996).

Many public-spirited contributions came from Baldrige Award winners, such as Florida Power and Light, which were required to disseminate information about their experiences and offered many tours and courses to public managers. When financial resources were necessary for the adoption of quality methods, business leaders provided testimony on the effectiveness and legitimacy of the techniques to legislative overseers (Berman, 1994).

The Desire for Productivity and Efficiency

Efforts to adopt quality techniques from the private sector were also motivated by the desire to increase productivity and reduce costs in the public sector. In this way, adoption is in concert with the observation made of the private sector that "it is quite possible that the most important contributions of quality management might fall under the familiar heading that economists label 'cost reduction' rather than 'quality improvement' in the conventional sense" (Winter, 1994, p. 95). Evidence for this assertion abounds. Following on the heels of the Grace Commission, which exposed the inefficiencies of the federal Office of Management and Budget (OMB), staff members "realize[d] the close-productivity-quality nexus that was emerging in the private sector" and convened a meeting of successful private sector organizations that had implemented TQM. Recommendations from this meeting resulted in the 1988 Executive Order mandating TQM, which was titled "Productivity Improvement Program for the Federal Government" (Burstein & Sedlak). The President's Quality Award, the parallel award to the Baldrige, is awarded "for use of quality management principles and practices to deliver excellent service to customers and reinvent their systems and operations to 'do more with less'" (10th Annual National Conference, 1997).

The National Performance Review/Reinventing Government Initiative provides another case in point. The very title of the initial report, *Creating a Government That Works Better and Costs Less,* reflects the desire to link quality and cost reduction. The NPR not only promised to save $108 billion by streamlining and improving processes and contracting but also called for an immediate reduction in the size of the federal workforce by 272,900 employees. Not surprisingly, the "works better" half of the equation was quickly overshadowed in the eyes of the public by the "costs less" half (Kettl, 1995, p. 18). Americans were quick to pick up on the cost savings goal—55% reported that the NPR was a genuine reform effort to save money by eliminating waste.[36]

In the state and municipal sectors, economic concerns also played a role in the adoption of private sector quality techniques. Jolted by tax revolts, states and cities began to look for ways to do more with less. Berman and West (1995) report that the desire for increased employee productivity was cited most frequently, by 88% of municipal respondents, as a motivating force for adopting quality techniques; budget pressures were cited by 79%.[37] Similarly, state agencies cited budget pressures and increased employee productivity among the top reasons for adoption (Berman, 1994). In both jurisdictions, citizen concerns with the quality of public services were significantly less important for adoption of quality techniques.

Quality Methods Are Sensemaking Activities

Public sector managers are embracing the quality techniques implicit in the phrases "world class service" and "meeting and exceeding customer expectations." Their enthusiasm, in light of the slim evidence about applicability and effect on organizational performance, suggests that quality methods may be sensemaking activities with great appeal. Weick (1997) tells us, "In an unknowable, unpredictable world, becoming a true believer can feel like a state of grace." Take, for example, this letter from a federal manager to the *New York Times:*

In addition to "icon," "diversity" and "closure," which Russell Baker cites (column, April 29), another word that seems to be on everybody's lips these days, particularly those in the Clinton Administration, is "reinvention." Not an hour goes by in my day at a certain Federal agency that the word is not uttered in E-mail, voice mail or team discussions. Reinvention, in all its diversity, is the icon we have come to worship, and there are no signs that closure will be reached any time soon. (Moyer, 1997).

Efforts to improve quality are solutions to socially constructed problems: low productivity, citizen dissatisfaction with government, declining tax revenues to support operations, and the desire to see operations shifted to the private sector. By adopting quality improvement techniques, public managers appear to be acting on their concerns about legitimacy. The phrase "reinventing government," when applied to particular projects, provides an account of government's recognition of public dissatisfaction with its performance as well as an account that actions are being taken to improve that performance. For managers coping with the complex accountability problems presented by ambiguous goals, uncertain technologies, shifting coalitions, and so on, activities related to improving quality are an important way to demonstrate accountability.

The appeal of quality improvement techniques for managers operating in fragmented environments with ambiguous goals is clear. First, the techniques help define a standard of performance. The SSA committed itself in the FY1995 federal budget "to meet world class standards of excellence in teleservice." To this end, the SSA participated in a multiagency benchmarking effort to determine the optimal waiting time for callers to its toll-free number. In order to staff the telephones to meet this standard of service, within the constraints of the budget and the personnel cap, the SSA trained many nonteleservice representatives to serve as "spikes" to staff the phones during peak call-in hours. A Deputy Commissioner at the SSA said that she decided to retire when she realized that "at the rate we were going, I was going to be a backup spike on the 800 number."

Although the Deputy Commissioner was speaking facetiously, the question of whether world-class service is an appropriate or even desirable standard for a public agency has never been addressed. The SSA will never be funded at the levels necessary to provide the same level of service offered by a private sector company competing on service. A more appropriate and realistic standard was defined by the deputy mayor of New York City, who said, "We should be the Motel 6 of the service industry, a damn good Motel 6, but not the Plaza Hotel." However, it is difficult to sell "Motel 6" to political authorizers and to citizens who are increasingly conditioned to believe that their service demands should set the standard for all production processes.

Second, quality improvement techniques identify a target to satisfy. The "customer" concept helps public managers to imagine the users of their goods and services and to direct their efforts toward them. This concept has not been obvious to many public managers, even in agencies with large volumes of service encounters. For example, the first survey of customer service that the SSA designed was directed toward its frontline employees, querying them on customer needs, preferences, expectations, and desired standards of quality. When confronted with the possibility that the survey should be administered to actual clients, the managers were surprised. They had a long history of taking good care of the public's interest and did not quite know how this effort was different.

The concept of a customer may be helpful in identifying targets to satisfy even when the organization does not have customers. A manager of a scientific shop in a federal agency rejected the TQM package offered to his employees, saying that it would never work:

Speaking under no pressure to follow the TQM route, philosophically I can live with this terminology but many scientists can not. Don't say to scientists that they are engaged in production, scientists don't want to be treated that way and our system has a tendency to do that. . . . Scientists feel insulted that their intellectual creativity is equated with nuts and bolts. (Kaboolian & Barzelay, 1990, p. 19)

However, this scientist-manager found the customer concept compelling, not for the internal activities of his unit, but for the dissemination of useful knowledge created by the scientists in his lab. As a result, he organized a team of scientists to think about the users of basic research in order to design information systems that package the results of creative processes in useful and digestible ways.

A third way in which the concept of a customer can be useful is in bridging the gap between performance and feedback. In a world of ambiguous and conflicting signals about what to do and how to do it, customer encounters are learning opportunities for public organizations. Service encounters represent an action set over which the public organization can exercise some control. These encounters provide almost instant feedback about organizational performance. The tight linkage between performance and reaction is in direct contrast to the loose linkage between performance and rewards created by the external environment.

"Customer orientation" as a quality technique can help guide process improvements and enhance accountability only if the customers are identified correctly. For example, there is a danger in looking at service encounters in order to identify customers when service to clients is not important to overseers. Because this has happened often, there is a robust debate among public management scholars about the characteristics of customers. On the one hand, critics argue that "customers" have less sovereignty than "owners"; therefore, citizens should not exchange their proprietary rights and role as the principals for mere customer standing (Fredrickson, 1993). On the other hand, others claim the primacy of collective action and politics over market transactions implied in "customer": "It is simply not true that the important end of a public organization effort is to make their individual clients happy" (Moore, 1997, p. 3). Nevertheless, in a recent survey of senior managers at state and local levels of government, nearly three fourths reported that

their organization refers to citizens as "customers."[38]

What the Examination of the Quality Movement in the Public Sector Says to the Private Sector

The description and analysis of the adoption and use of quality improvement techniques in public sector organizations questions the value of the "public sector exceptionalism" argument for analyzing public organizations. Whether public organizations are simply examples of organizations in uncertain and complex environments or are unique because of their public sector status, they provide the basis for hypotheses, useful to the study of all organizations, about why quality methods are adopted and where they might be useful. The examination of conditions, external and internal, should be central to studies of the adoption and effectiveness of quality methods in all organizations. A similar exercise can be performed for the patterns of diffusion of quality methods.

A second lesson for the private sector also comes from the careful study of characteristics of the external and internal environments of public organizations. The public sector increasingly is becoming a wholesaler rather than a retailer of goods and services (DiIulio et al., 1993, p. 32). Contracting with for-profit and nonprofit organizations for peripheral goods has always occurred. Today, the public sector is contracting for "core services of government," such as prisons, fire protection, security services, and courts. Contractors and procurement officers are now on the steep part of the learning curve, attempting to define goals, methods, and accountability mechanisms. "Transaction cost" is now part of the vocabulary of public sector managers. Once the glow of innovation fades, the coalition that values privatization begins to fragment, clients start to press for responsiveness, and ability to do the work in-house disappears, authorizers will begin to demand the levels and types of accountability from private organizations that they now do from public organizations. Of course, private organizations can exit from the market. However, the extent to which they depend on public work will condition how readily or easily they can exit and causes us to wonder how they will cope with the conditions now experienced by public organizations.

Notes

1. This chapter relies on Cole's distinction between the old and new paradigms outlined in Cole (1996).

2. This chapter addresses only the quality movements within the public sector in the United States. Extremely interesting insights regarding the diffusion and utility of quality methods in the public sector are provided by comparisons with efforts in the United Kingdom, Australia, and New Zealand. See, for example, GAO (1995).

3. For an example of a government-sponsored professional conference, see the program of the 10th Annual National Conference on Federal Quality, July 9-11, 1997, available on the Internet. The American Society for Quality Control and the Association for Quality and Participation are among the nongovernmental organizations that also sponsor conferences on quality in the public sector.

4. Trade associations sponsoring award programs include the National League of Cities and the Council of State Governments. Since 1988, the federal government has sponsored the Quality Improvement Prototype Award, the President's Quality Award, and the George M. Low Trophy (awarded to NASA contractors for quality and productivity). In 1992, state governments organized the State Quality Award Network for state and community quality award administrators. Many states also sponsor their own award programs. For more on the specifics of these programs, see Hunt (1993), pp. 89-141.

5. See the web page for the Alliance for Reinventing Government (http://www.clearlake.ibm.Com/Alliance) and the web page for the Council for Excellence in Government (http://www.excelgov.org.)

6. Executive Order 12637, "Productivity Improvement Program for the Federal Government," ordering a quality improvement program in every federal executive agency, was signed in April 1988. The guidelines for the new order were outlined in OMB circular A-132 dated April 22, 1988. The federal TQM effort was the result.

7. For a more complete analysis of QStP, see Kaboolian (1996).

8. See Article 21, "Quality Services Through Partnership." Exhibit 4, "Collective Bargaining Agreement Between the State of Ohio and OCSEA," March 18, 1994.

9. In fact, somewhat before the NPR, *The Citizens' White Paper* was issued by John Major's administration in the United Kingdom.

10. Labor-management partnerships at the agency level were required by Executive Order 12871 dated October 1, 1993. In addition to establishment of a National Partnership Council to set policy for the implementation of the agency partnerships, the order also required an expansion of bargaining to all permissible topics not expressly reserved to Congress or the president. The establishment of customer service standards was required by Executive Order 12862 dated September 11, 1993. Agencies had 6 months before reports on their service levels were due to the president.

11. Rainey remarks that Herbert Simon, in *Administrative Behavior,* was one of the first organizational theorists to recognize the importance of the political context of public organizations, but Simon concludes that public and private organizations are more similar than different. Rainey also cites Thompson (1962).

12. On empirical research comparing private and public organizations in the same industries, see Savas (1987), Atkinson and Halvorsen (1989), and Chubb and Moe (1990).

13. Recent political and administrative reform movements are seeking to address the competitiveness issue in the public sector. Called the "New Public Management" and based on public choice theory, this reform sees the allocation of public resources as an explicit competition in marketlike environments. Infused with microeconomic models, such reforms are thrusting public organizations into competitive markets for their goods and services and evaluating the organizations on market criteria. These reforms are taking place in Australia, New Zealand, Brazil, the United Kingdom, and the United States. For more on these reforms, see Kettl (1997).

14. A notable exception to this observation is Radin and Coffee (1993). This article is discussed in more detail below.

15. For a discussion of the problems of drawing boundaries to create samples of public organizations, see Kaboolian (1997).

16. The foundation of this debate is outlined by Woodrow Wilson in "The Study of Administration" (Wilson, 1987). For more contemporary statements of the debate, see Lynn (1996) and Moore (1995).

17. The choice between "bowing" and "strategizing" represents one important cleavage in the philosophies about management in the public sector; see, for example, Behn (1998) and Terry (1997).

18. I am indebted to my colleague, Arnold Howitt, for pointing out the utility to my argument of A. O. Hirschman's (1970) distinction.

19. However, it is certainly the case that the industry created to deal with bankruptcies can be depicted as interested in organizational failure.

20. Performance ambiguity presents a particular irony for organizations caricatured for their bureaucratic tendencies. As stated by Ouchi (1980), "When tasks become

highly unique, completely integrated, or ambiguous for other reasons, then even bureaucratic mechanisms fail" (pp. 134-135).

21. See Hibbing and Theiss-Morse (1996). In this way, citizen opinions about government are structured in a fashion similar to perceptions about service encounters.

22. For systematic studies of the adoption of quality methods, see Berman and West (1995) and Berman (1994).

23. Reforms in the post-World War II period began with the Hoover Commission during the Truman administration. MBO, introduced during the Nixon administration in 1973, was in effect until 1975; ZBB, introduced in 1977 during the Carter administration, was in effect until 1985. For a more detailed history, see GAO (1997), DiIulio et al. (1993), and Kettl and DiIulio (1995).

24. Council for Excellence in Government survey, 1995.

25. Council for Excellence in Government survey, 1997.

26. American Society for Quality Control/Gallup survey, July 1988.

27. *Business Week* telephone survey, 1995. Roper Center at University of Connecticut Public Opinion Archive, Accession No. 0228903.

28. American Society for Quality Control survey, 1991.

29. Council for Excellence in Government poll, 1997. Interestingly, 19% believe the government is bound to be ineffective no matter what types of reforms are made.

30. Louis Harris survey, 1989.

31. Council for Excellence in Government survey, 1997.

32. *Business Week* telephone survey, 1995. Roper Center at University of Connecticut Public Opinion Archive, Accession No. 0228903.

33. American Society of Quality Control/Gallup survey, July 1988.

34. This discussion borrows from Kaboolian and Barzelay (1990).

35. For more on the influence of consulting firms on the adoption of quality methods in the public sector, see Chapter 5, "Managing Leviathan: The Public Sector," in Mickelthwaite and Woolridge (1996).

36. NBC News, *Wall Street Journal* poll, September 19, 1993.

37. Berman and West (1995, p. 62) report anecdotal evidence that quality techniques did help alleviate budgetary pressures in cities that adopted them. However, as Winter (1994) points out, without a sample of nonadopters, it is not possible to make the general assertion that this is a causal relationship; also see Stupak (1993).

38. It is my preference to recognize the usefulness of the concept while cautioning against its limitations. It would be ludicrous to encourage prison guards to treat inmates like customers. That action would not be an effective way of either meeting the goal of the organization or satisfying the external environment. However, redesigning public production processes so that more citizens opt to use public facilities rather than withdraw to private spaces seems like a useful strategy that can both improve performance and meet the legitimacy needs of the organization.

References

Allison, G., & Moe, T. (1988, September). *The politics of structural choices: Toward a theory of public bureaucracy.* Paper presented at the annual meeting of the American Political Science Association.

Atkinson, S. E., & Halvorsen, R. (1989). The relative efficiency of public and private firms in a regulated environment: The case of the U.S. electric utilities. *Journal of Public Economics, 29,* 281-294.

Ban, C. (1996). *How do public managers manage?* San Francisco: Jossey-Bass.

Behn, R. D. (1998). What right do public managers have to lead? *Public Administration Review,* pp. 209-224.

Berman, E. (1994). Implementing TQM in state governments: A survey of recent progress. *State and Local Government Review.*

Berman, E. M., & West, J. P. (1995). Municipal commitment to total quality management: A survey of recent progress. *Public Administration Review.*

Bozeman, B. (1987). *All organizations are public: Bridging the public and private organizational theories.* San Francisco: Jossey-Bass.

Burns, T., & Stalker, G. M. (1961). *The management of innovation.* London: Tavistock.

Burstein, C., & Sedlak, K. The federal quality improvement effort: Current status and future agenda. *National Productivity Review,* pp. 122-133.

Choi, T. Y., & Behling, O. C. (1997). Top managers and TQM success: One more look after all these years. *Executive, 11*(1), 37-47.

Chubb, J. E., & Moe, T. M. (1990). *Politics, markets and America's schools.* Washington, DC: Brookings Institution.

Cohen, S., & Brand, R. (1993). *Total quality management in government.* San Francisco: Jossey-Bass

Cole, R. E. (1996). *The new quality paradigm.* Unpublished manuscript.

Dean, J. W., Jr., & Bowen, D. E. (1994). Management theory and total quality: Improving research and practice through theory development. *Academy of Management Review, 19.*

DiIulio, J. J., Jr., Garvey, G., & Kettl, D. (1993). *Improving government performance: An owner's manual.* Washington, DC: Brookings Institution.

DiMaggio, P. J., & Powell, W. W. (1983). The iron cage revisited: Institutional isomorphism and collective rationality in organizational fields. *American Sociological Review, 48,* 147-160.

Edelman, M. (1971). *Politics as symbolic action.* Chicago: Markham.

Final Report of the Disability Determination Process Reengineering Project. (1994).

Fredrickson, H. G. (1993, August). *Total quality politics.* Speech to 1993 Conference of the National Association of State Budget Officers, Reno, NV.

GAO. (1990, November). *Quality management scoping study: For internal GAO use only.* Unpublished report.

GAO. (1992, October). *Quality management survey of federal organizations* (GAO/GGD-93-9BR). Washington, DC: Government Printing Office.

GAO. (1995, May 2). *Managing for results: Experiences abroad suggest insights for federal management reforms* (GAO/GGD-95-120). Washington, DC: Government Printing Office.

GAO. (1997). *Performance budgeting: Past initiatives offer insights for GPRA implementation* (GAO/AIMD-97-46). Washington, DC: Government Printing Office.

Gore, A. (1993). *Creating a government that works better and costs less: The Gore report on reinventing government.* New York: Times Books.

Gore, A. (1997). Businesslike government: Lessons learned from America's best companies. *National Performance Review.*

Hackman, J. R., & Wageman, R. (1995). Total quality management: Empirical, conceptual and practical issues. *Administrative Science Quarterly, 40,* 309-342.

Hargrove, E. C., & Glidewell, J. C. (Eds.). (1990). *Impossible jobs in public management.* Lawrence: University Press of Kansas.

Hibbing, J. R., & Theiss-Morse, E. (1996). Cited in S. C. Craig (Ed.), *Broken contract? Changing relationship between Americans and their government.* Boulder, CO: Westview.

Hirschman, A. O. (1970). *Exit, voice and loyalty: Responses to decline in firms, organizations and states.* Cambridge, MA: Harvard University Press.

Hunt, V. D. (1993). *Quality management for government.* Milwaukee, WI: ASQC Quality Press.

Husock, H. (1996). *Improving Louisville's "City-CALL" citizen complaint system: CityCALL meets CityWORK.* John F. Kennedy School Case Program, C124-96-1355.0.

Kaboolian, L. (1996). *Changing the labor-management paradigm.* John F. Kennedy School of Government Case Program, C01-96-1311.0.

Kaboolian, L. (1997). Sociology. In D. F. Kettl & B. Milward (Eds.), *The state of public management.* Baltimore, MD: Johns Hopkins University Press.

Kaboolian, L., & Barzelay, M. (1990, October). *Total quality management in the federal sector: Discourse, practices and movement.* Paper presented at the annual meeting of the Association for Public Policy Analysis and Management (APPAM), San Francisco.

Kamensky, J. M. (1996). Role of the "reinventing government" movement in federal management reform. *Public Administration Review.*

Kettl, D. F. (1995). Building lasting reform: Enduring questions, missing answers. In D. F. Kettl & J. J. DiIulio, Jr. (Eds.), *Inside the reinvention machine: Appraising governmental reform.* Washington, DC: Brookings Institution.

Kettl, D. F. (1997). The global revolution in public management: Driving themes, missing links. *Journal of Policy Analysis and Management, 18,* 446-462.

Kettl, D. F., & DiIulio, J. J., Jr. (Eds.). (1995). *Inside the reinvention machine: Appraising governmental reform.* Washington, DC: Brookings Institution.

Lawrence, P. R., & Lorsch, J. W. (1967). *Organization and environment: Managing differentiation and integration.* Boston, MA: Harvard Business School Press.

Levin, M. A. (1994). The day after the AIDS vaccine is discovered: Management matters. *Journal of Policy Analysis and Management, 12,* 442-445.

Light, P. C. (1997). *The tides of reform: Making government work, 1945-1995.* New Haven, CT: Yale University Press.

Lynn, L. E. (1996). *Public management as art, science and profession.* Chatham, NJ: Chatham House.

March, J. G., & Olsen, J. P. (1978). Organizational choice under ambiguity. In O. Grusky & G. A. Miller (Eds.), *The sociology of organizations: Basic studies.* New York: Free Press.

March, J. G., & Olsen, J. P. (1986). Garbage can models of decision making in organizations. In J. G. March, R. Weissinger, & Baylon (Eds.), *Ambiguity and command* (pp. 11-35). White Plains, NY: Pittman.

Meyer, J. W., & Rowan, B. (1977). Institutionalized organizations: Formal structure as myth and ceremony. *American Journal of Sociology, 83,* 340-363.

Mickelthwaite, J., & Woolridge, A. (1996). *The witch doctors: Making sense of the management gurus.* New York: Random House.

Milakovich, M. E. (1995). *Improving service quality: Achieving high performance in the public and private sectors.* Delray Beach, FL: St. Lucie.

Moore, M. H. (1995). *Creating public value: Strategic management in government.* Cambridge, MA: Harvard University Press.

Moore, M. H. (1997, January). *Politics and the new public management.* Unpublished memo.

Moore, M. H., Kaboolian, L., Howitt, A., & Augusto, G. (1995). *Public value and customer service* [Unpublished memo]. Cambridge, MA: Harvard University, John F. Kennedy School of Government.

Moyer, R. E. (1997, May 2). Reinventing blather. *Letters to the Editor.*

NAoSBO. (1995, March). *Workforce policies: State activity and innovations.* Washington, DC: Government Printing Office.

Oakland, J. S. (1989). *Total quality management.* New York: Nichols.

Orren, G. (1997). In J. Nye, D. King, & P. Zelikow, *Why Americans don't trust government.* Cambridge, MA: Harvard University Press.

Osborne, D., & Gaebler, T. (1992). *Reinventing government: How the entrepreneurial spirit is transforming the public sector.* Reading, MA: Addison-Wesley.

Ouchi, W. G. (1980). Markets, bureaucracies and clans. *Administrative Science Quarterly, 25,* 129-140.

Perrow, C. (1970). *Organizational analysis: A sociological view.* Monterey, CA: Brooks/Cole.

Radin, B. A., & Coffee, J. N. (1993). A critique of TQM: Problems of implementation in the public sector. *Public Administration Quarterly,* pp. 42-54.

Rainey, H. (1991). *Understanding and managing public organizations.* San Francisco: Jossey-Bass.

Repenning, N., & Sterman, J. (1997, May). *Getting quality the old-fashioned way.* Paper presented at the Workshop of Integrating Social Science Theory and Research in Quality Improvement, Berkeley, CA.

Savas, E. S. (1987). *Privatization: The key to better government.* Chatham, NJ: Chatham House.

Sensenbrenner, J. (1991, March-April). Quality comes to city hall. *Harvard Business Review,* .

Sitkin, S. B., Sutcliffe, K. M., & Schroeder, R. G. (1994). Distinguishing between control and learning in total quality management: A contingency perspective. *Academy of Management Review, 19,* 537-564.

Starling, G. (1998). *Managing the public sector.* Fort Worth, TX: Harcourt Brace.

Stupak, R. J. (1993). Driving forces for quality improvement in the 1990s. *Public Manager,* pp. 32-35.

Swiss, J. E. (1992). Adapting total quality management (TQM) to government. *Public Administration Review, 52.*

Terry, L. (1997, November). *Administrative leadership, neo-managerialism and the public management movement.* Paper presented at the Fourth National Conference on Public Management Research, Athens, GA.

10th Annual National Conference on Federal Quality [Brochure]. (1997).

Thompson, J. (1962). Common and uncommon elements in administration. *Social Welfare Forum,* pp. 181-201.

Thompson, J. (1976). *Organizations in action.* New York: McGraw-Hill.

U.S. Department of Labor. (1996). *Report of the Secretary's Task Force on Excellence in State and Local Government Through Labor-Management Cooperation.* Washington, DC: Government Printing Office.

Wechsler, B., Berry, F. S., Park, W. S., & Tao, J. (1997, October). *Determinants of strategic choice: Proactive, political, and defensive models.* Paper presented at the Fourth National Public Management Research Conference, Athens, GA.

Weick, K. (1997). *Total quality management: A sensemaking perspective.* Unpublished manuscript.

Weiss, J. A. (1989). The powers of problem definition: The case of government paperwork. *Policy Sciences, 22,* 97-121.

Wilson, J. Q. (1987). *Bureaucracy: What government agencies do and why they do it.* New York: Basic Books.

Wilson, W. (1987). The study of administration. In J. M. Shafritz & A. C. Hyde (Eds.), *Classics of public administration.* Chicago: Dorsey.

Winter, S. G. (1994). Organizing for continuous improvement: Evolutionary theory meets the quality revolution. In J. A. C. Baum & J. V. Singh (Eds.), *Evolutionary dynamics of organizations.* New York: Oxford University Press.

Chapter 7

Quality Improvement

A Sensemaking Perspective

KARL E. WEICK

ost discussions of quality improvement programs such as Total Quality Management (TQM) assume a realist ontology (e.g., key performance indicators tell us how the world is operating), a rationalist epistemology grounded in objectivity (e.g., decision making based on facts), and a change strategy based on transformation (e.g., TQM is a quantum change). Suppose that, in the interest of theory development and practice improvement around themes of quality, these assumptions were altered and TQM were recast using the ideas that social construction tells us how the world is operating, rationality is an account rather than a tool, subjectivity is the feedstock of practice, and incremental change is the basis of renewal, these ideas being held together loosely by an emerging theory of sensemaking. What would the result look like? The following analysis is one attempt to answer that question.

My intent is to suggest to students of sensemaking that TQM is a good place to work out the intricacies of a sensemaking perspective, and to practitioners of TQM that their efforts often flounder because they fail to see how employees, including themselves, make use of interpretive practices. Sensemaking is a key activity when people try to enact a world where quality matters. To get to that conclusion, I first do a quick, selective overview of themes in quality management, organizing, and sensemaking that lend themselves to interconnections. Then, I move more slowly through discussion of the environment in which quality interventions unfold; the problems that that environment creates for information processing, fact gathering, and decision making; and the ways in which implementation of continuous improvement both meets the imperatives of quality and makes for good sensemaking. I conclude with a brief discussion of implications for practice that are suggested by the analysis.

AUTHOR'S NOTE: I am grateful to Kathleen Sutcliffe and David Obstfeld for their willingness to help me understand the intricacies of TQM. They should not be held responsible for the fact that I am a slow learner.

155

Conceptual Background

The Language of Quality Improvement

I understand TQM, following Dean and Bowen (1994, p. 396), as a set of mutually reinforcing principles that involves customer focus, continuous improvement, and teamwork. Having said that, it also seems clear that the phrase TQM itself prejudges appropriate means to improve quality. Those prejudgments are consequential for sensemaking because they provide the frame that limits interpretations and actions.

For example, the word "total" in the phrase Total Quality Management has the advantage of suggesting that all units are involved and no one can escape, but the disadvantage of suggesting a clear endpoint. It tempts people to say, as Lee Iacocca did in 1979, "We need to get this quality thing behind us and move on to other things." "Total" transforms a dynamic world into something that is artificially static. Something that is "total" has a spatial quality (e.g., embraces an entire system) and seems more suited to describe an entity than an ongoing flow of events. "Total" encourages a mind-set of structures rather than processes, of dichotomies (total vs. partial) rather than gradations. "Total" seems like a recipe for demoralization because it is next to impossible. Quality is never total because improvements unravel, become outdated, are forgotten, are translated during diffusion, and are dropped in favor of institutionalized improvisation. "Total" as in total quality is no more realistic than is optimal as in optimal rationality, accurate as in accurate perception, or absolute as in absolute conformance. "Total" is the language of lawyers and engineers and planners, who gloss over the realities of plea bargains and shims and updates. "Total" is a boilerplate for the investment community, not a manifesto for the operations community. "Total" is a bold but bald bid for external legitimacy that is unable to control internal judgments of irrelevance (Brown, 1989, p. 141).

I know, this borders on "trash talk." It seems to fly in the face of a proven track record of quality improvements, Baldrige winners, the mantra of six sigma, and an increasing number of services and technologies that do what they are supposed to do, the first time, and for longer periods. Those are outcomes worth applauding. My point is that they did not get there because interventions in the name of quality were total. They got there in spite of connotations of total. I think those connotations are of some consequence because they appear to be tacit causal factors that are assumed to be part of a quality package. Thus, to construct a program of total quality is to strive for a finite, discrete, bounded program with a clear endpoint consisting of structural changes that will succeed only if they hold together for everyone, are controlling for everyone, and admit neither exceptions nor deviations. No one would float a program with those specifications. And yet every effort after Total Quality implies something akin to that. It is that very impossibility that undermines expectations, thwarts the search for meaningful work, and makes people less willing to make explicit those tacit understandings that could make the quality system work (Nonaka & Takeuchi, 1995).

My point is not simply that "total" fosters cynicism. It may have that effect. My point is that it makes it harder to make sense of what is happening because so few observations fit it. "Total" tends to wipe out any explanations that take into account the transient or the momentary (e.g., this is a moment in a process rather than a fixed quality of organizational life). The bottom line of this linguistic harangue is the straightforward prediction that those who take seriously the word "total" in the phrase "total quality" are less likely to meet the Baldrige criteria than are those who ignore this description of their efforts. Those who strive for total quality are less likely to achieve it than are those who strive for ongoing, developmental, or progressive quality.

Some of the same problems are created by the word "management" in TQM. Again, my concern is that the word prejudges the issue by suggesting that TQM is managed (the phrase is not total quality "leadership," although this is what Xerox called its program); top down; controlled; controlling; and controllable; and not something that is executed or enacted or performed or achieved, but simply managed. The contrast between leadership and management has been a mainstay of the theory literature ever since Zaleznik (1990) pried the two terms apart and demonstrated that they were not synonymous. The contrast between managers and leaders is not trivial, because quality talks the talk of management yet relies on efforts that walk the talk of leadership. Talk of "vision," "transformation," "integrity," and "being an example" is leader talk, not manager talk.

To see the problems that "management" creates, consider just four contrasts between leaders and managers that Zaleznik (1990) mentions:

1. Managers assume that solid methods, organizational devices, and techniques of control will overcome human frailties and produce good results (p. 22). This confidence in form represents misplaced concreteness and diverts attention from substance, which is the focus of leaders.

2. Manager goals are passive, deeply entrenched in the structure of the organization, built from surveys of constituent needs, and framed to avoid both confrontation and the rise of strong feelings of support or opposition. Managers strive to make decisions that fall inside the "zone of indifference" (p. 24). Leaders, by contrast, adopt goals that actively shape ideas and tastes, innovate, and take risks.

3. Managers communicate in indirect, ambiguous signals because they fear that aggression will lead to chaos, whereas leaders communicate in clearly stated ideas, create a climate of ferment that intensifies individual motivation, and tend to direct their aggression toward ideas rather than people (pp. 24-25).

4. Managers relate to people according to the role the people play in a sequence of events or in a process [whereas] leaders, who are concerned with ideas, relate in more intuitive and empathetic ways. . . . Managers pay attention to how things get done, and leaders pay attention to what things mean to people. (pp. 27-28)

My point in sampling the contrast between leaders and managers is to show that the word "management" is not a neutral descriptor. To manage is to believe in "progress through the perfection of structures in order to control be-

havior" (Zaleznik, 1990, p. 39). It is that very focus on "control" that is the central point in Sitkin, Sutcliffe, and Schroeder's (1994) important argument that quality programs pay too little attention to organizing for learning. Another way to make the same point is that these programs pay too little attention to organizing for leadership or organizing for resilience (Wildavsky, 1991). Again, that bias in organizing cannot be attributed solely to the use of one word in a three-word label. However, that word "management" carries a great deal of consistent meaning and precludes a considerable range of organizational designs.

Finally, the word "quality" may shape interventions in unintended directions. Like the concept of effectiveness, the concept of quality means many things to many people, so its pursuit can raise uncertainty rather than reduce it. Quality has the unfortunate connotation that it applies to things more easily than to people, a limitation noted by Waterman (1995):

> Curiously, the word "quality" almost gets in the way [of total customer satisfaction]. It implies relevance only to widgets and manufacturing, and it has the potential to divert our attention from the real essence of total quality—serving the customer. (p. 243)

In a related observation, Waterman questions the value of a quality system because it implies that the relevant data are internal. Waterman quotes Rick Chandler of Motorola, who laments that "people have all sorts of charts and graphs 'proving' that they are meeting targets. But the data are internal. You've got to get out and find out what the customer wants" (p. 245). Reflecting on this, Waterman concludes that the job is not to please the boss—that is internal—but to please the customer.

Quality, understood as some process running the way it should, is also boring. Surprises and crises, on the other hand, are exciting. Although appeals to quality may tap positive feelings of pride, excellence, and distinctive merit, they also may foreshadow stifling sameness, contested measures, continued avoidance of the customer, and temptations to treat the organization as a closed system.

The label TQM is, in the final analysis, just that—a label. Considering that alone, the concerns expressed here may seem much ado about nothing. However, if one grants that words are all we have, that words gain their meaning from their connections with other words rather than with external objects (a correspondence theory of truth is untestable and therefore of little help), and that people learn what they think by seeing what they say, and learn what they want by seeing what they do, then it makes sense to linger over words, their connotations, and their surplus meanings that are taken for granted.

People use labels to organize and make sense retrospectively of what they have been doing. They use labels to consolidate some kind of identity. They use labels to demonstrate accountability and acceptable practice to others. To portray quality as a problem to be managed can, if taken seriously, set in motion the very forces that preclude its realization. Small wonder that the implementation of quality programs is the major issue in TQM practice (Kolesar, 1995). Implementation is not finished until it is "total" and is "managed," as if momentary episodes of chaos are tantamount to disaster rather than testimonials to the limits of anticipation in an unknowable and unpredictable world.

Remember, the point of this chapter is to introduce the idea of sensemaking and, in doing so, to display how it works, how it is deployed, and what it highlights. Sensemaking boils down to connections among words. And meaning, minimally, boils down to two elements and a relation (Weick, 1995, p. 110). Thus, customer dissatisfaction taken as one element and managers taken as a second element are meaningless until we connect them and discover that customer dissatisfaction haunts, offends, delights, escapes, and challenges managers. The range of acceptable elements and relations is culturally and institutionally limited, which means, when we hear a phrase like "Total Quality Management" and cringe at the controlling premises it contains, that we are not free to discard it capriciously and expect to retain an audience, credibility, or legitimacy.

If we are concerned with failures in implementation of quality programs, then one place to start is with the words that people impose on their actions, what those words conceal and highlight, and what happens when people take those words seriously as explanations for what they have done and as guides for what they are doing. The issue here is not one of words versus actions. Behaviors do not become actions until they are given a name, an account, or a justification. Once that happens, the tidy world of separable acts of walking and talking blur into one another. There is no walk until talk gets attached to it, and vice versa. And if people make sense of elapsed actions, then it is harder to walk the talk than it is to talk the walking that has occurred. Furthermore, if comfortable, taken-for-granted, automatic routines need to be redone in order for quality to improve, then people need linguistic latitude and latitude in performance to learn new ways of acting.

Taken literally and prescriptively, TQM forecloses more options than people may realize; it conduces toward a more stylized and narrower range of changes than may be intended; and it explains what is happening and prescribes what to do next with less stirring, less grounded rhetoric than is necessary. Correctives lie in the direction of attention to connotations, and a deliberate choice of labels that captures features of organizational design that will support rather than undermine the intent of the change (e.g., the label "management" is less imaginative than a quality change program needs for success). Correctives also involve an anticipation of what the likely consequences may be when people use specific labels to explain to themselves and others what they have been doing and will continue to do, and a plea for rich words that energize and rich connections that deepen meaning (Havel, 1992; Morrison, 1995).

The Organizing of Quality Improvement

The preceding effort to unpack the phrase "total quality management" was guided in part by the ideas that organizations are to be understood in terms of organizing, and action is to be understood in terms of sensemaking.

The two ideas are combined in this description: Organizing is "a continuous process of enactment in which notions of goals, purposes, or functions are used by actors as rhetoric to enhance their relative position or identity or to make their definition of the situation more compelling" (Brown, 1989, p. 139). This description suggests that to understand what makes for more or less success in efforts to infuse quality into an organization, the observer pays close attention to the ongoing streaming of events ("a continuous process"), actions that leave traces ("enactment"), words uttered in the service of negotiating and advancing one's interests ("enhance relative position or identity"), conversations and recurrent interaction sequences ("notions are used as rhetoric"), and social influences as the outcome of the organizing ("compelling definition of the situation"). The connotations of TQM that we worried about earlier were cause for worry because of their presumed effects on ongoing flows, actions, interactions, and the sense that would prevail temporarily.

To implement a quality program, events must be endowed with meaning.

> When uttering words, people endow what they do (including using language) with meaning: they *account* for what they have done (justification), for what they are doing (monitoring), for what they will do (planning). Thus, actions are constructed in conversation taking place between people, which gives meaning to physical movements and all kinds of events. (Czarniawska, 1997, pp. 41-42)

The word "account" is interesting because of its affinity to accounting, accountability, and accountable, all of which are concerned with giving good reasons (i.e., acceptable, legitimate reasons) for actions taken.

From the standpoint of sensemaking, what is crucial about reasons and rationality is that, in actual practice, they are "employed by social actors retrospectively as a rhetoric to account for actions that, from a rationalistic point of view, were chaotic and stumbling when performed" (Brown, 1989, p. 129). What is crucial in this view is the idea that rationality does not

instruct people in what action they should take. It is less a guide than an achievement. What constitutes a rational reason for actions that have taken place or are being enacted grows out of interaction and is applied retrospectively. Whatever value "quality" has as rhetoric may lie as much in its capacity to justify nonconventional, nonrational, chaotic, stumbling actions as in its capacity to produce efficiency. By contrast, think of labels such as "prudent actions," "circumspect actions," or "actions of foresight." The variety of actions admissible under those latter labels should be narrower, more homogeneous, and less capable of novel solutions. Conceivably, the phrase "quality improvement" could have staying power because, when it is used as a retrospective explanation, it fits a surprisingly broad range of adventuresome actions. And these broader ranging actions promote more learning more rapidly.

If rationality is seen as an account as well as a guide, there are other implications for quality improvement. The actions that actually improve quality may be much more disorderly and chaotic than they appear to be when rational rhetoric is imposed on them retrospectively. If the rational account rather than the disorderly practice is used as a prescription, then people will try to do orderly things that will not work and will avoid the more disorderly acts that actually work. If that is possible, then it also has implications for benchmarking. When teams visit other sites, they may be primed to look for well-rationalized practices and to ignore those practices that are less well rationalized. They will pay close attention to acts that look like they are the results of deliberation and ignore the acts that look like they are the result of improvisation. Their attention may be focused on precisely the wrong events.

However, if people understand that the rhetoric of rationality functions independently of the usefulness of actions, and that rational rhetoric is tied to concerns about legitimacy rather than concerns of efficacy, then they may be more inclined to experiment widely, take more risks, trust intuitions, and rely on tacit understanding, all of which may help people solve tougher quality problems more quickly because they are able to be more imaginative.

Sensemaking and Analysis

The specific Baldrige category where sensemaking most obviously comes into play is "information and analysis." This is the category concerned with the "scope, management, and use of data and information to maintain a customer focus, to drive quality excellence, and to improve . . . performance" (quoted in Dean & Bowen, 1994, p. 406). The Baldrige presumptions are that organizations that collect and analyze information will be more successful than those that do not and that decision making based on fact is better than decision making based on intuition. Both presumptions contain a grain of truth, but both also work because of other processes operating that have not yet been incorporated into Baldrige criteria. It is this tacit remainder, some of which is assembled under the label of sensemaking, that is crucial to success.

When people talk about "information and analysis," decision making based on facts, and key performance indicators, this is realist talk that encourages efforts to discover what is really happening (e.g., search for "the" root cause). However, information and analysis involve more than discovery. They involve issues of invention, communication, preformed worldviews, self-fulfilling prophecies, intuitions, consensual validation, construction, confusion, ignorance, and plausibility. Each of these affects what analysis means, what is declared a fact, and the stories about performance that are treated as prototypes. When they are imposed on the ongoing flow of events, they increase the number of patterns now seen as possible. TQM unfolds in a much richer field of possibilities when people have a mind-set that favors invention rather than discovery.

Practitioners trim away richness when they focus on decision making rather than sensemaking. When people at Motorola say "Our quality stinks" (Waterman, 1995, chap. 11), or when people at the Southern Pacific Railroad say "Our service is absolutely terrible" (Frailey, 1993, p. 62), these are statements of fact, but they are also an admission of ignorance. Quality may be terrible, but people do not know what they do not know. They do not know how it got that way, why it stays that way,

but more important, they are not sure what "it" is. "It" is up for grabs. The only thing we can say for sure about "it" is that its meaning will be invented rather than discovered.

The sensemaking context within which quality improvement is often initiated can be framed in terms of Goffman's (1974, p. 30) memorable image: We can tolerate the unexplained, but not the inexplicable. People turn to quality improvement in inexplicable hard times. A world that has taken on crisis proportions, sometimes with survival at stake (e.g., Southern Pacific Railroad in the early 1990s), is a confusing, unpredictable world that can be made sensible, momentarily, if its fractures are attributed to lousy quality. But saying so does not make it so. Quality may stink, but management may smell even worse, and it all may be just a run of rotten luck.

Quality is not a cool diagnosis that is right or wrong. Instead, it is a definition of the source of current trouble floated by people with enough power to make their definition of the situation salient, if not compelling. The fate of that definition, who buys it, who refuses it, and with what other definitions it has to contend are realities of quality improvement underlying information processing and analysis. The influence of sensemaking on the quality improvement process is hard to see because we have not had the language or concepts to spot it—or the nerve to enter a "hard" domain of engineering, technology, and economics—and argue that subjectivity and interpretations and stories and labels and words are just as influential as striving for zero defects.

To summarize the perspective we intend to carry forward, a concern with sensemaking assumes that

People are thrown into an unknowable, unpredictable world in which

They engage in an ongoing quest rather than a series of discoveries

Which they try to make sensible

So that they have a momentary direction

Which enables them to keep going.

This portrait is presumed to be as true for people at the top of the organizational hierarchy as it is for people at the bottom. It is out of this confused context that efforts to improve quality emerge. These efforts take their form from this scenario, and they unfold and are resolved within it. Total quality is a potent, legitimate frame that is a plausible means to impose order on confusion. Whether it is an accurate diagnosis of confusion is unknowable. I turn now to a more detailed unpacking of some of these assertions.

Early Stages in Sensemaking

Early moves in a TQM initiative often consist of taking the boundary between an organization and an environment, blurring it, and then treating entities formerly regarded as outsiders (e.g., suppliers, external customers, internal customers) as insiders who are now part of the organizational process (Spencer, 1994, p. 447). What sensemaking questions is the nature of the preexisting partitions and boundaries implied in these moves. That question is not trivial because the source of those boundaries and entities affects whether and how they can be changed.

Consider Southern Pacific Railroad (SP) in the early 1990s. Carman (1995) argued that at the time SP started its quality program, it was losing money; had no new sources of funds to tap; and was faced with hostile customers, marginal physical facilities, weak processes, nonintegrated railroads, and recalcitrant unions (p. 159). That translated into problems like this:

> Systemwide train delays attributable to waiting for locomotives began to approach 700 hours a day. Seven hundred hours, by the way, is the same as saying that 30 trains were set back a full 24 hours. . . . [The chief of marketing wrote to the Operating Dept. and said] we're losing business in the tens of millions of dollars at this point. Our service is absolutely terrible. The morning report of March 11 shows 28 trains holding, some since the 8th, setbacks [trains delayed after being made ready to depart] of 485 hours, and as I understand it, we are approaching 200 locomotives short. (Frailey, 1993, pp. 61-62)

What these people are talking about is "thrownness," unpredictability, and enactment.

Imagine that you are dropped into this ongoing flow of events at SP. This is what it would feel like:

1. You cannot avoid acting. Your actions affect the situation and yourself, often against your will.
2. You cannot step back and reflect on your actions. You are thrown on your intuitions and have to deal with whatever comes up as it comes up.
3. The effects of action cannot be predicted. The dynamic nature of social conduct precludes accurate prediction.
4. You do not have a stable representation of the situation. Patterns may be evident after the fact, but at the time the flow unfolds, there is nothing but arbitrary fragments capable of being organized into a host of different patterns or possibly no pattern whatsoever.
5. Every representation is an interpretation. There is no way to settle that any interpretation is right or wrong, which means that an "objective analysis" of that into which one was thrown is impossible.
6. Language is action. Whenever people say something, they create rather than describe a situation, which means that it is impossible to stay detached from whatever emerges unless you say nothing, which is such a strange way to react that the situation is deflected anyway. (Heidegger, paraphrased in Winograd and Flores, 1986, pp. 34-36)

The flow into which you have been thrown is not any more a "quality" problem than it is a problem of leadership, gender, or shamans. Nor is it even clear that "problem" is a useful way to label the flow. Thrownness also makes it hard to learn. Not only is there ongoing change, but there are also inherited labels, simplifications, misattributions, delayed effects of actions, and unanticipated consequences, all of which encourage superstitious learning (noncontingent events are seen as dependent on one another). Small wonder, in a condition of thrownness, that one seeks control; embraces programs that promise it; and adopts a mechanistic, functional mind-set to implement and justify the adoption of those programs. But "remedy" through control is illusory for a very simple reason.

Quantum theory and chaos theory suggest that the experience of thrownness should not surprise us. The world is less like a machine and more like patterns of relationships. These patterns are unknowable, because to measure something is to change it, as well as unpredictable, because very small differences in initial conditions can lead quickly to very large differences in the future state of a system (McDaniel, 1997). In an unknowable, unpredictable world, sensemaking is all we have. In a personal communication to me, McDaniel (May, 1996) put the point this way:

Because the nature of the world is unknowable (chaos theory and quantum theory) we are left with only sensemaking. Even if we had the capacity to do more, doing more would not help. Quantum theory helps us to understand that the present state of the world is, at best, a probability distribution. As we learn from chaos theory, the next state of the world is unknowable. And so we must pay attention to the world as it unfolds. Therefore, it is a good thing that we can't do more than sensemaking . . . because then we would only be frustrated by our inability to know. But believing enables actions which leads to more sense (sometimes) and taking action leads to more sense (sometimes) and sensemaking connects actions to beliefs (sometimes).

It is the combination of thrownness, unknowability, and unpredictability that makes having some direction, any direction, the central issue for human beings. Sensemaking is about navigating by means of a compass rather than a map. "Maps, by definition, can help only in known worlds—worlds that have been charted before. Compasses are helpful when you are not sure where you are and can get only a general sense of direction" (Hurst, 1995, p. 168). Hurst goes on to argue that maps are the mainstay of performance, whereas the compass and the compass needle composed of values are the mainstay of learning and renewal.

What possible bearing could this have on TQM? It speaks to what holds a TQM initiative together. Consider Alcoa's efforts to write a mission statement that captured what quality management meant to it:

The work began in May and the final articulation of the "first draft" was not arrived at until September. With communication to other senior level managers and reaction to their feedback, the final product was not ready for roll-out until January 1989. During those months, there was hardly a time when the Alcoa mission statement was not being actively worked on by the Operating Committee. "Forged" is the operative expression, for every single word and phrase was hammered out with great care. When they were finished, this group of the nine most senior Alcoa managers would have a document that each had a tremendous investment in, one that they expected would be the *compass* [emphasis added] to guide Alcoa into the future. (Kolesar, 1995, p. 199)

Values provide a direction. When people begin to move in that direction, they selectively notice, selectively ignore, and selectively impose constraints and opportunities that are the small structures that shape their further selections. That is all people have, but it is enough. What is noteworthy is how rudimentary the structuring is. It begins with some kernel that is elaborated into a cosmos. To produce that kernel, almost any old map, compass, value, or recipe will do. And that is part of what stands out in TQM when viewed as sensemaking. Quality is a kernel that easily expands into a cosmos.

Prescriptions for TQM are permeated with deep agonizing over Vision and Values, deep agonizing over the best problem-solving sequence to use (e.g., plan-do-check-act), and deep agonizing over the way to implement a quality program. That deep agonizing is useful because it encourages interaction and gives people something in common to talk about. But the specific vision, value, or problem-solving sequence that is the source of the agony is less crucial than the degree to which it provides a direction that animates people to begin enacting some order into the world. Kolesar (1995) says as much when he describes the framework for diagnosis that was used by consultants at Alcoa. Although they used a framework developed by Nadler-Tushman,

during the seminar we made the point that alternative diagnostic frameworks existed and that it was more important that one be used rather than which one. Our main purpose was to methodically expose all the elements of the enterprise that affected quality and that conversely would be affected by a move toward total quality management. (p. 212, n. 9)

The point about this Nadler-Tushman framework—or any framework—is that, as people use it to see what they are now saying, doing, and constructing, they begin to learn new preferences, intentions, goals, and identities, which eventuate in what looks like, in the Alcoa case, a conversion to quality as the one best way to go. In an unknowable, unpredictable world, becoming a true believer can feel like an orderly state of grace. It is also a transient state.

The point is, given the environment into which people are thrown at the time they appear to reach for quality improvement, *any* framework that they adopt will improve performance if it does three things:

1. Gets people into action
2. Gives people a direction (through values or whatever)
3. Supplies legitimate explanations that are energizing and enable actions to be repeated

These three are not as simple as they look. I have asserted that words matter because they are all we have. I have also asserted that, at times, any old words will do. Is this a contradiction? Not if we remember that any old words will do to animate behavior, but precise, emotionally charged words convert behavior into action when they infuse action with meaning. Sensemaking is about meaningful action. Words supply directions, accounts, and legitimacy, often in images provided by predecessors, powerful labelers, and by institutions. Quality is a story that holds events together in a plausible manner and allows self-fulfilling prophecies to be mobilized in ways that enact structure. What keeps this from being solipsistic is that others are doing the same thing, at the same time, around conflicting interests, often with more resources.

So, how does this set of ideas get a trainload of Monsanto tank cars filled with chemicals out of Southern Pacific's Houston classification yard and on its way to East St. Louis on time rather than 72 hours late? It does so by provid-

ing a compact explanation, portions of which can be converted into guides for action. To see this, look more closely at what SP did. They leased extra locomotives, an action that makes a priority visible, namely, to get the trains moving. The action begins to change the set of relationships that comprise the railroad. Three pairs of coordinated trains going north and south were put on a fixed schedule. The symbols for these six trains

"all end with the letter 'Q,' meaning Quality. These trains aren't notable for speed. By and large their elapsed times of 32 to 36 hours between East St. Louis and Houston are comparable to previous times over the 825-mile route. Interestingly, these six new trains became for a while the most reliable on the railroad. This is all about getting discipline back into the local operation, to get the trains out on time," says Bailey [Adriene Bailey, VP-Service Planning and Design]. "Schedules had shrunk in this corridor because of pressure from the terminals for more time to make up the trains. In response we squeezed the over-the-road time. Now we are being realistic." (Frailey, 1993, p. 60)

This is a typical moment in quality improvement. What is slightly different is the explanation of why it works. It works because it accepts thrownness, unknowability, and unpredictability. By creating six reliable trains, other trains can now be made up on a more regular basis, and needs for locomotive power can be anticipated. Visionary rhetoric may develop to explain these changes in operations, but what is crucial is that order is being enacted and labeled with language that is a basis on which a new common understanding can develop ("we are moving toward a scheduled railroad"). People act their way into more order and reliability (they focus on getting just six trains on schedule). They drape their actions with the rhetoric of rationality (we are "getting discipline back," we are "being realistic"). They adopt legitimizing rhetoric (these are the "Quality" trains). And they affirm agency by a tangible change, visible to employees and customers. The core idea here is that people act their way into meaning. The peripheral idea here is that an appeal to quality is one source of meaning that fits those actions. In the SP example, quality acts like a compass that provides a compelling direction and evokes action. Action makes both the producer and customer feel efficacious—the producer through creating a reliable schedule and the customers through having their need for a reliable shipping schedule noticed and met.

What this brief glimpse of sensemaking suggests for practitioners is that attempts at quality improvement may fail when directives restrict actions; when only large changes are permissible; when tired rhetoric for what is happening leaves people uninterested in making it happen again; when prescriptions stifle self-organizing; when people are forced to act like the world is more predictable than their limited powers of control and enactment can impose; when people are expected to know their customers and themselves beyond what is knowable; and when directions are overspecified, thereby discouraging adaptive action.

Sensemaking, Diagnosis, and Decision Making

Earlier, I mentioned that the Baldrige category closest to sensemaking is "information and analysis." I want to focus on two assumptions in that Baldrige category that may be counterproductive. First, I want to argue that diagnosis is often an outcome rather than an input. Second, I want to argue that decision making is not a one-off action, which means that it is often impossible to base decision making on facts. Both of these points may explain why practitioners who engage in extensive analysis fail to improve performance (Dean & Bowen, 1994).

Diagnosis as Misplaced Sensemaking

From the perspective of sensemaking, analysis is inseparable from performance, which means that the search for links between analysis and performance can be misleading. Performance may be necessary to discover the occasion for the performance (Follett, 1924, p. 60), implementation may uncover an intention (Weick, 1987), reaching a verdict during jury deliberations may define which evidence is rel-

evant (Brown, 1989; Garfinkel, 1967), fighting against the enemy may be necessary to learn the nature of the enemy (Isenberg, 1985), and it may be necessary to treat symptoms and notice their response in order to make a diagnosis (Starbuck, 1993). Sensitivity to reversals is not missing from TQM discussions. Many TQM programs are launched with a celebration of pilot projects initiated in outlying plants by people who were thought to be incapable of experimentation and craft. The problem is, after the celebration, people at headquarters lose sight of the fact that from then on it is pilot projects all the way down. It is all pilot projects simply because situations differ, routines vary, and people are fallible. Heavy use of cross-trained teams to customize quality interventions represents partial sensitivity to this point. I use the word "partial" because as quality programs gain momentum, there appears to be a subtle shift from the heavy reliance on exploration true of the initial projects, to more reliance on exploitation of lessons learned by other teams. This shift makes it easier for people to overlook anomalies in their own situation; put too much faith in the experience base; and overlook weak, mixed signals of trouble that are being accepted as routine. This is precisely the kind of normalization that led up to the *Challenger* disaster (Vaughan, 1996).

Diagnosis is a key part of TQM. In the early stages of his intervention at Alcoa, Kolesar (1995) stressed, at his first meeting with the Quality task force, that "diagnosis must precede and shape the specific actions and design to fit this company in this industry at this time. What are the specific organizational and performance problems at Alcoa for which this total quality is an alleged solution?" (p. 179). Although that prescription seems straightforward from the perspective of practice, it seems misleading from the perspective of sensemaking. The problem can be seen if we look more closely at the activity of diagnosis in medical settings. Starbuck (1993) suggests that good doctors do not base their treatments on diagnosis. They leave diagnosis out of the chain between symptoms and treatment because it discards too much information and injects random errors. There are many more combinations of symptoms than there are diagnoses, just as there are many more treatments than diagnoses.

The links between symptoms and treatments are not the most important keys to finding effective treatments. Good doctors pay careful attention to how patients respond to treatments. If a patient gets better, current treatments are heading in the right direction. But, current treatments often do not work, or they produce side-effects that require correction. The model of symptoms-diagnoses-treatments ignores the feedback loop from treatments to symptoms, whereas this feedback loop is the most important factor. (p. 87)

The same logic can be applied to academic research.

Academic research is trying to follow a model like that taught in medical schools. Scientists are translating data into theories, and promising to develop prescriptions from the theories. Data are like symptoms, theories like diagnoses, and prescriptions like treatments. Are not organizations as dynamic as human bodies and similarly complex? Theories do not capture all the information in data, and they do not determine prescriptions uniquely. Perhaps scientists could establish stronger links between data and prescriptions if they did not introduce theories between them. Indeed, should not data be results of prescriptions? Should not theories come from observing relations between prescriptions and subsequent data? (p. 87)

Starbuck reminds us that, when faced with incomprehensible events, there is often no substitute for acting your way into an eventual understanding of them. How can I know what I am treating until I see how it responds? To organize for diagnosis is to design a setting that generates rich records of symptoms, a plausible initial line of treatment, alertness to effects of treatments, and the capability to improvise from then on. Theories, diagnoses, strategies, and plans serve mostly as plausible interim stories that mix ignorance and knowledge in different proportions.

Isenberg (1985, pp. 178-179), following the work of Bursztjahn, Feinbloom, Hamm, and Brodsky (1981), has also discussed what he calls treating a patient empirically. Like Starbuck, he notes that a diagnosis, if it is arrived at at all, occurs retrospectively after the patient is cured. Isenberg then generalizes this

medical scenario to battlefield situations. This application fleshes out a much earlier statement by Janowitz (1959) that a combat soldier is not a rule-following bureaucrat who is

detached, routinized, self-contained; rather his role is one of constant improvisation. . . . The impact of battle destroys men, equipment, and organization, which need constantly and continually to be brought back into some form of unity through on-the-spot improvisation. (p. 481)

For Isenberg, the parallel between empirical medicine and empirical fighting is that in both cases,

tactical maneuvers (treatment) will be undertaken with the primary purpose of learning more about (diagnosing) the enemy's position, weaponry, and strength, as well as one's own strength, mobility, and understanding of the battlefield situation. . . . Sometimes the officer will need to implement his or her solution with little or no problem definition and problem solving. Only after taking action and seeing the results will the officer be able to better define the problem that he or she may have already solved! (pp. 178-179)

The idea that diagnosis is as much an outcome of problem solving as it is an input carries several implications for TQM. TQM interventions presume that people start with a defined problem, not that they will take action so that when all is said and done, they will finally know what their problem was. This presumption of starting with a defined problem forecloses the option of acting in order to discover what may have been the trouble. Recall that most of the problem-solving training that accompanies TQM starts with diagnosis (plan-do-check-act). What we need to remember is that diagnosis and theories discard information, which, in early stages of inquiry, may mean that potential remedies are ruled out before the process even starts. Those teams that focus on how symptoms respond to treatments and that create tight feedback loops to determine this should be more successful at process improvement than those teams that focus on diagnosis.

Although it is true that it is probably impossible to avoid some kind of immediate diagnosis or theorizing, it is possible to accelerate the speed with which one begins treatment and to start with multiple diagnoses in the interest of reducing data loss. Furthermore, teams that organize to generate a rich record of symptoms, a plausible initial treatment, alertness to effects of treatments, and the capability to improvise from there on should be more successful than those teams that do not. As we will see shortly, some of these problems of diagnosis are mitigated by a commitment to continuous improvement. Before we discuss that possibility, we first examine an issue closely related to the analysis-performance link, namely, decision making based on facts.

Decision Making as Abbreviated Sensemaking

As Dean and Bowen (1994) argue, "Decision making based on fact is the mantra for [the] aspect of the TQ philosophy, which emphasizes the collection and analysis of information about customer needs, operational problems, and the success of improvement attempts" (p. 406). What is troublesome about this mantra from the standpoint of sensemaking is the presumption that a decision is a discrete event. The literature on commitment, cognitive dissonance, and ethnomethodology (summarized in Weick, 1995, pp. 10-15) makes it clear that the postdecision period defines what the decision meant and the extent to which it even functions as a decision. It is during the postdecision period that the meaning of the decision crystallizes, often in the form of a mixture of regret, justification, and enhancement of the chosen alternative, while minimizing the value of the rejected alternatives. All of these activities define the meaning of the earlier decision. What this body of work also makes clear is that the setting for the decision—the extent to which the decision is volitional, public, and irrevocable—affects the degree to which people will concentrate on justification during this postdecision period. Thus, the importance of decision making stretches farther into the future than is implied by "decision making by fact." Facts are only one determinant of the outcome when compared with the social setting in which the decision itself was made.

But decision making also stretches earlier in time than is acknowledged by many TQM designs. Allinson (1993), in the context of efforts to explain maritime disasters such as the capsizing of the Roll On-Roll Off vessel the *Herald of Free Enterprise,* flags the common misperception that a decision is a one-off call, something that is made or done only once and not repeated. The concept

> of a decision as a one-off call by the captain on the bridge may well be proving a hindrance to the proper understanding of such disasters as the *Challenger* and British ferry disasters. If a decision is understood as a continuum of many acts, partial decisions, and, what is frequently neglected, conferences with others, it may be better understood why not one of the many causes acted to prevent this disaster from occurring. The concept of the decision as the snap of the camera shutter makes it a finished act: he made the decision, not me; it was his decision, not mine. But the notion of a decision as a continuum including all personnel who are partially responsible automatically spreads the moral responsibility so that everyone must take a share. No one's share is diminished, but everyone's share is enhanced. . . . It really would not matter which level intervened; what is important is that the accident was preventable. The very notion that actions possess causal efficacy can be influential in altering behaviour. (Allinson & Minkes, 1990, p. 187)

When attention is focused on "making" in decision making rather than on "decision," more relevant events are included, and the decision is spread across more time and more people. It is this very spread that suggests to me that the relevant activity is no longer meaningfully viewed as decision making but is more usefully described as sensemaking. In the early stages, people have no idea whether they are making a decision or not, whether a decision will be the culmination of their efforts to understand what is going on, or whether their sensemaking will enable them to keep going. Decisions are often declared rather than made, and they are as often interpretations of previous behavior as they are guides for future behavior. Drucker (1974) was alert to a similar point when he contrasted Western and Eastern decision making:

> The Westerner and the Japanese man mean something different when they talk of "making a decision." In the West, all the emphasis is on the *answer* to the question. Indeed, our books on decision making try to develop systematic approaches to giving an answer. To the Japanese, however, the important element in decision making is *defining the Question.* The important and crucial steps are to decide whether there is a need for a decision and what the decision is about. . . . The answer to the question (what the West considers the decision) follows from its definition. During the process that precedes the decision, no mention is made of what the answer might be. (pp. 466-467)

An important implication of Allinson's analysis is that, if you see a decision as a one-off activity, then the bucks stops with the decision maker. However, when the genesis of the decision is spread across time, the buck stops everywhere. It is that spread of responsibility for which TQM interventions aim. But in their narrow construction of what a decision means, they undermine efforts to get the buck to stop everywhere.

To summarize, from the standpoint of sensemaking, those people who push for decision making based on fact as a key provision of TQM typically construe that prescription too narrowly. They fail to locate the genesis of the decision early enough, and they stop watching the effects of decision making too soon. They miss the foreclosing of options as people make sense of ambiguity by steadily moving toward the conclusion that a decision is about to be made. And in the postdecision period, they miss the justification of the chosen alternative by means of perceptual and action adjustments that constrain what people can afford to see and do from then on. The mantra that actually seems to be operating is as much decision making by plausibility as it is decision making by fact. The decision is a plausible outcome of a plurality of inputs, and its meaning is defined belatedly in terms of plausible reasons that are socially acceptable and that cast the nominal decision makers as competent, consistent, efficacious people.

Paul Gleason, reputed to be one of the five best wildland firefighters in the world, has suggested to me that when fighting fires he prefers to view his leadership efforts as sensemaking rather than decision making. In his words, "A decision is something you polish. Sensemaking is a direction for the next period." When Gleason perceives himself as making a decision, he reports that he postpones action so he can get the decision "right," and that after he makes the decision, he finds himself defending it rather than revising it to suit changing circumstances. Both polishing and defending eat up valuable time and encourage blind spots. Instead, if Gleason perceives himself as making sense of an unfolding fire, then he gives his crew a direction for some indefinite period, a direction that by definition is dynamic, open to revision at any time, self-correcting, responsive, and with more of its rationale being transparent.

From the standpoint of sensemaking, those involved in TQM interventions may also face ambiguity similar to that faced by Gleason. But the combination of institutionalized rationality, pressure to be decisive, and the need to be seen as a good judge all combine to create a tendency for TQM efforts to be "decision making based on fact." That prescription may be self-defeating. It could seal off too many inputs too soon, in the same manner as does the premature imposition of a diagnosis or a theory.

By this time, the reader should have developed a feel for the sensemaking perspective, both the arguments that prop it up and the worries that animate it. With these as background, it is possible to move toward a conclusion by first discussing one aspect of TQM that seems to come closest to the spirit of sensemaking, the philosophy of continuous improvement. We then conclude with a brief suggestion of some prescriptions implicit in what has been said.

Continuous Improvement as Sensemaking

Midway through Winter's (1994) thoughtful juxtaposition of TQM and evolutionary theory, he notes that "quality management techniques facilitate a *disciplined* quest for process involvement" (p. 97). Whereas he underlines the word "disciplined," I would have underlined the word "quest." That difference is a clue to the thrust of my analysis. The image of a quest mixes together unpredictability, construction that is never finished, ongoing negotiation of meaning, multiple explanations rather than inexplicability, and pursuit of a goal that is continually reformulated and whose attainment can be known only when the process comes to an end. The quest for meaning, whether it be in an individual life or in the life of an organization,

> is a process that ends only when a life comes to an end. Rather than being defined at the outset, a "good life" acquires a performative definition through the living of it. A search looks for something that already exists (as in a "search for excellence"); a quest creates its goal rather than discovering it. (Czarniawska, 1997, p. 16; see also MacIntyre, 1985)

The notion of a quest treats goals as both the antecedent and the result of organizational action. The image of a quest—present both in Cavafy's poem "Ithaka," with which I concluded the second edition of the *Social Psychology of Organizing* (Weick, 1979, pp. 263-264), and in Bateson's (1972) observation that "an explorer can never know what he is exploring until it has been explored" (p. xvi), is consistent with earlier arguments that diagnoses and plans are outcomes; that cognition lies in the path of the action; and that sense and meaning, often to our dismay, are post hoc constructions that occur too late to do much about them. At best, we have guides, close attention, mindfulness, and feedback to shorten the span made sensible retrospectively and to soften the dismay.

Although this is not the route Winter would take to arrive at the conclusion, both he and I regard organizing for continuous improvement as the key element of quality management. That choice is not shared by everyone. Dean and Bowen (1994, p. 394), for example, regard customer focus as the key. From the standpoint of sensemaking, continuous improvement is central because it is ongoing, both preserves and doubts past experience, accepts thrownness, focuses on failure, decouples speed-accuracy

trade-offs, is grounded in specifics, and is best explained as a quest.

If sensemaking is about nothing else, it is about coping with flows, dynamics, change, and streams. Even when routines seem stuck or a relationship feels paralyzed, these are concerns with a change in change. To the extent that sensemaking is aligned with the condition of flow, it is more likely to convey a sense of accurate reception (Nord & Connell, 1993). The "continuous" in continuous improvement, whether writ small in terms of a single process, or writ large in terms of a quest to be pursued for the rest of the organization's life, is about starting somewhere, anywhere, and about keeping going in the face of surprise, ignorance, and learning. Continuous improvement is synonymous with adopting an attitude of wisdom, defined by Meacham (1990) as follows:

> The essence of wisdom . . . lies not in what is known but rather in the manner in which that knowledge is held and in how that knowledge is put to use. To be wise is not to know particular facts but to know without excessive confidence or excessive cautiousness. . . . To both accumulate knowledge while remaining suspicious of it, and recognizing that much remains unknown, is to be wise. . . . [T]he essence of wisdom is in knowing that one does not know, in the appreciation that knowledge is fallible, in the balance between knowing and doubting. (pp. 185, 187, 210)

If we shift attention from the word "continuous" to the word "improvement," then we add the important subtlety that, although change is continuous in the sense of being relentless, it is also continuous in the sense of incremental and evolutionary rather than transformational and revolutionary. The gradualist quality of improvement is much more controversial because it can be interpreted as conservative (Sullivan & Harper, 1996); suitable only for industry leaders (Kolesar, 1995, p. 206); and unsuited for large, interconnected systems (Lustick, 1980). All of these misgivings have a grain of truth. But there is also a grain of truth in the assumption that part of the past resembles part of the present. Ryle (1979) treats this pattern of resemblance/difference as the basis on which to treat all action as partly improvisational:

To be thinking what he is here and now up against, he must both be trying to adjust himself to just this present once-only situation *and* in doing this to be applying lessons already learned. There must be in his response a union of some Ad Hockery with some know-how. If he is not at once *improvising* and improvising *warily,* he is not engaging his somewhat trained wits in a partly fresh situation. It is the pitting of an acquired competence or skill against unprogrammed opportunity, obstacle or hazard. It is a bit like putting some *new* wine into *old* bottles. (p. 129)

In organizations, one mechanism for adaptive action is to simultaneously believe and doubt one's past experience (Weick, 1969, pp. 86-96; 1979, pp. 217-224). Belief affirms the resemblance of past to present, doubt affirms the difference, and the combination unifies the duality of exploitation-exploration (March, 1996). Action gets started because of resemblance-exploitation and gets updated because of difference-exploration. It is the seductive simplicity of either belief (exploitation) or doubt (exploration) that makes it so hard to implement both simultaneously.

The genius of "continuous improvement" is that it institutionalizes this simultaneity without calling attention to just how tough it can be to implement. In a way, those who commit to continuous improvement are always out of date and always in the dark. The present is not like the past, and what is ahead is like nothing seen before. That is the glass-half-empty rendition. The glass-half-full rendition is that part of the past is always being replayed in the present and, therefore, is available for exploitation and continuation into the future.

The point is that if an evolutionary system is represented using the notation of deviation amplifying and deviation counteracting feedback loops, the resulting system is unstable unless retained knowledge has opposite effects on variation and selection (Weick, 1979, pp. 132-133). If both variation and selection are constrained in the same way by the past, then there is a closed system where adaptation precludes adaptability. If neither variation nor selection is constrained by retention, then the system is open but must reinvent itself in the face of each new input—a condition where adaptability exhausts itself in the face of an inability to routinize.

Part of the stimulus to take a closer look at continuous improvement in the context of sensemaking came from Kathleen Sutcliffe's (personal communication, May, 1997) observation that part of the success that Southern Pacific had with quality improvement might be attributable to its insistence that the program *not* be called Total Quality Management but instead be called CQI, or "Continuous Quality Improvement" (Carman, 1995, p. 157). Recall my earlier mention of the success at SP that consisted of getting just six trains in the entire system to run on time, reliably, and calling them the "quality" trains. Conspicuous in the description of that success was mention that the trains, though now reliable, were still awfully slow (36 hours to go 825 miles = 23 mph). The Q trains were a demonstrable small change that could undergo additional changes from then on. Such a demonstration, in a demoralized, fearful system, can have the important consequence that it heightens perceptions of control and efficacy.

A commitment to continuous improvement may also work because it focuses attention on failures rather than successes, something that also seems to happen in the more successful high-reliability organizations (Weick, Sutcliffe, & Obstfeld, 1997). Schulman (1993), in the context of studies of the Diablo Canyon nuclear power station, observed that

there is widespread recognition that all of the potential failure modes into which the highly complex technical systems could resolve themselves have yet to be experienced. Nor have they been exhaustively deduced. In this respect the technology is still capable of surprises. In the face of this potential for surprise, there is a fundamental reluctance among higher management to put decision or action frameworks in place that are not sensitive to the possibilities of analytic error. (p. 364)

To interpret one's activities as continuous improvement is to accept the possibility of analytic error, the likelihood of unexpected failure modes, and the limitations of foresight. Equivalent cautions are not suggested by interpretations involving total quality or customer focus. To improve is to become better, which can only happen if one is aware that earlier it was worse.

Total quality obscures that kind of comparative thinking.

What gives an edge to these arguments is an impassioned commentary on continuous improvement, made companywide at Alcoa midway through its quality program, by CEO Paul O'Neill.

> "I believe we have made a major mistake in our advocacy of the idea of continuous improvement," he said. "Continuous improvement is exactly the right idea if you are the world leader in everything you do," he explained. "It is a terrible idea if you are lagging behind the world leadership benchmark. It is probably a disastrous idea if you are far behind the world standard. In too many cases we fall in the second and third categories." (quoted in Kolesar, 1995, p. 206)

O'Neill's frustration may make sense, considering what appears to be the slow pace of quality improvement at Alcoa. But to blame continuous improvement is to risk even worse problems. As Kolesar (1995) notes, although breakthrough improvements may be desirable, the way to get them is by continuous improvements that "enhance a firm's ability to carry off breakthroughs by adding greatly to its storehouse of product, process, and customer knowledge, and by adding to its ability to implement and maintain the breakthrough changes" (p. 208). Notice that incremental improvements are necessary both before ("implement") and after ("maintain") the breakthrough change. From the standpoint of sensemaking, imagine that as an Alcoa employee, you have invested extra time and effort in quality training and quality teams, you have used quality rhetoric to explain what you are doing and why it matters, and then hear your boss call these efforts a disastrous idea while the program is still being rolled out. The message that comes through is clear: Around here, it is short-term results, period.

O'Neill also may underestimate the power of many, simultaneous improvement projects, done in parallel, with specific innovations as by-products, that increase the general willingness to make tacit knowledge explicit. O'Neill, in his preoccupation with time, invokes and encourages a trade-off of speed for accuracy that could undermine the very goal he seeks. Fiske (1992, p. 884) has shown that when people feel under pressure for speed, they search for evidence that confirms their expectations, whereas when they feel under pressure to be accurate, their search for information is slower, more thorough, and less driven by confirmation of expectations. It is the very breakthrough innovations that O'Neill wants that he has neatly put out of reach. By asserting that he wants breakthroughs now, he puts pressure on people to search for data that confirm their prior expectations, expectations that presumably caused the problem in the first place. When O'Neill pulls the plug on continuous improvement, he encourages retrenchment and inertia rather than innovation.

Continuous improvement is not an explicit growth strategy and would never be mistaken for one. Nevertheless, given a quantum world in which small deviations can produce large novel structures, continuous improvement can be a source of innovation. Six reliable trains per day do alter operations in multiple, unpredictable ways. Those multiple effects may themselves be small. But that says nothing about their significance or what additional ideas and opportunities they trigger. From the standpoint of sensemaking, what is important is that action is under way. Action provides the raw material that needs to be explained. And in the explanation lies the potential for creating new routines and finding novel interpretations of what might be going on, as well as renewal. Whatever the rhetorical overlay, people practicing continuous improvement are more in tune with flows that embody their fate.

Practical Implications of Sensemaking for Quality Improvement

The preceding sections can be read as an attempt to make several tacit qualities of sensemaking more explicit. And in the course of making them explicit, there were hints—prescriptions is too strong a word given the nature of the evidence—of better and worse practice. For example, we discussed the following:

1. Thrownness: with the suggestion that making do and acceptance may be preferable to attempted control
2. Unknowable environments: with the suggestion that a capability for resilience is more helpful than a capability for anticipation
3. Enacted environments: with the suggestion that constraints are partly of one's own making and not simply objects to which one reacts, customers being just as susceptible to enactment as are one's own presumed limitations based on avoided tests of those presumptions
4. Quests: with the suggestion that questions never get fully answered, that discovering rather than discoveries is the best one can hope for, and that sense is something one authors, imposes, negotiates, and finds useful rather than truthful
5. Sensemaking: with the suggestion that plausibility rather than accuracy is the ongoing standard that guides improvements
6. Directions: with the suggestion that a compass may be as good as a map in a dynamic world
7. Past experience: with the suggestion that it should be simultaneously believed and doubted because one's present circumstance both resembles and is different from that past
8. Action: with the suggestion that it is more important to keep going than to pause because the flow of experience in which action is embedded does not pause
9. Retrospect: with the suggestion that so-called stimuli for action such as diagnoses, plans for implementation, and strategies are the products of action as much as they are the prods to action
10. Managing: with the suggestion that it is more about authoring an environment and bringing it to life with words than it is about a literal reading of someone else's words
11. Identity: with the suggestion that continuities in a system may be minimal and supplied mostly by values that provide what little coherence there is in an otherwise protean, mutable set of adaptations
12. Accounts: with the suggestion that these are fashioned for auditors and are imperfect, possibly misleading explanations for insiders of why events unfold the way they do

Thus, taking just what has been developed here, if one wanted to improve quality, then one would socialize people to make do, be resilient, view constraints as of their own making, value

quests, strive for plausibility, articulate directions, treat past experience with ambivalence, keep showing up, use retrospect to get a sense of direction, craft descriptions that energize, ground identity in a protean rather than singular self-image, and be wary of using rational accounts as job descriptions. Controversial as that list is, what makes it even more so is that there is no explicit mention of quality improvement in it.

The reason is simple. If a team enacted those 12 practices, they would never get into the position where "quality stinks." Instead, there would be continuous updating and co-evolution of producer-customer relationships. Furthermore, there would be continuous acting that continuously bumped into whatever constraints were generated by those relationships. Those actions and interruptions would be occasions for retrospective sensemaking. Thus, quality improvement would have been embodied in their continuous updating, whether it was called quality improvement or not.

If continuous implementation of those practices could have forestalled quality problems to begin with, then it is also possible that belated implementation can improve quality. This may already be happening. It is not uncommon to hear people say, when quality is described, "Oh, we are already doing that, we just don't call it quality." One interpretation of that comment is that people are already engaged in sensemaking grounded in action; and this is producing outcomes just like those we have come to associate with TQM. The common core, in both cases, is that people have moved toward designs that enable them to make better sense, not just better decisions.

References

Allinson, R. E. (1993). *Global disasters*. New York: Prentice Hall.
Allinson, R. E., & Minkes, A. L. (1990). Principles, proverbs, and shibboleths of administration. *Journal of Technology Management, 2,* 179-187.
Bateson, G. (1972). *Steps to an ecology of mind.* New York: Ballantine.
Brown, R. H. (1989). Bureaucracy as praxis. In R. H. Brown, *Social science as civic discourse* (pp. 123-142). Chicago: University of Chicago Press.

Bursztjahn, H., Feinbloom, A., Hamm, R., & Brodsky, A. (1981). *Medical choices, medical chances.* New York: Dell.

Carman, J. M. (1995). Quality improvement as survival strategy at Southern Pacific. In R. E. Cole (Ed.), *The death and life of the American quality movement* (pp. 157-174). New York: Oxford University Press.

Czarniawska, B. (1997). *Narrating the organization.* Chicago: University of Chicago Press.

Dean, J. W., Jr., & Bowen, D. E. (1994). Management theory and total quality: Improving research and practice through theory development. *Academy of Management Review, 19,* 392-418.

Drucker, P. E. (1974). *Management: Tasks, responsibilities, practices.* New York: Harper & Row.

Fiske, S. T. (1992). Thinking is for doing: Portraits of social cognition from daguerreotype to laserphoto. *Journal of Personality and Social Psychology, 63,* 877-889.

Follett, M. P. (1924). *Creative experience.* New York: Longmans, Green.

Frailey, F. W. (1993). Southern Pacific at the crossroads. *Trains, 9,* 48-63.

Garfinkel, H. (1967). *Studies in ethnomethodology.* Englewood Cliffs, NJ: Prentice Hall.

Goffman, E. (1974). *Frame analysis.* Harmondsworth, UK: Penguin.

Havel, V. (1992). A word about words. In V. Havel, *Open letters* (pp. 377-389). New York: Vintage.

Hurst, D. K. (1995). *Crisis and renewal.* Boston: Harvard Business School Press.

Isenberg, D. J. (1985). Some hows and whats of managerial thinking: Implications for future army leaders. In J. G. Hunt & J. D. Blair (Eds.), *Leadership on the future battlefield* (pp. 168-181). Dulles, VA: Pergamon-Brassey's.

Janowitz, M. (1959). Changing patterns of organizational authority: The military establishment. *Administrative Science Quarterly, 4,* 473-493.

Kolesar, P. J. (1995). Vision, valves, milestones: Paul O'Neill starts total quality at Alcoa. In R. E. Cole (Ed.), *The death and life of the American quality movement* (pp. 175-214). New York: Oxford University Press.

Lustick, I. (1980). Explaining the variable utility of disjointed incrementalism: Four propositions. *American Political Science Review, 24,* 342-353.

MacIntyre, A. (1985). *Aftervirtue* (2nd ed.). London: Duckworth.

March, J. G. (1996). Exploration and exploitation in organizational learning. In M. D. Cohen & L. S. Sproull (Eds.), *Organizational learning* (pp. 101-123). Thousand Oaks, CA: Sage.

McDaniel, R. R., Jr. (1997, Winter). Strategic leadership: A view from quantum and chaos theories. *Health Care Management Review,* pp. 21-37.

Meacham, J. A. (1990). The loss of wisdom. In R. S. Sternberg (Ed.), *Wisdom* (pp. 181-211). New York: Cambridge University Press.

Morrison, T. (1995). *The Nobel lecture in literature: 1993.* New York: Knopf.

Nonaka, I., & Takeuchi, H. (1995). *The knowledge-creating company.* New York: Oxford University Press.

Nord, W. R., & Connell, A. F. (1993). From quicksand to crossroads: An agnostic perspective on conversation. *Organization Science, 4,* 108-120.

Ryle, G. (1979). Improvisation. In G. Ryle, *On thinking* (pp. 121-130). London: Blackwell.

Schulman, P. R. (1993). The negotiated order of organizational reliability. *Administration & Society, 25,* 353-372.

Sitkin, S. B., Sutcliffe, K. M., & Schroeder, R. G. (1994). Distinguishing control from learning in total quality management: A contingency perspective. *Academy of Management Review, 19,* 537-564.

Spencer, B. A. (1994). Models of organization and total quality management: A comparison and critical evaluation. *Academy of Management Review, 19,* 446-471.

Starbuck, W. H. (1993). "Watch where you step!" or Indiana Starbuck amid the perils of academe (rated PG). In A. G. Bedeian (Ed.), *Management laureates* (Vol. 3, pp. 65-110). Greenwich, CT: JAI.

Sullivan, G. R., & Harper, M. V. (1996). *Hope is not a method.* New York: Random.

Vaughan, D. (1996). *The* Challenger *launch decision.* Chicago: University of Chicago Press.

Waterman, R. H., Jr. (1995). *What America does right.* New York: Penguin.

Weick, K. E. (1969). *The social psychology of organizing.* Reading, MA: Addison-Wesley.

Weick, K. E. (1979). *The social psychology of organizing* (2nd ed.). Reading, MA: Addison-Wesley.

Weick, K. E. (1987). Substitutes for corporate strategy. In D. J. Teece (Ed.), *The competitive challenge* (pp. 221-233). Cambridge, MA: Ballinger.

Weick, K. E. (1995). *Sensemaking in organizations.* Thousand Oaks, CA: Sage.

Weick, K. E., Sutcliffe, K. M., & Obstfeld, D. (1997). *Organizing for high reliability.* Unpublished manuscript, University of Michigan.

Wildavsky, A. (1991). *Searching for safety.* New Brunswick, NJ: Transaction Press.

Winograd, T., & Flores, F. (1986). *Understanding computers and cognition.* Norwood, NJ: Ablex.

Winter, S. G. (1994). Organizing for continuous improvement: Evolutionary theory meets the quality revolution. In J. Baum & J. V. Singh (Eds.), *Evolutionary dynamics of organizations* (pp. 90-108). New York: Oxford University Press.

Zaleznik, A. (1990). *The managerial mystique.* New York: Harper & Row.

PART III

Stages and Processes in Quality Improvement

Chapter 8

The Road to "Root Cause"

Shop-Floor Problem Solving at Three Auto Assembly Plants

JOHN PAUL MACDUFFIE

Introduction

In this paper, I present the results of a study comparing problem-solving processes at three North American auto assembly plants.[1] I focus on production-related, in-plant problems affecting quality (and to some extent productivity) that are not traceable to one clear-cut source. Problems of this kind are common to all manufacturing plants, cannot be easily resolved by applying a standard procedure or methodology, and require high levels of interaction and coordination across multiple departments or functional groups. As such, they reveal much about a plant's capability for process quality improvement—a capability that many companies have worked to develop during the quality revolution of the past fifteen years (Cole 1990, 1992b; Fine 1986; Juran 1988).

I studied three problem categories that require collaborative problem-solving: water leaks, paint defects, and functional electrical defects. All are readily noticeable by customers and are measured in the J. D. Power consumer surveys on vehicle quality. All are ubiquitous—no assembly plant in the world has suc-

ceeded in permanently eliminating these defects. Furthermore, all three problems have many possible sources.

For example, water leaks can result from gaps in the metal frame after it is welded in the body shop, which can be caused by poorly made of damaged stampings, misadjusted welding jigs or malfunctioning welding equipment. Or they can result if the sealer applied to the body before painting is either missing or inadequate—or if the rubber weatherstripping applied in the assembly department is poorly attached.

The paint process can be affected by small variations in the paint itself, the evenness of the spray from paint robots, or the temperature and humidity of the plant and the bake ovens. But the most elusive paint problems occur outside the paint booths. Painted bodies can be chipped or scratched by a worker's belt buckle, a tool set down in the wrong place, a misadjusted conveyer, or a redesigned jig. Misapplied sealer can prevent paint from adhering properly. Dirt can become embedded in paint because of inadequate cleaning after sanding, fibers coming off of gloves, unenclosed conveyor lines between

AUTHOR'S NOTE: From *Management Science, 43* (4), 1997, pp. 479-502. Reprinted by permission, The Institute of Management Sciences (currently INFORMS), 901 Elkridge Landing Road, Suite 400, Linthicum, MD 21090-2909 USA.

175

stages of the paint process, paint ovens that are not cleaned often enough, and countless other reasons.

Functional electrical defects affect the operation of interior and exterior lights, instrument panel, wipers, radio, power doors and windows, and air conditioning. Many result from missing or faulty electrical connections. Two connectors may be pushed together without quite locking in place, and may subsequently vibrate loose. Certain option combinations may pack so much equipment in the dashboard that wires have difficulty reaching their connectors. If electrical wiring is misrouted, a subsequent operation attaching parts may put a screw through a wire, creating a short-circuit.

These three problem categories can also be interrelated. For example, while heavy applications of sealer can help prevent water leaks, this increases the odds of mistakenly sealing over holes needed for fastening electrical wire harnesses. Furthermore, while each problem can result from either technical difficulties with automated equipment, failures of organizational systems, or human error, they most commonly result from a complex interaction of technical, organizational, and human factors.

I use my fieldwork observations here to develop, inductively, a set of insights about organizational influences on process quality improvement and the implications for how we think about problem-solving. Traditional models of problem-solving assume a structured process of problem identification and diagnosis, followed by solution generation and implementation (March and Simon 1957). Yet, as Simon (1973) has noted, "the problems presented to problem-solvers by the world are best regarded as ill-structured problems. They become well-structured problems only in the process of being prepared for the problem-solvers" (p. 186). Dealing with ill-structured problems, such as those studied here, requires "learning by doing" or "adaptive learning" (Adler and Clark 1991), in which the identification and diagnosis of problems emerges during the interaction among problem-solvers.

The adaptive learning required for process quality improvement draws increasing attention from both operations management and organi-

zational researchers. Operations management researchers have investigated the outcomes of adaptive learning, particularly the tradeoff between the "cost of learning" and the "cost of failure" in pursuing defect prevention under different production conditions (Fine 1986, Marcellus and Dada 1991). Organizational researchers focus on the adaptive learning process, including the "sensemaking" arising from social interaction during problem-solving (Weick 1979, Argyris and Schon 1978) and how cues from the physical environment affect problem-solving (Tyre and von Hippel 1993).

The observations presented below will link these concerns about outcome and process. In certain organizational contexts, problem-solving for process quality improvement may result in the misidentification of problems, faulty diagnoses, and inadequate solutions. This not only drives up the "cost of learning" but may also produce new problems, driving up the "cost of failure." Yet the organizational context for problem-solving can also create positive conditions for effective learning and potentially eliminate the cost/quality tradeoff for the majority of process improvement activities.

Research Questions

My fieldwork emphasizes the first three stages of the problem-solving process, following a commonly used model (e.g., March and Simon 1958, Imai 1986, Tyre 1989) that includes:

1. Problem definition
2. Problem analysis
3. Generation and selection of solutions
4. Testing and evaluation of solutions
5. Routinization—Development of new routines

I characterize these stages in the following way:

1. *Problem definition* occurs when a problem situation is perceived by organizational actors in light of established routines and subsequently defined in relation to those routines (Tyre 1989). The definition chosen will affect

all subsequent stages of the problem-solving process.

2. *Problem analysis* could also be described as "search activity." March and Simon (1958) see search— "aimed at discovering alternatives or consequences of action"—as the key variable in problem-solving activity, and as differentiating routinized or programmed activity (involving little or no search) from problem-solving.

3. The *generation and selection of solutions* is heavily influenced by the skills and knowledge that individuals bring to problem analysis, by the variety of perspectives brought by different individuals (representing different groups), by the way individuals and groups interact during the problem-solving process, and by organizational reward and control systems.

Then, for each of these stages, I ask the following questions:

1. *Problem definition*—What counts as a problem? What information on problems is gathered and how is it used? What kinds of problems are considered legitimate for problem-solving and which are not? How do resource constraints affect problem definition and decisions about which problems to solve?

2. *Problem analysis*—Who is involved in problem analysis? How broad (and/or deep) is the conceptual knowledge they bring to the analytical task? What strategy guides the analysis? What search techniques and methodologies are used?

3. *Solution generation and selection*—Who is involved in generating and selecting solutions? Do they share a common conception of the problem? What approach to generating solutions is used, in terms of techniques, group activities, boundary-spanning activities? What criteria are used for selection?

In addition to these stages of problem-solving, I will examine key attributes of the quality system within which problem-solving processes take place—in particular what organizational structure for quality improvement activities is chosen, what mix of people (with respect to functional or hierarchical position) is involved in such activities, and how the organization seeks to motivate problem-solving activities. I also briefly address issues of routinization and standardization.

Choice of Sites and Fieldwork Activities

My research sites for this study were three assembly plants in North America, one each from General Motors, Ford, and Honda.[2] I made inquiries about a total of nine sites at five companies (2 U.S.-owned and 3 Japanese-owned) and these companies were the ones that most quickly agreed to provide access. These three sites were chosen as most appropriate and most interested in the research after discussions at each company.

I spent one full week in the GM and Ford plants and five days, over two visits, at the Honda plant, all between January and October 1989. For reasons of confidentiality, I identify the plants only by company name; I have omitted or modified references that would indicate plant location, and have changed the names of any individuals who are mentioned in the case studies. At the GM plant, I carried out 23 interviews and attended four meetings—one work team meeting, two meetings of quality improvement groups, one informational meeting—as well as a daily quality audit meeting. At Ford, I carried out 19 interviews and attended three daily meetings—two meetings of quality improvement groups and one meeting of department heads—as well as a single meeting of two Employee Involvement groups and one meeting with representatives from another plant. At Honda, I interviewed 20 people and attended one meeting of a quality improvement group.

At all of these plants, I sought and received permission to walk around the plant, to talk with workers, team leaders (where applicable), quality analysts, engineers, and production managers, to observe work processes, and to gather relevant documentation (e.g., statistical data gathered to document problems, daily quality audits, minutes of quality circle meetings). In each plant, I asked about the same production

TABLE 8.1   Selected Characteristics of Plants in Problem-Solving Study

Characteristic	GM	Ford	Honda	Mean for US/NA	Mean for J/NA
Plant age	Built in 1980s	Built pre-1940 Retrofitted in 1980s	Built in 1980s	—	—
Union status	Unionized	Unionized	Nonunion	—	—
Productivity (hours/vehicle)	20-25	15-20	20-25	24.9	20.9
Quality* (defects/100 vehicles)	200-220	120-140	100-120	159	112
Water leaks	4.9	7.0	3.1	6.3	3.0
Paint defects	31.8	16.7	10.1	18.0	11.2
Electrical defects	36.5	16.7	20.1	25.8	16.7
Total automation (% automated prod. steps)	23%	35%	39%	30.6%	34.7%
Production organization (0 = mass prod; 100 = lean prod)	64	43	69	42	75
Production scale (vehicles per day)	700-900	900-1100	500-700	8	

SOURCE: International Assembly Plant Study, IMVP, MIT except for * = J. D. Power Initial Quality Survey (unadjusted).

problems, talked to people in the same kinds of jobs, and observed the same production processes and quality-focused group activities.[3]

Additional background information for these three plants is presented in Table 8.1, based on 1989 data from the International Assembly Plant Study,[4] including plant characteristics not investigated during the field visits, productivity (in hours per vehicle), and J. D. Power consumer-reported quality data for overall defects (per 100 vehicles) and for the three problems studied here.[5] Some variables are expressed as a range to preserve confidentiality. Averages for U.S.-owned and Japanese-owned plants in North America are included for comparison purposes.

The case summaries begin with background information about the plant and then describe the structure, composition, and motivational elements of the quality system. The accounts of problem-solving activity are organized into sections on problem definition and problem analysis/generation of solutions.[6] I then analyze the cases for evidence of consistency across stages within each case and of contrast across cases. The paper closes with a discussion of the implications, both theoretical and practical, for understanding process quality improvement as adaptive learning.

General Motors (GM) Plant

The GM plant is one of several built in the 1970s and 1980s using the team concept. All production workers are organized into teams of 15-20 members with an elected team coordinator. Unlike other GM plants that opened at the same time, the team concept has proved relatively successful, endorsed by a solid majority of the workforce in three local contract votes during the 80s. But this plant did not implement the manufacturing practices associated with lean production—reduced inventories, integrating quality inspection into production jobs—until the late 1980s. The technology in the plant is almost all mid-1970s vintage, with little investment in new technology since that time.

Of the three problem categories, paint defects were viewed as the most significant by the plant, followed closely by electrical defects, with water leaks a minor concern. This matches the relative ranking of these problems in the J.D. Power data for this plant. Compared to the other two plants, the GM plant had 90-215% more paint defects reported by consumers—in part a function of its relatively old paint booths—and 80-220% more electrical defects. These defect levels are also considerably worse than the Big Three average.

Quality System

Structure and composition. The plant has an elaborate structure of quality-related groups and roles. Each work team has a Quality Coordinator who samples a certain number of cars per day, keeps Statistical Process Control (SPC) charts, and attends the daily plant audit meetings (see below). Most quality activities are organized by department. Each department (e.g., weld, paint, assembly) has a Quality Analyst (QA)—an hourly person jointly appointed by union and management for a one year term to support quality improvement activities—and a Quality Improvement Team (QIT) that meets monthly. QITs are headed by a member of the top management group and include shift superintendents, engineers, and first-line supervisors. Under the QITs are Quality Action Teams (QAT), short-term task forces set up to address specific problems, nominally with hourly and management members, although an inspection of QAT minutes revealed low attendance by managers. Most cross-departmental problems are referred to a Plant Quality Council made up of senior management and top union officials, although some are handled at meetings of departmental QITs. No design engineers were stationed at the plant.

Motivation/incentives. At the corporate level, quality had certainly become a very important performance measure by the time of my visit. Plants were rated monthly on a GM corporate quality scale, based on a "surprise" audit, for internal comparisons. External comparisons with competitor's products were based on consumer-perceived defects identified in a survey commissioned by GM. The results of both internal and external comparisons were printed up monthly on pocket-sized index cards and distributed to all managers at or above department level. Bonuses for the top level of plant management (but not below) were affected by quality performance.

Within the plant, for lower-level managers, staff, supervisors, and production workers, the quality incentives were less clear. Workers perceived that managers in charge of production, at all levels, still placed the highest priority on meeting daily production targets. With respect to quality, department-level managers seemed most concerned about being charged with the cost of fixing quality defects in terms of their budget performance. Production workers were covered at that time by a corporate profit-sharing program, but the tie between plant-level quality performance and the formula used to calculate corporate profitability was unclear. In any case, GM had not paid a bonus to any production workers for three years because of losses at the corporate level (a period when top corporate officials continued to receive large bonuses—a fact pointed out to me by several employees). Thus while incentives to motivate the plant to achieve better quality performance certainly existed, they were unevenly distributed and not particularly strong in comparison with incentives to meet financial and production goals.

Problem Definition

Sources of data. GM primarily uses internal quality audit data for identifying quality problems. The audits that "count" are carried out by corporate auditors who visit the plant unannounced once a week. They follow a standard methodology and assign weights for various defects to get an overall score, which is compared with other GM plants and with cars made by other companies but sold by GM. The plant replicates these audit procedures daily for its own internal problem identification purposes.

At the time of the study, customer-based warranty data were collected at dealerships on a "defects per thousand vehicles" (DPTV) basis, but these were only reported to the plant after a delay of several months, so they played little role in the plant's problem-solving efforts. Also, the plant had established programs to emphasize that customers were the most important source of quality data. A few workers each night took a newly-built vehicle home for a thorough check and reported their findings at the next day's audit. Groups of workers visited dealers in other states to see what quality problems were reported. But the internal quality audits remained the primary source for both the data and incentives guiding most problem-solving activity.

Deciding what problems to solve: "Avoiding corporate" for design-related problems. One consistent frustration for groups identifying quality problems is the difficult in getting design-related changes made. This ultimately affects what is defined as a problem. There is a tendency to define problems in a way that allows the plant to deal with it independently, without lengthy and frustrating interactions with corporate designers.

The time involved in processing a design-related change, alone, is a disincentive. I was told that the typical engineering change involving parts design in this GM division takes 210 days to process. QIT members told me that designers have refused to respond to several persistent quality problems pressed by the plant. For example, the routing of the tube carrying window washing fluid to the back windshield brought it so close to several fasteners for other parts that it frequently got pinched or blocked. The QIT suggested an alternative routing but the designer insisted that the original routing was adequate and that any problems were the fault of the plant.

As a result of such experiences, groups at the plant often focus on problems that can be addressed without involving the corporate level. For example, the plant has had a persistent problem with a bracket on the brake pedal subassembly to which cables for both the cruise control and power brakes are attached. The

bracket often moves when the cruise control is used, resulting in misadjustment of the brakes. Engineers, supervisors, and operators I talked to agreed that the problem was a poor design—that the cruise control and brake cables shouldn't be attached to the same bracket, and that the bracket was in a bad location.

But the problem was defined in terms of the design of the clip holding the cruise control cable to the bracket, and a new, stiffer clip with a longer flange was ordered from the supplier. Upon investigation, I learned that this latter solution involved a small enough change in clip specifications that it could be worked out directly between the plant and the supplier, a process that took only 3 weeks. To define the problem in broader terms would require, it was claimed, a long struggle with designers in Detroit.

Deciding what problems to solve: "Unidentifying" problems due to cost concerns. The dominance of cost concerns often effectively precludes the identification of certain problems—or can lead to problems being "unidentified." One of the most common electrical problems serviced under warranty was the car horn either failing to operate or going off randomly—a highly visible problem for the consumer. The problem involved the wire connecting the horn button to the rest of the instrument panel wiring. First, this wire is connected and then the horn button is fastened to the steering wheel. The wire was generally cut long enough to allow a good connection to be made while the horn button was not yet fastened to the steering wheel, but it would bend and often get pinched when the horn button was fastened on. When the wire was shortened to avoid this pinching, the connection would often be pulled loose before the horn button was in place.

This problem was first formally registered in the plant's "5 Phase Problem Resolution Process" in October 1988. The initial response was to ask the operators involved to take extra care and to experiment with some different installation methods. By November, the QIT for the Trim Department proposed the use of a coiled wire with "memory," designed to spring back to a shorter length after being stretched. By

January 1989, the QIT worked with a supplier to test different "memory" wires, and found that it cut defects dramatically. That same month, a formal request for a design engineering change to the memory wire was sent to Detroit.

In April 1989, I was at the QIT meeting when the superintended announced that their request would not be approved because the cost— 94 cents per wire—was too much. An engineer at the meeting speculated that the design engineers might be examining wire with more "memory" capabilities than the plant needed—like the cord connected to a telephone handset which is stretched daily over several years—and said that such "overengineering" by designers was common. Unlike the superintendent of the department, who was angry about this outcome, most other QIT members seemed cynical, resigned, unsurprised by the lack of response. This horn problem persisted but it ceased being defined as a "resolvable" problem. The 5-Phase Problem Resolution sheet on this problem concludes the section on Problem Elimination with the statement "Re-design required for complete problem elimination."

Deciding what problems to solve: Striving for a common language. One prerequisite for problem definition is developing a common descriptive language that can be understood across departmental (and organizational) lines. I found two examples. I met with the Quality Analyst (QA) for the Paint Department while he was reviewing his daily audit of vehicles for paint "mutilations." I noted the highly picturesque language he used to describe these defects—boils, craters, bulls-eyes, sags, runs, orange peel, dings, mars, scratches, cracks, grind marks, powder bumps. He said the plant has been trying to make sure everyone uses the same language for describing paint problems—in the plant but also the dealers when they file out a warranty form for a repair. The paint QIT developed a form, complete with diagrams, that lists this terminology. This attention to language had resulted in more consistency in the reporting of types of defects. It had not helped much in achieving consistency in the standards individuals used in determining whether or not to report a defect.

The Final Line Quality Analyst also referred to the use of language in defining problems. She checks with the in-plant auditors daily to find out which problems might affect her area. Then she would visit the supervisor or work team most likely, based on her experience, to know what had happened. Often they would point her to some upstream process. After investigation, she would write up a problem statement describing where the responsibility lay. Much of the process, she explained, involved interpreting how different departments defined the problem. "Different people in different departments use different words for the same problem. I change the language around some to be sure the guys on my line can tell what I mean." In this case, the QA handles the "translation" problems caused by different terminology on her own. But this does not help eliminate the issue of inconsistent standards for identifying what is a problem. Both common language and common standards for defining a defect seem critical to effective problem definition.

Problem Analysis/Generation of Solutions

"Placing the blame" through the audit system. The in-plant audits are the basis for a twice-a-day ritual held in a special area in the front of the plant. The day's quality scores are announced by the Quality Analyst for each department, together with an explanation or defense of a bad score and applause for a good score. Several of the vehicles that were audited are parked around the speaker's podium and used to point out problems both during the audit meeting and throughout the day. All quality coordinators, supervisors, superintendents, and senior managers are expected to attend the meeting, and any visiting guests are invited.

The daily audit numbers are now perhaps the most important performance measure for the department, and the daily exposure of the departmental score only intensifies the concern about what this number will be. The audit system requires that every problem be assigned to a department, both to tally the departmental score and to allocate the costs of repair. Since not every problem can be easily attributed to a single department, the assignment of problems is often the focus of intense negotiations among Quality Analysts, supervisors, and department heads.

The Quality Analysts play a key role in problem analysis, since they are supposed to "root cause" problems (i.e., find out the real source of problems). The QAs do try to track down whatever information they can about problems, but since they do not have the time or resources for a full investigation, they usually rely on one of two approaches: 1) An automatic assignment of a problem to the department that should have spotted it (i.e., the repair or inspection group that usually finds problems in that part of the vehicle); or 2) Negotiating with representatives from other departments about where to assign a particular defect.

One example of the former approach emerged when I observed one of the plant's full-time auditors inspecting a vehicle. He found a paint defect—two small "dirt" spots on the hood ("dirt" refers to any foreign matter caught under the paint)—and, in checking the ticket, found they had been identified by inspectors at the end of the paint department but then "bought off" (i.e., passed through without repair) by the paint reprocess group at the end of the line. He told me this defect would be charged to the paint reprocess group that had failed to repair it.

When I asked how this would help with identifying the source of the dirt problem, he replied, "The reprocess guys are responsible. It's their job to catch this." This is a clear reflection of how the existing audit system still reinforces the "inspecting in" philosophy. Negotiating over where to assign the cost of defects is influenced partially by what is known about the problem, and partially by the number of defects already accruing to a given department that day (in the interest of insuring that no department looks too bad—or too good). In neither case is much effort made to identify the true source of a problem. Problem analysis, such as it is, is almost entirely concerned with assigning financial accountability, or as one QA called it, "placing the blame." The plant's production manager expressed his concern about this, say-

ing, "We spend too much time around here worrying about 'Who shot John?'."

Ford Plant

The Ford plant is the oldest I studied, built before World War II. It was completely retrofitted in the 1980s for a new product, and has been dedicated to that product ever since. It is in many ways a traditional mass production plant. There are no work teams. The number of job classifications, while reduced during the 80s, is still high—over 90 unskilled and over 20 skilled classifications. Relatively few employees are involved in Employee Involvement groups. The plant has made considerable efforts to reduce its use of buffers but inventories were large by lean production standards. But in the area of quality, the plant is closer to lean production policies.

Managers and workers alike spoke of a strong work ethic among employees, a "hands-on" attitude and high shop floor visibility from the management team, and a history of constructive (although not always cooperative) labor relations fostered by strong and long-serving plant managers and union officials. While employment has been stable for most of its history, the plant suffered massive layoffs in the early 1980s.

Of the three problems, electrical defects was viewed as the most serious, followed by paint chips and water leaks. These problems ranked first, third, and fourth, respectively, on the plant's "Top Ten" list of problems during my visit. Interestingly, the J. D. Power data show paint and electrical defects at the same level, both better than the U.S. average (and for the latter, matching the Japanese transplant average), with the incidence of water leaks worse than the U.S. average (and more than twice as high as the transplant average).[7]

Quality System

Structure and composition. Ford had recently reorganized the quality structure in all its plants, changing from department (e.g., weld, paint, assembly) to product "subsystem."

Eleven subsystems were defined, with a group assigned to each. Among the subsystems were all three of the problem categories I chose: water leaks, electrical defects, and paint problems. This shows how much Ford had reoriented their quality system to emphasize the inter-departmental nature of many quality problems.

Each subsystem group meets daily, and is chaired by a member of the plant's operations committee, made up of the plant manager and all department heads. Other members include a "vertical slice" of the plant organization: design engineers (sent from Detroit for a 2-year stint in the plant under a new program called QPRESS), process engineers, supervisors, and hourly workers. A full-time "coordinator"—often a process engineer—is assigned to each subsystem group as staff.

Each subsystem group collects a tremendous amount of data, using Statistical Process Control and Pareto graphs and "8D" charts, named after an eight-stage problem-solving process developed by W. Edwards Deming, the quality control guru used extensively by Ford. These graphs and charts are reviewed at the daily meetings but also form the basis of the Production Operations Report (POR) presented semi-annually to corporate staff during an in-plant review.

Ford has also created a new liaison role for quality improvement activities: the Zone Improvement Person, or ZIP. A ZIP is assigned to a subsection of a department, and authorized to take a variety of actions to prevent a quality problem from leaving their zone. ZIPs are permanent positions, filled by production employees who are paid a small hourly bonus, and are said to be popular assignments. ZIPs, working with supervisors, either generate or oversee much of the data-gathering activity in the plant.

Motivation/incentives. In many ways, the incentives to improve quality at Ford did not differ substantially from those at GM. Corporate-level audits were used to rank plants in terms of quality and performance on these audits, as well as the achievement of yearly quality improvement goals, factored into the calculation of yearly bonuses for top managers at the

plant. Rivalries with other plants, either those who built the same product or who were consistent contenders for divisional leadership, gave an extra competitive edge to these incentives. Production workers were subject to the same corporate-level profit-sharing as at GM, with the important distinction that Ford was paying out a substantial yearly bonus under this plan every year in the late 1980s. Another motivating factor was the memory of massive layoffs in the early 1980s, still vivid for many "old-timers" as a sobering break in the successful record of the plant from the time it opened. Both managers and workers attributed the commitment to both quality and productivity improvement in the plant to a strong desire to avoid such crises in the future.

Furthermore, Ford managers and workers alike seemed to perceive quality as central to their success in the mid-to-late 80s. Ford products were outscoring most GM and Chrysler products on quality during this time, although they still lagged Japanese companies. Finally, Ford's extensive reorganization of quality activities around vehicle subsystems meant that quality occupied more managerial attention here than at the GM plant.

Problem Definition

Sources of data. Ford had gone farther than GM in switching from internal to customer-based data as its primary source for identifying quality problems. This includes not only warranty claims reported through dealers but verbatim comments from mailed surveys and phone calls to new owners. The plant also still collects its own internal audit data.

The plant is still adjusting to the increased reliance on customer-based measures. One department superintendent told me that the problems identified during internal plant audits correspond much more closely with their sense of current and persistent quality problems than any of the customer-based measures. But, he said, if they focus on "drying up" the problems listed high on the internal audit, the customer measures improve as well. This suggests that the internal and customer data are ultimately identifying the same problems, but that the plant cannot always see the underlying link. This hidden link is a function of the time lag for the customer data, the use of different language by customers, and the way that dealers assign warranty codes for repairs. But it also reflects the skepticism with which manufacturing people view the quality perceptions of anyone outside the plant.

This skepticism is partially due to a common management reaction to the customer-identified problems— a nearly automatic acceptance of the customer definition of the problem, followed by an equally automatic data-gathering assignment. As one supervisor described this:

A hot item comes up on the NVQ (New Vehicle Quality) audit and management jumps on it, tells us to chart it. One time, we had some cars going to Taiwan and we had a report that the seat belts were rattling. So they told me to chart it ten times a day. But there's no way [at this point in the trim dept.] that you can tell if the belt will rattle, before the whole interior is in. But those are the charts that get started and continued. Problems that don't make the hit parade don't get charted.

Thus employees in this plant are often pulled between the customer-based data the corporation now wants them to rely on and the internal data that still makes more sense to them. As a result, problems are often "officially" defined, in reports of various kinds, in terms of the customer measures but people in the plant discuss them in terms of the internal measures.

Deciding what problems to solve: "Don't touch metal." As at the GM plant, problems are often defined—or left undefined—in terms of cost. In the sealer area, I heard about a persistent problem (since beginning production four years earlier) with the drip rail—the metal rim around the door opening that carries off rain water. A piece of weatherstripping over the outer lip of the drip rail prevents water from leaking into the car, but the lip is quite short, so that weatherstripping often will not seat well. The weatherstripping has been redesigned a few times, but the problem persists. It is made worse by the slightest variation in the thickness of the

sealer placed along the drip rail—too thin and the result is leaks, corrosion, wind noise, but too thick and the weatherstripping will pop off. I asked what it would take to solve the problem, and was told, "a longer lip." I asked if they had proposed this and was told, "No way—you don't touch metal."

This same response reportedly arose on other occasions too. Changes in the design of sheet metal parts is considered too expensive to change until a major model change—potentially eight years for this particular product.[8] The same is true for problems that would require a change of tooling to resolve. So the problem ceased to be defined in terms of the drip rail—instead, it was seen as a sealer or a parts (weatherstripping) problem. The shift here is subtle. "Water leak" is still the ultimate problem but the working definition—poor drip rail design vs. poor quality sealer or weatherstripping— frames the search for solutions powerfully. This may be one reason that water leaks continued to rank highest on the J.D. Power's consumer-derived defect list but was third on Ford's priority list (among these three problems) for in-plant improvement efforts.

At one subsystem meeting, someone remarked to me, "We just gather all the data and let Dearborn (corporate headquarters) decide what to do. Sometimes they decide it's cheaper to let the customer find the problem than for us to fix it." Clearly employees expect a certain percentage of the problems they identify to be ruled out-of-bounds for serious resolution because of cost concerns.

Deciding what problems to solve: The role of design engineers. At the Ford plant, unlike GM, design engineers are stationed in the plant, through the QPRESS program. As a result, manufacturing people report less frustration with design, better communication, and more optimism that design-related problems they find will be addressed. Still, many signs of the functional divide between design and manufacturing remain.

The QPRESS engineers, assigned to the plant for a two-year term, are keenly aware of their pioneer status. While most were glad to have some hands-on experience in the plant, they worried about the effects on their careers. Would this time at an assembly plant really count in their favor at promotion time? How much was their lack of visibility in Dearborn hurting them?

They protect themselves, in part, in the way they define problems encountered in the plant. Their analytic procedures categorized all problems as design-related, vendor-related, or plant-related. One QPRESS engineer told me that he was really only responsible for design-related problems, but that on occasion, to preserve good relations with plant engineers, he would spend some time on a "plant" problem. On the whole, he was critical of the plant for their failure to make more progress with their assigned problems. Yet, as far as I could tell, many of the "plant" problems had some design implications. By confining themselves to problems they felt were appropriate to their expertise, the QPRESS engineers appeared to hinder rather than facilitate process improvement for complex problems that could not be easily categorized.

Problem Analysis/Generation of Solutions

Definition as diagnosis. At first observation, the amount of attention to problem analysis at the Ford plant is very impressive. SPC and Pareto charts, the 8D problem-solving process sheets, and other data-based reports on quality are visible in profusion in meetings at all levels. But over the course of my visit, I began to notice that the data on quality problems were not treated very analytically. To define the problem in a certain category was, at the same time, to diagnose its cause. Based on past experience, most individuals, from production workers to management, seemed to feel that they understood the source of a problem immediately. Attention was therefore focused on choosing a solution.

My analysis of over fifty "8D" forms (the paper documentation for the Deming problem-solving process) proved revealing.[9] The section on problem definition was typically brief and generic, using stock phrases from the various quality reports. The section identifying the "root cause" was typically a more detailed description of the problem, with the "root cause" often implicit but with no evidence of any direct attempt to test these assumptions. The section on "actions taken" varied in length but was typically haphazard, with no indication that solutions were systematically considered, tried out, and then either accepted or rejected for implementation. Unlike the "root cause" section, actions were described with many details, bristling with specification numbers, name of new vendors or products that will be tried out, specialized terms for parts of the car. Occasionally, a general reference to some organizational action, such as an "operator awareness program" appeared as well. The section on verification was often scanty, listing "before" data only, or "before" and "after" data for the original problem—rather than "before" and "after" data for all the attempted solutions.

In general, the 8Ds appear to be used more to *report* on the activity level of the subsystem group, to show that the required processes are being fulfilled, rather than to *diagnose,* systematically, the "root cause" and possible solutions to a problem. When a problem recurs, seldom is it reanalyzed, and rarely are earlier actions reassessed. With past activities already documented and reported, the key is to generate new documentation, to provide proof of continued activity. Thus "continuous improvement" becomes less a process of incremental problem resolution than a process of energetic implementation of intuitively-selected solutions. Indeed, the profusion of data reports and charts, as a symbol for problem-solving activity, was a clear impediment to problem analysis, both because of the time spent generating them and because the sheer quantity tended to obscure rather than illuminate.

Accounting for long-term quality vs. short-term cost. A central, unresolved tension within the Ford system was apparent, between quality and cost. In my initial meeting, the comptroller said, "We can't continue to be all things to all people. We may need to spend more to keep improving our quality record." At first, I thought his comment reflected the traditional view of a tradeoff between cost and quality. But I came to understand his remark in another way—that the plant needs to be free to spend more money in some areas to make quality improvements that will, over time, save money in other areas. In other words, short-term cost concerns often constrain problem-solving activities that can lead, through defect reduction, to long-term quality *and* cost benefits.

I saw several examples during my visit. On the first day, I accompanied the electrical subsystem coordinator while he checked out a problem with wire harnesses in the instrument panel subassembly area. A supplier representative assigned to the plant joined us. The operator showed us the problem. At one location on the wire harness, a plastic block where several wires connect was near a plastic locator pin, used to situate the wire harness in the instrument panel. The block and locator pin were supposed to be taped at a 180 degree angle to one another but instead were taped incorrectly, in parallel, directly adjacent to each other. The operator therefore had to break the tape in order to make the connection and insert the locator pin. Without the tape, the chance of broken wires or loose and rattling connectors increases, so, as a makeshift remedy, the operator was fastening the wires down with a "chicken strap" (a thin plastic strip designed to lock as it is tightened) to hold the wires together. This was virtually impossible to do in the required cycle time.

Much of what ensued was impressive. The operator gave up his lunch hour to help explain the problem. The electrical coordinator carefully checked the inventory to determine the incidence of the problem; a whole pallet was incorrectly taped. The supplier representative, clearly accepted by plant personnel as part of the "team," busily researched the problem that day and reported his findings at the electrical subsystem meeting the next day. A speedy resolution seemed imminent.

But I learned later in the week that the supplier had discovered nothing in the Ford specifications for the part about how the wires should be taped and that, according to the contract, the cost of remedying the problem fell to Ford. A decision was made, therefore, that the specification would be adjusted but that until then, the

rest of the defective parts would be used, since it would cost too much to replace or rework them. So the problem did get fixed, but with Ford deciding that the loss of production time and the risk of loose wires in the instrument panel (both difficult to quantify) were easier to bear than the known cost of replacing the defective parts.

Here the effort to assign cost accountability took precedence over finding a way to minimize the quality impact of the problem. The accounting system was unable to balance the (measured) cost of replacing or reworking the faulty parts with the (unmeasured) cost of inspection, repair, and, potentially, a dissatisfied customer. These latter costs may be impossible to quantify. Nevertheless, decisions such as these send a powerful message to employees that quality is important but only as long as no additional costs are incurred.

Honda Plant

The Honda plant was still increasing its production volume (and thus its employment), and building only a single product. Like the other Japanese "transplants" in North America, it transferred practically all of the elements of the lean production system used by its sister plants in Japan: minimal repair area and in-process inventories, work teams and problem-solving groups, job rotation, extensive training, minimal status barriers, and bonus pay based on plant performance. The workforce was mostly young, single men from the surrounding agricultural area with no previous manufacturing experience.

Managers told me that most workers arrived with utopian notions of what it would be like to work in a Japanese plant and went through a difficult adjustment process in the first six months. At the time of my visit, the level of production at the plant had recently risen without an increase in the workforce, which reconfigured all jobs and increased the work pace, and I saw signs of some tension between workers and managers as this change was being implemented. On the whole, however, I found the workforce quite enthusiastic about Honda as a company, proud of the success of its products, and quite committed to Honda's quality philosophy. Indeed, I heard complaints from workers that managers did not consistently follow Honda's quality principles—and this misalignment in expectations about quality standards was the source of growing pains for the plant.

Of the three problem categories, paint defects dominated plant attention, with less concern about electrical defects. Water leaks had been a major quality focus in the preceding year but were felt to be under control at the time of my visit. This varies from the J. D. Power data, where paint defects are better than the Japanese average but electrical defects are worse.[10]

Quality System

Structure and composition. Most quality responsibilities are integrated into production jobs, with groups of coordinators responsible as liaisons for different aspects of quality, identified as Line Quality (LQ), Parts Quality (PQ), Vehicle Quality (VQ), and Quality Engineering (QE). LQ coordinators are assigned on the basis of the "zones" of 4-6 teams that make up departments. When problems are identified by team members, the team leader notifies the LQ coordinator, who then gathers information about the problem. If it is a parts problem, s/he contacts the PQ coordinator. VQ coordinators work in the final repair area, and relay information about problems back to the LQ coordinators, although LQ may also alert VQ about a problem that will show up post-process. QE is the group responsible for research on warranty claims, handling quality problems between the plant and the customer, quality testing, and long-term quality planning. Small group activities related to quality are structured in three different ways, depending on the nature of the problem. A one-time or infrequent occurrence that arises from sources within a single department is typically handled by production workers and team leaders, in conjunction with LQ and PQ coordinators. A more complex or more frequent problem in one single work area may be assigned to a New Honda (NH) Circle—an off-line, after-shift quality circle group. A problem that po-

tentially arises from sources in multiple departments can become a "project." A project requires a cross-departmental meeting—usually only one—typically organized by an LQ coordinator. A more serious or difficult-to-diagnose problem that spans departments may give rise to a "special project." These are assigned a leader and one or more "staff" members pulled off their regular jobs, and are time-limited—as soon as the project team presents an "action plan" to senior management, it disbands.

Motivation/incentives. Honda uses various means to motivate its employees to be concerned about quality. Plant-wide bonuses administered semi-annually to all employees are based in part on the degree to which quality goals for the model year were being achieved. These bonuses, calculated as a percentage of base pay, do not differentiate among individual employees, except for a portion that is tied to attendance. Pay for production workers also increased as a function of length of employment but was not linked to individual performance. This Americanized "seniority pay" provided incentives for associates (all employees at Honda are called "associates," regardless of position) to work at the plant long-term so that returns on company investments in training and quality awareness could bear fruit. More individual incentives were supplied through programs known collectively as REACH (Recognizing the Efforts of Associates Contributing at Honda).[11]

Problem Definition

Sources of data. Like Ford, Honda uses a mixture of customer-based and internal measures of quality. Warranty information isn't coded at the dealers. Rather, each warranty claim contains a page of written information about the problem and its repair that are further researched by QE. The internal quality system is relatively simple. The Honda sales organization that "purchases" vehicles from the plant carries out unannounced audits to check "fit and finish"; monthly at the beginning of each new model production and then every other month.

During daily production, VQ coordinators keep track of problems by listing them on a flipchart near their final inspection area. All day long, a steady stream of LQ and PQ coordinators, QE engineers, managers and team leaders come by to find out what is listed. Each department has one central area where quality, production, and cost information is tracked over time. Otherwise, quality charts are much less visible than at the Ford plant, although a higher percentage of charts are current and in use than at Ford.

"See it": Actual part, actual situation. Honda emphasizes having people actually see quality defects directly. LQ, PQ, and VQ coordinators, team leaders, and, at times, production workers will often go to another part of the plant to see a car with a defect. Persistent quality problems that are under investigation by QE are documented with sketches and photos as well as testing data. For particularly puzzling problems, the quality coordinators are sent to visit dealers to examine them first-hand. Honda has a saying for this, the plant manager told me: "actual part, actual situation." The philosophy is that when a person *sees* a quality problem, s/he is more likely to analyze it systemically, to communicate the problem more accurately to others in his/her team or work area, and to be motivated to find a preventive remedy.

Deciding what problems to solve: Too much quality? I heard many stories about Honda's willingness to make strenuous efforts to prevent defects from reaching the consumer. Interwoven in the corporate culture and often repeated, these stories helped reinforce the powerful idea that for Honda, quality and responsiveness to customer needs are the top priority. But there were costs associated with this strong culture around quality.

According to one American engineer, Japanese managers had a clear view about priorities for quality problems. "They [Japanese managers] take the view that we should find and fix all major quality problems first, and then fix as many of the minor problems as time permits," he said, noting that "major" and "minor" are defined in relation to how customers will react. In contrast, he said, "the Americans, once they buy

in, tend to become zealots." Showing me a barely visible spot of dirt under the paint on the roof, he said, "A Japanese manager would let this go—but most American workers wouldn't." As a result, this plant was known as the "pickiest" Honda plant, regularly reporting the highest defect rates in the company. At the time of my visit, only 19% of vehicles were passed "first-time through" all departments without needing some kind of repair—compared with 40-50% at other Honda plants. As one worker told me, "We build the best quality cars in the world, but it's only because we take so long on them."

This state of affairs was viewed with some concern by plant managers.[12] Honda had the goal of training its associates over time to distinguish between defects that were "customer acceptable" and those that were not. Indeed, at one point during my stay, I saw the plant manager marching a group of young quality coordinators out to the parking lot to re-examine a set of vehicles that they had pulled aside for minor defects that he believed were "customer acceptable." Yet managers feared that the effort to teach associates to calibrate precise levels of customer acceptability raised the risk of undermining their motivation and commitment to quality.

Deciding what problems to solve: Cost and consistency concerns. As at GM and Ford, there were clear cases at Honda in which cost concerns affected the choice of what problems to solve. For example, a VQ coordinator told me about water leak problems that could result from air bubbles getting into the white sealer used for body panel seams when changing from one sealer drum to another. A special project team had examined putting in a larger storage tank for sealer with a permanent piping system, so the supply could be replenished by adding sealer to the tank without disconnecting the sealer hoses. But their conclusion was that the one-time investment for this change would be too costly and that, instead, sealer associates would be urged to watch carefully for bubbles with each sealer drum change. Management seemed to believe that the remedy of associate attentiveness would be effective, if less fool-proof that the more capital-intensive solution.

Coordination with the plant in Japan making the same product also affected Honda's decisions about which problems to solve. For the new 1989 model, the weatherstripping for the quarter window (known as the quarter seal) was 10 mm too long, posing occasional installation problems. But, according to the assembly department manager, "we couldn't get the parts change justified through Japan." When the 1989 model was first introduced, with a relatively slow line speed, associates were generally able to complete the installation successfully. With the recent line speed increase, noted the department manager, "it's a lot harder to get the seals on—if there's a metal burr around the opening, the guys have to force the seal on, even hit it with a hammer."

But the sister plant in Japan was not having any problems with the quarter seal, so Honda's design engineers were skeptical about the diagnosis of a too-long seal, believing the problem might have some other source more directly under the control of the American plant. These engineers were unwilling to change the parts specification for all plants, or to allow a different parts specification at each of the two plants. The American managers and engineers voiced some frustration about this pattern, saying that Honda Japan was unsympathetic to their arguments that certain unique conditions at their plants (e.g., larger American hands, lots of trainees due to rapid growth) required unique solutions. Honda Japan was insisting on a consistency across plants, they felt, that was unrealistic and which deprived them of the independent right to solve quality problems as they saw fit.

Assigning responsibility, not blame. Quality problems are assigned to different departments, but with an important difference from the GM and Ford plants. One senior American manager told me, "The accounting system is deliberately designed to minimize the time spent figuring out who's to blame." Some Honda plants, he said, have a miscellaneous category for problems (such as water leaks) that can't easily be pinned to a specific department. But at this plant, the management team decided to assign

defects to *some* department (e.g., all body "deforms" assigned to the body shop, all paint chips to paint, and all water leaks to assembly) in the interests of calling attention to problems. The costs for these repairs, however, are covered from a plant-wide fund rather than charged to individual departments. As this same manager explained:

> The reason to want to fix the problem is so we don't lose a customer—not so costs won't accumulate. It doesn't really matter how it gets paid for. . . . If I find a problem and then piss off Tom by not fixing it or trying to blame him for it, then I have two problems. Honda's philosophy is that a problem with our product is a problem for the whole company, not for an individual or department.

According to one department head, this system disturbs some Americans, who feel there is not enough accountability in this system. "It doesn't help the rapport between departments," he said. Despite the absence of any accounting penalty for a high defect rate, some feel it would be more fair for defects to be attributed to the department that caused them. So far, Honda has resisted taking this approach.

Problem Analysis/Generation of Solutions

Breaking down status barriers: "Everyone builds cars." Honda attempts to encourage problem-solving across organizational boundaries by breaking down status barriers between organizational groups. Physically, the administrative and management offices have a completely open layout—rows of desks facing each other, without partitions or other physical dividers. All employees wear the same white overalls and often a Honda cap. There are no separate offices for managers, even the plant manager. The offices are generally empty; one manager called his desk "nothing but a giant inbasket." Most meetings take place in the cafeteria.

Managers and engineers also carry out a regular daily stint of work on the assembly line—30-60 minutes a day, four days a week, a reflection of the plant's philosophy that "everyone builds cars." I accompanied one QE engineer, who spent 45 minutes filling in for an absent operator on the line where the engine is readied for installation. He looked over the Operation Standard for the job, asked a few questions of the adjacent worker, and began. The job involved inserting and tightening some bolts, slipping a metal sleeve over some locator pins, and doing "marker checks"—checking a previous operation and marking "no defect" parts with an orange, green, or yellow marker. He said he liked the chance for some "hands-on" work. "I feel like I'm close to the action."

Temporary and permanent countermeasures. A key role for LQs was overseeing problem analysis and coming up with planned remedies—called "countermeasures" at Honda. The head LQ coordinator, Tom, in the Assembly Department told me how one problem—a fuel line pipe with a deformity in it—had been handled earlier that week. A production worker in the assembly department spotted the problem and contacted the team leader, who found the LQ coordinator for that zone. The LQ wrote down the Vehicle Identification Number (VIN) of the vehicle, inspected the problem first-hand, decided that the defect probably came from the supplier of the pipe, and called the PQ coordinator. The PQ was also shown the problem directly before calling the vendor to find out how many bad parts were in inventory. The LQ quickly examined the parts beside the line to determine how many were defective and discussed temporary "countermeasures" with the assembled group. In this case, the decision was to have the LQ, team leader, and one operator do "marker checks" on all OK parts.

If the problem comes from an upstream process rather than from a part, the LQs must decide whether the situation warrants bringing in someone from the upstream department to examine it first-hand. Tom gave the example of a gas tank coming to the assembly department from the weld shop with a serious deform. "Since I hadn't seen it before, I went to get the assistant manager and two associates from weld to come and see it. They were able to analyze the problem, which saved us from doing it. Also, they got the feedback at the same time."

The LQs may request multiple countermeasures to deal with a problem. For one water leak problem involving an unsealed gap in the inner wheel arch, Tom asked the paint LQ to do a temporary 100% inspection of the seal for that gap and the weld LQ to check the specifications of the robot applying welds in that area. LQs can face "a fair amount of animosity" in these situations, according to Tom:

> It's very sensitive. We don't want to tell them how to do their job or be too opinionated. We may not understand why they're having a problem. You can't assume you know the reason. If you don't have good communication skills, you don't last too long in these jobs.

The "five whys." Finding a permanent countermeasure involves the careful, iterative examination of possible sources and remedies of the problem—a process known as the "five whys." The answer to the first "why" is often based on the easily observable or familiar antecedents to its occurrence. An attempted solution based on this relatively automatic diagnosis is unlikely to be successful for long, because there are other "root" causes that are only uncovered with more "whys."

I learned about one case where the brakes in a car didn't work well during testing—a safety problem, ranked as the most serious of all quality problems. The first "why" revealed that a metal pin had fallen into a brake subassembly and was causing a jam. The second "why" led to an examination of the work stations where the subassembly was attached, to no avail. The next set of "whys" led to the supplier, and to material handling between the supplier and the plant.

Finally, a Japanese engineer, convinced that the pin looked familiar, successfully tracked it to an upstream machine, unrelated to the brake system. The pin had been replaced during routine maintenance, hadn't been thrown out, had fallen into the engine compartment, and eventually into the brake subassembly. The documentation of this problem-solving process, covering several pages, was augmented by a plastic envelope containing the mangled pin.

Simple experiments to test potential solutions for quality problems could be seen when walking around the plant. The plant was, at the time of my visit, struggling with one water leak problem brought about by a design change that eliminated the use of sealer around one part of the door. The fixture holding the front seat belt was moved forward, in this new design, directly onto the door post. Sealer on the door post was eliminated to guard against getting any on the seat belt, and replaced by a self-adhesive tape that wasn't sticking well. The LQ coordinator showed me an experiment involving the heating of this tape under a heat lamp to soften the adhesive before application. An SPC chart nearby showed the careful tracking of "before" and "after" data.

Many of the quality coordinators expressed the importance of having data to back up your proposed countermeasures. According to Philip, a VQ coordinator:

> When you come up with a countermeasure, anybody can challenge it. A bullshit countermeasure isn't worth a damn. You've got to have the data to show it is effective.

Spontaneous meetings, and "Y-gaya." When a problem is major, with no obvious countermeasure, the LQ can decide to designate it as a "project" and get VQ involved. The VQ typically calls an immediate cross-departmental meeting, paging whichever VQ, LQ, PQ, and QE coordinators s/he feels is appropriate; managers sometimes attend as well. "Meetings can get big," said one VQ, "but we find that they're a good way to let everyone know what's going on." Most meetings I saw were held in the audit area or in the break areas for teams near the line; some meetings are held right at the site of the problem. Honda has a term for these "spontaneous" meetings—"y-gaya," which translates as "act forthrightly," or as one American told me, "just do it." A key element of a "y-gaya" meeting is that anyone with relevant knowledge of a problem is included, regardless of rank. The norm for such meetings is that those closer to the problem speak first. "But the managers forget that sometimes," said one associate who had recently attended such a meeting. The degree to which such meetings actually achieve the kind of open communication across levels that facilitates problem-solving is heavily dependent on the behavior modeled by the senior managers and coordinators in the group.

Operations standards and process improvement: The tension between standardization and change. An approved countermeasure, to move from being temporary to being permanent, must be written into the operations standards for the relevant jobs. These standards are a key feature of Honda's approach to quality, both in insuring uniformity of process and in the problem-solving process. Workers are expected to adhere to these standards strictly, both within a team while rotating across jobs, and across shifts. Concerned about variation across shifts, the department managers had begun to require meetings of the LQ coordinators on each shift during the brief time they overlapped in the afternoon. I heard several complaints about the "rigidity" of this approach from American managers and associates. To them, it was natural for workers on different shifts to find their own favorite way of doing a job.

But from the company's perspective, each individual's "favorite way" introduces variation into the production process that can potentially cause defects. The tension between encouraging workers to find quality problems and suggest process improvements while also requiring that they adhere strictly to operations standards has been noted in studies of the Toyota Production System (e.g., Adler 1992, 1993). Managers and engineers at Honda often differentiated themselves from Toyota on this issue. One VQ coordinator, reacting to my comment about the high number of vehicles in repair one day, said, "we're not as reliable as Toyota, and we don't pin everything down as much, but that's because we are always doing new things." He felt that frequent process changes were an important component of Honda's flexibility and quality improvement, but that more repair was inevitable in that situation.

Yet for Japanese managers at the plant, the fact that process changes were frequent was all the more reason to specify tasks carefully after each change and then follow operations stan-

TABLE 8.2 Plant Case Studies—Contrast and Consistency Comparisons

Theme	GM	Ford	Honda
Quality system			
Structure	By department	By subsystem	By problem
Composition	Stable membership	Core members plus	As needed for problem
	No design engineers	Design engineers	Design engineers
Incentives	For managers only; no payout for workers from profit sharing	For managers; plus large payouts for workers from profit sharing	Plant-level performance bonuses for both managers and workers
Problem definition			
Sources of data	Internal	Internal and customer	Customer and internal
Categorization of problems	Plant vs. corporate	Plant vs. Design vs. vendor	Fuzzy, problem-centered
Problem framing	"Avoid corporate"	"Don't touch metal"	"See it"
Lens used	Cost	Cost/quality	Quality/cost
Problem analysis/generation of solutions			
Purpose	Accountability	Documentation	Diagnosis
Process	"Who shot John?"	Definition as diagnosis	Root cause
Scope of search	First-level cause	First-level cause	"Five whys"
Experiments	No systematic data	"After" data	"Before" and "after" data

dards precisely. Thus the mix of principles that govern Honda's quality efforts—insure that no defect gets to the customer and follow operations standards precisely, but introduce frequent design changes and continually fine-tune the production process—fits the new quality paradigm but is also quite difficult to implement and vulnerable to disruption. Quality standards can be set too high, incurring unnecessary costs. On the other hand, too much process change with insufficient attention to revising (and following) operations standards can introduce variability that can boost defect levels. As motivated associates set out to solve complex problems, animosities can emerge between departments if communication is not handled carefully. Yet if associates decide that it isn't worth the trouble to push for high levels of quality, the entire quality system can deteriorate. Given the down-side risks of slippage in the commitment to quality if employees perceive mixed messages from management, perhaps it is no surprise that the Honda plant seemed to err on the side of "too much quality."

Contrasts and Consistency in Problem Solving

The case studies reveal both similarities and differences in shop-floor problem solving for process quality improvement at these three plants. I have analyzed the case study data by looking for evidence of consistency within each case across stages of the problem-solving process and by contrasting pairs of cases for various themes (Eisenhardt 1989). (Table 8.2 summarizes this analysis.) In this section, I draw generalizable insights from the case material and demonstrate how the cases support certain propositions and prescriptions from the organizational behavior and quality improvement literature that are not often tested empirically.

Quality System—Structure-Composition and Incentives

The case studies reveal that different structural arrangements can be effective at promoting the boundary-spanning communication needed for problem solving. The GM quality system was least effective because it was almost entirely organized by department. The one cross-cutting group, at the senior management level, addressed the most obvious cross-functional problems but ultimately ended up arbitrating between the competing claims of responsibility from the departments. This suggests that cross-functional integration must occur at both lower and upper organizational levels.

The Ford and Honda approaches each have strengths and weaknesses. The Ford matrix structure of "subsystem" task forces and the Honda structure of "problem-centered" task forces both draw their members from "vertical" and "horizontal" slices of the organization. Both promote norms of allowing those with the expertise on a problem to speak. Both have "resident engineers" from the product design function available to participate in meetings and work on problems.

These two plants differ in the degree of permanence of their problem-solving groups and in the decision rules for group composition. The Ford approach gives the group a continuing focus (the subsystem) and a stable membership. The full range of problems related to a given subsystem is taken on, with problems that span subsystems handled on an ad-hoc basis. Core members are intended to remain the same over time, with guests invited for their expertise on a particular problem. This approach may be ideal for amassing both expertise and cumulative knowledge about subsystem problems over time. The repeated interaction across functional groups and hierarchical levels provides ample foundation for the development of a common language.

In contrast, the Honda approach establishes "spontaneous" groups that meet only until a problem is resolved, with members chosen for their relevance to that problem—potentially a quicker way to amass the right combination of resources for a given problem that the Ford approach. This may also avoid the stultifying group dynamics that can often accompany long-lasting committees with fixed membership. However, such groups will not have any "memory" about the incidence of past problems or the value of previous remedies. Furthermore, the fluid membership and short time duration of

these groups may only be possible in an organization with a strong culture and clear norms for communication processes (e.g., "those closest to the problem speak first"). Even with such a culture, it may take longer to develop a "common language" than in Ford's approach, since any one individual has a relatively brief exposure to other members of a given problem-solving group.

It is worth noting the multiplicity of quality-related structures at these plants (e.g., organized by team, department, cross-department, subsystem, problem focus). This multiplicity seems deliberately chosen, despite the potential for redundancy, because of its benefits for quality. Clearly not all of these structures are equally effective, and there will be variation in the efficacy of any given activity. But the redundancy may help create a climate of attentiveness to quality problems, establish the conditions for "opportunity framing" (discussed further below), and assure that no problems fall through the cracks.

While all three plants provide managers with incentives to improve quality, they differ substantially in the incentives for production workers, supervisors, and other lower-level staff and clerical employees. GM's profit-sharing plan was paying nothing to workers while corporate bonus plans continued to reward executives heavily. Ford's similar profit sharing plan had made large payouts (from $2500 to $7500) to workers, who tended to perceive the bonus as linked to quality improvement as much as (or more than) productivity. Honda had the most extensive set of incentive programs, applied to all employees and explicitly encouraging problem-solving. In contrast, the GM and Ford profit-sharing plans did not explicitly reward plant-level problem-solving, with bonuses that were tenuously linked (if at all) to plant performance in a given year.

Problem Definition/ Analysis—Sources of Data

The case studies suggest that both customer data and internal data, as well as the direct observation of defects where they occur, can provide valuable clues for problem-solving. The value of customer-based data is a function of how effectively it brings market-based information to bear on internal problem-solving processes—what Cole, Bacdayan, and White (1993) call the "market-in" principle—"bringing customer needs into every possible part of the organization, thereby heightening uncertainty." Cole (1990) also emphasizes the value of quality as a superordinate goal able to unite groups typically in conflict—different departments, different functions, or management and labor. Customer-based data help communicate the overarching nature of the quality goal, and are arguably more powerful when they reach plant problem-solvers directly (e.g., worker visits to dealers at GM and Honda; verbatim comments on warranty reports at Ford and Honda).

In contrast, the value of internal data should be a function of the proximity they allow between processes of problem definition and problem analysis. Here the Honda case points to the value of direct physical observation of a problem situation. This is similar to Tyre and von Hippel's work (1993) on the importance of the physical setting in prompting adaptive learning; and Leonard-Barton's (1991) finding that the examination of a physical prototype during design facilitates cross-functional communication and the development of a common language. Dialogue about problems located at the "actual place, actual situation" may both yield a common language and common understanding of what standards should be applied to deciding what will or won't be defined as a problem—something that proved elusive at the GM plant, despite the attention to problem terminology.

While customer data and internal data can differ, combining both kinds of data may result in better problem-solving outcomes than when relying solely on one data source. The two sources of data reveal cognitive differences between the customer perspective and the plant perspective, and the effort to make sense of these difference can yield insights to guide problem definition and analysis. In each of the cases, there are examples of different sources of customer data being combined—written de-

scriptions by customers of warranty problems (Ford and Honda); visits to dealers to talk with customers or see problems (GM and Honda); calls to new buyers (GM)—that offer more richness of information (Daft and Lengel 1986) and increase the probability of successfully bridging the cognitive gap between the customer and plant perspectives.

Richness of information may also be related to the speed of problem resolution. The Honda approach of "see the actual part in the actual situation" is clearly more costly in employee time than a written defect report. Yet if it allows the early elimination of defects, the preventive benefits may outweigh the costs. While time-based measures of problem resolution were not explicitly gathered for this study, my observations suggest that Honda developed both temporary and permanent countermeasures fastest, followed by Ford and then GM. Where "market-in" principles boost uncertainty, the effectiveness of problem solving may depend in part on its speed, consistent with Bourgeois and Eisenhardt's findings (1988) about high-velocity decision making.

Problem Definition: The Categorization of Problems

Recall that the problems investigated here were chosen because they commonly have multiple sources. This makes them particularly difficult to categorize—often important both for defining problems and establishing priorities for problem solving. Yet the quality system at the GM and Ford plants emphasized the strict categorization of problems either by department (GM) or as "design, vendor, or plant" (Ford). One consequence, at Ford, was that the resident QPRESS engineers felt they should investigate only "design" problems and leave "plant" problems to plant engineers, even though many problems involved both design and manufacturing. In contrast, Honda tried to avoid the strict classification of problems in various ways: the simple list of daily problems in the final repair area, the emphasis on seeing a problem *in situ* rather than sending it back to its supposed source, problem-centered temporary task forces composed of anyone with relevant expertise, and an accounting system that did not attempt to determine which department should be assigned the costs of a problem. This suggests the value of putting problems into "fuzzy" categories, to use a term drawn from the psychology literature on categorization.

The strict classification of complex problems into one category and not another exemplifies the "classical" view of categorization (Gardner 1987)—categories have defining or critical attributes that determine what items are members and what items are not; members possess these attributes, nonmembers do not, and there is no overlap between them (Smith and Medin 1981). In opposition to this view, Rosch and Lloyd (1978) have argued that the cognitive structure of categories is based not on "necessary and sufficient" criteria but rather on "prototypes"—objects that share the greatest number of attributes with other category members. Prototypes are mental representations that contain the most information about a category, are most easily learned, and are most quickly given as examples of a category. Other category members are located at varying distances from the prototype; their degree of similarity (or dissimilarity) to the prototype represents the degree to which they are members of the category. Thus categories and their boundaries are "fuzzy" rather than sharp. Many objects belong to more than one category, but are "better" members of the category in which they share the most attributes with the prototype.

The analogy to problem-solving is as follows. People can provide prototypical examples of certain problem categories (e.g., design or vendor, paint or electrical). When confronted with an actual problem, they compare its characteristics with these "prototypes" to decide how to classify it. Problems that resemble prototypes closely are easy to categorize, but other may be identified as "somewhere in between"—e.g., partly design and partly manufacturing, or partly electrical and partly water leak. This ambiguity about category is valuable information for finding the "root cause" of a problem. If quality systems force problems into one category or another, and problem-solving proceeds differently as a result, the benefits of rich, ambiguous data will be lost and the search for solutions may be misdirected. "Fuzzy" categories can help to preserve rich data about problems as they are communicated from one organizational member or group to another.

Problem Definition: Framing Problems as Opportunities

Problem analysis and solution generation, at both individual and organizational levels, are strongly affected, during problem definition, by whether problems are framed negatively, as liabilities or threats, or positively, as opportunities. For individuals, Dutton (1993) claims that an "opportunity frame" serves to give issues a "positive gloss" and to suppress certain undesirable threat effects. "Issues that are wrapped in opportunity frames are almost irresistible because of the positive 'charge' or emotion and sense of control that such issues evoke" (Dutton 1993, p. 200). This positive emotion is associated with more creativity, speedier decision-making, and a search for more integrative solutions to negotiations tasks (Isen and Means 1983).

At the same time, at the organizational level, Jackson and Dutton (1988) found that individuals have a hard time seeing organizational events as "opportunities" unless they can rule out any sense of threat—since threat is strongly associated with reduced search for external information and an increased likelihood of resorting to dominant, well-learned responses that may not be appropriate to the situation (Staw, Sandelands, and Dutton 1981). When threat can be ruled out, framing issues as opportunities can signal and legitimize ideas of proactiveness and innovation. "Opportunities" create what Eisenberg calls "strategic ambiguity"—allowing for "multiple interpretations while at the same time promoting unity" (1984, p. 231). Opportunity framing also looks forward rather than backwards, "refocusing collective effort from past and present towards the future" (Dutton 1993, p. 203). However, the organizational context must both motivate individuals to frame issues as opportunities and convince them that it is feasible or reasonable to do so.

Issues must be perceived as controllable, positive, and with potential gains.

There is ample evidence of both negative and positive framing in the three cases. Negative framing occurs when individuals or departments believe that they will be penalized if they are associated with a problem. The accounting system at GM, with its preoccupation with "Who shot John?" is a good example. The difficulty in getting a speedy and effective response from product designers in Detroit would also prevent GM plant personnel from believing that problems are "controllable" with high potential for "positive gain." Under these circumstances, the prospects of opportunity framing are low.

At Ford, the prospects are considerably higher. The cross-cutting subsystem structure, the creation of new lower-level liaison roles (ZIPs), the repeated use of quality as a superordinate goal capable of mustering broad support across organizational boundaries should all support the view of problems as opportunities. However, as at GM, there are mixed messages about the gains from finding problems, particularly those where quality remedies have short-term cost implications. The message from managers at one subsystem meeting—try new things but try not to make mistakes—is unlikely to suppress the sense of threat if failures do occur.

Honda clearly works hard to create opportunity frames for problem-solving, both in its philosophy—"a problem with our product is a problem for the whole company, not for an individual or department"—and its systems—"the accounting system is deliberately designed to minimize the time spent figuring out who's to blame." Several people at the plant told me their paraphrase of a famous saying of Soichiro Honda, the company founder: "It's OK to fail 99 times as long as you succeed on the 100th time." The importance given to quality legitimizes the actions of low-level LQs who "drag managers" to their department to see a problem. Yet clearly this is not an easy process. Being confronted with a problem still can be an emotionally-charged event, particularly if accompanied by a quick categorization or smug diagnosis of cause.

Sitkin (1992) points out the difficulty, and the value, of changing the way an organization views failure. While successes have the benefit of positive reinforcement, the absence of failure (or the suppression of evidence of failure) can weaken organizational resilience when facing uncertainty and resource constraints and can increase managerial overconfidence. Large failures can be devastating, but "small failures" can be an important way to learn, because the experience of failure prompts experimentation. As expressed by Lounamaa and March, "performance improvements are confounded but performance decrements contain information" (1989, p. 116). The benefits of "small failures," according to Sitkin, include: closer attention to potential problems, ease of recognition and interpretation of problems, the stimulus of search processes, greater tolerance for vulnerability, and more efficient problem-solving through practice. "Intelligent failures" can be facilitated when the organization's culture legitimizes "learning through failure" and when management emphasizes "failure management systems" rather than individual failure.

The public presentations made by NH Circle or "special project" group members at Honda serve an important function in legitimizing "intelligent failure" by providing a template for how "learning through failure" occurs. Robert Cole makes a similar observation based on recent field research in Japan:

> Typically, these problem-solving presentations include a history of the problem-solving activity, including a discussion of the blind alleys and failure modes that were pursued. Thus, they document a process by which failure and errors are overcome to produce success. In so doing, we see that errors and failures are treated as positive learning experiences. Top management officials, who often attend such sessions, associate themselves with an event in which learning from failure is a key theme (Cole 1992a, p. 12).

This is a good example of what Sitkin calls a "failure promotion system at the organizational level." Organizational practices that frame problems as opportunities help counteract certain natural psychological and information-processing tendencies in human beings, increasing the effectiveness of process quality improvement.

Problem Definition, Problem Analysis, Solution Generation: Quality Lens vs. Cost Lens

In all three cases, the problem-solving process was heavily affected by whether quality or cost is used as the "lens" during the definition and analysis of problems and potential solutions. For example, "customer acceptability" is a criterion used by Honda to establish which defects should be addressed first (or at all). This quality lens generates a decision rule that defects which are unacceptable to customers should always be addressed. To use Juran's terminology (1988), the "external costs of poor quality" are by definition too high if customers are unhappy, and thus from a cost-benefit perspective, it will always be worthwhile to incur some prevention costs. Similarly, minor defects that *are* acceptable to customers—more precisely, not unacceptable (or not noticed)—should not be addressed even if the cost of remedy is low. In this situation, the "costs of failure" are negligible and may exceed the "cost of prevention."

When problems and solutions are evaluated first with a cost lens, decision makers may decide, based on short-term calculations, that the "cost of prevention" is greater than the "cost of failure." Yet when managers think about quality and cost in a "no tradeoff" way—another kind of "opportunity framing"—they are more likely to accept the short-term cost of defect prevention activities that will improve both quality and productivity in the long term (Cole 1992b).

The case studies support this hypothesis in several ways. At GM, managers worried about the amount of time and energy directed towards finding out "who shot John." Pinning down cost responsibility interfered with using data about problems for careful "root cause" analysis and problem elimination. At Ford, cost concerns often justified the deferral or avoidance of actions that could reduce defects, in what employees often saw as a contradiction of the company's overall commitment on quality. Honda worked to develop an organizational culture that emphasized "quality first" while adopting an accounting system that deemphasized departmental preoccupation with the "cost of failure." Yet this did not mean that all quality defects were addressed immediately with no concerns for the cost of prevention. Cost was used not as a basis for deciding whether or not to fix a "customer unacceptable" defect but rather to determine the least costly remedy.

Problem Analysis/Generation of Solutions: The Standardization-Experimentation Cycle

Tyre (1989) and Tyre and Orlikowski (1994) have usefully challenged the notion of "continuous improvement" as an uninterrupted process of constant change. They note that most adaptive learning in the face of technological change follows a "punctuated equilibrium" model—rapid learning immediately after the change is made, followed by a longer period of routinization during which minimal (or no) changes are made. They cite ample literature, and their own findings, to suggest that this is a normal pattern of human and organizational behavior.

My observations confirm that adaptive learning alternates between periods of experimentation with process improvement and periods of relative stasis—if only because problem-solving activity is typically triggered by the appearance of a problem and stopped when a solution is found. However, these case studies also suggest the benefits for process quality improvement of organizational mechanisms that are "disequilibrating" (i.e., which limit the period of stasis by jarring individuals out of their routines and prompting them to return to experimentation). Imai (1986), writing about "kaizen" (the Japanese term for continuous improvement), emphasizes the crucial role of standardization in process improvement, in which extremely detailed and careful specification of the process is undertaken, far beyond what is necessary to keep the process running routinely. This specification provides a crucial base line of data against which all future improvement efforts will be evaluated. It also codifies whatever gains have been made since prior improvement efforts.

Whereas routinization implies process stability until some unforeseen event disturbs existing routines, standardization has a different meaning in a "problems as opportunities" culture. Completion of the specification process signals that the search for problems or possible performance enhancements can (and should) begin again. The idea that standardization should be the beginning rather than the end of the learning process is analogous to the use of the term "commencement" to mark the graduation of students from high school or college. Similar to opportunity framing, it orients the individual and the organization towards the future rather than the past, and strives to overcome the inertia that can accompany the end of a long and difficult passage by providing a reason to look ahead to the next challenge.

Particularly relevant here is the prevalence of experimentation in the case studies and the use of "before" and "after" data. Experimentation at the GM plant was limited and the use of data haphazard. As noted previously, data collection was often used for accountability and not for problem analysis or the generation of solutions. At the Ford plant, the emphasis on problem analysis to report that action was being taken meant that data was typically gathered after some remedy was tried but not before. Thus there was often no base line to evaluate whether the remedy in question was effective or to compare the merits of different remedies. At Honda, documentation of process improvement efforts always included "before" and "after" data, experimentation with different solutions was common, and complete standardization of the process was required before further improvements could be pursued.

Even when standardization is taken as a signal to begin new process improvement efforts, it does not mean that the same problem, job specification, or machine is addressed time after time. "Standardization as the beginning and not the end" should be understood as a goal that drives the constant *activity* of process improvement in some part of the plant's operations. Alternating cycles of experimentation and stasis are expected for any one process or step or piece of equipment. But across the plant, efforts are made to avoid any period of stasis through policies that promote constant search for the next opportunity for process improvement.

Conclusion

Problem-solving benefits from rich data that capture multiple perspectives on a problem and contain information about the physical context in which the problem occurs; problem categories that are "fuzzy," in the sense that problems are not forced into rigidly-defined groups but are perceived in terms of their degree of similarity (or dissimilarity) to complex problems observed previously; and organizational structures that facilitate communication across group boundaries and the development of a "common language" for discussing problems.

Also, when problems are framed as opportunities for learning and not liabilities to be avoided, problem-solving will benefit from the combination of positive attributions that boost motivation and the suppression of threat effects that can lead to reduced search and reflexive routine responses. Evaluating problems and potential solutions first in terms of quality criteria and only then in terms of cost creates a mindset that favors investments in process improvements, incurring short-term "costs of prevention" in order to reduce long-term "costs of failure"—the opposite effect from that of traditional accounting systems. Finally, when process standardization is understood as marking the beginning (and not the end) of further improvement efforts, the normal inertial tendencies of organizations with respect to adaptive learning can be partially overcome. These findings suggest the value of identifying and understanding the role of "disequilibrating" mechanisms and procedures used by an effective "learning organization" as a means of influencing the cognitive processes of its members.[13]

Notes

1. The case material presented here is selected from a longer, more comprehensive version of this paper to con-

form to space limitations. The long version is available from the author upon request.

2. My primary criteria for choosing the field sites were: 1) an agreement allowing extensive shop-floor access; 2) support for the project from corporate and plant-level management and, at GM and Ford, union officials (Honda is not unionized); 3) a readily observable level of problem-solving activity directed at quality improvement; 4) a reasonably high level of incidence for the three quality problems; 5) variation in company, production system (along a continuum from "mass production" to "lean production"), and quality performance; and 6) participation in the International Assembly Plant Study.

3. Many of these interviews were scheduled, semiformal sessions, while others were extended conversations accompanying my shop floor observations. Besides these interviews, I spoke briefly with many other individuals. I tape-recorded interviews held in offices and meeting rooms and also took extensive notes, recording key phrases and comments verbatim as much as possible. I took notes but did not tape interviews on the shop floor or in the cafeteria. I supplemented my notes soon after each interview and typed up field notes each night. I did not transcribe the interview tapes but referred to them when writing the fields notes.

4. The International Motor Vehicle Program at M. I. T. operated from 1985-90 and was sponsored by practically every automotive manufacturer in the world. The International Assembly Plant Study was carried out by John Krafcik and John Paul MacDuffie (see Krafcik 1988; Womack et al. 1990; MacDuffie and Krafcik 1992; MacDuffie 1991, 1995).

5. I first visited these plants in connection with data collection for the Assembly Plant Study. These visits, and similar trips to over thirty other assembly plants around the world, gave me a familiarity with automotive manufacturing, different types of production systems, and different approaches to quality that proved invaluable as a backdrop for the fieldwork on problem-solving.

6. On occasion, examples of problems outside the three primary categories are used to illustrate a particular point. Key themes in the cases are developed in parallel as much as possible, but themes unique to particular cases are also explicated when necessary.

7. This suggests, for electrical problems, that the plant was successful at repairing most defects before vehicles left the plant. Also, the incidence of water leaks, while high, was clearly not the plant's top quality priority—suggesting that the plant was willing to accept that level of water leaks or that customers were less concerned about water leak defects than about electrical problems.

8. I have no data on the actual costs of altering sheet metal design, but they may well be too high to justify a change in these circumstances. However, I saw no indication of any effort at Ford to assess the costs, in terms of customer perception, of quality problems that persist over the full life cycle of a product.

9. The eight sections of the report include 1) team contact information; 2) problem definition; 3) root cause; 4) actions taken; 5) action dates; 6) verification; 7) prevention; and 8) congratulate your team.

10. This emphasis on paint defects was unsurprising, given the belief at Honda that their superior "fit and finish" had been a major factor in the company's major surge in market share during the 1980s. In contrast, nearly half of the Honda electrical defects reported to J. D. Power involved the radio-cassette unit (compared with only $\frac{1}{4}$ of the Ford and (GM defects), a "stand-alone" component whose quality is mostly out of the control of the assembly plant. Thus paint defects were both more central in the company's self-definition of quality and seen as being more directly under assembly plant control than electrical defects.

11. The Kaizen program rewarded associates for process improvement suggestions and for involvement in the implementation of approved solutions. The Hawkeye Award was given for spotting, recording, and notifying coordinators about unusual quality problems, particularly those originating in upstream processes. The Safety Award was given for identifying ongoing and unusual safety-related problems. Finally, the NH Circle award was given to the group with the most impressive problem-solving process, quality improvement impact, cost-savings, and presentation to senior management. For all these awards, associates would gain points that could eventually be redeemed for prizes of various kinds, including (at the high end) a Honda vehicle. While Honda management originally expected that it would take five or more years for any associates to win a car, they have found that the most active associates have accumulated enough points for a car in $2\frac{1}{2}$ years. Special ceremonies for Milestone awards (i.e. lifetime point accumulation), Champion awards (i.e. most points during one calendar year), and Top Ten awards (i.e. ten associates with the most points in one calendar year) provided the additional incentive of social recognition and public praise.

12. The tendency for American workers to become, at first, overzealous about quality was reported at nearly every Japanese transplant I visited.

13. This research was supported by the International Motor Vehicle Program at MIT. The author is grateful to the managers and employees at the General Motors, Ford, and Honda assembly plants where this research was conducted.

References

Adler, P. S. and K. B. Clark, "Behind the Learning Curve: A Sketch of the Learning Process," *Management Sci.,* 37, 3 (1991), 267-281.

Argyris, C. and D. Schon, *Organizational Learning,* Addison-Wesley, Reading, MA, 1978.

Bourgeois, L. J. III and K. M. Eisenhardt, "Strategic Decision Processes in High Velocity Environments: Four Cases in the Microcomputer Industry," *Management Sci.,* 34, 7 (1988), 816-835.

Cole, R. E., P. Bacdayan, and B. J. White, "Quality, Participation, and Competitiveness," *California Management Rev.,* 35, 3 (1993), 68-81.

———, "U.S. Quality Improvement in the Auto Industry: Close but No Cigar," *California Management Rev.,* 32, 4 (1990), 71-85.

——, "Issues in Skill Formation and Training in Japanese Approaches to Automation," in Paul S. Adler (Ed.), *Technology and the Future of Work,* pp. 187-209, Oxford University Press, New York, 1992a.

——, "The Quality Revolution," *Production and Operations Management,* 1, 1 (Winter 1992b), 118-120.

Daft, R. L. and R. H. Lengel, "Organizational Information Requirements: Media Richness and Structural Design," *Management Sci.,* 32, 5 (1986), 554-571.

Dutton, Jane, "The Making of Organizational Opportunities: An Interpretive Pathway to Organization Change," in L. L. Cummings and Barry M. Staw (Eds.) *Research in Organizational Behavior,* 15 (1993), 195-226.

Eisenberg, E. M., "Ambiguity as Strategy in Organizational Communication," *Comm. Monographs,* 51 (1984), 227-242.

Eisenhardt, K., "Building Theories from Case Study Research," *Acad. Management Rev.,* 14, 4 (1989), 532-550.

Fine, C., "Quality Improvement and Learning in Productive Systems," *Management Sci.,* 32, 10 (1986), 1301-1315.

Gardner, H., *The Mind's New Science,* Basic Books, New York, 1987.

Imai, K., *Kaizen,* Free Press, New York, 1986.

Isen, A. and B. Means, "The Influence of Positive Affect on Decision-making Strategy," *Social Cognition,* 2, 1 (1983), 18-31.

Jackson, S. and J. Dutton, "Discerning Threats and Opportunities," *Admin. Sci. Quarterly,* 33 (1988), 370-387.

Juran, Joseph M., *Quality Control Handbook,* fourth ed., McGraw-Hill, New York, 1988.

Krafcik, J. F., "Comparative Analysis of Performance Indicators at World Auto Assembly Plants," M.S. thesis, Sloan School of Management, M.I.T., Cambridge, MA, 1988.

Leonard-Barton, D., "Inanimate Integrators: A Block of Wood Speaks," *Design Management J.,* 2, 3 (1991), 61-67.

Lounamaa, P. and J. March, "Adaptive Coordination of a Learning Team," *Management Science,* 33, 1 (1987), 107-123.

MacDuffie, J. P., "Beyond Mass Production: Flexible Production Systems and Manufacturing Performance in the World Auto Industry," Ph.D. dissertation, Sloan School of Management, M.I.T., Cambridge, MA, 1991.

——, "Human Resource Bundles and Manufacturing Performance: Organizational Logic and Flexible Production Systems in the World Auto Industry," *Industrial and Labor Relations Rev.,* 48, 2 (January 1995), 192-221.

—— and J. F. Krafcik, "Integrating Technology and Human Resources for High Performance Manufacturing: Evidence from the International Auto Industry," in T. A. Kochan and M. Useem (Eds.), *Transforming Organizations,* Oxford University Press, New York, 1992.

Marcellus, R. L. and M. Dada, "Interactive Process Quality Improvement," *Management Sci.,* 37, 11 (1991), 1365-1376.

March, J. G. and H. Simon, *Organizations,* John Wiley, New York, 1958.

Rosch, E. and B. B. Lloyd (Eds.), *Cognition and Categorization,* Erlbaum, Hillsdale, NJ, 1978.

Simon, H. A., "The Structure of Ill-Structured Problems," *Artificial Intelligence,* 4 (1973), 181-201.

Sitkin, S. B., "Learning Through Failure: The Strategy of Small Losses," in L. L. Cummings and B. M. Staw (Eds.), *Research in Organizational Behavior,* 14 (1992), 231-266.

Smith, E. E. and D. L. Medin, *Categories and Concepts,* Harvard University Press, Cambridge, MA, 1981.

Staw, B. M., L. E. Sandelands, and J. E. Dutton, "Threat-Rigidity Effects in Organizational Behavior: A Multi-Level Analysis," *Admin. Sci. Quarterly,* 26 (1981), 501-524.

Tyre, M., "Managing the Introduction of New Process Technology: A Study of Organizational Problem-Solving at the Plant Level," Ph.D. dissertation, Harvard Business School, Cambridge, MA, 1989.

—— and W. Orlikowski, "Windows of Opportunity: Temporal Patterns of Technological Adaptation in Organization," *Organization Sci.,* 5, 1 (1994), 98-118.

—— and von Hippel, "Locating Adaptive Learning: The Situated Nature of Adaptive Learning in Organizations," Working Paper #90-93, Sloan School of Management, M.I.T., Cambridge, MA, 1993.

Weick, K., *The Social Psychology of Organizing,* Random House, New York, 1979.

Womack, J., D. Jones, and D. Roos, *The Machine That Changed the World,* Rawson-MacMillan, New York, 1990.

Chapter 9

Getting Quality the Old-Fashioned Way

Self-Confirming Attributions in the Dynamics of Process Improvement

NELSON P. REPENNING
JOHN D. STERMAN

Managers, consultants, and scholars have increasingly recognized the value of considering an organization's activities in terms of processes rather than functions. The current popularity of the process approach stems from its ability to drive improvement within organizations (Garvin, 1995a). Starting with Total Quality Management (TQM) (Deming, 1986) and continuing with business process reengineering (BPR) (Hammer & Champy, 1993), many recent trends in management focus on the process rather than the function as the critical unit of analysis for improvement. The popularity of these approaches is one testament to the benefit of the process view; an-

other is the data. Many firms have made significant improvements in quality and productivity using quality improvement techniques. Easton and Jarrell (1998) find that firms that make a long-term commitment to quality improvement outperform their competitors in both profitability and stock returns. Hendricks and Singhal (1996) also find that firms that win quality awards (an assumed outcome of successful process improvement) outperform their counterparts in terms of share price.

Yet for every successful process improvement effort, there are many more failures (Ernst & Young, 1991, and General Accounting Office, 1991, report on failed quality improvement

AUTHORS' NOTE: Prepared for the National Research Council workshop on Improving Theory and Research on Quality Enhancement in Organizations. Support has been provided by the National Science Foundation, grant SBR-9422228, and the company described in this chapter. Many thanks to Tim Tiernan, Bill Colwell, Laura Cranmer, Dave Lazor, Vic Leo, Frank Murdock, Roger Saillant, and Ron Smith for their generous assistance. We thank Bob Cole, Dick Scott, and the workshop participants for helpful comments and criticisms, along with our colleagues Lotte Bailyn, John Carroll, Drew Jones, Steve Graves, Liz Krahmer, Tom Malone, Rogelio Oliva, Wanda Orlikowski, Scott Rockart, Julio Rotemberg, Ed Schein, Peter Senge, and seminar participants at MIT. For more information on the research program that generated this chapter, visit http://web.mit.edu/jsterman/www/.

Hammer & Champy, 1993, and White, , discuss failed reengineering efforts). n more puzzling, even initially successful rograms often fail to take hold. Kaplan (1990a, 1990b) and Sterman, Repenning, and Kofman (1997) describe the case of Analog Devices, a major semiconductor manufacturer, whose quality program led to substantial improvements in quality and productivity but was rewarded with declining profitability and a sharp decline in its share price, forcing a major layoff. Hendricks and Singhal (1996) find that large firms that win quality awards experience abnormally low returns in the 2 years preceding the award, providing some evidence of a "worse before better" dynamic even for successful improvement programs; and a study by the General Accounting Office (GAO, 1991) found that early Baldrige-award finalists did no better than comparable nonfinalists in sales growth or profitability. Scholars and managers alike have long realized the difficulty of making fundamental changes to the technology, processes, and structures of organizations, and the process focus does not appear to mitigate these difficulties. Although suggesting new and valuable improvement opportunities, process-focused improvement techniques still face the barriers that limit other organizational change efforts.

Resolving the improvement paradox is important for both managers and scholars. For managers, the ability to sustain learning and improvement is a source of competitive advantage and improved profitability (de Geus, 1988; Stata, 1989). For management and organizational theorists, process improvement efforts represent significant changes in both the structure and behaviors of the organizations that undertake them. Deeper understanding of successful process improvement initiatives can contribute to knowledge of organizational change more generally.

There is, however, a significant gap in the literature on process improvement. The physical design of manufacturing and service processes traditionally has been the domain of industrial engineering, operations research, and operations management (Chase & Aquilano, 1989). The quality movement grew out of the field of statistics (Deming, 1986; Shewhart, 1939),

whereas reengineering has its roots in information technology and computer science (Hammer & Champy, 1993). These frameworks focus on modifying the physical structure of the firm's processes and systems; less attention is paid to the concomitant organizational and behavioral changes required to improve performance. Michael Hammer, commenting on the technical approach of his best-selling book *Reengineering the Corporation,* said "I was reflecting my engineering background and was insufficiently appreciative of the human dimensions. I've learned that's critical" (White, 1996, p. 1).

In contrast, organizational scholars have focused primarily on the behavioral aspects of change. Successfully implementing change remains an open and important challenge in both the management and study of organizations, and it has generated a huge literature (for overviews, see Huber & Glick, 1993; Kanter, Jick, & Stein, 1992; Van de Ven & Poole, 1995). Dean and Bowen (1994) show that quality improvement research in the management literature stresses leadership, human resource issues, strategic planning, and other traditional foci of organizational research. Likewise, Hackman and Wageman (1995), working from an organizational theory perspective, analyze the conceptual underpinnings of the quality movement and suggest a research agenda to study its effectiveness. However, whereas physical theories largely ignore the behaviors of those working within the organization, organizational theories generally do not account for the physical structure of the organization and its processes. Dean and Bowen (1994) write, "Management theorists may have gone too far in emphasizing socio-behavioral over process and technical factors in explaining variation in performance. . . . Researchers rarely extended their theories to the social and technical aspects of organizational and process design" (p. 408).

There is a clear need for an interdisciplinary theory of process improvement that integrates the physical structure of improvement with an understanding of human decision making in organizations. To that end, in this chapter, we develop a framework to understand process improvement that accounts for both the physical structure of processes and the behaviors that people working in such systems are likely to display. In developing the physical component, we draw on the basic precepts offered by management science and the founders of the quality movement (Chase & Aquilano, 1989; Deming, 1986; Garvin, 1988; Ishikawa, 1985). On the behavioral side, we rely on experimental studies of human decision making (Hogarth, 1987; Kahneman, Slovic, & Tversky, 1982; Paich & Sterman, 1993; Plous, 1993; Sterman, 1989a, 1989b) and field study. The main tools for theory development are intensive case study research (Eisenhardt, 1989) and the development of dynamic models capturing the rich array of interdependencies and feedback processes in the organization and its environment (Forrester, 1961; Masuch, 1985; Richardson, 1991; Weick, 1979). Like the structuration literature (Giddens, 1984, 1993; Orlikowski, 1992, 1995), we stress the mutual, recursive causal links among technological artifacts (the physical structure), organizational structure, and the mental models of organizational actors that guide their behavior. We go beyond the structuration literature, however, in specifying an explicit feedback theory at the operational level and show how those feedback processes generate organizational dynamics.

The chapter is organized as follows. The next section develops the theory, followed by a section that describes two improvement initiatives we studied (readers requiring more details can consult Repenning, 1996a, 1996b). Then, the next section analyzes the initiatives using the framework, and the final section contains discussion and concluding thoughts.

The Theory

The Physical Structure of Improvement

A process is the sequence of activities that converts inputs into the desired outputs (Garvin, 1995b). Inputs can be raw materials, as in a manufacturing process, or information, such as customer requirements in a product development setting. Outputs are then finished products or completed product designs. The first construct in the model, Net Process Throughput, is the rate at which inputs are converted successfully into outputs (e.g., products manufactured per day or product designs completed per month). Net process throughput is determined by Gross Process Throughput less the rate of Defect Introduction. Work processes sometimes fail to convert inputs into the desired outputs; items produced incorrectly are termed Defects. "Defect" will be used as a generic term for any undesirable outcome of a conversion process (Schneiderman, 1988). For example, a product produced correctly but delivered late is defective if timely delivery is a desired attribute of the conversion process. Figure 9.1 shows the basic physical relationship between gross process throughput, the defect introduction rate, and net process throughput in the form of a causal diagram (Forrester, 1961; Richardson, 1991; Richardson & Pugh, 1981; Weick, 1979). An increase (decrease) in gross throughput causes an increase (decrease) in net throughput (ceteris paribus). Similarly, an increase (decrease) in defect introduction, ceteris paribus, causes a decrease (increase) in net throughput. Causal diagrams provide a compact and precise representation of interdependencies and are useful in describing the feedback structure of systems.[1]

Defects can often be corrected through rework (represented in Figure 9.2 by the flow Defect Correction). Defect correction increases net process throughput: Defective outputs, once fixed, become usable. The level variable Defects connecting the Defect Introduction rate and the Defect Correction rate represents the stock of defective products yet to be repaired. Sometimes, it is physically impossible or economically unfeasible to repair or rework defective products or services. In these cases, defective products are scrapped or end up in the hands of the customer. In either case, the firm incurs the cost of replacing the defective item or must compensate the customer for the defect. Such compensation may take the form of lower prices, a poor reputation, or lost market share, leading to reduced profitability, market value, revenue, and other costs. We define defect correction to include all remedial measures that a

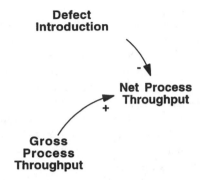

Figure 9.1.

NOTE: Net throughput for any process is gross throughput less the rate of defect introduction. Arrows indicate the direction of causality. Signs (+ or min) at arrow heads indicate the polarity of relationships: a "+" denotes that an increase in the independent variable causes the dependent variable to increase, ceteris paribus (and a decrease causes a decrease); that is, $Xria^{+}Y\_\_Y/\_X > 0$. Similarly, "min" indicates that an increase in the independent variable causes the dependent variable to decrease; that is, $Xria^{min}Y\_\_Y/\_X < 0$. See Richardson and Pugh (1981).

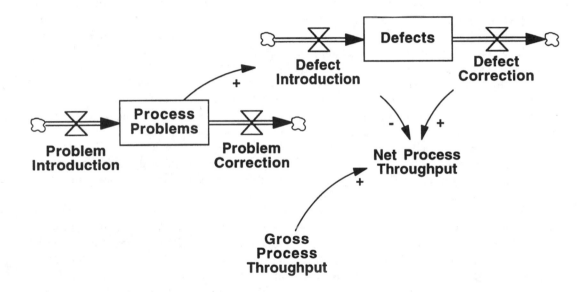

Figure 9.2. The Stock and Flow Structure of Defects and Process Problems

NOTE: This figure represents Defects and Process Problems as stocks (level or state variables) denoted by rectangles (Forrester, 1961). A stock is the integration (accumulation) of its inflows less its outflows, denoted by the straight arrows with valves.

firm can take to address the existence of defects, and thus the theory is general enough to include those cases where rework is impossible.[2]

A fundamental contribution of the founders of the quality movement was to recognize the distinction between correcting defects that have already been produced and preventing them from occurring (Deming, 1986). The causes of defects are Process Problems, also known as "root causes" in the quality literature (Ishikawa, 1985). Process problems are the features of the process, either physical or behavioral, that generate defects. The stock of process problems determines the Defect Introduction rate. For example, within a paint shop in a manufacturing operation we studied, some products were produced with small scratches. Correcting these defects required repainting. The process prob-

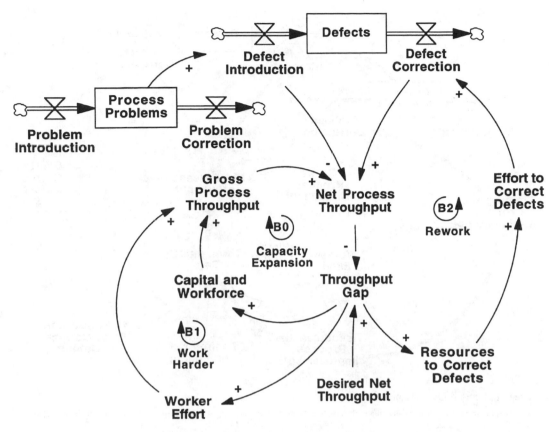

Figure 9.3. Negative feedbacks controlling throughput. The loop identifiers (e.g., B1) indicate whether a loop is a negative (balancing) feedback or a positive (self-reinforcing) feedback. See Richardson and Pugh (1981).

lem generating the flow of defects was found to be employees whose wrist watches, jewelry, or belt buckles scratched the work as they handled parts.

The stock of process problems is increased by Problem Introduction and reduced by Problem Correction. Process problems arise as equipment ages and wears, and as changes in products, processes, or customer requirements create conflicts with existing procedures, skills, and equipment. In the paint shop example, the process problem was eliminated by supplying employees with gloves to cover watches and rings and aprons to cover their belt buckles.

Explicitly portraying the stock and flow structure of processes gives insight into the importance of the distinction between defect correction and defect prevention. One process problem creates a continual inflow of defects,

forever reducing net process throughput unless each and every defect is corrected. Once a process problem is corrected, however, the stream of defect introduction is forever reduced. The challenge of process improvement is to shift attention from reducing the stock of defects to reducing the stock of process problems.

Responding to Throughput Pressure

Integrating the stock and flow structure with the behavioral processes governing the flows closes the feedback loops that determine the system's dynamics (Forrester, 1961; Richardson, 1991; Weick, 1979). Consider the feedback loops by which managers regulate process throughput. Managers assess the adequacy of

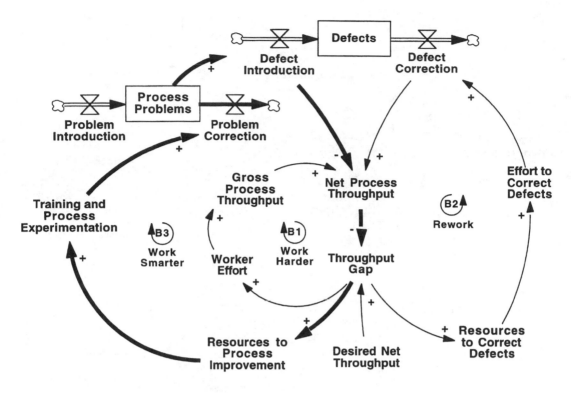

Figure 9.4. Second-Order Improvement

NOTE: Investing in improvement activity creates the negative Work Smarter loop (B3), which enhances net throughput by reducing process problems.

current throughput by comparing it to Desired Throughput, generating the Throughput Gap (Figure 9.3). Desired throughput is determined by the demand for the organization's products or services. For now, desired throughput is assumed to be exogenous; later, we show how throughput goals are actually endogenous, creating important additional dynamics.

First-Order Improvement

Faced with a throughput shortfall, workers and managers have three options: expand capacity, use existing capacity more intensely, or repair defective output. Each option forms a negative or balancing feedback loop whose goal is to eliminate the throughput gap by raising net process throughput toward the desired rate (Figure 9.3). First, managers can expand production capacity by hiring more workers and purchasing additional plants and equipment, boosting

gross process throughput through the balancing Capacity Expansion loop B0. However, expanding capacity takes time, is costly, and is generally not an option for managers responsible for day-to-day operations. We treat the capital stock and workforce as exogenous because these decisions are beyond the authority of the participants in the improvement programs we discuss below. For feedback models exploring capacity acquisition dynamics, see Forrester (1961), Mass (1975), and Lyneis (1980). For models of the interactions between process improvement and capacity, see Sterman et al. (1997) and Repenning (1997a, 1997b).

Second, to increase net process throughput, workers can Work Harder (balancing loop B1), increasing the utilization of existing resources. Effort can be increased through greater focus on task, shorter breaks, reduced absenteeism, and overtime. Third, managers can allocate resources to correct existing defects (the balancing Rework loop B2), for example, by repainting scratched parts or reworking faulty designs. Alternatively, quality standards can be lowered, "correcting" defects by redefining them, as, for example, when software is released with known bugs (often described to customers as "undocumented features").

Second-Order Improvement

Each of the first-order improvement feedbacks can close the throughput gap, but only at significant and recurring cost. A more effective solution is eliminating the process problems that generate defects (Deming, 1986). Such second-order improvements create the negative Work Smarter loop B3 (Figure 9.4), which closes the throughput gap by permanently eliminating the process problems that generate defects. Making such fundamental improvements requires managers to train their workforce in improvement techniques, release those workers from their normal responsibilities so that they may participate in improvement activities, and, most important, give them the freedom to deviate from established routines so that they may experiment with potential solutions. Experimentation and improvisation are fundamental to many quality improvement methods (Deming, 1986; Wruck & Jensen, 1994). Weick (1993) and Orlikowski (1996) go further and argue that improvisation is central to successful organizational change in general.

The Self-Reinforcing Nature of Improvement

First- and second-order improvement processes are strongly coupled. The most basic interactions arise because resources are finite. Line workers have limited time, which must be allocated among production, defect correction, and process improvement. Managerial attention is also limited and must be allocated to competing activities (March & Simon, 1958/1993). Process-oriented improvement programs, because they cut across traditional organizational boundaries, intensify demands for senior management attention. Improvement activities require management time to motivate employees, guide training, review results, and mediate conflicts. Resource constraints create two negative links: as Worker Effort rises, Training and Process Experimentation suffer. Likewise, Resources to Process Improvement fall when management increases Resources to Defect Correction (Figure 9.5).

The new links close two important feedbacks, the self-reinforcing Reinvestment loops R1a and R1b (Figure 9.5). Unlike the loops described so far, the Reinvestment loops are positive feedbacks that tend to reinforce whichever behavior currently dominates. Successful process improvement increases net throughput by reducing defect generation. As the throughput gap falls, workers have more time to devote to training and experimentation, leading to still more improvement (loop R1a). Similarly, if the organization succeeds in reducing defect generation, less time and effort are needed for correction, freeing resources for fundamental improvement, speeding the elimination of process problems, and driving defects down still further (loop R1b): The loops operate as virtuous cycles. Conversely, if defects increase, worker effort rises and more resources are allocated to defect correction. Improvement effort falls. Process problems accumulate at a faster rate, leading to still more defects: The reinvestment loops operate as vicious cycles. For example, deferring preventive maintenance to repair unexpected equipment breakdowns can lead to more breakdowns and still greater pressure to reassign maintenance mechanics from preventive to reactive work (Carroll, Sterman, & Markus, 1997).

Another link between first- and second-order improvement arises because improvement activity can disrupt production. The experimentation and improvisation required to generate and test ideas for improvement take time and often reduce potential throughput. Machines must usually be taken off-line to conduct experiments, and inevitably, many of these experiments will fail, reducing throughput. These short-run costs of process improvement effort are captured by the negative link from Training and Process Experimentation to Gross Process Throughput. The strength of this link depends on the slack available. If experiments can be run when machines are normally idle, then the link is weak and the cost of experimentation is low.

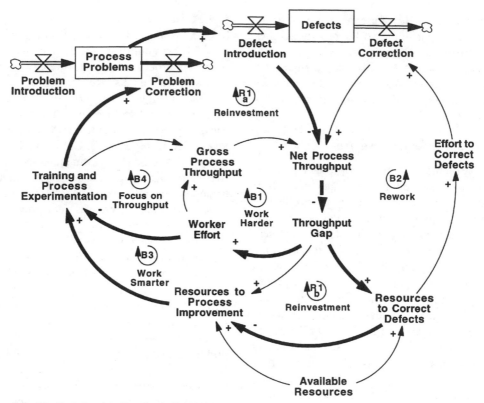

Figure 9.5. The Reinforcing Feedback Created by Finite Resources

NOTE: As more time is devoted to defect correction, less is available to correct process problems, leading to still more defects and still less time for improvement. Note also the balancing Focus on Throughput loop: Workers can meet throughput goals by cutting back on improvement activity.

In round-the-clock operations where there is little scheduled downtime or where work weeks are already long, the link is strong and the trade-off between improvement and throughput is severe. The link creates another balancing feedback that helps workers reach their production goals. Workers can close the throughput gap not only by Working Harder (B1) and by doing more Rework (B2), but also by Focusing on Throughput (B4) and reducing the time spent on process improvement. The availability of slack determines the importance of these loops and plays a critical role in the dynamics of improvement.

Interactions of Physical Structure and Behavioral Decision Making

What determines whether the reinforcing reinvestment loops operate as vicious or virtuous cycles? The answer is determined in large measure by the mental models of the managers about the causes of low process throughput. Managers must choose one of two basic options to close a throughput gap: first-order activities including working harder (B1), reworking defects (B2), and focusing on throughput by neglecting other activities (B4); or working smarter through second-order improvement efforts to reduce process problems (loop B3).

Behavioral Biases Against Fundamental Improvement

The high leverage point for improvement is allocating effort to reducing the stock of process problems, not defect correction or capacity expansion. But there are at least four reasons, rooted in basic cognitive processes, why correction often takes precedence over prevention. First, defects are more salient and tangible than process problems, and people have repeatedly been shown to give too much weight to available and salient features of the environment (Kahneman et al., 1982; Taylor & Fiske, 1975). In a manufacturing setting, for example, the stock of defective products is a pile sitting somewhere on the production floor. It is literally in the way. In contrast, process problems are often invisible. Processes consist of the activities and relationships that create tangible products, and they cannot be discerned easily from the products themselves (Orlikowski, 1995). Indeed, many quality improvement tools are designed to ferret out root causes from observations of the defects they create. In the paint shop example, a defect is a scratched product sent to the "rework hospital" and visible to all, whereas the underlying process problem (a transfer line requiring workers to bend over the work, thus bringing their belt buckles into contact with the parts) is harder to observe and diagnose.

Second, defect correction and process improvement work at different speeds. Process improvement takes time: to document the current process, diagnose root causes, experiment with possible changes, implement solutions, train participants in the new procedures, and so on. The delays between the start of an improvement program and results are long, ranging from months to years, depending on the complexity of the process (Schneiderman, 1988). Defects, however, usually are identified easily and repaired quickly. Choosing to eliminate process problems often entails a short-term reduction in throughput as resources are reallocated from throughput and defect correction to improvement. Faced with this worse-before-better trade-off, managers and workers under pressure to close a throughput gap are likely to choose correction over prevention, even if they understand that doing so suppresses the symptoms without curing the disease.

Third, correction efforts have a more certain outcome than do prevention efforts. A defective product is easily identifiable, and it is usually clear when the defect has been corrected. In contrast, process problems are more complex and their characterization more ambiguous. It is often unclear whether and how a proposed process change will, in fact, result in fewer defects. Risk aversion is a basic feature of human decision making, and people have also been shown to be ambiguity averse (Einhorn & Hogarth, 1985). Faced with a throughput gap, most managers will prefer the more certain gain of correction efforts to the ambiguous, uncertain, and delayed yield of an investment in prevention.

Fourth, eliminating process problems, although preventing future defects, does nothing to eliminate the stock of defects already generated. The stock of defective outputs represents a substantial and tangible investment in materials, labor, and capital. Most accounting systems report the value of the inputs to each product, making it easy to assess the benefit of investing in correction: If the value of a repaired product is $Y and its scrap value is only $X, it is worth investing anything up to $Y - $X to correct the defect. In contrast, assessing the value of defect prevention is more difficult. As one manager in our study said, "Nobody ever gets credit for fixing problems that never happened." The well-known sunk cost fallacy (Arkes & Blumer, 1985; Staw, 1976, 1981; Thaler, 1980) reinforces the bias toward correction. Decision makers often continue a project beyond the economically rational point when they have already made a substantial investment of time, money, and emotion. Here, the sunk cost fallacy means that managers often favor defect correction rather than defect prevention, to, as they see it, recoup past investments in defective outputs, even though these investments are sunk costs.

Biased Attributions About the Causes of Low Throughput

Differences in information availability, salience, and time delays bias managers against fundamental improvement. But the situation is worse. In choosing whether to pursue first- or second-order improvement, managers must make a judgment about the causes of low process throughput. If managers believe that the cause lies in the physical structure of the process, they will focus their efforts on process improvement. However, if low throughput is thought to result from lack of worker effort or discipline, then managers will increase produc-

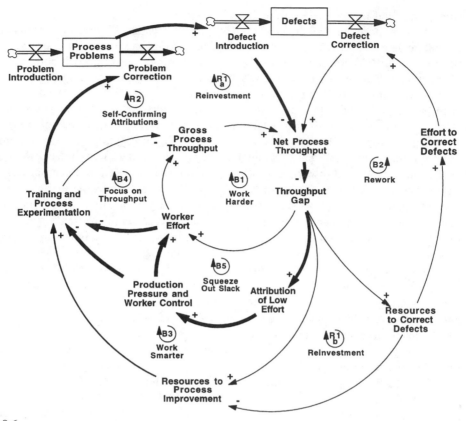

Figure 9.6.

NOTE: Managers who attribute the throughput gap to worker shirking will increase production pressure and monitoring in an attempt to Squeeze out Slack (B5). Throughput rises in the short run, but production pressure pulls resources away from improvement activity, leading to erosion of process capability and still lower throughput (reinforcing loop R2).

tion pressure or the strength of process controls to close the throughput gap. The "cues to causality" that people use to make causal attributions include temporal order, covariation, and contiguity in time and space (Einhorn & Hogarth, 1986). Attributing low throughput to inadequate worker effort is consistent with all of these cues: Worker effort immediately precedes the production of an item, production is highly correlated with worker effort, and workers and the items they produce are highly contiguous in time and space. In contrast, process problems typically precede low throughput with much longer and often unobservable delays, the correlation between process problems and low throughput is frequently unobservable, and process problems can be far removed in time and space from the detection of the defects they create. Thus, managers are likely to attrib-

ute a throughput shortfall to the attitudes and dispositions of the workforce even when the true causes are systemic features of the environment, such as process problems. Many studies show that attributing the cause of a problem or behavior to individuals rather than the systems in which they are embedded is a pervasive and robust phenomenon—the so-called fundamental attribution error (Ross, 1977).

If managers believe that the workforce is underutilized, then the intendedly rational response is to Squeeze Out Slack by increasing Production Pressure and Worker Control (loop B5 in Figure 9.6). Production pressure includes higher throughput objectives, overtime, and faster line speed. Managers can also increase the strength of controls on the workers. Worker control aggregates three ideas: (a) the level of detail with which protocols for employee conduct are specified, (b) how closely management monitors adherence to those protocols, and (c) the penalties imposed for departing from procedure. For example, in a product development organization we studied, a project manager whose subsystem was behind schedule was required by his boss to call in every hour with a status report until the prototype met the specifications. A senior manager in a firm we studied calls such behavior "getting quality the old fashioned way."

But although increasing production pressure has the desired effect in the short run, it also yields a long-run side effect. Workers under greater scrutiny from management and greater pressure to make production goals have less time to attend improvement team meetings and are less willing to undertake experiments that might reduce throughput temporarily. With less effort dedicated to process improvement, fewer process problems are corrected, and the defect introduction rate rises. Process throughput falls, and managers are forced to increase production pressure and controls still further. These links create the Self-Confirming Attribution loop R2, a reinforcing feedback that drives the organization to higher levels of production pressure and fewer resources dedicated to process improvement.

As production pressure and controls increase, they may also begin to conflict. Caught between ever higher throughput goals and the need to comply with stricter controls, workers may cut corners and play games with metrics to appear to meet all of their objectives. Conflicting objectives force workers to make ad hoc, undocumented, or even surreptitious changes to the process so that they can both meet throughput objectives and satisfy the control structure. The organizational literature contains many examples, ranging from simple "workarounds" on the manufacturing floor (Orlikowski & Tyre, 1994) to changing the standards for O-ring tolerance on the space shuttle (Wynne, 1988). Clearly, not all workarounds are harmful. Pressure can sometimes spur a creative solution to vexing problems. But to the extent that they face time pressure and multiple, incompatible objectives, workers will be tempted to erode standards, cut corners, fail to follow up on and resolve problems, and fail to

document their work. Even if creative workarounds solve the initial problem, they can create new ones when downstream processes are not updated to reflect the new upstream process. In a firm we studied, manufacturing engineers facing the imminent launch of a new product made ad hoc changes to parts and tooling to resolve problems, but they were too busy to report the changes to the design engineers. The changes solved the immediate problem, but they also created new ones because design engineers would then develop new parts based on the erroneous drawings, perpetuating problems in the next-generation product (Jones, 1997). As shown in Figure 9.7, such ad hoc changes increase the number of process problems.

Often, workers will keep their workarounds secret from management and manipulate metrics to appear to be in compliance with objectives when, in fact, they are not. In one firm we studied, product development managers improved the reported product development time not by making fundamental improvements in the product development process but by shifting from risky and time-consuming breakthrough products to faster and easier line extensions. The reported product development time fell, but at the cost of reducing the rate of innovation, threatening the competitiveness of the firm. These links create two additional positive feedbacks, the Process Integrity and Double Bind loops R3 and R4, which inadvertently erode production capacity by introducing new process problems as a side effect of management's attempt to boost throughput.

Misperceptions of Feedback and Self-Confirming Attributions

Thus, managers who attribute low process throughput to insufficient worker effort increase production pressure and worker monitoring. Whereas these actions boost throughput in the short run, they also cause process capability to erode further. An important question arises here: As the long-term consequences of boosting production pressure become apparent, would managers not realize that the true cause of low process throughput was low process

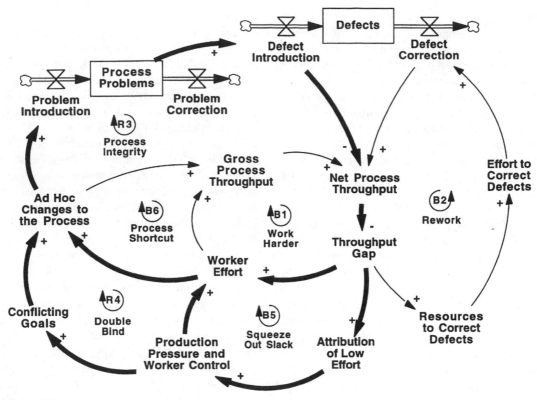

Figure 9.7.

NOTE: Production pressure and control over worker effort conflict, forcing workers to find workarounds, eroding process integrity, and leading to still more production pressure and still tighter controls (reinforcing loops R3 and R4).

capability rather than lazy employees? To the contrary, the initial attribution of low worker effort can become strongly self-confirming, leading managers to ratchet up the pressure still further, until the organization is trapped by low throughput, high costs, and insufficient resources for improvement.

Consider the short-run response of the system to production pressure. As shown in Figure 9.6, managers attributing low throughput to inadequate worker effort respond by increasing production pressure and monitoring workers more closely. Throughput increases. But why? At first, workers will Work Harder and spend less time on non-work-related activities (loop B1). If these efforts are not sufficient, workers also reduce the time they spend on training and fundamental improvement to Focus on Throughput (loop B3). What do managers conclude? In most settings, managers cannot observe all of the activities of the workers; hence

they cannot determine how much of the additional throughput is due to increased work effort and how much to cutting back on training, improvement, or maintenance. For example, suppose that there is a throughput gap requiring an extra 6 hours of productive effort per person per week. Managers, believing that employees are simply not working hard enough, increase production pressure and monitoring. Workers will focus their activities, cutting their breaks and other nonproductive time. Suppose that these responses yield only 2 hours per person per week in effective work effort. To close the remaining throughput gap, workers may gradually reduce the time they spend on process improvement, training, and experimentation until they free up the needed 4 hours per week. Managers observe that throughput rises by the equivalent of 6 hours of productive effort. However, because the managers do not fully observe the reduction in training, experimentation, and improvement effort (they fail to account for the Focus on Throughput loop), they overestimate the impact of their get-tough policy on productivity—in our example by as much as a factor of three. To the extent that managers are unaware of the process shortcuts that workers take to meet their goals, the throughput gains resulting from production pressure provide powerful evidence confirming the managers' suspicions that workers were not giving their full effort. Managers quickly learn that boosting production pressure works: Throughput rises when they turn up the pressure.

Note that workers may unwittingly conspire in strengthening the managers' attributions. Faced with intense production pressure and the resulting goal conflicts, workers are naturally reluctant to tell supervisors that they cannot meet all of their objectives. The more effectively workers are able to cover up the process shortcuts that they take to meet their throughput targets (loop B6), the less aware managers will be of the long-run costs of production pressure. Unaware that improvement activity, maintenance, and problem solving have been cut back, throughput appears to rise without requiring any sacrifices, reinforcing management's attribution that the workers really were lazy: Squeezing out slack is the right thing to do.

The long-run effects of production pressure also reinforce managers' belief that the workers are the problem. The time required for increased production pressure and worker control to boost throughput via the Work Harder, Focus on Throughput, and Squeeze Out Slack loops is much shorter than the time required to detect the resulting erosion in process capability as the reinforcing Reinvestment, Process Integrity, and Double Bind loops lead to more process problems, lower throughput, more shortcuts, and less improvement effort. The erosion of process capability caused by production pressure is delayed, gradual, and diffuse. It is distant in time and space from its cause. Managers are unlikely to attribute the cause of a throughput gap to the pressure they placed on workers months or even years before. Instead, they are likely to conclude that the workers have once more become lazy, requiring another increase in production pressure. Boosting production pressure to elicit full effort from the slothful workers generates powerful evidence to reinforce and confirm the managers' initial, but incorrect, attribution that the workers just need a kick in the pants. Recall the project manager who was required to provide hourly status reports on a balky prototype: Soon afterward, the problem was solved, confirming the boss's belief that he had acted appropriately—indeed, had decisively taken charge of the situation—even though the team was already working around the clock and his calls drained precious time from their efforts to solve the problem.

The feedback structure described above explains how managers erroneously learn that increasing production pressure and worker control is a successful strategy: Each time they do it, throughput improves in the short run, even as it erodes in the long run. Such misperceptions of feedback have been observed repeatedly in a wide variety of systems with even modest levels of dynamic complexity. Dynamic complexity arises in systems with multiple feedback processes, time delays, stocks and flows, and nonlinearities (Brehmer, 1992; Funke, 1991; Sterman, 1989a, 1989b). Laboratory experiments show that as the dynamic complexity of a system grows, decision-maker performance deteriorates relative to optimal; indeed, decision makers are often outperformed by simple decision rules (Diehl & Sterman, 1995; Paich & Sterman, 1993). The misperceptions of feedback and dysfunctional dynamics to which they lead arise for two basic reasons (Sterman, 1994): First, our cognitive maps are grossly oversimplified, tending to omit feedbacks and the other elements of dynamic complexity; and second, we are unable to use our cognitive maps to correctly infer the dynamics of the system or its likely response to policies and perturbations. These problems interact: The more complex the cognitive map, the less accurate are our mental simulations of its behavior. In the case of improvement programs, the structure of the system provides information feedback that can lead managers systematically to ever stronger, self-confirming, but erroneous beliefs about the source of low throughput.

But the misperceptions of feedback operating here are even more insidious. As increased production pressure and ad hoc workarounds inadvertently create new process problems, net throughput falls. Faced with a persistent throughput gap, managers may feel compelled to further increase production pressure and worker control. However, the stress of the constant crisis, extended overtime, ever more aggressive throughput objectives, and conflicting goals eventually causes fatigue and burnout among workers, lowering productivity and quality. Absenteeism and turnover rise, eroding skills and lowering gross throughput still more. Workers may grow to resent the control exerted by management and the lack of trust behind it, leading to an increasingly hostile and adversarial relationship between superiors and subordinates, workers and management. Workers ultimately have no choice but to evade or subvert management's controls, play games with performance metrics, and shirk to relieve an intolerable workload. What begins as a false attribution by management that workers are slothful, undisciplined, and untrustworthy becomes reality. Managers' worst fears are realized as a consequence of their own actions.

Over time, the physical environment adapts to both reflect and perpetuate these self-reinforcing attributions. Managers who have come to believe that production pressure is an effective way to improve throughput will often resort to technology to further increase their control over the workforce. Such technological solutions can take the form of time cards, detailed work reporting systems, video surveillance, or software that measures the key stroke rate of data entry operators. Workers often become increasingly sophisticated in circumventing technological controls, further confirming managers' belief that the controls were necessary and, perhaps, even need to be augmented—another reinforcing feedback.

So it is that initially erroneous attributions about the capabilities and motives of the workforce can soon become embedded in the routines, culture, and even the physical structure of the organization, perpetuating the cycle. Consistent with technological structuration theory (Orlikowski, 1992), mental models, behavior, and the physical structure of the system mutually reinforce one another to generate or-

ganizational dynamics. As Churchill said, "We shape our buildings; thereafter they shape us."

The Case Studies

A variety of field studies document the dynamics described above (Carroll et al., 1997; Krahmer & Oliva, 1996; Repenning, 1996a, 1996b). We focus here on two. The field research was performed within one division of a major American manufacturer. The division manufactures electronic components that are then integrated into the final product at the company's main assembly facilities. The division is quite large, with more than 2 billion dollars in annual sales, and it has many major manufacturing facilities. Two process improvement initiatives were studied. The first was targeted at reducing the cycle time of the manufacturing process—the Manufacturing Cycle Time (MCT) initiative—and the second was designed to improve the efficiency, speed, and reliability of the product development process—the Product Development Process (PDP) initiative.

Methodology

The main tool for theory development was intensive case study research (Eisenhardt, 1989). Both initiatives were completed at the time the research was undertaken. Although the company has undergone numerous change initiatives in the past 15 years, the MCT and PDP initiatives were chosen for several reasons. The MCT initiative was very successful. During the course of the effort, the division cut average cycle time from more than 15 days to approximately 1 day. The division's experience with MCT continues to influence how other improvement efforts are implemented and managed throughout the company. The PDP initiative was selected because it was influenced heavily by the success of MCT. The same senior executive launched both initiatives, viewed PDP as a logical extension of the success of MCT, and tried to use many of the same strategies that had been so successful in the MCT initiative. The two initiatives represent a rare opportunity to control for the effect of senior leadership.

The primary data collection method was semistructured interviews. More than 60 interviews were conducted with participants in the two initiatives. Most levels within the organization were represented, from the general manager of the division to development and operations engineers who do product engineering or run production lines. The researcher visited two different manufacturing facilities and the product development headquarters. Interviews lasted between 45 and 90 minutes and were all recorded on tape. Each interview began with the subject describing his or her background with the organization and relevant previous experience. Participants were then asked to give a detailed account of their experience with the initiative. Subjects were asked to assess the key successes and failures of the initiative and to offer their personal hypotheses for their causes. Finally, subjects were asked to describe any lessons learned and to speculate on what they would do differently if they were to participate in a similar initiative in the future.

The interviews were supplemented with extensive collection of archival data. We were given access to a wide range of promotional and training material associated with each initiative, such as pamphlets, newsletters, instructional books, and video- and audiotapes. The historical performance data were also reviewed. In the case of the MCT effort, extensive data on actual cycle times, product quality, productivity, and other operational variables were available. Fewer data were available for the PDP effort.

The data were summarized in the form of two detailed case studies (Repenning, 1996a, 1996b). The cases describe the history of the initiatives, drawing on the quantitative data, archival materials, and recollections of participants. Both cases make significant use of quotations taken from the recorded interviews. Participants were given the cases to review their quotations for accuracy but were not allowed to change the content. They were also asked to review the entire case for accuracy. The cases are available from the first author upon request.

The research was also supported by a company team that was formed specifically for this study. Participants were drawn from multiple levels and played several important roles. They provided access to key players in each of the initiatives, explained and interpreted the organization's unique language, and met with the first author on a regular basis to review the case documents for accuracy and completeness and to assess the relevancy of the theory being developed.

Manufacturing Cycle Time (MCT)

State of the System Prior to the Initiative

Prior to MCT, the division's plants were operated like those of other companies whose business requires substantial capital investment and labor expense. Line supervisors were charged with keeping each piece of equipment and each laborer fully utilized. The performance measurement and evaluation system emphasized direct labor performance (roughly defined as the number of units produced per person per day) and gave supervisors a strong incentive to keep high levels of work-in-process (WIP) inventory to ensure that breakdowns and quality problems at upstream machines did not force downstream machines to shut down. A large portion of each plant's floor space was dedicated to holding WIP inventory. As an operations manager recalled, "Before [MCT,] if you were to walk out onto the floor and ask a supervisor how things were going, he would say 'Great, all my machines are running' and you would see tons of WIP sitting around."

High WIP levels hobbled plant performance in several ways. First, carrying WIP was expensive—between 60% and 80% of the division's total costs derived from purchased components. Second, a high level of WIP delayed quality feedback—a machine could produce a large batch of defective parts before the defect was discovered by a downstream operation. Third, it was difficult for the plants to change the production schedule on short notice—high WIP meant a long cycle time. Last-minute changes were accommodated through expediting, which destabilized the production floor by forcing operators to do more machine set-ups and changeovers, reducing lot size, and increasing production pressure. High WIP levels and expediting were adaptations through which the system had evolved to be tolerant of quality and reliability problems.

Launching the Initiative

The MCT initiative was launched by a new general manufacturing manager (GM) who had previously worked for a leader in the electronics industry. He recalls his first step:

> We analyzed [for a sample product] the time elapsed between when a part came in the back dock until the time it left the shop floor, and asked the questions "How long did it take?" and "What was the value-added?" We found out it took 18 days to make the product, and we were adding value to the product 0.5% of the time.

Based on this analysis, the GM concluded that substantial improvement could be made by focusing on the time that products spent in between operations as opposed to the conventional focus on reducing the time that parts spent on a particular machine. Communicating this idea took some effort:

> Many people thought of cycle time as the cycle time of the equipment. They were looking at reducing the time a part spent on a particular piece of equipment from 20 seconds to 10 seconds. My feeling was, when you are at 18 days, big improvements are not going to come from focusing on individual machines.

The GM spent much of his time visiting the division's plants to show how focusing on cycle time and value-added percentage could lead to improvement. He recalls that people in the plants always

> wanted to give me presentations in the conference room, and I would say "No, let's go out to the floor." . . . I wanted to show them examples of what I was talking about. I might look at the shipping labels in the warehouse. If it were May, I would usually find parts that had been received the previous August, and I would ask, "If you aren't using this stuff until May, why has it been sitting here since last August?"

These trips stimulated interest in the effort. His senior position enabled the GM to command the attention of the plant managers; his message was sufficiently interesting that, at least in some cases, he was able to keep it. Following these visits, a few plants undertook an intense period of experimentation. Early efforts focused on developing appropriate metrics for cycle time and value-added percentage. Improvement began almost immediately. As one plant manager recalls,

> In the first year, we started with simple counts at different times during the day, and we started to plot them and to try and understand what was happening. Very quickly, our creative engineering personnel came up with clever ways to control the buffers that helped make big improvements.

In the first year, cycle time at that plant fell by more than 50%.

MCE Analysis

In the middle of the second year, a four-person group was created at division headquarters to promote the initiative throughout all the plants. The group began by institutionalizing a measurement system based on the experiments performed at the early adopter facilities. Each plant was required to calculate a metric called Manufacturing Cycle Efficiency (MCE), defined as the ratio of value-added time (time in which a function or feature was being added to the product) to total manufacturing cycle time. The early results were not encouraging. As another plant manager recalled, "When we first started to calculate MCE, the numbers were so low [less than 1%] we really wondered how relevant they were." The process, however, proved valuable. A staff member recalled,

> You had to walk through the shop floor and ask the question "Is this value added?" for every step in the process. By the time you were finished, you had flow charted the entire process and really highlighted all the value-added stations. . . . After calculating MCE, we really started to understand the process flow of our products. We knew where value was being added, and, more importantly, where value was not being added.

Within a year, the MCE efforts helped cut the average cycle time for the division to less than 5 days, down from the initial 15-day average.

Theory of Constraints

Two years into the initiative, with the MCE analysis well under way in most facilities, the corporate staff focused on shop floor management as the next opportunity for reducing cycle time. The MCE effort had focused on the structure of the process by eliminating non-value-added operations and identifying unneeded buffer inventories. To achieve further reductions in cycle time, the plant staff needed better tools for process design and day-to-day management. Two challenges arose. First, the manufacturing processes were very complex, and scheduling them was difficult. The division used a group of simulation specialists to help with process design and to develop scheduling and coordination strategies. Second, implementing new scheduling routines required the understanding and participation of manufacturing engineers, machine operators, and material handlers. A supervisor recalls,

At the time, people thought, "This is important because it's important to the general manufacturing manager," but they didn't necessarily feel in their gut that it was important because they didn't understand what was behind it. . . . We needed more than just a definition of MCT or MCE. People needed a better understanding of how the shop floor really worked.

The corporate group became interested in the offerings of the Goldratt Institute, which taught the shop floor management philosophy Theory of Constraints (TOC), developed by founder Eli Goldratt (Goldratt & Cox, 1986). The attraction of the Goldratt group was twofold. They offered a scheduling and coordination strategy, and, perhaps more important, they offered a training program focused on developing intuition through hands-on experience with a computer simulator. The supervisor of the manufacturing simulation group recalled,

I called it "Shop Floor Scheduling and Coordination Awareness 101." If you wanted to concentrate in 3 days everything you would want to understand about the dynamics of the shop floor and how to keep the line running, this was it.

The division made a substantial commitment to disseminating the Goldratt training. Within 6 months, almost every manufacturing engineer and supervisor within the division had participated in a 2-day TOC class. In the following year, the division developed a hands-on, board game version of the simulator and used it to train almost every operator and material handler within the division. In addition, line supervisors made TOC training a part of their daily operations. One supervisor who experienced substantial success using TOC recalls,

We started by teaching each of the work teams how to manage their line using TOC. . . . The classes were useful, but I felt the real learning came from working with them on their lines on the floor. I would coach them through making actual decisions. I'd let them make the decisions, and then we would talk about the results.

Over time, TOC was widely accepted in the division and continues to play an important role in managing the plants. Responsibility for managing the production floor also shifted to the machine operators, as another supervisor observed: "Essentially, all the inventory management is now done by the operators themselves. They do all the counting, the majority of the analysis, and contribute to the scheduling."

By almost any measure, the MCT effort was very successful. Between 1988 and 1995, the average manufacturing cycle time fell from approximately 15 days to less than 1 day, product quality improved, and revenue, profit, and cash flow all increased significantly. The manufacturing process became less elaborate and more flexible. Many facilities are now able to change their production schedule on a daily basis, something that was impossible before MCT. Finally, the reduction in WIP created enough extra floor space within existing plants that two of five planned new facilities were not needed, saving hundreds of millions of dollars in capital expenditures.

Product Development Process (PDP)

Designing a New Development Process

The second initiative, focused on improving the division's product development process, was initiated in large part due to the success of MCT. The general manufacturing manager who launched MCT was promoted to general manager of the division. He launched the PDP initiative by forming a dedicated task force charged with designing and implementing a new development process: "We need a development process that is fast, is the best in the industry, and it needs to increase throughput by 50% in 2 years. And everyone must adhere to the same process."

The task force was composed of representatives from the major functions within the organization. The team spent nearly 2 years designing the new process, including (a) hiring an outside consultant to provide basic methodology, (b) benchmarking other companies, and (c) documenting the current process and determining how many recurrent problems had come to be part of the process. As a team member summarizes,

> We spent a substantial amount of time looking at what other people did, how they structured their processes, and the problems they had. We looked at . . . the current state of our process and tried to net out a process that had all the things we wanted and . . . allowed us to do things much more quickly.

The New Product Development Process

PDP was not the first attempt to improve the development process. Over the preceding 10 years, many attempts had been made to speed product development, but with mixed results. At the time PDP was launched, two separate improvement initiatives were already in progress. The PDP team consolidated benchmarking results, learning from the earlier efforts, and the input of people throughout the company into a detailed new product development process for the division. Three key elements distinguished the process from prior practice.

First, PDP was a "one pass" development process. Historically, projects were initiated with ambiguous customer requirements, and as a result, many physical prototypes were created as the requirements for the final product were updated. Developing multiple prototypes was time-consuming and expensive. To combat this "build and bust" cycle, PDP required detailed documentation of customer requirements before the design process began. When the requirements were established, engineers would then do the majority of the design work using computer engineering and design tools. The combination of detailed, up-front documentation of customer requirements and use of computer design would allow new products to be developed with one physical prototype and little rework, saving time and engineering resources.

A second goal of PDP was to propagate learning through the use of the "bookshelf." The division did not share technological learning well, causing substantial effort to be duplicated. The bookshelf was to be an engineering library of technologies, modules, and subsystems. Every time a new technology was used, it was the designer's responsibility to bookshelf that technology by fully documenting its uses, capabilities, and limitations, and then placing it in the library. To complement the bookshelf, PDP also specified a "wall of innovation." Projects using new and unproven technologies often fell behind schedule or suffered from quality problems. The wall of innovation was the point in the development project beyond which every project had to be based on technologies that had already been placed on the bookshelf, and it was designed to prevent projects from proceeding too far in the development cycle with technologies that had not been tested appropriately.

Third, the PDP process was designed to increase discipline. The process was divided into six major phases, and at the end of each phase, development teams were required to undergo a "phase exit quality review" before proceeding to the next step. The reviews, conducted by senior managers, required development teams to assemble detailed documentation on the state of the project. One important role of the phase exit quality reviews was to enforce the wall of innovation: Managers were supposed to prevent teams from proceeding to the next phase until each of the technologies they planned to use was documented and placed on the bookshelf. Between reviews, projects were to be run using standard project management techniques such as work plans, Gantt charts, and project management software. By using project management tools, engineers would be more accountable, more efficient, and better able to meet critical milestones.

Pilot Development Projects

The design team tested the new process on a number of pilot projects. The pilots were chosen to serve two purposes: (a) They provided an opportunity for the team to identify and correct problems in the process, and (b) if they were successful, the pilot projects could be used as examples to drive the process through the organization. The first pilot project chosen was a high-profile product critical to the corporation's image and financial success.

But the first pilot suffered because much of the support infrastructure required for the new tools was not in place. Engineers did not have computers powerful enough to use the new CAD/CAE/CAM software, and once the computers were obtained, the rest of the organization was not able to accept their output because of software incompatibility. In addition, learning how to use the tools imposed a substantial burden on the already overworked engineers. One engineer recalled,

> I had some background in CAD/CAE from my master's program, and I still stayed at work until midnight every night for a month learning how to use the tools and trying to figure out how to get my work done. . . . Some of the older engineers, even with training, they just have a [computer] sitting on their desks gathering dust.

Another engineer said,

> The value of the tools was way overestimated. . . . We never had time to take the courses and get the equipment we needed to really make this stuff work. . . . It was really exhausting trying to learn how to use the tools and do the design at the same time.

The project also required the use of new and unproven technologies. As the first test of the new process, the bookshelf of documented designs was nearly bare. As a consequence, engineers were not able to achieve the one-pass design dictated by the PDP process. Instead, much of the design was reworked substantially late in the development cycle, increasing work pressure and stress on members of the pilot project team.

To meet the project schedule and specifications, many of the engineers working on the pilots abandoned much of the methodology. One recalled, "We crashed through the wall of innovation and never looked back." The effect of these problems on the morale of the engineers was significant. Every interviewee reported being frustrated with the process. Many felt that management had defined a development process and then immediately gave the engineering staff a project and time line that could not be accomplished using it. A common sentiment was expressed by an engineer who said, "I believe PDP is a good process. Some day, I'd really like to work on a project that actually follows it."

Results

Evaluating the success of the PDP initiative is difficult. The time delays are sufficiently long that by the fall of 1995, only the first pilots had reached the launch phase. There are little quantitative data with which to evaluate the success of the initiative. The lack of data caused by the long cycle times for development projects is a key feature of the feedback structure governing the success of the program and not just a problem for researchers. Without rapid feedback on results, people formed judgments about the effectiveness of PDP through anecdote, rumor, and personal experience. Indeed, despite the lack of hard data, many people developed strong feelings as to the successes and failures of the effort. Everyone believed that the process as designed was good but that the division as a whole did not follow it. The GM rated the effort as a 50% success. The executive in charge of the initiative believes that they achieved 80% to 90% of their objective for the use of new tools, and less than 20% of their objectives for documenting customer requirements, using project management, and developing a more rigorous and repeatable process. Members of the design team also believe that the effort failed to achieve its objectives, but they hoped it would provide a catalyst for future improvements. Among the engineers interviewed, not one believed that the initiative had influenced his or her job materially.

Analysis

PDP and MCT provide good examples of the paradoxical nature of process improvement efforts. PDP was launched by a senior executive, had substantial funding, and was designed and implemented by a cross-functional, co-located team. World-class development processes were used as models, and a substantial investment was made in roll-out and training. Yet it was, at best, a partial success. In contrast, the MCT initiative was extremely successful even though it was launched by a lower-level executive, had only a four-person staff and a modest training budget, involved no benchmarking, and spent little money on promotion or internal marketing. In this section, the framework developed in the theory section is used to diagnose and explain the differing results of the two initiatives.

Manufacturing

The Reinforcing Nature of Improvement

Prior to the MCT effort, manufacturing suffered from many of the dynamics outlined in the theory section. A supervisor at one plant discussed the difficulty of finding time for preventive maintenance:

> Supervisors never had time to make improvements or do preventive maintenance on their lines. . . . They had to spend all their time just trying to keep the line going, but this meant it was always in a state of flux, which, in turn, caused them to want to hold lots of protective inventory,

because everything was so unpredictable. It was a kind of snowball effect that just kept getting worse.

A manager at a different plant also reflected on the difficulty of finding time for improvement:

> In the minds of the [operations team leaders,] they had to hit their pack counts. This meant if you were having a bad day and your yield had fallen . . . you had to run like crazy to hit your target. You could say, "You are making 20% garbage—stop the line and fix the problem," and they would say, "I can't hit my pack count without running like crazy." They could never get ahead of the game.

Both examples can be mapped into the framework (Figure 9.8). Process throughput is determined by the number of machines currently broken (not operative or producing defective product). There are several corrective actions available to improve throughput. Broken machines can be repaired (the Rework loop B2). Alternatively, operators can run their remaining machines longer or faster via the Work Harder loop B1, and they can refuse to stop their machines for maintenance or problem solving to Focus on Throughput (loop B4). In either case, the time allocated to corrective efforts directly reduces the time available for prevention. When workers spend more time repairing broken machines, they have less time for preventive maintenance. In addition, because preventive maintenance usually requires stopping working machines, time spent running machines to compensate for those that are broken also reduces preventive maintenance. These links create the reinforcing Reinvestment loops R1a and R1b, which drove the system until machines were so unreliable that they had to be run constantly to hit throughput objectives, eliminating time for preventive maintenance and making the machines even less reliable.

The Attribution Error and Work Pressure

Why did the manufacturing system tend toward low performance rather than high performance? The answer lies in the high level of work pressure. Prior to the MCT effort, manufacturing managers reported being under con-

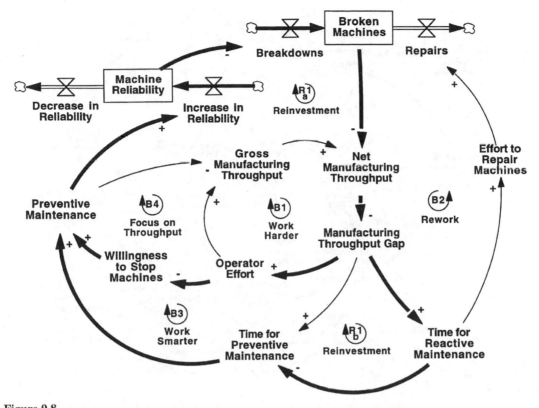

Figure 9.8.

NOTE: As breakdowns reduce throughput, more time is spent in reactive maintenance at the expense of preventive maintenance, leading to still more breakdowns.

stant pressure to hit throughput objectives. One recalled, "Supervisors who missed their targets knew they were going to get beat up by their managers." The aggressive throughput objectives were designed to increase the plant's efficiency and squeeze slack from the manufacturing system. Implicit in these objectives was the assessment that such slack existed, and that if people simply worked harder, process capability would improve. The addition of these decision rules closes the balancing Squeeze Out Slack feedback B5 (Figure 9.9). Increasing throughput pressure appeared to work—in the short run, the situation did improve. However, such actions were self-defeating. Additional production pressure reduced the willingness of operators to shut down machines for preventive maintenance and continuous improvement, leading to more machine breakdowns and product defects. The self-reinforcing feedbacks dominated the dynamics, and the operation spi-

raled down to a state of low uptime, throughput, and quality.

Ad Hoc Process Changes

During the pre-MCT period, manufacturing supervisors and operators also worked under an increasingly constraining measurement system. For example, the finance organization required plants to report equipment and labor utilization rates on a daily basis. As one manager recalled, plant staff reacted by "making sure everybody was busy all the time to make labor efficiency." Previous programs to reduce WIP inventory created a direct conflict with the objectives of high machine and labor utilization. Operators and supervisors reacted by making ad hoc changes to the manufacturing process that allowed them to appear to satisfy both objectives. Many surreptitiously accumulated secret WIP inventories so that they could keep their

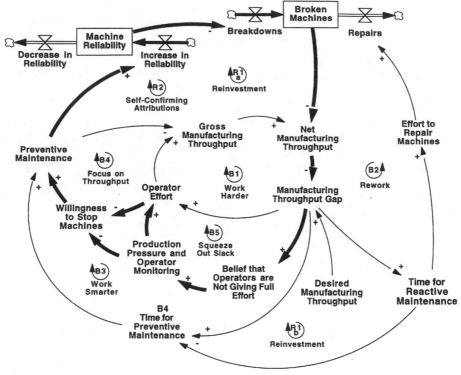

Figure 9.9.

NOTE: Boosting throughput objectives reduces the willingness of workers to stop machines for maintenance or to correct problems, leading to still more breakdowns and production pressure.

machine running, even if its output was not needed. A manager explains,

> Supervisors at that time were evaluated on labor performance on a daily basis. It didn't take long for them to develop a buffer in front of their line so that if the schedule called for 700 and their line was fully utilized at 800, they could still run 800 units every day and still make their labor performance.

The feedback structure is shown in Figure 9.10.

Managers react to a throughput gap by scrutinizing machine utilization more often and increasing the pressure to hit pack counts to Squeeze Out Slack (loop B5). Those working on the production line then experience a conflict between the higher throughput objective and the imperative to reduce cycle time and improve quality. Workers react to the conflict by taking Process Shortcuts, such as holding secret caches of WIP, which allow them to satisfy their

utilization objectives and still appear to meet their inventory reduction goals (loop B6). However, increasing WIP lengthens the manufacturing cycle time, delaying the detection of defective product and reducing the capability of the manufacturing process. Management responds by further tightening controls and increasing production pressure. These links cause the self-reinforcing Process Integrity feedback to drive the manufacturing system to higher levels of WIP and production pressure.

Breaking the Cycle

The feedback structure described above explains why the manufacturing organization suffered from excessive WIP inventory, low equipment reliability, low product quality, and high levels of work pressure. A critical feature of the MCT initiative was the radical reconceptualization of the underlying cause of these problems. First, the general manufactur-

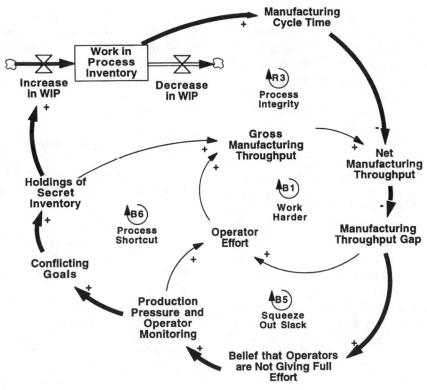

Figure 9.10.

NOTE: As throughput objectives conflict with cycle time reduction goals, workers began to hold secret caches of inventory, lengthening cycle time and reducing process capability.

ing manager challenged the conventional wisdom with his simple analysis of cycle time and value-added percentage. He recalls, "When I laid this [the cycle time analysis] out for everybody . . . they were astonished." The new analysis called into question people's basic understanding of the manufacturing process. A plant manager recalls,

> We had a gut feel that our cycle times were going to be pretty long . . . but what really got us was that even with the very crude definitions of value-added time we were using—they are much stricter now—we had astoundingly low cycle efficiencies [the ratio of value-added to total production time].

Faced with the fact that value was being added to the products less than 0.5% of the time, managers could no longer attribute the low capability of the manufacturing process to the substandard efforts of supervisors and operators.

The development of new understanding of poor performance that was focused on the manufacturing system rather than on those working within it continued through the TOC phase. By working with the TOC computer simulators, managers realized that their actions were as much a cause of low performance as the efforts of employees on the line. One area manager recalled,

> It [TOC] allowed you to step back and understand the shop floor as a system rather than as a bunch of process areas, particularly if you worked inside of one. Even though your training would lead you to make decisions one way, it led you to a new intuition that helped you make decisions differently.

These reframings were critical to the success of MCT because they provided managers with a new conception of the cause of low process capability, thus breaking the self-confirming attribution cycle. The initial data analysis and the TOC training pointed to physical attributes and managerial behaviors as the cause of low capability rather than the attitudes and skills of the workforce. One manager summed up his explanation of the success of the MCT effort by saying,

> There are two theories. One says, "There's a problem, let's fix it." The other says, "We have a problem, someone is screwing up, let's go beat them up." To make improvement, we could no longer embrace the second theory, we had to use the first.

The general manufacturing manager also believed that finding systemic rather than attitudinal causes for problems was critical to success. When asked what skills and talents he possessed that allowed him to make improvements where others had failed, he recalled the following experience:

> At [a previous employer,] I was a plant manager. One of the things I'll never forget as long as I live . . . the guy I took over from blamed his people for everything [and] . . . there was really one guy in particular who he thought was the whole reason for the poor performance of the plant. So I didn't say anything or do anything for about 2 or 3 months. Finally, I gave the guy more responsibility . . . as much responsibility as he'd take. He ended up being one of the best people in the plant. I guess that was probably the turning point for my thinking.

Active experimentation is a critical part of many improvement methodologies. However, a prerequisite for experiment-based methodologies is accepting that significant process problems exist and can be corrected by solutions that are as yet unknown. Prior to the MCT initiative, supervisors and operators were forced to make ad hoc departures from standard operating procedures to satisfy conflicting objectives, but once the reinforcing attribution cycle had been broken, open experimentation could become part of the MCT effort. Experiments add a higher level of rigor to the improvement process and increase the chances of making favorable process changes. Openness means that harmful side effects are more likely to be anticipated. By making the results public and observable, rather than hiding them, the organization is able to adopt the benefits of any new learning more rapidly.

Experimentation was the fundamental mechanism of improvement. Increasing the level of experimentation meant a decrease in the level of control that managers exerted over the process. The plant manager from a facility that was an early adopter of many of the MCT techniques described the new environment:

> If somebody had a better idea about how to manage the buffer, they could try it. . . . Everything we tried, we picked up from our own people . . . everything from the Toyota Production System's kanban to doing statistical process control on buffer sizes.

In addition to allowing the experiments to take place, the penalty for trying something that did not work was reduced, a further reduction in the control that managers exerted over the process. The same plant manager continued,

> The best thing we did was that we didn't kill anybody when they shut down the line, and that happened a lot during this period of time as we experimented with new buffer management systems. We certainly shut it down more than we would have otherwise, but we were willing to do this in order to make more improvements.

Product Development

Despite large apparent differences between manufacturing and product development, the feedback structures governing improvement in both are strikingly similar (Figure 9.11).

Similar to the experience in the manufacturing area before MCT, product development managers had come to believe that the cause of low process capability was the "undisciplined" nature of the development engineers. A senior manager on the PDP design team recalls,

> We found . . . [the existing development process] was . . . poorly documented and poorly disci-

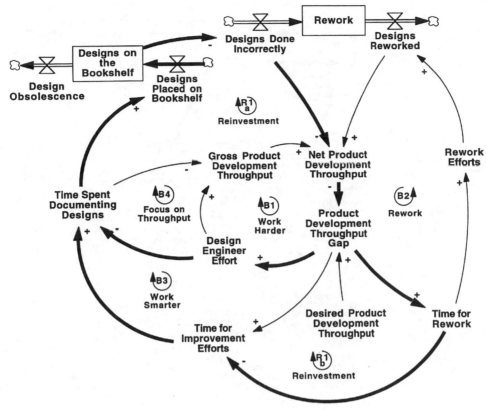

Figure 9.11.

NOTE: Development engineers under pressure to meet deadlines failed to document and share their designs. Without this learning, design error rates remained high, reinforcing schedule pressure and limiting time for future improvement.

plined. . . . Engineers, by trade, definition, and training, want to forever tweak things. . . . It's a Wild West culture. . . . [With PDP,] we were trying to instill some rigor, repeatability, and discipline into the process.

A chief engineer explains his diagnosis:

We went through a period where we had so little discipline that we really had the "process du jour." Get the job done, and how you did it was up to you. . . . It allowed many of the engineering activities to go off on their own, and as long as they hit the key milestones, how they got there wasn't that important.

To increase discipline, engineers were directed to follow PDP, including learning how to use the new CAD/CAM system, doing failure mode and effects analysis (FMEA), and docu-

menting their work for the bookshelf (the Work Smarter loop B3). However, the large costs of delivering a new design late created incentives to meet deadlines—incentives succinctly described by a development engineer, who said, "The only thing they shoot you for is missing product launch . . . everything else is negotiable." Correction efforts—reworking flawed designs, loop B2—took precedence over preventing problems in subsequent projects. Resources were limited because engineers were responsible for completing both existing designs and process improvement activities, such as learning how to use the computer tools and placing designs on the bookshelf. Increasing the strength and number of product development throughput objectives, for example, via the phase exit quality reviews, imposed additional work pressure on engineers (the Squeeze Out Slack loop B5 in Figure 9.12). Because the

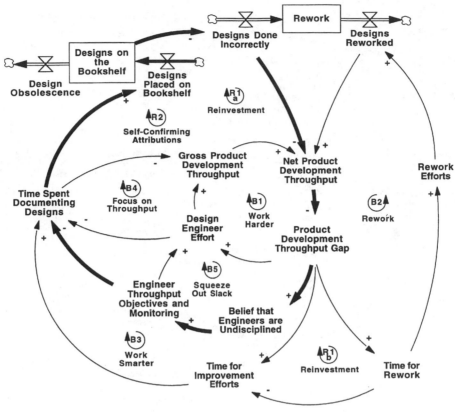

Figure 9.12.

NOTE: The belief that engineers simply needed to work harder led to aggressive throughput goals that could be met only if the engineers failed to document and share their designs, perpetuating low design productivity.

engineers were already working as many hours per week as they could, the time required for rework came directly at the expense of time for improvement, causing the Reinvestment loops to work as vicious cycles and dominate the dynamics.

To meet project deadlines and still comply with reporting requirements, engineers cut back the time spent documenting their designs to prepare for their design review meetings (the negative link from Throughput Objectives and Monitoring to Time Spent Documenting Designs was strong). But because fewer designs could be properly documented and posted to the bookshelf, the cumulative stock of knowledge available to help avoid error did not grow, perpetuating low design productivity. As the PD organization continued to fall behind, managers imposed still more control, unintentionally limiting the ability of the organization to imple-

ment the bookshelf and other key elements of the PDP initiative. The lack of long-term results only reinforced managers' belief that the engineers were undisciplined (via the Self-Confirming Attributions loop R2).

PDP Did Not Break the Cycle

Whereas MCT was successful in changing managers' assessment of low process capability, PDP was not. PDP's focus on discipline and project management did not represent a fundamental change in the core beliefs of senior managers. The result was a further increase in control, which gave engineers even less freedom to experiment and improve the process. The conflict between the attributions of the managers and the experience of the engineers is most obvious in their comments concerning project management, a key component of the PDP initiative that failed to achieve widespread use. Engineers reported that they had no problem with project management techniques per se, but the combination of their assigned engineering tasks and all of the project management and documentation work was more than they could possibly accomplish. One engineer said, "People had to do their normal work as well as keep track of the work plan. There just weren't enough hours in the day, and the work wasn't going to wait." Another expressed a similar sentiment:

> Under this system, . . . the new workload was all increase. . . . In some cases, your workload could have doubled. . . . Many times, you were forced to choose between doing the physical design and doing the project and administrative work. To be successful, you had to do the design work first, but the system still required all this extra stuff.

How did engineers accommodate the substantial increase in workload imposed by the new process? An engineer from a PDP pilot project explains: "How do we catch up? We stayed late. Most of the team was working from 7:00 a.m. to 8:00 p.m. and on weekends. A lot of people worked right through the Christmas vacation." One chief engineer suggested that managers were actually creating the situation they were trying to prevent:

> I believe that P[rogram] M[anagement] is not an issue in and of itself. The problem with PM is that sometimes management chooses to adhere to it, and sometimes it chooses not to adhere to it. . . . When we set out the disciplines of PDP, we said, "There it is, it's a very disciplined, rigid program, go follow it." Then, in the very next breath, we would say, "I want you to ignore all that and bring this project home in half the time." That just didn't go down very well.

In stark contrast, many managers attributed the failure to the basic attitudes and culture of the engineering staff. The executive in charge of PDP said, "A lot of the engineers felt that it was no value add[ed] and that they should have spent all their time doing engineering and not filling out project worksheets. It's brushed off

as bureaucratic." When pressed further for an explanation of the engineers' resistance to project management, he continued,

> Program management and the disciplines associated with it continue to be a problem, in my opinion, in most Western cultures. The people that are particularly rigorous and disciplined, the Japanese and the Germans, tend to be so by cultural norms. I can't tell you if it's hereditary or society or where it is they get it, but the best engineers are those that tend to be the most disciplined, not as individual contributors but as team-based engineers. So, there's a strong push back from the Western type of engineers for much of this.

Such attributions, here generalized to entire nations and ethnic groups, are typical of the fundamental attribution error. As these attributions are shared and repeated, they become institutionalized. They become part of corporate culture and, as suggested by the quote above, can strengthen widely held stereotypes and prejudices in society at large.

Ad Hoc Process Changes

The conflict between trying to get work done and following PDP was pronounced. Almost every engineer expressed feelings similar to the one who said, "I believe PDP is a good process. Some day, I'd really like to work on a project that actually follows it." As in manufacturing prior to MCT, the conflict between the throughput goals and process adherence goals forced participants to work around the process. These departures took the form of neglecting documentation, not placing technologies on the bookshelf, or not filling out a detailed work plan. Another chief engineer gives an example:

> Writing [computer] code on the back of an envelope is a lot faster than documenting it. Of course, the quality of code went up if you documented it and fixed things that might require rework later, but that only shows up in speed after the fact.

Another manager observed, "In the long run, [inadequate documentation] prevented us from being able to deploy the reusability concepts that we were looking for." These behaviors

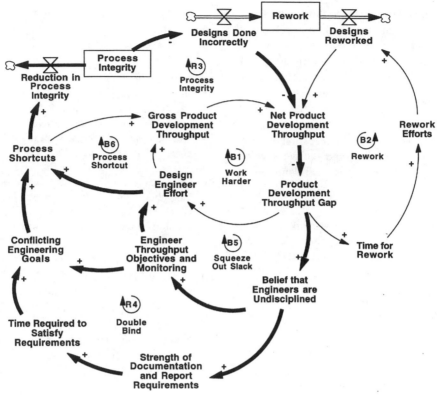

Figure 9.13.

NOTE: Managers, believing that engineers were undisciplined, increased throughput objectives and specified additional reporting and documentation requirements. To resolve the conflict, engineers cut corners, reducing the integrity of the process, leading to still more defects and still lower productivity. Management's belief that engineers were undisciplined was reinforced.

create a structure very similar to that found in the pre-MCT manufacturing environment (see Figure 9.13). Upon observing low process capability, managers' belief that engineers are undisciplined is confirmed. They react by increasing pressure to hit product launch dates while simultaneously stiffening documentation and reporting requirements. The increase in production pressure and process control leads to a conflict in the objectives of the engineers. They react to the conflict by taking shortcuts and working around the process, causing the self-reinforcing Double Bind and Process Integrity loops to operate as vicious cycles. Another engineer summed up the effect that work pressure had on the success of PDP:

> To be perfectly honest, I really don't think PDP changed the way engineers did their jobs. In many ways, we worked around the system. Good, bad,

or indifferent, that's what happened. We had a due date, and we did whatever it took to hit it.

Discussion

The framework presented provides some insight into the differing levels of success of MCT and PDP, and it also identifies some key differences between the two initiatives that led to the different outcomes. However, a basic question remains unanswered: Why were the strategies that were used in MCT not used in PDP? If the successful MCT effort was predicated on developing a better understanding of the system among the frontline managers and encouraging their experiments to improve it, why was this approach abandoned in the PDP effort? If the same senior-level executive kicked off both initiatives, and the MCT effort preceded PDP, why was the MCT strategy not replicated in the PDP effort? The answers to these questions lie in the different physical structure of the two processes and the resulting unanticipated interactions between them.

Differential Time Delays

Manufacturing and product development work at different speeds. In both functions, the short-term positive effects of increasing control and work pressure can be observed quickly—people work harder, they spend more time at their jobs, or they follow the process more closely. However, there is a significant difference in the times required to observe the negative, long-term effects. At its worst, the average cycle time in manufacturing was less than a month, whereas product development projects typically took more than 3 years. These different delays affected the ability of management to break the vicious cycle of self-confirming attributions.

In the MCT program, only a few months passed before the reinforcing loops R1-R3 began producing observable improvement. In addition to quickly confirming the value of the new strategy—a behavioral effect—early results also increased potential throughput—a physical change. Extra manufacturing capacity played an important role in the continued success of MCT for at least three reasons. As capacity grew, production pressure fell, and the plants could devote an increasing level of resources to improvement and still hit their production targets. Second, additional capacity makes operations more robust to the variability and disruptions caused by experiments. Third, slack resources also mitigate the "worse before better" trade-off associated with improvement initiatives. For example, preventive maintenance requires shutting down operable machines. With excess capacity, this can be done without missing the production schedule.

In contrast to the short time delays in manufacturing, a year or more was required to observe and reap the potential benefits of PDP. In the meantime, managers were under continual pressure to improve throughput. Under such production pressure, it was difficult to undertake experiments and make investments with long-term payoffs such as the bookshelf. Furthermore, even if these dynamics were fully understood by engineers and project supervisors, it would have been difficult to convince senior leadership to be patient, as the executive in charge of PDP remarked:

> Imagine at the end of the year, the general manager going up in front of the president and saying, "We missed our profitability numbers because we spent extra money developing our new design process that won't be fully deployed and rolled out till 5 years from now, but wasn't that a good move?"

The long cycle time for improvement in product development lengthened and deepened the short-run throughput sacrifice caused by reallocating resources to process improvement, and, as a consequence, product development was more likely to suffer from self-confirming attribution errors.

As these attributions are repeatedly confirmed, they become embedded in the organization's norms and culture. Management, more firmly convinced that engineers as a group lack discipline and fail to understand the realities of business, increasingly focuses new improvement efforts on compliance with ever more detailed procedures and ever more stringent reporting requirements. Engineers become cynical about the value of new improvement programs and suspicious of management's motives. Dilbert cartoons appear on cubicles (Adams, 1996). The vicious cycles of self-confirming attributions dominate the dynamics. New improvement efforts are more and more likely to fail.

The Relationship Between Manufacturing and Product Development

As in most large firms, the improvement initiatives in manufacturing and product development were undertaken independently. Such decomposition is almost inevitable: Both manufacturing and product development are large organizations in their own right with facilities located around the world and multiple, semiautonomous departments. However, manufacturing and product development are intimately intertwined with one another. These linkages were not appreciated or attended to in the improvement strategy.

Because of the inherently shorter time delays for improvement in manufacturing, the MCT effort progressed faster than PDP. In addition, PDP was started 2 years after MCT, and largely in reaction to MCT's success. The excess capacity created by MCT's success could be used only if the development organization could generate new products to bring in additional business. The general manager said,

> When I started out, I was only the manufacturing manager, so I did everything I could to fix the manufacturing side. When I became the general manager [in 1991], I realized that, in part because of what we had done in manufacturing, our plants were half empty. If we couldn't [generate new business], we were going to have empty plants, which meant unaffordable plants.

The demand facing the manufacturing plants was constrained by the slow rate of product introduction, so early improvements in manufacturing generated slack, allowing the plants to hit their production targets using less than 100% of their available resources. Excess capacity meant that manufacturing managers could both satisfy their production objectives and achieve their improvement targets. No difficult choices had to be made. In contrast, when PDP started, product development was the bottleneck on the demand for the division's products—demand could grow only to the extent that new products could be designed and launched. Product developers faced an acute trade-off between improvement and throughput: Investing in improvement activity directly reduced the time available to bring new products to market. Under intense pressure to use the excess capacity created by MCT, the development organization aggressively sought new business, increasing production pressure on the developers and weakening the reinforcing reinvestment loops

that are fundamental to sustained improvement. As one manager said,

> There was tremendous pressure to grow, and there was tremendous pressure for new products, new technology, and new customers. We were trying to sell very, very aggressively to the outside. So, we would get ourselves in situations where we would have a success with an outside customer which translated into a resource problem for the engineers. We typically never said no.

Thus, the very success of MCT intensified the problems faced by PDP.

The feedback structure linking manufacturing and product development is shown in Figure 9.14.

The Reinvestment in Manufacturing loop R-M is a high-level representation of the self-reinforcing feedbacks driving improvement in manufacturing. Given product demand, initial improvement boosts potential manufacturing throughput. Fewer resources are needed to meet production schedules. The extra resources can be reinvested in experimentation and process improvement, decreasing the level of process problems, further enhancing production capacity, and freeing up even more resources for improvement. An identical structure exists in product development, shown as loop R-PD. Manufacturing and product development are linked because excess capacity depends on the potential throughput of the manufacturing operation relative to product demand. In turn, product demand is augmented as new products are developed and introduced to the market. The two loops differ in that the delays between improvement effort and results are much longer in product development than in manufacturing.

In the case of MCT and PDP, rapid progress in manufacturing, coupled with slow improvements in product development, enabled the manufacturing organization to reinvest its initial productivity gains in further improvement, strengthening loop R-M. As plant utilization fell, management urgently sought ways to use the excess capacity created by successful improvement to prevent morale-shattering layoffs that would undercut the gains of MCT. The development organization faced enormous pres-

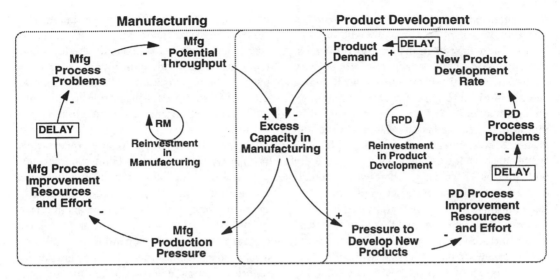

Figure 9.14. Linkages Between Manufacturing and Product Development

sure to get new products to market. Development engineers did not have time to experiment and improve the process, perversely slowing the rate of new product introduction and leading to still more pressure. The initial success in manufacturing led to still more success while simultaneously choking off gains in product development. Ultimately, the self-reinforcing imbalance between production capacity and the ability to generate demand did lead to layoffs in manufacturing.

The positive feedbacks coupling manufacturing and product development arise to some degree in most firms. Manufacturing, with its shorter cycle times and comparatively low complexity, generally has a shorter improvement half-life than does product development (Schneiderman, 1988). In most firms, the quality revolution came first to manufacturing and only later spread to product development (Cole, Chapter 4, this volume), and improvement techniques continue to be more highly developed in manufacturing. Thus, quality improvement in most firms is likely to come earlier and more rapidly in manufacturing. But the more successfully a firm improves manufacturing, the faster capacity will grow. Unless demand grows rapidly as well, improvement will create excess capacity, leading to pressure for layoffs and destroying commitment to further improve-

ment—few people want to work themselves into the unemployment line (Repenning, 1997a, 1997b, and Sterman et al., 1997, provide theory and examples). However, the linkages between manufacturing and product development virtually ensure that excess capacity will arise: The more successfully manufacturing improves, the faster excess capacity builds up. At the same time, excess capacity creates powerful pressure to develop new products. The time available to redesign the product development process shrinks further, limiting process improvement and slowing the growth of demand. Excess capacity grows further. The more effectively these reinforcing feedbacks spin the virtuous cycle of process improvement in manufacturing, the more likely the same loops will operate as vicious cycles in product development.

Robust Strategies for Improvement

Although the PDP initiative had many of the ingredients for success, unanticipated interactions between manufacturing and product development prevented the effort from breaking the self-confirming attribution error dynamics that had thwarted previous programs. The interaction between the manufacturing and product development processes is subtle and could not have been easily anticipated by management given the organization's structure and the tools available to design improvement programs. Prior to the dramatic changes in productivity created by the MCT effort, the organization had been able to bring development and manufacturing capacity into rough balance through hiring and capital expansion. Manufacturing and product development were effectively decoupled because each was operating at full capacity with high work pressure. There was little evidence to indicate the existence of the strong, latent couplings between functions. Furthermore, improvement initiatives had always been undertaken and managed separately. Independent management of the programs seemed a wise strategy given two apparently loosely coupled organizations, each with its own needs, staff, training organization, culture, and history.

Decomposition is a time-honored strategy for solving complex problems (Simon, 1969). The structure of large organizations is predicated on such a strategy as different functions are defined and compartmentalized. And decomposition often works. It led to the undeniably successful MCT effort, and although it did not accomplish all of its objectives, PDP was also responsible for at least one important change within the development organization—the widespread use of CAD/CAM/CAE tools. However, functionally based organizations often optimize the pieces at the expense of the organization's objectives.

The process view underlying many improvement techniques derives much of its power by cutting across traditional functional boundaries (Garvin, 1995b). But the very ability of improvement techniques to make dramatic improvements means that they can destabilize relationships between processes upon which other organizational structures and routines are predicated. Structures and routines that slowly co-evolved to high effectiveness can become dysfunctional as other processes upon which they depend change faster than they can adapt. Organizational routines far from the locus of improvement efforts can be invalidated even when they appear to be unrelated to the process being reengineered. Successfully improving a process can alter the strength of critical feedback loops created by the couplings among processes. Feedbacks that previously stabilized the organization can be weakened, whereas previously dormant loops can become dominant, pushing the organization into new dynamic regimes for which existing structures, mental models, and experience are ineffective or even harmful.

Despite the advantages of the process view, in practice, process-oriented improvement techniques are not capable of identifying the multiple, delayed, and nonlinear consequences of their use. Many are predicated on a static view of the world in which different process problems are assumed to be separable and, as result, can be attacked independently. They are good at identifying unneeded activities but weak at identifying latent feedback processes that may become dominant only when the reengineered process is deployed. There is a clear need to develop robust process improvement and change strategies that enable managers to understand these complex dynamics and design policies to prevent harmful side effects of improvement. Such strategies would account for both the physical and behavioral aspects of improvement efforts and the interrelationships of the different processes involved.

Elements of such robust strategies can be found. McPherson (1995) and Krahmer and Oliva (1996) describe the case of the Network Systems Division of Lucent Technologies, documented as a part of our research, which successfully improved both product development and manufacturing using strategies very different from those promoted in the PDP effort. Sitkin, Sutcliffe, and Schroeder (1994) propose a contingency theory of improvement that also may help account for the different physical and organizational structure of manufacturing and development processes. Repenning (1997a, 1997b) develops the beginnings of such strategies through the analysis of game theoretic and behavioral simulation models. Carroll et al. (1997) discuss a successful effort at the Du Pont Corporation to boost maintenance productivity and equipment reliability using a management flight simulator as the key tool to communicate insights and develop shared mental models.

Implications for Research and Practice

Process improvement programs have both physical and behavioral dimensions, but past scholarly work has focused on one at the expense of the other. In contrast, practitioners of quality improvement offer both technical and organizational tools, but they provide no explicit theoretical framework to support their suggestions.

Our work suggests that the work of designing better processes cannot be disentangled from the work of implementing them. A complete theory of process improvement requires the integration of both operations research and organizational theory. Models and tools to develop real-world intuition behind these systems proved critical in the successful initiative, and operations research and management science have much more to contribute in this area. Early efforts, including the development of simulation games and management flight simulators, are promising. Participatory simulations were critical in the MCT effort, and such management flight simulators have proved successful in many applications (Morecroft & Sterman, 1994). For organizational scientists, the analysis suggests that future studies of organizational change need to consider explicitly the physical environment in which the change is taking place. Time delays, feedback processes, and interdependencies all play an important role in determining the outcome of a change effort.

The ideas presented here also offer a complementary perspective to many of the ideas advocated by practitioners. In many ways, the PDP effort was more consistent with much of the current thinking on organizational change and process improvement than was MCT. However, the MCT effort was substantially more successful. Two key differences account for the different outcomes. First, whereas PDP focused on laying out a specific process and creating structures to make participants adhere to that process, the MCT effort focused on improving managers' and operators' understanding of the dynamics of the manufacturing system. PDP drew on many of the currently popular change strategies, but none of these was sufficient to overcome managers' flawed understanding of the dynamics of the development system. Second, the interaction of the behavioral processes with the physical structure of product development and with other activities in the organization created feedback processes that counteracted the intended effects of the program. Whereas managers often focus on the *detail* complexity of their organization, it is often the *dynamic* complexity that is more daunting. Future change efforts need to be focused on improving managers' understanding of the feedbacks between the structure and behavior of the processes they are trying to improve.

Notes

1. Causal loop diagrams are not intended to provide mathematical specification of the relationships, which may be linear or nonlinear, or of any time delays between cause and effect. Specifying a formal mathematical model is often the next step in testing the theories embodied in causal diagrams. For examples of formal feedback models of quality improvement programs, see Repenning (1997a, 1996b) and Sterman et al. (1997).

2. Of course, inspection processes are imperfect and subject to both Type I and Type II errors. Defective outputs can inadvertently end up in the hands of the customer, and good products are sometimes mistakenly rejected as defective.

References

Adams, S. (1996). *The Dilbert principle.* New York: HarperCollins.

Arkes, H. R., & Blumer, C. (1985). The psychology of sunk cost. *Organizational Behavior and Human Decision Processes, 35,* 124-140.

Brehmer, B. (1992). Dynamic decision making: Human control of complex systems. *Acta Psychologica, 81,* 211-241.

Carroll, J., Sterman, J., & Markus, A. (1997). Playing the maintenance game: How mental models drive organization decisions. In R. Stern & J. Halpern (Eds.), *Debating rationality: Nonrational elements of organizational decision making* (pp. 99-121). Ithaca, NY: ILR.

Chase, R. B., & Aquilano, N. J. (1989). *Production and operations management* (5th ed.). Homewood, IL: Irwin.

de Geus, A. (1988, March-April). Planning as learning. *Harvard Business Review,* pp. 70-74.

Dean, J. W., & Bowen, D. (1994). Management theory and total quality: Improving research and practice through theory development. *Academy of Management Review, 19,* 392-418.

Deming, W. E. (1986). *Out of the crisis.* Cambridge: MIT Center for Advanced Engineering Study.

Diehl, E., & Sterman, J. D. (1995). Effects of feedback complexity on dynamic decision making. *Organizational Behavior and Human Decision Processes, 62,* 198-215.

Easton, G., & Jarrell, S. (1998). The effects of total quality management on corporate performance: An empirical investigation. *Journal of Business, 71,* 253-307.

Einhorn, H. J., & Hogarth, R. M. (1985). Ambiguity and uncertainty in probabilistic inference. *Psychological Review, 92,* 433-461.

Einhorn, H. J., & Hogarth, R. M. (1986). Judging probable cause. *Psychological Bulletin, 99,* 3-19.

Eisenhardt, K. M. (1989). Building theories from case study research. *Academy of Management Review, 14,* 532-550.

Ernst & Young. (1991). *International quality study—Top line findings and international quality study—Best practices report.* Milwaukee, WI: Ernst and Young/ American Quality Foundation.

Forrester, J. W. (1961). *Industrial dynamics.* Cambridge: MIT Press.

Funke, J. (1991). Solving complex problems: Exploration and control of complex systems. In R. Sternberg & P. Frensch (Eds.), *Complex problem solving: Principles and mechanisms* (pp. 185-222). Hillsdale, NJ: Lawrence Erlbaum.

Garvin, D. A. (1988). *Managing quality.* New York: Free Press.

Garvin, D. (1995a, September-October). Leveraging processes for strategic advantage. *Harvard Business Review,* pp. 77-90.

Garvin, D. (1995b). *The process of organization and management* (Working Paper #94-084). Boston: Harvard Business School Press.

General Accounting Office. (1991, 2 May). *US companies improve performance through quality efforts* (GAO/ NSIAD-9-190). Washington, DC: Government Printing Office.

Giddens, A. (1984). *The constitution of society: Outline of the theory of structure.* Berkeley: University of California Press.

Giddens, A. (1993). *New rules of sociological method* (2nd ed.). Stanford, CA: Stanford University Press.

Goldratt, E. M., & Cox, J. (1986). *The goal: A process of ongoing improvement* (rev. ed.). Croton on Hudson, NY: North River Press.

Hackman, J., & Wageman, R. (1995). Total quality management: Empirical, conceptual, and practical issues. *Administrative Science Quarterly, 40,* 309-342.

Hammer, M., & Champy, J. (1993). *Re-engineering the corporation.* New York: HarperCollins.

Hendricks, K. B., & Singhal, V. R. (1996). Quality awards and the market value of the firm: An empirical investigation. *Management Science, 42,* 415-436.

Hogarth, R. M. (1987). *Judgment and choice: The psychology of decision* (2nd ed.). New York: Wiley.

Huber, G. P., & Glick, W. H. (1993). *Organizational change and redesign: Ideas and insights for improving performance.* New York: Oxford University Press.

Ishikawa, K. (1985). *What is total quality control?* Englewood Cliffs, NJ: Prentice Hall.

Jones, A. P. (1997). *Sustaining process improvement in product development: The dynamics of part print mismatches.* Unpublished master's thesis, Massachusetts Institute of Technology, Cambridge.

Kahneman, D., Slovic, P., & Tversky, A. (Eds.). (1982). *Judgment under uncertainty: Heuristics and biases.* Cambridge: Cambridge University Press.

Kanter, R. M., Jick, T. D., & Stein, R. A. (1992). *The challenge of organizational change.* New York: Free Press.

Kaplan, R. (1990a). *Analog devices: The half-life system* (Case 9-191-061). Boston: Harvard Business School Press.

Kaplan, R. (1990b). *Analog devices: The half-life system* (Teaching Note 5-191-103). Boston: Harvard Business School Press.

Krahmer, E., & Oliva, R. (1996). *Improving product development interval at AT&T Merrimack Valley Works.* Case history available from authors, MIT Sloan School of Management, Cambridge, MA 02142.

Lyneis, J. M. (1980). *Corporate planning and policy design.* Cambridge, MA: Productivity Press.

March, J. G., & Simon, H. A. (1993). *Organizations* (2nd ed.). Oxford, UK: Basil Blackwell. (Original work published 1958)

Mass, N. J. (1975). *Economic cycles: An analysis of underlying causes.* Cambridge: MIT Press.

Masuch, M. (1985). Vicious cycles in organizations. *Administrative Science Quarterly, 30,* 14-33.

McPherson, A. (1995). *Total quality management at AT&T.* Unpublished master's thesis, Massachusetts Institute of Technology, Cambridge.

Morecroft, J., & Sterman, J. (Eds.). (1994). *Modeling for learning organizations.* Portland, OR: Productivity Press.

Orlikowski, W. J. (1992). The duality of technology: Rethinking the concept of technology in organizations. *Organization Science, 3,* 398-427.

Orlikowski, W. J. (1995). *Action and artifact: The structuring of technologies in use* (Working Paper WP 3867-95). Cambridge: MIT Sloan School of Management.

Orlikowski, W. J. (1996). Improvising organizational transformation over time: A situated change perspective. *Information Systems Research, 7*(1), 63-92.

Orlikowski, W. J., & Tyre, M. J. (1994). Windows of opportunity: Temporal patterns of technological adaptation. *Organization Science, 5,* 98-118.

Paich, M., & Sterman, J. (1993). Boom, bust, and failures to learn in experimental markets. *Management Science, 39,* 1439-1458.

Plous, S. (1993). *The psychology of judgment and decision making.* New York: McGraw-Hill.

Repenning, N. (1996a). *Reducing manufacturing cycle time at Ford Electronics.* Case study available from author, MIT Sloan School of Management, Cambridge, MA 02142.

Repenning, N. (1996b). *Reducing product development time at Ford Electronics.* Case study available from author, MIT Sloan School of Management, Cambridge, MA 02142.

Repenning, N. (1997a). *Drive out fear (unless you can drive it in): The role of agency in process improvement efforts.* Working Paper available from the author, MIT Sloan School of Management, Cambridge, MA 02142.

Repenning, N. (1997b). *Successful change sometimes ends with results: Exploring the improvement paradox.* Working Paper available from the author, MIT Sloan School of Management, Cambridge MA 02142.

Richardson, G. P. (1991). *Feedback thought in social science and systems theory.* Philadelphia: University of Pennsylvania Press.

Richardson, G. P., & Pugh, A. (1981). *Introduction to system dynamics modeling with DYNAMO.* Cambridge: MIT Press.

Ross, L. (1977). The intuitive psychologist and his shortcomings: Distortions in the attribution process. In L. Berkowitz (Ed.), *Advances in experimental social psychology* (Vol. 10, pp. 174-214). New York: Academic Press.

Schneiderman, A. (1988, April). Setting quality goals. *Quality Progress,* pp. 55-57.

Shewhart, W. (1939). *Statistical method from the viewpoint of quality control.* Washington, DC: U.S. Department of Agriculture.

Simon, H. A. (1969). *The sciences of the artificial.* Cambridge: MIT Press.

Sitkin, S., Sutcliffe, K., & Schroeder, R. (1994). Distinguishing control from learning in total quality management: A contingency perspective. *Academy of Management Review, 19,* 537-564.

Stata, R. (1989). Organizational learning: The key to management innovation. *Sloan Management Review, 30*(3), 63-74.

Staw, B. M. (1976). Knee-deep in the big muddy: A study of escalating commitment to a chosen course of action. *Organizational Behavior and Human Performance, 16,* 27-44.

Staw, B. M. (1981). The escalation of commitment to a course of action. *Academy of Management Review, 6,* 577-587.

Sterman, J. D. (1989a). Misperceptions of feedback in dynamic decision making. *Organizational Behavior and Human Decision Processes, 43,* 301-335.

Sterman, J. D. (1989b). Modeling managerial behavior: Misperceptions of feedback in a dynamic decision making experiment. *Management Science, 35,* 321-339.

Sterman, J. D. (1994). Learning in and about complex systems. *System Dynamics Review, 10,* 291-330.

Sterman, J., Repenning, N., & Kofman, F. (1997). Unanticipated side effects of successful quality programs: Exploring a paradox of organizational improvement. *Management Science, 43,* 503-521.

Taylor, S. E., & Fiske, S. T. (1975). Point of view and perceptions of causality. *Journal of Personality and Social Psychology, 32,* 439-445.

Thaler, R. (1980). Towards a positive theory of consumer choice. *Journal of Economic Behavior and Organization, 1,* 39-60.

Van de Ven, A., & Poole, M. S. (1995). Explaining development and change and organizations. *Academy of Management Review, 20,* 510-540.

Weick, K. E. (1979). *The social psychology of organizing* (2nd ed.). New York: Random House.

Weick, K. E. (1993). Organizational redesign as improvisation. In G. P. Huber & W. H. Glick (Eds.), *Organizational change and redesign.* New York: Oxford University Press.

White, J. B. (1996, November 26). Re-engineering gurus take steps to remodel their stalling vehicles. *Wall Street Journal,* p. 1.

Wruck, K. H., & Jensen, M. C. (1994). Science, specific knowledge, and total quality management. *Journal of Accounting and Economics, 18,* 247-287.

Wynne, B. (1988). Unruly technology: Practical rules, impractical discourse and public understanding. *Social Studies of Science, 18,* 147-167.

Chapter 10

The Effects of Total Quality Management on Corporate Performance

An Empirical Investigation

SHERRY L. JARRELL

Introduction

The emergence of Total Quality Management (TQM) has been one of the most significant recent developments in U.S. management practice. The focus on the development of TQM systems in the U.S. appears to have begun around 1980 in response to global competition, primarily in U.S. manufacturing companies facing competition from Japan. By the mid to late 1980s, the U.S. TQM movement had developed significant momentum, in part due to the creation of the Malcolm Baldrige National Quality Award by Congress in 1987 and participation in the Award by leading companies such as AT&T,

Motorola, Texas Instruments, Westinghouse, and Xerox.

Exactly what constitutes TQM is the subject of debate. In this article, we define TQM to be a management system which substantially addresses the criteria of the Malcolm Baldrige National Quality Award (NIST, 1994). Although a complete definition of TQM is beyond the scope of this article, some of the key characteristics include:[1]

- Emphasis on processes and their management and improvement. Widespread systematic organizational focus on quality improvement, cycle-time reduction, and waste (cost) reduction. Adoption of a prevention focus.

AUTHORS' NOTE: The authors would like to thank the companies that participated in the interviews. We would also like to thank the Editor and two anonymous referees for comments which substantially improved the manuscript. In addition, we would like to thank the following for comments and suggestions: George Benson, George Benston, William Golomski, Mark Holder, Tom Hustad, Phillip Lederer, Albert Madansky, Harry Roberts, Vinod Singhal, and Marc Zenner. Finally, we would like to thank Melissa J. Smith and Karin Sparf Chill for excellent research assistance. This research was partially supported by NSF grants numbers SBR-9523962 (Easton) and SBR-9523003 (Jarrell), a grant from the conference "Field Studies in Quality Management" at the Simon School of Business, University of Rochester, March 1993, and by summer research grants from the Graduate School of Business, University of Chicago and the School of Business, Indiana University.

From *Journal of Business, 71*(2), 1998, pp. 253-307. Reprinted with permission of the University of Chicago Press, 5801 South Ellis Avenue, Chicago, IL 60637.

- Efforts to apply the process concept and the emphasis on improvement throughout the company, including to product development and business support processes.

- Emphasis on customer focus. This includes emphasis on customer requirements and customer satisfaction to define product quality ("customer-defined quality") as well as a focus on customer service and integration with customers ("customer partnerships").

- Emphasis on the deployment of systematic analysis and fact-based decision making driven by objective data and information ("management-by-fact"). This includes focus on deployment and tracking of metrics.

- Widespread employee involvement in quality improvement, often through teams. Emphasis on employee development through training.

- Explicit emphasis on cross-functional management, including both cross-functional improvement and cross-functional participation in key processes (e.g., new product development).

- Emphasis on supplier quality and service and on supplier involvement and integration ("supplier partnerships") such as involvement in joint quality improvement or in new product development.

- Recognition of TQM as a critical competitive strategy and thus as a primary concern of *all* levels of management, including senior management. The role of senior management in providing leadership for the development and deployment of the TQM system is a natural consequence of recognition that TQM is a critical competitive strategy.

There is considerable controversy concerning the effectiveness of TQM and research examining its impact is only beginning to emerge. Most of this research is based on cross-sectional surveys that examine the association between manager perceptions of the impact of TQM and model constructs based on questionnaire items that are intended to capture various aspects of the deployment of TQM. There is little empirical research that attempts to determine the impact of TQM on corporate performance by directly examining publicly available financial data. Of these studies, most do not focus directly on TQM, but rather on related events such

as winning a quality award (e.g., Hendricks and Singhal, 1996) or achieving ISO-9000 registration (e.g., Anderson, et al., 1995). For a critical review of existing research on TQM that measures performance using publicly available financial data, see Easton and Jarrell (1997).

This study examines the impact of TQM on financial performance for a sample of 108 firms. The study is based on a comprehensive research methodology which combines: (1) interview-based research to identify a sample of firms which have, in fact, made serious efforts to implement TQM systems in a majority of their business, and (2) an empirical analysis of publicly available financial data using an improved benchmark and control methodology (Jarrell, 1991) for isolating the impact of the adoption of TQM. We believe that the methodology developed in this study for examining the impact of a complex management phenomenon is an improvement over approaches generally taken in the literature and represents one of the contributions of this article.

Overview of the Research Methodology

The basic approach used in this study adapts the event study methodology, commonly used in empirical corporate finance, to examine the impact of TQM on firm financial performance. In this study, the "event" corresponds to the beginning of serious efforts to deploy a comprehensive TQM system. The impact of TQM is assessed by examining the unexpected changes in financial performance for a five-year period following the beginning of deployment of the TQM system.

In most event studies in empirical finance, both the event and when it occurred can be unambiguously defined without much difficulty (e.g., the announcement of a merger). In this study, however, determining both whether and when an event has occurred is more difficult. First, whether or not a firm has seriously pursued TQM cannot be determined by relying on the firm's public pronouncements. Many firms claim to be implementing TQM when, in fact, they have made essentially no changes (other than in their public rhetoric). In other cases, TQM has been implemented in only a small fraction of their business. Second, firms seldom publicly announce the beginning of the deployment of their TQM systems. In fact, there is often no completely unambiguous start date. Rather, there is a period during which the firm's activities focus and efforts begin in earnest.

The lack of publicly available information about firms' implementations of TQM, the unreliability of their public statements, and the ambiguity of the start date of their TQM implementations are addressed in this study by interviews of a senior quality executive at each of the potential sample firms. Potential sample firms were first identified through public information sources as described in the next section. Interviews were then used to determine: (1) whether a firm has, in fact, seriously pursued development of a TQM system; (2) the approximate extent of development and deployment of the firm's approaches; and (3) the approximate date that serious efforts began. The interviews were conducted by a former Senior Examiner for the Malcolm Baldrige National Quality Award. The interview methodology is discussed in detail later.

The use of in-depth semi-structured interviews to select the sample firms is an important difference between this study and typical studies based on questionnaires. The key reasons are that the interviews are interactive, flexible, and allow in-depth discussion and focused probing. This permits considerable verification of the information obtained and allows for clarification of terminology and adjustment for the specific knowledge and experience base of the interview subject. In addition, interviews conducted by an interviewer trained in evaluation against a TQM "standard" (the Baldrige Award Criteria) allow external rather than respondent self-assessment of the company's TQM system against a well-developed operational definition.

In contrast, questionnaire-based approaches generally allow self-selection into the sample and rely on the managers' perceptions without critical evaluation. It is also very difficult in survey-based research to address the large variation in interpretation of terminology in different companies and it is frequently unclear how respondents actually operationalize the questions. As a result, most questionnaire-based research is fairly superficial. These research issues are discussed further in Easton and Jarrell (1997). Interview-based approaches, of course, also have disadvantages. These include dependence on the skill and knowledge of the interviewers, the difficulty of precise replication of the methodology, and the inability to examine the data collection instrument used.

In this study, interviews are also used to divide the sample firms into two groups based on the development of their TQM systems. The performance for these two groups is then compared. This provides an intra-sample validation of the overall research method since, if TQM positively impacts performance, the more advanced firms should perform better than the less advanced firms.[2]

The event study approach is another important difference between this study and cross-sectional studies which examine association between performance and the reported use of various practices (e.g., employee participation). Such cross-sectional studies generally do not attempt to determine when the practices were initiated or to examine performance changes associated with actual implementation. The failure to focus specifically on performance changes associated with the actual changes in management practices greatly increases the possibility of confounding factors. Further, such studies provide weak evidence concerning causality, even when statistically significant associations are observed, because the direction of causality is often unclear. In many cases, it is at least as plausible that, because of the availability of additional resources, improved performance drives the more extensive use of the "progressive" practices typically examined in these studies as it is that the progressive practices caused the improved performance. While it is impossible to *prove* causality through observational studies (including this one), studies which focus as tightly as possible on the period of the management changes and which use a carefully developed control methodology clearly provide far more compelling evidence than those that do not.

The control methodology used to develop the performance measures is another critical research issue. To assess the impact of TQM, the company's actual performance would ideally be compared to what the performance would have been had the company not implemented TQM (i.e., a perfect "clone" but with no TQM). Since this is not possible, a benchmark performance measure must be constructed which on average captures what the performance would have been without TQM. In this study, performance is assessed using both accounting-based variables and daily stock returns over a five-year period following the event. The performance measures are constructed somewhat differently for the accounting and stock return variables. For the accounting variables, the primary approach consists of two components. First, a firm's *unexpected performance* is measured by the difference between the firm's actual performance and an analyst's forecast made just prior to the event. Second, the event firm's unexpected performance is compared to the unexpected performance of a carefully matched control portfolio of three firms that do not appear to have implemented TQM. The control firms are matched to the event firm based on industry, time period, analysts' projections of future performance, and, to the extent possible, on market size, debt to equity ratios, and a market risk factor. The impact on performance is then measured by the *excess unexpected performance,* the difference between the unexpected performance of the event firm and the unexpected performance of its control portfolio.

The use of analysts' forecasts in the accounting performance variables is important because such forecasts incorporate an expert's evaluation of the future impact of the firm's particular circumstances. It is these forecasts that allow the performance measure to adjust for firm-specific exogenous factors that are likely to affect future performance, including factors influencing the endogenous decision to implement TQM. The failure to control for such factors can introduce potentially significant bias into the results. Such factors may not be apparent in the firm's historical financial data (e.g., emerging foreign competition, the expiration of a patent,

developing labor issues, or pending regulatory or tax changes).[3]

The use of the control portfolios is also critical to correct for subsequent exogenous events during the post-event period (e.g., a recession). Since the control portfolio is also matched on the analyst's projection of future performance, the research design provides an additional control against systematic differences between the event and control firms in bias in the analysts' forecasts.[4]

The idea of assessing performance relative to a prediction of future performance (i.e., the unexpected performance) is a fundamental idea in financial theory. It is intrinsic in any analysis based on stock returns because stock prices are derived from the market's consensus forecast of expected future performance. Ideally, market consensus forecasts would have been used here. However, these are not directly available.[5] Analysts forecasts, which represent an expert assessment, are used instead to proxy for market expectations.[6]

In contrast to the methodology used here, traditional approaches in the empirical finance literature use pre-event firm performance or post-event industry average performance as the control benchmark. Both of these approaches are unsatisfactory. The pre-event performance benchmark fails to control for subsequent exogenous macroeconomic events. The post-event industry benchmark assumes that the firm, had it not adopted TQM, would have performed like the typical firm in the industry. This fails to address the endogeneity of the decision to implement TQM. Some more recent approaches are based on fitting structural models and comparing actual performance to the model's prediction (see, for example, Healy, Palepu, and Ruback, 1992). While superior to the pre-event performance or post-event industry benchmark methods, such approaches generally assume that the structural equation is the same across event firms and is unaffected by subsequent exogenous events. They further assume that all of the factors likely to affect future performance, including those associated with the decision to implement TQM, are evident in the pre-event financial performance data used to estimate the structural equation. Thus, they do not adequately control for bias due to endogeneity of the decision to implement TQM.[7]

The method developed in this paper is used to assess performance of the TQM firms for appropriately scaled variables based on net income, operating income, and sales. Unfortunately, analysts' forecasts are not available for some other variables of interest (e.g., variables based on inventory levels or number of employees). For these variables, performance is measured by *excess actual performance,* the difference between the actual performances of the event firm and the control portfolio. While the evidence provided by these variables is much less compelling than when analysts' forecasts are available, we believe the results do contain some useful indications, particularly in the context of the overall analysis.

The impact of TQM is also evaluated using with-dividend continuously-compounded daily stock returns. Because the stock price incorporates the market's forecast of a firm's future performance, it is not appropriate to use analysts' forecasts when examining stock returns. It is important, however, to control for the impact of post-event exogenous events. Thus, the performance measure for stock returns is based on the *excess actual returns,* the difference between the returns of the event firm and its control portfolio. For this measure to be valid, it is important that the event firms and control portfolios are well-matched in terms of non-diversifiable risk. This is achieved as a result of the method of matching control firms discussed above which includes consideration of expected future performance, market size, debt to equity ratios, and a market risk factor. Thus, the matched control portfolios control for both post-event exogenous events and non-diversifiable risk.

Despite the similarity in methodology, this study differs from typical empirical finance event studies in some important ways. First, this study does not focus on the impact of information events ("announcements") on the capital market. While we examine stock returns, we use them for a different purpose—as a comparatively "clean" overall performance measure. Second, the event dates are not determined from public information, but rather from private information obtained through interviews. Third,

the phenomenon of interest (the deployment of TQM) does not occur at a discrete point in time like a typical "announcement," but rather occurs over a period of at least several years. Thus, we do not expect stock price reactions around event time zero. Instead, we examine a five-year period following the beginning of the implementation of TQM. While some of the benefits of TQM, such as certain types of cost reductions, can be obtained relatively quickly, many others, such as improvements in new product development or increased market share due to increased customer satisfaction, require at least several years to become evident in the firm's accounting data. Many benefits of TQM may even occur after the five-year post-event period that we examine. Further, during the period that the firms in this sample began implementing TQM, the capital markets had little basis for assessing TQM's impact; the evidence is only now beginning to emerge. Thus, it is not unreasonable to expect that the impact on stock return performance will occur throughout the five-year post-event period as the results (positive and negative) of TQM implementation accrue and become evident in the firms' accounting data.

In interpreting this study, it is important to understand that we are attempting to examine transient performance effects due to introduction of a new management "technology." In a theoretical setting where managers always instantaneously select the optimal strategy for maximizing firm performance based on the available information set, a firm's decision to implement TQM or not would always be deterministically driven as the optimal response to exogenous variables. After controlling for all of these exogenous variables, there would be no observable effect due to TQM. This theoretical argument is not unique to TQM; it also applies to other management decisions, including restructuring decisions (e.g., mergers), which are frequently the focus of similar research examining their performance impact.

These assumptions, of course, are unrealistically strong. Managers do not always make optimal decisions and certainly do not always do so instantaneously. What managers seek are strategies for moving their companies towards a dynamically changing optimum. Potential strategies include implementation of TQM (among many others — including restructuring). It is of interest to examine whether or not such strategies generate value for the companies that implement them. The performance impact can be examined only because of deviations from the theoretical setting described above. These deviations should be transient as competitive pressure drives the economic system towards optimality.

Data Sources and Sample Design

Candidate event firms were initially identified through publicly available information sources. The search was intended to be comprehensive, but not exhaustive. The primary sources were the ARS full-text database of on-line annual reports from Nexis/Lexis (since 1987), the Businesswire full-text database of press releases (since 1986), Standard and Poor's Corporate Register of Directors (1993), and the U.S. GAO (1991) Report's list of Baldrige Award site-visited companies.

The study was conducted in two phases. The pilot phase was based on annual report searches for the key words "total quality management," "just-in-time" or "JIT," "Baldrige," "Deming," "Juran," and "Crosby." These searches identified 274 firms. Relevant excerpts were then reviewed to select only the firms whose annual reports clearly indicated implementation of at least one specific quality management approach (e.g., SPC, JIT, quality training, improvement teams, etc.)

Review of the annual report searches resulted in a list of 78 firms. These firms were contacted to set up an interview with a senior manager familiar with the development of the firm's quality management systems. Of the 78 firms, 59 were interviewed. In 11 cases, firms were not interviewed because it became clear in trying to set up the interview that the firm was not actually implementing TQM. In the remaining 8 cases, the request was refused. Of the 59 firms interviewed, 15 were eliminated because

the interviews did not indicate serious efforts to implement TQM in a majority of their business. An additional 5 firms were eliminated because the required performance data were not available. The remaining 39 firms formed the pilot sample. Interviews for the pilot sample were conducted between January and March, 1993.

In the second phase of the study, additional candidate firms were sought from a variety of sources. First, an additional 54 firms were selected after a second review of the original 274 firms identified through the annual report searches. Second, new firms were sought through additional searches and sources. The Businesswire database was searched for references to quality awards. Searches were also made for quality-related executive titles. The annual report database was searched for "quality" within five words of "vice president" or "director" and the Businesswire database was searched for "total" or "continuous" within three words, and "focus" and "satisfaction" within five words, of "vice president" or "director." These searches identified 89 firms. The 1993 Standard and Poor's Register of Directors and Executives was searched for "quality" within five words of "vice president" or "director," identifying 71 firms. Finally, lists of site-visited firms from the GAO study and lists of the institutional affiliations of Baldrige Award Examiners for the years 1989 to 1993 (available from the Baldrige Award Office) were reviewed, identifying 67 additional firms. Thus, 281 new candidate firms were identified in the second phase of the study.

As in the pilot phase of the study, the information on these firms was reviewed for evidence of specific quality management approaches. This resulted in a list of 129 firms which were then contacted for interviews. Of these, 117 agreed to be interviewed. Of the 12 firms that were not interviewed, 6 declined to participate and 6 obviously did not have TQM programs. Of the firms that were interviewed, 38 were eliminated because the interviews did not confirm serious efforts to implement TQM in a majority of the business and 10 were eliminated because the required performance data were not available. This resulted in 69 additional event firms. These interviews were conducted between August, 1993 and January, 1994.

In summary, information on over 500 firms was reviewed to identify potential sample firms. Of these, a total of 207 were approached for interviews. Fourteen firms declined to participate giving an overall response rate of 93%. In trying to set up the interviews, 17 firms were determined not to have a TQM system. A total of 176 firms were actually interviewed and 53 firms (30% of those interviewed) were eliminated because their efforts to implement TQM did not appear to be adequate. An additional 15 firms were eliminated because the required performance data were unavailable. This process resulted in 108 event firms in the final sample (see Appendix 10.1).

The Value Line Investment Survey was used as the source of analysts' forecasts, the primary source of the accounting data, and to select the control firms. For the measures based on the Value Line analysts' forecasts, performance is examined for years 1, 2, and the average of years 3-5 following the event. Long-term data were available for 100 of the 108 events. The COMPUSTAT database compiled by Standard and Poor's was used for data which Value Line does not report (inventory levels and the number of employees). Daily stock returns were obtained from the database compiled by the Center for Research in Security Prices (CRSP) at the University of Chicago.

Interview Methods

Each candidate sample firm was contacted, first by a letter describing the project and then by telephone, to set up an interview with a senior manager familiar with the development of the company's quality management systems (generally a vice president or director of quality). The interviews generally lasted about 45 minutes and were conducted by George S. Easton, a former Senior Examiner for the Malcolm Baldrige National Quality Award. The objective of the interview process was to develop a time-line of the development of the company's TQM systems, to determine what key ap-

proaches were used, and to assess the actual extent of deployment through in-depth probing in a few areas. The interviews were semi-structured and allowed flexibility in the topics discussed. The managers were promised complete confidentiality concerning the interview content.

The interview process occurred in two phases. The objective of the first phase was to elicit from the manager, with minimal prompting, the major milestones in the development of the company's TQM approaches. Questions were asked as necessary to establish the level of detail desired and to determine as specifically as possible the dates of the events surrounding the beginning of the TQM approaches. Questions about approaches or methods not mentioned by the manager were avoided in order not to influence the manager's description. These impromptu descriptions are very revealing about the aspects of the development of the TQM system that the manager believes are important and what the key drivers of the company's system actually are; that is, how the company "thinks" about its TQM systems.

The second phase of the interview process was intended to fill in any important gaps and to probe some key areas in order to assess actual levels of deployment. The list of interview topics given in Appendix 10.2 was used to prompt the interviewer. The objective was not to discuss every topic, but rather to discuss in detail a few areas as appropriate for the company's approaches and the expertise and experience of the manager being interviewed. If not adequately addressed by the initial description of the time-line, four areas were always covered: production, customer satisfaction measurement, supplier management, and new product development and design. In general, the extent of deployment of approaches mentioned was assessed by asking specific questions concerning the number of employees involved, the training they have received, and the dates of the various events mentioned. Other questions used to determine the actual extent of deployment included asking what were the most important barriers to implementation, what would you do differently if you were to begin implementing this approach again, what lessons were learned, and what changes or improvements have been made since the initial approach. When the approaches described have actually been deployed, there is generally a rich "story" surrounding them and it is fairly easy for a knowledgeable interviewer to determine if significant deployment has actually occurred.

Companies were included in the sample if, based on the interviews, they appear to have made serious efforts to implement TQM approaches in the majority of their business. Deployment must be in a majority of the company (as measured by sales) in order for there to be any reasonable expectation that the results could be observable in the company's overall financial data. The standard of "serious efforts" for inclusion in the sample is quite low; it is not a requirement that the company's efforts resulted in a comprehensive and well-integrated approach.

Companies were eliminated from the sample for a variety of reasons. In many cases, the reason was that the TQM efforts were deployed in only a small fraction of the company. Other reasons ranged from a lack of evidence of any significant deployment efforts to confusion of TQM with other approaches (such as quality improvements due solely to automation).

The start dates for the sample companies were chosen, based on the time-line developed from the interview notes, to be about six months after the beginning of the first major initiative. This initiative was usually the deployment of widespread quality training. In some companies, however, other initiatives marked the beginning of their TQM systems, such as major changes in customer satisfaction measurement or new product development, widespread deployment of SPC, or deployment of a quality management systems assessment process (e.g., Baldrige-based assessment). The start date was chosen to be six months after the beginning of the first major initiative because most such initiatives take substantial time to roll out. For example, it is not uncommon for widespread training initiatives to take over a year to complete in a large company and there is usually an additional lag before substantive organizational or operational changes occur.

The start date determines when the analysts' forecasts were made that are used in the performance measures. In order for the difference between the actual post-event performance and the analyst's forecast to capture the unexpected performance due to TQM, the forecasts should be made prior to the analyst's incorporating knowledge about the firm's TQM initiatives. This suggests selecting an early event time zero to ensure that the analyst is not aware of the TQM initiative. However, too early an event time zero truncates the postevent period, which is limited to five years, and may result in a failure to capture the main performance improvement due to TQM. The selection of event time zero to be six months after the initial deployment of the first major initiative compromises between these conflicting objectives.

Despite the fact that event time zero was selected to be six months after the beginning of the first major initiative, there are several reasons that it is unlikely that the analysts' forecasts are affected. They include: (1) there is almost never any public information available about the initiatives until later than this period; (2) any claims made by management about their intentions contain little substantive information about whether or not serious efforts to implement TQM will actually be made; (3) during the period we are studying, TQM was new and thus there would be little or no basis for updating the forecasts; and (4) the texts accompanying the Value Line analysts' forecasts were also reviewed and in no case was there any mention of the firm beginning a quality-related initiative. More importantly, however, any such leakage into the analysts' forecasts biases against finding an effect due to TQM, and thus makes the results of this study conservative.

The companies that were retained for the sample were divided into a group of 44 firms with more advanced TQM systems and a group of 64 firms with less advanced TQM systems by making a rough estimate, based solely on the interviews, of what the firm's score would be in terms of the approach and deployment (not results) areas of the Baldrige Criteria. It should be noted that the interviews focused only on the approaches taken and the extent of their deployment and not on operational or financial results.

The firms selected as more advanced had estimated scores above 450 out of 1000 possible points. This represents considerable success developing and deploying a TQM system. The median score of companies which apply for the Baldrige Award is generally below 500.

The key differences between the more advanced and less advanced firms were in the scope of the issues addressed by their TQM systems and the extent of deployment of their approaches. Some of the firms in the less advanced group had successfully deployed basic approaches such as quality training and improvement teams, but had then not further developed their quality management systems. Others had developed approaches which address a broader scope of the Baldrige Criteria but had only limited deployment. In contrast, firms in the more advanced group had better deployment of the basic approaches together with the deployment of a broader scope of systems. These companies typically have had multiple major phases in the development of their TQM systems whereas less advanced firms typically have only completed one major phase. For example, a typical advanced firm might start with an initial phase focused internally an SPC and quality improvement teams, followed by a second phase which might focus on design quality, internal self-assessment, or customer satisfaction measurement (and feedback of such information into the company's internal processes). Subsequent phases would then focus on approaches and issues not already addressed.

Analysis Methods

This study examines statistical evidence against the null hypothesis that implementation of TQM does not improve corporate performance. Performance is measured by accounting variables, primarily focusing on net income, operating income, sales, and inventory, and by with-dividend continuously-compounded stock returns. As discussed in an earlier section, in order to be convincing, the performance measures must: (1) take firm-specific factors into account, including those associated with the (endogenous) decision to implement TQM; and (2) compensate for post-event macroeconomic or industry-specific developments that are likely to affect firm performance. The approach used here was developed by Jarrell (1991) to address these issues.

Control Portfolio Selection

All of the performance measures examined rely on matched control portfolios. For each event firm, a control portfolio of three firms that do not appear to have implemented TQM is formed by matching them to the TQM firm on the basis of industry, calendar time, projected performance, and, to the extent possible, market size, debt to equity ratios, and a market risk factor (the Value Line "safety" ranking).[8] Matching on industry and calendar time is designed to control for various economic and regulatory influences. The industry classifications are defined by the Value Line Investment Survey and verified with the Standard Industrial Classification (SIC) code. The matching included a detailed review of product lines as described by Value Line, so the matching realized is substantially better than provided by using the Value Line industry classifications or SIC codes alone.

The "projected performance" matching of the control firms to the event firms is based on the Value Line "timeliness" rank. The timeliness rank summarizes the analyst's assessment of the firm's expected stock price performance over the next twelve months relative to the other firms covered by Value Line.[9] Whenever possible, firms were selected whose timeliness rank at the time of the event differed by no more than one from the event firm rank. These firms were then narrowed to three control firms per event, first by choosing those closest in size to the TQM firm and then (if more than three remain) those whose debt to equity ratio and Value Line safety rank are closest to the TQM firm. Size is measured by the market value of debt plus the market value of equity and preferred stock as reported by the Value Line during event year zero.

Matching on the basis of the timeliness rank incorporates into the control portfolios as much information as possible about the expected performance of the TQM firms. Because the control firms are selected to have an outlook similar to that of the event firm, such matching has the potential to control for effects such as systematic differences in forecast accuracy between firms forecast to perform every well and those forecast to perform poorly. The existence of this type of bias is plausible. For example, due to the phenomenon of regression towards the mean, analysts' forecasts may be systematically too high for firms that are expected to perform very well and systematically too low for firms that are expected to perform poorly. In such a case, failure to control for projected performance could introduce bias into the results, especially if the sample has a high concentration of firms that are expected to either perform very well or very poorly.[10] Similarly, matching that considers the timeliness rank also minimizes the effects of any systematic differences in responses to subsequent economic events between firms with very positive and very negative outlooks.[11]

Accounting Variables: The Primary Performance Benchmark Method

The primary performance benchmark compares each event firm's corresponding control firm's performance to Value Line analysts' forecasts made prior to the event. Specifically, for event firm i for post-event year t, then *unexpected performance* $U_i^E(t)$ is

$$U_i^E(t) = P_i^E(t) - F_i^E(t),$$

where $P_i^E(t)$ is the actual performance of TQM firm i for post-event year t, and $F_i^E(t)$ is the Value Line analyst's forecast of that performance made prior to the event. The unexpected performance $U_i^{Cj}(t)$ for the firms in the control portfolio is similarly defined:

$$U_i^{Cj}(t) = P_i^{Cj}(t) - F_i^{Cj}(t),$$

where $P_i^{Cj}(t)$ is the actual performance and $F_i^{Cj}(t)$ is the forecast performance for period t for control firm j corresponding to event i. The unexpected performance $\overline{U}_i^{Cj}(t)$ for the control portfolio is the average of the unexpected performance for the three control firms:

$$\overline{U}_i^{Cj}(t) = \tfrac{1}{3} \sum_{j=1}^{3} U_i^{Cj}(t).$$

For the accounting variables, the primary measure examined for evidence of the impact of TQM on firm performance is the *excess unexpected performance $XU_i(t)$*, the difference between the unexpected performance of the event firm and the unexpected performance of the corresponding control portfolio. Thus,

$$XU_i(t) = U_i^E(t) - \overline{U_i^{C}(t)}.$$

Value Line analyst's forecasts are given for one year ahead, two years ahead, and the average of years three to five ahead. Thus, the excess unexpected performance cannot be calculated separately for post-event years 3, 4, and 5. Instead, following the analyst's forecasts, the long-term performance measure is based on unexpected average performance for years three to five. Specifically, for event firm i, the unexpected average annual performance $\overline{U}_i^E(3{:}5)$ for post-event years three to five is

$$\overline{U}_i^E(3{:}5) = \overline{P}_i^E(3{:}5) - \overline{F}_i^E(3{:}5),$$

where $\overline{P}_i^E(3{:}5) = (P_i^E(3) + P_i^E(4) + P_i^E(5))/3$ and $\overline{F}_i^E(3{:}5)$ is the analyst's forecast of the average annual performance over years three to five. Unexpected average performance for years three to five is calculated for each control firm in the same manner. Paralleling the development above, the excess unexpected average performance for years three to five is then calculated.

Accounting Variables: When Forecasts Are Unavailable

Value Line analysts' forecasts are not available for variables based on inventory levels and the number of employees. For these variables, *excess actual performance* is examined.[12] The excess actual performance $X_i(t)$ for event i for post-event time t is

$$X_i(t) = P_i^E(t) - \overline{P}_i^C(t),$$

where $\overline{P}_i^C(t) = \frac{1}{3}\sum_{j=1}^{3} P_i^{Cj}(t)$. Note that $P_i^E(t)$ and $P_i^{Cj}(t)$ are the actual performance for the event and control firms as defined in the previous section. In addition, excess average performance for both a five-year pre-event and a five-year post-event period is examined; that is

$$\overline{X}_i^{\text{pre}} = \frac{1}{5}\sum_{t=-5}^{-1} P_i^E(t) - \frac{1}{5}\sum_{t=-5}^{-1}\overline{P}_i^C(t),$$

and

$$\overline{X}_i^{\text{post}} = \frac{1}{5}\sum_{t=1}^{5} P_i^E(t) - \frac{1}{5}\sum_{t=1}^{5}\overline{P}_i^C(t).$$

Finally, the difference between the post- and pre-event excess average performance is also examined:

$$D_i = \overline{X}_i^{\text{post}} - \overline{X}_i^{\text{pre}}.$$

Stock Returns

The impact of TQM is also examined using with-dividend continuously-compounded daily stock returns. As discussed in an earlier section, it is not appropriate to use analysts' forecasts in conjunction with stock returns. Thus, the stock return performance measure is the *excess cumulative daily return*. The excess cumulative daily return $XCR_i(t)$ for event i at post-event day t is

$$XCR_i(t) = CR_i^E(t) - \overline{CR}_i^C(t),$$

where $CR_i^E(t)$ is the post-event cumulative daily return at day t for event firm i and $\overline{CR}_i^C(t)$ is the average of the cumulative returns at day t for firms in the corresponding control portfolio. Thus, $\overline{CR}_i^C(t) = \frac{1}{3}\sum_{j=1}^{3} CR_i^{Cj}(t)$, where $CR_i^{Cj}(t)$ is the post-event cumulative return at day t for firm j of the control portfolio C for event i. The cumulative returns $CR(t)$ are defined similarly for the event and control firms: $CR(t) = \sum_{t'=1}^{t} r(t')$ where $r(t')$ is the with-dividend continuously-compounded daily stock return for day t' following event time 0. The excess average monthly stock returns for the pre- and post-event period and the difference of the differences are also examined, where the monthly returns are calculated by cumulating the with dividend continuously-compounded daily returns for the month.

As described above, the control portfolio methodology matches control and event firms as closely as possible, with the result that the event and control firms are closely matched on systematic risk. However, the stock returns analysis was also repeated using beta excess returns. The results, which are not presented here, are similar indicating that differences in systematic risk between the events and controls are not driving the stock return results.

Results

This section describes the results for both the accounting measures and stock returns. All results are for either excess unexpected or excess actual performance (depending on the availability of analysts' forecasts) of the TQM firm in comparison to the matched non-TQM control portfolio. The analysis of the accounting variables focuses on net income, operating income, and inventory scaled by measures of firm size based on sales, assets, or number of employees. Results for sales-to-assets are also presented. Results are given for the full sample of 108 TQM events and for the subsamples of event firms with more advanced and less advanced TQM systems. The analysis is repeated using only the 93 manufacturing firms. We examine manufacturing firms separately because the early development of U.S. TQM was primarily in manufacturing companies and, as a result, the methods of TQM are better developed in this context.

Summary statistics for the full sample of 108 TQM event firms are given in Tables 10.1-10.3. Event year zero, the beginning of the firm's TQM implementation, spans the years 1981 to 1991 (Table 10.1). The sample firms represent 32 different industries (Table 10.2) and range in market size from $76 million to $73 billion with a mean of $5.4 billion (Table 10.3).

TABLE 10.1 Distribution of the Year of
Implementation of TQM

Year of Implementation	Number of TQM Firms
1981	1
1982	3
1983	9
1984	11
1985	7
1986	15
1987	17
1988	10
1989	17
1990	15
1991	3
Total	108

TABLE 10.2 Distribution of the TQM Firms by
Industry

Industry	No. Firms
Aerospace	4
Air Transport	1
Auto and Truck	3
Auto Parts	3
Banking	2
Building Materials	1
Chemicals	12
Computers and Peripherals	10
Diversified	3
Electric Utilities	2
Electronics/Electrical Equipment	12
Financial Services	1
Food Processing	1
Furniture and Home Furnishings	1
Home Appliances	2
Household Products	1
Machine Tools	1
Machinery	5
Medical Supplies	2
Metals and Mining	1
Office Equipment and Supplies	4
Oilfield Services	1
Packaging and Containers	2
Paper and Forest Products	5
Petroleum	1
Precision Instruments	3
Publishing	1
Semiconductors	11
Steel	1
Telecommunications	4
Tire and Rubber	2
Trucking and Transport Leasing	5
Total	108

TABLE 10.3 TQM Firm and Control Firm Market
Size

Market Size[a]	TQM Firms	Non-TQM Control Firms
Mean Size	$ 5.4 billion	$ 2.4 billion
Median Size	$ 1.5 billion	$ 0.9 billion
Minimum	$75.9 million	$47.6 million
Maximum	$73.3 billion	$35.0 billion

a. Market size is the market value of equity (including preferred
stock) plus the market value of total debt. Both the debt and equity
variables are taken from the Value Line Investment Survey
published during event year zero.

Statistical Analysis Methods

All tables, except for Tables 10.10 and 10.19,
report the medians of the performance measures. The medians are used because, especially
for the accounting variables, the data are not
normally distributed. Deviations from the normal distribution include the presence of outliers, wide tails, and, for some variables, skewness. Medians are extremely robust to these
types of problems. The tables for the accounting
variables also present sign-test p-values testing
the one-sided null hypothesis that TQM does
not improve performance against the alternative
that performance is improved. Sign-tests were
used because they are non-parametric and thus
robust to the kinds of deviations from the normal distribution described above. Wilcoxon
signed-rank tests were not used because this test
assumes that the distribution of the data is symmetric, an assumption violated by the accounting data. When there is skewness, the test is not
valid and can be inconsistent with the actual
medians (e.g., the sample median can be negative, while the Wilcoxon test indicates that the
center of symmetry of the distribution is positive).

The tables also compare the results for the
less advanced and more advanced TQM firms.
Wilcoxon rank-sum tests were used to test the
null hypothesis that the distribution of the performance measure for the more advanced firms
is not stochastically larger than that of the less
advanced firms (against the alternative that it is
stochastically larger). A distribution $F(x)$ is

stochastically larger than a distribution $G(x)$ if $F(x)$ gee $G(x)$ for all x, but $F(x)$ not $G(x)$. Unlike the Wilcoxon signedrank test, the Wilcoxon rank-sum test does not assume that the distributions are symmetric or that, under the null hypothesis, the two distributions are identical. Wilcoxon rank-sum test are also used for several other comparisons between subsamples. The specific hypotheses are described in the table legends.

For the cumulative daily stock return data in Tables 10.9, 10.12, 10.18, and 10.21, Wilcoxon signed-rank tests are used rather than sign tests. The reasons are: (1) normal probability plots do not indicate departure from symmetry; (2) there is much empirical evidence indicating that daily stock returns are reasonably close to normally distributed; and (3) Wilcoxon signed-rank tests are more powerful than sign tests when the underlying distribution is symmetric.

Tables 10.10 and 10.19 present analysis of the cumulative daily stock return data based on the assumption that the stock returns are multivariate normal. Thus, sample means are reported. The p-values in these tables use test statistics that are based on estimates of the variances and covariances between firms whose event year zero is the same calendar year. Thus, comparison of these tables with Tables 10.9 and 10.18 allows an assessment of the impact of any correlation due to industry and event-year clustering.

Accounting Variables: Excess Unexpected Performance

Table 10.4 shows the results for excess unexpected performance for net income/sales (NI/S), net income/assets (NI/A), operating income/sales (OI/S), operating income/assets (OI/A), and sales/assets (S/A). For the full sample of firms, the table shows that the median excess performance is positive for all of the variables for the average of years 3-5 indicating that, for all of the variables examined, more than half of the event firms performed better in comparison to the analysts' forecasts than did the matched control portfolios. This improvement for years 3-5 is significant at the 1% level

for OI/A, at the 5% level for NI/S and NI/A, and at the 10% level for S/A. Performance is also improved for all the variables in years 1 and 2 except for OI/S and OI/A where there is a decline in performance in year 2. While the results for years 1 and 2 are generally not statistically significant, this provides some evidence against the idea that implementing TQM hurts short-term performance. Note that the improvement is much larger for years 3-5 than for years 1 and 2 for all of the variables except OI/S, consistent with the hypothesis that the most important impact of implementing TQM is on longer-term performance.

For the firms with more advanced TQM systems, except for OI/S, the results for years 3-5 are uniformly better than for the firms with less well-developed systems. For the more advanced firms, in spite of the much smaller sample size ($n = 44$); the years 3-5 performance improvement is significant at the 1% level for OI/A and S/A, at the 5% level for NI/A, and at the 10% level for NI/S. The results are also better for the years 3-5 performance than for the year 1 and 2 performance for all variables except OI/S. For the more advanced firms, the improvement in year 1 is significant for all of the variables and significant in year 2 at the 10% level for NI/S. For the less advanced firms, while all of the medians for years 3-5 are positive, none of the variables are significant. There is no indication that short-term performance is improved for the less advanced firms and, in fact, there may be some evidence that it declines for OI/S.

The p-values for the Wilcoxon rank-sum test indicate that the improvement for the years 3-5 performance for the more advanced firms in comparison to the less advanced firms is significant at the 1% level for S/A, the 5% level for OI/A, and the 10% level for NI/A. The difference in year 1 performance is significant at the 5% level for NI/S, NI/A, and OI/A and at the 10% level for S/A. The difference in year 2 performance is significant at the 10% level for NI/S and OI/S.

In summary, Table 10.4 provides strong evidence of overall improvement in longer-term performance for these accounting variables for the full sample of TQM events. This improvement is stronger for the more advanced firms,

TABLE 10.4 Excess Unexpected Performance for the Accounting Variables

Variable	Year	Full Sample			Less Advanced TQM Firms			More Advanced TQM Firms			
		Median	p-sgn	n	Median	p-sgn	n	Median	p-sgn	n	p-wrs
NI/S	1	0.26%	0.11	108	−0.03%	0.55	64	0.54%	0.03	44	0.04
	2	0.25%	0.19	108	−0.03%	0.55	64	0.54%	0.09	44	0.09
	3-5	0.60%	0.03	100	0.47%	0.11	56	1.12%	0.09	44	0.12
NI/A	1	0.39%	0.11	108	−0.04%	0.65	64	0.83%	0.01	44	0.02
	2	0.49%	0.07	108	0.40%	0.13	64	0.52%	0.23	44	0.22
	3-5	0.91%	0.03	100	0.37%	0.17	56	1.86%	0.05	44	0.06
OI/S	1	0.03%	0.50	108	−0.43%	0.92	64	0.58%	0.06	44	0.11
	2	−0.12%	0.78	108	−0.47%	0.92	64	0.10%	0.38	44	0.10
	3-5	0.04%	0.46	100	0.16%	0.45	56	−0.01%	0.56	44	0.30
OI/A	1	0.46%	0.11	108	−0.17%	0.73	64	1.27%	0.01	44	0.04
	2	−0.12%	0.16	108	0.02%	0.55	64	−0.12%	0.67	44	0.54
	3-5	1.52%	0.01	100	0.37%	0.17	56	2.98%	0.01	44	0.04
S/A	1	1.72%	0.05	108	0.46%	0.35	64	3.86%	0.03	44	0.10
	2	1.17%	0.25	108	0.05%	0.55	64	2.82%	0.15	44	0.36
	3-5	4.89%	0.07	100	0.03%	0.55	56	8.40%	0.01	44	0.01

NOTE: Medians and p-values for the excess unexpected performance for net income/sales (NI/S), net income/assets (NI/A), operating income/sales (OI/S), operating income/assets (OI/A), and sales/assets (S/A). The medians are expressed as percentages. Results are reported for both the full sample of 108 events and for the subsamples of 64 event firms with less advanced TQM systems and 44 event firms with more advanced TQM systems. The data and forecasts used to construct the performance measures were obtained from Value Line. The columns labeled p-sgn contain p-values for the one-sided sign test of the null hypothesis H_0 : true median ≤ 0 against the alternative H_A : true median > 0. The sample sizes are given in the columns labeled n. The column labeled p-wrs contains p-values for the one-sided Wilcoxon rank-sum test of the null hypothesis that the underlying distribution of the more advanced firms is not stochastically larger than that of the less advanced firms.

and weaker for the less advanced firms, with performance for the less advanced firms, for the most part, not statistically different than the controls. The longer-term performance is stronger than the short-term performance. For the full sample, there is no evidence that short-term performance is hurt by the implementation of TQM. There is, in fact, evidence that even the short-term performance for the more advanced TQM firms is improved.

Accounting Variables: Excess Actual Performance

Table 10.5 shows excess actual net income/employees (NI/E) and operating income/employees (OI/E) for a period from five years before the event to five years after the event. For the full sample, there appears to be an overall declining trend in NI/E preceding the event and a generally improving trend following the event, resulting in positive (but not sig-

nificant) median performance for year five. At the bottom of each panel, the table also shows the excess average year −5 to −1 performance, the excess average year 1 to 5 performance, and the difference between the pre-event and post-event period excess average performance. The median average performance is negative for both the pre- and post-event periods. The median difference between the pre- and post-event period averages is positive but not statistically significant.

For OI/E, the performance varies around zero through year 1 following the event. For years 2-5, there is an improving trend with significant positive performance at the 5% level in years 3 and 5. Note that, due to the availability of the data, the sample size decreases over years 2-5, making it more difficult to obtain statistical significance for the longer-term data. For year 5, the median improvement in operating income for the event firms in comparison to the control firms is approximately $3,000 per employee. The median post-event period aver-

TABLE 10.5 Excess Actual Net Income per Employee and Operating Income per Employee

Variable	Year	Full Sample			Less Advanced TQM Firms			More Advanced TQM Firms			
		Median	p-sgn	n	Median	p-sgn	n	Median	p-sgn	n	p-wrs
NI/E	−5	−0.48	0.82	98	−0.50	0.79	57	−0.47	0.73	41	0.50
	−4	−0.41	0.86	100	−0.35	0.70	57	−0.72	0.89	43	0.73
	−3	−0.77	0.95	102	−0.50	0.70	59	−0.92	0.98	43	0.68
	−2	−0.02	0.58	105	−0.02	0.45	62	−0.15	0.73	43	0.63
	−1	−1.16	0.99	108	−0.53	0.92	64	−1.54	0.97	44	0.64
	0	1.20	0.95	108	−1.56	0.97	64	−1.16	0.67	44	0.13
	1	−0.83	0.93	108	−1.02	0.95	64	−0.47	0.67	44	0.04
	2	−0.46	0.78	105	−1.88	0.85	61	0.16	0.56	44	0.04
	3	−0.17	0.54	90	−1.39	0.72	47	0.13	0.38	43	0.33
	4	−0.27	0.59	71	−1.28	0.76	33	0.29	0.44	38	0.34
	5	0.70	0.22	61	−0.70	0.65	27	0.84	0.11	34	0.35
	−5 to −1	−0.72	0.86	108	−0.68	0.73	64	−0.78	0.85	44	0.66
	1 to 5	−0.30	0.68	108	−1.43	0.87	64	0.47	0.33	44	0.03
	Difference	0.29	0.19	108	−0.04	0.55	64	0.88	0.09	44	0.03
OI/E	−5	0.44	0.22	84	0.24	0.39	51	0.83	0.24	33	0.28
	−4	−0.23	0.67	85	−0.16	0.61	51	−0.78	0.70	34	0.43
	−3	−0.07	0.58	87	0.31	0.50	53	−0.70	0.70	34	0.64
	−2	−0.44	0.62	90	−1.14	0.66	56	−0.07	0.57	34	0.38
	−1	0.22	0.42	93	0.26	0.55	58	0.22	0.37	35	0.31
	0	−0.26	0.62	94	−0.67	0.74	58	0.74	0.43	36	0.19
	1	−0.18	0.62	94	−1.33	0.82	58	2.68	0.31	36	0.08
	2	1.39	0.17	92	−0.24	0.55	56	2.68	0.07	36	0.06
	3	2.78	0.02	78	2.03	0.18	43	3.63	0.02	35	0.18
	4	2.04	0.22	61	−2.86	0.77	29	2.52	0.06	32	0.09
	5	3.03	0.05	51	1.27	0.27	24	4.83	0.06	27	0.25
	−5 to −1	0.07	0.34	93	0.16	0.45	58	0.06	0.37	35	0.27
	1 to 5	1.19	0.09	94	−1.28	0.74	58	3.68	0.00	36	0.01
	Difference	0.46	0.34	93	−0.22	0.74	58	2.63	0.09	35	0.03

NOTE: Medians and p-values for the excess actual performance for net income/# employees (NI/E) and operating income/# employees (OI/E) for event years −5 to 5. The rows labeled "−5 to −1," "1 to 5," and "Difference" give the results for the average pre-event period performance, the average post-event period performance, and the difference of the pre-event period and post-event period averages, respectively. The units for the medians are $1,000s per employee. Results are reported for both the full sample of 108 events and for the subsamples of 64 event firms with less advanced TQM systems and 44 event firms with more advanced TQM systems. The data were obtained from COMPUSTAT. The columns labeled p-sgn contain p-values for the one-sided sign test of the null hypothesis H_0 : true median ≤ 0 against the alternative H_A : true median > 0. The sample sizes are given in the columns labeled n. The column labeled p-wrs contains p-values for the one-sided Wilcoxon rank-sum test of the null hypothesis that the underlying distribution of the more advanced firms is not stochastically larger than that of the less advanced firms.

age is positive and statistically significant at the 10% level. The median difference in the pre-post averages is positive, but not significant.

For the more advanced TQM firms, a similar but stronger pattern occurs. The median excess NI/E turns positive in year 2 and, with a p-value of 0.11, is almost significant at the 10% level in year 5. The median excess NI/E in year 5 is approximately $840. The median post-event period average is positive, but not significant. The median difference in the pre-post averages, however, is positive and significant at the 10%

level, providing some evidence of improvement between the pre- and post-event periods. For OI/E, the performance is significantly positive at the 5% or 10% level for years 2-5 following the event with a median excess OI/E of $4,830 in year 5. The median post-event period average is about $3,680 and is significant at the 1% level. The median difference in the pre-post averages is about $2,630, and is significant at the 10% level. In contrast, for the less advanced firms, excess NI/E is negative, although improving, throughout the post-event period. The

TABLE 10.6 Excess Actual Sales per Employee

Variable	Year	Full Sample			Less Advanced TQM Firms			More Advanced TQM Firms			
		Median	p-sgn	n	Median	p-sgn	n	Median	p-sgn	n	p-wrs
S/E	−5	−4.36	0.96	98	−4.63	0.97	57	−4.09	0.73	41	0.14
	−4	−7.37	0.97	100	−8.71	0.99	57	−3.50	0.62	43	0.09
	−3	−7.38	0.99	102	−8.38	0.99	59	−7.02	0.89	43	0.16
	−2	−5.03	0.99	105	−5.64	0.99	62	−1.50	0.82	43	0.26
	−1	−8.07	1.00	108	−8.07	1.00	64	−6.59	0.85	44	0.17
	0	−6.80	0.99	108	−9.56	0.99	64	−3.30	0.85	44	0.10
	1	−11.01	0.98	108	−16.96	0.99	64	−1.63	0.67	44	0.07
	2	−5.74	0.91	105	−8.70	0.98	61	3.84	0.44	44	0.04
	3	−5.90	0.77	90	−15.68	0.93	47	2.15	0.38	43	0.03
	4	−1.89	0.68	71	−15.45	0.98	33	4.06	0.13	38	0.03
	5	−3.33	0.70	61	−12.18	0.88	27	2.63	0.43	34	0.07
	−5 to −1	−6.23	0.99	108	−7.43	0.99	64	−3.04	0.85	44	0.14
	1 to 5	−5.60	0.95	108	−8.59	0.98	64	−0.37	0.56	44	0.04
	Difference	−2.43	0.81	108	−4.84	0.92	64	1.10	0.44	44	0.12

NOTE: Medians and p-values for the excess actual performance for sales/# employees (S/E) for event years −5 to 5. The rows labeled "−5 to −1," "1 to 5," and "Difference" give the results for the average pre-event period performance, the average post-event period performance, and the difference of the pre-event period and post-event period averages, respectively. The units for the medians are $1,000s per employee. Results are reported for both the full sample of 108 events and for the subsamples of 64 event firms with less advanced TQM systems and 44 event firms with more advanced TQM systems. The data were obtained from COMPUSTAT. The columns labeled p-sgn contain p-values for the one-sided sign test of the null hypothesis H_0 : true median ≤ 0 against the alternative H_A : true median > 0. The sample sizes are given in the columns labeled n. The column labeled p-values for the one-sided Wilcoxon rank-sum test of the null hypothesis that the underlying distribution of the more advanced firms is not stochastically larger than that of the less advanced firms.

excess OI/E fluctuates around zero and is not statistically significant. For both of these variables, the median pre-post averages and their median difference are not significant. The post-event average excess performance and the difference in the pre-post averages is greater for the more advanced than for the less advanced firms with significance at the 3% level or better for both variables.

Table 10.6 shows the excess actual sales per employee (S/E). For the full sample, the median excess S/E during years 3-5 is negative ranging from −$1,890 to −$5,900. The results for years 3-5 for the more advanced firms are positive although not statistically significant. For the less advanced firms in years 3-5, S/E is clearly negative. For the more advanced firms, S/E is significantly better than for the less advanced firms for years 1 to 5 with significance at the 10% level for years 1 and 5 and at the 5% level for years 2-4. For both the full sample and the more advanced firms, there appears to be an overall improving trend during the post-event period. The median pre- and post-event averages are

negative for both the less and more advanced firms, and thus for the full sample. For the more advanced firms, the median difference in the pre- and post-event averages is positive but not significant. The median post-event excess average performance is greater for the more advanced firms than for the less advanced firms ($p = 0.04$).

Table 10.7 shows the excess percent change in sales, assets, and employees between years 0 and 4. The table shows that, in comparison to the control firms, the event firms grew for all three measures. This was also the case for both the less advanced and more advanced firms. All of the results are significant with strong significance ($p = 0.00$) for the full sample. For the more advanced firms, the percent growth in sales was significantly better than for the less advanced firms at the 5% level. Interestingly, the percent growth in the number of employees was smaller for the more advanced firms than for the less advanced firms.

Table 10.8 gives the results for excess actual performance for total inventory to sales (I/S)

TABLE 10.7 Excess Percent Year 0 to 4 Change in Sales, Assets, and Employees

Variable	Full Sample			Less Advanced TQM Firms			More Advanced TQM Firms			
	Median	p-sgn	n	Median	p-sgn	n	Median	p-sgn	n	p-wrs
%ΔS	10.39%	0.00	72	5.54%	0.08	33	13.92%	0.01	39	0.04
%ΔA	13.25%	0.00	72	12.98%	0.04	33	15.61%	0.00	39	0.35
%ΔE	8.61%	0.00	71	9.23%	0.02	33	6.12%	0.07	38	0.84

NOTE: Medians and p-values for the excess percent change in sales (%ΔS), assets (%ΔA), and number of employees (%ΔE). Results are reported for both the full sample of 108 events and for the subsamples of 64 event firms with less advanced TQM systems and 44 event firms with more advanced TQM systems. The data were obtained from COMPUSTAT. The columns labeled p-sgn contain the p-values for the one-sided sign test of the null hypothesis H_0: true median ≤ 0 against the alternative H_A: true median > 0. The sample sizes are given in the columns labeled n. The column labeled p-wrs contains p-values for the one-sided Wilcoxon rank-sum test of the null hypothesis that the underlying distribution of the more advanced firms is not stochastically larger than that of the less advanced firms.

and total inventory to cost-of-goods-sold (I/CGS).[13] For the I/S variable, the median excess actual performance for the full sample is negative during the post-event period, indicating lower inventory levels for the sample firms than for the controls (an improvement). The results are significant at the 5% level for years 0, 2, and 3. The more advanced firms show a similar but stronger pattern, with significantly reduced I/S levels for years 0-4. For the less advanced firms, there is no clear pattern. The excess I/S levels for the more advanced firms are significantly lower than for the less advanced firms for all post-event years except year 5. The median excess post-event average I/S levels are also significantly negative negative for the full sample ($p = 0.06$), and strongly significantly negative for the more advanced firms ($p = 0.00$). The excess post-event average inventory levels are also significantly lower for the more advanced firms than for the less advanced firms ($p = 0.02$). The excess I/S for both the full sample and the more advanced firms is also negative during the pre-event period and there is some suggestion that excess I/S levels increase during the pre-event period, and subsequently decrease during the post-event period. The median differences in the pre-post averages, however, are positive, although not significant. For I/CGS for the full sample, there is a similar pattern.

In summary, the results for net income, operating operating income, and sales per employee indicate improved performance in comparison to the controls for the more advanced firms in the post-event period. The median performance throughout the post-event period for all of these variables is greater for the more advanced firms than for the less advanced firms with a significant difference for excess S/E. Excess inventory is lower for the event firms than for the controls during the post-event period for both of the inventory variables examined. The inventory results are stronger for the more advanced firms.

Excess Cumulative Daily Stock Returns

Table 10.9 shows the results for the excess cumulative with-dividend continuously compounded daily stock returns. The cumulative returns begin in July of event year zero. For the full sample, the median excess cumulative return is 21.02% in year five. The improvement is strongly significant ($p = 0.00$). For the more advanced firms, the median excess cumulative returns are 17.28%, 18.48%, and 22.11% for years 3, 4, and 5, respectively, with $p = 0.00$ for all three years. The excess cumulative returns for the more advanced firms are also positive and significant at the 5% level for years 1 and 2. The excess cumulative returns are not statistically significant for the less advanced firms for years 1 through 4. Year 5 performance, however, is positive and significant ($p = 0.10$). The differences between the excess cumulative returns for more and less advanced firms are significant at the 5% level for years 2 through 4, and at the 10% level for year 1. Thus, consistent

TABLE 10.8 Excess Actual Total Inventory/Sales and Total Inventory/Cost-of-Goods-Sold

Variable	Year	Full Sample			Less Advanced TQM Firms			More Advanced TQM Firms			
		Median	p-sgn	n	Median	p-sgn	n	Median	p-sgn	n	p-wrs
I/S	−5	−1.02%	0.11	95	0.47%	0.66	54	−1.77%	0.01	41	0.07
	−4	−0.94%	0.03	95	−0.38%	0.34	54	−2.86%	0.01	41	0.10
	−3	−0.95%	0.06	98	−0.22%	0.60	57	−2.36%	0.01	41	0.02
	−2	−0.76%	0.12	101	−0.38%	0.45	60	−1.79%	0.06	41	0.11
	−1	−0.81%	0.08	103	−0.71%	0.22	61	−1.19%	0.14	42	0.06
	0	−0.64%	0.04	103	−0.11%	0.30	61	−1.43%	0.02	42	0.03
	1	−0.52%	0.22	103	0.86%	0.70	61	−1.95%	0.04	42	0.01
	2	−0.88%	0.04	100	−0.06%	0.45	58	−1.51%	0.01	42	0.05
	3	−1.58%	0.04	85	−0.11%	0.56	44	−1.84%	0.01	41	0.04
	4	−1.18%	0.20	68	1.29%	0.86	31	−2.13%	0.02	37	0.07
	5	−0.06%	0.45	58	0.33%	0.79	25	−0.60%	0.24	33	0.13
	−5 to −1	−1.04%	0.08	103	−0.03%	0.50	61	−2.90%	0.02	42	0.02
	1 to 5	−0.93%	0.06	103	0.29%	0.60	61	−1.59%	0.00	42	0.02
	Difference	0.03%	0.58	103	−0.12%	0.40	61	0.27%	0.78	42	0.56
I/CGS	−5	−1.29%	0.04	85	−0.66%	0.39	51	−3.66%	0.01	34	0.07
	−4	−1.33%	0.04	85	−0.27%	0.50	51	−3.65%	0.01	34	0.05
	−3	−0.90%	0.05	88	−0.06%	0.55	54	−6.07%	0.01	34	0.00
	−2	−0.43%	0.34	91	0.95%	0.70	57	−3.20%	0.11	34	0.03
	−1	−1.43%	0.03	93	−1.05%	0.18	58	−4.74%	0.05	35	0.01
	0	−1.19%	0.04	94	−0.22%	0.35	58	−4.13%	0.02	36	0.01
	1	−0.94%	0.13	94	0.69%	0.65	58	−3.72%	0.02	36	0.01
	2	−1.03%	0.17	92	0.02%	0.55	56	−1.70%	0.07	36	0.06
	3	−1.23%	0.21	78	0.83%	0.73	43	−2.77%	0.05	35	0.04
	4	−0.12%	0.50	61	1.29%	0.93	29	−1.92%	0.11	32	0.10
	5	0.01%	0.71	51	0.38%	0.73	24	0.01%	0.65	27	0.23
	−5 to −1	−1.43%	0.11	93	0.24%	0.65	58	−4.74%	0.01	35	0.01
	1 to 5	−0.87%	0.13	94	−0.48%	0.45	58	−2.28%	0.07	36	0.03
	Difference	0.19%	0.66	93	−0.09%	0.45	58	0.43%	0.84	35	0.68

NOTE: Medians and p-values for the excess actual performance for total inventory/sales (I/S) and total inventory/cost-of-goods-sold (I/CGS) for event years −5 to 5. The rows labeled "−5 to −1," "1 to 5," and "Difference" give the results for the average pre-event period performance, the average post-event period performance, and the difference of the pre-event period and post-event period averages, respectively. The medians are expressed as percentages. Results are reported for both the full sample of 108 events and for the subsamples of 64 event firms with less advanced TQM systems and 44 event firms with more advanced TQM systems. The data were obtained from COMPUSTAT. The cost-of-goods-sold (CGS) used here is the sum of the COMPUSTAT "cost of goods sold" and "selling, general, and administrative expense" data items. Note: in the COMPUSTAT database, "cost of goods sold" is often not reported separately from "selling, general, and administrative expense." The columns labeled p-values for the one-sided sign test of the null hypothesis H_0 : true median ≥ 0 against the alternative H_A : true median < 0. The sample sizes are given in the columns labeled n. The column labeled p-wrs contains p-values for the one-sided Wilcoxon rank-sum test of the null hypothesis that the underlying distribution of the more advanced firms is not stochastically smaller than that of the less advanced firms.

with the accounting variables, the cumulative stock returns indicate improved long-term performance for the TQM firms, with stronger results for the more advanced TQM firms.

Table 10.9 also shows the median pre- and post-event period excess average monthly returns and the median difference of the pre-post averages. For both the full sample and sub samples of less and more advanced firms, the excess average pre-event monthly returns are negative. For both the full sample and the more advanced

firms, the post-event excess average return is strongly positive ($p = 0.00$). The median difference in the pre-post averages is strongly significantly positive for both the full sample and the more advanced firms ($p = 0.00$). For the less advanced firms, the pre-post difference is positive and significant at the 10% level. The post-event excess average monthly returns and the pre-post difference averages are significantly larger for the more advanced firms ($p = 0.06$ and $p = 0.09$, respectively).

TABLE 10.9 Excess Cumulative Percent Daily Stock Returns

Variable	Year	Full Sample			Less Advanced TQM Firms			More Advanced TQM Firms			
		Median	p-sr	n	Median	p-sr	n	Median	p-sr	n	p-wrs
Excess	1	3.19%	0.05	107	1.55%	0.28	63	4.72%	0.02	44	0.10
Cumulative	2	3.82%	0.18	106	−2.80%	0.66	63	9.41%	0.02	43	0.05
Returns	3	3.91%	0.10	103	−1.72%	0.78	60	17.28%	0.00	43	0.00
	4	6.04%	0.02	87	−1.43%	0.67	46	18.48%	0.00	41	0.00
	5	21.02%	0.00	69	14.20%	0.10	32	22.11%	0.00	37	0.20
Excess Average	−5 to −1	−0.24%	0.98	106	−0.30%	0.83	63	−0.22%	0.98	43	0.59
Monthly	1 to 5	0.25%	0.00	108	0.13%	0.16	64	0.36%	0.00	44	0.06
Returns	Difference	0.50%	0.00	106	0.36%	0.07	63	0.66%	0.00	43	0.09

NOTE: Medians and p-values values for the excess cumulative percent with-dividend continuously compounded daily stock returns for event years 1 to 5. The rows labeled "−5 to −1," "1 to 5," and "Difference" give the results for the average monthly returns for the pre-event period, the post-event period, and the difference of the pre-event period and post-event period average monthly returns, respectively. The monthly returns are calculated by cumulating the daily returns in the month. Results are reported for both the full sample of 108 events and for the subsamples of 64 event firms with less advanced TQM systems and 44 event firms with more advanced TQM systems. The columns labeled p-sr contain p-values for the one-sided Wilcoxon signed-rank test of the null hypothesis H_0: true median ≤ 0 against the alternative H_A: true median > 0. The sample sizes are given in the columns labeled n. The column labeled p-wrs contains p-values for the one-sided Wilcoxon rank-sum test of the null hypothesis that the underlying distribution of the more advanced firms is not stochastically larger than that of the less advanced firms.

TABLE 10.10 Excess Cumulative Percent Daily Stock Returns: Covariance-Based Analysis

Variable	Year	Full Sample			Less Advanced TQM Firms			More Advanced TQM Firms			
		Mean	p-cv	n	Mean	p-cv	n	Mean	p-cv	n	p-2
Excess	1	3.37%	0.17	97	1.17%	0.40	56	6.36%	0.11	41	0.23
Cumulative	2	4.48%	0.17	97	−0.71%	0.55	57	11.88%	0.04	40	0.09
Returns	3	7.26%	0.11	99	−3.79%	0.67	57	22.26%	0.00	42	0.01
	4	12.91%	0.04	86	−1.83%	0.57	46	29.87%	0.00	40	0.01
	5	24.21%	0.01	69	15.71%	0.15	32	31.55%	0.00	37	0.20

NOTE: Averages and p-values for the excess cumulative percent with-dividend continuously compounded daily stock returns. Results are reported for both the full sample of 108 events and for the subsamples of 64 event firms with less advanced TQM systems and 44 event firms with more advanced TQM systems. The columns labeled p-cv contain p-values for the one-sided test of the null hypothesis H_0: $\mu \circledR 0$ against the alternative H_A: $\mu > 0$. The estimates of the standard deviations of the means used in the test statistics are based on estimates of the variance-covariance matrices for events in the same year. The variance-covariance estimates are calculated from five years of monthly returns, where the monthly returns are calculated by cumulating the daily returns in the month. The sample sizes are given in the columns labeled n. The column labeled p-2 contains p-values for the one-sided two-sample test of the null hypothesis H_0: $\mu_{more} \leq \mu_{less}$ against the alternative H_A: $\mu_{more} > \mu_{less}$, where μ_{less} and μ_{more} are the true means of the less advanced and more advanced firms, respectively.

Table 10.10 shows analysis of the excess cumulative returns based on the assumption that the distribution of the stock returns is multivariate normal. This analysis corrects for any correlation between the excess returns for firms with the same event year zero. There is very little industry and event-year clustering in the sample, and thus it would appear unlikely that such correlation would have any impact on the results. Comparison of Table 10.10 to Table 10.9, however, allows direct assessment of any such impact. The two tables show that the results are essentially the same, with similar patterns in the levels of significance, verifying that correlation due to event-year clustering does not have consequential impact on the results.

TABLE 10.11 Long-Term Performance for the Accounting Variables for TQM Firms With Positive and Negative Excess Percent Change in Employees

Variable	Excess %ΔE	Full Sample			Less Advanced TQM Firms			More Advanced TQM Firms			p-wrs
		Median	p	n	Median	p	n	Median	p	n	
NI/s	−	0.76%	0.29	30	−0.26%	0.60	14	1.75%	0.26	16	0.16
	+	0.57%	0.03	41	0.71%	0.01	19	0.40%	0.42	22	0.68
			0.59†			0.85†			0.33†		
NI/A	−	0.63%	0.43	30	−0.98%	0.79	14	2.51%	0.23	16	0.02
	+	1.65%	0.01	41	0.53%	0.08	19	1.86%	0.07	22	0.31
			0.79†			0.96†			0.36†		
OI/S	−	0.95%	0.29	30	−1.01%	0.60	14	1.86%	0.23	16	0.21
	+	−0.02%	0.62	41	0.08%	0.50	19	−0.15%	0.74	22	0.40
			0.54†			0.74†			0.42†		
OI/A	−	2.28%	0.29	30	−2.03%	0.79	14	3.18%	0.11	16	0.03
	+	2.50%	0.01	41	0.23%	0.32	19	3.12%	0.01	22	0.10
			0.88†			0.93†			0.70†		
S/A	−	−2.21%	0.71	30	−22.49%	0.91	14	6.33%	0.40	16	0.01
	+	4.57%	0.06	41	−0.04%	0.68	19	9.95%	0.01	22	0.03
			0.95†			0.93†			0.80†		
NI/E	−	−0.28	0.71	30	−1.53	0.91	14	0.29	0.40	16	0.15
	+	0.79	0.50	41	0.87	0.50	19	−0.07	0.58	22	0.54
			0.71†			0.87†			0.37†		
OI/E	−	1.51	0.42	26	−5.73	0.97	11	5.05	0.06	15	0.09
	+	2.04	0.25	35	1.99	0.41	18	2.04	0.31	17	0.21
			0.76†			0.81†			0.48†		
S/E	−	−2.58	0.71	30	−11.27	0.91	14	0.13	0.40	16	0.29
	+	−1.78	0.62	41	−17.62	0.97	19	6.26	0.14	22	0.04
			0.45†			0.34†			0.70†		

NOTE: Medians and *p*-values for the accounting performance variables. For net income/sales (NI/S), net income/assets (NI/A), operating income/sales (OI/S), operating income/assets (OI/A), and sales/assets (S/A), the median excess unexpected performance for post-event years 3-5 are reported (expressed as percents). For net income/# employees (NI/E), operating income/# employees (OI/E) and sales/# employees (S/E), the median excess actual performance for post-event year 4 are reported expressed in units of $1,000s per employee. The rows labeled − and + correspond to events with negative and positive year 0 to 4 excess percent change in employees, respectively. Results are reported for both the full sample of 108 events and for the subsamples of 64 event firms with less advanced TQM systems and 44 event firms with more advanced TQM systems. The data were obtained as described in Tables 10.4 and 10.5 for the corresponding variables. Except as indicated by †, the columns labeled *p* contain *p*-values for the one-sided sign test of the null hypothesis H_0: true median ≤ 0 against the alternative H_A: true median > 0. The sample sizes are given in the columns labeled *n*. The *p*-values labeled † are for Wilcoxon rank-sum tests of the null hypothesis that the underlying distribution for the events with negative excess percent change in employees is not stochastically larger than that for the events with positive excess percent change in employees. The column labeled *p*-wrs contains *p*-values for the one-sided Wilcoxon rank-sum test of the null hypothesis that the underlying distribution of the more advanced firms is not stochastically larger than that of the less advanced firms.

Downsizing

This section examines whether or not the observed positive performance for the TQM firms might be explained by downsizing that took place in conjunction with or during the same period as the deployment of TQM. There appears to be little consensus concerning a uniform definition of the term "downsizing." It is also debatable the extent to which some downsizing-like activity is a natural consequence of the development of quality management systems. Empowerment of employees, one of the principles of TQM, is likely to lead to elimination of some levels of management and supervision over time. The effects of downsizing are examined here by examining the relationship between performance and percent changes in the number of employees. We believe that this captures what is commonly meant by downsizing—major reductions in the number of employees.

TABLE 10.12 Excess Cumulative Percent Daily Stock Returns for TQM Firms With Positive and Negative Excess Percent Change in Employees

Variable	Excess %ΔE	Full Sample			Less Advanced TQM Firms			More Advanced TQM Firms			
		Median	p	n	Median	p	n	Median	p	n	p-wrs
1	−	−0.68%	0.33	30	−3.03%	0.72	14	9.75%	0.10	16	0.13
	+	1.90%	0.12	40	−	0.32	18	4.12%	0.13	22	0.31
			0.69†			0.86†			0.36†		
2	−	−2.49%	0.75	29	−12.89%	0.96	14	4.01%	0.18	15	0.03
	+	2.41%	0.37	40	−5.93%	0.72	18	7.73%	0.16	22	0.20
			0.84†			0.87†			0.56†		
3	−	4.83%	0.52	29	−15.02%	0.98	14	17.28%	0.04	15	0.01
	+	3.78%	0.06	40	−2.92%	0.41	18	17.71%	0.07	22	0.09
			0.84†			0.98†			0.36†		
4	−	4.55%	0.18	29	−9.27%	0.92	14	34.86%	0.01	15	0.00
	+	8.00%	0.02	40	0.88%	0.24	18	12.07%	0.03	22	0.21
			0.68†			0.95†			0.21†		
5	−	21.27%	0.05	29	7.74%	0.51	14	34.29%	0.01	15	0.10
	+	20.78%	0.01	40	24.03%	0.04	18	17.95%	0.04	22	0.59
			0.56†			0.86†			0.17†		

NOTE: Medians and p-values for the excess cumulative percent with-dividend continuously compounded daily stock returns. The rows labeled − and + correspond to events with negative and positive year 0 to 4 excess percent change in employees, respectively. Results are reported for both the full sample of 108 events and for the subsamples of 64 event firms with less advanced TQM systems and 44 event firms with more advanced TQM systems. The cumulative returns data were calculated from the daily returns database compiled by the Center for Research in Securities Prices (CRSP) at the University of Chicago. Except as indicated by †, the columns labeled p contain p-values for the one-sided Wilcoxon signed-rank test of the null hypothesis H_0 : true median ≤ 0 against the alternative H_A : true median > 0. The sample sizes are given in the columns labeled n. The p-values labeled † are for Wilcoxon rank-sum tests of the null hypothesis that the underlying distribution for the events with negative excess percent change in employees is not stochastically larger than that for the events with positive excess percent change in employees. The column labeled p-wrs contains p-values for the one-sided Wilcoxon rank-sum test of the null hypothesis that the underlying distribution of the more advanced firms is not stochastically larger than that of the less advanced firms.

In order for the data to support the hypothesis that downsizing drives the results: (1) a large number of the event firms should be downsizing in comparison to the controls; (2) the firms that do not downsize should not show significant positive performance; and (3) the firms that do downsize in comparison to their controls should show significant positive performance consistent with downsizing driving the results, especially when compared to the firms that do not downsize.

Requirement (1) is not supported by the data. Overall, both the event firms and the control firms grow in terms of the number of employees during the post-event period. The median percent change in employees between years 0 and 4 is 5.4% for the event firms and 1.0% for the controls. For the more advanced events only, the four-year percent growth in employees is 2.1% for the event firms and 1.0% for the controls.

For the less advanced events, the percent growth in employees is 9.2%, while the growth in control portfolios is again 1.0%. Thus, the number of employees grows for most firms in the sample and most event firms grow faster than their control portfolios. This is consistent with the results for excess percent change in employees given in Table 10.7.

Requirements (2) and (3) above are examined by comparing the performance of events with negative excess percent change in employees to those with positive excess percent change in employees. Tables 10.11 and 10.12 give the results for the accounting variables and stock returns, respectively. Examination of these tables shows that the required patterns are not evident. Specifically, requirement (2) is not supported by the data. The vast majority of the performance measures for the events that do not downsize are positive and frequently signifi-

TABLE 10.13 Excess Unexpected Performance for the Accounting Variables—Manufacturing Firms Only

Variable	Year	Full Sample			Less Advanced TQM Firms			More Advanced TQM Firms			
		Median	p-sgn	n	Median	p-sgn	n	Median	p-sgn	n	p-wrs
NI/S	1	0.14%	0.27	93	−0.07%	0.65	58	0.53%	0.09	35	0.08
	2	0.29%	0.15	93	0.08%	0.45	58	0.97%	0.09	35	0.06
	3-5	0.72%	0.01	87	0.64%	0.06	52	1.23%	0.05	35	0.10
NI/A	1	0.35%	0.20	93	0.03%	0.55	58	0.94%	0.09	35	0.05
	2	0.51%	0.01	93	0.40%	0.12	58	0.59%	0.02	35	0.09
	3-5	1.65%	0.01	87	0.52%	0.11	52	2.26%	0.01	35	0.02
OI/S	1	−0.13%	0.58	93	−0.50%	0.96	58	0.70%	0.05	35	0.14
	2	−0.27%	0.89	93	−0.48%	0.96	58	0.07%	0.50	35	0.12
	3-5	0.33%	0.26	87	0.16%	0.44	52	1.66%	0.25	35	0.11
OI/A	1	0.91%	0.11	93	−0.34%	0.65	58	1.29%	0.01	35	0.08
	2	0.03%	0.50	93	−0.01%	0.55	58	0.03%	0.50	35	0.49
	3-5	2.22%	0.00	87	0.62%	0.11	52	3.28%	0.00	35	0.01
S/A	1	1.15%	0.15	93	0.46%	0.45	58	6.35%	0.09	35	0.13
	2	1.80%	0.15	93	0.05%	0.55	58	5.35%	0.05	35	0.19
	3-5	4.57%	0.10	87	−0.62%	0.66	52	8.54%	0.01	35	0.01

NOTE: Medians and p-values for the excess unexpected performance for net income/sales (NI/S), net income/assets (NI/A), operating income/sales (OI/S), operating income/assets (OI/A), and sales/assets (S/A) for the manufacturing events only. The medians are expressed as percentages. Results are reported for both the entire sample of manufacturing events and for the subsamples of manufacturing firms with less advanced and more advanced TQM systems. The data and forecasts used to construct the performance measures were obtained from Value Line. The columns labeled p-sgn contain the p-values for the one-sided sign test of the null hypothesis H_0 : true median ≤ 0 against the alternative H_A : true median > 0. The sample sizes are given in the columns labeled n. The column labeled p-wrs contains p-values for the one-sided Wilcoxon rank-sum test of the null hypothesis that the underlying distribution of the more advanced firms is not stochastically larger than that of the less mature firms.

cant. In particular, the results for the excess cumulative stock returns in Table 10.12 show significant (at the 5% level) positive excess returns for years 4 and 5 for both the full sample of firms that did not downsize and the more advanced firms that did not downsize. Thus, there is evidence of a positive association between the implementation of TQM and performance for firms that do not downsize.

Finally, requirement (3) is also not supported by the data. There is no clear pattern of improved performance for the firms with negative excess percent change in employees over those with positive excess percent change in employees and none of the corresponding p-values comparing the "negative" and "positive" firms is significant. For the accounting variables for the full sample shown in Table 10.11, a positive difference is observed for only two of the eight performance variables. It is interesting to note that for both the accounting measures and the stock returns, for the less advanced subsample, the performance for events with a negative excess percent change in employees is worse (ex-

cept for S/E) than for those with a positive excess percent change in employees. For the more advanced events, the opposite tends to the case.

Results for the Manufacturing Firms Only

The analysis described above was repeated omitting the 15 events (indicated in Appendix 10.1) corresponding to predominantly vice companies. Tables 10.13-10.21 present the results. These results are not specifically discussed here. Overall, however, the results for the manufacturing firms alone are stronger and have increased statistical significance.

Other Variables and Research Issues Examined

A number of other factors and research issues were also examined.

TABLE 10.14 Excess Actual Net Income per Employee and Operating Income per Employee—Manufacturing Firms Only

Variable	Year	Full Sample			Less Advanced TQM Firms			More Advanced TQM Firms			
		Median	p-sgn	n	Median	p-sgn	n	Median	p-sgn	n	p-wrs
NI/E	−5	0.28	0.37	84	0.13	0.50	51	0.36	0.36	33	0.42
	−4	0.25	0.59	85	0.42	0.50	51	−0.41	0.70	34	0.65
	−3	0.44	0.80	87	0.05	0.50	53	−0.58	0.94	34	0.65
	−2	0.19	0.23	90	0.03	0.34	56	0.29	0.30	34	0.47
	−1	−0.49	0.89	93	−0.14	0.74	58	−1.35	0.91	35	0.55
	0	−1.20	0.89	93	−1.24	0.88	58	−1.19	0.75	35	0.11
	1	−0.82	0.85	93	−0.95	0.88	58	−0.40	0.63	35	0.06
	2	0.07	0.50	91	−1.66	0.66	56	0.41	0.37	35	0.06
	3	0.29	0.37	78	−0.23	0.56	44	0.40	0.30	34	0.36
	4	0.79	0.40	63	−1.28	0.64	31	1.44	0.30	32	0.26
	5	1.85	0.11	54	0.70	0.50	25	2.74	0.07	29	0.41
	−5 to −1	0.03	0.50	93	0.17	0.45	58	−0.19	0.63	35	0.57
	1 to 5	0.50	0.34	93	−1.26	0.74	58	1.31	0.09	35	0.03
	Difference	0.27	0.27	93	0.07	0.45	58	0.71	0.25	35	0.06
OI/E	−5	0.44	0.22	84	0.24	0.39	51	0.83	0.24	33	0.28
	−4	−0.23	0.67	85	−0.16	0.61	51	−0.78	0.70	34	0.43
	−3	−0.07	0.58	87	0.31	0.50	53	−0.70	0.70	34	0.64
	−2	−0.44	0.62	90	−1.14	0.66	56	−0.07	0.57	34	0.38
	−1	0.22	0.42	93	0.26	0.55	58	0.22	0.37	35	0.31
	0	−0.13	0.58	93	−0.67	0.74	58	0.89	0.37	35	0.14
	1	−0.05	0.58	93	−1.33	0.82	58	3.38	0.25	35	0.05
	2	1.41	0.15	91	−0.24	0.55	56	3.02	0.05	35	0.04
	3	2.80	0.01	77	2.03	0.18	43	3.94	0.01	34	0.13
	4	2.19	0.18	60	−2.86	0.77	29	2.65	0.04	31	0.05
	5	3.03	0.05	51	1.27	0.27	24	4.83	0.06	27	0.25
	−5 to −1	0.07	0.34	93	0.16	0.45	58	0.06	0.37	35	0.27
	1 to 5	1.25	0.07	93	−1.28	0.74	58	3.79	0.00	35	0.00
	Difference	0.46	0.34	93	−0.22	0.74	58	2.63	0.09	35	0.03

NOTE: Medians and p-values for the excess actual performance for net income/# employees (NI/E) and operating income/# employees (OI/E) for event years −5 to 5 for the manufacturing events only. The rows labeled "−5 to −1," "1 to 5," and "Difference" give the results for the average pre-event period performance, the average post-event period performance, and the difference of the pre-event period and post-event period averages, respectively. The units for the medians are $1,000s per employee. Results are reported for both the entire sample of manufacturing events and for the subsamples of manufacturing firms with less advanced and more advanced TQM systems. The data were obtained from COMPUSTAT. The columns labeled p-sgn p-values for the one-sided sign test of the null hypothesis H_0: true median ≤ 0 against the alternative H_A: true median > 0. The sample sizes are given in the columns labeled n. The column labeled p-wrs contains p-values for the one-sided Wilcoxon rank-sum test of the null hypothesis that the underlying distribution of the more advanced firms is not stochastically larger than that of the less advanced firms.

Analysts' Forecasts

In order to provide some empirical validation for the use of Value Line analysts' forecasts, the mean-squared errors (MSEs) of the analysts' forecasts were compared to the MSEs of forecasts made by simple AR 1 models. The AR 1 models were estimated for each firm using the time series of annual values obtained from COMPUSTAT for the 11 years prior to and ending with event year zero (i.e., $t = -10$ to $t = 0$).

Forecasts were then made for postevent years 1 to 5. For years 1 and 2, the MSE of the forecast is the average squared difference between the forecast and the realized value. In order to parallel the long-term forecasts provided by the Value Line analysts, the AR 1 forecasts for years 3-5 are averaged and compared to the average value of the realized values for years 3-5 by computing the average of the squared differences. The MSEs for the Value Line analysts' forecasts were computed in a similar manner

TABLE 10.15 Excess Actual Sales per Employee—Manufacturing Firms Only

Variable	Year	Full Sample			Less Advanced TQM Firms			More Advanced TQM Firms			
		Median	p-sgn	n	Median	p-sgn	n	Median	p-sgn	n	p-wrs
S/E	−5	−4.07	0.88	84	−4.06	0.92	51	−4.09	0.64	33	0.17
	−4	−6.76	0.96	85	−8.71	0.98	51	−3.53	0.70	34	0.08
	−3	−7.36	0.99	87	−8.38	0.99	53	−7.10	0.89	34	0.15
	−2	−6.69	1.00	90	−6.69	0.99	56	−5.04	0.89	34	0.21
	−1	−8.18	1.00	93	−10.13	1.00	58	−4.86	0.84	35	0.11
	0	−6.38	0.98	93	−10.82	0.98	58	−2.29	0.84	35	0.05
	1	−10.35	0.95	93	−16.01	0.98	58	−0.87	0.63	35	0.04
	2	−5.82	0.90	91	−9.58	0.96	56	1.71	0.50	35	0.03
	3	−4.38	0.63	78	−14.60	0.85	44	2.63	0.30	34	0.03
	4	−1.78	0.60	63	−10.71	0.96	31	4.06	0.11	32	0.03
	5	−0.44	0.55	54	−8.75	0.79	25	2.96	0.36	29	0.07
	−5 to −1	−6.83	0.99	93	−7.43	0.99	58	−4.38	0.91	35	0.11
	1 to 5	−2.70	0.93	93	−6.61	0.96	58	−0.76	0.63	35	0.03
	Difference	−0.45	0.73	93	−7.38	0.93	58	2.73	0.25	35	0.03

NOTE: Medians and p-values for the excess actual performance for sales/# employees (S/E) for event years −5 to 5 for the manufacturing firms only. The rows labeled "−5 to −1," "1 to 5," and "Differences" give the results for the average pre-event period performance, the average post-event period performance, and the difference of the pre-event period and post-event period averages, respectively. The units for the medians are $1,000s per employee. Results are reported for both the entire sample of manufacturing events and for the subsamples of manufacturing firms with less advanced and more advanced TQM systems. The data were obtained from COMPUSTAT. The columns labeled p-sgn contain p-values for the one-sided sign test of the null hypothesis H_0 : true median ≤ 0 against the alternative H_A : true median > 0. The sample sizes are given in the columns labeled n. The column labeled p-wrs contains p-values for the one-sided Wilcoxon rank-sum test of the null hypothesis that the underlying distribution of the more advanced firms is not stochastically larger than that of the less advanced firms.

TABLE 10.16 Excess Percent Year 0 to 4 Change in Sales, Assets, and Employees—Manufacturing Firms Only

Variable	Full Sample			Less Advanced TQM Firms			More Advanced TQM Firms			
	Median	p-sgn	n	Median	p-sgn	n	Median	p-sgn	n	p-wrs
%ΔS	7.40%	0.02	69	5.25%	0.24	31	11.37%	0.02	38	0.10
%ΔA	7.53%	0.01	69	8.33%	0.08	31	7.22%	0.04	38	0.53
%ΔE	7.44%	0.03	69	13.68%	0.04	31	1.53%	0.21	38	0.80

NOTE: Medians and p-values for the excess percent change in sales (%ΔS), assets (%ΔA), and number of employees (%ΔE) for the manufacturing events only. Results are reported for both the entire sample of manufacturing events and for the subsamples of manufacturing firms with less advanced and more advanced TQM systems. The data were obtained from COMPUSTAT. The columns labeled p-sgn contain p-values for the one-sided sign test of the null hypothesis H_0 : true median ≤ 0 against the alternative H_A : true median > 0. The sample sizes are given in the columns labeled n. The column labeled p-wrs contains p-values for the one-sided Wilcoxon rank-sum test of the null hypothesis that the underlying distribution of the more advanced firms is not stochastically larger than that of the less advanced firms.

using data and forecasts obtained from Value Line. Missing values in the COMPUSTAT pre-event data caused loss of a number of firms in the calculation of the AR 1 MSEs. For comparability, such missing firms were also deleted from the calculation of the Value Line MSEs.

Table 10.22 shows the efficiencies of the AR 1 forecasts relative to the analysts' forecasts. The efficiency is defined as the ratio of the MSE of the analysts' forecasts to the MSE of the AR 1 forecasts. Efficiencies of less than 100% show superior performance of the Value Line

TABLE 10.17 Excess Actual Total Inventory/Sales and Total Inventory/Cost-of-Goods-Sold—Manufacturing Firms Only

Variable	Year	Full Sample			Less Advanced TQM Firms			More Advanced TQM Firms			
		Median	p-sgn	n	Median	p-sgn	n	Median	p-sgn	n	p-wrs
I/S	−5	−1.02%	0.14	85	0.57%	0.71	51	−3.66%	0.01	34	0.04
	−4	−1.25%	0.04	85	−0.29%	0.39	51	−3.59%	0.01	34	0.04
	−3	−1.11%	0.05	88	0.34%	0.66	54	−4.84%	0.00	34	0.00
	−2	−1.09%	0.10	91	−0.30%	0.50	57	−3.10%	0.03	34	0.04
	−1	−1.11%	0.07	93	−0.71%	0.26	58	−3.65%	0.09	35	0.02
	0	−0.76%	0.05	93	−0.07%	0.35	58	−3.76%	0.02	35	0.01
	1	−0.52%	0.27	93	1.03%	0.74	58	−4.66%	0.05	35	0.00
	2	−0.94%	0.07	91	−0.06%	0.45	56	−2.93%	0.02	35	0.02
	3	−2.06%	0.07	78	−0.11%	0.56	44	−2.85%	0.01	34	0.02
	4	−1.89%	0.22	63	1.29%	0.86	31	−2.80%	0.03	32	0.04
	5	−0.03%	0.55	54	0.33%	0.79	25	−0.87%	0.36	29	0.11
	−5 to −1	−1.19%	0.07	93	0.08%	0.55	58	−3.69%	0.01	35	0.00
	1 to 5	−0.93%	0.11	93	−0.42%	0.65	58	−2.72%	0.01	25	0.01
	Difference	0.24%	0.66	93	−0.09%	0.45	58	1.40%	0.84	35	0.63
I/CGS	−5	−1.29%	0.04	85	−0.66%	0.39	51	−3.66%	0.01	34	0.07
	−4	−1.33%	0.04	85	−0.27%	0.50	51	−3.65%	0.01	34	0.05
	−3	−0.90%	0.05	88	−0.06%	0.55	54	−6.07%	0.01	34	0.00
	−2	−0.43%	0.34	91	0.95%	0.70	57	−3.20%	0.11	34	0.03
	−1	−1.43%	0.03	93	−1.05%	0.18	58	−4.74%	0.05	35	0.01
	0	−1.27%	0.03	93	−0.22%	0.35	58	−5.18%	0.01	35	0.01
	1	−0.69%	0.65	58	−4.11%	0.01	35	0.00			
	2	−1.03%	0.15	91	0.02%	0.55	56	−1.91%	0.05	35	0.05
	3	−1.52%	0.18	77	0.83%	0.73	43	−2.78%	0.03	34	0.04
	4	−0.15%	0.45	60	1.29%	0.93	29	−1.96%	0.08	31	0.08
	5	0.01%	0.71	51	0.38%	0.73	24	0.01%	0.65	27	0.23
	−5 to −1	−1.43%	0.11	93	0.24%	0.65	58	−4.74%	0.01	35	0.01
	1 to 5	−0.92%	0.11	93	−0.48%	0.45	58	−2.50%	0.05	35	0.02
	Difference	0.19%	0.66	93	−0.09%	0.45	58	0.43	0.84	35	0.68

NOTE: Medians and p-values for the excess actual performance for total inventory/sales (I/S) and total inventory/cost-of-goods-sold (I/CGS) for event years −5 to 5 for the manufacturing events only. The rows labeled "−5 to −1," "−1 to 5," and "Difference" give the results for the average pre-event period performance, the average post-event period performance, and the difference of the pre-event period and post-event period averages, respectively. The medians are expressed as percentages. Results are reported for both the entire sample of manufacturing events and for the subsamples of manufacturing firms with less advanced and more advanced TQM systems. The data were obtained from COMPUSTAT. The cost-of-goods-sold (CGS) used here is the sum of the COMPUSTAT "cost of goods sold" and "selling, general, and administrative expense" data items. Note: in the COMPUSTAT database, "cost of goods sold" is often not reported separately from "selling, general, and administrative expense." The columns labeled p-sgn contain p-values for the one-sided sign test of the null hypothesis H_0 : true median ≥ 0 against the alternative H_A : true median < 0. The sample sizes are given in the columns labeled n. The column labeled p-wrs contains p-values for the one-sided Wilcoxon rank-sum test of the null hypothesis that the underlying distribution of the more advanced firms is not stochastically smaller than that of the less advanced firms.

forecasts. The analysis was conducted separately for the control firms and for the event firms because the MSEs for the event firms contain a bias component due to their subsequent implementation of TQM. The results for the control firms do not include this bias component. Because the accounting data contain outliers and other deviations from normality and MSEs are very sensitive to these problems, a "robust efficiency" was also computed after trimming the largest 5% of the squared deviations.

Table 10.22 shows clear superiority of the analysts' forecasts. For the usual efficiency (based on the standard MSEs), there is no instance of superior performance of the AR 1 forecasts. For the robust efficiencies, there are only three instances (out of 30) where the AR 1 forecasts had superior performance. Most of the robust efficiencies are well below 70%.

TABLE 10.18 Excess Cumulative Percent Daily Stock Returns—Manufacturing Firms Only

Variable	Year	Full Sample			Less Advanced TQM Firms			More Advanced TQM Firms			
		Median	p-sr	n	Median	p-sr	n	Median	p-sr	n	p-wrs
Excess	1	2.71%	0.11	92	1.55%	0.33	57	2.72%	0.06	35	0.16
Cumulative	2	5.40%	0.17	91	−0.17%	0.55	57	9.74%	0.04	34	0.09
Returns	3	5.79%	0.05	89	−0.70%	0.60	55	17.44%	0.00	34	0.00
	4	7.14%	0.01	75	−1.07%	0.59	43	33.31%	0.00	32	0.00
	5	23.51%	0.00	61	19.07%	0.11	30	31.21%	0.00	31	0.10
Excess											
Average	−5 to −1	−0.33%	0.98	91	−0.30%	0.83	57	−0.47%	0.99	34	0.70
Monthly	1 to 5	0.34%	0.00	93	0.17%	0.11	58	0.52%	0.00	35	0.05
Returns	Difference	0.55%	0.00	91	0.41%	0.04	57	0.94%	0.00	34	0.04

NOTE: Medians and p-values for the excess cumulative percent with-dividend continuously compounded daily stock returns for event years 1 to 5 for the manufacturing events only. The rows labeled "−5 to −1," "1 to 5," and "Difference" give the results for the average monthly returns for the pre-event period, the post-event period, and the difference of the pre-event period and post-event period average monthly returns, respectively. The monthly returns are calculated by cumulating the daily returns in the month. Results are reported for both the entire sample of manufacturing events and for the subsamples of manufacturing firms with less advanced and more advanced TQM systems. The columns labeled p-sr contain the p-values for the one-sided Wilcoxon signed-rank test of the null hypothesis H_0 : true median ≤ 0 against the alternative H_A : true median > 0. The sample sizes are given in the columns labeled n. The column labeled p-wrs contains p-values for the one-sided Wilcoxon rank-sum test of the null hypothesis that the underlying distribution of the more advanced firms is not stochastically larger than that of the less advanced firms.

TABLE 10.19 Excess Cumulative Percent Daily Stock Returns: Covariance-Based Analysis for the Manufacturing Firms Only

Variable	Year	Full Sample			Less Advanced TQM Firms			More Advanced TQM Firms			
		Mean	p-cv	n	Mean	p-cv	n	Mean	p-cv	n	p-2
Excess	1	2.87%	0.23	82	0.76%	0.44	50	6.15%	0.16	32	0.25
Cumulative	2	4.83%	0.18	82	0.71%	0.46	51	11.59%	0.09	31	0.16
Returns	3	9.90%	0.07	85	−0.99%	0.54	52	27.04%	0.00	33	0.02
	4	15.67%	0.03	74	−0.42%	0.52	43	37.99%	0.00	31	0.01
	5	28.64%	0.00	61	16.16%	0.15	30	40.72%	0.00	31	0.12

NOTE: Averages and p-values for the excess cumulative percent with-dividend continuously compounded daily stock returns for the manufacturing events only. Results are reported for both the entire sample of manufacturing events and for the subsamples of manufacturing firms with less advanced and more advanced TQM systems. The columns labeled p-cv contain p-values for the one-sided test of the null hypothesis H_0 : $\mu \leq 0$ against the alternative H_A : $\mu > 0$. The estimates of the standard deviations of the means used in the test statistics are based on estimates of the variance-covariance matrices for events in the same year. The variance-covariance estimates are calculated from five years of monthly returns, where the monthly returns are calculated by cumulating the daily returns in the month. The sample sizes are given in the columns labeled n. The column labeled p-2 contains p-values for the one-sided two-sample test of the null hypothesis H_0 : $\mu_{more} \leq \mu_{less}$ against the alternative H_A : μ_{more} μ_{less}, where μ_{less} and μ_{more} are the true means of the less advanced and more advanced firms, respectively.

Firm Size and Calendar Year

Possible effects of firm size and year of TQM implementation were also examined. There were no clear differences in performance between event firms in the lower half of the size distribution and those in the upper half or be-

tween events which occurred in 1987 or earlier and those which occurred after 1987.

Quality Awards

To determine if the results might be biased by selection of potential firms for the sample

TABLE 10.20 Long-Term Performance for the Accounting Variables for TQM Firms With Positive and Negative Excess Percent Change in Employees—Manufacturing Firms Only

Variable	Excess %ΔE	Full Sample			Less Advanced TQM Firms			More Advanced TQM Firms			p-wrs
		Median	p	n	Median	p	n	Median	p	n	
NI/S	−	1.12%	0.17	28	0.32%	0.50	13	2.26%	0.15	15	0.13
	+	0.62%	0.02	35	0.71%	0.02	18	0.55%	0.31	17	0.60
			0.55†			0.81†			0.34†		
NI/A	−	1.00%	0.29	28	−0.30%	0.71	13	2.76%	0.15	15	0.03
	+	2.08%	0.01	35	1.23%	0.12	18	2.13%	0.02	17	0.16
			0.82†			0.94†			0.52†		
OI/S	−	1.19%	0.29	28	−2.39%	0.71	13	2.06%	0.15	15	0.20
	+	0.08%	0.50	35	−0.17%	0.59	18	0.14%	0.50	17	0.13
			0.66†			0.77†			0.59†		
OI/A	−	2.37%	0.17	28	−3.14%	0.71	13	3.28%	0.06	15	0.03
	+	2.86%	0.02	35	0.36%	0.41	18	6.33%	0.01	17	0.04
			0.91†			0.94†			0.80†		
S/A	−	1.74%	0.57	28	−26.74%	0.87	13	6.41%	0.30	15	0.02
	+	1.40%	0.16	35	−2.65%	0.76	18	9.07%	0.02	17	0.04
			0.90†			0.92†			0.71†		
NI/E	−	−0.35	0.71	28	−1.79	0.87	13	0.41	0.50	15	0.16
	+	2.10	0.25	35	2.16	0.41	18	2.10	0.31	17	0.44
			0.87†			0.90†			0.57†		
OI/E	−	1.51	0.42	26	−5.73	0.97	11	5.05	0.06	15	0.09
	+	2.35	0.20	34	1.99	0.41	18	2.35	0.23	16	0.12
			0.82†			0.81†			0.60†		
S/E	−	−0.94	0.57	28	−7.08	0.87	13	0.25	0.30	15	0.24
	+	−1.78	0.63	35	−14.16	0.95	18	4.44	0.17	17	0.05
			0.31†			0.35†			0.56†		

NOTE: Medians and p-values for the accounting performance variables for the manufacturing events only. For net income/sales (NI/S), net income/assets (NI/A), operating income/sales (OI/S), operating income/assets (OI/A), and sales/assets (S/A), the median excess unexpected performance for post-event years 3-5 are reported (expressed as percents). For net income/# employees (NI/E), operating income/# employees (OI/E) and sales/# employees (S/E), the median excess actual performance for post-event year 4 are reported expressed in units of $1,000s per employee. The rows labeled − and + correspond to events with negative and positive year 0 to 4 excess percent change in employees, respectively. Results are reported for both the entire sample of manufacturing events and for the subsamples of manufacturing firms with less advanced and more advanced TQM systems. The data were obtained as described in Tables 10.4 and 10.5 for the corresponding variables. Except as indicated by †, the columns labeled p contain p-values for the one-sided sign test of the null hypothesis H_0 : true median < 0 against the alternative H_A : true median > 0. The sample sizes are given in the columns labeled n. The p-values labeled † are for Wilcoxon rank-sum tests of the null hypothesis that the underlying distribution for the events with negative excess percent change in employees is not stochastically larger than that for the events with positive excess percent change in employees. The column labeled p-wrs contains p-values for the one-sided Wilcoxon rank-sum test of the null hypothesis that the underlying distribution of the more advanced firms is not stochastically larger than that of the less advanced firms.

based on quality-award-related search criteria, the analysis was also rerun deleting all firms that were identified as a result of quality awards. The results are essentially unchanged, showing the same patterns of significance as for the full sample. In addition, a separate analysis was performed for the 39 events collected as a part of the first phase (Jarrell and Easton, 1997) of the study, which were not based on any searches relating to quality awards, and the 69 events collected in phase two. The results of these analyses are also consistent. This stability lends further validity to the overall analysis and results.

Less- and More-Advanced Firms Intra-Sample Validation

The differences in performance between the more advanced and less advanced subsamples

TABLE 10.21 Excess Cumulative Percent Daily Stock Returns for TQM Firms With Positive and Negative Excess Percent Change in Employees—Manufacturing Firms Only

Variable	Excess Δ%E	Full Sample			Less Advanced TQM Firms			More Advanced TQM Firms			
		Median	p	n	Median	p	n	Median	p	n	p-wrs
1	–	−0.79%	0.39	28	−3.13%	0.70	13	2.70%	0.15	15	0.17
	+	1.90%	0.14	34	1.07%	0.29	17	2.72%	0.17	17	0.30
			0.74†			0.83†			0.48†		
2	–	−7.24%	0.76	27	−15.64%	0.97	13	6.71%	0.17	14	0.03
	+	5.20%	0.33	34	−5.44%	0.71	17	10.06%	0.12	17	0.17
			0.86†			0.89†			0.62†		
3	–	4.83%	0.48	27	−17.15%	0.98	13	17.44%	0.02	14	0.00
	+	5.89%	0.05	34	−0.70%	0.34	17	18.75%	0.05	17	0.08
			0.85†			0.99†			0.41†		
4	–	6.50%	0.17	27	−13.45%	0.93	13	36.83%	0.01	14	0.00
	+	10.66%	0.02	34	2.84%	0.22	17	18.14%	0.02	17	0.12
			0.72†			0.96†			0.31†		
5	–	23.59%	0.06	27	3.97%	0.54	13	41.07%	0.01	14	0.09
	+	22.81%	0.00	34	24.54%	0.05	17	21.02%	0.02	17	0.37
			0.69†			0.87†			0.35†		

NOTE: Medians and p-values for the excess cumulative percent with-dividend continuously compounded daily stock returns for the manufacturing events only. The rows labeled – and + correspond to events with negative and positive year 0 to 4 excess percent change in employees, respectively. Results are reported for both the entire sample of manufacturing events and for the subsamples of manufacturing firms with less advanced and more advanced TQM systems. The cumulative returns data were calculated from the daily returns database compiled by the Center for Research in Securities Prices (CRSP) at the University of Chicago. Except as indicated by †, the columns labeled p contain p-values for the the one-sided Wilcoxon signed-rank test of the null hypothesis H_0 : true median ≤ 0 against the alternative H_A : true median > 0. The sample sizes are given in the columns labeled n. The p-values labeled † are for Wilcoxon rank-sum tests of the null hypothesis that the underlying distribution for the events with negative excess percent change in employees is not stochastically larger than that for the events with positive excess percent change in employees. The column labeled p-wrs contains p-values for the one-sided Wilcoxon rank-sum test of the null hypothesis that the underlying distribution of the more advanced firms is not stochastically larger than that of the less advanced firms.

of TQM firms represent a very important intrasample validation of the overall research design. Because, however, the development the firms' TQM systems occurs over a multi-year period, it is possible that the subsequent development of a firm's TQM system could be influenced by financial performance early in the post-event period. If this were the case, this might create a kind of "TQM survivorship" bias where firms that had positive early financial results would be more likely to continue the kinds of efforts necessary to develop an advanced TQM system. There are a number of reasons why this is not likely. This hypothesis assumes that managers expect early overall financial success from their TQM initiatives, that early success does not diminish the perceived need

for major organizational change, and that early success drives development of an advanced system as defined by the Baldrige Award Criteria rather than just a continuation of initial efforts.

This issue was also examined empirically by conditioning on zero excess average year 1 and 2 stock returns, and examining whether or not the difference in performance between the more advanced and less advanced firms persists in years 3 and 4. Two subsamples were constructed, one of the more advanced firms and the other of the less advanced firms, with zero median year 1 and 2 excess average stock returns. For these subsamples, the year 3 and 4 performance of the more advanced firms continues to be significantly better than for the less advanced firms. This analysis provides evi-

TABLE 10.22 Efficiencies of AR 1 Forecasts Relative to Value Line Analysts' Forecast for the Accounting Variables

Variable	Year	Control Firms			Event Firms		
		Eff	r-Eff	n	Eff	r-Eff	n
NI/S	1	44.44%	54.21%	299	5.33%	30.76%	98
	2	25.01%	36.25%	288	1.65%	30.96%	96
	3-5	1.84%	71.41%	248	0.00%	41.18%	84
NI/A	1	47.63%	50.35%	299	20.72%	55.06%	98
	2	30.50%	37.90%	288	5.72%	49.32%	96
	3-5	4.11%	92.48%	248	0.09%	82.70%	84
OI/S	1	75.47%	77.96%	259	83.51%	66.18%	85
	2	34.94%	37.70%	249	37.03%	82.96%	84
	3-5	35.51%	94.83%	212	7.53%	79.70%	72
OI/A	1	72.61%	82.46%	259	96.25%	68.19%	85
	2	43.09%	52.28%	249	63.07%	114.90%	84
	3-5	61.11%	188.40%	212	13.58%	110.44%	72
S/A	1	50.57%	66.11%	299	79.37%	75.39%	98
	2	65.71%	50.31%	288	51.24%	53.90%	96
	3-5	83.12%	95.02%	248	40.07%	75.41%	84

NOTE: Efficiencies (Eff) and "robust" efficiencies (r-Eff) for AR 1 time series forecasts for net income/sales (NI/S), net income/assets (NI/A), operating income/sales (OI/S), operating income/assets (OI/A), and sales/assets (S/A) for post-event years 1, 2, and the average of years 3-5. The efficiencies are expressed as percents. The efficiency is calculated as the mean-squared error of the Value Line analysts' forecasts divided by the mean-squared error of the time series forecasts. The "robust" efficiencies are calculated in a similar fashion except that the mean-squared errors are replaced by 5% trimmed mean-squared errors (the mean-squared error obtained after omitting the largest 5% of the squared errors). The performance measures and forecasts used to calculate the mean-squared errors for the analysts forecasts were obtained from Value Line. The performance measures used to calculate the AR 1 forecasts were obtained from COMPUSTAT. The AR 1 model was estimated for each firm based on 11 years of data prior to and ending with event year 0 (i.e., t_{-10} to t_0).

dence against the hypothesis that "feedback" due to early financial performance is the driver of the difference in the results for the more and less advanced firms.

Conclusion

The major finding of this study is clear evidence that the long-term performance of firms that implemented TQM is improved. We believe that evidence of improvement is particularly strong when the overall analysis is considered. Specifically, both the results based on the excess unexpected performance of the accounting variables and excess cumulative stock returns are consistent. We also view the overall stronger performance of the more advanced TQM firms, which were identified independently by interviews, as both an important test of the research methodology and compelling evidence that management methods which comprise TQM

are associated with improved performance. In addition, the results are even stronger when the analysis is limited to just manufacturing firms. The study has also examined whether downsizing, which might have occurred in conjunction with the implementation of TQM, could explain the positive performance we observed. This hypothesis is not supported by the data.

While no observational study can prove a causal relationship, this study is based on a carefully developed research methodology designed to provide as compelling evidence as possible on the impact of the adoption of TQM on corporate financial performance. Specifically, a carefully controlled event study approach is used rather than cross-sectional analysis, the sample of TQM firms is selected based on in-depth interviews not self-selected based on mail survey responses or public pronouncements, an established operational definition of a TQM system is the basis for selection (the Baldrige Award Criteria), and the approach is further validated by comparison of the more and less advanced TQM firms. In addition, there is a plausible causal mechanism for the observed improvement performance—TQM, after all, does focus specifically on generating quality and operational improvements. Further, the management changes associated with the development of a TQM system are sufficient in scope that it is plausible that their effects are observable in overall corporate performance. Finally, even under the most unfavorable interpretation, the results of this study clearly provide evidence against the proposition that implementation of TQM actually hurts corporate performance.

It is important, however, to recognize limitations on the generalizability of the results. This study examines whether or not TQM is associated with an improvement in financial performance for companies that made serious efforts to implement TQM. This was done by comparing actual performance with a carefully constructed benchmark of what performance would have been without TQM. The finding that TQM improves performance for the companies that implement it, however, cannot necessarily be generalized to a prescription that the companies that did not implement TQM would also have improved performance if they had. It is possible that there are enabling factors that would make TQM effective in some companies and ineffective in others. The decision to implement or not implement TQM may be based on managers' knowledge of these factors.

Appendix 10.1: Sample of TQM Firms

TQM Firm	Year of Implementation	TQM Firm	Year of Implementation
ADC Communications	1987	George A. Hormel & Co.	1986
Advanced Micro Devices	1988	IBM	1989
Air Products	1987	Integrated Device Technology	1989
Albany International Corporation	1987	Intel	1985
Alcoa	1990	International Paper	1985
Allied Signal Inc.	1991	James River	1986
Amdahl Corporation	1984	Johnson Controls	1986
American Express[s]	1989	Kulicke and Soffa	1988
Analog Devices	1987	Lubrizon Corporation	1988
Applied Materials	1985	Lyondell Petroleum	1989
Ark Best Corporation[s]	1984	Micron Technology	1988
Armstrong World Industries	1983	Millipore Corporation	1986
Arvin Industries	1986	Minnesota Mining & Manufacturing (3M)	1984
AT&T[s]	1988	Molex Inc.	1986
Baldor Electric Co.	1987	Moog Inc.	1989
Banc One Corporation[s]	1986	Morton International	1991
Bausch & Lomb	1989	Motorola Inc.	1983
Baxter International	1985	Nashua Corporation	1981
Black & Decker	1990	National Semiconductor	1990
Boise Cascade	1990	Pacific Telesis[s]	1989
Cameron Iron Works Inc.	1984	Perkin Elmer Corporation	1984
Carolina Freight Corporation[s]	1984	PPG Industries	1986
Carpenter Technology Corporation	1987	Proctor & Gamble	1987
Caterpillar	1983	Raychem Corporation	1987
Ceridian	1984	Roadway Services[s]	1989
Chevron	1987	Rockwell International Corporation	1986
Chrysler	1985	Rogers Corporation	1983
Conner Peripherals	1989	Rohr Industries	1989
Consolidated Freight[s]	1990	Scotsman Industries	1990
Corning Glass	1984	Sealed Air Corporation	1989
Cummins Engine	1983	Snap-on Tools	1986
Dana Corporation	1984	Square D	1987
Diebold Inc.	1990	Standard Register	1989
Digital Equipment	1989	Sterling Chemical	1990
Dun & Bradstreet[s]	1991	Storage Technology	1988
DuPont	1987	Sun Microsystems	1988
Eastman Kodak Co.	1983	Tektronix Inc.	1989
Ethyl Corporation	1986	Teradyne	1990
Federal Express[s]	1986	Texas Instruments Inc.	1982
Firestone Tire	1982	Thomas & Betts	1987
First Chicago[s]	1985	Timken Company	1983
Fluke (John) Mfg Co Inc.	1990	Union Camp Corporation	1987
Ford Motor	1984	Union Carbide	1988
FPL Group[s]	1986	Unisys	1988
Gaylord Container Corporation	1990	United Technologies	1984
General Datacomm	1987	Varian Associates Inc.	1987
General Motors	1985	VLSI Technology	1989
Goodyear Tire	1990	Westinghouse Electric Corporation	1982
Goulds Pumps	1989	Weyerhaeuser Co.	1989
Grumman	1988	Whirlpool Corporation	1990
GTE Corporation[s]	1986	WPL Holdings Inc.[s]	1987
Hanna (M.A.) Co.	1990	Xerox Corporation	1983
Harris Corporation	1986	Yellow Corporation[s]	1990
Hewlett Packard Company	1983		
Hillenbrand Inds Inc.	1987		

NOTE: "s" indicates a predominantly service company.

Appendix 10.2: Interview Topics

General Category	Specific Approach	General Category	Specific Approach
Training	Senior management training		Flowcharting
	Awareness training		Plan-do-check-act
	Training of other management		Seven basic QC tools
	levels		Seven management tools
	Workforce basic training		Root-cause analysis
	Technical training		
	Training for engineering	Involvement and	
		morale	Suggestion systems
Teams	Workforce improvement teams		Employee quality recognition
	Natural work-group teams		Employee morale survey
	Cross-functional teams		
	Vertical teams	Design and	
	Work cell teams	engineering	Design-for-manufacturability
	Self-managed teams		Concurrent/simultaneous
	Project-oriented teams		engineering
	Management teams		Design of experiments
			Taguchi methods
Customers	Customer satisfaction surveys		Quality function deployment
	Customer complaint tracking		
	Customer audits	Production	SPC
			JIT/cycle time reduction/SMED
Organizational			Activity-based costing
structures	Senior management quality council		Work cells
	Departmental quality councils		
	Specific location quality councils	Suppliers	Supplier tracking
	Internal quality consultants		Supplier certification
			Supplier quality audits
Planning/values	Written quality values and/or		Supplier training
	mission statement		Joint supplier teams
	Hoshin planning/policy deployment		Ship-to-stock/production
	Formal benchmarking		relationships
	Quality/customer satisfaction		Supplier integration into product
	measures reported to senior		development
	management		
		Crosby	Quality Improvement Teams
Audits	Quality assurance audits		Error Cause Removal system
	ISO-9000		Corrective Action Teams
	Baldrige self-assessments		Cost of Quality/Price of Non-
	Other management systems audits		Conformance
			Measure and display
Team processes			QES training
and tools	Problem-solving process		Zero defects days

Notes

1. See Easton (1995) for a discussion of the characteristics of U.S. TQM.

2. The validity of this comparison as an intra-sample validation is discussed further later in the paper. Because the decision to continue TQM implementation is endogenous, early financial success during the post-event period could influence the subsequent development of the firm's TQM system. The empirical analysis indicates that this phenomenon does not drive the results of the comparison between the more advanced and less advanced firms.

3. Adjusting for endogeneity of the decision to implement TQM (or any similar management decision) requires prediction of what performance would have been had the same firms not implemented the changes. Thus, the performance measures used in this study must account for variables which are associated with the decision to implement TQM that would affect future performance even if TQM was not implemented. There are a variety of other approaches that might be taken other than the use of analysts' forecasts. For example, one might try to build econometric models that include exogenous variables thought to be associated with the choice to implement TQM. Actual performance of the event company could then be compared to the model's prediction. Forecasts based on such statistical models, however, have several disadvantages relative to analysts' forecasts (see footnote 5). They are generally not developed on a firm-by-firm basis, do not incorporate information from sources other than the time series of accounting data, and are subject to errors caused by model building, outliers in the data, etc.

4. What is required is that the difference between the analysts' forecasts for the event firm and for the control portfolio is unbiased for the market consensus forecast of the expected difference. This means that the control portfolio methodology corrects for any systematic bias in the analysts' forecasts, provided such biases apply, on average, equally to the event and control firms (under the null hypothesis of no effect due to TQM).

5. The IBES market consensus forecasts are not used because they are limited to short-term earnings per share forecasts and are not time-stamped in a way that allows reliable determination of when the forecasts were made relative to the event times. This study requires long-term forecasts and examines variables other than earnings per share.

6. In addition to the theoretical basis discussed here, there is also considerable empirical evidence that analysts' forecasts are effective proxies for market expectations (e.g., see Schipper, 1991, and Brown, 1993). There is also evidence that analysts' forecasts are superior to time-series forecasts, at least for simple time-series models. Brown, et al. (1987) find that the forecasting ability of Value Line analysts is superior to univariate time-series models. Brown and Rozeff (1978) compare the earnings predictions of Value Line analysts and forecasts in Standard and Poor's Earnings Forecaster to those from three different time series models, including random walk and Box-Jenkins models, and find that Value Line analysts produce more small annual forecast errors and fewer large annual forecast errors. Finally, Brown et al. (1987), who examine Value Line forecasts, and Fried and Givoly (1982), who examine forecasts from Standard and Poor's Earnings Forecaster, find that one-year-ahead analyst forecasts have a greater association with excess stock returns over the next year than do one-year-ahead earnings forecasts made by time-series models. These studies support the view that analyst expectations are a better proxy for market expectations than forecasts from time-series models. A later section also provides empirical evidence validating the Value Line forecasts for the sample of event and control firms used in this study.

7. This remark also applies to the approach suggested by Barber and Lyon (1995). Their paper examines several methods from event studies using accounting-based measures, and concludes that test-statistics are only well-specified when sample firms are matched to control firms of similar pre-event performance.

8. Eighteen control firms were interviewed to provide some verification that the control firms have not made significant efforts to implement TQM. All were determined to be appropriate controls. It would be impractical to interview the entire control sample. In addition, especially for larger firms, failure to detect TQM-related efforts through the searches performed provides considerable evidence that these firms have not made significant TQM efforts. More importantly, however, contamination of the control portfolio by firms that have implemented TQM should bias the results against finding an effect associated with TQM.

9. The timeliness rank is scaled from 1 to 5 (1 corresponds to the highest projected performance) and is updated approximately every quarter. Value Line indicates that the rank is based on three criteria: (1) the firm's industry-adjusted price-earnings ratio from the previous twelve months relative to the last ten years; (2) the year-to-year change in the quarterly earnings of the stock compared with that of all Value Line stocks; and (3) an earnings "surprise" factor.

10. Analysis of the forecasts for the control firms (which, with respect to this issue, are not contaminated by the effects of implementing TQM) does show a very slight, but not statistically significant, pattern of overestimation for firms with low timeliness ranks (strong expected performance) and underestimation of performance for firms with high timeliness ranks (poor expected performance). This, however, should not be interpreted as a justification for not using the analysts' forecasts since the bias associated with the high and low timeliness ranks is very small and is not statistically significant. Further, it is much smaller than would occur when matching to firms with very different timeliness ranks, and is corrected by the matching strategy used here. Finally, the average timeliness rank of the event firms is 3.08, so there is no concentration of firms in the sample with very high or very low timeliness ranks.

11. A specific example further illustrates these issues. The event firm United Technologies (UT), a diversified company, has a TQM starting year of 1984. At that time, UT's timeliness rank was 1, the highest rank. According to the analyst, "The key here is technological integration. Unlike the typical conglomerate, UT isn't simply equal to the sum of various unrelated parts." The analyst goes on to say

that "Whatever it may have once been, UT is now a large and diverse company with a clear business strategy." If the timeliness rank is ignored in matching the controls, ITT Corp. (timeliness rank 4) would replace Kaman Corp. (timeliness rank 2). While ITT is a better match than Kaman in terms of size, it is a far worse one in terms of the analyst' assessment of future prospects. Specifically, ITT's "top priority is to become a major force in telecommunications, through its new digital telephone switch, the System 12." While the "System 12 is succeeding oversees," it is "incompatible with the current generation of equipment used here." The analyst concludes that "success in this country will not come overnight," "the telecommunications thrust is expensive," and that ITT "will probably step up its divestiture activity." In contrast, for Kaman "1984 is shaping up as a record year" as a result of "record gains from both the diversified and industrial distribution divisions." For example, examining the operating margin, UT and all three of the original control firms (including Kaman) ended up performing worse than their year 3-5 forecasts. UT's performance was about 2% worse than the average of the control portfolio. ITT's performance, however, was substantially better than forecast (unlike any of the three original control firms), so the substitution of ITT for Kaman would make the performance of UT appear worse (2.5% worse than the control portfolio instead of 2% worse). While this result is anecdotal and thus may be due merely to random variation, it is also possible that the conditions that resulted in ITT's poor timeliness rank make it a poor control for the forecast error of a firm expected to perform very well.

12. As discussed in the second section, we believe the validity of analysis based on excess actual performance is considerably weaker than that based on excess unexpected performance. We nevertheless examine these variables because of their close link to the methods of TQM. In the context of the other analysis presented, we believe these variables do provide some useful indications.

13. COMPUSTAT's cost-of-goods-sold (CGS) often includes selling, general, and administrative expenses (SGA). When this is the case, the corresponding COMPUSTAT SGA variable is missing. To correct for this inconsistency, the variable used here (which we refer to as CGS) is actually the sum of COMPUSTAT's CGS and SGA variables. Also note that, for the I/S variable, the five firms with missing data for all years are service firms. For the I/CGS variable, the fourteen firms with missing data for all years are service firms — only one service firm remains. Thus, the results in Table 10.8 are very similar to the results for the manufacturing firms alone (Table 10.17).

References

Anderson, S. W., Daly, J., and Johnson, M. F. 1995. The value of management control systems: Evidence on the market reaction to ISO 9000 quality assurance certification. Working paper, University of Michigan Business School, Ann Arbor, MI.

Barber, B. M., and Lyon, J. D. 1995. Detecting abnormal operating performance: The empirical power and specification of test-statistics. *Journal of Financial Economics* 41 (No. 3): 359-399.

Brown, L. D. 1993. Earnings forecasting research: Its implications for capital markets research. *International Journal of Forecasting* 9: 295-320.

Brown, L. D., Hagerman, R., Griffin, P., and Zmijewski, M. 1987. Security analyst superiority relative to univariate time-series models in forecasting quarterly earnings. *Journal of Accounting and Economics* 9: 61-87.

Brown, L. D., and Rozeff, M. 1978. The superiority of analyst forecasts as measures of expectations: Evidence from earnings. *Journal of Finance* 6: 1-16.

Easton, G. S. 1995. A Baldrige examiner's assessment of the U.S. total quality management. In R. E. Cole (ed.), *The Death and Life of the American Quality Movement.* New York: Oxford University Press.

Easton, G. S., and Jarrell, S. L. 1997. The emerging academic research on the link between total quality management and corporate financial performance: A critical review. Forthcoming in M. J. Stahl (ed.), *Topics on Total Quality.* Malden, MA: Blackwell Publishers.

Fried, D., and Givoly, D. 1982. Financial analysts' forecasts of earnings: A better surrogate for market expectations. *Journal of Accounting and Economics* 4: 85-108.

Healy, P., Palepu, K., and Ruback, R. 1992. Does corporate performance improve after mergers? *Journal of Financial Economics* 31: 135-175.

Hendricks, K. B., and Singhal, V. R. 1996. Quality awards and the market value of the firm: An empirical investigation. *Management Science* 42 (No. 3): 415-436.

Jarrell, S. L. 1991. Do Takeovers Generate Value? Non-Stock Price Evidence on the Ability of the Capital Market to Assess Takeovers. Unpublished dissertation, Graduate School of Business, The University of Chicago.

Jarrell, S. L., and Easton, G. S. 1997. An exploratory empirical investigation of the effects of total quality management on corporate performance. In P. Lederer and U. Karmarkar (eds.), *The Practice of Quality Management.* Norwell, MA: Kluwer Academic Publishers.

NIST. 1994. *Malcolm Baldrige National Quality Award 1995 Award Criteria.* National Institute of Standards and Technology, U.S. Department of Commerce.

Schipper, K. 1991. Commentary on analysts' forecasts. *Accounting Horizons* 5: 105-121.

United States General Accounting Office. 1991. Management practices: U.S. companies improve performance through quality efforts. (GAO/NSIAD-91-190).

Chapter 11

Organizational Quality as a Cultural Variable

An Empirical Investigation of Quality Culture, Processes, and Outcomes

KIM S. CAMERON
CAROLE K. BARNETT

Although an extensive literature exists on quality techniques and procedures, the relationship between quality at the organizational level and performance is still poorly understood. Disagreement exists, for example, regarding whether quality programs enhance organizational performance or merely deflect energy and resources away from more potent activities (Schaffer & Thompson, 1992). Unresolved issues exist related to organizational quality, such as its relationship to cost (e.g., Cole, Bacdayan, & White, 1995; Juran, 1992) and customer satisfaction (e.g., Anderson & Sullivan, 1992; Fornell, 1992); its dimensionality (Garvin, 1988); and its key processes or elements (e.g., Barnett, 1994; Khurana, 1994).

Surveys of Quality

To be sure, some investigations have produced evidence that particular techniques are important predictors of product or service quality. For example, Quality Circles, certain organizational structures and processes, "lean" manufacturing techniques, and particular quality control procedures have been found to be associated with improved product quality, productivity, morale, and efficiency (Flynn, Schroeder, & Sakakibara, 1993; Garvin, 1988; Reynolds, 1988). Well-known surveys conducted by the General Accounting Office (1991), the Profit Impacts on Marketing Strategies (PIMS) (Buzzell & Gale, 1987; Buzzell & Weirsema, 1981), and the Delta Consulting

AUTHORS' NOTE: This manuscript was prepared for the Workshop on Improving Theory and Research on Quality Enhancement in Organizations sponsored by the National Science Foundation and the Air Force Office of Scientific Research, September 6-7, 1996, and March 16-17, 1997.

Group (1993) have also found positive relationships between quality and organizational performance (including employee-related indicators, operating indicators, customer indicators, and financial indicators). In particular, one survey found that 91% of corporate CEOs whose firms had implemented quality programs thought that customer satisfaction improved, 88% thought that internal processes improved, 86% thought that employee satisfaction improved, and 76% thought that financial performance improved (Delta Consulting Group, 1993).

On the other hand, contrary findings have also emerged regarding the relationship between quality and organizational effectiveness. For example, surveys across several countries have reported that most quality initiatives fail to achieve their objectives. A great many firms have labeled TQM a failure and are actually cutting back their quality budgets (*Behavioral Sciences Newsletter,* 1992; Ernst & Young, 1993; *Wall Street Journal,* 1992). Larcker and Ittner (1997) reported that only 29% of managers could link quality initiatives to accounting returns such as ROA and ROI, and only 12% could link quality to stock price returns. Criticisms of quality programs have become widespread in the popular press, labeling them as an outdated management fad of the 1980s because, it is argued, most quality efforts have faltered (Harari, 1993; Szwergold, 1992).

In the organizational sciences literature, the evidence for a positive association between aspects of quality and organizational benefits is also lacking. For example, Powell's (1995) survey of the organizational studies literature on TQM led him to conclude that most organizational features commonly associated with quality programs do not yield significant performance benefits to organizations. Westphal, Gulati, and Shortell (1996, 1997) found that the main effect of total quality management programs on health care organizations was an enhancement of legitimacy in the industry, not enhanced operational outcomes (e.g., economic and human resource benefits). The point is, conclusive empirical evidence is lacking regarding whether a positive or a negative relationship exists between organizational quality and organizational performance.

Definitions of Quality

Among the inhibitors to more extensive empirical investigations of organizational quality and effectiveness are the differences in the way quality has been defined and approached. One difficulty, as pointed out by Weick (Chapter 7, this volume), is that the term *quality* is a diffuse, multidimensional *construct,* and little consensus exists regarding how it is to be measured or operationalized. No objective referent exists, and no one definition is completely comprehensive or correct (Cameron, 1981). For example, in the 1970s and 1980s, the organizational sciences literature treated quality as a *predictor* of overall organizational effectiveness (Campbell, 1977; Conrad & Blackburn, 1985). Quality referred to the rate of errors or defects in goods-producing organizations (Crosby, 1979), to institutional reputation in higher education organizations (Webster, 1981), to renown and talent in arts organizations (Tschirhart, 1993), to recovery levels in health care organizations (Scott, Flood, Ewy, & Forrest, 1978), and so on. In every case, quality was *one* of the desired attributes of the outcomes produced by organizations, and it was always used as a qualifier in describing some product or service (i.e., high-quality products, high-quality education, high-quality art, high-quality health care). It was merely an attribute of what organizations were interested in accomplishing.

On the other hand, another stream of quality writing—usually associated with quality gurus such as Fiegenbaum (1961), Crosby (1979), Deming (1986), and Juran (1989)—expanded the focus of quality to include organizational processes and practices beyond those directly related to attributes of products or services and to the processes that produce them. A distinction was invented that differentiated a "big Q" approach to quality from a "little q" approach (Greene, 1993; Juran, 1989). The former refers to quality as an overall, encompassing culture of the organization, and the latter refers to specific tools, techniques, activities, or product and service attributes within an organization. Little q is associated with quality as an attribute of a product or a process. Big Q is associated with the culture and overall functioning of the organiza-

TABLE 11.1 Major Definitions of Quality

Approach	Definition	Example
Transcendent	"Quality is neither mind nor matter, but a third entity independent of the two . . . even though Quality cannot be defined, you know what it is" (Pirsig, 1974).	Innate excellence Timeless beauty Universal appeal
Product-based	"Quality refers to the amounts of the unpriced attributes contained in each unit of the priced attribute" (Leffler, 1982).	Durability Extra desired attributes Wanted features
User-based	"Quality is fitness for use" (Juran, 1974). "Quality consists of the capacity to satisfy wants" (Edwards, 1968).	Satisfied customers Meets needs Fulfills expectations
Production-based	"Quality means conformance to requirements" (Crosby, 1979).	Reliability Adherence to specifications Variation within tolerance limits
Value-based	"Quality means best for certain conditions . . . (a) the actual use and (b) the selling price" (Fiegenbaum, 1961).	Performance at an acceptable price Value for the money spent Affordable excellence
System-based	"[Quality is] a system of means to economically produce goods or services which satisfy customers' requirements" (Japanese Industrial Standard Z8101, 1981).	Using accepted quality procedures Quality processes Integrated approach
Cultural	"[Quality] means that the organization's culture is defined by and supports the constant attainment of customer satisfaction through an integrated system of tools, techniques, and training" (Sashkin & Kiser, 1993).	Management philosophy Lifestyle Mind-set

SOURCE: Cameron and Whetten (1996).

tion. The phrase "total quality management" (TQM) is often used synonymously with big Q quality.

Table 11.1 summarizes seven different approaches to quality typical of the current quality literature. They include the *transcendent approach* (e.g., innate beauty), the *product-based approach* (e.g., reliability), the *user-based approach* (e.g., customer satisfaction), the *production-based approach* (e.g., no defects), the *value-based approach* (e.g., high utility for low cost), the *system-based approach* (e.g., integrated processes), and the *cultural approach* (e.g., a mind-set or philosophy) (see Garvin, 1988, for an extended discussion of the first five definitions). Each approach generates different assumptions about and different criteria for assessing quality, and each is emphasized in a different portion of the quality literature. A common theme in the first five definitions is a focus on quality as an attribute of products and services (little q). The last two definitions focus on quality from a more comprehensive, organization-level perspective (big Q or TQM).

The approach that is addressed least in the scholarly literature is the cultural approach. Whereas an extensive literature exists on the topic of organizational culture (see Cameron & Quinn, 1998; Martin, 1992; Schein, 1985; Trice & Beyer, 1993), empirical work on *quality* culture as a dimension of organizational culture is scarce, and knowledge about the relationships between quality as a cultural phenomenon and organizational performance is largely absent.

Consequently, this study seeks to investigate quality from a cultural perspective, and it examines the relationships between quality culture and organizational effectiveness. This is an exploratory investigation by design, and its major objective is to raise awareness of the cultural perspective in quality research.

Specifically, four research questions form the basis for this study.

1. What differences among organizations' quality cultures can be detected?
2. What quality practices or processes are associated with differences among organizations' quality cultures?
3. What quality practices are associated with differences between highly effective organizations and others?
4. What quality practices account for differences between organizations that improve in their effectiveness over time compared to those that remain stagnant or decline in effectiveness?

To better understand these four questions, a brief discussion is necessary of quality culture as a phenomenon for investigation, and a brief definition is provided for organizational effectiveness in the context of this study.

The Construct of Quality Culture

Quality culture is a subset of the overall culture of an organization. It refers to the predominant definition, paradigm, set of values, or overall approach to quality in the organization. It is, therefore, more narrow in focus than organizational culture. In the big Q or TQM sense, it represents an organizational mind-set or unobserved understructure that may be reflected by a set of processes and practices. It is illustrated by the following assertion of George Bush (Malcolm Baldrige National Quality Award Application Guidelines, 1992):

> Quality management is not just a strategy. It must be a new style of working, even a new style of thinking. A dedication to quality and excellence is more than good business. It is a way of life, giving something back to society, offering your best to others. (p. 1)

Quality culture, then, represents more than just a set of tools, procedures, or technologies. It represents a way of thinking about and defining quality. It has just begun to be investigated in the scholarly literature, and only rudimentary conceptual development has occurred to date. For example, Garvin (1988), Shiba, Graham, and Walden (1993), Sitkin, Sutcliffe, and Schroeder (1994), and Reed, Lemak, and Montgomery (1996) are authors who have identified differences in general orientations toward quality in organizations. The most commonly identified orientations distinguish between internal, company, or operations orientations and external, customer, or market orientations. Cameron (1992) formulated a model of quality culture in which both internal and external orientations were included. Three different orientations toward quality were described in that typology. These orientations emerged as a result of interviews and surveys in more than 200 manufacturing and service organizations from 1986 through 1995 (e.g., Cameron, Freeman, & Mishra, 1993; Cameron & Peterson, 1995). Different organizations were found to have recognizable differences in their cultures of quality.

Table 11.2 summarizes the attributes of the three dominant types of cultures. Not every single one of the listed attributes was necessarily present in each quality culture, but most were found to be present. These attributes illustrate the general differences typical of each culture type. No organization was characterized by only one single quality culture, but in most organizations, one culture dominated the others in emphasis.

The Chronological Development of Quality Culture

Consistent with the viewpoints of authors such as Ansoff (1979), Miles and Kimberly (1980), Cameron and Whetten (1981), Garvin (1988), and Treacy and Wiersema (1993)—who proposed that different cultures or orientations tend to develop over time in organizations—different quality cultures also seem to have emerged developmentally over the past few decades. Through the 1970s, for example, most

TABLE 11.2 A Model of Quality Cultures: Three Stages

Error detection
  Regarding products
    Avoid mistakes
    Reduce waste, rework, repair
    Detect problems
    Focus on outputs
  Regarding customers
    Avoid annoying customers
    Respond to complaints efficiently and accurately
    Assess satisfaction after the fact
    Focus on needs and requirements
Error prevention
  Regarding products
    Expect zero defects
    Prevent errors and mistakes
    Hold everyone accountable
    Focus on processes and root causes
  Regarding customers
    Satisfy customers and exceed expectations
    Eliminate problems in advance
    Involve customers in design
    Focus on preferences or "nice to have" attributes
Continuous creative quality
  Regarding products
    Constant improvement and escalating standards
    Concentrate on things gone right
    Emphasize breakthroughs
    Focus on improvement in suppliers, customers, and
      own processes
  Regarding customers
    Expect lifelong loyalty
    Surprise and delight customers
    Anticipate expectations
    Create new preferences

North American and Western European organizations were characterized by a quality culture labeled *error cause removal* (Cole, Chapter 4, this volume). Garvin (1988) used the labels *inspection era* and a subsequent *statistical control era* to describe the same phenomenon. In Garvin's inspection era, quality is associated with detecting mistakes and errors in products and services; in the statistical control era, quality is associated with reducing errors and controlling variation through statistical procedures. Organizations dominated by an error cause re-

moval culture approach quality as a problem to be solved or as a set of potential obstacles to be avoided. With regard to products, these organizations tend to emphasize inspecting and detecting errors, avoiding mistakes, reducing waste, and finding and fixing defects. Quality control auditors examine and test products and services after they are produced. The emphasis is on output uniformity and staying within specified tolerance limits. Quality professionals in organizations focus on counting, measuring, and auditing.

With regard to customer orientation, a major focus is on avoiding dissatisfaction or irritation among internal and external customers in service delivery. There is a general orientation toward addressing customer complaints quickly and accurately to reduce the incidence of customer disapproval. The emphasis is on giving customers what they need—that is, meeting demands and requirements—and the extent to which customer needs are met is assessed after the service has been provided.

The primary disadvantages of this approach to quality are that quality is inherently reactive, defensive, and protective. Action and improvement are driven by customer complaints, errors and defects, and externally generated requirements. The correlation between cost and quality is positive (i.e., the higher the quality, the higher the cost), hence, it is an expensive way to achieve high quality. The defect rate is always assumed to be substantial because no amount of inspection can eliminate all errors (Deming, 1986; Huff, 1994).

During the decade of the 1980s, a transition to an *error prevention culture* occurred in many firms in North America and Western Europe.[1] Costs were recognized as being too high and quality too low, especially with regard to Asian competitors. Tolerance for defects and general customer satisfaction with domestic products and services plummeted as high-quality, low-cost products and services became readily available (e.g., Cole, 1993). The defensive, reactive approach to quality typified by error detection became recognized as too costly.

A new *error prevention culture* emerged in which quality was approached as a problem to be tackled aggressively. It was identified by Garvin (1988) as a *quality assurance era* in which quality techniques and philosophies were expanded beyond the production of outputs to "total quality control." Top management began to take responsibility for ensuring quality in all parts of the organization (Fiegenbaum, 1983). This shift represented a change in the general orientation toward quality to proactivity instead of reactivity and to avoiding mistakes instead of correcting them after the fact. Regarding products, this new orientation focused on achieving zero defects (perfection) by doing work right the first time, and by emphasizing root (common) causes of problems instead of treating symptoms or special (unique) causes of problems. All workers were assumed to be accountable for quality, not just end-of-the-line inspectors. Organizational design and measurement systems concentrated on processes more than on outputs. Quality professionals in firms emphasized planning, program design, and process mapping.

With regard to the customer orientation, the mind-set shifted toward pleasing and satisfying customers, not just avoiding annoying them, and toward providing value-added service that creates customer trust and loyalty. Customer expectations were sometimes exceeded, not just satisfied. Customer preferences (not just requirements) were obtained in advance of product and service design and delivery, and customer satisfaction was monitored continually after the service was provided. Customer training occurred so that expectations could more closely match company capability, and customers were involved in the design of the organization's products and services.

An advantage of this approach to quality is that as a shift to an aggressive, proactive orientation occurs in the organization, the correlation between cost and quality becomes negative (Huff, 1994; Schonberger, 1986). Firms avoid the costs of rework, repair, inspection, and customer dissatisfaction. The error prevention culture makes it possible to expect that products and services can be produced with zero defects. The main disadvantage, however, is that quality is limited to the organization's own processes

and activities—excluding customers and suppliers—and it is static in its orientation.

A third quality culture emerged during the late 1980s and early 1990s labeled here as *continuous creative quality culture.* Garvin's (1988) strategic quality management era shares some characteristics with this stage. Garvin described this era as one in which quality is defined from the customer's point of view, and the organization's strategy and culture become centered on quality. The business strategy and the quality strategy become inseparable. Similarly, continuous creative quality culture—which was found in only a relatively few organizations—not only emphasized quality as the central business policy of the organization, but quality itself took on a new definition as well. Continuous improvement (small, incremental changes) was coupled with innovation (large, breakthrough changes) in the pursuit of better products and services. Current standards of performance, as well as levels of performance, were constantly rising or improving. The focus shifted to designing, producing, and measuring "things gone right" in addition to avoiding "things gone wrong." Products were not only designed to be produced defect-free, but they were designed so as to achieve additional, unexpected benefits (e.g., recyclable, user-friendly, less costly, safer). Quality professionals in the organization emphasized education, training, coaching, and system design. Helping to improve suppliers' and customers' quality became as important as improving the firm's own work processes and outcomes.

With regard to customer orientation, the focus was on generating lifelong loyalty among customers. That is, customers remained committed to the organization because it created new preferences and expectations that no other organization addressed. This was done by surprising and delighting customers, solving problems for them that they did not expect anyone to solve, and engaging in extra-mile restitution when aberrations or mistakes occurred. Customer expectations were anticipated before being verbalized, and customer excitement replaced customer satisfaction as the primary goal.

An advantage of this third type of quality culture is not only that errors and defects are avoided, but that improvement and innovation become part of everyday work. Escalating standards motivate organizational learning and improvement. Suppliers' and customers' performances are enhanced, not just the organization's own performance, as a result of this approach. In addition to doing the work right the first time, each employee is charged with improving his or her own work processes and outputs on a continuous basis. (Also see Weick, Chapter 7, this volume, for a discussion of continuous quality improvement.)

These three stages in the model represent something of a progression from a less advanced quality culture to a more advanced quality culture. Error detection represents a less advanced quality culture than does error prevention, which is less advanced than continuous creative quality.

Previous research on organizational downsizing investigated the relationship between these stages of quality culture and the success of organizational downsizing (Cameron, 1992, 1995; Cameron et al., 1993). The three quality culture types were assessed in approximately 100 manufacturing and service organizations, and it was found that the more advanced the quality culture, the more successful the organizations were in maintaining high performance after downsizing. High performance was indicated by product defect levels, financial performance over 5 years, customer satisfaction, and ratings of organizational effectiveness. Downsizing organizations that were dominated by a continuous creative quality culture scored highest on all outcome measures. Preliminary evidence exists, in other words, that the quality culture of an organization, at least under conditions of downsizing, has a positive relationship to its performance.

A Definition of Organizational Effectiveness

In previous work on effectiveness (Cameron, 1986; Cameron & Whetten, 1983, 1996), it was argued that, like quality, organizational effectiveness is a multidimensional, ambiguous construct without precise or consensual criteria for measurement. In each separate investigation, effectiveness must be defined (i.e., bounded) based on seven critical questions: What level of analysis is being used? What time frame is being employed? Whose perspective is being accepted? What domain of activity is being considered? What is the purpose of the assessment? What type of data are being gathered? and What is the referent against which effectiveness is judged? In organizational studies, the terms *effectiveness* and *performance* may be used synonymously providing that it is clear that the boundaries established by these seven questions are the same.

In this investigation, effectiveness was assessed at the organization level over a 3-year time frame—1990 through 1992. The perspectives of upper and middle managers inside the organizations as well as knowledgeable outside managers were used, and perceptual judgments form the primary basis of evaluation. More specifically, effectiveness in this study was indicated by a combination of achieving lower defect rates; higher levels of improvement; a greater degree of implementation of the Malcolm Baldrige National Quality Award (MBNQA) criteria (i.e., the U.S. government's quality award); and superior ratings of effectiveness by organization employees and outside experts compared to four standards: the industry average, the organization's best competitors, customer expectations, and the organization's own past performance. Highly effective organizations, in other words, perform better than other organizations in their industry, than their best competitors, than their customers expect of them, and than their own past performance.

Organizational effectiveness differs from quality culture in that effectiveness refers to organizational outcomes and accomplishment. Quality culture refers to an orientation, a mind-set, an overall definition, or a general approach to quality that guides action in the organization. Investigating the relationship between quality culture and effectiveness is the focus of this study.

Methodology

A total of 64 strategic business units and semiautonomous businesses within a large, multinational corporation served as the source of data for this investigation. The types of organizations included in the study were assembly, parts, distribution, European headquarters, land services, lighting, marketing, medical systems, new product development, retail sales, and stamping and casting businesses. Each of these organizations represents a business unit with full authority to establish strategy, implement quality procedures, make organizational changes, and hire and fire employees.[2] Unfortunately, whereas each business unit is independent in terms of strategy deployment, performance indicators such as profit and loss, productivity, and customer satisfaction are not compiled at this level in the corporation. Because the kinds of outputs produced by each of these units differ markedly (e.g., products, reports, staff support, sales), only aggregated corporate measures are accumulated. Therefore, common objective performance indicators (e.g., productivity, costs, errors) are unavailable at the business unit level, so perceptual data on outcomes were obtained from managers in each organization.

An overall corporate quality philosophy was shared by each of these business units, but the level of adoption and buy-in among the various units varied markedly. Some of these units had a general reputation inside the corporation of performing well, whereas others had a reputation of performing less well. One aim of this investigation was to determine if these performance differences could be explained by differences in quality culture as well as by the quality processes and practices implemented in these organizations. Therefore, quality culture, organizational effectiveness, and quality processes and practices were all assessed at the organization (business unit) level of analysis by means of a survey instrument.

Sample

On a monthly basis over a period of 3 years—1990, 1991, and 1992—upper mid-level managers in each of the 64 organizations completed a 120-item survey assessing quality culture, organizational effectiveness, and the process and practices associated with quality. The same managers did not respond to the survey in each month; instead, a subsample of managers at the same hierarchical level in the corporation completed the survey each month during the 3-year period. In 1990, 126 managers provided data; in 1991, 338 managers provided data; and in 1992, 431 managers provided data, for a total of 895 respondents. The number of respondents per organization ranged from 4 to 104. These respondents each participated in a weeklong executive program focused on quality and managerial and organizational effectiveness. Functions represented by these managers included control, employee relations, engineering, finance, manufacturing, marketing, operations, production, purchasing, quality, research, and sales. No significant differences were found among the different respondent groups on a month-by-month basis or in terms of function, personal demographics (e.g., age, tenure, salary), or quality experience. Moreover, the reliability coefficients for respondents rating their own organization's performance ranged between .44 and .97, indicating an acceptable level of intraorganizational reliability. Therefore, there is no reason to assume that a systematic bias exists in the respondent samples across the 3-year period.

Gathering data across a 3-year time period makes it possible to assess changes in culture and effectiveness over time. We were interested, in other words, in exploring not only the static relationship between quality culture and effectiveness but also the extent to which quality culture changes over time, and what might account for differences between organizations that improve in their effectiveness over time compared to those that remain stagnant or decline in effectiveness. In other words, the study includes three major analyses: (a) identifying the major predictors of quality culture differences, (b) examining the relationships between quality culture and organizational effectiveness, and (c) identifying the major predictors of changes in quality culture and organizational effectiveness over time.

Variables

Survey questions were developed to assess quality culture, effectiveness, and predictors. A substantial portion of the predictor variables were based on the practices, processes, and activities specified in the 1995 Malcolm Baldrige National Quality Award (MBNQA) application criteria.[3] These criteria are claimed to be a comprehensive set of indicators of quality processes (Reimann, 1988). Specific items assessed leadership; information collection, analysis, and use; quality planning; the management of human resources; quality assurance and the use of quality tools; organizational structure; and approaches to cost containment and efficiency. They serve as the major indicators of quality culture and practices that are predictive of effectiveness. The rating scale ranged from 1 (strongly disagree) to 6 (strongly agree).

To assess quality culture, the underlying definitions and orientations of organization members toward quality needed to be uncovered. Therefore, descriptive scenarios were developed that describe the value orientation, attributes, and approach to production and to customers that typify each different quality culture. Respondents were asked to divide 100 points among four scenarios based on the extent to which each scenario was similar to the respondent's own organization. A scenario that was most similar to the respondent's own organization was assigned the most points, and fewer points were assigned to scenarios that were less similar. These scenarios are reported in the appendix. Scenarios that received the highest number of points reflected the dominant quality culture in the organization, although each organization was expected to have some emphasis on more than one culture type.

Organizational effectiveness was assessed in three ways. One was by having respondents compare various aspects of their organization's performance with four standards: the industry average, the performance of their best competitor, the level of expected performance by customers, and their own past performance. Ratings ranged from 1 (much lower) to 6 (much higher), and an average score was computed for each organization. (The level of reliability coefficient among ratings of the four comparison standards is $r = .87$, suggesting that computing an average effectiveness score is an appropriate procedure.[4])

A second way that effectiveness was assessed was by having respondents report several specific results of organizational performance—that is, the amount of rework, missed deadlines, waste, excess, grievances and employee complaints, absenteeism, customer complaints, levels of customer satisfaction, speed of new product introduction, customer loyalty, and consistency and reliability of performance. Scores on these various results variables were averaged together so that each organization was given a single results score. Such averaging was appropriate inasmuch as the reliability coefficient among these various measures of results is .83.

The third method for assessing effectiveness was to obtain the rank orderings of six knowledgeable, external (unattached), corporate-level, senior executives in the parent company who were familiar with the general performance of all of the organizations in this study. Each of these executives ranked the businesses from high to low depending on their evaluation of the effectiveness of each organization. Therefore, organizations were arrayed on the basis of the average ranking received by these outsiders. The purpose for collecting these external executive rankings was to provide a method for calibrating the validity of the organization members' ratings.

Organizations were rank-ordered on the basis of the scores they received on these three types of effectiveness ratings—(a) comparisons with the industry average, the performance of

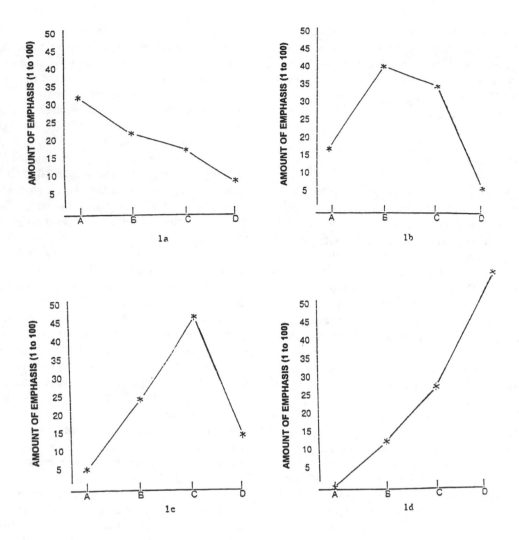

Figure 11.1. Four Examples of Quality Culture Profiles in the Sample

Note. A = No change, status quo; B = Find and fix, error detection approach; C = Prevent errors, focus on processes; D = Continuous improvement, creative quality.

the organization's best competitor, the level of expected performance by customers, and the organization's own past performance; (b) reports of performance results by organization members and (c) external executive rankings of performance. The average Spearman rank-order correlation among these sets of rankings is .58 ($p < .001$), suggesting a reasonable degree of consistency between the ratings of internal respondents and the ratings of independent external executives.[5] Therefore, an overall effectiveness score was assigned to each organization.

Analyses

Quality culture plots were generated for each organization in the sample by averaging across the ratings of quality culture by members of each organization. Figure 11.1 provides an example of four different quality culture plots from the sample of 68 organizations. In Plot A, for example, the organization is dominated by a status quo approach to quality—little attention is being paid to quality, quality is not systematically pursued by the organization, and quality improvement is part of neither the strategy nor the goals of top management. Plot B shows an organization dominated by the error detection culture, Plot C shows an organization dominated by a error prevention culture, and Plot D shows an organization dominated by the continuous creative quality culture. Culture plots were generated for each organization over each of the 3 years. No organization's dominant quality culture changed from one type to another between the beginning of 1990 and the end of 1992. That is, quality culture plots for each organization stayed relatively stable over the 3-year period.

After computing a quality culture plot for each organization, the dominant culture type was identified for each unit. If equal numbers of points were given to two different quality cultures, the organization was classified by the more advanced culture type. One set of analyses discriminated among the organizations characterized by these different quality culture types. Discriminant analyses used the quality processes and practices assessed on the survey as predictors to identify the main differences among quality culture types. Scores were averaged across the 3-year period.

A second set of analyses differentiated organizations with the highest effectiveness scores from those with the lowest effectiveness scores. Organizations were grouped into one of three categories based on their average effectiveness score—high, moderate, and low levels of effectiveness. Average scores on quality processes and practices were used to explain the differences among high and low performers.[6]

Third, organizations that improved in their effectiveness scores over the 3 years were also differentiated from those that remained stable or deteriorated. Discriminant analysis procedures identified the major predictors of improvement in organizational effectiveness

over time. Predictor variables were lagged by a year in order to identify which organizational processes and practices in the previous year led to improvement in effectiveness in a later year.

Fourth, organizations with the highest effectiveness scores that *also improved* were compared to highly effective organizations that *did not improve* over the 3 years. The intent was to identify clearly the variables accounting for improvement in the best firms as differentiated from merely identifying high versus low levels of performance. The major predictors of the best organizations that also got better were thus identified using discriminant analyses. Again, lagged predictors were used in these analyses.

Results

The first research question asked what differences in quality cultures could be detected in these organizations. Given a common corporate quality philosophy, were unique subunit cultures present? Figure 11.2 identifies the average overall plot for all 68 organizations over the 3-year period. This plot can be interpreted as the parent corporation's overall quality culture profile. However, individual business units also had developed their own unique quality cultures, similar to the ones displayed in Figure 11.1. Four of the organizations had a status quo culture type[7] (similar to Figure 11.1a), 8 had an error detection culture type (similar to Figure 11.1b), 50 of the organizations had an error prevention culture type (similar to Figure 11.1c), and 6 had a continuous creative quality culture type (similar to Figure 11.1d). Clearly, the dominant quality culture type in this organization is the error prevention orientation. This contrasts with an error detection culture that dominated this corporation's two largest U.S. competitors in 1992 and that is typical of the average manufacturing firm in North America and Western Europe (Cameron, 1992; also see Cole, Chapter 4, this volume).

Table 11.3 reports discriminant analysis results that differentiate among the four types of

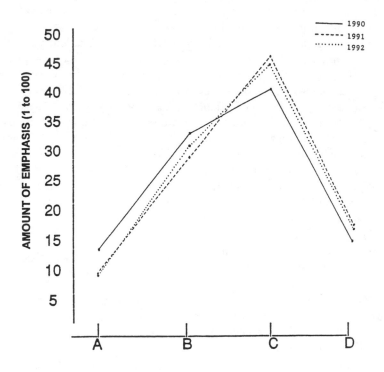

Figure 11.2. Average Overall Corporate Quality Culture Profiles: 1990-1992

Note. A = No change, status quo; B = Find and fix, error detection approach; C = Prevent errors, focus on processes; D = Continuous improvement, creative quality.

quality cultures. The question being addressed in this analysis is Research Question 2: "What quality practices or processes are associated with differences among organizations' quality cultures?" Only two of the three discriminant functions are statistically significant, so only two are reported in the table.

The first discriminant function separates the two quality cultures that are less advanced—status quo and error detection—from the two cultures that are more advanced—error prevention and continuous creative quality. The major theme highlighted in this function is the emphasis on fostering and recognizing innovation and new ideas for improvement in the more

advanced quality cultures. These advanced quality cultures encourage more originality and discovery than do organizations with other quality cultures. They also have developed a unique sense of mission as an organization. The less advanced quality cultures are characterized primarily by more errors and defects than the organization's own goals specify and than customers expect, suggesting that an advanced quality culture may be positively related to high-quality performance. Advanced quality cultures rarely redo work because of mistakes, and their customers are increasing in loyalty.

The second discriminant function separates the first and fourth quality cultures—status quo

TABLE 11.3 Discriminations Among Four Quality Culture Types

Eigenvalue	% of Variance	Canonical Correlation	Chi-Square	df	Significance
.212	68.9	.42	197.52	66	.000
.065	21.2	.25	64.46	42	.015

Variables	Coefficient
Function 1	
Creative thinking and innovation encouraged	−.542
Organization has a special, unique mission and pride	−.498
Rarely redo work	−.466
New ideas for improvement are used in decisions	−.458
Collect data on new ideas for improvement	−.433
More errors and defects than own goals and customers expect	.428
Increasing number and loyalty of customers	−.387
Day-to-day decisions influenced by quality data	−.370
Employees have access to competitors' performance data	−.363
Function 2	
System for translating customer expectations into standards	.572
Top managers committed to quality	.521
Top managers ask employees for ways to improve quality	.518
Monitor customer complaints	.464
Improving kinds of data collected on quality	.386
Quality improvement teams report regularly	.313

	Centroid		
Group	Function 1	Function 2	% Correctly Classified
Status quo quality culture	.148	−.458	
Error detection quality culture	.625	.080	43
Error prevention quality culture	−.100	.191	
Continuous creative quality culture	−1.118	−.124	

and continuous creative quality—from the second and third culture types—error detection and error prevention. This function makes less sense than the first function (and accounts for only 21% of the variance) inasmuch as it combines the two least similar quality cultures (status quo and continuous creative quality). The major theme that emerges from this function is that organizations with error detection and error prevention cultures place emphasis on having a well-developed system for monitoring customer expectations, employee opinions, customer complaints, and team reports. This is not to say that, especially, the continuous creative quality culture does not emphasize information collection, only that this is a dominant attribute of error detection and error prevention.

To clarify the relationship between quality culture and organizational effectiveness that is implied in the first discriminant function, simple correlations were computed between the four quality culture types and the average organizational effectiveness measure. Table 11.4 reports the mean scores and correlations. The statistically significant differences among means and correlation coefficients indicate that the more advanced stages of quality culture—namely, error prevention and continuous creative quality—are positively related to effectiveness, whereas the less advanced quality

TABLE 11.4 Correlations Between Quality Culture and Effectiveness

Quality Culture	Correlation With Average Effectiveness Measure	Mean Effectiveness Score
Status quo—no orientation toward quality	−.24	3.58
Error detection culture	−.19	3.41
Error prevention culture	.20	3.72
Continuous creative quality culture	.22	3.97

TABLE 11.5 Discriminations Among Organizations With High and Low Levels of Effectiveness

Eigenvalue	% of Variance	Canonical Correlation	Chi-Square	df	Significance
1.78	100	.80	217.4	5	.000

Variables	Coefficient
Use Pareto processes (quality tools)	.872
Use statistical process control (quality tools)	.694
Use step-by-step problem-solving process (quality tools)	.669
Quality data are available in usable form	.417
Collect data on unit costs	.414
Performance appraisal holds everyone accountable for quality	.409
Collect data on global competitors' quality	.403
Use cross-functional teams (quality tools)	.397
Use process improvement methods (quality tools)	.392
Collect data on things gone wrong	.387
Collect information on adverse factors (complaints, errors, etc.)	.381
Use data in decision making regarding unit costs	.381
Regular assessments of quality improvement by top management	.375
Use data in decision making on global competitors' performance	.361
Use of Kaizen processes (quality tools)	.359
Top management uses information on quality performance	.342
Use several types of assessments (benchmarking, audits, surveys)	.330

Group	Centroid	% Correctly Classified
High performers	.803	90
Low performers	−2.200	

cultures—namely, status quo and error detection—are negatively related to effectiveness. These results are consistent with past research (e.g., Cameron, 1995) and with the first discriminant function.

A more thorough analysis of the quality practices and processes that explain differences in organizational effectiveness was conducted using additional discriminant analyses. In addition to differences in quality culture type, differences were investigated between the quality processes and practices typical of high- and low-performing organizations. Table 11.5 reports the results of these analyses. The six organizations scoring the very highest in effectiveness were compared to the six organizations scoring the very lowest in effectiveness. The reason for selecting six in each group was to accent the factors that accounted for the high and low performance by eliminating very similar and only moderately effective organizations. Research Question 3 serves as the basis for

TABLE 11.6 Discriminations Among Organizations That Improved in Effectiveness Versus Those That Deteriorated or Stagnated

Eigenvalue	% of Variance	Canonical Correlation	Chi-Square	df	Significance
2.23	61.9	.83	167.13	94	.000
1.37	38.1	.76	70.91	46	.010

Variables	Coefficient
Function 1	
Use data collected on things gone wrong	.262
Collect data on unit costs	.242
Use several types of assessments (surveys, benchmarking, audits)	.241
Collect data on customer complaints	.229
Collect data on things gone right	.221
Collect data on customer satisfaction levels	.220
Top managers communicate the importance of quality	.211
Function 2	
Use of statistical process control	.371
Expect best quality in the world in this decade	.303
Official communication always contains quality messages	.290
Clear short- and long-term quality plans in place	.257
Collect data on things gone wrong	.254
Ongoing quality training provided	.235
Good coordination, communication, teamwork across units	.221
Regular assessments of quality improvement by top management	.210
Ongoing monitoring of needs for quality improvement	.210

	Centroid		
Group	Function 1	Function 2	% Correctly Classified
Improved in effectiveness	1.26	−1.35	
Declined in effectiveness	−2.33	− .35	91
Remained the same	.60	1.34	

these analyses, namely, "What quality practices and processes are associated with differences between highly effective organizations and others?"

The results suggest that two main categories of variables explain differences in organizational effectiveness: (a) the use of standard quality tools (e.g., statistical process control, Pareto processes, 8-D decision processes, process improvement methods) and (b) the collection and use of information on quality. When organizations implement the widely known tools that traditionally have been associated with quality processes, and when they gather and use data on quality—the costs of quality; adverse indicators of quality (e.g., errors, complaints); and competitors' quality performance—organi-

zational effectiveness is significantly higher than in organizations that do not use these tools and that do not collect and use quality-related information. The analyses also show that effectiveness is enhanced if the data being gathered are obtained by using multiple processes (e.g., surveys, benchmarking, audits) and are made available to employees in a useable form.

Table 11.6 reports the analyses associated with the fourth research question, namely, "What quality practices are associated with differences between organizations that improve in their effectiveness over time compared to those that remain stagnant or decline in effectiveness?" The table identifies the significant predictor variables that explain *improvement* in effectiveness over time. Table 11.6 compares 14 organizations that improved in their effectiveness scores over time with 37 that did not improve (stagnated) and the 13 that deteriorated.

Table 11.6 shows two discriminant functions. The first separates organizations that deteriorated in effectiveness versus those that improved or remained the same. The second discriminant function is less meaningful in that it separates organizations that did not change in effectiveness over the 3-year period from organizations that either improved or deteriorated—that is, the stagnant versus the changing organizations. The first discriminant function clearly shows that the collection of information lies at the heart of improvement in effectiveness. Improving organizations collect data on quality-related indicators (e.g., TGW, unit costs, TGR, customer satisfaction), and they use a wider variety of data collection methods than do nonimproving organizations. Organizations that deteriorated in effectiveness over time did not gather information on quality, nor did they use a variety of methods for information collection. Gathering information on quality, in other words, appears to be the most important predictor of organizational improvement over time.

To accent the difference between *achieving* high levels of effectiveness and *improving* effectiveness over time, a final analysis was conducted in which highly effective organizations that also improved were differentiated from highly effective organizations that did not improve. Table 11.7 reports discriminant analysis results comparing the three most effective organizations that improved in effectiveness over the 3-year period to the other three organizations that had especially high effectiveness scores but did not improve.

Two central themes underscore the discriminant function separating improving high performers from nonimproving, high-performing organizations. They are (a) the importance of rewarding and involving all employees in the quality effort, and (b) the importance of gathering and sharing quality data. Holding every employee accountable for personal quality improvement and then rewarding and recognizing individuals as well as teams for customer service is one major predictor of improvement in

highly effective organizations. In addition, the availability of quality-related data on competitors and customers, shared through stories and examples, also explains improvement in highly effective firms.[8]

Summary and Conclusions

We began this chapter by identifying the ambiguity that surrounds the relationships between quality programs and organizational performance. Whereas evidence exists that initiating quality improvement programs may have a positive impact on organizational effectiveness, equally compelling evidence has been reported that organizational performance does not improve as a result of quality initiatives. One reason for this discrepancy may rest with the specific processes or procedures being implemented. For example, the American Quality Foundation's (1992) survey of companies initiating quality improvement programs found that more than 945 quality tactics, tools, and techniques had been employed. The nonsystematic, "shotgun" approach to improvement implied by this extraordinarily large number of quality tactics suggests that a positive relationship between quality and effectiveness must be guided by more carefully selected quality processes and practices.

Of course, it is unlikely that all nonpositive performance effects can be attributed to a nonsystematic implementation of quality initiatives. Instead, it is more likely that the absence of improvement in organizational effectiveness is associated with the lack of underlying or fundamental change in organizations striving for quality improvements. Imposing onto an organization one more quality program or procedure is unlikely to produce sustained organizational improvement. This is consistent with the arguments of numerous authors (e.g., Cameron & Quinn, 1998; Denison, 1990; Huber, Sutcliffe, Miller, & Glick, 1993; Trice & Beyer, 1993) who identified the absence of change at the foundational organizational culture level as a critical deterrent to organizational improvement, no matter which change technique or tactic was applied. In other words, a change at the cultural level is needed to sustain almost any major organizational improvement initiative (Beyer & Cameron, 1997).

This argument is similar to that advanced by Frederick W. Taylor (1912) in explaining to members of the U.S. Congress the power of his scientific management revolution. He argued that the power of this approach resides in the organizations' culture—the changes in thought patterns and general orientations—rather than in the systems or techniques being applied:

> Scientific management is not any efficiency device, not a device of any kind for securing efficiency; nor is it any bunch or group of efficiency devices. It is not a new system for figuring costs; it is not a new scheme of paying men; it is not a piecework system; it is not a bonus system; it is not a premium system; it is no scheme for paying men; it is not holding a stop watch on a man and writing things down about him; it is not time study; it is not motion study nor an analysis of the movement of men and saying, "Here is your system; go use it." Now, in its essence, scientific management involves a complete mental revolution on the part of the working man engaged in any particular establishment or industry. . . . Without this complete mental revolution on both sides (workers and managers), scientific management does not exist. That is the essence of scientific management, this great revolution.

We argue here that, as with scientific management, the quality culture possessed by an organization may be among the most important factors in explaining the relationship between implementing quality initiatives and organizational effectiveness. Whereas we have identified key quality processes and practices that are associated with high and improving organizational performance, a mental and values revolution may be the key to quality success rather than merely initiating one more quality technique or process. Unfortunately, quality culture as a subset of overall organizational culture has seldom been considered in the literature, so this study is an introduction to and preliminary investigation of quality as a cultural variable.

The model of quality culture introduced in this chapter has parallels in the quality eras outlined by Garvin (1988), and it enjoys a great deal of face validity among executives who have struggled to manage quality initiatives in their organizations. The model outlines three types of quality cultures—error detection, error prevention, and continuous creative quality—with a fourth culture type being an absence of a quality orientation—status quo. These types of quality culture represent something of a progression from a less advanced culture to a more advanced culture. Data from 64 strategic business units support the notion that more advanced quality cultures predict higher rates of organizational effectiveness and quality achievement.

Organizations that perform at the highest levels of effectiveness, in other words, tend to possess quality cultures that prevent errors before they occur, hold everyone in the organization accountable for quality improvement, focus on processes more than outcomes, constantly raise standards and use improvement as a superordinate goal, surprise and delight customers and solve problems for them before they request them, and create new standards and new customer preferences through innovation and never-ending improvement. The quality culture reflected by these attributes is significantly more likely to produce organizational performance that exceeds industry averages, competitors' performance, and the organization's own past performance.

Specific quality processes and procedures differentiate the three types of quality cultures. In particular, the empirical results suggest that the error detection quality culture is characterized by a higher number of errors and defects than are the more advanced culture types, and that it is a culture that is characterized by a well-developed system for gathering and monitoring quality information. The error prevention quality culture is characterized by that same well-developed system for gathering and monitoring quality information, but it also shares an emphasis on innovation, creativity, and a unique mission with the continuous creative quality culture. Fewer mistakes and errors typify this quality culture compared to the error detection culture. The continuous creative quality culture recognizes and encourages innovation and new ideas for quality improvement, and it achieves substantially better quality results than the less advanced quality cultures. In other words, a shift seems to occur from less advanced to more advanced quality cultures in terms of (a) greater error rates and lower levels of organizational effectiveness at less advanced quality culture levels, (b) consistent emphasis on gathering and monitoring quality data at all quality culture levels, but a greater degree of *use* of those data at the advanced levels, and (c) more emphasis on innovativeness and on a unique organizational mission at more advanced quality culture levels.

Supplementary analyses focused on identifying which quality processes and practices are most closely associated with organizational effectiveness and improvement, and they uncovered two recurring themes. The first is that quality improvement and effectiveness are associated with information-gathering activities focused on quality in the organization—especially the collection and use of quality data related to competitors' performance, customer expectations, and employee ideas. Relying on a wide variety of methods for obtaining the data (e.g., customer surveys, audits, interviews, focus groups, benchmarking, professional surveys) and making the data available to all employees in usable form are also important predictors of high and improving effectiveness.

The second recurring theme related to the balance between using standardized quality tools (e.g., statistical process control, quality function deployment, rational problem-solving formulas, process improvement methods)—all designed to create more control over quality processes and outcomes—and encouraging and rewarding innovation, creativity, new ideas, originality, and invention in producing quality improvements—often designed to supersede controls and foster change and innovation. Consistent with the argument made by Sutcliffe, Sitkin, and Browning (Chapter 13, this volume), maintaining a balance between the tensions of preserving control, on one hand, and fostering originality, on the other hand, is a predictor of high levels of effectiveness and improvement in quality performance.

One of the important, and as yet uninvestigated, puzzles that remains concerns the process by which organizations move from a less advanced level of quality culture to a more advanced level. Whereas idiosyncratic cases have been observed where quality cultures shift from one level to another in organizations, no systematic investigation has been conducted of that process. The time frame involved; the incentives and change levers that are most influential; the extent of congruence between mind-set or orientation and the actions actually pursued by the organization; and the identification of the fine-grained, unobserved attributes of each culture type are among the important issues to be investigated in order to better understand quality as a cultural variable. Continuing to define and investigate quality as merely a set of established techniques and procedures—namely, customer focus, teamwork, supplier partnerships, process management, use of statistical and scientific tools (see Hackman & Wageman, 1995)—is not likely to help resolve the ambiguity and confusion that permeates the organizational studies literature. The effects and outcomes of quality defined in traditional ways are simply too contradictory. Hackman and Wageman (1995) went so far as to advance "a relatively gloomy projection about the future of total quality management. TQM, in our view, is far more likely gradually to lose the prominence and popularity it now enjoys than it is to revolutionize organizational practice" (p. 338). Without a serious attempt to investigate quality as a cultural phenomenon, as a subset of organizational culture, we concur with this pessimistic prediction. On the other hand, we are optimistic that in light of these preliminary findings, quality culture may be an important theoretical and practical construct that can significantly improve organizational effectiveness and performance.

Appendix

Variables Assessed in the Survey	Means		
	1990	*1991*	*1992*
Status quo quality culture	13.02	9.61	9.26
Error detection quality culture	31.86	27.73	28.92
Error prevention quality culture	39.72	45.50	44.34
Continuous creative quality culture	15.30	17.21	16.88
Leadership			
Commitment to highest-quality work, service, products	5.01	5.40	5.30
Frequently and clearly communicate importance of quality	5.00	5.10	5.08
Ask employees how to improve quality	4.04	4.40	4.37
Day-to-day decisions influenced by quality data	4.10	4.32	4.28
Official communications always mention quality improvement	4.03	4.19	4.15
Regular assessments of quality improvement	3.86	3.98	4.09
Information gathering, analysis, and use			
Many aspects of work are benchmarked	3.76	3.84	4.11
Quality improvements made as a result of benchmarking	3.85	4.01	4.21
Survey organization members	4.10	3.79	4.03
Interview organization members	3.66	3.63	3.69
Rely on suggestions of employees	3.84	3.91	4.09
Establish teams to report regularly	4.13	4.01	4.16
Seek senior management's ideas	3.42	3.75	3.86
Analyze outside organization's performance	3.99	3.92	3.96
Monitor customer complaints	4.85	4.88	4.96
Use outside consultants and researchers	3.50	3.43	3.47
Collect ongoing data on customer expectations	4.17	4.64	4.50
Collect ongoing data on customer satisfaction levels	4.84	4.96	4.93
Collect ongoing data on employee attitudes and morale	3.73	3.88	4.15
Collect ongoing data on domestic competitors' performance	4.33	4.22	4.26
Collect ongoing data on global competitors' performance	4.16	3.94	4.03
Collect ongoing data on supplier quality	4.36	4.22	4.26
Collect ongoing data on things gone wrong	4.67	4.58	4.60
Collect ongoing data on things gone right	4.15	4.02	4.29
Collect ongoing data on unit costs	4.43	4.09	4.30
Collect ongoing data on timeliness of our work	4.15	4.25	4.38
Collect ongoing data on new ideas for improvement	4.11	4.33	4.48
Use data in decision making regarding customer expectations	4.23	4.45	4.44
Use data in decision making regarding customer satisfaction levels	4.50	4.63	4.66
Use data in decision making regarding employee attitudes	3.41	3.70	4.01
Use data in decision making regarding domestic competitors	3.84	3.71	3.97
Use data in decision making regarding global competitors	3.80	3.50	3.84
Use data in decision making regarding supplier quality	4.14	3.91	4.06
Use data in decision making regarding things gone wrong	4.30	4.24	4.30
Use data in decision making regarding things gone right	3.80	3.76	4.01
Use data in decision making regarding unit costs	4.14	3.93	4.19
Use data in decision making regarding timeliness of our work	4.00	4.13	4.37
Use data in decision making regarding new ideas for improvement	3.96	4.22	4.41
Types of data collected are improving	4.35	4.53	4.56
Steps taken to shorten time to collect, analyze and disseminate	3.86	4.26	4.17
Use several types of assessments	4.35	4.61	4.79
Quality data are in usable format	3.37	3.78	3.71
Information collected on adverse indicators of quality	4.48	4.52	4.54
Stories and examples of quality widely shared	3.28	3.42	3.73

(Continued)

	Means		
Variables Assessed in the Survey	1990	1991	1992
Quality planning			
Plans in place to exceed best competitors' performance	3.53	3.83	3.97
Customers, suppliers, and employees involved in planning	4.00	4.27	4.36
Number one priority is improving quality	4.24	4.72	4.68
All employees involved in quality improvement efforts	4.34	4.34	4.54
All employees know and use quality philosophy	3.63	3.84	3.92
Clear short- and long-term quality plans in place	3.43	3.40	4.03
Human resource management			
All employees charged to improve quality	4.34	4.39	4.59
All employees have received quality training	3.65	3.69	4.00
Ongoing quality training provided	3.10	3.18	3.42
Well-defined reward and recognition for quality improvement	3.09	3.19	3.55
Encourage creativity and innovation related to quality	4.11	4.47	4.58
Rewards for good ideas for quality improvement	3.70	3.80	4.08
Performance appraisal holds everyone accountable for quality	3.87	4.04	4.30
Rewards and recognition for improvement	3.24	3.50	3.66
Quality assurance			
System for translating customer expectations into standards	3.39	3.64	3.76
System for meeting customer expectations in designing products	3.56	3.80	3.87
System for reducing time to do work	3.28	3.72	3.84
Informed answer to: How do you know you are improving quality?	2.89	3.32	3.46
Everyone has access to competitors' quality performance data	2.86	2.97	3.15
Staff and support services totally involved in quality	3.29	3.71	3.74
Ongoing audits of staff and support service quality	2.93	3.39	3.37
Ongoing monitoring of needs for quality improvement	3.24	3.64	3.66
Customer satisfaction			
Employees empowered to solve customer problems on the spot	3.65	3.94	3.95
Information on customer complaints provided to those responsible	3.96	4.16	4.22
Decisions indicate customer caring	4.47	4.73	4.77
Awards, ceremonies, recognition given for customer service	3.41	3.38	3.68
Awards, ceremonies, recognition given to customer service teams	3.36	3.30	3.71
Quality management			
Quality gets higher priority than budget	2.88	3.17	3.48
Willing to make radical changes to achieve quality	3.25	4.03	4.07
Quality training and development gets high priority	3.42	3.95	4.06
Resources available for personal development	4.17	4.49	4.61
Quality improvement carries over into personal life	3.50	3.55	3.90
Everyone is clear regarding internal and external customers	4.31	4.53	4.73
Everyone knows the score all the time	3.46	3.53	3.82
Do not require reports that are not used	3.54	3.10	3.17
Constantly reducing costs without hurting quality	3.44	3.85	3.85
Doing more with less is prerequisite to success	4.64	4.64	4.68
Structure does not inhibit quality	3.28	3.74	3.85
Adequate tools, equipment, materials	3.61	3.98	4.07
Good communication, coordination, teamwork	3.71	4.23	4.16
Special sense of mission and pride	3.99	4.37	4.42
Easy for customers to give feedback	4.27	4.27	4.27
Quality tools			
Use of statistical process control	3.14	3.32	3.49
Use of quality function deployment	2.52	2.63	2.70
Use of design of experiments	2.52	2.60	2.69
Use of eight-step problem-solving process	3.54	3.51	3.82

Variables Assessed in the Survey	Means		
	1990	*1991*	*1992*
Use of Pareto processes	3.22	3.42	3.73
Use of fault tree or root cause analysis	3.14	3.29	3.42
Use of Kaizen or continuous improvement processes	2.66	2.20	2.52
Use of cross-functional teams	4.61	4.49	4.60
Use of process improvement methods	3.41	3.83	4.06
Use of suggestion systems	3.41	3.56	3.40
Quality results			
Lower errors and defects than industry average	4.26	4.28	4.16
Lower errors and defects than best competitor	3.19	3.03	3.17
Lower errors and defects than customers expect	2.98	3.04	3.03
Lower errors and defects than own goals specify	2.89	2.88	2.95
Higher rate of quality improvement than industry average	4.00	4.01	4.06
Higher rate of quality improvement than best competitor	3.27	3.44	3.41
Higher rate of quality improvement than customers expect	3.14	3.22	3.12
Higher rate of quality improvement than own goals specify	3.02	3.12	3.00
Higher organizational effectiveness than industry average	3.96	4.16	4.22
Higher organizational effectiveness than best competitor	3.14	3.25	3.43
Higher organizational effectiveness than customers expect	3.22	3.45	3.45
Higher organizational effectiveness than own goals specify	3.13	3.14	3.25
Extreme customer loyalty	3.00	3.05	2.96
Rarely do rework	2.91	3.26	3.17
Missed deadlines are uncommon	3.41	3.68	3.70
Minimal absenteeism	4.63	4.64	4.70
Little waste and excess	3.58	3.83	3.78
Consistent and reliable work	4.38	4.50	4.49
Expect best quality in the world in this decade	4.45	4.64	4.91
Decline in grievances, complaints, absenteeism, violations	4.03	4.24	4.47
Decreasing time for new products, services, ideas	4.12	4.23	4.50
Increasing number and loyalty of customers	3.80	3.84	4.23

Examples of Scenarios for Assessing Quality Culture

We haven't thought much about our approach to quality. Not much has changed from past practice. We do things about the same as we have always done them.

We focus on finding our mistakes and correcting them accurately and efficiently. We place an emphasis in inspecting and auditing our work for defects. We try to avoid antagonizing our customers, so we focus on meeting their needs and responding quickly to their complaints.

We focus on preventing mistakes before they occur by searching for root causes of problems. We place an emphasis on making sure that the processes we use are clearly mapped and well-functioning. We serve our customers by satisfying their preferences and sometimes exceeding requirements, and we try to do the job right the first time.

We focus on consistently exceeding the standards of performance expected of us. We place emphasis on surprising and delighting our customers by going beyond what they request. We focus on continuous improvement in everything we do, so that no current performance level is satisfactory. We are constantly pursuing creative breakthroughs in quality performance.

Notes

1. Empirical assessments of quality culture in more than 100 organizations in North America and Western Europe were conducted by the first author as part of several executive development, consulting, and research projects. This was the decade when U.S. manufacturing firms were most blatantly being hurt by the invasion of Japanese rivals (especially in automobiles and consumer electronics), who had significantly lower costs and higher quality than did U.S. firms, and it was the decade in which the American quality movement was officially launched with the Malcolm Baldrige National Quality Award. Not only did quality culture profiles (as assessed in these various projects) begin to shift as the decade of the 1980s progressed, but awareness and importance of quality began to escalate as well in many organizations.

2. Among the advantages of studying strategic business units within a single parent organization are that criteria of measurement, language and definitions, and assessment procedures are more comparable than they would be if business units were in disparate organizations or disparate industries. Consequently, managers' ratings of effectiveness, culture, and organizational practices are likely to be comparable. Among the disadvantages, however, are that a lack of independence exists among units; a potential restriction in the range and variety of quality cultures might exist; and common indicators of organizational effectiveness (e.g., productivity, revenues, defect levels, costs) are not collected at this level of analysis.

3. The Malcolm Baldrige National Quality Award criteria change slightly each year, including the labels used to describe each of the seven dimensions. The 1997 dimension names were changed quite substantially compared to the dimension names used in the MBNQA process from 1988 through 1995. The questionnaire items in this study used the 1995 MBNQA labels and criteria.

4. These ratings are different from the standard perceptual assessments of effectiveness. Generally, overall ratings of effectiveness are obtained based on generalized impressions of organization members (e.g., see Cameron, 1978). The reliability of such ratings is suspect, however, because no objective or external referent is present upon which to base the ratings. To overcome this difficulty, effectiveness ratings in this study were obtained by asking respondents to compare their own organization's performance to specific standards (e.g., industry average, last year's performance), not merely general impressions. Therefore, these ratings are more likely to reflect reliable judgments than are ratings without referents.

5. More conservative levels of correlation are acceptable when using Spearman rank-order correlations rather than Pearson correlation coefficients. Therefore, where the correlation coefficient is somewhat lower for the effectiveness variable than for other multi-item variables, the level of acceptable (Nunnally, 1975).

6. Because of their ipsative rating scale, the quality culture variables were not included in the discriminant analyses that analyzed differences among levels of effectiveness scores nor improvement in effectiveness scores.

7. In organizations dominated by a status quo quality culture, quality was ignored, for the most part, as a key issue for the organization. Little or no emphasis was placed on quality improvement activities, and organizations focused on other areas as part of their strategic competence. Quality was simply not an area of priority.

8. The small number of organizations included in these analyses make the results only suggestive, not definitive. However, the results are quite consistent with previous analyses of high levels of effectiveness and improvement, so it may be fair to conclude that a fairly consistent pattern of predictors is associated with high-scoring improvers.

References

Anderson, E., & Sullivan, M. (1992). The antecedents and consequences of customer satisfaction for firms. *Marketing Science, 12,* 125-143.

Ansoff, H. I. (1979). *Strategic management.* London: Macmillan.

Barnett, C. (1994). *Organizational learning and continuous quality improvement in an automotive manufacturing organization.* Unpublished doctoral dissertation, University of Michigan.

Beyer, J. M., & Cameron, K. S. (1997). Organizational culture. In D. Druckman & J. Singer (Eds.), National Research Council.

Buzzell, R. D., & Gale, B. T. (1987). *The PIMS principles: Linking strategy to performance.* New York: Free Press.

Buzzell, R. D., & Weirsema, F. D. (1981). Model changes in market share: A cross-sectional analysis. *Strategic Management Journal, 2,* 27-42.

Cameron, K. S. (1981). Construct and subjectivity problems in organizational effectiveness. *Public Productivity Review, 7,* 105-121.

Cameron, K. (1986). A study of organizational effectiveness and its predictors. *Management Science, 32,* 87-112.

Cameron, K. S. (1992, August). *In what ways do organizations implement total quality?* Paper presented at the annual meeting of the Academy of Management, Las Vegas.

Cameron, K. S. (1995). Downsizing, quality, and performance. In R. E. Cole (Ed.), *The fall and rise of the American quality movement.* New York: Oxford University Press.

Cameron, K. S., Freeman, S. J., & Mishra, A. K. (1993). Downsizing and redesigning organizations. In G. P. Huber & W. H. Glick (Eds.), *Organizational change and redesign.* New York: Oxford University Press.

Cameron, K. S., & Peterson, M. (1995). *The culture and climate for quality.* Ann Arbor: University of Michigan School of Education.

Cameron, K. S., & Quinn, R. E. (1998). *Diagnosing and changing organizational culture.* Reading, MA: Addison Wesley Longman.

Cameron, K. S., & Whetten, D. A. (1981). Perceptions of organizational effectiveness over organizational life cycles. *Administrative Science Quarterly, 26,* 525-544.

Cameron, K., & Whetten, D. (1983). *Organizational effectiveness: Multiple models.* New York: Academic Press.

Cameron, K., & Whetten, D. (1996). Organizational effectiveness and quality: The second generation. In J. R. Smart (Ed.), *Higher education: Handbook of theory and research.* New York: Agathon.

Campbell, J. P. (1977). On the nature of organizational effectiveness. In P. S. Goodman & J. M. Pennings (Eds.), *New perspectives of organizational effectiveness.* San Francisco: Jossey-Bass.

Cole, R. E. (1993). Learning from learning theory: Implications for quality improvements of turnover, use of contingent workers, and job rotation policies. *Quality Management Journal, 1,* 9-25.

Cole, R. E., Bacdayan, P., & White, J. B. (1995). Quality, participation, and competitiveness. In R. E. Cole (Ed.), *The fall and rise of the American quality movement.* New York: Oxford University Press.

Conrad, C. F., & Blackburn, R. T. (1985). Program quality in higher education. In J. R. Smart (Ed.), *Higher education: Handbook of theory and research* (pp. 283-308). New York: Agathon.

Crosby, P. (1979). *Quality is free.* New York: New American Library.

Crosby, P. (1992). Does the Baldrige Award really work? *Harvard Business Review, 70,* 127-128.

Delta Consulting Group. (1993). *Ten years after: Learning about total quality management.* New York: Author.

Deming, W. E. (1982). *Quality, productivity, and competitive position.* Cambridge: MIT Press.

Deming, W. E. (1986). *Out of the crisis.* Cambridge: MIT Press.

Denison, D. R. (1990). *Corporate culture and organizational effectiveness.* New York: John Wiley.

Fiegenbaum, A. V. (1961). *Total quality control.* New York: McGraw-Hill.

Fiegenbaum, A. V. (1983). *Total quality control* (2nd ed.). New York: McGraw-Hill.

Flynn, B., Schroeder, R., & Sakakibara, S. (1993). *A framework for quality management research: Definition and measurement.* Working paper, University of Iowa.

Fornell, C. (1992). A national customer satisfaction barometer. *Journal of Marketing, 56,* 6-21.

Garvin, D. A. (1988). *Managing quality: The strategic and competitive edge.* New York: Free Press.

General Accounting Office. (1991). *Management practices: U.S. companies improve performance through quality efforts.* Washington, DC: Government Printing Office.

Greene, R. T. (1993). *Global quality: A synthesis of the world's best management methods.* Homewood, IL: Business One Irwin.

Hackman, J. R., & Wageman, R. (1995). Total quality management: Empirical, conceptual, and practical issues. *Administrative Science Quarterly, 40,* 309-342.

Harari, O. (1993). Ten reasons why TQM doesn't work. *Management Review, 82,* 33-38.

Huber, G. P., Sutcliffe, K. M., Miller, C. C., & Glick, W. H. (1993). Understanding and predicting organizational change. In G. P. Huber & W. H. Glick (Eds.), *Organizational change and design.* New York: Oxford University Press.

Huff, L. (1994). *Tradeoffs between quality and productivity: Cross-category differences in the relationship between perceived quality and productivity.* Unpublished doctoral dissertation, University of Michigan.

Hunt, V. D. (1992). *Quality in America: How to implement a competitive quality program.* Homewood, IL: Irwin.

Juran, J. M. (1951). *Quality control handbook.* New York: McGraw-Hill.

Juran, J. M. (1989). *Juran on leadership for quality.* New York: Free Press.

Juran, J. M. (1992). *Juran on quality by design.* New York: Free Press.

Khurana, A. (1994). *Quality in the global color picture tube industry: Managing complex production processes.* Unpublished doctoral dissertation, University of Michigan, Ann Arbor.

Larcker, D., & Ittner, C. (1997, Winter). Measuring nonfinancial assets. *Wharton Alumni Magazine,* pp. 7-12.

Macduffie, J. P., & Kracik, J. F. (1992). Integrating technology and human resources for high performance manufacturing. In T. Kochan & M. Useem (Eds.), *Trans-*

forming organizations. New York: Oxford University Press.

Malcolm Baldrige National Quality Award Application Guidelines. (1992). Washington, DC: U.S. Department of Commerce.

Martin, J. (1992). *Cultures in organizations: Three perspectives.* New York: Oxford University Press.

Miles, R., & Kimberly, J. R. (1980). *The organizational life cycle.* San Francisco: Jossey-Bass.

Peterson, M., Cameron, K., & Associates. (1995). *Total quality management in higher education: From assessment to improvement.* Ann Arbor: University of Michigan, Center for the Study of Higher and Postsecondary Education.

Powell, T. C. (1995). Total quality management as competitive advantage: A review and empirical study. *Strategic Management Journal, 16,* 15-37.

Porter, M. E. (1980). *Competitive strategy: Techniques for analyzing industries and competitors.* New York: Free Press.

Reed, R., Lemak, D. J., & Montgomery, J. C. (1996). Beyond process: TQM content and firm performance. *Academy of Management Review, 21,* 173-202.

Reimann, K. W. (1988). The Malcolm Baldrige National Quality Award. Speech given at the Executive Education Center, University of Michigan.

Reynolds, R. B. (1988). *An investigation into the effectiveness of quality circles applications in the United States.* Unpublished doctoral dissertation, University of Georgia.

Schaffer, R. H., & Thompson, H. A. (1992). Successful change programs begin with results. *Harvard Business Review, 70,* 80-89.

Schein, E. H. (1985). *Organizational culture and leadership.* San Francisco: Jossey-Bass.

Scott, W. R., Flood, A. B., Ewy, W., & Forrest, W. H. (1978). Organizational effectiveness and the quality of surgical care in hospitals. In M. Meyer (Ed.), *Environments and organizations* (pp. 290-305). San Francisco: Jossey-Bass.

Shiba, S., Graham, A., & Walden, D. (1993). *A new American TQM.* Portland, OR: Productivity Press.

Schonberger, R. J. (1986). *World class manufacturing.* New York: Free Press.

Sitkin, S., Sutcliffe, K., & Schroeder, R. G. (1994). Distinguishing control from learning in total quality management: A contingency perspective. *Academy of Management Review, 19,* 537-564.

Szwergold, J. (1992). Why most quality efforts fail. *Management Review, 81,* 5.

Taylor, F. W. (1912). Report to the U.S. Congress in Washington, DC.

Treacy, M., & Wiersema, F. (1993). Customer intimacy and other value disciplines. *Harvard Business Review, 71,* 84-93.

Trice, H. M., & Beyer, J. M. (1993). *The cultures of work organizations.* Englewood Cliffs, NJ: Prentice Hall.

Tschirhart, M. (1993). *The management of problems with stakeholders.* Unpublished doctoral dissertation, University of Michigan.

Webster, D. S. (1981, October). Methods of assessing quality. *Change,* pp. 20-24.

Westphal, J. D., Gulati, R., & Shortell, S. M. (1996). The institutionalization of total quality management: The emergence of normative TQM adoption and the consequences for organizational legitimacy and performance. *Academy of Management Proceedings, 56,* 249-253.

Westphal, J. D., Gulati, R., & Shortell, S. M. (1997). Customization or conformity? An institutional and network perspective on the content and consequences of TQM adoption. *Administrative Science Quarterly, 42,* 366-394.

Chapter 12

Quality as a Cultural Concept

Messages and Metamessages

TOMOKO HAMADA

Quality can be defined in many ways, and its meanings may shift over time. This chapter argues that the construction and interpretation of a term such as "quality" has a social existence that is guided by a person's *habitus* and is embedded in time and space. In the present context, habitus is defined as the pragmatic reasoning schema that an individual quality researcher uses to make sense of reality. In plain English, we call it "the feel for something," "knack," or "custom" (Bourdieu, 1977). In the following section, I provide an ethnological analysis of four perspectives or culture models that researchers use to study quality. The primary objective of ethnology is to uncover general cultural principles, those rules (which I call "metamessages,") that govern human behavior.

The first section discusses three types of organizational culture models currently being used to conduct research on issues of quality: (a) the integration model, (b) the differentiation model, and (c) the fragmentation model (Martin, 1992). I will try to reveal habitus in each of the three approaches. The objective of analyzing the habitus that underlies the three models is to illustrate how the same world of quality culture can be seen quite differently by different researchers because of the various ontological and epistemological orientations each scholarly

tradition takes to the field. I then discuss a fourth perspective on organizational culture that is also culture-bound: an anthropological perspective. I attempt to bring to light the presuppositions inherent in an objectivist construction of any study subject. This part is essentially an anthropological discussion of the so-called etic (outsider's) view of organizational culture.

The second part of this chapter is a case history on the emic (insider's) perspective and habitus. From my perspective as a Japanese anthropologist, this part strengthens my argument that not only do quality meanings differ across space and according to the perspective of the researcher but also that the meanings held by the research subjects (the organization's insiders) can also shift over time. The case in point is the three-stage shift in the Japanese business elite's quality definitions over the past three decades. I describe how Japanese top management's sensemaking activities (see Weick, Chapter 7) in the 1970s, 1980s, and 1990s have been bound by their unique cultural perspectives. Then, I show how the shift in their metamessages is related to changes in socioeconomic and political currents. Finally, I describe in more detail the late-1990s definition of quality promoted by business executives of large firms in Japan. This new rhetoric of quality is currently backed by Japan's leading industrial organizations, the government, and top executives of large firms, but it may or may not be shared by other sub-groups of Japanese society.

Quality Culture

Organizational culture studies have produced a variety of culture models that can be applied to many research targets. In this section, I discuss the application of three such organizational culture models to quality issues—integration, differentiation, and fragmentation (Martin, 1992).

The Integration Model

The first of the quality culture models is the integration model. The integration perspective seeks organizationwide consensus and emphasizes sharing a cognitive view of quality. For example, Cameron and Barnett (1996) define the culture of quality as an organization's orientation toward quality. According to them, an organization's quality culture refers to the predominant definition, model, set of values, and overall approach to quality. Therefore, it is more narrow in focus than organizational culture and concerns the unobservable understructure or basic presupposition that guides thinking and action related to quality (see Cameron and Barnett, Chapter 11).

Several basic premises (metamessages) are present in their definition of culture: Culture is organizational and, therefore, a collective phenomenon. As a normative orientation, it is learned and at least partly shared by its members. It is the key to behavior, with tangible consequences. This definition of culture contains a viewpoint similar to that of the "cultural engineering" school, which applies the concept of culture as a variable that creates a specific organizational outcome (see Deal & Kennedy, 1982; Kilmann, 1985).

This position was also expressed in the early core of most popular texts on corporate culture (e.g., Deal & Kennedy, 1982; Peters & Waterman, 1982; Sathe, 1985). They treated culture as a shared normative orientation. Scholars who support this position discuss such topics as strong or weak cultures, and a homogeneity of value orientations among their members. The implication of this literature is the assumption that a companywide set of norms and values can become the cause of organizational behavior and performance. Table 12.1 shows some instances of this position.

If one takes this position in analyzing quality culture, an organization's quality orientation may be measured and assessed through interviews, surveys, and other research techniques. Like early attempts by anthropologists to categorize "the patterns of cultures" (see Benedict, 1959), quality researchers may create a typology of quality cultures in order to assess organizational shifts from one cultural pattern to another. Later in this chapter, I show how this approach applies to a specific situation involving the subculture of Japanese top management.

The Differentiation Model

In contrast to the integration perspective, a differentiation perspective defines the organization as being filled with inconsistencies, with consensus occurring only within the boundaries of subcultures. The differentiation perspective acknowledges subcultural inequality and explores the dynamics of power, conflict, and normative orientation. Ambiguity is channeled, so it does not intrude on the clarity that exists within these subcultural boundaries. Trice and Beyer (1984), Louis (1983, 1985), Gregory (1983), and Smircich (1983) define culture as distinctive to a particular group, and the group boundaries also define the limits of the culture. In this model, there is cohesion only within subcultures.

In the quality movement, there is a popular assumption that management can create and clarify organizational ambiguity, and that management can change norms and values among members in order to achieve desired behavioral outcomes. This view is fueled by the enormous importance that American managers and management scholars attribute to top management leadership. Differentiation scholars, however, view management as only one subculture, albeit

TABLE 12.1 Metaphors of Culture in the Integration Model

Culture as	Major Ideas	Proponents
Clan	Socializing collective goals	Ouchi and Wilkins (1985): "We take the paradigmatic view of culture, and call it a clan" (p. 469).
Value system	Shared beliefs and values	Davis (1984): "The pattern of shared beliefs and values that give the members of an institution meaning and provide them with the rules for behavior in their organization" (p. 1).
Social cohesion	Values, beliefs, norms, emotions, sentiment	Ray (1986): "The top management team aims to have individuals possess direct ties to the values and goals of the dominant elite in order to activate the emotion and sentiment which might lead to devotion, loyalty, and commitment to the company" (p. 294).
Ideal form	Affective attachment Historical creation	Gagliardi (1990): "Organizational culture can be seen as the idealization of a collective experience of success in the use of a skill and the emotional transfiguration of previous beliefs" (p. 5).

a powerful one, of organizational culture. In order to explain the reason for subculture differentiation, some scholars have examined subcultures' connections to the wider society. Whereas integration culture researchers are concerned mostly with specific agents such as trade associations, trade unions, and governmental agencies, which serve as a supportive infrastructure for quality management, differentiation scholars argue that the organization must operate within the context of a larger society and that subcultures within an organization are linked to groupings in the larger society. They point out local-global connections and the relationship between cultural reproduction and power. For example, Van Maanen and Barley (1984, 1985) state that occupational, ethnic, gender, and sociological variations may create competitive definitions of reality, and these multiple realities may be reinforced by new innovations and technology. From this viewpoint, quality can be enacted quite differently by different subcultures, each of which is linked to different sociopolitical groups in the wider society.

Placement of the organization within a larger sociocultural environment derives from a long tradition in the social sciences: In sociology, Durkheim (1933) and Weber (1947) provided important analyses of the relationship between culture and industrialization. Marx's historical materialism also deals with the relationship between the mode of production and the superstructure. In anthropology, many studies compare national systems of work organization and philosophy (e.g., Ong, 1987; Polanyi, 1957; Sahlins, 1972). In management science literature, Hofstede's typology of national cultures has been particularly influential (Hofstede, 1984).

Current total quality management (TQM) statements fail to argue persuasively why workers should share their ideas with managers if the adoption of innovation and new methods are likely to threaten a worker's job. Ishikawa (1985) was correct to point out that if management wanted to satisfy the customer, it had to first satisfy the worker. Although the key U.S. developers of total quality philosophy in the 1970s and 1980s stressed the importance of value-sharing, they failed to address the larger cultural context of American society in which the management-worker relationship has been more confrontational, and where the social contract between the two has been in flux. During the 1980s, American management adopted quality concepts in order to cut costs and regain international competitiveness. Their adoption of quality improvement practices often paralleled organizational restructuring and employment loss.

Differentiation studies question who benefits and who suffers from organizational changes (see Burawoy, 1979; Collinson, 1992; Kunda, 1992). The fact that some TQM cases have occurred simultaneously with or resulted in downsizing and layoffs makes the effect of TQM a serious concern for workers and other stakeholders.

In contrast to the U.S. economy, the Japanese economy expanded rapidly in the 1970s and 1980s along with quality management practices. During that period, the Japanese managed to improve productivity without displacing surplus workers. The policy among larger Japanese firms was to avoid layoffs, promote internally, reward long years of service, and use seniority-based wage scales. In retrospect, these practices made it easier for Japanese management and workers to develop a core organizational culture of quality and gave Japanese workers reason to believe that managers could be trusted partners.

The differentiation model brings the important consideration of power and politics of cultural representation to the quality research agenda. The model's proponents sometimes argue that the quality movement has failed to deliver on its democratic promise to create more egalitarian institutions. Differentiation scholars criticize the current quality culture rhetoric for supporting participatory management and bottom-up decision making, saying that these discourses ignore the fact that "culture" already reflects a hotbed of differences in American organizations. According to this position, the linkage between job security, wage increases, quality enhancement, and corporate profits is where the barriers to quality transformation seem to lie: If quality improvements mean the sacrifice of workers' jobs and wage stagnation, why should employees support quality transformation advocated by managers?

Another contribution of this "cultural perspective" is the notion that the organization should not be described in traditional terms (with an organizational chart, flow diagrams, and so on) but in terms that explain "how things really work around here." The organization should be seen not as a system with a rigid and static structure but as an evolving bioecological network. And the real worlds of people should be the object of inquiry. If the quality researcher takes this position, it is safe to assume, at least in the initial stages of investigation, that consensus on quality may be less prevalent than managers would wish. If the researcher takes the differentiation perspective, he or she may find little consensus on quality within the organization, no matter what the management wishes to advocate.

The Fragmentation Model

The cultural fragmentation perspective focuses on ambiguity and lack of shared meaning as the essence of organizational culture. According to this perspective, organization is fluid and incomplete: No stable organizationwide or subcultural consensus exists. Nothing is certain; only webs and shades of meanings exist.

The fragmentation model introduces the concept of organizational ambiguity, which recognizes the absence of broad agreements in complex organizations today (Martin, 1992; Meyerson & Martin, 1987). It hypothesizes that a construct such as "quality" holds fuzzy meanings, and there may be confusion, inconsistencies, and gaps in the collective understanding of the term. Whereas the differentiation model calls attention to the demarcation between contending definitions by different groups in an organization, the fragmentation model examines ambivalence and confusion among groups in the organization. It recognizes multiple self-identities and multiple memberships that blur boundaries between subcultures. From this perspective, organizational reality is composed of cognitive fragments: The members never understand one another completely; they share

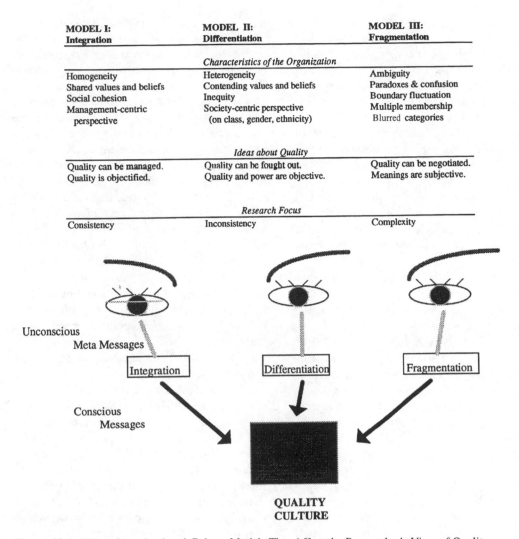

MODEL I: Integration	MODEL II: Differentiation	MODEL III: Fragmentation
Characteristics of the Organization		
Homogeneity	Heterogeneity	Ambiguity
Shared values and beliefs	Contending values and beliefs	Paradoxes & confusion
Social cohesion	Inequity	Boundary fluctuation
Management-centric perspective	Society-centric perspective (on class, gender, ethnicity)	Multiple membership Blurred categories
Ideas about Quality		
Quality can be managed. Quality is objectified.	Quality can be fought out. Quality and power are objective.	Quality can be negotiated. Meanings are subjective.
Research Focus		
Consistency	Inconsistency	Complexity

Unconscious
Meta Messages

Integration · Differentiation · Fragmentation

Conscious
Messages

**QUALITY
CULTURE**

Figure 12.1. Three Organizational Culture Models That Affect the Researcher's View of Quality

information partially, and they execute tasks based on the limited outlook and subjective comprehension of reality.

Taking this perspective, a new quality research agenda may involve analyses of cognitive confusion, information underload, bottlenecks, blind spots, and unexpected consequences of quality deployment. Such research may lead us to believe that the meaning of quality cannot be understood without taking into consideration the position and history of the individuals and groups doing the interpreting and enacting.

Each of the three research perspectives sees quality quite differently. See Figure 12.1 for a summary.

A Fourth Model: Quality Culture as a Contextualizing Process

Most contemporary anthropologists view culture as a process rather than as an innate, homogeneous, simple, and categorizable entity such as an integrated culture, a differentiated culture, or a fragmented culture. They also tend to treat culture as if it were a root metaphor: From this perspective, the organization does not have a culture to manipulate; rather, it *is* a culture. Organizational culture is not just another piece of the puzzle, it *is* the puzzle. Culture from this viewpoint can be defined as an emergent, collective *process* of meaning configuration. Organization is seen as a contextualizing process that encompasses cognitive, psychological, political, economic, social, biological, ecological, and symbolic relationships. All facets of the organization become relevant to the extent that they are part of a constructed process of meaning creation.

A number of anthropologists (Abu-Lughod, 1986; Geertz, 1973, 1983; Kondo, 1990; Ong, 1987), cultural historians (Anderson, 1991), scholars of cultural studies (Bhabha, 1990), and sociologists (Giddens, 1984; Strauss, 1991, 1993) view culture as the process of creating and reproducing symbols, meanings, and practices through the interactions of a group's members. Many have treated culture as a site of eruptive self-other differentiation in an ethnoscape (Appadurai, 1996).

The argument presented here is closely related to Karl Weick's research on sensemaking in this volume. Weick says that much of human behavior can be explained in terms of the individual's need to make sense of a situation and to appear as a competent actor within it. According to him, individuals employ a variety of interpretive scripts in order to make sense of their existential realities. He notes that as situations become more highly institutionalized, people accept existing social scripts instead of creating original scripts, and many individuals follow routines and performance programs for everyday actions rather than inventing new action schemes.

In relation to Weick's perspective on individual sensemaking, it is important to point out that individuals need a social "code" or grammar in order to create individualized scripts, no matter how creative and idiosyncratic they may be. Individual interpretive activities require socially acquired coding and encoding competence. Historically and culturally developed sense-making procedures, practices, or methods are made available to us as resources and constraints into which we have been socialized. We mutually construct ourselves through the management of meaning. Culture provides a dynamic system for coding and decoding symbolic activities over time. Thus, sensemaking is not an individual-level activity but largely a cultural activity. The following four analogies about individual sensemaking may be instructive: (a) A person who hears jazz music today can tell immediately that it is jazz. Johann Sebastian Bach, however, might have heard the same jazz music as nothing but a jumble of noise. (b) A high school student knows how to multiply numbers because she knows mathematical rules. (c) Mr. Zorba can communicate in Greek with his fellow Greeks but not with Mr. Zhou who speaks only Chinese. (d) In order to engage in meaningful social interaction and make sense of social realities, one needs to learn, consciously or unconsciously, a social and symbolic "grammar."

Homo sapiens are predisposed to make conscious choices. Through cultural evolution, some of the choices become hardened into habitus, then into precepts, and then into laws or codes for behavior, and, if the predisposition is strong enough, into societal or universal beliefs. Strong inner feelings and historical experience cause certain actions to be preferred and to be considered natural, as collective precepts support such normative orientation.

Humans are, however, creative agents. The strength of commitment to institutionalized ideas (such as quality management) can wane as we acquire new knowledge and experience, with the result that certain rules may lose inviolability, old codes may be revoked, and formerly suppressed behavior may be set free and become more salient. For the same reason, new codes may need to be devised, first perhaps with contention, confusion, and ambiguity, with the potential of being made sacred in time. Ideational movement is from precanonical to canonical, in which a particular voice about quality becomes less ambiguous and more dominant over time, and other voices and alternative interrelations get muted so that groupwide cognition and behavior coordination begins. Then, in the movement from postcanonical to new precanonical, another new voice emerges, sometimes in opposition to existing canonical discourse, which, in turn, leads to the construction of new definitions of reality and alternative interrelations.

Ong (1987) describes this process as follows:

> Cultural change . . . is not understood as unfolding according to some predetermined logic [of development, modernization, or capitalism] but as the disrupted, contradictory, and differential outcomes which involve changes in identity, relations of struggle and dependence, including the experience of reality itself . . . in situations wherein groups and classes struggle to produce and interpret culture within the industrializing milieu. (p. 23)

Quality movement gurus all suggest that in order to create desirable performance, an organization's members must experience almost a religious-like conversion to a new quality model (see Deming, 1985, 1986, 1993; Ishikawa, 1982, 1985; Juran, 1974, 1988, 1989). The organizational canon must change, and new values must be internalized, they argue.

For the new quality canon to move into a dominant and legitimized position, the subject must internalize the norms and ideology attached to the canonical meaning. Gramsci's (1996) concept of hegemony is useful in analyzing this legitimization process. He states that once the canon becomes internalized, it will no longer require policing because the subject will willingly perform what is prescribed. If such a conversion is not possible, various forms of noncompliance, sabotage, and tacit opposition may emerge, if not outright resistance.

The contextualizing approach calls attention to historical experiences and unforeseen circumstances. Through enculturation in particular traditions such as quality culture, people internalize a previously established system of meanings and symbols that they use to define their world, express their feelings, and make their judgments. Every person begins immediately, through a process of conscious and unconscious learning and interaction with others,

to internalize, or incorporate, a cultural tradition. The anthropological model described above sees quality organization as an evolving process in which the individual agent creatively and dialogically uses social grammar, plans, recipes, rules, and constructions to weave collective intelligence and cosmology. Because of anthropologists' interest in the cultural process, anthropological studies of organizational culture tend to be more configurational, holistic, and longitudinal in orientation than the previously discussed three approaches, which are more typological, specific, and synchronic. What is more, the anthropological model tends to be more comparative, at least implicitly, because its vista includes both industrial and nonindustrial settings across time and space and because its interest includes the observation of all facets of organization to the extent that they are used to create a meaningful context for coordinated action.

The Contextual and Historical Study of Shifting Meanings of Quality

I have argued that the meaning of quality is created relationally and that the same organizational reality can be interpreted and studied polysemically by different researchers because of their habitus. In this section, I shift gears and investigate the organizational insiders' construction of the meaning of quality. I will focus on one subculture of organization—top management. My materials come from Japanese executives, and yet the theoretical issues concerning the emic contextuality of quality definition remain the same. This section illustrates how the definition of quality presented by this subgroup has changed rather dramatically and dialogically from the 1970s to the 1990s. I describe three quality models and their three metamessages on quality management over the three decades in relation to the Japanese business environment. Following that discussion, I turn to the late-1990s definition of Japanese quality management and the discourse by business executives, government officials, and business consultants in Japan. It is still too early to judge whether the 1990s definition of quality put forth by management will be understood, shared, and/or supported by other subgroups and stakeholders of Japanese organizations.

The Three Models

In this volume, Robert Cole describes the early years of quality concepts, when, between 1955 and 1980, leading manufacturers in Japan shifted their management philosophy from the old model that emphasized conformity to requirements to a new model that reflected the firm's companywide commitment to customer needs. Since then, Japanese management has gone through many fads on quality deployment. However, it is safe to say that major components of Japan's total quality movement in the 1970s and 1980s included such key assumptions as companywide involvement; leadership by top management; statistical process control; continuous incremental improvement (*kaizen*) with the goal of zero defects; just-in-time inventory control (*kanban*); small group activities (quality circles); customer focus; participatory decision making; cross-functional collaboration; formal and informal reward systems; and management-by-fact, thorough documentation, data analysis, and continuous assessment. Japanese firms' relentless pursuit of market orientation and companywide improvement for customer satisfaction have been well documented (see Cole, Chapter 4, this volume).

In the late 1990s, Japanese management rhetoric on corporate excellence seems to be undergoing another change, this time from quality for customer satisfaction to ecological excellence. Building on their strengths in market orientation, large firms' top executives are now turning to ecological quality and using such culture-bound metaphors as *kyosei* (coexistence or symbiosis) as their corporate message. Whereas some successful large firms are already incorporating environmental quality into their operational processes and cost calculations, others are downsizing and struggling to survive in the current period of economic stagnation. Whether the new environmental concerns will move the

increasingly differentiating Japanese society to new heights of quality is open to further investigation.

However, the current shift in managerial rhetoric is reminiscent of the changes that took place in Japan before TQM took off in the late 1970s and 1980s, when managerial thinking moved away from mere compliance to companywide quality enhancement. In a similar manner, Japanese managers are now stressing the firm's need to move away from mere compliance with legal requirements on such things as carbon dioxide emissions and recycling codes. They would rather advance their corporations through more proactive, process-oriented, companywide ecological quality systems. Table 12.2 shows the three different models that Japanese top management has used to implement quality concepts during the three historical periods.

New Concepts of Quality in the 1990s: Quality Is Ecology

The new quality model was born in tandem with the wider socioeconomic trends of the 1990s, both internationally and domestically. Internationally, the ideas for the new global environmental standards emerged primarily as a result of two international events: the Uruguay Round of the GATT negotiations, begun in 1986, and the international conference on the environment held in Rio de Janeiro in 1992. The GATT talks addressed the need to avoid or remove nontariff barriers to trade, whereas the Rio conference established the world's commitment to protection of the environment. The 1997 conference on the environment held in Kyoto, Japan, further accelerated public awareness of the urgent need for international cooperation for environmental control, particularly over global warming and acid rain issues.

The quality standards of corporate environmentalism are directly linked with the set of ISO 14000 standards, which are discussed in detail later. The standards are a blueprint for promoting world trade while encouraging and assisting corporations to be environmentally

TABLE 12.2 Quality Models in Japanese Firms Since the 1950s

Themes and Values		
Model 1: 1950s-1960s	Model 2: 1970s-1980s	Model 3: 1990s-2000s
Conformance to requirements	**Customer satisfaction**	**Environmentalism**
Defect detection	Process orientation	System orientation
Quality specialist	Companywide cross-functional cooperation	Companywide globally cross-regional cooperation
Specification	Statistical control	Environmental accounting and auditing
		Waste and energy cost reduction
	Waste reduction	Flow analysis and product life cycle
	Zero defects	Community outreach
Reactive	Conformance to requirements	Proactive in response to customer needs
	Proactive in response to customer needs	Proactive in response to environmental needs
	Reactive to environmental needs	

Metamessages		
Survive	Support economic growth	Limit growth
Catch up with the West	Global expansion	Work ecologically
Feed the nation	Double income	Live in harmony with nature
Maintenance	Quantity of life	Improve quality of life
Operate as a hierarchy	Think as a team, corporate community	Think as a global community
		Organization as biosocial organism

Socioeconomic Trends		
Recovery from war	Market expansion	Global investment
Economic take-off	Trade surplus and trade friction	Transnational corporation
Concerted push to expansion	Industrial expansion	Multiple values
Low-tech industries	High technology	Electronic technology
Basic manufacturing	More advanced manufacturing	Commerce, manufacturing
	Increasing affluence	Multiple-value society
	Industrial pollution	Environmental regulations
	Bubble economy	Economic stagnation

responsible. The first phase of the standards was implemented in 1996. Although there have been other standardization and auditing mechanisms (BS7750 in England, and the eco-management and audit scheme [EMAS] and the environmental management system [EMS] in the European Union), the ISO 14000 series is currently the most talked-about set of standards in Japan.

Like many advanced nations, Japan has developed its environmental plans in reaction and response to past mistakes. Japan experienced a series of environmental disasters, particularly in the 1960s and 1970s, when the quest for international market expansion took off. Major envi-

ronmental pollution in the 1970s resulted in citizens' deaths from mercury and cadmium poisoning. The first antipollution law was passed in 1967, and the first white paper on *kogai* (public hazards) was published by the government in 1970. *Kankyo-cho,* the Environment Agency (EA), was established in 1971. Immediately after the establishment of *kankyo-cho,* 14 environmental laws and regulations in the 1970s set strict industrial standards for air quality, water, noise, and automobile carbon dioxide emissions.

In 1993, a new comprehensive environmental law was enacted, and in 1995, the Japanese government announced "green procurement programs." The government, which contributes to 10% of Japan's gross domestic production, began purchasing recycled paper, energy-saving automobiles, and environmentally friendly office equipment. Today, the government favors environmentally sound firms for public projects. In 1997, the container and package recycling law was established, and in 1998, the environmental assessment law took effect. In addition, new laws to promote new energy sources and waste treatment are in the pipeline.

During the same period, society's view of the corporation has also shifted. After the so-called bubble economy of the late 1980s burst, and during the subsequent economic recessions of the 1990s, Japan experienced several devastating incidents that shook the public confidence. They included the great Hanshin earthquake; the sarin gas poisoning of subway passengers by a religious cult, *Aum Shinrikyo*; the O-157 food poisoning of school lunches; and a series of clashes and confrontations between local communities and the central government over the selection of sites for nuclear and industrial waste treatment. These occurrences, as well as a series of political and banking scandals, shook the Japanese faith in the safe, efficient, harmonious, and prosperous society and its ever-expanding economy. Citizens' trust in the government bureaucracy-big business complex to guide the nation's economic course was strained, as bankruptcies and layoffs hit newspaper headlines. As Japan entered into the era of financial uncertainty in the postindustrial turmoil, social critics began to cast doubt upon the conventional managerial principle for unlimited growth and maximum utilization of natural resources.

When the ISO 14000 plan was announced in 1996, the Japanese government's reaction was swift. It quickly established the ISO/TC207 Committee and created environmental standards as integral parts of the JIS (Japan Industrial Standard). Meanwhile, many Japanese manufacturers' initial response to the series of environmental laws and regulations was similar to their response to the old quality model of compliance. Companies tried to create production processes to satisfy legal requirements in

the most cost-effective way and defined environmental quality as meeting product specifications. Most environmental quality management was handled by specialists. This practice was analogous to the 1970s quality management model that defined quality as adherence to product specification rather than to the companywide commitment to customer satisfaction in the 1980s (see Table 12.1).

The 1990s marked the beginning of Japan's global manufacturing for select successful industries, where multiple steps of the manufacturing process—from raw material procurement, parts assembly, and final production to consumer marketing and product disposal—are handled by different units in different parts of the world. Very often, raw material procurement and purchase of energy begin in a developing country, whereas the labor-intensive process of parts manufacturing is done in another country, and final products are shipped to the market in a developed country.

The ISO 14000 series represents the new corporate goals of implementing environmental quality management systems, environmental audits, environmental performance evaluations, product life cycle assessments, and new-product labeling across different units of operation. Understandably, Japanese multinationals are at the forefront of implementing ISO standards and auditing unit performance for environmental excellence. Their activities comprise a strategic environmental quality program for global economic penetration: Today's corporate strategy requires a more lateral, more interconnected configuration of quality that extends to many different continents.

The ISO 14000 Series of Environmental Quality Standards

Businesses that meet the requirements may seek ISO 14000 certification or self-declare their compliance with the ISO 14000. Each firm seeking ISO 14000 certification must complete a self-assessment, implement new production methods, and undergo auditing by external auditors. The company that seeks ISO 14000 will do the following:

- Define corporate excellence in terms of environmental issues
- Create international standards of excellence
- Undergo third-party auditing in addition to governmental inspections
- Advance product life cycle analysis
- Consolidate and simplify reporting
- Create new technology and production methods that are environmentally sound

ISO 14000 is a management system benchmark. The standard describes a process; it does not set norms. The new definitions of quality encompass not only the manufacturing process but also the life cycle of the product, from its raw material procurement, production, sale, and consumption to final disposal.

At present, there are concerted efforts for corporate environmentalism by Japan's upper echelon, particularly by large industrial associations and organizations such as *keidanren,* the Japanese Federation of Economic Organizations. *Keidanren* sent a large number of delegates to the Rio environmental conference, and the *Keizai-doyu-kai,* a leading Japanese employers' association, declared in 1990 the principle of corporate *kyosei* (symbiosis) as the basic business principle for the future. The following are the symbiosis principles announced by the *Keizai doyu-kai* as the foundation of their business philosophy:

1. What one takes out of nature must be returned to nature in a form that nature can reabsorb it by itself.
2. Do not take more than nature needs to revitalize itself.
3. Organize economic activities within the limits of nature and help nature revitalize itself.
4. Resources taken out of nature must be used most effectively. One must constantly improve (*kaizen*) in order to save energy, to recycle, to manage waste, and to reduce costs.
5. Incorporate quality control of waste in the designing and manufacturing processes so that final products and industrial wastes can be easily dismantled, dissolved, or recycled without causing undue environmental burden.
6. Business must share the social and economic costs of eliminating environmental stresses caused by manufacturing, products, industrial waste, and recycled items.

7. Business must take responsibility for nurturing all lives, both human and nonhuman.
8. Each individual employee must contribute to environmental conservation through appropriate corporate and civil activities.
9. Corporate profits must be equitably distributed.
10. All business activities must be implemented and audited according to the *kyosei* principles.

Although the initiative for the earlier ISO 9000 standards taken first by export-oriented electronics and electric companies was not necessarily followed by firms in other non-export-oriented industrial sectors, the ISO 14000 environmental standards have been enthusiastically greeted by firms in a wide variety of industrial sectors, regardless of their international market orientation. A 1996 government survey indicates that the ISO 14000 standards are being adopted by transportation firms, utilities, and commercial businesses, for example. Thus, it is reasonable to assume that corporate environmentalism is likely to spread. Because the standards are so new, however, it will be some time before it can be determined that this management ideology will be shared by other stakeholders in Japan.

Analysis of the Kyosei Principle and Its Metamessages

The new corporate environmentalism is accompanied by new narratives and words such as *kyosei,* which means "living together." The term *kyosei* began to appear in corporate mission statements in the early 1990s. *Kyosei,* the biological-ecological principle for harmonious co-existence, has been adopted by some of Japan's leading companies, including Canon, Fujitsu, and NEC. The naturalistic and biological connotation of symbiosis evokes Shintoist and Buddhist worldviews that consider human beings part of nature. Symbiosis is a relationship between two organizations in which one or both profit.

While "mutualism"[2] and "commensalism"[3] are also possible symbiotic relations, current corporate activities can be more aptly described as "parasitism," in which one organism (human) benefits and, in doing so, harms the other organism (other beings on the earth). Unlike the more optimistic description set forth by Mauro Guillén (1994), I see the *kyosei* concept as essentially promoting a parasitic relationship in which *Homo sapiens* live as parasites and feed on the other organisms. The host of this parasite is the earth biosphere. The important point is that a parasite usually tries not to kill its host. If the host dies, so might the parasite.[4] From this perspective, the new concept of sustainable development advocated by management can be understood as an ideology for not destroying the earth while pursuing economic activities that might be harmful to the environment, up to a certain point.

Quality Deployment

Whereas many Japanese firms and Japanese quality experts originally resisted the adoption of the ISO 9000 standards when they were first introduced,[5] the reaction of Japanese firms to the new ISO 14000 standards was enthusiastic. The 14000 series is being adopted by firms in diverse industrial sectors, in nonmanufacturing industries, and by local governments and communities. By June 1997, less than a year after the 14000 series' announcement, 330 Japanese firms had already received external auditors' approval of their environmental quality efforts. Firms have responded much more quickly than they did to the ISO 9000 series. Of these 330 firms, about half are in the electronics industry, and 13.6% are in general machinery.

Already, notable cases of environmental activism have been reported at large firms such as Seiko Epson, Mitsui Metal and Mining, Mitsubishi Chemical, Kirin Brewery, Morinaga Dairy, and Toyoko Group. Each firm has devised its own strategy and focus of environmental investment. For example, Kirin Brewery operates under three Rs—recycle, reuse, and reduce—backed up by two As—assess and audit—throughout its brewery operations, marketing, and bottle/can recycling. Morinaga Dairy, on the other hand, focuses on energy costs and CO_2 emissions. In 1993, the company shifted fuel from oil to liquid natural gas and liquid propane gas in order to reduce CO_2 emissions by 6,000 tons in that year. In 1994-1995, the company targeted the reduction of environmental problems related to air pollution, water pollution, noise pollution, and vibration. One of the largest chemical manufacturers in the world, Mitsubishi Chemical, launched the so-called responsible care program for product safety, public health, environmental protection, and occupational safety. The company has integrated monetary assessment, auditing systems, and management of all of the processes based on the total product life cycle model, from the development of environmentally safe chemical materials to final disposal. The list of Mitsubishi subsidiaries that have signed "the Ethics of Corporate Responsibility" is now published annually and is available for public scrutiny. Toyoko Riken has developed the following eight steps for developing an ecologically active organization:

1. Publicly declare the corporate commitment to environmental improvement.

2. Create quantifiable, operational, and financial data on each unit and each level of operation based on set targets, strategies, and limits.

3. Undertake recycling and waste management projects.

4. Invest in research and development for energy saving, 100% recycling of parts and materials, and product cycle assessment.

5. Create a new performance evaluation system based on the amount of contribution to environmental preservation. Incorporate environmental auditing systems in personnel evaluation, cost appraisal, product development, waste management, and marketing strategies.

6. Systematize environmental impact assessments by using measurable indicators and collecting longitudinal data. Establish environmentally oriented financial and accounting standards, and use them as economic indicators of productivity and profitability.

7. Build new marketing and publicity strategies for promoting the public understanding of corporate transformation. Provide environmental education services and gain public confidence in the new corporate policy initiatives.

8. Contribute to regional and community environmental efforts through voluntary and philanthropic activities.

The new corporate environmentalism that began in the mid-1990s sparked much debate because it was not intended to set particular product standards. Rather, it is a systematic approach to corporate quality enhancement using a series of new indicators and cost accounting. It entails far more than mere legal compliance. Corporate environmentalists and progressive corporate leaders are urging voluntary, industry-led activities, stating that it is up to business, not the government, to define environmental excellence. They advocate a position that business should integrate environmental issues at every level and in every part of the company, instead of seeking mere compliance with a set of product or service standards. The industrial leaders who are familiar with *kaizen* (continuous incremental improvement) methods, zero defects, small group activities, statistical control, and the four steps of PDCA (plan, do, check, act) have begun incorporating ecological management ideology into conventional business operations. Their rhetoric and practices for an environmental management system (EMS) have several notable characteristics:

1. New key words have been invented for this ideology; these include zero waste (rather than zero defect, which was used in the quality enhancement model); zero emission (rather than zero inventory); flow analysis (rather than process analysis); sustainable development (rather than productivity enhancement); and in-process technology (rather than pulling system).

2. The new management lexicon frequently uses analogies to biology rather than to engineering. For example, the total product life cycle, from procurement and manufacturing to disposition and recycling, is frequently compared to the flows of the arteries and veins of the human body. Biotechnological terms such as "bioremediation" are used.

3. EMS auditing is not limited to the factory's in-house manufacturing process. EMS targets the whole life cycle process, from the initial procurement of raw materials to production, sales and marketing, consumption, and final disposal and recycling.

4. Just like the total quality manufacturing process that aimed at zero defects and zero rejects, the new EMS emphasizes in-process improvement at every step for zero emissions, zero waste, and zero pollution. The quality check occurs not at the end of the line but at every phase of the production process. In an ideal situation, all inputs into the system (raw material, energy, other resources) must be 100% utilized, producing no industrial waste. Any by-products or waste should be converted to reusable materials for the same or other manufacturing processes. The QC method of production, waste disposal took place just before the final product was shipped out of the factory.

5. The new quality system also pays attention to the procurement of raw materials and the use of energy and natural resources. It may involve innovative product designs for complete decomposition and recycling after consumption. EMS can streamline the complete life cycle process for cleaner production, zero emissions, cost reduction, and new business creation.

Figure 12.2 illustrates the EMS concept for in-process environmental quality control and continuous improvement, or *kaizen*, in the manufacturing plant. With EMS, it is important to calculate quality costs at every step of the product life cycle by using the PDCA system of quality management. The EMS for environmental quality is not limited to manufacturing but can also be applied to many different sectors, including consumers, households, community organizations, governments, and public service agencies.

EMS also changes the concept of cost accounting. Like the quality movement for customer satisfaction, where improving quality originally meant incurring costs, today's environmental skeptics believe that ecology does not pay off for the corporate bottom line. On the other hand, top management and new environmental gurus believe that environmental quality may actually enhance corporate profitability because EMS efforts will result in reduced waste, lower energy consumption, fewer legal

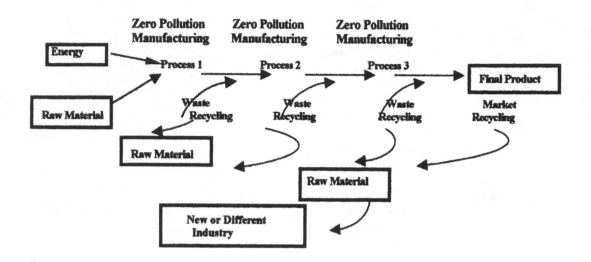

Figure 12.2. EMS In-Process Improvement for Cleaner Production

costs, more customer satisfaction, new eco-business opportunities, an enhanced corporate image, more effective system coordination, and global-level assessment and auditing of material and product flows. In other words, green can become gold. The Japanese government predicts that the ecology-oriented business will expand to a hefty 3.5-trillion-yen growth industry by the year 2010.

If these gurus are right, one can clearly see why management would want to use the environmental quality management strategy. A comparison of the three models—the quality model for compliance, the model for customer satisfaction, and the model for ecology—finds the following similarities and differences.

Similarities. In many respects, the environmental quality concepts described above are an extension of Japanese corporate ideology. Both corporate environmentalism and the quality movement for customer satisfaction emphasize the manifested commitment of top management, total companywide efforts, unit-level participation, small group activities, and the need to eliminate waste and defects. They also use new forms of cost calculation, statistical control, and process coordination. Both movements see that interventions and behavioral modification take place holistically, at multiple levels. The corporate environmental statement, just like the traditional statement of profit and loss, can be published in annual reports and other public documents. Convinced that corporate environmentalism makes good financial sense, Japanese firms, and particularly multinationals, have begun to provide a basis on which to evaluate corporate performance in environmental areas in the same way that corporate financial disclosure allows analysts to evaluate a company's financial performance.

In Japan, where energy is expensive, the business norm that waste is cost is culturally ac-

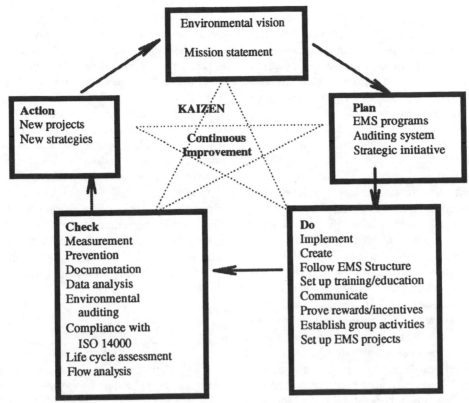

Figure 12.3. Quality Environmental Management System (EMS) as a *Kaizen* Process of PDCA

cepted by industrialists. In addition, symbiosis is a very vague and therefore malleable concept (just like the quality concept) that is, nevertheless, compatible with the Japanese traditional and indigenous cosmology, which tends to integrate noneconomic and economic activities and does not endorse an anthropocentric view of man against nature.

Differences. In the 1970s and 1980s, Japan's large firms continued productivity enhancement and relentless cost reduction in order to export to advanced industrial societies and to increase international competitiveness. Big business was considered good, and the bigger the better. Ever-increasing market share expansion was the name of the game. The 1990s movement in large Japanese companies, in contrast, concerns how to transform Japanese companies from efficient, cost-effective, *customer*-friendly organizations into environmentally efficient, cost-effective, and *nature*-friendly or-

ganizations. The new quality meaning is significant because it links the deeply held managerial principles for cost reduction and profit maximization with the socially acceptable ecological mind-set and legal restrictions prevalent in Japanese civil society at large. The concepts of the limits of growth and *kyosei* as the parasitic relationship are new to this quality model. Japanese top managers now seem to be thinking about eco-business, because by saving energy, keeping air clean, and recycling, they will reduce costs, streamline complex organizational processes internationally, and tighten global corporate control.

It is important to note that the move from the second model for customer satisfaction to the third model for ecological excellence is the result of a reconfiguration and recontextualization of the original meanings rather than a total replacement of the old scheme with the new one. The meaning transformation is conducted by recontextualizing the existing cultural equipment, such as corporate practice for statistical control, companywide efforts, auditing, and market orientation, and ideologically useful and culturally compatible images and narratives (such as *kyosei* and coexistence). In such metamessage negotiation, the preexisting store of knowledge (*kaizen, kanban,* zero defect, in-process technology, and PDCA) is docked with components of new narratives for growth within limits, corporate responsibility, eco-business, and so forth.

Quality transformation involves developing a new behavior pattern that is reinforced by positive feedback. If it is successful, these new behavior patterns become habitual, and "refreezing" takes place (Lewin, 1951). Refreezing means locking the new behavior pattern into place so that it eventually becomes the dominant way of doing things. In a state of total acculturation and hegemonic movement (Gramsci, 1996), social reality appears given, natural, and nonnegotiable, although in principle, it is arbitrary and negotiable. Once a particular schema about quality becomes part of the everyday lexicon and organizational habitus, the quality culture may become a "psychic prison" or "blinder" (Morgan, 1986). Whether the new corporate rhetoric for ecological excellence will take root and refreeze the Japanese mind is open for further longitudinal investigation.

A growing body of research on "culture as an emergent phenomenon" concludes that much of human cognition is context specific and cannot be separated from the field of collective activity (Hirschfeld & Gelman, 1994). The unfolding of new institutional arrangements, both formal and informal, often parallels the formation of distinctive metamessages as an adaptation to particular environmental pressures and group dynamics. Culture provides a context in which such symbolic actions take place. Over the years, Japanese managers have constructed different social meanings of quality and, in doing so, have made sense of their new competitive environment in the world. Whether this new managerial rhetoric for ecological quality will be shared by other members of the organization, such as workers, is yet to be tested.

Clearly, it takes imagination and emotional tension to detach oneself from one's habitus, whether one is an outside researcher or an inside power holder. Although one can always find an exotic principle in other people's cultures, such as foreign management practices, it is more difficult to see that one's own culture is a subjective but nonindividual system of internalized structures of perception, conception, and action. In studying quality, we need to pay attention to this "feel for things" because culture defines the unchosen habitus of all choices that managers and researchers make.

Quality research is a historically constructed cognitive activity. The researcher must begin with rigorous cultural reflection on what he or she means by quality—when and where the definition is made, according to what reference points, and according to whose metamessages.

Notes

1. Martin (1992) first categorized the three distinct organizational culture perspectives and advocated the combining of all three models in organizational culture research. The objective of this chapter, on the other hand, is to illustrate how the same organizational phenomenon such as quality can be researched quite differently because of the metamessages that individual researchers have adopted and bring specifically to the quality research field.

2. Mutualism is a relationship in which two species benefit from each other. For example, the tickbird eats the ticks that infest the warthog's skin. In the process, the warthog gets rid of parasites and is warned of approaching dangers by the cries of the tickbird. Likewise, a bee or hummingbird sips nectar from a blossom while also fertilizing the flower with pollen from other, similar plants. In the process, the bee or bird gets food, and the plant is helped to reproduce.

3. Commensalism is a symbiotic relationship in which one organism benefits and the other is neither helped nor harmed. The barnacle that hitches a ride on a whale is an example of commensalism. Whereas the barnacle gets transportation and a steady supply of food, the whale is generally not affected by this association.

4. Considering humans as parasites is not a new idea. For example, according to ancient Chinese folklore, P'an Gu, the first being, hammered the universe into shape about 2,229,000 B.C. As he worked, his breath became the wind and the clouds, his voice became the thunder, his veins the rivers, his flesh the earth, his hair the grass and trees, his bones the metals, his sweat the rain, and the insects that clung to his body the human race. The earliest celestial emperors, says Chinese legend, struggled to turn P'an Gu's lice into civilized men.

5. In 1997, 7 years after the ISO 9000 industrial standards were introduced in 1991, more than 4,000 Japanese firms had received ISO certification. Although the initial reason for seeking certification was market driven, the 9000 standards are now recognized as an effective management tool for organizational streamlining and quality enhancement. Statistical data from Japan Quality Assurance show that a majority of Japanese firms that applied for and received ISO 9000 certification for quality enhancement in the early 1990s (582 firms) were heavily concentrated in electric and electronics industries, which had a large export market. Companies that wanted to penetrate the advanced industrial markets, such as the European Union, may have been more likely than others to adopt the global quality standards.

References

Abu-Lughod, L. (1986). *Veiled sentiments: Honor and poetry in Bedouin society*. New York: Oxford University Press.

Anderson, B. (1991). *Imagined communities*. London: Verso.

Appadurai, A. (1996). *Modernity at large: Cultural dimensions of globalization*. Minneapolis: University of Minnesota Press.

Benedict, R. (1959). *Patterns of culture*. Boston: Houghton Mifflin.

Bhabha, H. K. (1990). *Nation and narration*. New York: Routledge.

Bourdieu, P. (1977). *Outline of a theory of practice* (R. Nice, Trans.). New York: Cambridge University Press.

Burawoy, M. (1979). The anthropology of industrial work. *Annual Review of Anthropology, 8*, 231-266.

Collinson, D. L. (1992). *Managing the shop floor: Subjectivity, masculinity and workplace culture*. New York: Walter de Gruyter.

Davis, S. (1984). *Managing corporate culture*. Cambridge, MA: Ballinger.

Deal, T., & Kennedy, A. (1982). *Corporate cultures: The rites and rituals of corporate life*. Reading, MA: Addison-Wesley.

Deming, W. E. (1985). Transformation of Western style of management. *Interfaces, 15*(3), 6-11.

Deming, W. E. (1986). *Out of the crisis*. Cambridge: MIT Press.

Deming, W. E. (1993). *The new economics for industry, government, education*. Cambridge: MIT Press.

Durkheim, E. (1933). *The division of labor in society*. New York: Free Press.

Gagliardi, P. (Ed.). (1990). *Symbols and artifacts: Views of the corporate landscape*. Hawthorne, NY: Walter de Gruyter.

Geertz, C. (1973). *The interpretation of cultures*. New York: Basic Books.

Geertz, C. (1983). *Local knowledge: Further essays in interpretive anthropology*. New York: Basic Books.

Giddens, A. (1984). *The constitution of society*. Berkeley: University of California Press.

Gramsci, A. (1996). *Prison letters* (H. Henderson, Trans. & Intro.). Chicago: Pluto.

Gregory, K. (1983). Native-view models: Multiple cultures and culture conflicts in organizations. *Administrative Science Quarterly, 28*, 359-376.

Guillén, M. F. (1994). *Models of management: Work, authority, and organization in a comparative perspective*. Chicago: University of Chicago Press.

Hirschfeld, L. A., & Gelman, S. A. (Eds.). (1994). *Mapping the mind: Domain specificity in cognition and culture*. Cambridge: Cambridge University Press.

Hofstede, G. (1984). *Culture's consequences*. Beverly Hills, CA: Sage.

Ishikawa, K. (1982). *Guide to quality control*. White Plains, NY: Quality Resources.

Ishikawa, K. (1985). *What is total quality control? The Japanese way*. Englewood Cliffs, NJ: Prentice Hall.

Juran, J. A. M. (1974). *The quality control handbook* (3rd ed.). New York: McGraw-Hill.

Juran, J. A. M. (1988). *Juran on planning for quality*. New York: Free Press.

Juran, J. A. M. (1989). *Juran on leadership for quality*. New York: Free Press.

Kilmann, R. (1985). *Beyond the quick fix: Managing five tracks to organizational success*. San Francisco: Jossey-Bass.

Kondo, D. (1990). *Crafting selves: Power, gender, and discourses of identity in a Japanese workplace*. Chicago: University of Chicago Press.

Kunda, G. (1992). *Engineering culture: Control and commitment in a high-tech corporation*. Philadelphia: Temple University Press.

Lewin, K. (1951). *Field theory in social science: Selected theoretical papers* (D. Cartwright, Ed.). New York: Harper and Brothers.

Louis, M. (1983). Organization as culture-bearing milieux. In L. Pondy, P. Frost, G. Morgan, & T. Dandridge (Eds.), *Organizational symbolism* (pp. 39-54). Greenwich, CT: JAI.

Louis, M. (1985). An investigator's guide to workplace culture. In P. Frost, L. Moore, M. Louis, C. Lundberg, & J. Martin (Eds.), *Organizational culture* (pp. 146-159). Beverly Hills, CA: Sage.

Martin, J. (1992). *Cultures in organizations: Three perspectives*. Oxford, UK: Oxford University Press.

Meyerson, D., & Martin, J. (1987). Cultural change: An integration of three different views. *Journal of Management Studies, 24*, 623-647.

Morgan, G. (1986). *Images of organization*. London: Sage.

Ong, A. (1987). *Spirits of resistance and capitalist discipline: Factory women in Malaysia*. Albany: State University of New York Press.

Ouchi, W. G., & Wilkins, A. L. (1985). Organizational culture. *Annual Review of Sociology, 11*, 457-483.

Peters, T., & Waterman, R. (1982). *In search of excellence: Lessons from America's best-run companies*. New York: Harper & Row.

Polanyi, K. (1957). The economy as instituted process. In K. Polanyi, C. Arensberg, & H. Pearson (Eds.), *Trade and market in the early empires.* Glencoe, IL: Free Press.

Ray, C. A. (1986). Corporate culture: The last frontier of control. *Journal of Management Studies, 23,* 287-296.

Sahlins, M. (1972). *Stone Age economics.* Chicago: Aldine-Atherton.

Sathe, V. (1985). *Culture and related corporate realities: Text, cases and readings on organizational entry, establishment, and change.* Homewood, IL: Irwin.

Smircich, L. (1983). Concepts of culture and organizational analysis. *Administrative Science Quarterly, 28,* 339-358.

Strauss, A. (1978). *Negotiations: Varieties, contexts, processes and social order.* San Francisco: Jossey-Bass.

Strauss, A. (1991). *Creating sociological awareness: Collective images and symbolic representations.* New Brunswick, NJ: Transaction.

Trice, H., & Beyer, J. (1984). Studying organizational cultures through rites and ceremonials. *Academy of Management Review, 9,* 653-669.

Van Maanen, J., & Barley, S. (1984). Occupational communities: Culture and control in organization. In B. Staw & L. Cummings (Eds.), *Research in organizational behavior* (Vol. 6, pp. 287-366). Greenwich, CT: JAI.

Van Maanen, J., & Barley, S. (1985). *Cultural organization: Fragments of a theory.* In P. Frost, L. Moore, L. Louis, C. Lundberg, & J. Martin (Eds.), *Organizational culture* (pp. 25-33). Beverly Hills, CA: Sage.

Weber, M. (1947). *The Protestant ethic and the spirit of capitalism* (T. Parsons, Trans.). London: Allen & Unwin.

PART IV

Conditions and Contingencies
Affecting Quality Development

Chapter 13

Tailoring Process Management to Situational Requirements

Beyond the Control and Exploration Dichotomy

KATHLEEN M. SUTCLIFFE
SIM B. SITKIN
LARRY D. BROWNING

Scholars have recently distinguished two fundamentally different types of process improvement approaches that are reflected in two parallel but independent streams of research on organizational effectiveness and change. The first stream emphasizes the need for continuous improvement and efficiency, focusing on customer-responsive, highly reliable processes for the delivery of products and services (e.g., quality management methods, business process reengineering). The second stream emphasizes anticipating disjunctive change requirements, focusing on the need to adopt flexible, "boundaryless," learning-oriented processes. Taken together, the streams capture two simultaneous and opposing pressures for organizational evolution.

The dominant (perhaps even exclusive) assumption in this work has been that the two approaches reflected in the two research streams are antithetical and that organizations can be most effective by striking a balance between the two (March, 1995). As March (1995) observes, this dilemma is

> well known to students of rational choice (where it is represented by the problem of balancing search and action), by students of evolution (where it is represented by the problem of balancing variation and selection), and by students of institutional change (where it is represented by the problem of balancing change and stability). (p. 432)

Yet even with such an acknowledgment of the need to consider reliability and learning simultaneously, there has been no conceptual framework proposed to begin to systematically examine this phenomenon. Several questions critical to developing such a framework remain

AUTHORS' NOTE: The authors gratefully acknowledge support from the National Science Foundation (Grant Nos. SBR-94-96229 and SBR-94-20461) and the U.S. Air Force (Grant No. USAF-F49642-97-P-0083) for the program of research on which this chapter is based. Portions of this chapter were previously presented at the ORSA/TIMS meeting in Detroit, October 1994.

315

unarticulated and, thus, unaddressed: What is meant by "balance"? Is balancing the only way to think about the two approaches? What tensions exist between the two that can help to clarify whether there are some conditions for which balancing is not the best solution? What are the implications of these tensions for organization design and management? Articulating a conceptual framework to begin to answer these questions is the goal of this chapter. Specifically, in this chapter, we conceptualize process management in a less bifurcated way than has been the case in the literature to date by integrating past theory and recent empirical research.

Distinguishing Process Requirements

The need for dramatically improved reliability (e.g., the capacity to produce collective outcomes of a certain minimum quality repeatedly) has driven the recent scholarly interest in process improvement methods, such as quality management (e.g., Dean & Bowen, 1994) and high-reliability organizations (e.g., Weick & Roberts, 1993). Goals associated with increased reliability are the reduction of unwanted variance and the desire to improve existing capabilities and technologies. Concurrent with rising demands for reliability, scholars have noted how the world confronting organizations is increasingly characterized as discontinuous, uncertain, and chaotic (D'Aveni, 1994; Nonaka & Takeuchi, 1995). These scholars argue that uncertain conditions favor organizations that are flexible and can adapt quickly to changing conditions. Therefore, organizations are faced with simultaneous demands to become both more reliable and more adaptable. To understand these dual (and perhaps competing) pressures and their effect on organizational processes, there has been a rising interest in studying how organizations can respond predictably to the demands of an unpredictable world. Researchers have begun to examine how organizations become more adept at ensuring reliability while learning and innovating con-

cerning products, services, and administrative structures and processes.

The implications of this changing competitive landscape have led to a similar set of ideas being proposed almost simultaneously by several groups of scholars. These researchers have argued that the essence of process management (e.g., quality management and related change efforts) involves dual core goals—reliability and learning—and that distinct types of processes (i.e., control-oriented and exploration-oriented) are related to each of those goals. For example, issues of process management and how they relate to the distinctions just outlined can be found in our own work (Sitkin, 1992; Sitkin, Sutcliffe, & Schroeder, 1994; Sutcliffe, Sitkin, & Browning, 1997), as well as in the work of March (March, 1991, 1995) and his colleagues (e.g., Levinthal & March, 1993; March, Sproull, & Tamuz, 1991; Tamuz, 1987, 1994), Eisenhardt (1993) and her colleagues (e.g., Brown & Eisenhardt, 1995; Eisenhardt & Tabrizi, 1995), and others (e.g., Henderson & Clark, 1990; Sterman, Repenning, & Kofman, 1997).

Most prior work in this area has suggested that these fundamentally distinct goals (reliability and learning) are antithetical in that the pursuit of one is presumed to preclude the pursuit of the other. Much of the organizational literature still suggests that organizations face a choice: to compete by being highly reliable in exploiting that which they already know and are known for, or to compete by being a leader in exploring new, breakthrough technologies or systems. By focusing on *either* the enhanced delivery of product, service, and/or performance reliability *or* the enhancement of organizational learning capacity, these approaches at best implicitly assume that the pursuit of reliability or learning is a trade-off.

There is a growing recognition by scholars and practitioners that we need to move beyond framing this choice in either/or terms. A few analyses have recognized that not only can these dual goals coexist but also that the processes associated with each of these goals is present to some extent in all organizational settings. Pushing this argument further, it has been proposed that the simultaneous consideration of the dual goals is associated with increased effectiveness in that competitive conditions will require the simultaneous pursuit of two metaprocesses—reliability-focused control processes and learning-focused exploration processes—or, at a minimum, will favor those organizations that are able to master the apparent inconsistency suggested by their simultaneous pursuit (March, 1995; Sitkin, 1992; Sutcliffe et al., 1997). Thus, this argument goes, organizational survival will increasingly hinge on the capacity to balance control-based performance reliability and exploration-based resilience.

Although a recognition of the need for balance has been reflected in past work, the purpose of this chapter is to begin to go beyond this recognition by identifying the alternative logics underlying different kinds of balance—thus setting the stage for additional in-depth work on the issue in the future. In the next section, we review the evolution of organizational process models, showing the underlying logics of models that view processes in singular or binary terms. We also propose a third type of model that reflects the simultaneous presence and interaction of control and exploration approaches, in what is referred to here as a "dual" approach. After introducing the notion of dual process models, the third section of the chapter answers the question, What does it mean in a concrete sense for organizations to balance or integrate the use of control-oriented and exploration-oriented approaches? We draw together theory and data to explore in more detail the conditions under which control and exploration involve zero-sum trade-offs, are orthogonally related, or are synergistic and result in mutually greater gains, and we also discuss the implications of this conceptualization for future research on organizational process management.

Evolution of Organizational Process Models

Work on organizational processes has been scant compared with other forms of organizational study. Most macro-organizational research over the past 20 years has been dominated by a focus on structure and function, rather than process. One reason for this is that processes tend to be harder to perceive than structures such as departments, functions, or tasks. Specifically, organizational processes have tended to be unnoticed and unnamed in the literature because our attention has been focused on individual departments and their goals rather than on sets of interrelated work activities that cross formal boundaries and involve a variety of organizational members.

It is useful to focus on organizational process when discussing organizations and their future adaptability because it allows us to concern ourselves with the specific managerial and employee action sets that might be associated with differing conditions. More specifically, it allows us to distinguish between processes concerned with the improvement of existing production processes and stable value chains (reliability-enhancing processes) and processes concerned with defining or redefining real or potential value chains (innovation/learning-enhancing processes). Attempts to classify organizational processes are made more difficult because the available database is inadequate. Nevertheless, researchers during the past 30 years have proposed several classification schemes to describe organizational processes. For example, March and his colleagues (e.g., Cyert & March, 1963; March & Simon, 1958) distinguish between problem-driven and slack-driven search processes; Quinn (1980) distinguishes between synoptic and incremental strategic decision-making processes; Burns and Stalker (1961) contrast mechanistic and organic organizational processes; and Ouchi (1977, 1979, 1981) describes input, behavioral, and output control processes.

The recent classification of organizational processes into the dual categories noted above (i.e., control vs. exploration) grew out of the growing interest in adaptive processes and organizational learning. However, this typology is not entirely without precedent because it mirrors one of the central and enduring paradoxes in organization theory concerning the trade-off between efficiency and flexibility (Thompson, 1967). Organization theorists have argued that bureaucracy enhances efficiency but impedes flexibility, the implication being that organizations cannot achieve both. We discuss the distinctions between control and exploration below before moving on to a more in-depth discussion of the relationships between the two.

There are two key distinctions between control and exploration. First, control emphasizes systematically clarifying that which is shared or convergent, whereas exploration emphasizes systematically discovering that which is unforeseen and divergent. Second, control stresses the clear, the articulated, and the specific. In contrast, exploration stresses the emergent, the suggestive, and the general.

In a recent review of process management perspectives and implications for organizational design, Denison (1997) builds a hierarchical framework that distinguishes three fundamental organizational process modalities. Denison's framework is helpful in terms of translating reliability-focused control and resilience-focused exploration goals into types of actions available to organizational managers and other members. Specifically, Denison distinguishes the need to *design* a facilitating infrastructure, *manage* the interaction among units and individuals, and *implement* the designs through practices that accomplish the work to be done. By parsing the processes into three modes—designing, managing, and implementing—Denison's scheme helps to clarify how actions taken in pursuit of control or exploration can be distinguished.

Designing for control involves the pursuit of reliability by articulating clear, specific, shared understandings that will govern activities. If reliability is to be achieved, it is crucial that goals not be divergent, responsibilities not be fuzzy, and criteria to be met in products or services be unequivocal. The designer's role in control-oriented processes is to be sure that goals and responsibilities are clear and shared; schedules and criteria for performance are specific and understood; and that any general understandings about the purpose, tasks, or roles are as concrete as possible. Design for exploration, in contrast, emphasizes the opposite: distinct and independently defined goals, fuzzy expecta-

tions, and performance criteria carried out by independent operating units.

Managing for control and exploration exhibit equally distinctive practices. Given a well-defined set of goals, plans, and performance expectations, a control orientation stresses tightly coupled action plans and close coordination across operating units and individuals. Because the thrust of control-oriented processes is to more carefully hone in on established targets, systems and procedures to reduce needless variation are an essential part of managing for control. In contrast, the pursuit of the fuzzier goals and emergent expectations associated with an exploration orientation fosters the use of parallel processes and the development of innovative ideas (Bendor, 1985; Cohen, March, & Olsen, 1972). The management of exploration processes, in other words, involves the active generation of greater variance as the only route to discovery and capacity building (Sitkin, 1992).

Implementing refers to doing work in a way that supports the underlying goals for which a process is being used. The implementation practices that support control include conforming to work, product, and service specifications—and even tightening those specifications as a result of experience. Research on learning curves illustrates this approach (Epple, Argote, & Devadas, 1991). In contrast, when practices are implemented that support exploration, these efforts involve challenging accepted standards and specifications rather than conforming to them, and looking for new and novel opportunities rather than avoiding or minimizing risky activities.

But the question still remains, how are control and exploration linked? Table 13.1 distinguishes three models for thinking about the relationship between control-oriented and exploration-oriented organizational processes. The models can be distinguished along several dimensions: their primary goal, the relationship between goals, and the strategic and management challenges posed by the implementation of that model. In the following paragraphs, we discuss each model in terms of these dimensions.

TABLE 13.1 The Evolution of Organizational Process Models

	Singular	*Binary*	*Dual*
Control focus	• Increase reliability and predictability • Exploit existing capabilities • Conformity	• Increase reliability and predictability • Exploit existing capabilities • Conformity	• Increase reliability and predictability • Exploit existing capabilities • Conformity
Exploration focus	NOT RECOGNIZED	• Increase resilience and flexibility • Explore new capabilities • Risk-taking	• Increase resilience and flexibility • Explore new capabilities • Risk-taking
Relationship between control and exploration	None because there is no exploration focus to consider	Both apply to different circumstances and thus are unrelated	Balance must be struck between the two because both are relevant to varying degrees under different circumstances
Strategic challenge	Simplification of mission	Recognition of contingent missions	Acknowledgment of simultaneous pursuit of dual missions
Management challenge	Implementation of solutions	Differentiation of solutions	Identification of distributive solution

Singular Organizational Process Model

The "singular" model has dominated until quite recently in that almost all of the literature and much practice concerning quality management and other process improvement methods have reflected a singular, monolithic view. Dating back to the early 20th-century scientific management movement, this approach has emphasized the achievement of control by stressing the importance of variance reduction, whether that logic was applied to formal procedures, norms, practices, personnel, or other features of organizations. This conceptualization of organizational processes typically ignores the possibility that significant contingency factors may be relevant to whatever processes are being proposed.

As Sitkin et al. (1994) describe, much of the TQM movement in the United States has adopted this singular stance, suggesting that the tenets and practices of quality management are universally applicable (but see Cole, Chapter 4, in

this volume, concerning how this attribute of the American TQM movement may not apply to Japanese quality management efforts). This is illustrated in some of our earlier research on the forcing of a singular, control-oriented model of TQM on a basic research laboratory, in which efforts to achieve zero-defect research was described by employees as "quality through conformity" (Sitkin & Stickel, 1996).

The implications of this approach for management practice are twofold. First, the organization's strategy is likely to reflect a clear, focused emphasis on reliability by reducing unwanted, unanticipated, and unexplainable variance in performance and by focusing attention on meeting stated milestones and achievement targets. Once clarified, the key strategic challenge is to simply articulate the mission so that it is applicable and implementable throughout the organization. Given the assumption of a clear, singular, strategic goal, the critical managerial challenge is to carry out that goal through disciplined implementation. Proponents of this approach are likely to stress the importance of clear and comprehensive measures and motivational procedures, all keyed tightly to the core, unified strategic goal. If there is a central theme in this work, it concerns the value of high levels of control through standard routines and procedures to achieve the goal of high reliability.

Binary Organizational Process Model

A central distinction in organization theory is made between situations described as certain, analyzable, routine, and predictable and those situations described as uncertain, unanalyzable, nonroutine, and unpredictable. For example, Thompson (1967) discusses the much more complex and open-ended coordination requirements needed when action interdependencies cannot be specified a priori. Williamson (1975) describes the difficulties associated with contractually specifying transaction expectations under uncertain conditions. Scholars from a wide variety of disciplinary perspectives have long recognized that technical transformation processes that are well understood present organizational members with a fundamentally different challenge than do processes that are poorly understood (Perrow, 1967). An implication of this distinction is that whereas more certain activities can be accomplished through the use of systematic, routine, rational, bureaucratic procedures, uncertain conditions require a more flexible, experimental, and improvisational approach.

We drew on this distinction in our theorizing about the quality management perspective, its practices, and related outcomes by developing a binary model of quality management. Most process management programs had been advocated as universally applicable to all organizational activities with virtually no attention to the nature of situational or task uncertainty. Thus, we proposed a binary model as an alternative to the standard singular models that dominated to that point. Our thinking was based on the familiar contingency theory notion that problematic outcomes may result when organizational systems are poorly attuned to contextual requirements.

This led to the hypothesis that highly uncertain conditions would require an alternative to standard process management practices (i.e., standard quality control practices) and also to the hypothesis that matching process management techniques to situational requirements would enhance their effectiveness. In our contingency-based model, we suggested that rational cybernetic control approaches (e.g., engineering approaches) fit best in highly certain situations, whereas experiential, learning-oriented, improvisational approaches fit best in highly uncertain situations. The central point is that taking situational uncertainty into account and tailoring process methods to the nature of uncertain situations allows for a more accurate and quicker diagnosis of the problems, as well as more effective problem resolution through the use of situationally appropriate quality practices.

The hypothesized benefits of control-oriented process management practices in routine/certain situations is relatively straightforward, and there are numerous empirical examples of improved process accuracy (e.g., reduced error rates), process efficiency (e.g., reduced costs), and process cycle time (e.g., reduced time to complete a process) (Hackman & Wageman, 1995). In contrast, there is little or no empirical support for the idea that traditional process management practices lead to improvements under less certain, nonroutine situations. In fact, it has been generally accepted in organization theory that highly uncertain organic situations lack structure, and that process management is futile under such conditions (e.g., Burns & Stalker, 1961). Contrary to this received wisdom, in our earlier work, we proposed that actively implementing *appropriate* process management can be helpful in carrying out work in uncertain and nonroutine conditions and that this idea had been missed in mainstream process management thinking.

We explored how process management practices could be designed and tailored to uncertain situations to enhance performance and pointed out that there are at least two benefits of using process management tactics in uncertain situations. First, process management tactics may help people cope with unclear and changing environments because such practices help to more rapidly build intuition and flexibility (Sitkin, 1992; Weick, 1984, 1985). Second, process management tactics may simultaneously "provid[e] enough structure so that people will create sensemaking, avoid procrastination, and be confident enough to act in these highly uncertain situations, which easily lead to paralyzing anxiety and conflict" (Eisenhardt & Tabrizi, 1995, p. 88).

Dual Organizational Process Model

Neither the singular nor the binary model examines the relationship between the two types of process. The two either do not recognize that two distinct processes exist (singular model) or merely distinguish them in a traditional contingent choice sense (binary model). The third type of model shown in Table 13.1, the dual process model, reflects that organizations cannot typically focus on only one type of goal (as a simple contingency) but that they must do both simultaneously to remain adaptable under differing conditions. As Stacey (1992) observed,

> When you look at the world or organizing through new lens, you do not see "either/or" choices. Instead you see "both/and" choices. Successful organizations—that is, continually innovative organizations—cannot choose between tight, formal control systems and structures on one hand and loose, informal processes that provoke learning on the other . . . they must do both at the same time. (p. 19)

The nature of the situation and the nature of the relationship between the control-oriented and exploration-oriented processes is crucial in determining the effectiveness of organizational adaptation efforts. Even when earlier binary models recognized both the control and exploration approaches, standard assumptions about their relationship (e.g., that they were negatively related in a zero sum trade-off) side-stepped the need to deal with their relationship. Thus, the recognition and awareness of both

types of processes is not sufficient; rather, this approach stresses how the decision of how to balance the two approaches necessarily involves considering potential trade-offs in resource and attention allocation. However, this issue has never been addressed explicitly or analyzed systematically in the organizational process literature. In the next section, we outline the basic contours of a framework for examining the various forms that the relationship between control and exploration can take, and the implications of those relational forms for managerial actions and organizational effectiveness.

Balancing Control and Exploration in Organizations

Although some previous work has acknowledged the need for balance, none has actually explored the nature of that balance or the tensions and impediments that balancing dual processes poses for organizations and their members. Although one potential implication of using the term "balance" is to suggest equality between the two types of processes, that is not how we use the term here. Instead, our use of the notion of balancing focuses on the need to actively consider both types of process and to determine what an appropriate balance should be, contingent upon situational conditions. We wish to highlight that balancing is active and lies along a continuum. Furthermore, understanding the nature of balancing requires that we specify distinct ways that the two processes might be related to each other.

Past work has tended to only look at balancing these processes in terms of trade-offs, and calls for balance have typically taken a singular form by suggesting that the more one turns attention to learning-enhancing exploration, the more that concern comes at the expense of a focus on reliability-enhancing control (and vice versa). However, this general logic reflects just one of the three potential types of relationships (antithetical) that we describe below.

Table 13.2 shows the characteristics associated with each of three logical alternatives in

TABLE 13.2 Clarifying the Control/Exploration Relationship

	Relationship Between Control and Exploration	
	Antithetical (Negative)	*Orthogonal (Independent)*
Description of relationship	Zero-sum game with negative feedback loops, in which each approach can be increased only by decreasing attention or resources devoted to the other.	The two approaches coexist independently of each other, with no feedback loops. Increased attention to learning in one part of the organization does not detract from the emphasis on control in another part of the organization.
Strategic challenge	Balanced choice	Understanding and respecting differences
Management challenge	Identification of distributive solution	Protection of nonequivalent solutions

how the two processes can be related to each other. The first explores conditions under which they are negatively associated ("antithetical"), the second explores conditions under which they are unrelated ("orthogonal"), and the third explores conditions under which they are positively related ("synergistic"). The antithetical perspective assumes that process choices occupy a fixed attention/resource space, and that the choice to pursue control or exploration is a zero-sum game. The orthogonal perspective reflects the notion that there are conditions in which the two types of processes might be pursued independently of each other, draw on different and noncompeting resource pools, and thus be viewed as orthogonal contributors to an organization. The synergistic model refers to conditions under which the effective pursuit of reliability and learning are mutually supportive, such that doing one better simultaneously enhances the ability to do the other.

As we examine each of these three models below, we structure our discussion around three key points. First, we discuss the logic underlying the relationship between control-oriented and exploration-oriented processes. Second, we illustrate how that relationship can be manifested by drawing upon case study data gathered as part of a longitudinal field study of 10 organizations cited as having exemplary quality

management programs. Third, we raise several challenges posed by each model.

The Antithetical Perspective on Balancing Processes

Scholars who have recognized that balance is needed commonly hold the view that the relationship between control and exploration is antithetical. That is, the two processes are presumed to exist in a kind of zero-sum world in which one pursues the novel at the expense of ensuring reliable improvement, and pursues incremental improvement by sacrificing a willingness to innovate. The following quotation from March (1995) illustrates:

A system that specializes in [control] will discover itself becoming better and better at an increasingly obsolescent technology. A system that specializes in exploration will never realize the advantages of its discoveries. . . . Exploration and [control] are linked in an enduring symbiosis. . . . Each interferes with the other . . . [and] organizations persistently fail to maintain an effective balance between the two. (pp. 432-433)

In an earlier examination of this issue, the distinction between small wins (Weick, 1984) and small losses (Sitkin, 1992) stressed how the pursuit of one reduced the capacity to pursue the other. As routines and systems become more focused on amplifying and developing a single strength, several things can result: Flexibility decreases, myopia increases, and exploratory learning and adaptation are curtailed (Miller, 1993)—a potentially problematic combination under conditions such as environmental decline, turbulence, uncertainty, or complexity. Illustrating this point, simulation studies have demonstrated that enhancing reliability under conditions of uncertainty or rapid change can put fast-learning firms at a disadvantage by foreclosing opportunities to discover other good alternatives (Levinthal & March, 1981; March, 1988, 1995).

Although the presumption has been that the pursuit of one process inevitably takes place at the expense of the other, in our research, we found that this presumed pattern was not always observed. If the logic underlying the antithetical model is that control and exploration processes involve a trade-off in attention or other resources, then firms facing antithetical situations could either recognize them as such and act appropriately for a zero-sum choice or they could mistakenly think about the situation as involving orthogonal or synergistic relations and, thus, take a course of action inappropriate for the situational attributes. In our research, we found examples of each of these possible courses of action.

The first example concerns a semiconductor equipment manufacturer that faced dramatically increased demand for its products from customers who preferred to get products on time with defects rather than receiving higher-quality products late or in smaller quantities. This firm had been engaged in a significant learning-oriented effort to enhance its production capabilities, focusing not just on capacity and reliability but also on broader exploration capabilities. When confronted with the demands for sheer production volume, it recognized the unavoidable trade-off for managerial attention, staffing, and facility expansion—and chose to abandon its exploratory efforts in the short-term. Company executives told us that they assumed that they would be able to resume exploratory activities when future industry

shifts occurred without hampering their long-term viability. Thus, they recognized the situation as fundamentally antithetical and chose to "re-balance" control and exploration by investing all of their resources in control. They could have chosen otherwise and kept some level of exploratory efforts going, if they had determined that their competitors threatened to be better prepared for the next competitive wave in their industry.

The second example, drawn from a premier hotel chain, concerns the successful transformation of front desk operations at one of its properties. This property, already noted as excellent on nearly all quality indicators and also known as a leading innovator in the chain, developed new arrangements to enhance its quality services and to build the property's organizational capacity for continued learning. In effect, it wanted to pursue synergistic process improvements by melding its reliability focus with its effort to increase individual and subunit learning. To achieve this goal, it implemented self-managing teams throughout the property. Its front desk operation was exemplary among all of the subunits measured across a variety of indicators. Yet success began to have untoward effects, as front desk staff received promotions, were transferred to other units (sometimes to gain broader experience and other times to facilitate transfer of learning from the front desk operation to other hotel subunits), or used success as an opportunity to move on to other personal or professional pursuits. As turnover increased, front desk performance declined (it moved from first place to last place on most performance measures).

Our analysis suggests that the basis for reliability rested in the focused attention and shared knowledge of the front desk team members. The organization failed to realize that the pursuit of learning came at the expense of control. Key leaders anticipated that promotions and transfers would benefit individual employees, other units, and the property as a whole but did not realize that these resource reallocations undermined the single-minded reliability focus that had been the underpinning of the front desk's initial success. Even one transfer would have hurt the operation's reliability but not so much as to be noticeable. However, high levels of turnover pushed to the forefront the degree to which its pursuit of learning in this case involved a direct zero-sum trade-off with its pursuit of control-oriented reliability.

The trade-offs associated with the antithetical condition arise because inadequate resources are available to carry out both processes effectively. The examples cited above suggest that in an ideal world it is desirable to pursue both control and exploration processes. However, when managerial attention, employee knowledge, time to expand human and physical capacity, and other resources are limited, difficult choices have to be made. Thus, a key condition under which antithetical relationships emerge is when control and exploration processes do not need to be actively intertwined, but where they do draw upon common underlying—and limited—resource pools.

Failures of the antithetical approach provide rich fodder for post hoc critiques, which may explain why salient examples of zero-sum trade-offs have been so often alluded to in the past. Antithetical relations have often been associated with negative outcomes; however, in the case of the semiconductor equipment manufacturer, it was the timely recognition and strategic response to an antithetical situation that led to positive outcomes (at least in the short term).

The issues associated with trade-offs between control and exploration raise important implications for researchers (and managers as well). One key issue involves simply recognizing when control and learning are competing for limited resources. In the two cases cited, the key differentiating factor was the extent to which key leaders were able to discern important nuances in the situation they faced. The ability to perceive strategic situations clearly and accurately (Sutcliffe, 1994) may play an important role in appropriately tailoring resource use to the more complex and subtle demands of dual process requirements. Thus, when the two processes are in opposition, the key strategic choice is to determine the most appropriate distribution of critical resources between the pursuit of reliability goals and learning goals.

Second, creatively identifying distributive options and matching them to the politics and cultural norms of the situation are critical managerial skills. For example, as the language of empowerment becomes widely accepted, it can become more difficult to acknowledge those situations where it does not fit, unless leaders can offer other, more culturally acceptable frames for these tough choices. Justice researchers have studied what are referred to as "distributive outcome" situations and have found that acknowledging the validity of opposing claims, treating both losers and winners with respect, and helping to put the tough choices into a broader strategic context can be critically important in gaining acceptance of decisions made under antithetical conditions. Like the distributive situations described by justice researchers, when in antithetical conditions, impression management skills become especially important.

The Orthogonal Perspective on Balancing Processes

The conceptualization of control and exploration processes as orthogonal rests on the assumption of slack resources that permit attention and resources devoted to one type of process not to come at the expense of the other. Much like divisions operating in a pooled interdependence arrangement (Thompson, 1967), where operations and outcomes associated with one do not substantially affect the functioning or outcomes of the other, the two processes may draw on the same resource base but do not need to interact to do so. The distinction between orthogonal and antithetical process relationships hinges on the degree to which pooled interdependency is coupled with resource scarcity or munificence. When resources are scarce, one must make trade-offs in who gets to use the limited resources, and thus antithetical relations arise because resource use by one precludes use by the other. In contrast, when resources are ample, such trade-offs do not need to be made, and the two processes can coexist without interaction or interference.

Even though most past work on control and learning processes has either ignored the balance issue or focused on the antithetical form, there are several streams of related research that can inform an analysis of the orthogonal condition. Perhaps most prominent is the large body of work that has examined the multidivisional organizational form to describe the conditions under which organizations will create quasi-independent operating units or divisions. Whether units are differentiated based on products, geography, or other reasons, the two key factors identified in this work are that the processes used require no coordination, and that there are sufficient resources to accommodate some inefficiencies associated with cross-divisional duplication. These same conditions apply to orthogonal relations between processes.

Several other streams of work are also relevant to our understanding of orthogonal processes. Daft's (1982) notion of "dual core" organizations is also parallel to the orthogonal model's emphasis on the independence of distinct organizational goals and processes. A similar set of ideas is reflected in work on "preservative" acquisitions (Haspeslagh & Jemison, 1991), in which firms recognize the need to keep a newly acquired subsidiary separate because its value comes from its unique processes and perspective, which could be lost if the previously independent organizations fully merged their operations.

Orthogonal relations can be handled either by structurally partitioning control and learning-oriented activities (e.g., by creating a separate R&D laboratory) or by developing the capability to carry out both types of processes and using switching rules to handle the transitions between them. Our first example illustrates how switching rules can enable a work unit to achieve reliability while also pursuing organizational learning. In a high-technology manufacturing company, several cross-functional product development teams designed a process they referred to as "shelf technology" production. Their routine work focused on the design of new products to meet specific internal and external customer needs. However, when opportunities arose to develop new designs that went beyond customer requirements, these design teams recognized that the situation could be constructively seen as an opportunity to de-

couple their customer request-driven efforts from their creation of new product features unrelated to current customer needs. Teams did both kinds of design work but switched their goals and the processes used to achieve them depending upon whether they needed to meet specifications and time lines or "simply" create a preliminary technology or feature to the point where it could be retrieved at a later date. What permitted their creation of shelf technologies was the availability of adequate resources to continue to reliably meet current customer demands, while also allowing teams to explore.

In the second example, a heavy equipment maintenance unit of an educational institution faced the problem of how to proactively handle an expected increase in workload. The popularity of participatory management, self-managed teams, and empowerment seduced the organization's management to adopt a synergistic approach when its previously orthogonal approach was better suited to the situation. The unit was reorganized into a self-managing team, and employees were required to explore new mechanisms to work with external stakeholders while also maintaining timely and reliable service—all while workloads increased and personnel levels stayed the same. The idea was that direct contact with external stakeholders, extensive intragroup interaction, and increased exploration of new ways of organizing their work would improve not only their control over routine tasks but also their exploration and adoption of new ideas and processes. They tried simultaneously to operate a high throughput repair production line and to create a learning organization. The unit's performance declined quickly and dramatically in both reliability and learning terms because members' skills, interests, and task demands were ill-suited to the synergistic approach they had been encouraged to adopt. Service to key customers declined, and team members became so confused and defensive that learning all but ceased. Although the team members had been informed that they could expand their resource base as needed to continue to perform their critical function, they never acted as though these resources were available to them. Virtually all team members reported that the old system seemed very well-suited to the task and was very effective. Unfortunately, they came to blame each other and management for the performance problems rather than ever being able to clearly point to the inappropriate situational diagnosis and linking of orthogonal processes as the root source of their difficulties.

The logic underlying the orthogonal model is that control and exploration processes do not involve any interdependencies and thus do not imply the need for trade-offs. Acting appropriately under orthogonal conditions can take two forms. At a minimum, it involves ensuring that the two distinct processes are understood for what they are and respected for those differences and that sufficient resources are available to allow them to operate independently and distinctly. This may be accomplished by structural partitioning or process switching. If the firm is to gain learning insights across the two distinct processes, it also requires cross-process linkages that permit the diffusion of information and insight without forcing conformity. Thus, the strategic challenge for organizations is to appropriately recognize distinct process capabilities and needs and how those distinctions link to organizational reliability and learning goals. The managerial challenge in such arrangements is to promote a respect for the range of differences implied by distinct processes—because these are often accompanied by different cultures, structures, and personnel—and to ensure that linkages are put in place that transfer critical learning without permitting the desire for hegemony to override the interest in tapping the potential benefits of diversity.

The Synergistic Perspective on Balancing Processes

For the synergistic perspective, greater control and greater exploration are mutually reinforcing in that each process facilitates and contributes to the effectiveness of the other. Table 13.2 portrays the synergistic view as a systems perspective, conceptualizing the relationship in terms of joint optimization across both processes for both the short- and long-term. Whereas both the antithetical and the orthogonal views focus on the core differences between control and exploration and recognize their low level of interdependence, a synergistic view stresses their complementarities and interdependencies.

Brown's (1991) description of "research that reinvents the corporation" at Xerox Corporation highlights how the joining of short-term production problems and long-term, futuristic research can serve to benefit both of these functions by creating a shared sense of pioneering ideas—solutions that simultaneously serve immediate product development problems while also unearthing long-term research problems in fundamentally new ways. A strikingly similar example can be seen in the argument, used by several leading business schools, that engaging leading scholars in teaching and work with organizations in the field serves to fill a unique role by identifying problems and solutions that would not be otherwise apparent to either the scholar or the practitioner. Both Xerox and the universities are using a synergistic logic.

A question to be asked is, How can synergy be achieved? As noted throughout this chapter, reliability and its accompanying performance enhancements are important in the short-term and are often an effective strategy under conditions of stability. But under conditions of change, resilience is typically more important than reliability. However, reliability and resilience are mutually reinforcing. According to *Webster's Third New International Dictionary,* resilience is defined as (a) the capability of a strained body to withstand a shock without permanent deformation or rupture or (b) an act of springing back. Effective coping and adaptability in the long-term rest on the resilience of an organization, its units, and its members.

Research suggests that resilience in individuals is enhanced by experiences that allow for the exercise of judgment, discretion, and imagination; by the ability to make and recover from mistakes; and by observing role models who demonstrate these behaviors (Kobasa, 1979; Sternberg & Kolligian, 1990). The attributes of exploratory processes coupled with control processes are likely to instantiate the conditions necessary to bring about resilience. Control processes often hinge on the co-location of decision-making authority with those who are most likely to have the relevant and specific knowledge necessary to make a decision and resolve a problem (Wruck & Jensen, 1994). At the same time, control hinges on individual training, experience, and the development of specialized knowledge. As individuals gain control over key task behaviors and exercise discretion in performing those behaviors, they develop a sense of competence. As a sense of competence increases, individuals are better able to respond effectively in unfamiliar or challenging situations, and effective action subsequently reinforces a sense of competence. Resilience is an outcome of the self-reinforcing nature of this cycle.

The process underlying resilience at the team and organizational levels is similar and is facilitated as these units come to better understand their collective capabilities, competencies, and identities. Researchers increasingly acknowledge that collective beliefs can have a very positive effect on performance (Wood & Bandura, 1989). In particular, collective beliefs about the efficacy of the group and beliefs about the group's capacity for action (response repertoires) (Sutcliffe & Bunderson, 1996; Weick, 1988) may be particularly important for cultivating resilience and for achieving the synergies associated with control and exploratory processes in the long-term.

The basis for this line of thinking is derived from the idea that it takes a complex sensing system to register and regulate complexity (Weick, 1979). Specially trained, multifunctional teams may develop better sensing and coping capabilities—especially when they perceive that they have the ability to act (Westrum, 1991). As the capabilities for action increase, work groups that perceive many possibilities for action may be better able to grasp variations in their environments. The more an entity sees in any situation, the greater the likelihood that it will see specific changes that need to be made. Jointly believing that a work group has capacity and that this capacity makes a difference reduces defensive perception; allows the members to see more; and, as they see more, increases the likelihood that they will see where they can intervene to make a difference. Explor-

atory processes coupled with control processes build resilience and also enhance longer term capabilities through their effect on registering and handling dynamic and complex decision environments and through their effect on motivation and persistence in handling obstacles and adversities.

Two cases from our data illustrate how to build synergistic capacity and the problems associated with the missed opportunity for synergy. Our first example is drawn from a highly regarded high-technology manufacturing company that was trying to achieve control over complex manufacturing processes while also trying to develop new products and processes. In its fast-moving, highly competitive sector, it was essential that new ideas be leveraged whenever possible to enhance both productivity and innovation. As an advanced practitioner of quality management, this firm was quite skilled at taking even the newest learning breakthroughs and routinizing them to gain maximum benefit. One example of this involved its adaptation of Failure Mode Effects Analysis (FMEA) techniques. In particular, its use of FMEA involved gathering broad, in-house expertise in a single room and applying an especially rigorous analytical process to new product design and launch. Using this approach to product analysis, it created a profile of opportunities and threats as well as a broader range of possible futures. By combining selective elements from its dual arsenals of reliability-enhancing and learning-enhancing tools, it created a process by which both goals could be simultaneously and more effectively achieved. First, it was able to draw on deep knowledge about routine problems in innovative ways by combining routine knowledge from different experts in nonroutine ways. Second, it built the future learning capacities of both the individuals involved and the organization as a whole by creating previously unrecognized knowledge linkages and action repertoires. Finally, these techniques were used to anticipate and resolve specific product problems in a way that enhanced the reliability of product design and process engineering.

The second example illustrates the problems associated with the missed opportunity for synergy. In an office equipment company, efforts to bring the discipline of quality management were applied to training world-class scientists in a basic research laboratory. The company's renowned quality program had led to a strong belief by corporate leaders in the importance of enhancing reliability and control throughout the organization, including the research labs. Historical culture clashes between the laboratory and the corporation's central office had led to a mutual distrust and win-lose approach typical of the antithetical approach. Because both sides (central office trainers and laboratory research scientists) came to the training prepared for a battle, the disruption that followed was surprising only in its intensity (Sitkin & Stickel, 1996). What appeared to be a classical antithetical situation later emerged more clearly as a missed opportunity for synergism. Specifically, it later became clear that the training focused on terminology and analytic techniques that allowed scientists and business managers to communicate more effectively about shared ideas and opportunities. The training program design, once adapted to foster synergism, began to help scientists to see business unit input as an opportunity for novel ideas or problems. In parallel, business unit managers who once saw science as a tax on their profitability began to see the value of more rigorous, data-based decision making and analysis. The situation was potentially synergistic from the outset, but because it was initially viewed in purely antithetical terms, it took nearly 10 years before training could be effectively offered to the laboratory and before scientists and business unit managers could work together constructively.

There is little research examining the competencies, investments, and performance trade-offs of trying to balance the pursuit of both types of processes. However, some recent empirical research is consistent with the essence of the synergistic argument, bolstering the contention that each of the approaches to balance presents a viable option and should be examined and compared more systematically. The strategic challenge in synergistic conditions is to generate insight into the interdependencies associated with the simultaneous relevance of high reliability and highly effective learning, often associated with fast-moving, highly complex situations. For managers facing synergistic conditions, the creation of truly integrative solutions that limit the rejection of one or another process is the crucial but difficult challenge.

Recently, researchers have found that an integrated control/exploration approach to innovation-enhancing processes may be critical for fast and flexible adaptation (Cardinal, 1995; Eisenhardt & Tabrizi, 1995; Henderson & Clark, 1990; Simon, 1995). That is, the acquisition of skills and accomplishments in each domain (control and exploration) appears—at least under some conditions—to enhance the likelihood of succeeding in the other domain. More generally, the resilience of organizations and their members for withstanding change and ambiguity appears to be facilitated by the simple pursuit and balancing of the two overarching processes and associated practices. Thus, firms may need to pursue reliability while simultaneously paying attention to the development of new competencies (i.e., innovation-enhancing processes) if they are to remain viable over both the short and long term.

References

Bendor, J. B. (1985). *Parallel systems.* Berkeley: University of California Press.
Brown, J. S. (1991). Research that reinvents the corporation. *Harvard Business Review, 69,* 102-111.
Brown, S. L., & Eisenhardt, K. M. (1995). Product development: Past research, present findings, and future directions. *Academy of Management Review, 20,* 343-378.
Burns, T., & Stalker, G. M. (1961). *The management of innovation.* London: Tavistock.
Cardinal, L. B. (1995). *Technological innovation in the pharmaceutical industry: Managing research and development using input, behavior, and output controls.* Working paper.
Cohen, M. D., March, J. G., & Olsen, J. P. (1972). A garbage can model of organizational choice. *Administrative Science Quarterly, 17,* 1-25.
Cyert, R. M., & March, J. G. (1963). *A behavioral theory of the firm.* Englewood Cliffs, NJ: Prentice Hall.
D'Aveni, R. A. (1994). *Hypercompetition: Managing the dynamics of strategic maneuvering.* New York: Free Press.
Daft, R. L. (1982). Bureaucratic vs. nonbureaucratic structure and the process of innovation and change. In

S. Bacharach (Ed.), *Research in the sociology of organizations* (Vol. 1, pp. 129-166). Greenwich, CT: JAI.

Dean, J. W., & Bowen, D. E. (1994). Management theory and total quality: Improving research and practice through theory development. *Academy of Management Review, 19,* 392-418.

Denison, D. R. (1997). Toward a process-based theory of organizational design: Can organizations be designed around value chains and networks? In J. Walsh & A. Huff (Eds.), *Advances in strategic management* (Vol. 14, pp. 1-44). Greenwich, CT: JAI.

Eisenhardt, K. M. (1993). High reliability organizations meet high velocity environments: Common dilemmas in nuclear power plants. In K. H. Roberts (Ed.), *New challenges to understanding organizations* (pp. 117-136). New York: Macmillan.

Eisenhardt, K. M., & Tabrizi, B. N. (1995). Accelerating adaptive processes: Product innovation in the global computer industry. *Administrative Science Quarterly, 40,* 84-110.

Epple, D. E., Argote, L., & Devadas, R. (1991). Organizational learning curves: A method for investigating intra-plant transfer of knowledge acquired through learning by doing. *Organization Science, 2,* 58-70.

Hackman, J. R., & Wageman, R. (1995). Total quality management: Empirical, conceptual, and practical issues. *Administrative Science Quarterly, 40,* 309-342.

Haspeslagh, P., & Jemison, D. (1991). *Managing acquisitions.* New York: Free Press.

Henderson, R. M., & Clark, K. B. (1990). Architectural innovation: The reconfiguration of existing product technologies and the failure of established firms. *Administrative Science Quarterly, 35,* 9-30.

Kobasa, S. C. (1979). Stressful life events, personality, and health: An inquiry into hardiness. *Personality and Social Psychology, 37,* 1-11.

Levinthal, D., & March, J. G. (1981). A model of adaptive organizational search. *Journal of Economic Behavior and Organization, 2,* 307-333.

Levinthal, D. A., & March, J. G. (1993). The myopia of learning. *Strategic Management Journal, 14,* 95-112.

March, J. G. (1988). *Decisions and organizations.* New York: Basil Blackwell.

March, J. G. (1991). Exploration and exploitation in organizational learning. *Organization Science, 2,* 71-87.

March, J. G. (1995). The future, disposable organizations, and the rigidities of imagination. *Organization, 2,* 427-440.

March, J. G., & Simon, H. A. (1958). *Organizations.* New York: Wiley.

March, J. G., Sproull, L. S., & Tamuz, M. (1991). Learning from samples of one or fewer. *Organization Science, 2,* 1-13.

Miller, D. (1993). The architecture of simplicity. *Academy of Management Review, 18,* 116-138.

Nonaka, I., & Takeuchi, H. (1995). *The knowledge-creating company.* New York: Oxford University Press.

Ouchi, W. G. (1977). The relationship between organizational structure and organizational control. *Administrative Science Quarterly, 22,* 95-113.

Ouchi, W. G. (1979). A conceptual framework for the design of organizational control mechanisms. *Management Science, 25,* 833-848.

Ouchi, W. G. (1981). Markets, bureaucracies, and clans. *Administrative Science Quarterly, 25,* 129-141.

Perrow, C. (1967). A framework for the comparative analysis of organizations. *American Sociological Review, 32,* 194-208.

Quinn, J. B. (1980). *Strategies for change: Logical incrementalism.* Homewood, IL: Irwin-Dorsey.

Simon, R. (1995). *Levers of control.* Boston: Harvard Business School Press.

Sitkin, S. B. (1992). Learning through failure: The strategy of small losses. In B. M. Staw & L. L. Cummings (Eds.), *Research in organizational behavior* (Vol. 14, pp. 231-266). Greenwich, CT: JAI.

Sitkin, S. B., & Stickel, D. (1996). The road to hell: The dynamics of distrust in an era of quality. In R. M. Kramer & T. R. Tyler (Eds.), *Trust in organizations: Frontiers of theory and research* (pp. 196-215). Thousand Oaks, CA: Sage.

Sitkin, S. B., Sutcliffe, K. M., & Schroeder, R. G. (1994). Distinguishing control from learning in total quality management: A contingency perspective. *Academy of Management Review, 19,* 537-564.

Stacey, R. D. (1992). *Managing the unknowable: Strategic boundaries between order and chaos in organizations.* San Francisco: Jossey-Bass.

Sterman, J. D., Repenning, N. P., & Kofman, F. (1997). Unanticipated side effects of successful quality programs: Exploring a paradox of organizational improvement. *Management Science, 43,* 503-521.

Sternberg, R. J., & Kolligian, J. (1990). *Competence considered.* New Haven, CT: Yale University Press.

Sutcliffe, K. M. (1994). What executives notice: Accurate perceptions in top management teams. *Academy of Management Journal, 7,* 1360-1378.

Sutcliffe, K. M., & Bunderson, J. S. (1996, August). *Competence learned: Developmental processes in organizational teams.* Paper presented at the annual meeting of the Academy of Management, Cincinnati, OH.

Sutcliffe, K. M., Sitkin, S. B., & Browning, L. D. (1997). Perspectives on process management: Implications of research on 21st century organizations. In C. Cooper & S. Jackson (Eds.), *Handbook of organizational behavior* (pp. 207-229). Chichester, UK: Wiley.

Tamuz, M. (1987). The impact of computer surveillance on air safety reporting. *Columbia Journal of World Business, 22*(1), 69-77.

Tamuz, M. (1994). Developing organizational safety information systems for monitoring potential dangers. In G. E. Apostolakis & T. S. Win (Eds.), *Proceedings of PSAM II* (Vol. 2, Section 71, pp. 7-12). Los Angeles: University of California Press.

Thompson, J. D. (1967). *Organizations in action.* New York: McGraw-Hill.

Weick, K. E. (1979). *The social psychology of organizing* (2nd ed.). Reading, MA: Addison-Wesley.

Weick, K. E. (1984). Small wins: Redefining the scale of social problems. *American Psychologist, 39*(1), 40-49.

Weick, K. E. (1985). A stress analysis of future battlefields. In J. G. Hunt & J. D. Blair (Eds.), *Leadership on the future battlefield* (pp. 32-46). McLean, VA: Pergamon.

Weick, K. E. (1988). Enacted sensemaking in crisis situations. *Journal of Management Studies, 25,* 305-317.

Weick, K. E., & Roberts, K. (1993). Collective mind in organizations: Heedful interrelating on flight decks. *Administrative Science Quarterly, 38,* 357-381.

Westrum, R. (1991). *Technologies and society: The shaping of people and things.* Belmont, CA: Wadsworth.

Williamson, O. E. (1975). *Markets and hierarchies.* New York: Free Press.

Wood, R., & Bandura, A. (1989). Social cognitive theory of organizational management. *Academy of Management Review, 14,* 361-384.

Wruck, K., & Jensen, M. (1994). Science, specific knowledge, and total quality management. *Journal of Accounting and Economics, 18,* 247-287.

Chapter 14

Speed and Quality in New Product Development

An Emergent Perspective on Continuous Organizational Adaptation

ANDREW B. HARGADON
KATHLEEN M. EISENHARDT

Now here, you see, it takes all the running you can do, to keep in the same place. If you want to get somewhere else, you must run at least twice as fast as that!
—Lewis Carroll's Red Queen in *Through the Looking Glass*

Now more than ever, managers face the need for speed. At the same time, the recent emergence of the quality movement reflects the recognition that now, more than ever before, quality has become critical to effective competition. Yet from the tortoise and the hare to images of "quick and dirty" solutions, the implicit assumption is that quality and speed are mutually incompatible goals. This assumption holds for all aspects of organizational life, but perhaps nowhere with more acute awareness—and proffered solutions—than in new product development.

Traditionally, speed and quality were seen as trade-offs. The way to be fast was to focus early on a single design concept, minimize the engineering analysis, and engage in less thorough testing, but the result was lower quality. This approach to speed was fine when quality was unimportant. Conversely, the way to high product quality was through longer planning stages, increased analysis, and more thorough testing, resulting in longer project schedules. Again, this approach to quality was acceptable when speed was unnecessary. But ultimately, these approaches fail to recognize the importance of matching speed *and* quality and fail to understand the underlying barriers to achieving both, including lack of confidence, ineffective cognitive processing, and poor conflict resolution. More recently, the answer to achieving both speed and quality in product development lay in rationally laying out the product development process and then compressing or overlapping its component stages. New research, however, suggests that this approach may be nearing its limit, particularly in highly uncertain contexts, and that the next set of answers may lie in fundamentally different understandings of the development process.

The purpose of this chapter is to describe this new perspective, which we term an "emergent model" of rapid product development, in which developers simultaneously achieve speed and quality in their new product development process by using tactics that strengthen their ability to learn quickly and act confidently in uncertain conditions.

New Product Development Speed and Quality

New product development is often the primary means by which organizations adapt themselves to a changing environment (Brown & Eisenhardt, 1995; Dougherty, 1992; Womack, Jones, & Roos, 1991). For instance, Hewlett-Packard transformed from an instruments company to a computer-based one through new product development. Similarly, Intel changed from a memory company to a microprocessor firm through product development (Burgelman, 1991). Yet the pace of technological change and level of competition have increased in recent years to the point where organizations must not only continually adapt by developing new products, they must also do so at a pace that matches the market. For some markets, rapid product development has become a strategic advantage. For others, it is just the price of admission, and many organizations must now be able to develop new products rapidly simply to survive in rapidly changing markets (e.g., Eisenhardt, 1989; Stalk & Hout, 1990).

Evidence for the importance of rapid product development to success is compelling. Vesey (1991) reported on a study of high-technology products, showing that products that were 6 months late in entering the market, but were within budget, earned 33% less over a 5-year period than they would have earned if they had been on time. Entering the market on time, even 50% over budget, reduced a firm's profitability by only 4% for that product. Moreover, fast product development is usually more productive and lower cost because lengthy time in product development tends to waste resources on peripheral activities, changes, and mistakes (Clark & Fujimoto, 1991; Stalk & Hout, 1990).

But speed is no longer enough. To compete successfully today, most organizations must simultaneously achieve rapid *and* high-quality product development cycles. As new technologies and markets emerge, it is no longer sufficient to be the first out of the gate with a cutting-edge, yet flawed product. Quick-fix solutions like reduced testing or lower standards can often backfire because market demands for quality have grown in lock-step with demands for speed (Feigenbaum, 1990; also see Cole, Chapter 4, this volume). This became painfully clear to Intel managers when a bug, or flaw, was found in its Pentium processor after it was released on the market. Although the bug affected only a tiny percentage of its customers, the damage to Intel's reputation was disproportionately larger than it had been for similar mistakes in previous products as news of the mistake spread in "Internet time," magnifying the fallout from that error. But the absence of flaws is not the only measure of product quality. Garvin (1988) outlines eight dimensions of quality—performance, features, reliability, conformance, durability, serviceability, aesthetics, and perceived quality—and many organizations are now often pressed to meet or exceed customer expectations on all dimensions of quality. As a result, without both quality and speed in new product development, organizations stand little chance of competing in rapidly changing environments.

Two Assumptions in Product Development Research and Strategy

But how do project teams reduce development time while maintaining quality products? A great deal of research has gone into answering this question and into creating the many useful insights that have resulted in dramatically increased speed and quality in new product development in many organizations. These increases have come through streamlining the development process, cutting out unnecessary delays, overlapping interdependencies, and increasing the efficiency of the teams and technologies involved. Yet although whole industries have dramatically rationalized their development cycles to improve speed and quality, just as the Red Queen recognized, such tactics no longer provide advantage. As increasing numbers of firms adopt these proven strategies for achieving both speed and quality, where will the new insights come from to compete in the future once the development process is outsourced, compressed, and overlapped to the limit? There is evidence that firms in highly competitive industries are already reaching the limits of this current approach, and a fundamentally new understanding of the product development process has to emerge to guide the next wave of research and strategy.

It is useful, then, to step back and consider some basic assumptions about the product development process that are inherent in traditional approaches. Like Kuhn's (1962) scientific paradigms, these assumptions are part of the underlying framework that has directed *where* we look for influences on product development performance, *how* we interpret and explain what we find, and *what* actions we take to improve the process based on these interpretations. In particular, several assumptions have influenced most attempts to resolve the tension between developing products quickly and developing quality products. One assumption is that product development is subject to rational planning, and a second is that product development is a process of linear problem solving in which developers begin with a broad problem definition and narrow continuously toward a single, optimal solution. These assumptions, as described below, are evident in much of the product development literature and can also be seen as underlying much of the quality movement's approach toward achieving quality and speed in new product development.

The perspective of product development as a rational plan emphasizes that upper management can accelerate development projects without sacrificing quality by carefully planning the requirements of the project and then simplifying the stages of the development process, com-

pressing, overlapping, or arranging them in parallel wherever possible (for a review of this literature, see Brown & Eisenhardt, 1995). Research in this perspective focuses on the product, market, and organizational aspects of successful (and failed) development projects, and it develops recommendations for facilitating early planning and decision making and for streamlining and simplifying the development process (e.g., Clark & Fujimoto, 1991; Gupta & Wilemon, 1990; Millson, Raj, & Wilemon, 1992; Nonaka, 1991; Stalk & Hout, 1990; Womack et al., 1991). This approach has dramatically improved the product development processes of many organizations. Yet rational planning assumes that managers have access to all of the information necessary to make appropriate decisions and plan accordingly and that this information will not change significantly between decisions and their implementation. As the speed and quality of competitors increase, and as uncertainties in markets and technologies multiply, this assumption may reach its useful limits in guiding future development projects.

The assumption that product development follows a linear problem-solving path from problem definition to detailed solution can be seen in some of the earliest work on the development process, stage model research (for a review of this research, see Wolfe, 1994). This approach attempted to divide the product development process into sequential component phases, typically including concept development, product planning, engineering design, detailed design, and pilot production (e.g., Clark & Fujimoto, 1991; Ulrich & Eppinger, 1995; Wheelwright & Clark, 1992b). These stages characterize the new product development process as a sequence of predictable steps in which the development team narrows in on and then defines a single, optimal solution. The stage model of product development has become a central organizing framework for researchers and practitioners alike to look at and talk about the development process (e.g., Clark & Fujimoto, 1991; Ulrich & Eppinger, 1995; Wheelwright & Clark, 1992b). Strategies for increasing speed while maintaining quality include compressing the time of each stage, running stages in parallel, overlapping the execution of successive stages, and rewarding participants for meeting each stage of the accelerated schedules (Eisenhardt & Tabrizi, 1995). Stages are shortened or overlapped through elimination of unnecessary activities, efficient sequencing of remaining activities, and increased investment in predevelopment planning (Clark & Fujimoto, 1991; Cordero, 1991; Gupta & Wilemon, 1990; Rosenau, 1988; Stalk & Hout, 1990; Takeuchi & Nonaka, 1986). Like the assumption that product development can be planned rationally, the assumption that it unfolds in a linear fashion from broad problem to narrow solution, from stage to stage, has enabled significant improvements in the management of the process. However, increasing evidence suggests that there are dangers to following this process when facing uncertain conditions.

As the focus shifted during the 1980s from "inspecting quality in" to "building quality in" to, finally, "designing quality in," the quality movement migrated upstream from the factory floor to address the product development process (Hackman & Wageman, 1995; Juran & Gryna, 1988). Its roots in improving manufacturing processes built heavily upon the same assumptions of rational planning and linear problem solving in organizational processes, particularly in its approaches to identifying and eliminating error by reducing variance in those processes (e.g., Deming, 1986; Ishikawa, 1985; Juran & Gryna, 1988). Following this perspective, simplification and streamlining of work processes are the predominant objectives of quality initiatives in organizations (Conference Board, 1991; Hackman & Wageman, 1995).

In the quality literature, quality and speed are mutually attainable if the development process can be planned and managed to eliminate the time and money spent in costly rework (Juran & Gryna, 1988; Roa et al., 1996). To accomplish this goal, emphasis is placed on investing heavily in the early stages, where product definition and "gate zero" set the initial direction for the project and where managerial control is at its highest (Roa et al., 1996). For example, Quality Function Deployment (or the House of Quality) emerged as a detailed plan-

ning tool that would account for all dimensions of product quality, manufacturing requirements, and customer responses (e.g., Hauser & Clausing, 1988). The quality literature views the later stages of the development process as implementation stages, analogous to a production line, with the goal of zero implementation defects: "get it right the first time." Emphasis during these stages is on conformity to plan and reduced variance in performance. Roa et al. (1996), for instance, recommend that managers rely on the "tollbooth" process, which, at the end of each development stage, reviews a project's status relative to its initial goals and makes a decision to continue or abort the project. Thus, the recent attention that the quality movement has focused on product development has served to reinforce the underlying assumption that it is a process subject to rational planning and linear problem solving.

Yet recent studies of high-technology markets question the assumption that adequate planning and foresight are possible, let alone desired, in markets characterized by shifting needs and technological capabilities (Brown & Eisenhardt, 1997; Eisenhardt & Tabrizi, 1995). The power of rational planning—although appealing and, at times, very effective—has its limits. As Starbuck (1993) and Weick (1995) suggest, it is too easy for managers to forget that "it is what they do, not what they plan, that explains their success . . . and having made this error, they then spend more time planning and less time acting. They are astonished when more planning improves nothing" (Weick, 1995, p. 58). Recent work has also questioned the validity of assuming that the development cycle unfolds in a linear fashion, moving in one direction from broad to narrow in the search for a solution and from concept to detail in the specification of that solution. For instance, Wolfe (1994) argues that the organizing framework provided by a stage model "can be deceiving as innovation is often not simple or linear, but is, rather, a complex iterative process having many feedback and feedforward cycles" (p. 411) (see also Tornatzky & Fleischer, 1990). When development teams are forced into situations demanding highly accelerated schedules or uncommon quality goals, heavy investments in planning and seemingly irreversible decisions may inhibit teams from being open and responsive to information that emerges throughout the development process. Furthermore, failure is being increasingly recognized as a crucial aspect of the learning process in new product development (Leonard-Barton, 1995; Sitkin, 1992; Sutton & Hargadon, 1997). The notion that product development can be planned and managed with minimal error may be dangerous because by avoiding failure, it may also avoid the very opportunities to learn and adapt quickly. As development cycles accelerate, blind assumptions of rational planning and linear problem solving may not only outlast their usefulness, they may also prevent organizations from reaching the next step in rapid, yet high-quality product development.

An Emergent Model of New Product Development

Until recently, linear and sequential decision making and rational planning were recognized as flawed but still viable assumptions in guiding the management of new product development. As uncertainty surrounding development projects increases, however, so do the dangers of assuming that planning is possible and that decisions are final. And more and more organizations are attempting to develop products under these highly uncertain conditions. This uncertainty is a result of the interaction of many factors, including the needs to incorporate the latest technological features, globalize products and operations, and exploit simultaneously economies of scale and customization of products for local markets and even individual customers. Uncertainty has also increased because organizations have achieved faster development cycles and increased the standards for quality, increasing the odds that little mistakes can have large consequences. Small changes in the road ahead mean one thing at 60 miles per hour and something wholly different at 120. The complexities of shifting markets and technologies coupled with the already accelerated pace of product development means that many of to-

day's organizations must rapidly develop quality products under conditions of high uncertainty.

This chapter offers an alternative perspective on the development process, what we are calling the emergent process, that integrates speed and quality under highly uncertain conditions. To do so, we introduce two propositions that replace the past assumptions of linearity and rational planning. First, product development is an emergent process in which new knowledge and understandings unfold through action in an uncertain and shifting environment rather than being planned ahead. Second, this emergent process requires a nonlinear process of problem solving that allows the development team to move flexibly both forward in exploring unforeseen opportunities and backward in revising past decisions and commitments if the new conditions and understandings justify doing so. These two propositions, discussed below, recognize that within accelerated product development projects requiring the highest quality possible, learning and reacting quickly in response to new knowledge and shifting terrain is critical to maintaining both speed and quality.

The first proposition, that new product development is an emergent process, draws upon recent research in a variety of fields, including product development (Brown & Eisenhardt, 1997; Eisenhardt & Tabrizi, 1995; Hargadon & Sutton, 1997; Quinn, 1985; Sutton & Hargadon, 1996), improvisation (Bastien & Hostager, 1988; Moorman & Miner, 1994; Weick, 1993), cognitive psychology (Meacham, 1990; Payne, Bettman, & Johnson, 1988; Sternberg, 1990), and strategic choice (Eisenhardt, 1989; Eisenhardt & Zbaracki, 1992). The key assumption is that the product development process involves navigating through continuously shifting markets and technologies and so cannot be planned. For instance, in high-technology markets, new technologies and new technology standards can easily change between the time a project has begun and when it hits the market. Similarly, a competitor's offerings may devalue the quality, in terms of customer satisfaction, of a new product before it has even been released. As in successful improvisation, the ability to take in real-time feedback from the environment is critical to evaluating past decisions and initiating new action (Bastien & Hostager, 1988; Moorman & Miner, 1994; Weick, 1993). The assumptions of rational planning, although providing structure and direction to the development process, may prevent the team from recognizing changes in the environment that expose the inaccuracies of earlier decisions.

The second proposition builds from the first in arguing that new product development is often a nonlinear process of problem solving. Information uncovered later in the development process may reveal inadequacies in one or more previous decisions that, to maintain quality and speed, require quick and easy revision. Weick (Chapter 7, this volume) describes how, in problem solving, even the problem definition is often uncertain until after one (or more) solutions have been attempted (see also Isenberg, 1985; Starbuck, 1993). In this way, small changes in the understanding of project conditions may have dramatic effects in determining best available outcomes: For example, detailed subsystem design may reveal unanticipated flaws requiring a new system architecture; a key technology may underperform in the field, radically changing the price-performance assumptions of the product; or user testing of advanced prototypes may suggest that the project is solving the wrong problem. To achieve the highest quality and speed under these uncertain conditions, developers must be able to improvise, act quickly based on real-time feedback, and choose the appropriate course of action (Bastien & Hostager, 1988; Moorman & Miner, 1994; Weick, 1993). The assumption that decision making in new product development moves linearly and sequentially from concept and problem definition through detailed design until ultimately narrowing to a single best solution can artificially lock the development team into an increasingly narrow range of alternatives, preventing team members from quickly and easily revising earlier decisions when the next best available solution falls outside of the initial assumptions of the project.

Organizations that repeatedly create innovative product designs, and do so with aggressive development schedules, often share a set of distinctive practices that allows them to achieve

quality and speed simultaneously. These practices reflect the emergent approach to the development process and are discussed below and listed in Table 14.1. The following sections describe, using an emergent and nonlinear perspective, how organizations are able to accelerate the product development cycle while maintaining quality first by looking at actions within a single project and, second, by looking at how these organizations manage a range of products over time.

Managing for Speed and Quality Within a Single Project

Product development projects that have accelerated schedules yet maintain product quality share a number of practices that occur at the project level. These practices include heavy reliance on prototyping, frequent project milestones, the use of multifunctional teams, and strong project leadership. Using an emergent perspective on new product development, we describe each of these practices in detail below.

Prototyping. Prototyping involves building and testing iterations of the product, or component parts of the product, as its design evolves over the course of the project. The common image of a prototype is of a detailed model replicating the finished product, but prototypes can be simple sketches, scale drawings, or rough cardboard and glue models. They can also be finely machined details representing a small but critical corner of the product. The basic purpose of prototyping is to provide a quick, inexpensive way to test a design or a variety of designs.

Prototyping speeds the project schedule by accelerating the learning that occurs throughout the development process (Eisenhardt & Tabrizi, 1995; Leonard-Barton, Bowen, Clark, Holloway, & Wheelwright, 1994). Similar to situated learning (e.g., Brown, Collins, & Duguid, 1989; Lave & Wenger, 1991), learning-by-doing through multiple prototypes is a quicker way to learn than through less participative and more cognitive strategies. In addition, design iterations shorten the process by improving the confidence of development teams. Teams that have

TABLE 14.1 Tactics for Achieving Speed and Quality in New Product Development When Facing High Uncertainty

	Definition	Implications for Speed	Implications for Quality
Within-project tactics			
Frequent prototyping	The building and testing of multiple iterations of the product, or parts of the product, in order to refine the design	• Accelerates learning process through learning-by-doing • Increases decision-making speed and confidence • Facilitates communication	• Improves decision making through testing of alternatives • Identifies problems and misassumptions early in project • Facilitates communication
Short milestones	Structured review points for evaluating the progress and future direction of development project	• Creates opportunities to consider emergent problems and opportunities earlier • Creates sense of urgency and sense of completion • Provides structure to process	• Creates opportunities to consider emergent problems and opportunities earlier in process • Provides formal opportunities for midcourse correction as result of learning
Multifunctional teams	Project team made up of representatives from range of functions necessary for successful design and manufacture of product	• Increases identification and resolution of cross-functional problems earlier in project • Speeds hand-off between functions • Increases commitment to project	• Identifies problems earlier in process, when changes are easier and less costly • Improves identification and evaluation of wider range of alternatives
Strong leadership	Leadership involves setting goals for the project, communicating those goals, and getting the resources necessary to achieve those goals	• Keeps project focused • Provides common goals and values for rapid resolution of conflicts • Provides necessary resources to maintain schedule (e.g., prototyping budget)	• Single vision promotes integrity of product design • Provides necessary resources to ensure quality (e.g., for prototyping, multifunctional team)
Across-project tactics			
Leverage	New products use existing designs, components, and manufacturing processes from organization's past projects	• Speeds development by recombining existing components of past products • Builds on existing expertise in organization • Frees project resources from redundant design work to focus on true innovation	• Builds on well-developed components • Reduces (unnecessary) novelty and risk of project • Focuses project resources on key areas of uncertainty
Technology brokering	Project imports innovative product and process technologies from other industries and organizations	• Speeds innovation by adapting and recombining existing solutions from outside industry or organizations • Accelerates learning and decision making surrounding uncertainty of innovation	• Increases quality by building on well-developed technologies from outside organization and industry • Uses existing technologies, materials, and suppliers
Frequent experimentation	Organization supports a range of development projects, ranging in levels of commitment and completion, to test market and technology assumptions	• Speeds learning and decision making about market and technological possibilities • Increases willingness to attempt smaller, riskier, or simpler products because less depends on each	• Improves decision making by testing alternative product and market plans • Increases ability to rapidly shift resources to more successful projects, reduces commitment to failing options
Modularity	Design strategy that emphasizes modularity in product architecture and common modules across development projects	• Increases speed by early explication of product architecture and components • Allows parallel development of independent modules • Facilitates leveraging of modules between projects	• Increases quality by forcing early identification and definition of product architecture • Facilitates leveraging and brokering to create new combinations of existing modules

337

created multiple iterations will be less likely to procrastinate because they worry that they are missing better alternatives. As a result, they are more likely to settle on a design, or they may have more confidence to revise old decisions in light of conflicting evidence (Eisenhardt, 1989). Frequent prototypes also accelerate development schedules by rendering in tangible form many of the goals and assumptions regarding the product. As a result, misunderstandings or conflicts can be communicated and understood more easily across functional boundaries (Leonard-Barton, 1995; Schrage, 1993).

Not only does prototyping enhance speed, but it also improves the quality of the final design. Prototyping entails building and testing critical aspects of the product early enough in the development cycle to eliminate mistakes and refine the design. Quality improves because multiple iterations continually test the designers' assumptions about the product and, through user testing, the market. Furthermore, judging the worth of any one design iteration is difficult in unpredictable settings. Multiple iterations make such judgments easier because comparing alternatives makes strengths and weaknesses much more apparent (Eisenhardt, 1989; Payne et al., 1988). And prototyping serves to integrate the work of different functional groups, identifying problems early so that resulting solutions can include the perspectives of a wider range of functional groups and even customers (Leonard-Barton, 1995).

Frequent milestones. Milestones represent formal review points that occur throughout the development project. Frequent milestones do not imply comprehensive planning. Rather, they suggest frequent reassessment of the current state of progress (Eisenhardt & Tabrizi, 1995). In this way, milestones act as scheduled interruptions that focus attention on accumulated problems and offer a formal opportunity for their resolution (Okhuysen & Eisenhardt, 1997). Milestones also provide a sense of order and routine that serves as a counterpoint to the more freewheeling and even chaotic activities of iteration and testing that accompany prototyping (Bastien & Hostager, 1988; Weick, 1993).

Frequent milestones accelerate the product development cycle by providing opportunities to recognize mistakes early in the process when they are easier to correct. In contrast, with widely spaced milestones, problems are spotted later, when it is usually hard to readjust. Project progress can stall or go off track because of limited or incorrect direction, and misunderstandings can arise because of lack of communication and coordination of activities among developers. Frequent milestones also shorten development time because they are motivating, both by creating a sense of urgency for developers (e.g., Gersick, 1988) and, in their achievement, by giving people a sense of accomplishment (Langer, 1975; McClelland, 1961; Weick, 1984). In addition, frequent milestones provide a structure to an adaptive process that can fail if it becomes unstructured and chaotic (Waldrop, 1992).

Frequent milestones maintain or improve quality, particularly in uncertain situations, because they are an effective way of checking current progress against evolving understandings of markets and technologies (Gersick, 1994). In addition, program quality benefits when frequent milestones prevent prolonged effort and investment by the developers in one direction that may result in increased commitment toward an inappropriate course of action (Cialdini, 1993; Staw & Ross, 1989). Frequent milestones also increase quality in the final designs by promoting coordination and communication among different parts of the development team through the structured interactions of review meetings and progress reports.

Multifunctional teams. Multifunctional teams are made up of representatives from the range of organizational functions whose expertise is necessary to develop a new product successfully. These teams typically include marketing, design and engineering, and manufacturing but may also include members from finance, field support and maintenance, and even key suppliers or customers. The rationale behind multifunctional teams is to ensure that the experience and requirements of each function are incorporated into the product design early in the process. The use of multifunctional teams reflects the notion that product development does not follow a certain path through the organization, moving sequentially from marketing to design to manufacturing but, instead, is a highly iterative process that continually uncovers and solves problems requiring the knowledge and cooperation of many different functions at the same time.

The use of multifunctional teams is closely linked to rapid product development cycles (e.g., Clark & Fujimoto, 1991; Quinn, 1985; Stalk & Hout, 1990) because the different stages of the development process rely on differing blends of organizational expertise. Problems that arise in the course of product development projects are often the result of conflicts between functions, such as a conflict between features and manufacturability, that are discovered only as the development project unfolds over time. Multifunctional teams, by integrating and linking technical, marketing, and manufacturing activities throughout the project, often discover these problems earlier and resolve them more easily (e.g., Gold, 1987; Imai, Nonaka, & Takeuchi, 1985). Furthermore, involving more functions early in the process reduces the wait time between steps (Stalk & Hout, 1990). The time that it takes to move between design and prototype manufacturing, for example, is likely to be reduced when manufacturing people are already present on the team (e.g., Cordero, 1991; Gupta & Wilemon, 1990; Mabert, Muth, & Schmenner, 1992). Multifunctional teams can also boost project speed by aligning the loyalty and commitment of individuals toward the successful completion of the project.

Multifunctional teams improve product quality while maintaining speed by identifying problems earlier in the process when changes are easier and less costly to fix (e.g., Gold, 1987; Imai et al., 1985). And the solutions generated by multifunctional teams will consider a wider range of organizational needs and take advantage of a wider range of organizational capabilities. Furthermore, Wheelwright and Clark (1992b) describe how multifunctional teams are better able to produce designs composed of components and subsystems that are well integrated, meaning the functions of the product not only fit together but also support one another. In this way, multifunctional teams enable product quality by enhancing overall product integrity.

Strong project leadership. Powerful leadership helps improve quality and speed in product development by keeping the process both supported and focused. Powerful leadership involves setting the goals and values of the development project, communicating those goals, and providing the team with the necessary resources to achieve those goals.

Strong project leadership accelerates the development process because the highly iterative and experiential process of design can easily lose its focus if the product team loses sight of the big picture. Such leadership accelerates the speed of product development by maintaining a disciplining vision that keeps the chaos of experiential product development under control (Brown & Eisenhardt, 1995). A powerful leader is also better able to secure the resources that the team needs to execute the design task and thus maintain speed. Clark and his colleagues (Clark, Chew, & Fujimoto, 1987; Clark & Fujimoto, 1991) have provided evidence for the importance of a powerful leader to the pace of a development project. They used the term "heavyweight" to describe project leaders who report to high levels within the hierarchy, have high status within the organizations, and have direct responsibility for many aspects of the project. They found that projects managed by heavyweight managers had a 9-month advantage over projects run by managers with little influence.

Strong leadership also improves product quality because of the singular vision and values communicated by the leadership. As problems and conflicts emerge through the course of the development project, it is this vision that sets the expectations for quality, communicates the overall values of the project, and determines what trade-offs, if any, can be made. Strong leadership also helps to maintain quality by maintaining the integrity of the product design—how the individual components and subsystems of the product work together (Wheelwright & Clark, 1992b). Strong leadership helps promote this integrity by maintaining the focus of multifunctional teams, by providing direction during the frequent milestones, and by providing the resources necessary to pursue multiple prototypes.

Managing for Speed and Quality Across Multiple Projects

Organizations that consistently and successfully engage in rapid and high-quality product development projects rely on more than the practices described above. These firms also make use of synergies that become visible, and possible, when considering more than one development project. For many firms, product development is an ongoing process involving a range of development projects at any one time and often a sequence of development projects following common product lines or development teams. When looking at the relationships between these projects over time, we have seen successful organizations engaging in a set of practices that exploits potential synergies between projects, such as leveraging past designs, pursuing current technology brokering, and conducting futuristic experimentation. We describe each of these practices in detail below.

Leverage. The idea behind leverage is striking the appropriate balance between exploiting the past and exploring or creating the future (Brown & Eisenhardt, 1997). Often, only one or a few components of innovative products are truly new to the organization; significant portions are existing and relatively well-known components and technologies. Product development teams can gain speed and quality by reusing, or leveraging, these existing designs, components, and manufacturing processes from the organization's past projects for use in new projects.

Leveraging accelerates the product development process by recombining component designs, specific parts, and manufacturing processes that were already established for previous projects. Leveraging also improves speed by exploiting the existing expertise of developers who worked on past projects and are familiar with the existing components and how

those components fit into the larger systems being designed. This experience allows them to rapidly identify opportunities to leverage and to avoid problems that they experienced with these technologies or processes in the past. Leveraging past designs also frees up development team resources that would have been used on redundant design efforts in order to focus on true innovation.

Leveraging supports quality in the development process by creating new combinations of previously developed components. The leveraged aspects of the product have already been developed and tested in previous projects and markets, reducing the uncertainty of how these components will work in the product and how they will be accepted by the market. Furthermore, leveraging increases product quality in the same way it allows for faster projects, by freeing up resources to focus on those aspects of the product that are more complex or that must be new.

Technology brokering. Whereas leveraging describes how developers can reuse existing components from the organization's past projects, technology brokering describes a process of recognizing and adapting technologies from outside the organization and often the industry (Hargadon & Sutton, 1997; Kodama, 1992). Technology brokering allows product development teams to innovate quickly and with quality by building on existing and well-developed technologies, adopting and adapting them to fit new situations in which they *become* innovative solutions. Where development teams do not need innovations, they can save time and improve quality by leveraging past designs; where they need innovations, they can save time and improve quality by brokering those solutions from outside the organization and industry.

Technology brokering helps to create innovative products rapidly because the development team is adopting technologies that are already well developed and in use elsewhere. Firms that innovate through technology brokering often work in a wide range of industries, as consultants or as multidivisional firms, and thus are able to work with and learn about a wider range of technologies than are those firms that work within one or only a few industries. From their position spanning multiple industries, technology brokers are the first to see the opportunities that lie in matching technologies within one industry and market needs within another (Burt, 1992; Hargadon & Sutton, 1997). This reduces time not only in the design cycle but also in locating and managing the manufacturing process because these existing technologies are often already supported by a network of suppliers and other resources. Technology brokering also accelerates development projects because it accelerates the learning and decision making surrounding the uncertainty of innovations. Significant aspects of the innovation are already in use elsewhere, and developers can judge more quickly their technological performance and market acceptance than they can designs that did not explicitly use existing technologies.

Technology brokering, like leveraging, supports quality in the development process by creating new combinations of previously developed components. Many of the uncertainties inherent in developing new technologies can be avoided by adopting and adapting technologies that already exist in other industries. The brokered aspects of the product have already been developed and tested in previous industries and uses, reducing the uncertainty of how these components will be designed and how they will work. By exploiting existing technologies, technology brokering can leverage the expertise and infrastructure of existing manufacturers, materials suppliers, and even customers (Von Hippel, 1988). Furthermore, developers can predict more accurately the technological performance of the innovations than they can designs that were built from scratch.

Both technology brokering and leveraging accelerate new product development without sacrificing quality because they are routines that exploit principles similar to those used by organisms and systems for rapid and flexible adaptation to changing environments. These principles are described by the concept of genetic algorithms, which characterizes adaptation through reproduction as the recombination of existing (and presumably well-developed and successful) traits (Brown & Eisenhardt,

1997; Bruderer & Singh, 1996; Holland, 1992). Creating new product designs by recombining existing and successful components from past products and from outside industries represents a strategy for rapid and effective adaptation because much of the uncertainty surrounding individual components has been reduced through previous use. The uncertainty that remains surrounds the interaction between these components, which can be explored through prototyping early in the development projects because these components already exist in approximate forms.

Experimentation. Organizations that experiment across multiple development projects do so by ensuring that, at any time, a number of projects are exploring new technologies or new uses (Brown & Eisenhardt, 1997; Wheelwright & Clark, 1992a). These experimental projects differ from more central products in a number of ways. First, the primary goal is to provide learning, not revenue, to the organization. Second, these projects are often built from existing modules of other projects with only minor modifications. This allows the organization to rapidly develop alternative configurations while avoiding the costs of a full-blown development project. And third, should these projects prove successful in the market, their innovative features can be recombined and incorporated into more central projects.

Experimentation increases the speed of an organization's product development projects by accelerating the learning and decision-making process surrounding market and technological opportunities. It does so in the same way as prototyping at the project level, providing the organization with learning-by-doing and increasing the communication between functional groups and project teams through real and common experiences. By maintaining a range of development projects and products that test alternative technologies and markets, experimenting organizations develop valuable knowledge and experience (Cohen & Levinthal, 1994). In addition, because experimentation consists of multiple, small-scale products and projects, developers may be more willing to test alternative designs or markets that would be too risky for larger projects. Similarly, without the resources of larger projects, developers must often experiment with many small projects by simplifying the designs and by leveraging past products, both enabling rapid development schedules.

Experimentation increases quality as well as speed by allowing the firm to probe the future, continually testing the firm's assumptions by developing experimental projects and making sense of the shifting market by viewing the results of those tests. Again, like the frequent prototyping that occurs at the individual project level, quality benefits from improved decision making by allowing managers to test alternative product strategies in the market. Similarly, experimentation helps identify technological problems before significant investment is made in full-scale production, and the organization can learn as much information from these failures as from the successes (Sitkin, 1992). Multiple projects are also a way to hedge against the tendency of individual projects to focus narrowly on one of a few technology and market strategies and to have difficulty redirecting themselves quickly. Firms can maintain quality more easily yet adapt to a changing environment by supporting a range of nascent projects and investing additional resources behind those products and technologies that perform well. For example, Galunic and Eisenhardt (1996) observed how one large, multidivisional firm continuously adapted by supporting a range of projects by different divisions, using different technologies, that competed with each other in the market. The decision of which technologies or markets to pursue, and under which division, was made by the market. As one project team or another proved successful, they were rewarded with more resources.

The Pivotal Role of Modularity

Modularity describes the process of breaking products, and projects, into relatively independent components that can be assigned and pursued independently. These independent components become the essential elements in recombination, which occurs when leveraging solutions from past projects or brokering technologies across industry boundaries, and hence exploit the advantages to speed and quality that result from adaptation through recombination. The previous sections described activities that could be parsed neatly between those occurring within a single project and those that build on interdependence between multiple projects over time. The concept of modularity does not fit neatly into this distinction because the benefits that modularity provides occur at both the individual project level and across multiple projects.

Within a single project, modularity describes the ways in which a development project can be divided that allow for the parallel development of different components, or subsystems, of a project. The development team separates subsystems of the ultimate product along those boundaries that have relative certainty. For instance, by determining in advance a small set of dimensions common to the base and display of a portable computer (the hinge and latch locations and overall dimensions), the project team can now pursue each module independently of the other. These modules often have their own prototyping requirements, milestones, and leaders, and themselves can be broken into smaller subsystems. Modularization accelerates product development and improves quality by allowing many tasks to be pursued in parallel rather than sequentially, requiring attention early in the project to the relationships between components, introducing a loose structure to the project that defines areas of certainty and predictable solutions and areas of uncertainty and innovation, and making it easier to drop features to meet schedule.

Across multiple projects, modularity is the practice of ensuring that the components determined by within-project modularity remain common across projects. This not only allows for common processing across parallel development projects but also facilitates using successful modules from past projects in creating new ones. Organizations that manage each product development project as the combination of individual modules can more easily leverage past modules into current projects as well as exploit technology brokering to incorporate features from outside industries to replace existing components. In this way, modularity accelerates the development process by allowing firms to piece together already well-developed modules and strategically direct their innovative efforts to fewer components. It also provides for higher quality by allowing design teams to exploit existing product components or technologies, whether from inside the firm through leveraging or outside the firm (and industry) through technology brokering.

Exploiting modularity across multiple projects depends on an organization's ability to maintain the knowledge and experience surrounding past modules and the ability to recombine these modules in new ways (Brown & Eisenhardt, 1998; Garud & Nayyar, 1994; Hargadon & Sutton, 1997). Organizations that successfully recombine their existing knowledge depend on a number of internal routines for recognizing and sharing valuable knowledge across project teams and over time (Hargadon & Sutton, 1997). For example, one firm depends heavily on brainstorming meetings to bring designers from outside projects together to discuss potential solutions for one project (Sutton & Hargadon, 1996). Larger firms use a range of electronic communication, from e-mail to complex databases of past solutions, to help share knowledge across the firm. And often, teams or individuals with relevant expertise will be reassigned to assist in creating new products that are the new combinations of their past experiences.

A Balanced Approach to Managing for Quality and Speed

Assumptions of rational decision making and linear problem solving have led to significant advances in the speed and quality of the product development process. Yet as uncertainty increases because of shifting technologies and markets, and increased expectations for speed and quality, these assumptions may no longer provide a sufficiently accurate model of the development process. The rise in research depicting product development as an emergent process suggests that further solutions for increasing quality and speed lie in addressing the learning, improvisational, and nonlinear aspects of the development process. To move to the next level, a balance must be struck between the structure of rational planning and linear problem solving, on one hand, and the freedom of learning and improvisation, on the other.

Rational planning and sequential activities provide structure so that people will create sensemaking, avoid procrastination, and be confident enough to act in highly uncertain situations (Brown & Eisenhardt, 1997; Weick, 1995). Yet developers must also recognize that the decisions made and directions chosen are fallible and subject to revision. In this way, successful design teams must maintain an attitude of wisdom, what Meacham (1990) defines as acting with knowledge while simultaneously doubting what one knows (see also Sutton & Hargadon, 1996; Weick, 1993). Developers must be willing to rapidly build intuition and revise past assumptions, particularly when new knowledge and understanding reveals the need to initiate dramatic changes to cope with a changing environment. The emergent model of new product development recognizes the need for balance between planning and learning and between decisions and doubting and that achieving greater speed and quality in new product development results from the right combination of these two approaches.

It should be noted that many of the activities associated with rapid, high-quality product development can themselves become problematic if their contributions to project speed and product quality are pursued without this balance. For example, too much prototyping can be problematic if a rigid and aggressive schedule provides too little time between prototypes to learn from each and revise the design accordingly. Similarly, frequent milestones may distract the development team from the work at hand by requiring team members to prepare and present their work too often, and it may increase the attention to short-term, presentable results at the expense of exploring other potential options. Finally, multifunctional teams, created to reduce the "silo" effect of functional differentiation, can have the opposite effect when development projects become too inward-focused. Team members can lose contact with their functional peers and with opportunities for learning and leveraging from other projects, and competition between projects can become harmful when it leads to different technology and market strategies. These activities contribute to speed and quality when they are managed from an emergent perspective of new product development, with a balanced appreciation, on one hand, for the benefits of planning and structured implementation and, on the other, for the benefits of emergent learning and improvising.

Discussion and Conclusion

This chapter has described an emergent model of new product development that enables fast yet high-quality development projects in the face of uncertainty. The model relies on a perspective of product development as a process of experiential learning, of navigating through a fog of shifting markets and technologies. Two assumptions of product development in the face of uncertainty inform this perspective: that it is an emergent and learning process and that the problem solving that occurs throughout is often nonlinear. Based on these assumptions, we outlined a variety of approaches for achieving both speed and quality in product development at the project and organization levels. At the project level, these include prototyping, frequent milestones, multifunctional teams, and strong project leadership. At the organizational level, we described leveraging, technology brokering, and experimentation. We also described modularity in design, an approach that has benefits both within and across projects.

The increasing market demands for innovative products coupled with the rising expectations for quality at the cutting edge of technology mean that organizations face a greater need than ever before to improve their product development process. The available alternatives range from following the same path and making the same assumptions, but running faster, to revisiting assumptions about the product develop-

ment process and searching for a new path. That new path can reveal a more dynamic model of organizational innovation, one that accounts for the learning and improvisation that occur as the process unfolds.

References

Bastien, D. T., & Hostager, T. J. (1988). Jazz as a process of organizational innovation. *Communication Research, 15,* 582-602.

Brown, J. S., Collins, A., & Duguid, P. (1989). Situated cognition and the culture of learning. *Educational Research, 18,* 32-42.

Brown, S. L., & Eisenhardt, K. M. (1995). Product development: Past research, present findings, and future directions. *Academy of Management Review, 20,* 343-378.

Brown, S. L., & Eisenhardt, K. M. (1997). The art of continuous change: Linking complexity theory and time-paced evolution in relentlessly shifting organizations. *Administrative Science Quarterly, 42*(1), 1-34.

Brown, S. L., & Eisenhardt, K. M. (1998). *Competing on the edge: Strategy as structured chaos.* Boston: Harvard Business School Press.

Bruderer, E., & Singh, J. V. (1996). Organizational evolution, learning, and selection: A genetic algorithm-based model. *Academy of Management Journal, 39,* 1322-1349.

Burgelman, R. A. (1991). Intraorganizational ecology of strategy making and organizational adaptation: Theory and field research. *Organization Science, 2,* 239-262.

Burt, R. S. (1992). *Structural holes: The social structure of competition.* Cambridge, MA: Harvard University Press.

Cialdini, R. B. (1993). *Influence: The psychology of persuasion.* New York: Quill.

Clark, K. B., Chew, W. B., & Fujimoto, T. (1987). Product development in the world auto industry. *Brookings Paper on Economic Activity, 3,* 729-781.

Clark, K. B., & Fujimoto, T. (1991). *Product development performance: Strategy, organization, and management in the world auto industry.* Boston: Harvard Business School Press.

Cohen, W. M., & Levinthal, D. A. (1994). Fortune favors the prepared firm. *Management Science, 40,* 227-251.

Conference Board. (1991). *Employee buy-in to total quality.* New York: Author.

Cordero, R. (1991). Managing for speed to avoid product obsolescence: A survey of techniques. *Journal of Product Innovation Management, 8,* 283-294.

Deming, W. E. (1986). *Out of the crisis.* Cambridge: MIT Center for Advanced Engineering Study.

Dougherty, D. (1992). Interpretive barriers to successful product innovation in large firms. *Organization Science, 3,* 179-202.

Eisenhardt, K. M. (1989). Making fast strategic decisions in high velocity environments. *Academy of Management Journal, 32,* 543-576.

Eisenhardt, K. M., & Tabrizi, B. N. (1995). Accelerating adaptive processes: Product innovation in the global computer industry. *Administrative Science Quarterly, 40,* 84-110.

Eisenhardt, K. M., & Zbaracki, M. J. (1992). Strategic decision making. *Strategic Management Journal, 13,* 17-37.

Feigenbaum, A. V. (1990, March). Management of quality: The key to the nineties. *Journal of Quality & Participation,* pp. 14-19.

Galunic, D. C., & Eisenhardt, K. M. (1996). The evolution of intracorporate domains: Changing divisional charters in high-technology, multidivisional corporations. *Organization Science, 7,* 255-282.

Garud, R., & Nayyar, P. R. (1994). Transformative capacity: Continual structuring by intertemporal technology transfer. *Strategic Management Journal, 15,* 365-385.

Garvin, D. (1988). *Managing quality.* New York: Free Press.

Gersick, C. J. G. (1988). Marking time: Predictable transitions in group tasks. *Academy of Management Journal, 31,* 9-41.

Gersick, C. J. G. (1994). Pacing strategic change: The case of a new venture. *Academy of Management Journal, 37,* 9-45.

Gold, B. (1987). Approaches to accelerating product and process development. *Journal of Product Innovation Management, 4,* 81-88.

Gupta, A. K., & Wilemon, D. L. (1990). Accelerating the development of technology-based new products. *California Management Review, 32*(2), 22-33.

Hackman, J. R., & Wageman, R. (1995). Total quality management: Empirical, conceptual, and practical issues. *Administrative Science Quarterly, 40,* 309-342.

Hargadon, A. B., & Sutton, R. I. (1997). Technology brokering and innovation in a product development firm. *Administrative Science Quarterly, 42*(2), 716-749.

Hauser, J. R., & Clausing, D. (1988, May-June). The house of quality. *Harvard Business Review,* pp. 63-75.

Holland, J. H. (1992). *Adaptation in natural and artificial systems* (2nd ed.). New York: Wiley.

Imai, K., Nonaka, I., & Takeuchi, H. (1985). Managing the new product development process: How Japanese companies learn and unlearn. In R. Hayes, K. Clark, & P. Lorenz (Eds.), *The uneasy alliance: Managing the productivity-technology dilemma* (pp. 337-375). Boston: Harvard Business School Press.

Isenberg, D. J. (1985). Some hows and whats of managerial thinking: Implications for future army leaders. In J. G. Hunt & J. D. Blair (Eds.), *Leadership on the future battlefield* (pp. 168-181). Washington, DC: Pergamon-Brassey's.

Ishikawa, K. (1985). *What is total quality control? The Japanese way.* Englewood Cliffs, NJ: Prentice Hall.

Juran, J. M., & Gryna, F. M. (1988). *Juran's quality control handbook* (4th ed.). New York: McGraw-Hill.

Kodama, F. (1992, July-August). Technology fusion and the new R & D. *Harvard Business Review.*

Kuhn, T. (1962). *The structure of scientific revolutions.* Chicago: University of Chicago Press.

Langer, E. (1975). The illusion of control. *Journal of Personality and Social Psychology, 32,* 311-328.

Lave, J., & Wenger, E. (1991). *Situated learning.* Cambridge, UK: Cambridge University Press.

Leonard-Barton, D. (1995). *Wellsprings of knowledge.* Boston: Harvard Business School Press.

Leonard-Barton, D., Bowen, H. K., Clark, K. B., Holloway, C. A., & Wheelwright, S. C. (1994, September-October). How to integrate work and deepen expertise. *Harvard Business Review.*

Mabert, V. A., Muth, J. F., & Schmenner, R. W. (1992). Collapsing new product development times: Six case studies. *Journal of Product Innovation Management, 9,* 200-212.

McClelland, D. A. (1961). *The achieving society.* New York: Van Nostrand.

Meacham, J. A. (1990). The loss of wisdom. In R. J. Sternberg (Ed.), *Wisdom: Its nature, origins, and development* (pp. 181-211). Cambridge, UK: Cambridge University Press.

Millson, M. R., Raj, S. P., & Wilemon, D. (1992). A survey of major approaches for accelerating new product development. *Journal of Product Innovation Management, 9,* 53-69.

Moorman, C., & Miner, A. S. (1994). *Walking the tightrope: Improvisation in new product development.* Working paper, University of Wisconsin.

Okhuysen, G. A., & Eisenhardt, K. M. (1997). *Creating opportunities for change: How formal problem solving interventions work.* Working paper, Stanford University.

Payne, J., Bettman, J., & Johnson, E. (1988). Adaptive strategy selection in decision-making. *Journal of Experimental Psychology, 14,* 534-552.

Quinn, J. B. (1985, May-June). Managing innovation: Controlled chaos. *Harvard Business Review,* pp. 73-84.

Roa, A., Carr, L. P., Dambolena, I., Kopp, R. J., Martin, J., Rafii, F., & Schlesinger, P. F. (1996). *Total quality management: A cross functional perspective.* New York: John Wiley.

Rosenau, M. D., Jr. (1988). Faster new product development. *Journal of Product Innovation Management, 5,* 150-153.

Schrage, M. (1993). The cultures of prototyping. *Design Management Journal, 4*(1), 55-65.

Sitkin, S. B. (1992). Learning through failure: The strategy of small losses. In B. M. Staw & L. L. Cummings (Eds.), *Research in organizational behavior* (Vol. 14, pp. 231-266). Greenwich, CT: JAI.

Stalk, G., & Hout, T. M. (1990). *Competing against time: How time-based competition is reshaping global markets.* New York: Free Press.

Starbuck, W. H. (1993). Strategizing in the real world. *International Journal of Technology Management, 8,* 77-85.

Staw, B. M., & Ross, J. (1989). Behavior in escalation situations: Antecedents, prototypes, and solutions. In L. L. Cummings & B. M. Staw (Eds.), *Research in organizational behavior* (Vol. 9, pp. 39-78). Greenwich, CT: JAI.

Sternberg, R. J. (Ed.). (1990). *Wisdom: Its nature, origins, and development.* Cambridge, UK: Cambridge University Press.

Sutton, R. I., & Hargadon, A. B. (1996). Brainstorming groups in context: Effectiveness in a product design firm. *Administrative Science Quarterly, 41,* 685-718.

Sutton, R. I., & Hargadon, A. B. (1997). *The attitude of wisdom.* Manuscript in preparation.

Takeuchi, H., & Nonaka, I. (1986, January-February). The new product development game. *Harvard Business Review,* pp. 137-146.

Tornatzky, L. G., & Fleischer, M. (1990). *The process of technological innovation.* Lexington, MA: Lexington Books.

Ulrich, K. T., & Eppinger, S. D. (1995). *Product design and development.* New York: McGraw-Hill.

Vesey, J. T. (1991). The new competitors: They think in terms of speed and market. *Academy of Management Executive, 5*(2), 23-33.

Von Hippel, E. (1988). *The sources of innovation.* New York: Oxford University Press.

Waldrop, W. M. (1992). *Complexity: The emerging science at the edge of order and chaos.* New York: Simon & Schuster.

Weick, K. E. (1984). Small wins: Redefining the scale of social problems. *American Psychologist, 19*(1), 40-49.

Weick, K. E. (1993). The collapse of sensemaking in organizations: The Mann Gulch disaster. *Administrative Science Quarterly, 38,* 628-652.

Weick, K. E. (1995). *Sensemaking in organizations.* Thousand Oaks, CA: Sage.

Wheelwright, S. C., & Clark, K. (1992a, March-April). Creating project plans to focus product development. *Harvard Business Review,* pp. 70-82.

Wheelwright, S. C., & Clark, K. (1992b). *Revolutionizing product development: Quantum leaps in speed, efficiency, and quality.* New York: Free Press.

Wolfe, R. A. (1994). Organizational innovation: Review, critique, and suggested research directions. *Journal of Management Studies, 31*(3), 405-431.

Womack, J. P., Jones, D. T., & Roos, D. R. (1991). *The machine that changed the world: The story of lean production.* New York: Harper & Row.

Chapter 15

Quality Improvement Practices and Innovative HRM Practices

New Evidence on Adoption and Effectiveness

CASEY ICHNIOWSKI
KATHRYN SHAW

I n the past 15 years, employers have increasingly adopted more innovative human resource management practices (HRM) and increasingly adopted quality improvement (QI) practices. Although a great deal has been written about the value of both of these sets of practices, there is very little empirical analysis comparing the effectiveness of these alternative strategies. Moreover, the evidence on productivity effects often comes either from aggregate data, which may suffer from estimation biases, or from case studies that are limited in scope. Our objectives herein are to use a unique data set from the steel industry to evaluate the effectiveness of QI and HRM practices in raising product quality and worker productivity as well as to understand the conditions surrounding the adoption of these two sets of practices.

To evaluate the effectiveness of QI and HRM practices, we made personal visits to steel plants to gather production and management data pertaining to one particular type of production process. The type of production process is a "finishing line" in the steel industry, and we have gathered longitudinal data from 35 lines of this particular type that are owned by 16 different companies. Because these data compare production performance across lines that produce the same product in approximately the same manner, the data are particularly suited for performance comparisons across lines (or across firms). And by obtaining longitudinal time-series data for each line, we are able to examine the conditions that affected the adoption of QI and HRM practices in the steel industry as well as their interactions with the success of these programs. The advantage of this data set is that it bridges the gap between the case study analysis, which obtains evidence for an individual firm, and the cross-firm analysis, which uses surveys of practices and effectiveness.

This chapter is organized as follows. First, we define the terms QI and innovative HRM practices, and then we describe the data set and

AUTHORS' NOTE: This chapter was prepared for the NRC/NSF Workshop on Improving Theory and Research on Quality Enhancement in Organizations, Berkeley, CA, May 16-17, 1997.

347

equations that we use to estimate their impact. Next, the estimated performance effects are presented. Then, we ask the question, are QI and HRM substitutes or complements? Following that, we review the evidence on the sequential adoption of these practices in the steel industry. Then, in the final section, we summarize our conclusions.

What Is the Difference Between QI and Innovative HRM Practices?

The objectives of the two alternative management strategies are quite different, and the mechanisms for implementing the strategies are also different. We describe each in turn, and we summarize the practices underlying these strategies in Table 15.1.

The overall goals of QI are to focus on meeting customer needs by producing a high-quality product, where quality is built in by using continuous process improvement to prevent product defects. This process of quality control differs from the traditional approach of the inspection and correction of defects after production. To achieve these goals, a quality improvement (QI) program should have the following features or practices (Dean & Bowen, 1994, pp. 394-395; Hackman & Wageman, 1995, pp. 312-314):

1. Cross-functional teams to identify and solve quality problems
2. Training in problem-solving skills and in process analysis to enhance team effectiveness by guiding the process of solving quality problems (e.g., flow chart, fishbone diagram)
3. Direct contact with customers to identify customer requirements
4. Statistical methods to monitor performance and identify areas for improvement (e.g., SPC, control charts)

The overall goals of a program of innovative HRM practices are to get workers to work smarter, work harder, make better decisions, and do problem solving both on and off the line.

Thus, a system of the most innovative HRM features should contain the following practices:

1. Enhanced communication and information sharing so that employees understand the impact of their contribution and the effects of changing market conditions and the firm's relative position in the market
2. Careful recruiting and selection to obtain highly skilled workers with the ability and interest in solving problems
3. Flexibility in job design to enable workers to use a range of skills as they do operations jobs, limited maintenance, or problem solving
4. The use of problem-solving teams off the line that enables workers to improve the potential performance of the line by contributing and implementing their suggestions regarding productivity enhancements and cost controls as well as quality improvements
5. Enhanced training in operations, maintenance, interpersonal skills and motivation, and problem-solving skills
6. An implicit offer of employment security so that workers feel as though they are valued and trusted employees and will not "engineer themselves out of a job"
7. Gainsharing, or a multidimensional incentive pay plan, that is a function of many outcomes, such as the quantity and quality of the product, safety conditions, and the profitability of the firm

In Table 15.1, we contrast these two strategies by summarizing the practices that make up the QI and HRM systems, but before examining the contrasting differences, let us consider why these two management approaches could be considered "systems" of complementary practices. To form systems, we posit that the individual practices that compose each system all reinforce one another to reach the overall goals that were stated above for the HRM and QI strategies.[1]

Regarding the QI system, the overarching philosophy of QI is to focus on building in quality rather than correcting defect problems. This philosophy or objective is implemented through the use of problem-solving teams addressing quality issues, training in problem-solving techniques, training in statistical process control,

TABLE 15.1 Practices Underlying the Alternative Strategies

	QI Practice	HRM Practice
Problem-solving teams		
For quality improvement	Yes	Yes
For productivity/cost control	No	Yes
Enhanced training		
For problem solving	Yes	Yes
For improved operator performance	No	Yes
SPC	Yes	Maybe
Customer visits	Yes	Maybe
Employment security	Maybe	Yes
Enhanced communication	No	Yes
Careful employee selection	No	Yes
Job design—enhanced flexibility	No	Yes
Incentive pay plan	No	Yes

and a customer focus. If any one of these practices is eliminated, the value of the remaining practices would diminish. For example, if training in problem-solving techniques is eliminated, the value of team meetings is diminished dramatically. Similarly, if employees do not know the customers' preferences, the value of team meetings that are aimed at solving customer quality problems is diminished. Finally, if SPC techniques are not available to monitor quality, the need for improvements and the impacts of changes are indeterminant. Thus, these practices are complements in the overall system of QI.

Turning to the innovative HRM system, all of the practices listed in Table 15.1 could be considered interactive elements of the innovative HRM system. The reason why all elements are valuable is that they form complements in inducing workers to perform to higher standards both on the production line and off the line in problem-solving teams. Note that one primary element of an innovative HRM system is problem-solving teams, but in this case, these teams tackle productivity problems and cost containment problems in addition to the QI issues. And as workers participate on these teams, other practices are very helpful in designing the optimal HRM system. For example, carefully screening workers to select those who have higher levels of ability and interpersonal

team-building skills for improved performance on teams will enhance production line and problem-solving performance. Moreover, firms would also wish to select workers who tend to be motivated to respond to challenges and to have positive "can do" attitudes. Next, jobs should be designed to incorporate more flexibility in duties, including operators who do some maintenance tasks, and possibly rotation across jobs. Rotation, or greater breadth in duties, provides operators with greater information to bring to the team sessions and further opportunities for synergistic improvements in quality during production work. Employment security raises the levels of trust between operators and managers, introduces a long-term commitment to the firm, and thus increases the value that the individual places on the future of the firm and his or her expectations of receiving future benefits for hard work now. Information sharing offers greater production line information, financial information, and information on market conditions so that individuals will have the knowledge necessary for higher performance on teams and on the line. Greater levels of training will have these same effects.

Finally, gainsharing, or some form of incentive pay, is often a key element of the most advanced HRM system for two reasons. First, gainsharing can serve as an additional motivating force, in addition to the intrinsic factors described above. Second, gainsharing offers employees a WIFM, or "What's in it for me?" outcome. After working hard on the line and in teams, production workers ought to share in the rewards.

Now that we have defined the QI and HRM systems in Table 15.1, note that many practices that are part of the HRM system are omitted from the QI system, or are given "no" designations in the table. These omitted practices could be considered complements to the QI system, but they were not emphasized in the original agenda for the TQM strategy and, therefore, are given "no" designations. For example, a QI program is likely to be more effective when there is enhanced communication. In a traditional environment of low communication, the worker does his or her job with limited information on the productivity or quality of production off the line, the financial performance of the firm, or the characteristics of the market and the competitors. Information sharing is not a necessary part of a QI program, but some sharing would certainly be a very desirable element.

The last practice listed in Table 15.1 is incentive pay, and on this topic, the TQ philosophy has clearly stated that incentive pay plans should not be a part of QI programs (this is especially true of Deming) (Dean & Bowen, 1994, p. 402; Hackman & Wageman, 1995, p. 317). Deming, in particular, felt that the individual worker's motivation for participating in a QI program should originate from the worker's intrinsic motivation rather than from extrinsic rewards. Deming was very much against pay on the basis of individual performance appraisal, believing that the group or system produced superior performance, not the individual. However, other researchers have been less adamant on this point. Moreover, in many applications of QI, including ours in the steel industry, pay for performance is based on group standards, not individual standards, and therefore need not undermine group performance.

Given the differences in QI and HRM that are summarized in Table 15.1, a primary objective of this study is to determine whether QI programs, as they are implemented today, really are complements to the HRM strategy outlined in Table 15.1. If they are complements, it may be wise to widen our description of QI to include more practices than were commonly introduced and to recognize that when manufacturing firms adopt a QI strategy they may find it very wise to introduce more innovative HRM practices.

Overall, our goals are to use these alternative definitions of the QI and innovative HRM systems to address the following questions:

1. How do these two alternative strategies affect production performance? How do they affect productivity and product quality?
2. Do these two alternative strategies act as complements or substitutes? That is, do they tend to coexist as complements, or do some firms choose QI and other firms choose innovative HRM because these two approaches are substitute strategies for maximizing the value of the firm?
3. In considering the introduction of QI and innovative HRM processes, what is the typical, or possibly optimal, sequence of the adoption of these practices, and how do they interact?

These questions are addressed sequentially in the following sections, but first, we must describe the data set.

The Data and the Variable Definitions

Highly publicized case studies of the success of new forms of work organization and employee involvement initiatives have added considerably to the interest in employee involvement among U.S. managers by giving greater credence to the idea that new work practices can help improve economic performance.[2] However, systematic investigations of the effects of innovative HRM practices among larger samples of businesses show more mixed results. Levine and Tyson (1990) provide a review of these studies and show that although some studies do find positive performance effects of Quality Circles, work teams, and other similar measures of employee participation, the overall record on the performance effects of these practices is mixed.

We set out to develop a data set that could be used to do the best possible job of identifying the performance effects of management practices. In the past, researchers tended to use data (on performance) that pertained to either the industry or the firm, but the drawback of these aggregate data is that it is never possible to control for all variables that might affect productivity and also be correlated with management practices. Therefore, we sought to obtain very disaggregate data, pertaining to one particular type of production line, so that we might appropriately control for all variables that could affect performance and HRM or QI usage. Using personal plant visits, we collected a data set on the performance and work practices for a sample of U.S. steel production lines. The data pertain to one very specific type of steel finishing line, and thus, this sample eliminates many sources of heterogeneity that confound attempts to make convincing productivity comparisons with more aggregate industry-level or firm-level data. Through site visits and extensive interviews with managers, production supervisors, and line employees, we collected precise data on performance measures, HRM practices, and the technology of the production lines. The sample used in the analysis includes data from 35 U.S. production lines covering 16 companies.[3] The productivity analysis below is based on a panel sample of up to 2,081 monthly observations—or an average of about 5 years of monthly observations on a given U.S. finishing line. This unique sample of homogeneous U.S. production facilities enables the direct comparisons of productivity differentials, although it clearly suffers from obtaining information from only one industry and one process within that industry.

The Measurement of the QI and HRM Variables

As described above, the data for the QI and HRM variables were obtained by personal plant visits and then by a series of follow-up calls to verify data or to fill in missing data. We must emphasize that the responses regarding these questions refer to the practices that are actually in use on the line, not to practices that may be in use at the plant level. Moreover, our information comes from the area managers, engineers, and HRM specialists whom we questioned (and when discrepancies occurred, we as researchers met to determine the most accurate response based on all of our interview evidence), and data were often validated by archival data. When callbacks were necessary, we called area managers or area engineers.

Table 15.2 displays the mean values of the QI, HRM, and performance variables that are described below. When the variable listed is a dummy variable, no standard deviation is displayed below the mean.

We obtained four measures of QI practices in response to the following series of questions: "Was a total quality management program tried at this plant? What was tried? When was the program tried? Do you think the quality program was successful?" Given an adequate verbal description of some features of the QI program, we created a dummy variable for the existence of a QI program and coded the dates that it existed. In addition, we coded a dummy variable, QI_SUC=1, when the manager felt that the program had been successful, although we made no attempt to code the reasons for the success. Finally, a substantial number of lines had more than one program in existence; therefore, we have two sets of QI variables: QI1 and QI_SUC1 for the first program tried in our data period, and QI2 and QI_SUC2 for the second program tried. Looking at Table 15.2, nearly half of the lines tried a QI program, and of those that tried, about half were judged to be successful.

In separate interviews, we also measured the use of specific practices that would be key elements of most QI programs. These practices (and the dummy variables formed from these) are the use of Statistical Process Control (SPC); the use of customer visits by production workers (CUST); the use of training in team practices or SPC (TEAMTRAIN); and the use of problem-solving teams (TEAM). These variables will be used below to interpret our QI results.

Regarding the HRM variables, based on a very extensive survey instrument, we made the

TABLE 15.2 Variable Means and Definitions

Variable	Mean	Definition
QI variables		
QI1	0.48	First QI program in place
QI2	0.19	Second QI program
QI_SUC1	0.24	Successful QI1 program
QI_SUC2	0.13	Successful QI2 program
TEAM	0.35	Production workers are on some off-line teams
TEAMTRAIN	0.42	Training in team skills (either problem solving, SPC, or other)
SPC	0.35	Production workers use SPC
CUST	0.21	Production workers visit customers
QICHARS	0.58	One or more QI characteristics (TEAM, TEAMTRAIN, SPC, CUST)
HRM variables		
HRM	0.27 (0.58)	HRM index (ranges −1.00 to 1.00)
TEAMHIGH	0.25	High percentage of workers in problem-solving teams
TEAMMANY	0.14	Workers are on multiple teams
TRAINEXT	0.14	Extensive off-line operations training
TRAINLOW	0.22	Low-level off-line operations training
SECURITY	0.30	Job security pledge
INFO	0.60	Information sharing of production or financial information
MEETMAN	0.53	Managers meet regularly with production workers to discuss line performance
ROTATE	0.084	Workers rotate across jobs
FEWJOBCLAS	0.14	Small number of production jobs
RECRUIT	0.09	Careful screening in recruitment
COMPINC	0.20	Company-level incentive pay
GAINSHARING	0.11	Production line gainsharing plan for incentive pay
YEARBUILT	63.07 (10.03)	Year line was built
Productivity variables		
YIELD	0.94 (.041)	Prime yield as percentage of tonnage produced
UPTIME	0.92 (.044)	Time line runs as a percentage of scheduled time

NOTE: Standard deviations are in parentheses. All variables are dummy variables except YIELD, UPTIME, HRM, and YEARBUILT.

decision to focus on 26 key HRM variables that describe the seven practices that were listed in an earlier section. However, our objective is to attempt to measure the extent to which the lines have an innovative environment, an environment that would be conducive to improved employee decision making and performance. Thus, we combine our 26 HR variables to form an index of the extent of innovative HRM use, calling this index merely "HRM."

We used three alternative methods to form our HRM index, and the outcomes of all of the methods were very highly correlated. Two of the methods are multivariate classification procedures: nominate scaling and Guttman scaling.[4] These procedures assume that one or more underlying dimensions are responsible for generating the individual HRM practices at a line, so that the lines can be ranked according to the underlying dimension or dimensions. In the case of our finishing lines, the underlying dimension might be the extent to which lines have introduced progressive HRM practices that are intended to elicit valuable yet hard-to-observe cooperative behaviors from workers. At the high end of this underlying scale will be finishing lines with cooperative labor-management relations and multiple innovative HRM policies, whereas at the bottom end of the scale will be finishing lines with adversarial labor relations and an uncooperative workforce. Our third classification method is simply to add up all of the practices in use and rescale as an index. All three methods use the 26 underlying HRM practice variables, and all three indexes that are developed are very highly correlated. In the work reported below, we use the nominate scale as our most desirable scaling method, but all of the analysis would be unchanged if other scales were used. The index has a range of -1.0 to 1.0, where moving up the index reflects more innovative practices.

The Measurement of the Performance Variables

To test whether management practices raise performance, we require precise data and definitions of performance levels. The steel lines that we include in this sample produce tons of flat-rolled steel using a continuous production process that runs 24 hours a day (except for maintenance periods). The lines take very long sheets of steel that are about 4 feet wide and about 1/8 inch thick and run them through a treatment process. These sheets of steel are so thin that they are coiled in huge, 12-ton coils, and these coils are loaded onto the line at the entry end and are then welded to the sheet of steel that is already running through the line. The steel is then processed through the line, recoiled at the end, and cut. To understand this process, we toured each line with an experienced engineer, area operations manager, or superintendent. These tours gave us a detailed understanding of the nature of the production process, as well as the opportunity to discuss the best ways to measure and compare the performance outcomes of different finishing lines.

The *overall objective of these lines is to produce high-quality tons of steel.* Because this is a very specific production process, we can develop a very specific model of this process. To understand this model, we begin by defining the production of steel tons and then adding a definition of quality tons.

The potential output of tonnage that is produced by the line i in each month t, or output Q_{it}, is a function of three things: the amount of tonnage loaded onto the line, or steel input, I_{it}; the speed of the line, s_{it}; and the number of hours that the line is scheduled to run that month, h^s_{it}:

$$\text{Potential } Q_{it} = \gamma \, (I_{it} \cdot s_{it} \cdot h^s_{it}), \qquad (1)$$

where the quantity in parentheses in Equation 1 is the volume of steel through the line in month t, and γ is an estimate of the density of steel. Thus, the potential output is determined by the capacity of the line (and, therefore, the sizes of coils that are loaded on the line); the speed of the line; and the amount of scheduled running time. All of these factors are a function of the size of the input coil and the nature of the capital or technology on the line, and therefore, innovative HRM or QI practices have relatively little impact on these factors.

There are two ways in which workers can have a significant impact on quality tons produced: They can raise either "uptime" or "prime yield." The actual steel produced on the line differs from potential production defined in Equation 1 because the line does not run during all of its scheduled hours. In particular, the line will stop running because of unscheduled delays or line stops arising from problems on the line, such as equipment failure or poor product quality. Thus, actual tons of production is a function:

$$\text{Actual } Q_{it} = (1 - d_{it}) \qquad (2)$$
$$[\gamma(I_{it} \cdot s_{it} \cdot h^s_{it})],$$

where d_{it} represents delays, or the fraction of scheduled hours that are lost because of unscheduled line stops, and $(1 - d_{it})$ is uptime. Once the technological parameters of the line are specified and coil size is determined by technology and product demand conditions, actual production depends upon the amount of time that the line is running. *Actual production depends entirely on uptime, which is readily influenced by the actions of operators.*

In addition to producing tons of output, steel lines want to produce quality tons. To define quality tons produced by the line, augment Equation 2:

$$\text{Actual quality } Q_{it} = Y_{it}(1 - d_{it}) \quad (3)$$
$$[\gamma(I_{it} \cdot s_{it} \cdot h^s_{it})],$$

where Y is prime yield, or the percentage of tons that come off the line that meet the customer's specifications. All steel produced on these lines is produced for a specific customer—none is produced for inventory. Each particular customer requires a specific steel chemistry (e.g., the extent to which the steel is formable) and a specific surface quality for its steel. When these quality specifications are not met for the intended customer, the lower-quality steel that is produced must either be reworked, placed in inventory for a different customer, or put into scrap. All of these outcomes are far less profitable uses of the steel, and moreover, the loss of the steel does not provide the customer with the product demanded in a timely fashion. Therefore, prime yield is an excellent measure of product quality. Prime yield is measured in percentage terms, with a mean value of about 94% in our data set and a range of 41% to 100%. Therefore, we multiply actual tons off the line by the percentage that is prime yield to get the volume of quality tons that are produced on the line.

Equation 3 demonstrates that there are two primary ways of raising the volume of quality tons that is produced—raise the uptime of the line and raise the prime yield of the line. Therefore, these are our two primary measures of performance. The potential tons that are produced on the line depend on the size and capital stock of the line, so we do not model potential tons.

Models to Estimate the Performance Effects of the Alternative Management Practices

We aim to compare the productivity and product quality gains for two types of practices: QI and innovative HRM practices. Our sample de-

sign, focusing on one very specific type of production process, was developed so that we could make valid production comparisons across companies and lines having very different practices. Thus, we have sought to make our cross-sectional comparisons valid through sample design and extensive control variables. In addition, we have time-series data for each line, which enables us to look at "before-after" effects of QI and HRM practices. These before-after effects have the advantage of controlling implicitly for important, unobserved, line-specific differences, such as managerial quality, and thus we will estimate these fixed effects models to do this, as described below. Note, however, that the cross-sectional analysis remains very important because there is more variation in the data across lines than there is within lines over time and because we have sought to introduce excellent cross-sectional controls. The primary objective of the econometric analysis below is to make the best use of both types of information—of the longitudinal and cross-sectional differences in uptime—and to compare the alternative longitudinal and cross-sectional estimators of the productivity effects of HRM policies.

Empirical Models

The productivity of workers on the line is improved when they find ways of increasing uptime; therefore, our measure of worker productivity is uptime. Increases in uptime will increase tonnage, or productivity. Our model of uptime is the following:

$$UPTIME_{it} = f(QI_{it}, HRM_{it}, \quad (4)$$
$$CAPITALD_{it}, VINTAGE_{it}, INPUT\_$$
$$QUALITY_{it}, MAINTENANCE_{it}) + u_{it},$$

where u_{it} is assumed initially to be independently and identically distributed with mean zero.

The dependent UPTIME variable in Equation 4 is equal to $(1 - d)_t$, measuring the percentage of scheduled operating time that the line actually runs. It has a mean of .928 and a standard deviation of .047 in the sample of 2,081 "line-month" observations used in the empirical analyses. It ranges from a low of .398 to a high of 1.0. The QI and HRM variables are the QI1, QI2, and HRM variables described in a previous section.

Our objective is to measure the impact of management practices, QI and HRM, on worker performance, so in our regressions, we must control for any other factors that might affect performance and could be correlated with the use of the key managerial practices. We have chosen our sample of steel finishing lines because they are very homogeneous lines that all use the same basic process to treat the steel—therefore, we are able to implicitly control for many factors that could affect performance by choosing very comparable lines. However, pieces of equipment on the line may vary across the different lines. Through our on-site inspections of the production lines and our discussions with experienced operations managers, we identified and collected a comprehensive set of data on technological features of the lines that affect their productivity. The prime yield and uptime equations include up to 25 controls for detailed features of the line that affect performance.

The first set of controls in Equation 4 is a set of dummy variables that indicates the presence of specific features of the capital equipment. This vector of dummies, called CAPITALD, is a set of nine dummy variables indicating the presence of specific features of the equipment along the line that could complicate the production process, making delays more likely, or streamlining operations and thereby reducing delays. Also included is a variable for periods when new equipment was being installed on a line, because these periods tend to have relatively high levels of delays, and a dummy variable for the degree of computer automation of the line. VINTAGE measures the year that the line started operations and the current age of the line in period t, because finishing lines with older capital stocks should tend to have more equipment failures. In addition to these measures of vintage, we also include a dummy variable indicating whether the line is in the first 12 months of operations and a 1-to-12 time counter for the first 12 months of operations. Lines just beginning operations have high levels of delays during startup periods. INPUT_QUALITY is an in-

dex of the quality of the steel input. According to people we interviewed, lower-quality steel input tends to cause more line delays. Finally, some lines may have low levels of unscheduled delays simply because they schedule more downtime for maintenance work, and the variable MAINTENANCE measures the number of annual 8-hour maintenance shifts at the line.

The equation for prime yield matches that of uptime:

$$YIELD_{it} = (QI_{it}, HRM_{it}, \qquad (5)$$
$$CAPITAL_{it}, VINTAGE_{it}, INPUT\_$$
$$QUALITY_{it}, MAINTENANCE_{it},$$
$$YDUMMY_{it}) + e_{it} .$$

In addition to the variables in Equation 4, a set of four dummy variables, YDUMMY, is added to control for the five different ways that the firms in our sample measure prime yield.[5]

Econometric Methodology

The econometric models that we will estimate begin with the cross-sectional model, where we merely rewrite Equations 4 and 5 to highlight the econometric methodology.

$$P_{it} = \gamma'M_{it} + \beta'X_{it} + \varepsilon_{it} , \qquad (6)$$

where performance, P, represents either productivity or prime yield, the $\mathbf{M}$ is the vector of QI and HRM management variables, and the $\mathbf{X}$ is the additional set of controls in Equations 4 and 5.

In estimating the impact of management practices on productivity, we want to reduce possible selection biases arising from nonrandom selection of HRM practices. The ideal data set would be experimental data in which the selection of these practices is made randomly. However, without an experimental design that ensures random assignment, we must use our nonexperimental data to mimic the desired experimental comparison. In this section, we describe fixed effects models in light of our concern with nonrandom selection issues.

The most likely reason for the nonrandom choice of the innovative practices versus the less innovative practices is that high-quality lines choose the most innovative practices, where high quality could refer to either better management or better technology. Thus, we introduce an unobserved, line-specific quality variable, α_i, in our performance regression.

$$P_{it} = \gamma' M_{it} + \beta' X_{it} + \qquad (7)$$
$$\alpha_i + \varepsilon_{it} .$$

Estimates of γ in Equation 7 will be biased if we omit the unobserved line-specific determinants of productivity if they are correlated with choice of management practices; that is, if $\alpha_i \neq 0$ and $E(\alpha_i \cdot M_{it}) \neq 0$. For example, if the innovative HRM environment exists only in high-quality lines, then estimates of gam are biased upward if alp$_i$ is omitted. Because the sample contains longitudinal data and information on lines that changed their QI and HRM systems, we can control for this potential source of bias with a fixed-effects specification. This can be expressed as follows:

$$(P_{it} - P_{i.}) = \gamma' (M_{it} - M_{i.}) +$$
$$\beta' (X_{it} - X_{i.}) + (\varepsilon_{it} - e_{i.}), \qquad (8)$$

where the terms subscripted with "i." indicate line-specific time series means

$$(\text{e.g., } P_{i.} = \sum_{j=1}^{T} P_{ij}/T).$$

The fixed effects models also include changes in any X variables that might be correlated with changes in management practices.

The advantage of fixed effects estimation is that it controls for standard types of selection bias that would result if different quality lines adopted different HRM practices. The disadvantage of fixed effects estimation is that it uses only the information from HRM "changers" in estimating the effects of HRM practices. All cross-sectional information is eliminated in the estimation. Recognizing that the information from HRM changers is limited because HRM changes are not common events, the data collection protocol for this study was developed to obtain convincing cross-sectional performance comparisons.

Production Quality and Productivity: Regression Results

The estimated effects of management practices are displayed in Table 15.3 for prime yield (in columns 1-4), and for uptime (in columns 5-8). Fixed effects estimates for Equation 8 and OLS (ordinary least squares) results for Equation 6 are presented for each dependent variable.

Regarding the production of high-quality products, the results of Table 15.3 suggest that QI practices have a positive effect on product quality, as measured by prime yield. Prime yield is unaffected by QI practices in the OLS models, but QI practices raise prime yield in the fixed effects models. Because the fixed effects results look only at changers, these results tell us that lines that introduce QI practices do experience quality gains. The zero QI effects for the OLS models may tell us that QI practices tend to be introduced at "bad" (or below average) lines, so the omitted variable bias of omitting unobserved line quality will bias downward the coefficients on QI. Alternatively, it may be that when comparing across all the lines that have introduced QI practices, there is no average effect arising from their introduction.

Regarding productivity, or uptime, QI practices produce perversely negative or insignificant results. Looking at the results in columns 6 and 8 that contain the HRM variable as well, the first QI program has no effect on productivity, and the second QI program would seem to have a negative effect overall.

Innovative HRM practices have persistently positive effects across all of our regression results, and effects that are more sizable than returns to QI practices. Given the coefficient values for prime yield and for uptime, an increase in the HRM index from the bottom tier to the upper tier implies gains that are more than twice that of QI system effects (for prime yield). Moreover, the OLS and fixed effects results produce essentially the same coefficient values, suggesting that the "controls" in the OLS model seem to be doing a good job of controlling for

TABLE 15.3 Yield and Uptime Regressions

	Prime Yield				Uptime			
	1	*2*	*3* *Fixed* *Effects*	*4* *Fixed* *Effects*	*5*	*6*	*7* *Fixed* *Effects*	*8* *Fixed* *Effects*
	OLS	*OLS*			*OLS*	*OLS*		
QI1	.0027	.0026	.025**	.020**	−.0068**	−.0044	.0064*	.0043
	(.0027)	(.0026)	(.003)	(.003)	(.0028)	(.0027)	(.0035)	(.0036)
QI2	−.0051	−.0033	.014**	.012**	−.0043*	−.0049*	−.013**	−.013**
	(.0027)	(.0026)	(.003)	(.003)	(.0026)	(.0025)	(.003)	(.003)
HRM		.039**		.024**		.015**		.016**
		(.003)		(.003)		(.002)		(.004)
N	1,750	1,750	1,750	1,750	2,081	2,081	2,081	2,081
R^2	.602	.632	.158	.181	.413	.434	.073	.078
SSR	1.1857	1.0971	1.0306	1.0024	2.338	2.2908	2.1013	2.0881

NOTE: Standard errors are in parentheses. The OLS regressions contain 29 control variables for line speed and speed-squared, width and width-squared; and nine variables to indicate specific pieces of equipment; age of piece of equipment; extent of computer control; line-age and line-age squared; startup learning curves; year built and built-squared; input quality; scheduled maintenance; four product market dummies; managerial tenure and tenure-squared; and changes in capital value during the introduction of new equipment. The fixed effects regressions contain 10 of these variables that vary over time within lines.

*Significant at the .05 level; **significant at the .01 level.

unobserved line quality that might affect productivity. The coefficients on the **X** control variables are also virtually the same across the models, implying that the cross-sectional model appears to have a very reasonable set of control variables that proxies for omitted line quality. In particular, *t* tests cannot reject the hypothesis that the coefficients on the **X** variables in the fixed effects model are equal to the corresponding coefficients in the OLS model for 7 of the 10 controls.

To assess the impact of QI on performance, we also asked managers, "Do you think the quality program was successful?" and we find some very interesting results using these responses. Of those lines with QI programs, 55% said that they thought their programs were successful, although this success was not defined by the interviewer.

When the QI_SUC1 and QI_SUC2 dummies, for QI success in each program, are added to the performance regressions in Table 15.4, we find some startling results. Successful QI programs have very positive effects on prime yield (in the OLS and fixed effects models), but they have very little effect on the productivity

outcomes (although productivity does rise for QI_SUC1 in the fixed effects results).

Thus, our regression results corroborate the managers' opinions: Those QI programs that managers thought were successful clearly are successful—product quality rose as a result of the programs. That is, the QI programs labeled a success have much higher prime yields (or product quality), even though our data-gathering process produced no inherent correlation between the managers' responses and the hard data. These results suggest that the managers' views appear to be very accurate, or conversely, that our regression results appear to produce very sensible performance estimates that are corroborated by the managers' views.

The results in Table 15.4 can also be used to compare the average return to investing in QI (represented by the coefficients on QI1 and QI2) to the return to investing in successful QI programs (represented by the coefficients on QI_SUC1 and QI_SUC2). The successful programs raise performance 20% to 50% more than average in the fixed effects regressions, and in the OLS regressions they raise it from zero effect to a positive and sizable effect. Throughout,

TABLE 15.4 Yield and Uptime Regressions: QI Success

	Prime Yield				Uptime			
	1 OLS	2 Fixed Effects	3 OLS	4 Fixed Effects	5 OLS	6 Fixed Effects	7 OLS	8 Fixed Effects
QI1	.0026 (.0026)	.020** (.003)			−.0044 (.0027)	.0043 (.0036)		
QI2	−.0033 (.0026)	.012** (.003)			−.0049* (.0025)	.013** (.003)		
QI_SUC1			.0142** (.0028)	.024** (.003)			−.0032 (.0024)	.013** (.003)
QI_SUC2			.0043** (.0020)	.018** (.002)			−.0011 (.0020)	.001 (.003)
HRM	.039** (.003)	.024** (.003)	.031** (.003)	.010** (.003)	.015** (.002)	.016** (.004)	.015** (.002)	.008* (.004)
N	1,750	1,750	1,750	1,750	2,081	2,081	2,081	2,081
R^2	.632	.181	.638	.212	.434	.078	.432	.076
SSE	1.0971	1.0024	1.0793	0.9633	2.2908	2.0881	2.2984	2.0946

NOTE: Standard errors are in parentheses. The OLS regressions contain 29 control variables for line speed and speed-squared, width and width-squared; and nine variables to indicate specific pieces of equipment; age of piece of equipment; extent of computer control; line-age and line-age squared; startup learning curves; year built and built-squared; input quality; scheduled maintenance; four product market dummies; managerial tenure and tenure-squared; and changes in capital value during the introduction of new equipment. The fixed effects regressions contain 10 of these variables that vary over time within lines.

*Significant at the .05 level; **significant at the .01 level.

the magnitudes of the gains to QI are quite reasonable and yet fairly sizable. The gains imply that mean prime yield will rise from the average of 94% to a range of 95.2% to 96.4% following QI introduction. These are sizable and economically valuable gains.

Given the evidence on QI success, we must wonder, why are some QI programs successful while others are not? This question is explored in the next section as we raise the issue of complementarities between QI and HRM strategies.

QI and Innovative HRM Practices: Complements or Substitutes?

When managers are considering the adoption of either the QI or the innovative HRM approach, they must address the question, "Are these strategic approaches substitutes or complements?" If they are complements, then introducing innovative HRM practices raises the returns to the QI practices, and thus, the manager ought to consider the joint adoption of these practices. In fact, if a manager adopts only the QI system, he or she will not earn the full returns to QI because the returns can be enhanced with the adoption of innovative HRM practices. If they are substitutes, that means that they are distinct approaches and thus can be adopted independently at any time.

If the QI and innovative HRM systems are strategic approaches that are substitutes for one another, then we would expect to see that (a) managers select either one path or the other as they seek to maximize shareholder value; and (b) the underlying practices that support the strategies are distinctly different. As we examine these issues, we want to return to the theoretical question, do the individual elements of a high-performance work system reinforce the

TABLE 15.5 Correlation Matrix

	HRM	QI_SUC2	QI_SUC1	QI2	QI1
HRM	1.00				
QI_SUC2	0.235	1.000			
QI_SUC1	.078	0.036	1.00		
QI2	0.136	0.73	−0.095	1.000	
QI1	−0.002	0.374	0.55	0.510	1.00

objectives of the QI program and thus enhance the value of the QI program? If they do, these practices are complements; if they do not, they are substitutes.

The performance results of Tables 15.3 and 15.4 demonstrate that QI and innovative HRM practices appear to have distinct effects on prime yield and on uptime, *implying that these are identifiably different managerial strategies.* Note that in columns 2 and 4, when HRM is added to the regressions containing QI, there are few changes in the coefficients on the QI variables. If the HRM and QI variables were highly correlated, these coefficient estimates would be unstable because of the multicolinearity, and it would be difficult to label these different strategies.

Although our regression results are able to identify distinct differences in the impact of QI and HRM practices, these QI and HRM systems are positively correlated, as is evident in the correlations of Table 15.5. The second QI program, QI2, is more likely to be put in place with a more innovative HRM system, as indicative of the positive correlation between the QI2 and HRM. And in all cases, *QI programs that are successful, as judged by managers and confirmed by our regression results, are more likely to be joined with more innovative HRM practices* (as shown by the more positive correlations between HRM and QI_SUC1 and QI_SUC2).

The next way of assessing whether the strategies are substitutes or complements is to look at the underlying practices and see whether they are distinctly different or closely overlapping. Thus far, we have looked for empirical correlations between QI and HRM, but as we look at the underlying practices, we are reminded of the theoretical reasons for possible complementarities that were laid out in Table 15.1. In that table, we showed that the QI and HRM strategies are characterized by different practices, but also that the QI practices tend to be a subset of the practices in use in the innovative HRM system.

In Table 15.6, we present the distributions of the underlying practices for the subsamples of the lines adopting the QI strategy versus those adopting the innovative HRM strategy. The four QI subsamples are the QI1 = 1 and the QI2 = 1 subsamples and the two subsamples of successful QI practices. To create the High HRM subsample, we choose those 22% of lines having the highest HRM index value (and thus corresponding to HRM systems for "High Teams" and "Highest HRM" in the next section). The column values show the proportion of the lines having the individual practices (or show the mean values of the dummy variables).

The objective is to compare the theoretical distributions of the underlying practices that were specified in Table 15.1 to the actual distributions of practices shown in Table 15.6. In comparing these two tables, it is quite interesting that the distributions match very closely. That is, the QI systems are highly likely to adopt the four key practices—teams, team training, SPC, and customer visits by operators. In row 11, we construct the variable called QICHARS, which is set equal to 1 when the production line has at least one of the four QI characteristics listed in the lines above it. The means for QICHARS show that 91% of QI2 lines have one

TABLE 15.6 The Distribution of Individual Practices Underlying the QI Strategies[a]

	1	2	3	4	5	6
Variable	Entire Sample	QI1 = 1	QI2 = 1	QI_SUC1	QI_SUC2	HIGH HRM
YIELD	0.94	0.93	0.94	0.93	0.93	0.95
UPTIME	0.92	0.91	0.92	0.91	0.93	0.93
QI1	0.48	1.00	1.00	1.00	1.00	0.42
QI2	0.19	0.40	1.00	0.14	1.00	0.29
QI_SUC1	0.24	0.50	0.18	1.00	0.27	0.15
QI_SUC2	0.13	0.27	0.66	0.14	1.00	0.29
Underlying QI variables						
TEAM	0.35	0.48	0.70	0.34	0.69	0.76
TEAMTRAIN	0.42	0.47	0.61	0.45	0.92	1.00
SPC	0.35	0.50	0.72	0.38	0.73	0.87
CUST	0.21	0.27	0.49	0.21	0.74	0.49
QICHARS	0.58	0.74	0.91	0.70	1.00	1.00
Underlying HRM variables						
TEAMHIGH	0.25	0.26	0.30	0.33	0.45	0.92
TEAMMANY	0.14	0.15	0.26	0.052	0.39	0.63
TRAINEXT	0.14	0.18	0.31	0.11	0.46	0.65
TRAINLOW	0.22	0.23	0.33	0.21	0.50	0.92
SECURITY	0.30	0.27	0.49	0.020	0.38	0.45
INFO	0.60	0.52	0.68	0.40	0.67	0.74
MEETMAN	0.53	0.58	0.81	0.54	0.86	0.86
ROTATE	0.084	0.094	0.093	0.19	0.14	0.26
FEWJOBCLAS	0.14	0.050	0.070	0.10	0.11	0.50
RECRUIT	0.09	0.00	0.00	0.00	0.00	0.42
COMPINC	0.20	0.19	0.32	0.24	0.48	0.69
GAINSHARING	0.11	0.00	0.00	0.00	0.00	0.53
YEARBUILT	63.07	62.60	64.55	61.78	64.61	72.18
Sample size	2,081	993	399	499	265	450

a. The columns show the proportion of each subsample that has adopted the relevant practice.

or more of these practices, and 100% of QI_SUC2 success lines have one or more of these practices.

However, the lines with the QI strategies are much less likely to adopt the HRM practices. Relative to the High HRM system, the QI systems have lower levels of training; less widespread team use; more job classes and less rotation across jobs; and, most important, very little incentive pay.

Of course, in looking at the last column for the High HRM subsample, it is not surprising to see that most of the lines in this subsample have adopted most of the underlying HRM practices.

After all, the High HRM systems category was formed by looking for large numbers of underlying HRM practices. However, this is not true of the QI systems. These systems were designated "QI plans" from managers' responses, not from examining underlying practices. Thus, it is very revealing that they do line up so well with the practices designated by the theory.

On the basis of Table 15.6, we see that the QI strategy and the High HRM strategy appear to be quite distinct strategies and thus would appear to be substitutable strategies as managers choose their preferred approaches. However, the correlations data in Table 15.5 implied that there is some positive correlation between the adoption of these two alternatives, suggesting perhaps that they are often complements. To resolve this issue, we turn to a discussion of the adoption of QI and HRM strategies in our data.

The Sequential Adoption of Alternative Management Practices

The question that we are addressing in this section is, What can we learn about the adoption of HRM and QI practices that will enhance our understanding of the interactions between these two systems? We begin with evidence from our plant visits and then look at the distributions in the data.

To obtain our data and to understand the functioning of the QI and HRM systems, we personally visited 45 production lines that form the basis for this study. These visits are especially helpful to us in understanding the adoption of practices, because adoption is inherently difficult to measure or to model. For example, given our 5 years of data (on average) for 35 lines, some of these lines will change their practices, but many will not. Thus, we cannot reach conclusions about adoption by observing lines going through a series of practices over time. Instead, we must combine the evidence that we have from lines that change practices with the evidence that we have on the reasons for the distributions of practices across lines.

On the basis of our interview information, we reach three conclusions regarding adoption that are supported by the distribution of the practices across lines. Before showing the distributions, we state our observations:

1. In older brownfield facilities, the adoption of a QI strategy is often the first step toward the adoption of more innovative HRM practices over time.
2. In older brownfield facilities, the success of a QI strategy raises the probability of adopting innovative HRM practices.
3. In new greenfield facilities, the adoption of a formal QI strategy is unlikely; instead, an informal QI strategy is completely embedded in the larger, innovative HRM strategy.

These points emphasize the differences between "brownfield" and "greenfield" facilities, which we define somewhat differently from most. In our sample, brownfield facilities are those with an older plant and an existing workforce, whereas greenfield facilities are those with a new workforce and either an old or a new plant. The distinguishing factor is the tenure of the workforce, not the production line, because lines with new workforces can readily introduce new personnel practices as they hire the workers. Brownfield facilities must bear heavy transition costs to change personnel practices, and that is why we claim that QI is a first, transitional step.

For supporting evidence regarding these three points, turn to the distribution of practices in Table 15.7. This table shows the distribution of the underlying practices for four HRM systems: Traditional (having no innovative practices); Information Sharing (focusing on information sharing with some very low-level use of teams); High Teams (having very high worker involvement in all types of teams); and Highest HRM (having all the practices of High Teams but adding forms of incentive pay). These systems were formed by looking for natural breakpoints in our innovative HRM index.[6]

To compare greenfield to brownfield lines, the bottom row in Table 15.7 shows the proportion of the lines that are greenfield for each

TABLE 15.7 The Distribution of QI and Individual Practices Underlying Innovative HRM Systems[a]

Variable Name	HRM System			
	Traditional	Info Sharing	High Teams	Highest HRM
QI1	0.36	0.60	0.71	0.00
QI2	0.062	0.25	0.50	0.00
QI_SUC1	0.20	0.32	0.25	0.00
QI_SUC2	0.01	0.14	0.50	0.00
TEAM	0.01	0.43	1.00	0.41
TEAMTRAIN	0.01	0.45	1.00	1.00
SPC	0.01	0.41	0.65	1.00
CUST	0.01	0.24	0.55	0.41
TQCHARS	0.01	0.84	1.00	1.00
HRM	−0.31	0.44	0.78	1.00
TEAMHIGH	0.01	0.11	0.86	1.00
TEAMMANY	0.00	0.00	0.79	0.41
TRAINEX	0.00	0.00	0.83	0.41
TRAINLOW	0.00	0.045	0.86	1.00
SECURITY	0.01	0.47	0.057	1.00
INFO	0.59	0.53	0.55	1.00
MEETMAN	0.01	0.80	0.76	1.00
ROTATE	0.00	0.063	0.15	1.00
FEWJOBCUTS	0.00	0.063	0.15	1.00
RECRUIT	0.00	0.00	0.00	1.00
COMPINC	0.01	0.10	0.46	1.00
GAINSHARING	0.00	0.00	0.19	1.00
YEAR BUILT	57.86	62.74	71.05	73.76
GREENFIELD	0.00	0.00	0.40	1.00
Number of observations	729	902	263	187

a. The columns show the proportion of each subsample that has adopted the practices, except for the YEARBUILT and HRM rows, which display the mean values.

subsample. Looking at those numbers, we see that all of the Highest HRM lines are greenfield; 40% of the High Teams lines are greenfield; and the other, less innovative HRM systems have no greenfield lines. (Although not displayed, note that only 12% of the lines having QI practices are greenfield lines).

The evidence supporting Point 1 above is shown in line 1 of Table 15.7: QI is very clearly one of the first practices that is adopted by lines having Traditional HRM systems. What is most startling is that this is nearly the only practice adopted by Traditional lines. As we move up the HRM systems progression, QI adoption grows until it reaches 71% for High Teams in column 3. A QI strategy certainly seems to precede movement to the innovative HRM, as described in Point 1, in that the rates of early adoption of QI are much higher than the adoption rates of HRM practices.

Regarding Point 2, successful adoption of QI clearly leads to the adoption of a more innovative HRM system. Looking at column 3, among the High Teams system, 25% were successful with their first QI program, and 75% were successful with the second QI program. These rates of success clearly exceed the success rates of the less innovative HRM systems in columns 1 and 2. Our interview evidence reinforced this point: Having produced documented success with a quality program, line managers and production workers were ready to move on to the next innovation. Note also that failure with a first QI program that was poorly supported could be followed by success in a second program and then lead to innovative HRM adoption.

Regarding Point 3, the data in column 4 show that the lines with the Highest HRM have no QI programs, and our interview evidence explains this odd fact. All of the lines in the Highest HRM system are greenfield lines, and at startup, the owners or managers made the decision to make QI one element of their overall management strategy (an element that is essential for success but that is embedded in their overall HRM strategy). All of these lines emphasize a quality focus and attention to the customer. But in addition, they choose to develop complementary policies that encourage workers to work smarter as they make decisions on the job and to focus on productivity and cost reduction as they solve problems off the line. All of these lines use SPC and team training practices, but their formal and informal teams focus on a range of topics in addition to their quality emphasis. Note, though, that not all greenfield lines have taken this approach. Those lines that adopted the High Teams approach at startup are more likely to have a QI program.

The points made here describe QI as a first evolutionary step toward the adoption of more participatory work practices. The key question is, Why was QI the first step? There are two reasons. First, managers became aware of the TQM strategy before they became aware of the participatory HRM approach, simply because TQM was the first strategy that readily migrated from Japan to the United States (for a description of TQM migration, see Cole, 1999). Second, QI was the easiest strategy for steel plants to adopt, and it readily addressed an acknowledged problem: the need to raise quality. QI was the easiest to introduce because it introduced only marginal changes in workplace practices, requiring that workers meet off line and be trained in new problem-solving skills. It did not require extensive training, the sharing of financial information, job rotation, or the recruitment of different types of workers. It provided a shared goal of solving problems that all could acknowledge, and solving those problems would not entail the reduction of employees (as productivity problems might). Therefore, for some, it became a first step toward successful change.

Finally, we return to the question, Are QI and innovative HRM strategies complements or substitutes as managers select strategies? The distribution of practices shown in Table 15.6 suggested that they are substitutes because QI systems clearly have a set of distinct practices. However, in that table, we also see that the QI practices are used by the higher HRM systems, thus accounting for some positive correlation between the QI and HRM strategies in Table 15.5. Moreover, our analysis of the evolutionary adoption of these practices suggests that QI and HRM are complements. Steel lines begin by adopting QI because these practices are essential elements of a broader strategy of participatory management. This is true for our Highest HRM lines, where a QI philosophy is informally embedded in their participatory practices, and it is also true for our High Teams lines, where QI teams are clearly a formal part of that HRM system.

Although our analysis suggests that lines in our particular sample of steel producers would gain from movement up the HRM hierarchy, it is unlikely that all lines will overcome the costs to such movement. It is costly for brownfield lines to overcome entrenched practices and make such moves, particularly if they involve the negotiation of incentive pay. Others have pointed out that the longer a firm is involved with QI practices, the greater the likelihood that it will adopt incentive pay schemes (Hackman & Wageman, 1995, p. 318). Our sample results are certainly consistent with that conclusion.

Conclusion

In this study, we examined the adoption and effectiveness of QI and innovative HRM practices in a sample of steel finishing lines. The advantages of using this sample are that we obtained excellent production performance data that are likely to be very comparable across lines in the analysis of performance differences and that we could visit all of these steel plants, thus providing a very detailed understanding of this environment. The drawback, of course, is that the narrow focus might not produce conclusions that are applicable outside the steel industry, although the general nature of our results suggests to us that they could be very applicable in much of heavy manufacturing.

Using these data, we first examined the effects of QI and innovative HRM practices on production performance, and we reached the remarkable conclusion that QI practices do raise production quality but have little effect on worker productivity. Thus, we found evidence that QI programs do what they set out to do—raise product quality. Moreover, when managers identify their QI program as successful, they are correct: These programs do produce higher product quality. We also found that more innovative HRM practices raise product quality as well as worker productivity.

Given these results, the question naturally arises, Are QI and HRM strategies complements or substitutes? Our initial evidence suggests that they are substitutes. The practices underlying QI—teams, team training, SPC, and customer focus—are clearly in greater use by QI programs than they are by innovative HRM systems, and innovative HRM systems intro-

duce many practices that are not adopted by QI programs. Thus, the strategies appear distinct.

However, as we examined the patterns of adoption, we concluded that QI and participatory HRM are often complementary strategies. Among older brownfield facilities, QI is often a first step that, if successful, leads to the adoption of more general participatory practices. Among newer greenfield facilities, QI is often informally embedded in an extensive system of innovative HRM practices. Thus, it would seem that the key practices that form a QI system are an integral part of an innovative HRM system, so that at some level, the two are indistinguishable. However, the all-encompassing emphasis of QI—to build in quality to meet customer needs—is just one element of the innovative HRM set of objectives.

Notes

1. See Hackman and Wageman (1995), Dean and Bowen (1994), and Lawler, Mohrman, & Ledford (1992), and the original sources of the QI agenda cited therein (Deming, Juran, and Ishikawa).

2. For example, one of the most widely cited cases is that of the NUMMI plant in Fremont, California. Various analysts document dramatic improvement in productivity and quality after the introduction of Japanese organizational practices (Krafcik, 1988; Womack, Jones, & Roos, 1991).

3. In total, we visited 45 U.S. lines at 22 different locations. Four of the 45 U.S. lines visited had only recently begun operations or had not yet started operating and so could supply no productivity information. Of the remaining 41 lines, 36 could provide comparable information for estimating the performance models. Subsequently, one of these lines went out of business and could not answer our callbacks.

4. See Ichniowski, Shaw, and Prennushi (1997) for further description of these methods.

5. Because we enter four dummy variables, the yield regressions are effectively fixed effects regressions comparing the effects of the X variables within the set of lines that measures yield in the same manner. Of course, when line-specific fixed effects are entered later, these dummy variables cancel in the regressions. The four different dummies have to do with different ways of measuring scrappage or reworks.

6. See Ichniowski et al. (1997) for further description.

References

Cole, R. (1999). *Managing quality fads: How American business learned to play the quality game.* New York: Oxford University Press.

Dean, J. A., Jr., & Bowen, D. (1994). Management theory and total quality: Improving research and practice through theory development. *Academy of Management Review, 19,* 392-418.

Hackman, J. R., & Wageman, R. (1995). Total quality management: Empirical, conceptual, and practical issues. *Administrative Science Quarterly, 40,* 309-342.

Ichniowski, C., Shaw, K., & Prennushi, G. (1997). The effects of human resource management practices on productivity. *American Economic Review, 87,* 291-313.

Krafcik, J. (1988). Triumph of the lean production system. *Sloan Management Review, 30,* 41-45.

Lawler, E. E., III, Mohrman, S. A., & Ledford, G. E. (1992). *Employee involvement and QI: Practices and results in Fortune 1000 Companies.* San Francisco: Jossey-Bass.

Levine, D. I., & Tyson, L. D. (1990). Participation, productivity and the firm's environment. In A. S. Blinder (Ed.), *Paying for productivity: A look at the evidence.* Washington, DC: Brookings Institution.

Womack, J., Jones, D., & Roos, D. (1991). *The machine that changed the world.* New York: Harper & Row.

Chapter 16

The Incentives of Quality and the Quality of Incentives

Quality Improvement and Incentive Pay for Frontline Workers

KATHRYN SHAW

O ver the past 20 years, firms have increasingly realized that it usually pays to build in quality. That is, it is more profitable to build quality into the product during production than it is to rework the product after production or to accept rejects from customers (and thus lose customers). As a result of these changes, quality levels have risen across most industries, and some fairly standard procedures have been developed to monitor and improve quality—procedures such as statistical process control and the use of problem-solving teams. Nevertheless, programs for continuously improving quality vary widely. In this chapter, we address the role that group-based financial incentives can have in supporting quality programs.

In the early years of the modern quality movement, little attention was given to financial incentives. In fact, the most common recommendation was that incentive pay be avoided.

As summarized below, incentive plans can have many undesirable effects. At the same time, quality programs make a number of demands on frontline workers and provide them with increased autonomy to raise or lower company performance. Given these changes, team-based incentive can often be important complements to other elements of a quality program.

Before turning to our analysis, we must address this question: Why are we focusing on the connection between quality programs and incentive pay? One reason is that quality programs are embedded in much of modern manufacturing (and other sectors). Many early Total Quality Management (TQM) programs had mixed success, perhaps, in part, because of insufficient attention to incentives. At the same time, the philosophy of building in quality has become widely incorporated in the mission statements of firms. These quality programs differ widely among workplaces and over time.

AUTHORS' NOTE: Comments from Bob Cole and the participants of the National Science Foundation Workshop on Integrating Social Science Theory and Research in Quality Improvement are gratefully acknowledged.

367

An underlying theme of our analysis is that quality initiatives are constantly evolving; moreover, incentive pay is now increasingly introduced as an important element of newer quality plans.

This chapter analyzes the value of incentive pay in a quality improvement (QI) environment. We describe the ways in which incentive pay plans can raise the effectiveness of QI but also emphasize that in some environments the costs of adding a pay plan outweigh the benefits. We begin by defining our terminology, and in the next section, we outline the problems of traditional incentive pay schemes. Then, we turn to explanations of ways that carefully designed incentive schemes can address many of these problems. In addition, the principles of the quality movement can help solve problems within incentive pay plans. In the next section, we provide evidence that incentive plans and quality programs can be complements and raise performance. However, we conclude by pointing out that many organizations have not yet adopted incentive pay either because the costs outweigh the benefits or because they are slow to make this transition.

Defining Terms

What is "incentive pay"? Given our focus on quality programs, we discuss incentive pay plans that relate a portion of employees' pay to the quality of the output produced (as well as a function of other factors, such as measures of creativity). The four most common forms of incentive pay in workplaces with quality programs are (a) quantity-focused incentives, in which pay is a function of the volume of the output that is of a certain quality level; (b) gainsharing, in which pay depends on the quality and quantity of output and a set of other factors, such as cost reduction or safety; (c) profit sharing, in which the returns from quality improvements are assumed to translate into higher profits; and (d) team-based bonuses, in which sizable bonuses are paid for achieving quality and other targets. In all cases, we are referring

to incentive pay that is team based rather than arising from individual evaluations.

We focus on the motivation of frontline workers in a manufacturing environment or other environment with repetitive work (e.g., customer service representatives). In these settings, most variation is not within an individual worker's control; thus, individual assessments are less common and less valuable. In addition, quality programs have their longest history of use in settings where many tasks are repetitive.

Thus, we do not discuss incentives for product design or for managers. Moreover, we do not discuss incentives for skill acquisition such as pay-for-knowledge, although these pay plans can be important for the success of a quality program (Ledford, 1991). We also give little emphasis to symbolic incentives such as awards, although we acknowledge their value in many cases. We do not address the incentives that the product market can provide when a plant is more likely to maintain employment if quality improves. To the extent that job security has declined, the incentives provided by the threat of layoffs may be increasingly important. Finally, we ignore individual-level incentives and the role that innovative versions such as 360-degree reviews can play in a quality-oriented workplace. All of these incentives can be important, but we are limiting the scope of this chapter.

What is a "quality program"? The quality programs we discuss are based on an ever-evolving philosophy of organizationwide efforts for quality improvement (QI), a set of management principles and structures, and/or a set of problem-solving tools (Cole, 1995). There is no single definition of "the quality movement" that captures all of its dimensions. What all the definitions have in common is a belief in continuous improvement based on employee involvement, the tools of statistical process control and other means to analyze data, and an organizationwide quality focus. All versions of QI stress that the quality and innovation goals of the organization must be taken as seriously as the quantity goals stressed by traditional U.S. management. Because QI by construction stresses continuous improvement, including of itself, QI has a dynamic aspect that leads any single definition to become obsolete over time.

Check the Numbers: The Adoption of Incentive Pay

Before turning to the various reasons why incentive pay can add to a quality program, consider first the empirical evidence on the adoption of incentive pay. After all, one indication of the value of incentive pay is whether it is increasingly being adopted, and if so, by whom. Several recent surveys show fairly low levels of adoption in the past. At the same time, most evidence indicates that adoption rates are rising. (These findings are all tentative because the surveys largely had only modest response rates, included nonrandom sample of firms, and relied on self-reports from a single informant.)

In a 1993 national survey of large employers, those with active TQM programs were not disproportionately heavy users of innovative reward programs (Lawler, Mohrman, & Ledford, 1995, p. 57). The survey covered four dimensions of innovative human resource practices: training, information sharing, employee empowerment through Quality Circles and other participation groups, and reward programs. Employers who reported that they had implemented TQM programs had, as expected, more training, information sharing, and employee involvement than did other employers. In contrast, they had virtually identical amounts of innovative rewards programs such as profit sharing and team-based pay. A smaller survey of 56 American companies also found no relation between quality programs and "progressive" compensation practices such as team-based pay, group incentives, skill-based pay, and an all-salaried workforce (Waite, Newman, & Krzystofiak, 1994).

Other recent studies find a positive correlation between some forms of incentive pay and a flexible, team-oriented work environment. For example, in 1992, Paul Osterman surveyed establishments with 50 or more employees and obtained a response rate of 66% (for a sample

size of 875) (Osterman, 1994). He found that about 55% of establishments used TQM, 50% of manufacturing plants used teams, and 45% of manufacturing plants used both TQM and teams. Regarding pay practices, more than 45% of establishments had some form of group incentive pay plan (profit sharing, bonuses, or gainsharing). In addition, the correlation between these pay plans and the use of flexible work practices (including teams) was significantly positive for the practices that are most prevalent. Similarly, 32% of the respondents to a 1992 survey of the British Institute of Management who reported that they had an active TQM program also reported that quality indicators were included in their bonus or performance measurement system (Snape, Wilkinson, & Redman, 1995).

Several authors have pointed out that incentive pay is increasingly a part of a quality program. In their review assessment of TQM, Hackman and Wageman (1995) state that "a large majority of organizations using TQM modify their performance measurement and reward systems so that achievement of specific quality goals can be assessed and rewarded" (p. 317). They rely on a Conference Board Survey finding that 85% of TQM organizations have developed such programs. Hackman and Wageman conclude that "the longer an organization has been involved with TQM, the greater its reliance on incentives to motivate work toward quality improvement goals" (p. 318). This claim was based on a 1991 Peat Marwick survey that found that 60% of organizations with 5 or more years of TQM experience explicitly rewarded the achievement of quality goals using group-based rewards. Similarly, a survey of 130 companies conducted by the Council for Continuous Improvement and the Wyatt Co. finds that roughly one fifth of all respondents were planning to adopt skill-based pay, team-based pay, or a group-based pay plan (profit sharing, gainsharing, or stock-based awards) (Labbs, 1994). For skill- and team-based pay, these plans for adoption are much higher than current rates of usage (Lawler et al., 1995). A 1992 survey by the American Quality Foundation and Ernst & Young also found that although 16% of responding companies emphasized overall quality in senior management assessments, respondents expected that proportion to rise to 58% in the near future (Willett, 1993; see also Snell & Dean, 1994).

These survey results all date from 1992 or before, and all practices are likely to be more prevalent today, although they are not likely to be in use in the majority of firms. Osterman reports that in his 1992 survey 71% of the TQM programs had been introduced in the 5 years prior to his survey. Anecdotal evidence from case studies or smaller surveys suggests that adoption rates continued to grow in the 1990s.

The Original Quality Movement Ignored or Rejected Incentive Pay

The early proponents of the modern quality movement tended to either ignore or reject the use of incentive pay.[1] The reasons varied by author; here, we briefly summarize their main points. Although these critiques apply to all workplaces, the first four are particularly relevant to workplaces that are transforming to a quality emphasis. Following our summary of these critiques, in the next section we discuss the potential value of incentive pay in quality programs.

You Get What You Pay for

The early authors on TQM were concerned that some forms of incentive pay were too effective and, therefore, should be avoided. For example, if the incentive scheme rewarded workers for tons of output produced, the firm would get rising tonnage levels but at the cost of reductions in many other dimensions of performance, such as quality. The incentive can also undermine the goal of using problem solving to raise quality.

If the incentive system is based on a supervisor's performance evaluation, it is possible to reward quality as well as quantity, but individ-ual evaluation undermines the teamwork that is necessary for a quality improvement process. Moreover, if a company rewarded reported quality, individuals would be punished for divulging defects. (MacDuffie, 1995, gives case study evidence of the problems of rewarding measured quality in auto plants.) Substantial case study evidence suggests that simple incentive schemes often have these undesirable side effects.

Because incentive plans were often subject to these problems, quality gurus such as Deming and Crosby recommended the elimination of incentive pay. Their critique of narrow incentive plans held extra urgency because the move to a quality-oriented environment implied that the proportion of value that was correlated by quantity (as opposed to quality and innovation) was declining.

Creativity: Extrinsic Incentives Can Hurt

Some writers focused on their preferred methods of motivating workers, called intrinsic incentives, and gave little attention to extrinsic motivators, such as financial rewards. Theories of intrinsic incentives posit that people have an innate desire to produce work of which they are proud. In many workplaces, quality improvement programs offered frontline workers their first opportunity to produce work and show initiative. Quality programs offer employees the personal satisfaction of solving problems successfully as well as the recognition among their peers for having succeeded. Thus, quality programs motivate by offering employees respect and the opportunity to make a difference.

Moreover, pay plans that emphasize extrinsic rewards have the potential to "crowd out" intrinsic motivation. In a number of studies, people paid to solve puzzles were less creative and worked less on the puzzles during their free time than did people who were not paid for the task (Calder & Staw, 1975; Deci & Ryan, 1985). As creativity became integrated into the job description of even assembly-line workers, this critique of extrinsic incentives became increasingly important.

BOX 16.1: AT&T Universal Card Case[2]

Management at AT&T decided that outstanding customer satisfaction would be the hallmark of its new credit card subsidiary, Universal Card Service (UCS). To achieve this goal, they instituted a thorough and complex system of performance measurement. The system measured market outcomes such as customer satisfaction. In addition, it included dozens of workplace outcomes such as courtesy (as measured by trained quality inspectors listening in) and the time required to pick up calls. These measures were selected because management believed that they led to customer satisfaction. Measures were reported, and problems were addressed daily. Incentive bonuses for the workforce were tied to achievement of 90% of the goals each day.

This system led to rapid achievement of the customer satisfaction goals, winning the Baldrige quality award, and phenomenal growth in market share. Employee satisfaction remained fairly high, in part because of high pay.

Initially, many workers were unhappy because low scores on measures such as courtesy, as measured by a quality staff, were recorded in the worker's permanent file. This source of dissatisfaction was lessened when low performance was considered an opportunity to learn and was not recorded individually. In addition, over time, frontline workers (not the quality staff) had more involvement in measuring courtesy.

When goals were routinely met, became obsolete, or were discovered not to be relevant, management wanted to change the goals. Changing the goals involved raising the bar (changing the level of an existing goal) or dropping old goals and adding new ones.

Employees correctly perceived that either of these changes would reduce take-home pay. They resented such pay cuts. The result was that the company stopped updating its goal levels or mix. At the end of the case study period, AT&T Universal Card Service enjoyed high levels of customer satisfaction but had a stagnant pay system that was not motivating innovation or continuous improvement.

Output Restriction: Ratchet Effects Arise

In some settings, incentive plans have the perverse effect of causing workers to attempt to restrict output. The reason for this is that many pay plans have a ratchet effect: Once the goals are met, the goals are raised. For example, in piece-rate settings, this is reflected in lower rates per piece (see the references in Levine, 1992). Juran (1988), for example, emphasized that employees sometimes do not want to share their "knacks" with engineers or managers. In general, output restrictions arise when the workers have more information than managers and behavior cannot be perfectly observed (Gibbons, 1987). The desire to restrict output is amplified if employees feel that higher productivity may lead to layoffs. (The AT&T Universal Card Service example, Box 16.1, describes how a company with a quality focus ran into trouble when it tried to ratchet up the quality goals.) As with the previous problems, the emphasis on continuous improvement in workplaces with active quality programs made the problem of output restriction increasingly important.

"That's Not My Job": Reward Performance Outside an Individual Worker's Control

The quality gurus Deming and Juran both stressed that many incentive pay schemes provided incentives for dimensions of performance that were largely outside the span of control of the individual employee (see Juran, 1988, and Scholtes, 1990, on Deming). Both objective schemes, such as piece rates, and subjective schemes, such as merit pay based on supervisors' subjective performance ratings, often reward outputs of the system not controlled by the worker.

"Incentives" of this form lead to payments that are largely random. This randomness increases risk, which most workers do not like. Most employees also perceive this randomness to be unfair. Once again, in the move to continuous improvement and systemwide changes implied that in a quality-oriented workplace, the already low fraction of variation accounted for by individual attentiveness and exertion would further decrease.

Free Riding: Low-Power Incentives Result From Team-Based Pay

A natural response to the problem of rewarding performance within a worker's or workgroup's span of control is to reward group performance. Typical plans include plantwide gainsharing or profit sharing. These plans also can reward multiple dimensions of performance such as product quality, further improving the fit with a QI philosophy.

Unfortunately, these plans can give rise to free riding. Free riding occurs when each employee recognizes that he or she has an individually rational incentive to exert little effort in response to the incentive, because he or she can free ride on the hard work of others. Moreover, when these schemes incorporate quality and other goals, they become increasingly complicated, which can lower their effectiveness.

Bundling: Incentives Can Improve the Quality Program

The concerns just raised need to be addressed when considering the adoption of an incentive

plan, but they need not be fatal. In fact, well-designed incentive plans can largely overcome these concerns so that the incentive pay serves as an important complement to the QI program. In this section, we discuss the complementary nature of incentives and the QI program, first with some general comments and then with some direct rebuttals to the concerns raised above. Our rebuttals offer some key reasons why incentive pay should be considered.

The prescriptive literatures on organizational design typically emphasize the importance of aligning the rights to make decisions with incentives to make good decisions. This premise reappears in the prescriptive compensation and employee involvement literatures (e.g., Lawler et al., 1995); expectancy theory in psychology; exchange and work design models of sociology and organizational behavior (e.g., Pfeffer, 1994); and the rational models of economics, agency theory, and transaction cost economics (e.g., Wruck & Jensen, 1994). The move to a quality-oriented organization involves substantial changes in decision-making rights, as frontline employees collect more data, analyze it, and suggest and implement improvements. *Thus, the design of the incentive plan should change to address the new design of the organization. Specifically, managers should modify incentives to align frontline workers' goals with their new authority—that is, to reward quality and improvement.*

The arguments presented above weaken the case for incentives, and several arguments noted below strengthen the case for incentives. At the same time, we find the goal of aligning incentives with decision making and information to be a sensible starting point.

An additional value of incentive plans is that they enable the manager to substitute "motivation" for "control." In a traditional environment of hourly pay, workers have never played an active role in problem solving, and they often do not trust managers and do not believe that managers value their input. Thus, when a QI plan is introduced, employees may have little desire to participate in the plan and often do not respond to intrinsic incentives. As a result, the manager needs to "control" the employees to achieve participation in QI plans—the manager needs to require their attendance at meetings and to monitor their behavior. Such control is antithetical to the QI concept of voluntary employee participation. Thus, in firms that have difficulty in enticing QI participation and would not want to control it, an incentive scheme can provide the motivation that eliminates the need for behavioral controls.[3]

Finally, in designing appropriate incentives, it is important to recognize that the effectiveness of the incentive can depend critically on what other human resource (HR) practices are also in use and what QI practices are in use. This complementarity between pay and quality practices is part of a larger set of complementarities among HR practices that researchers have identified (Milgrom & Roberts, 1995).

HR practices can complement one another for a number of reasons. Consider the firm that is planning to introduce off-line problem-solving teams for the frontline employees. Under what conditions are these teams most likely to be effective? First, when employees are well-trained in both technical and problem-solving skills so that they can offer good suggestions and can work well in problem-solving sessions. Second, when employees have information about the financial and production sides of the firm so that they understand the context in which they solve problems and are motivated to do so. Third, when they tend to rotate across different jobs so that they see a variety of viewpoints and alternative approaches and can present a fresh approach to a new job. Fourth, when they have been hired through careful screening so that they have the basic technical and interpersonal skills that are needed for problem solving. Fifth, when they have some job security so that they do not feel that their suggestions can engineer them out of a job. And finally, when they have appropriate forms of incentive pay so that they will have the additional motivation to perform well in their problem-solving sessions.

This example suggests that adoption of one practice can enhance the return to other practices. This example spans multiple innovative HR practices: enhanced training, information sharing, job rotation, careful selection of employees, employment security, and incentive pay. Although each of these practices may be costly, and thus each firm will not adopt all of the practices, there are some very basic reasons for complementarities. (Levine, 1995, and Ichniowski, Shaw, & Prennushi, 1997, review the theory and evidence on complementarities.)

This section provides theoretical arguments concerning why quality programs and incentive pay can have similar complementarities. For each topic below, we make the argument that *properly designed* incentives can result in strong complementarities between incentive pay and the quality program (see Ichniowski and Shaw, Chapter 15). Then, in the next section, we emphasize that the quality program can be used to develop a better incentive pay plan.

You Get What You Pay for: How Multifactor Incentives Can Help

In traditional manufacturing workplaces, workers are rewarded for the quantity production off the lines, such as tons of steel. These incentives can undermine quality by encouraging workers to skimp on maintenance and to ignore problems that reduce quality.

As a result, firms are shifting to multifactor incentives, or gainsharing, in which workers are rewarded for many factors, such as product quality, reduction of customer rejects, safety, and cost reduction. If it is not possible to choose so few factors, profit sharing may be desirable (although the problem with it is that profits vary with factors that are beyond a worker's control, such as the business cycle). Such plans can readily be developed to focus on product quality, and thus to enhance the QI program. For example, at NUMMI, rewards exist for plantwide levels of productivity and quality measured both within the plant and based on customers' responses. (NUMMI is a Toyota-GM joint venture that has been widely cited as one of the exemplary quality improvement programs in the United States; Adler, Goldoftas, & Levine, 1998.) Rewarding both quantity and quality reduces many of the perverse incentives of focusing on only one of these. Boxes 16.2 and 16.3

Box 16.2: The Evolution of Pay Systems in the Steel Industry

As conditions in the U.S. steel industry have changed over time, the optimal pay plan has also changed. The traditional union contracts in the industry were developed in the 1940s during the period of rapid steel demand. In these contracts, jobs were divided into specific job classes for the determination of base pay. At the time, managers supported the use of job classes in order to identify the routines required for volume production. In addition to base pay, incentives were paid for tonnage off the line. Once again, at the time of high demand for steel, tonnage was the driving factor.

In the 1990s, pay plans have evolved to focus more heavily on the quality of output and on other dimensions of production performance. The integrated steel industry now focuses its production on flat-rolled steel (as compared to bar products) where high quality is essential, because the steel is often produced for the automobile and appliance markets. As a result, incentive pay remains a substantial portion of take-home pay, but the focus is on the production of quality tons rather than simply volume of tons. At the same time, integrated producers have been increasingly adopting QI practices over the past 10 years or more. The QI programs often offer recognition awards (such as gifts or prizes). In addition, most QI programs also increase employee pay in the short run and in the long run, when lines hit their goal of increasing tons of high-quality production on the line.

---

describe the evolution of incentives in steel plants, from a narrow measure of tons produced to more complicated plans.

Creativity: How Incentive Plans Can Help

In the early quality movement, proponents emphasized the power of intrinsic rewards that come from doing a good job and therefore result in more creative problem solving. Moreover, they noted that these intrinsic incentives can be crowded out by extrinsic incentives.

These trade-offs are important because organizational success is usually a function of multiple inputs (e.g., attention to quality, creativity, and effort) and multiple outcomes (e.g., productivity, product quality, innovation). Because the relationship between inputs (such as creative suggestions) and outputs (such as quality) is complex, workplaces with active quality programs should reward both inputs and outputs. And, because many inputs and outcomes cannot be measured well at the individual level, plans should reward both individuals and workgroups. To reward inputs, firms often

choose to use bonuses, gifts, or awards offered for successful suggestions or successful team projects (Knouse, 1995). Although firms are traditionally less likely to offer gainsharing plans than to offer recognition rewards, a multifactor incentive plan can complement the traditional plan: one rewards outputs and the other rewards inputs. Thus, rewards for creativity, such as team awards, can readily coexist with rewards for outcomes that come from extrinsic pay plans.

In addition, extrinsic pay plans can be valuable in addition to the intrinsic or symbolic rewards that motivate many people to be creative. The reason is that *people are heterogeneous.* Whereas some people respond best to intrinsic rewards, others are more responsive to financial rewards, perhaps because they are less wealthy or have more expenses, or because they are simply motivated by different factors. Moreover, each individual may also respond to different incentives on different days. On some days, the recognition is the primary goal, whereas on others (as near Christmas), the bonus is important. Thus, heterogeneity in individual tastes suggests that firms should offer a variety of incentives in order to make a quality program most

---

Box 16.3: Gainsharing in the Steel Industry

Charter Steel is a minimill steel company that is known for its innovative QI and human resource practices and its gainsharing plan. The company is a privately held, nonunion steel mill located in Wisconsin that employs 650 people. The practices that it has introduced have evolved over time.

Charter's gainsharing plan makes pay a function of five factors that reflect the contribution of three divisions. The number one factor is safety (as measured by reduction in OSHA case rates), and the second is quality (as measured by reduction of customer claim dollars). The other three factors are measured by division and combine cost reduction with improvements in productivity (adjusted for quality). This pay plan was developed by a cross-functional team composed of members from different levels of the company. Most important, it made use of the quality improvement procedures that were already in use in the plant: the training in team processes and the team facilitators.

The gainsharing plan is constantly evaluated and updated through the ongoing use of the Gain Sharing Maintenance Team. Their job is to evaluate the factors in the plan and to update them as needed. Moreover, perhaps a larger element of their job is to communicate the details of the plan and its performance to current and new employees. They do so through ongoing orientations and team meetings.

The Charter plan is not unique and is not limited to a nonunion environment. Other steel companies that have adopted similar gainsharing plans include North Star Steel and IN-KOTE and IN-TEK, both of which have worked with the United Steel Workers of America to develop their plans.

---

successful.[4] Moreover, employees who value monetary rewards will recognize that creative problem solving will raise those monetary rewards in the long run.

For example, at NUMMI, the rewards for plantwide levels of productivity and quality are complemented by rewards for suggestions, whether these suggestions are made by an individual or by a workgroup. Virtually all assembly-line workers have their name on at least one suggestion each year. This number is biased upward by the fact that groups of workers or low-level managers sometimes put the name of a worker on a suggestion even when he or she made little contribution. Moreover, not all of the suggestions require high levels of creativity. Nevertheless, the near-universal participation suggests that creativity norms can be enhanced by a well-run quality program, and that recognition programs can coexist very successfully with incentive pay plans (Adler et al., 1998).

Output Restriction: Targets Can Have Build-in Improvements

Standard incentive programs lead to the ratcheting up of goals and to output restriction by frontline workers.

Fortunately, incentive pay plans can be designed so that employee pay rises naturally over time as performance rises. One obvious pay plan is to make pay a linear function of quality of production, so that as it rises, pay rises continually. If it is difficult to set the initial goals to be both challenging and achievable, then it may make sense to institutionalize the ratchet in a way that is consistent with a philosophy of continuous improvement. That is, it makes more sense to reward improvement with a bonus based on, say, percentage decline in defects than it does to set an absolute goal and then reduce the goal the following year. Although these have similar material incentives in the long run, the former does not appear to punish improvement, whereas the latter reeks of the bad faith that so often led to output restriction in traditional incentive plans.

The principles of continuous improvement can also be built into the incentive system by focusing goals in terms of improvement or in terms of metrics relative to ever-increasing competition. For example, at NUMMI, bonuses are based in part on high relative scores in the J.D. Powers measures of initial customer satisfaction. As competitors improve, NUMMI must improve as well. This incentive minimizes the ratchet effect and promotes high effort.

In some cases where it is difficult to find a naturally rising goal, the problem-solving process can be used to agree on a fair process for setting goals and updating them, and for informing workers in advance of the changes, as discussed in the next section on bundling.

Aligning Jobs and Incentives: Reward Aspects Inside a Workgroup's Control

Pay plans that reward on the basis of variables that are largely outside the workers' span of control will lower workers' expected value of pay, will be perceived as unfair, and can be less effective. Moreover, in environments where employees come from a tradition of fixed incomes, it is much harder to implement incentive pay plans because the new plans will tend to retain a significant portion of base pay that is not at risk. The drawback with such an outcome is that employees will then respond less to the plan because the incentives are small.

Fortunately, incentives can match the broader span of control found in a quality-oriented workplace. Well-designed incentives focus on the factors *within a workgroup's span of control*. In a QI workplace, workers have more control over the entire production process than is true in a traditional workplace that lacks quality improvement teams. In such a setting, pay for performance is typically both more effective and more likely to be considered fair, and thus will enhance the QI objectives.

Moreover, in a QI environment, gainsharing may be perceived by workers as very desirable. A successful quality program can save a modest-sized company millions of dollars, leading to higher rewards for managers (through salary, bonus, and stock options). There is both theory and evidence that frontline employees will find this allocation of the benefits of their effort and ideas as unfair, and that they are likely to withdraw effort from the quality program (Cowherd & Levine, 1992). Much has been written about how extrinsic incentives can crowd out intrinsic incentives; at the same time, lack of extrinsic incentives leading to perceptions of inequity can also hurt both creativity and intrinsic motivation. When employees work hard to increase the performance of their unit, they expect to see their compensation grow as well.

Free Riding: QI Employees Who Value Incentives Will Reduce Free Riding

Free riding occurs when an incentive pay plan applies to a large group of workers, so that each individual worker has little impact on the payout and thus has an incentive to get by on the effort of others.

The good news is that workplaces with effective quality programs often have peer pressure that can reduce free riding.[5] Group incentives offer employees monetary rewards for their effort. As described above, members of QI teams often put extra effort into their team activities, effort beyond that required for their day-to-day jobs. In exchange for the extra effort, employees often want to share the rewards. They will ask managers "What's in it for me?" (WIFM). When group-based incentive systems are offered to distribute rewards for effort, the QI frontline employees have every incentive to punish free riders, so the incentive pays out for the extra effort.

Moreover, an environment that is supportive of QI is also an environment that reduces free riding. The best way to reduce free riding is to use peer pressure: When one employee sees another slacking off in his effort, he punishes the shirker in some way. Workers are more likely to exert such peer pressure when they work in an innovative HRM environment that reinforces the value of hard work through indoctrinating values, carefully selecting hard-working employees, training the employees well so that they can make a difference in their jobs, and rotating the workers across jobs.[6] These practices all raise the likelihood that workers will not shirk or free ride, and they also are practices that are very valuable in a QI program.

In Sum, Bundling Raises the Effectiveness of QI

We have shown a number of ways in which well-designed incentive plans can promote the goals of a quality program. Pay plans can reward multiple outcomes, including the quality of output and of suggestions. These rewards can serve as a complement to the recognition awards that employees often get in QI programs. And financial incentive plans even reward creativity in the long run through higher profits and returns to gainsharing. Overall, incentive pay can reward workers for their problem-solving efforts in the short run and in the long run. We turn next to the ways in which a QI program can raise the effectiveness of incentive pay plans.

Bundling: A QI Program Can Raise the Effectiveness of Incentive Pay

The conclusion that we reached above is that a well-designed incentive plan can complement a QI plan. Conversely, the quality improvement procedures can help develop and improve the incentive plan. A large number of the concerns with incentive pay are that such plans can work very well but are difficult to implement successfully. Given a quality improvement plan that is in place, the QI methods should also be applied to the incentive plan, typically through an ongoing compensation team. (In a unionized environment, many of these activities already occur through the collective bargaining process.)

The goal of the compensation team is to produce a pay plan that is constantly evolving to address problems with incentive plans that were listed above and to adjust to changes in the environment. For example, the team would meet to continually evaluate and update the factors that enter the gainsharing plan. They might, for example, decide to introduce safety into the gainsharing formula and reduce the payoff from cost reductions. The team would also meet to set appropriate goals for gainsharing, thereby avoiding the arbitrary ratcheting up of targets. In addition, they would search out unintended consequences of the pay plan and attempt to eliminate them. For example, they would search out and reduce the exogenous risk that arises in some forms of incentive pay plans, as when pay is a function of variables over which the employees have too little control. Thus, overall, this QI process improves the effectiveness of the pay plan and improves employees' perceptions of its fairness.

NUMMI provides an example of the interaction between the QI process and the incentive pay plan that is in place. At NUMMI, the union participated in setting up and adjusting the incentive plan over time. Employees find the measures of quality more credible because the union is able to monitor them.

Moreover, the HR practices associated with a QI plan can increase the value of incentives. For example, the QI plan improves workgroups' influence over their workplace. This change implies that paying for group performance will have a better fit between scope of control and metric used for the incentives. The longer time horizons encouraged by high investments in training and (frequently) in assurances that the employer will try to avoid layoffs can increase employees' cohesiveness—that is, the value they place on each others' good opinions. This increased cohesiveness increases the effects of norms of high effort—workers are more willing and able to reward hard-working colleagues and to sanction free riders. A related argument comes from game theory: As the odds of repeated play of the "game" of providing high or

---

Box 16.4: Varian X-Ray Tube[9]

In the 1980s, Varian X-Ray Tube Products introduced a significant QI program that had a dramatic impact on production line performance. Varian produces very high-quality X-ray tubes (for scanners or mammography equipment) that must meet quality targets—targets that increased in the 1980s. Thus, they did three things to raise performance: (a) reduced layers of management to flatten the organization and introduced work teams with an emphasis on empowerment; (b) assigned employees to product groups to bring them closer to the customer; and (c) introduced QI methods, such as training in SPC and problem-solving skills and general skills training, and hired more qualified people to implement teamwork. The outcome was that production yield rose substantially, to 90%.

However, by the 1990s, they assessed their position and realized that to remain competitive, they must increase yield closer to 100%, and they decided that it was time to introduce an incentive pay plan. They settled on a simple plan of creating a bonus pool for each quality tube produced, and using this pool to replace the annual 3% merit pay increases that all production employees had been receiving. Varian had the HR manager meet with small groups of employees to discuss the plan and describe the payouts. Employees had important concerns—about losing money, paying for the mistakes of others, and losing base pay over time. Management addressed some concerns and yet also pointed out that it is inevitable that the mistakes of others will affect pay because all must be responsible for raising product quality. The plan was then implemented in 1995, and constant updates were provided to employees.

The outcome of the incentive plan was dramatic: Yield rose rapidly to 94%, accompanied by increases in customer satisfaction and market share. How did this happen? Under the QI plan, employees had already been given the tools to improve quality. Every tube was tracked carefully from production to customer, and teams could easily be formed to investigate problems. Once incentives were in place, this activity accelerated, with teams tracking down defective suppliers and altering production arrangements. The human resources manager summed it up with the following assessment: "They even share their trade secrets with each other now. It's also interesting to see how well they work in teams and how conscious they are of the fact that each one's actions affect the others."

---

low effort increases, it becomes more likely that the outcome of high effort by all workers coupled with high pay from the employer becomes sustainable. The long time horizon also increases employees' willingness to invest in learning the intricacies of even fairly complex pay schemes.

Is Incentive Pay Effective?

As we review the effectiveness of pay schemes, we are focusing on whether they offer an important boost to a quality focus—or on whether incentive pay schemes and quality programs are complementary. We do not seek to review the broader literature that asks about the effectiveness of incentive pay independent of quality programs, although much of it is mentioned along the way.

There are three sources of evidence on the effectiveness of incentive pay: case studies, empirical analysis of particular types of pay plans, and empirical analysis of HR systems that include incentive pay. We consider each of these in turn. But note that we now often review literature that assesses the impact of problem-solving teams when combined with incentive pay, not the impact of QI with incentive pay. The reason for introducing results on problem-solving teams is that they often encompass a QI initiative.

Case Study Evidence

The case study evidence includes summaries of glowing success stories, often producing a positive picture of success with incentive pay plans. Of course, the firms studied in case studies are not chosen randomly by the researcher. The firms with successes are most likely to be written about either because researchers are aware of them or because companies wish to publicize their successes. Reports of failures occur at a much reduced rate.

There are numerous case studies that make the point that incentive pay introduces a key component to a quality program.[7] They state that incentive pay takes the program to a higher level of success, or in some cases, that incentive pay is the primary reason for the success of a quality plan. For example, in the case of Varian X-Ray Tube Products—highlighted in Box 16.4—their incentive program yielded substantial results when combined with their quality program (Kluge, 1996). More dramatically, Imberman (1996) makes the claim that for many companies, incentive pay is the key element to its success with the quality program, and he cites a large number of companies who had this experience.[8]

Although the case studies are not studies of random firms, they can be valuable reading because the level of detail is both valuable and convincing. The cases are particularly numerous in the trade press of the quality, productivity, and engineering journals, as in those cited above. Many more are available in the general business journals. Included in these are some very well-known cases of company turnarounds that involved incentive pay as one component of HR change, as in the NUMMI example (Adler, Goldoftas, & Levine, 1997, 1998).

Evidence From Baldrige Award Winners

The annual Malcolm Baldrige Award, named in honor of the former Secretary of Commerce, recognizes companies in the manufacturing, services, and small business sectors for general excellence and quality achievement. The award is administered by the Department of Commerce and the American Society for Quality. The application for the award requires a detailed description of the applicant's quality program, with points awarded based on the design of the program, the level of employee involvement, the role of continuous improvement, and customer satisfaction. More than 1 million copies of the award have been distributed, suggesting that the criteria are widely used as a benchmark of a well-designed quality program. Many state awards and private supplier certifications are based largely on the Baldrige criteria.

The criteria in the Baldrige Award were drawn from an array of sources, with heavy reliance on the quality gurus noted above. The resulting criteria provide little attention to incentives. Only 15% of the total points are given for human resource policies in total. This 15% is broken down into human resource planning (2%), work systems (4.5%), employee training (5%), and employee well-being (2.5%). The 4.5% on work systems, in turn, includes work and job design and compensation and recognition programs. Thus, as a rough approximation, perhaps 2% of the Baldrige criteria apply to incentive programs.[10]

In contrast to what is proposed in typical quality management theory and what enters the Baldrige Award criteria, in practice Baldrige Award winners pay a great deal of attention to the use of incentives. One pair of researchers interviewed a number of Baldrige winners. They noted that the winners tended to empower employees to make a difference and to reinforce individual and team commitment to quality with a wide range of rewards and reinforcements (Blackburn & Rosen, 1993).

In a complementary study, Hewitt Associates surveyed over 1991 and 1992 the perfor-

TABLE 16.1

Sample	Author(s)	HR Practices	Outcome
Apparel-making business units	Dunlop and Weil (1996)	Bundle of HR practices including gainsharing, training, communication, teamwork	Higher productivity of workgroups, especially when combined with better information systems and distribution support
All industries, 968 Compustat firms	Huselid (1995)	Two HR indexes—"Skills and work organization" and "motivation" (incentive pay)	Performance higher for those with higher HR index values
Steel finishing lines (United States and Japan)	Ichniowski et al. (1997)	Clusters of incentive pay, problem-solving teams, training, information sharing	Productivity and quality is highest among the plants with the highest HR factors
Auto production plants, worldwide	MacDuffie (1995)	Indexes of job design (including teams) and HR practices (including incentive pay)	Performance highest when these practices are combined with just-in-time practices
All industries, quality award recipients	Hendricks and Singhal (1994)	TQM factors of Baldrige Award, often including incentive pay	Stock prices rise with quality award outcomes
All industries	Easton and Jarrell (1998)	System of teamwork, training, and some pay factors	Stock prices rise after system implemented
Michigan manufacturing	Cooke (1994)	Gainsharing, problem-solving teams	Value-added rose with incentive pay

mance and reward programs of 13 Malcolm Baldrige Award winners. They found that several themes run through the award winners' compensation programs: "Reward and recognition programs are well integrated with quality initiatives. Much attention is given to execution. Recognition and celebration are emphasized. Variable reward programs are designed to encourage teamwork and employee involvement" (Braddick, Pfefferle, & Gandossy, 1993).

These interviews and surveys, coupled with the existing case study research, makes clear that Baldrige winners have implemented a wide array of incentive programs, coupled with supporting human resource policies that ensure that employees find improvement in their best interest. (For other recent cases, see also Walter, 1995, and Rohan, 1994.) Employees receive both monetary and nonmonetary rewards for

their ideas, and these rewards are directed at both individuals and teams.

Evidence on the Effectiveness of Particular Types of Pay Plans

Moving beyond the case studies, we turn to empirical work in which researchers analyze performance data across many firms to assess the effectiveness of incentive pay. Unfortunately, it is very difficult to provide convincing empirical evidence on this question. Some researchers have conducted surveys of firms, but in this case, it is hard to obtain measures of productivity that are comparable across firms, and it is hard to control for the other factors that affect productivity and might be correlated with incentive pay. Other researchers have obtained production data from firms and assessed the effectiveness of pay plans within an industry, but this is limited to only a few industries.

Most studies have only poor measures of organizational performance. For example, Wageman and Baker (1997) and Nalbantian and Schotter (1997) provide experimental evidence of the effectiveness of group-based pay. Kim (1996) describes a survey in which there is an association among gainsharing, employee involvement, and productivity. In the 1992 survey of the British Institute of Management mentioned above, managers rated their quality programs as more successful when quality indicators were included in the bonus or performance measurement system for frontline workers. No such relation appeared for quality awards for managers (Snape et al., 1995). In a field setting, Cooke (1994) shows that when gainsharing, profit sharing, and problem-solving teams are combined, value added rises in Michigan manufacturing establishments.

Evidence on the Effectiveness of Combinations of HR Practices

In recent years, some well-regarded empirical research examines the effectiveness of the adoption of clusters of complementary HR practices, where these clusters of practices often include incentive pay plans and quality improvement programs.

Given the theories reviewed here about the bundling of practices, empirical research on the effectiveness of HR practices must look at the effectiveness of clusters of these practices. In Table 16.1, we offer a summary of this work. (For more details, see the review articles of Ichniowski et al., 1997, Kling, 1995, and Levine, 1995). In each of these research projects, the researchers attempted to ascertain the effects of HR practices after they had introduced control variables for other influences that could affect performance. The individual industry studies tend to have better control variables but less breadth to their analysis. The evidence across all of these projects suggests positive

outcomes from the use of teams, incentive pay, and other supportive practices.

Discussion of Evidence

In the empirical studies above, ranging from the case studies to the cross-industry studies, the authors tend to reach two conclusions. First, innovative practices tend to be adopted in unison. This bundling makes it difficult to study the effects of any single policy or practice. Second, the overall evidence is that sets of innovative practices—spanning problem-solving teams and incentive pay—raise workers' performance levels. The result of these two facts is that we cannot isolate the independent effects of QI and incentive pay.

Why Are Firms Slow to Adopt Incentive Pay?

The evidence and theory above suggest that incentive pay plans can often be important components of a quality program. At the same time, many firms do not have such pay plans. Why are they so slow to adopt incentive pay?

In general, there are two sets of reasons why firms do not adopt incentives. The first set of factors leads the costs to outweigh the benefits, so incentives are not efficient. The second set of factors is made up of institutional constraints that stop firms from adopting pay plans that are otherwise likely to be cost-effective.

Pay plans will be ineffective when no simple incentive plan can be devised. In workplaces where the production of quality products is very complicated, so that employees face a wide variety of tasks on and off the line, the optimal pay plan may be hourly pay combined with modest profit sharing (Holmstrom & Milgrom, 1991). Case study evidence and common sense suggest that gainsharing pay plans should be relatively simple to be effective. When employees have long-term horizons, having several pay plans with one to three components each appears workable. As plans become more complicated or when turnover is high, employees cannot ascertain how their performance affects their pay. Moreover, complicated plans are costly to monitor. In a highly variable environment, hourly pay coupled with profit sharing is often sensible, and gainsharing plans may be harmful.

Even when a simple plan is possible, the process of change need not be simple. As noted above, in many cases, managers must change multiple practices to move to a quality-oriented workplace. Most managers are willing to innovate only at the margin. Changing an organization so that people have appropriate incentives, as well as other supporting practices, can be costly and require significant up-front investments. However, the evidence presented above implies that successful programs do change multiple practices.

Another reason that some workplaces avoid incentive plans is that the specific features of an effective incentive pay plan depend on the details of the workforce, the production technology, the product market, and the history of the organization. As a consequence, getting the details of a plan wrong can kill the value of any plan. Recognizing this, managers may avoid introducing appropriate plans.[11]

The difficulties with getting the parameters of the pay plan approximately correct are strongest when the organization first shifts to a new management system. Thus, it may be hard to avoid a period when the pay plan lags behind the other organizational changes.

The first set of obstacles impedes changes that might not be cost-effective. In addition, for several reasons, managers may not implement cost-effective changes. For example, in many organizations, managers do not have incentives to adopt incentive pay and a quality program. The adoption of innovative HR practices requires significant up-front investments and a long-term payoff horizon.[12] Many managers respond more to their own incentives to maximize short-run profits than to their incentives to maximize their company's long-term value (Levine, 1995, chap. 5; Porter, 1992). Appropriate incentives for employees to improve quality may await appropriate incentives for executives to invest in the organization's capabilities, even in ways that are difficult for investors to monitor.

(Kaplan and Norton's "balanced scorecard" for measuring organizational performance and investment in its capabilities can play a role here if the scorecard includes an element that indicates how well a manager "provides incentives for employees to innovate and produce high quality"; Kaplan & Norton, 1996, p. 1391.)[13]

Imperfections in capital markets can worsen the problem of short horizons. For example, when a firm is currently unprofitable, it may not be able to raise the funds to invest in structuring an innovative pay plan.

Finally, it is often difficult to change managerial practices, and changes in compensation schemes can be particularly threatening. Many workers and managers resist putting their pay at risk, particularly if they fear that managers will manipulate the measures or formula. Prospect theory and an array of evidence suggest that people are particularly leery of changing practices that have worked for them for many years, particularly if the changes have a reasonable chance of reducing real and (especially) nominal pay. Moreover, workers often do not have the time or money to invest in new methods. Therefore, because change is difficult to achieve, the adoption of innovative HR practices is much more likely in greenfield plants than in brownfield plants (Ichniowski & Shaw, 1995; Snell & Dean, 1994).

More generally, for most large organizations, the current quality program is one in a series of management innovations that attempted to convince workers to share their ideas (for minimal or negative rewards). Virtually all large U.S. organizations have experimented with many programs such as quality of worklife, Quality Circles, total quality management, non-TQM quality programs ("Quality 2000"), employee empowerment, team-building, and reengineering, often with multiple variations. In each instance, managers typically promised a fundamental shift in how the organization was managed, with a new focus on empowering frontline employees. In each case, the most common scenario was initial excitement by many employees and a burst of productivity as employees shared a set of accumulated good ideas. This burst was then followed by increased cynicism when employees realized that a faster work pace or more layoffs were more likely than true empowerment or higher pay. Thus, the lack of serious consideration to incentives in most quality programs was part of a consistent pattern of organizational (non-) change efforts.

Conclusion

The early quality gurus found fault with existing incentive pay plans and often recommended that having no material incentives was better than the current choices. This perspective ignored the possible positive effects of material incentives and the need to compensate frontline workers for the extra work involved in a quality program. The result is that quality improvement programs may flounder because of lack of incentives. It is particularly telling that QI programs are more likely to introduce incentive pay over time (Hackman & Wageman, 1995). Quality programs offer the intrinsic rewards of recognition and respect, but when employees work hard in problem-solving teams, they also want to know "what's in it for me." Moreover, workers are heterogeneous: Some respond well to intrinsic incentives, but others respond better to the extrinsic incentives of pay increases—they want to be paid for their extra effort and for the resulting improvements.

QI programs can also improve the effectiveness of incentive pay plans. The QI programs offer intrinsic rewards, such as recognition and pride, that induce higher levels of hard-to-measure efforts, such as investment in learning on the job. Because greater learning on the job can raise the returns to extrinsic pay plans, the intrinsic complements the extrinsic. QI programs also raise most employees' span of control. Whereas a typical hourly employee influences only line output (through his or her production effort), the hourly employee at a quality-oriented workplace also contributes to long-run profitability through the off-line teams. This broader span of control raises employees' response to the profit incentive plan and can increase their desire and capability to sanction peers who free ride and to reward colleagues who provide high levels of effort.

Finally, the QI program can be used to fine-tune the features of the incentive pay plan that is in place. No incentive pay plan is perfect, and each must be tailored to the particular needs of a workplace and workforce. The QI process can be used to predict problems or solve problems and reshape the incentive plans.

Unfortunately, there is little empirical evidence on the value of these pay plans in a QI environment. Case study evidence tends to showcase the value of incentive pay and is persuasive in the details that are described, but self-selection among case studies may lead to unrealistically few failures being reported. The broader empirical evidence does show that bundles of innovative HR practices that include incentive pay and QI practices appear to raise performance levels.

Incentive pay is not right for every quality program, and adoption rates are likely to remain low due to the high costs of changing past practices. Many obstacles can impede the integration of QI and incentives. In some complex production environments, there is no simple incentive pay plan that is functional. In other environments, the managers and frontline workers are resistant to change. Managers often have short time horizons and avoid the up-front investments of introducing new HR practices, particularly when practices must be bundled, as when training is combined with incentive pay. Finally, frontline workers fear putting their pay at risk.

In spite of these many obstacles, it is likely that the quality improvement plans that create sustained success are those that align decision making with incentives. Frontline employees must know that hard work, high quality, and creativity will lead to higher compensation for themselves and their peers, not to downsizing or job loss.

Notes

1. For other research making this same point, see Youndt, Snell, Dean, and Lepak (1996), Hackman and Wageman (1995), and Snape et al. (1995). Scholtes (1990)

reviews and elaborates on the critiques of traditional incentives from the perspective of quality guru W. E. Deming. Knouse (1995) gives a thoughtful overview of many of the critiques and solutions proposed here.

2. This box is drawn from the Harvard Business School case "AT&T UCS."

3. For further discussion on the structure and value of incentives as an alternative to behavioral controls, see Baker, Gibbons, and Murphy (1993) and Eisenhardt (1989).

4. This heterogeneity of incentive plans must be balanced by the fixed cost of running a plan and by the extra complications that each plan creates for both managers who must administer the plan and employees who must keep track of the various plans.

5. This value of employee effort can be shared either through forms of production incentives (quality of output) or through the creation of a bonus pool that is periodically divided among the employees. Thus, an incentive plan may provide a boost to the effectiveness of quality programs that began well but are floundering (Hackman & Wageman, 1995). In other production environments where the quality program has never been successful, the pay plan may make a difference. If there is a history of traditional HR practices and close supervision of employees, bonus pay plans may offer a needed first step in overcoming the distrust that can exist in such environments.

6. See Kandel and Lazear (1992) for a model of peer pressure as a means of reducing free riding.

7. For articles on compensation, recognition rewards, and QI, see the trade journals of ASQC (*Quality Progress*) and the human resource fields (*Personnel Journal*), as well as the book by Knouse (1995). Such descriptions are also embedded in the cases that can be found in places like *Harvard Business Review* and in op-ed pieces (Gross & Safier, 1995).

8. The companies included in his list are Xerox, Kaiser Aluminum, General Tire, General Electric, Rowe Furniture, Whirlpool, and Josens.

9. This summary is extracted from Kluge (1996).

10. The criteria address incentives for managers implicitly. Applicants must explain how the leadership system focuses on and reinforces the organization's quality goals (Criteria 1.1 and 1.2). Again, measuring incentives' importance is approximate, but we can allocate roughly 2% of the total Baldrige points as measuring incentives to managers. Thus, managerial incentives are roughly as important as incentives for frontline employees.

11. This chapter has not tried to describe all of the contingencies involved in the optimal pay plan, but has merely laid out several general principles (such as making pay a function of factors over which the workers have some control). Other principles exist in the literature (such as payout from the plan at frequent intervals). These factors have been described elsewhere at length. See, for example, Beck (1992), Markham, Scott, and Little (1992), and Masternak and Ross (1992), as well as the cases in Knouse (1995).

12. The selling of quality programs was greatly enhanced when quality guru Crosby (1979) claimed, "Quality is free!" In some passages, Crosby clarified his claim, explaining that quality is free in present-value terms but has some up-front costs. Nevertheless, the idea of something for (almost) nothing apparently enhanced quality programs' attractiveness.

13. A comprehensive quality program can also provide a number of positive externalities that are not captured by the enterprise. For example, the high levels of training at QI employers benefit other employers after employees quit. In addition, the high levels of employment security at employers with quality programs can stabilize aggregate demand during recessions, helping other companies. The high level of quality at a company improves the industry's and nation's overall reputation for quality, benefiting even producers without effective quality programs. Because of these and other externalities, the free market may underprovide substantive workplace redesign, including incentives (Levine, 1995).

References

Adler, P. S., Goldoftas, B., & Levine, D. I. (1997). Ergonomics, employee involvement, and the Toyota production system: A case study of NUMMI's 1993 model introduction. *Industrial and Labor Relations Review, 50,* 416-437.

Adler, P. S., Goldoftas, B., & Levine, D. I. (1998). Model changes in the Toyota production system. *Organization Science.*

Baker, G., Gibbons, R., & Murphy, K. J. (1993). *Subjective performance measures in optimal incentive contracts.* Working paper no. W4480, Cambridge, MA.

Blackburn, R., & Rosen, B. (1993). Total quality and human resources management: Lessons learned from Baldrige Award-winning companies. *Academy of Management Executive, 7*(3), 49-66.

Braddick, C., Pfefferle, M., & Gandossy, R. (1993). How Malcolm Baldrige winners reward employee performance. *Journal of Compensation and Benefits, 9*(3), 47-52.

Calder, B. J., & Staw, B. M. (1975). Self-perception of intrinsic and extrinsic motivation. *Journal of Personality & Social Psychology, 31,* 599-605.

Cole, R. E. (Ed.). (1995). *The death and life of the American quality movement.* New York: Oxford University Press.

Cooke, W. N. (1994). Employee participation programs, group-based incentives, and company performance: A union-nonunion comparison. *Industrial & Labor Relations Review, 47,* 594-609.

Cowherd, D. M., & Levine, D. I. (1992). Product quality and pay equity between lower-level employees and top management: An investigation of distributive justice theory. *Administrative Science Quarterly, 37,* 302-320.

Crosby, P. B. (1979). *Quality is free.* New York: McGraw-Hill.

Deci, E. L., & Ryan, R. M. (1985). *Intrinsic motivation and self-determination in human behavior.* New York: Plenum.

Dunlop, J. T., & Weil, D. (1996). Diffusion and performance of human resource innovations in the U.S. apparel industry. *Industrial Relations, 35*(3), 334-355.

Easton, G., & Jarrell, S. (1998). The effects of total quality management on corporate performance: An empirical investigation. *Journal of Business, 71*, 253-307.

Eisenhardt, K. M. (1989). Agency theory: An assessment and review. *Academy of Management Review, 14*(1), 57-74.

Gibbons, R. (1987). Piece-rate incentive schemes. *Journal of Labor Economics, 5*(4, pt. 1), 413-429

Gross, S., & Safier, S. (1995). Unleash the power of teams with tailored pay. *Journal of Compensation and Benefits, 11*, 27-31.

Hackman, J. R., & Wageman, R. (1995). Total Quality Management: Empirical, conceptual, and practical issues. *Administrative Science Quarterly, 40*, 309-342.

Hendricks, K., & Singhal, V. (1994). *Quality awards and the market value of the firm.* Working paper, College of William and Mary.

Holmstrom, B., & Milgrom, P. (1991). Multitask principal-agent analyses: Incentive contracts, asset ownership, and job design. *Journal of Law, Economics, and Organization, 7*, 24-52.

Huselid, M. (1995). The impact of human resource management practices on turnover, productivity and corporate financial performance. *Academy of Management Journal, 38*, 635-672.

Ichniowski, C., & Shaw, K. (1995). Old dogs and new tricks: Determinants of the adoption of productivity-enhancing work practices. *Brookings Papers on Economic Activity: Microeconomics*, pp. 1-65.

Ichniowski, C., Shaw, K., & Prennushi, G. (1997). The effects of human resource practices on productivity. *American Economic Review, 87*, 291-313.

Juran, J. M. (1988). *Juran on planning for quality.* New York: Free Press.

Kandel, E., & Lazear, E. (1992). Peer pressure and partnerships. *Journal of Political Economy, 100*, 808-817.

Kaplan, R. S., & Norton, D. P. (1996). *The balanced scorecard.* Boston: Harvard Business School Press.

Kim, D.-O. (1996). Factors influencing organizational performance in gainsharing programs. *Industrial Relations, 35*, 227-243.

Kling, J. (1995). High performance work systems and firm performance. *Monthly Labor Review, 118*, 29-36.

Kluge, R. H. (1996). An incentive compensation plan with an eye on quality. *Quality Progress, 29*, 65-68.

Knouse, S. B. (1995). *The reward and recognition process in total quality management.* Milwaukee, WI: ASQC Press.

Labbs, J. J. (1994). Specialized pay programs link employees' TQM efforts to rewards. *Personnel Journal, 73*(1), 17-18.

Lawler, E. E., III, Mohrman, S. A., Ledford, G. E., Jr. (1995). *Creating high performance organizations: Practices and results of employee involvement and total quality management in* Fortune *1000 companies.* San Francisco: Jossey-Bass.

Ledford, G. E. (1991). Three case studies on skill-based pay. *Compensation and Benefits Review, 23*(2), 11-23.

Levine, D. I. (1992). Piece rates, output restriction, and cohesiveness. *Journal of Economic Psychology, 13*, 473-479.

Levine, D. I. (1995). *Reinventing the workplace: How business and employees can both win.* Washington, DC: Brookings Institution.

MacDuffie, J. P. (1995). Human resource bundles and manufacturing performance: Organizational logic and flexible production systems in the world auto industry. *Industrial and Labor Relations Review, 48*, 197-221.

MacLeod, B. (1988). Equity, efficiency, and incentives in cooperative teams. *Advanced Economic Analysis of Participatory Labor Managed Firms, 3*, 5-23.

Markham, S. E., Dow, K. D., & Little, B. L. (1992). National Gainsharing Study: The importance of industry differences. *Compensation & Benefits Review, 24*(1), 34-45.

Masternak, R., & Ross, T. (1992). Gainsharing: A bonus plan or employee involvement. *Compensation & Benefits Review, 24*, 46-55.

Milgrom, P., & Roberts, J. (1995). Complementarities and fit: Strategy, structure, and organizational change in manufacturing. *Journal of Accounting & Economics, 19*(2-3), 179-208.

Nalbantian, H., & Schotter, A. (1997). Productivity under group incentives: An experimental study. *American Economic Review, 87*, 314-341.

Osterman, P. (1994). How common is workplace transformation and who adopts it? *Industrial and Labor Relations Review, 47*, 173-187.

Pfeffer, J. (1994). *Competitive advantage through people.* Cambridge, MA: Harvard Business School Press.

Porter, M. (1992). *Capital choices.* Washington, DC: The Council on Competitiveness Report, and Boston: Harvard Business School Press.

Rohan, T. M. (1994, January 3). Culture change wins the Baldrige. *Industry Week*, pp. 41-42.

Scholtes, P. R. (1990). An elaboration on Deming's teachings on performance appraisal. In G. McLean, S. Damme, & R. Swanson (Eds.), *Performance appraisal: Perspective on a quality management approach.* American Society for Training and Development.

Shapiro, R. D., Watkins, M. D., & Rosegrant, S. (1997, July 3). *Measure of delight: The pursuit of quality at AT&T Universal Card Services (A)* (Product No. 694047). Cambridge, MA: Harvard School of Business.

Snape, E., Wilkinson, A., & Redman, T. (1995). Cashing in on quality? Pay incentives and the quality culture. *Human Resource Management Journal, 6*(4), 5-17.

Snell, S., & Dean, J. (1994). Strategic compensation for integrated manufacturing: The moderating effects of jobs and organizational inertia. *Academy of Management Journal, 37*, 1109-1140.

Wageman, R., & Baker, G. (1997). Incentives and cooperation: The joint effects of task and reward interdependence on group performance. *Journal of Organizational Behavior, 18*, 139-158.

Waite, M. L., Newman, J. M., & Krzystofiak, F. J. (1994). Associations among performance appraisal, compensation, and total quality programs. *Psychological Reports, 75,* 524-526.

Walter, I. S. (1995). Linking quality with employee rewards: An evolutionary tale of a Baldrige Award winner. *Journal of Compensation & Benefits, 11*(3), 38-42.

Willett, D. (1993). Promoting quality through compensation. *Business Quarterly, 58,* 107-111.

Wruck, K. H., & Jensen, M. C. (1994). Science, specific knowledge, and total quality management. *Journal of Accounting & Economics, 18,* 247-287.

Youndt, M., Snell, S., Dean, J., Jr., & Lepak, D. (1996). Human resource management, manufacturing strategy, and firm performance. *Academy of Management Journal, 39*(4), 836-866.

Chapter 17

Human Resource Policies and Quality

From Quality Circles to Organizational Transformation

THOMAS A. KOCHAN
SAUL RUBINSTEIN

T he study of quality and human resources has progressed over time from a narrow focus on how these two sets of practices affect each other to the study of how the combined effects of quality, human resource, and other organizational practices are producing fundamental transformations in American corporations. Indeed, the need to understand how quality practices relate to the broader changes occurring in organizations today motivated the National Science Foundation and a consortium of private sector organizations organized by the American Society for Quality to create the "Transformation to Quality Organizations" research program that is supporting much of the work presented in this book. The implicit hypothesis underlying this program seems to be that quality can serve as an agent or catalyst for transforming organizations. We will explore this hypothesis in this chapter by reviewing the evolution of research that examines the link

among quality, human resource, and organizational practices.

But we want to do more than review the evidence. We also seek to lay out a set of ideas for moving to the next stage of work on this topic. Specifically, we argue for expanding the array of outcomes against which quality programs, human resource practices, and organizational transformations are evaluated. We need to examine the effects of these transformations in practices on the basic social contract in employment relations and on the multiple stakeholders affected by these practices. We believe that this is the next intellectual debate for work in this area, and so we will offer some very tentative thoughts on how to frame research that might address this debate.

Our approach is to review the evidence in rough historical sequence of its development, starting with early work on Quality Circles, moving through the evidence generated by

AUTHORS' NOTE: Support for this research is provided by the National Science Foundation, the Alfred P. Sloan Foundation, and the MIT International Motor Vehicle Program. The views expressed are solely those of the authors.

done in various industries, and ending in some of our current work under way at the Saturn Corporation. Throughout, we focus on how quality practices relate to four other sets of organizational practices: (a) human resource systems, (b) production systems, (c) labor management relations, and (d) corporate governance arrangements. As concerns about how these practices affect quality outcomes are raised, organizational transformations occur that challenge deeply embedded power relationships and structures; ideologies regarding the roles of workers, unions, managers, and shareholders; and the legal doctrines governing employment relations and corporate governance. Thus, we end with a discussion of how to address these broader issues by arguing for a deeper analysis of the politics of organizational learning and diffusion of innovations. Because much of our own work over the years has been in the automobile industry, we draw heavily on the evidence and lessons generated from this sector.

A Historical Perspective

If the terms *organizational transformation* and *quality* had been used in the same sentence in the 1970s, the modern-day quality movement would have never gotten started. As Cole (1999) notes, the modern quality movement began in earnest in the late 1970s and early 1980s with the movement from a traditional quality control and inspection model to an approach that emphasized the role of quality practices as part of a line worker's and manager's responsibilities. One of the first manifestations of the quality movement was the introduction of Quality Circles in American firms. One of the features of many of these early programs was that they would be narrowly constructed supplements or add-ons to existing structures and power relationships. In unionized settings, for example, these efforts would often be governed by collective bargaining language that essentially said, "Nothing in this program will alter or reduce the rights of management or workers otherwise contained in provisions of the collec-

tive bargaining agreement." In other words, the initial conception of Quality Circles and/or their sister quality of working life programs was that there would be off-line weekly or biweekly group problem-solving meetings focused on incremental improvements in production methods, worker attitudes and skills, and the relationships among workers and supervisors that might affect performance (both quality and productivity) and the quality of the working environment and lives of employees (Bluestone, 1981). If either the gatekeepers of management rights and power or union rights and power as specified in contracts or in nonunion settings of production managers and human resource specialists had thought these initiatives would lead to significant changes in work structures, devolution of decision-making power to frontline employees, or other organizational changes, they would have defeated efforts to introduce these initial programs. Indeed, many did just that as they saw the potential for altering traditional structures and power relationships.

Yet as is summarized below, over time, the evidence has become clear that Quality Circles and, later, total quality management (TQM) programs (Feigenbaum, 1961; Ishikawa, 1982, 1985; Juran, 1964; Juran & Gryna, 1988) had little effect and could not be sustained in organizations unless they addressed and changed existing structures, power relations, human resource practices, and production systems. In short, the biggest effects on performance are seen when quality practices are embedded in and part of a broader organizational transformation. This is the hypothesis underlying much of the research and experimentation going on today that relates quality and human resource management.

We should note that the effects of quality as a tool for transforming organizations developed here rest heavily on research that focuses on improvement in production and service delivery processes, such as error detection and reduction, reliability, scrap reduction, and so on, and less on quality in product design, engineering, aesthetics, or technological leadership. These latter quality features may be less dependent on the complementary organizational changes and features emphasized here than those in the former category. For example, Chrysler's successful rebound in the 1980s was due in large part to its successful development and marketing of the minivan and its improvements in product design. Yet Chrysler made most of the organizational changes discussed here only in selected plants (MacDuffie & Pil, 1997). Thus, the transformative effects of quality practices may depend, in part, on the strategies that a firm adopts to improve its image as a quality producer and its market position.

What's at Stake?

Why should we care about the relationships of human resource practices to quality practices? The most common answer found in the management literature on this subject is that quality is an important organizational goal and outcome (Dean & Bowen, 1994; Spencer, 1994). More recently, as we will review below, quality and human resource practices are being seen as "complementarities" that, when tied together appropriately, have a greater impact on quality performance than do their separate effects. The industrial relations literature on this subject adds a second reason. For workers and firms to achieve mutual gains in advanced industrialized countries, firms must compete on the basis of quality and innovation rather than cost minimization (Kochan, Katz, & McKersie, 1986; Kochan & Osterman, 1994; Piore & Sabel, 1984). Therefore, employees have a stake in getting firms to emphasize quality equal to the stake that firms have in getting employees to take quality seriously. The hypothesis implied in this literature is that more joint gains can be negotiated into employment contracts and sustained in settings where quality is an important objective and organizational feature. Moreover, for employees, quality of the products and services produced by their individual and collective efforts is an important source of personal satisfaction and identity. Finally, there is a public interest stake as well. For the American economy to compete at high and improving living standards in a world with widely varying (and significantly lower) labor

costs, we must be successful at sustaining a competitive advantage based on innovation, quality of goods and services, and responsiveness of differentiated and changing customer preferences. Thus, quality is important to the interests of multiple stakeholders in organizations and in society. It is the broad perspective that we believe should shape research in this area.

The Evidence: From Quality Circles to Organizational Transformation

Early Evidence: The Rise and Fall of Quality Circles

As noted above, early efforts to introduce new approaches to quality improvement took the form of off-line Quality Circles or quality of working life improvement efforts (Guest, 1979). The auto industry began experimenting with these efforts in earnest in the 1970s, after various highly publicized reports about rising worker dissatisfaction with their working conditions (U.S. Department of Health, Education, and Welfare, 1983). These early programs provided a test of whether interventions that focused solely on introducing quality practices without changing existing human resource practices or organizational structures would have a significant effect on performance and be sustainable over time. The evidence from these early experiments was not encouraging. Several empirical studies of the effects of these early efforts in the auto industry found only marginal effects for these interventions on quality and no significant effects on productivity (Katz, Kochan, & Gobeille, 1983; Katz, Kochan, & Weber, 1985). Other evaluation studies (Goodman, 1979) also found marginal effects on performance for several large-scale experiments in other industries aimed at improving both quality of working life and organizational performance. These same studies, however, found that the traditional employment and labor relations system features were producing a cycle of low trust, high conflict, and rigid work rules that had significant negative effects on both quality and productivity. The implication was that stronger interventions that addressed the features of the traditional systems would be needed to make a significant difference on quality, productivity, and other dimensions of manufacturing performance.

Given this early evidence, it is not surprising that studies in the 1980s found relatively high attrition and failure rates for Quality Circles (Lawler & Mohrman, 1985; Walton, 1979). But during the 1980s, intensifying economic pressures on American industry, particularly on manufacturing industries exposed to competition from Japan, stimulated a broader set of changes in employment and production practices. At the same time, the human resource management literature was gradually beginning to discover that the system effects of practices were greater than the effects of individual practices. In one of the first such studies, for example, Cutcher-Gershenfeld (1991) found that the combined effects of employee participation (Quality Circles), use of work teams, and other elements of a transformed labor-management relationship produced significantly higher levels of quality and productivity than did the individual effects of any single organizational innovation. As is reviewed below, this result has now been replicated in a number of studies, leading to the recognition that quality improvement and human resource practices need to be viewed as embedded in a larger organizational system.

Embeddedness of Quality Practices

Human resource, work organization, and production systems. Over the past decade, a number of empirical studies have been conducted within specific industries that have demonstrated that quality practices have a significant effect on performance when embedded in a larger set of innovations in traditional human resource management, work organization, and production systems. Although one of the weaknesses of this line of research is that the prac-

tices included vary across studies, most use as their conceptual frame of reference the difference between traditional, Taylorist, or Fordist versus transformed, flexible, lean, or high-commitment-oriented practices. The traditional, Fordist, and control models involved tight and narrowly specified individual job descriptions with individual fixed pay rates assigned to each job, clear lines of demarcation among jobs and between the roles of workers and supervisors, and a separation of the conception from the execution of work. In unionized settings, the labor management relationship was carefully delineated by detailed contract terms protecting management's right to manage; workers' rights to enforce the contract through grievance procedures; and the union's right to serve as the exclusive channel for negotiating changes in the contract governing wages, hours, and working conditions.

The alternative transformed, high-commitment, or flexible employment systems generally involved breaking down many of the detailed rules and individual jobs by giving greater emphasis to teamwork, job rotation or combination, pay for knowledge or skills, labor-management consultation or joint administration of direct employee participation, and significant investments in training along with stronger employment security commitments and/or contractual guarantees. The traditional production system focused on achieving control and high volume of standardized goods through long production runs, sufficient inventory buffers to ensure continuous production flows, and quality control through use of specialists and inspection of samples of the goods produced. Lean production embeds responsibility for quality into the jobs of frontline workers and teams, emphasizes minimization of in-process inventory and buffers in order to lower costs and keep the pressure on the production system to solve problems, and emphasizes flexible technologies suitable for handling greater variation in product characteristics. Efforts to implement these changes were inevitably motivated in part by the need to improve quality and productivity; therefore, these change efforts also incorporated some or all of the quality improvement tools associated with the TQM movement (Hackman & Wageman, 1995), as well as many of the changes in organizational symbols and rhetoric associated with efforts to embed a stronger quality culture and interpretive language in the organization as noted by Cameron and Barnett (Chapter 11), Hamada (Chapter 12), and Weick (Chapter 7) in this volume.

Again, work in the auto industry set the pattern for the approach and the results that were then used to justify implementing similar changes in employment practices and work systems in other sectors. MacDuffie and Krafcik (MacDuffie, 1995; MacDuffie & Krafcik, 1989, 1992) provided the clearest and most influential evidence of the effects of "bundling" human resource, work organization, and flexible or lean manufacturing practices together to achieve higher levels of quality and productivity. The first evidence came from comparing the differences at NUMMI, Toyota's plant in Japan, Honda's Ohio plant, and several traditionally structured and managed auto plants in the United States. The fact that Toyota, NUMMI, and Honda all achieved high quality (number of defects per car reported by customers) and high productivity (hours per car) sent a clear message to the American auto industry that dramatic changes were needed. Subsequently, using data from a worldwide survey of auto assembly plants, MacDuffie (1995) showed that the bundling of flexible human resource, work organization, and production practices produced higher levels of quality and productivity than achieved in plants employing traditional Fordist or mass production practices and systems. The implication of this work was that quality improvement had to be built into the organizational practices and systems.

Projects in other industries have produced similar results. For example, Ichniowski and Shaw (Chapter 15, this volume) summarize their results for the steel industry. In their earlier work, they demonstrated the existence of strong complementarities across human resource, work organization, and flexible production practices in the steel industry and found that the highest levels of productivity and quality were obtained when these practices were combined to include careful selection of the workforce; high levels of investment in training, team-based work systems, and employee involvement in problem-solving processes; and employment security (Ichniowski, Shaw, & Prennushi, 1995). Similar results were demonstrated in industries such as clothing (Dunlop & Weil, 1996), telecommunications (Batt, 1995), machining (Kelley, 1996), and computers (Repenning & Sterman, Chapter 9, this volume). (See Ichniowski, Kochan, Levine, Olson, & Strauss, 1996, for a review.)

From vertical control to horizontal networks. High-quality manufacturing requires greater levels of internal coordination upstream and downstream in the production process, in which each unit is treated by the others as a customer or supplier. This form of organization provides the capacity to solve nonroutine problems, improve quality, and lower costs. However, it requires extensive information sharing, decentralization, and rapid mutual adjustment (Shimada & MacDuffie, 1986). MacDuffie (1995) has argued that, in these systems, workers' tacit knowledge of their tasks become linked to those in other units, and informal networks become key for coordination. Furthermore, he states that the important knowledge leading to innovation tends to be boundary spanning. Trist (1981), challenging the traditional theory of bureaucratic scientific management, argued that the function of supervision in these systems is to manage the boundaries, not control the people.

The automotive industry in particular has required greater levels of coordination between customers and suppliers (Womack, Jones, & Roos, 1991). These suppliers can be both external and internal, requiring highly effective levels of communication and coordination within an organization in which semifinished product flows from one department to the next. Each department adds value and then transfers product, treating the downstream department as its customer, and the receiving department must behave as though it is getting product from its upstream supplier (Ishikawa, 1985). Vital to such systems are upstream and downstream communications, customer-supplier coordination, and on-line problem solving (Aoki, 1990). The role of supervision in these work systems has increasingly become one of facilitating relationships between teams and departments in the production chain.

Recent work in the airline industry also shows the importance of cross-functional coordination to service quality and productivity equivalent to the upstream and downstream coordination in production systems. Gittell (1996) found that the quality and efficiency of turnarounds (the process of landing, unloading, loading, and taking off of an airplane) is significantly affected by the degree to which the different occupational groups (pilots, flight attendants, ticket agents, mechanics, baggage handlers, etc.) share information, communicate, and work together to solve problems as they arise.

Taken together, the manufacturing and service industry results are highlighting the importance of horizontal coordination in organizations. This, in turn, is leading us, along with many other researchers, to give greater attention to the role of networks in organizations and to network theories and methods in research on these topics.

In his conceptualization of Japanese firms, Aoki (1988, 1990) provides a concise theoretical argument for why communication and coordination as one might expect to find in a dense social network is critical to high-quality performance. He points to the significance in Japanese firms of nonhierarchical, horizontal communications and coordination networks in adjusting to change. In creating this capacity, he stresses the importance of workers' communicative abilities, information flow, and an organizational learning view of the firm. Information and coordination play key roles in Aoki's J-form model of the Japanese firm. Horizontal coordination that occurs through information exchanges substitute for the hierarchical control systems built into the traditional American corporation (Aoki, 1990). Horizontal coordination and information sharing are encouraged in Japanese firms by organizational design features and human resource practices that break from the American legal and managerial traditions of separating planning and supervision from those who execute the work. Among these features are job rotation; enterprise unions that include blue-collar, white-collar, and managerial employees; extensive use of teams; and other problem-solving processes that support the sharing of knowledge that is essential to improving work unit and organizational performance. Aoki suggests that this conception of the firm may fit those environments in which markets demand product variety; where the technology can be informed by and made more productive with worker knowledge; where the market conditions support a premium on quality, innovation, and rapid response to changing consumer preferences; and where the regulatory environment supports those organizational features.

Granovetter (1973, 1985, 1992) has similarly argued the importance of understanding economic activity as embedded in networks of social relationships. Baker (1992) suggests that "all known network organizations evolved unplanned or resulted from the redesign of a non-network organization." He further suggests that the distinguishing feature of network organizations is the high degree of integration across units.

Thus, both recent empirical and theoretical work suggests that networklike communications structures and processes are critical to the achievement of high levels of quality in manufacturing and service organizations where there is a high degree of interdependence among tasks and/or functions. Yet the full implications of this insight have not yet been realized by most of the organizational behavior or management researchers studying TQM and related practices. That is, the transformations required to fully develop and realize the benefits from a networked organization require a rather fundamental reallocation of decision-making power and a rethinking of one of the major precepts of the TQM literature. The change process shifts from one controlled by a top-down strategy (Hackman & Wageman, 1995) to one involving multiple groups that share power and must coordinate their activities and solve problems across horizontal as well as vertical boundaries. In these settings, top-down change models lose their predictive power and practical effects.

The role of labor-management relations. The nature of labor management relations is a powerful yet underresearched part of the larger system in which quality transformation efforts are embedded. Team-based production systems pose significant challenges for organized labor (Kochan et al., 1986; MacDuffie, 1995) because they often break down traditional job classifications, replace individual incentive systems or fixed pay rates tied to individual jobs with contingent pay based on group performance, and minimize seniority rights. However, the role of unions in high-performance manufacturing, or lean production, has been less well researched than has the role of management or the behavior of teams. Our work at Saturn has led us to propose a new theory of the role of the union in these systems, namely, the union as a social network that facilitates communication and problem solving in ways that contribute directly to high performance.

At Saturn, the union and management have put in place a co-management system in which union representatives and managers work as partners up and down the hierarchy and across the key functional roles, such as human resources, finance, marketing, manufacturing and engineering, and supplier relations. In our work at Saturn, we found that the local union had created a dense social network among its representatives in which business issues and production problems were being discussed along with more traditional union and labor management issues. These social relationships served as information and knowledge resources on which union representatives could draw in their co-management roles. A network analysis of these relationships (Rubinstein, in press) found that (a) the union representatives were actively communicating with each other and with their nonrepresented management counterparts, and (b) the higher the levels of communication among these union and management representatives, the higher the first-time quality and quality improvement achieved in the units for which they were responsible. In fact, the evidence showed that the union representatives were communicating more frequently than their management counterparts and that the union communication patterns were a stronger predic-

tor of performance than those of the managers. Thus, the local union at Saturn had built a dense social network that contributed significantly to quality performance in this team-based production system and co-managed organization. But whether this theory and role generalize to other union-management settings is still an open question, and one that needs to be examined in future research. Our findings at Saturn do, however, fit well with the literature on organizational networks. In this case, it is the local union and the co-management system at Saturn that serve as the catalysts for producing the network structure and process.

Organizational governance. Our work at Saturn has led us to explore the role of governance systems as they relate to quality performance and organizational transformations. As noted above, Saturn's original organizational design called for a labor-management partnership from the shop floor to the strategic levels of decision making. Over time, as this design was implemented, a co-management structure and process was put in place at the work unit and middle management levels as well. As we followed these developments, it became evident that the parties at Saturn were experimenting with a fundamentally different organizational form, one that took on many of the characteristics implied by those who have been writing about stakeholder models of organizations. In our view, a stakeholder firm is one that is designed to achieve the joint objectives of parties with different interests (Kochan & Rubinstein, forthcoming). To achieve these objectives requires an organizational design and governance process that generates and sustains high levels of employee effort and commitment and a means of allocating equitably the rewards achieved by the organization. At Saturn, as in other organizational forms that resemble stakeholder firms such as law or consulting partnerships (Landers, Rebitzer, & Taylor, 1996), the stakeholders participate directly and with significant power in the strategic production and distributional decisions.

However, the Saturn case also points out some features in society and organizations that limit the potential to implement a stakeholder model. The type of co-management governance process embedded in Saturn challenges prevailing norms, ideologies, and public policies about labor-management relations, the role of unions, managerial rights, and the primacy of the principle of shareholder maximization as the underlying goal of the American corporation. Thus, full-fledged stakeholder models such as Saturn are likely to be rare and difficult to sustain in the absence of changes in these broader norms, ideologies, policies, and the power relations among those with a stake in these issues. Therefore, the question for researchers ought to be twofold: Are hybrid or partial models of stakeholder firms that do not require as direct a frontal assault on these broader forces capable of achieving the same performance results as the full stakeholder model? and How can change in the broader forces be achieved to create a more supportive environment for organizations that seek to embody stakeholder principles?

Thus, whereas the specific features of Saturn's organizational design and governance structure reflect the labor-management history and setting of the U.S. auto industry, we believe that they may also illustrate some generalizable principles about the evolution of quality practices from their narrow, Quality Circle heritage to the current interest in their potential for transforming organizations. The proposition suggested by Saturn is that for quality to reach its full potential as a transforming agent, changes will be needed in traditional governance structures, managerial and labor ideologies, and public policies that define and regulate the role of the corporation in society. As Hackman and Wageman (1995) note, this may be a limiting condition for quality practices, given the likely resistance to these types of transformations in American organizations and society. We explore this issue in more detail below as we discuss the role of organizational learning and diffusion of quality practices and related organizational innovations.

Organizational Learning and Diffusion

One of the central questions posed by researchers in the human resource and industrial relations field reflects the influence of the economics profession in our discipline. That is, if these quality practices and related organizational innovations are so good at improving organizational efficiency, why are they so slow to diffuse across the economy (Osterman, 1995)? The fact is, we have no good parsimonious answer to this question (see Ichniowski et al., 1996, for a discussion of alternative explanations). We are not alone in searching for answers to this question. Indeed, a whole new subfield has arisen in recent years around the concept of "organizational learning."

The problem of organizational learning and diffusion of innovation is a critical issue for both contemporary industrial relations theory and policy (Cole, 1989; Locke & Jacoby, 1995) and organization theory (Hackman & Wageman, 1995; Nonaka, 1991; Senge, 1990; Sitkin, Sutcliffe, & Schroeder, 1994). Researchers have struggled with the problems of diffusion for decades, first focusing on the adequacy of the work systems models (Walton, 1975, 1979), and later on the necessary support and commitment of top management and union leadership. Furthermore, Kochan and Cutcher-Gershenfeld (1988) found that in order to sustain and institutionalize innovation, the union leadership must be involved in strategic-level decisions that affect economic performance, accompanied by workforce participation at the shop floor. Cole (1989) stressed the importance of national institutions such as professional associations, labor-management relations policies and norms, and cross-firm ties as critical factors explaining differences in the diffusion across firms in different countries.

The politics of learning and diffusion. Although the growing literature on learning and diffusion provides a useful starting point in a search for the answers to the questions posed above, intensive studies of organizational and technological decision making (Thomas, 1994) and our own work at Saturn lead us to suggest the need to add another perspective to this literature, namely, a focus on the politics of learning and diffusion. If the basic finding of this research is that for quality practices to have a significant effect they require organizational transformations that involve shifts in power relations, challenge prevailing ideologies and norms, and may even challenge long-standing legal doctrines, then "learning" and "diffusion" will be hotly contested political processes. Heckscher (1996) begins to get at this phenomenon in his description of "successful failure," in which innovation fails to diffuse even after meeting its goals. He ascribes various causes to this pattern, including resistance by managers who are threatened by or do not fully understand the innovation, inadequate succession planning, provincial competition between functional units that are motivated to reject anything "not invented here," and an inability to give up established control systems during a transformation effort. Thomas (1994), for example, documented the role of political considerations in the choice of technologies, even in the face of justification and rhetoric couched in rational financial and engineering analyses and terminology.

The politics of learning and diffusion are especially likely to be important in settings where the transformations take their broadest form, challenge deeply embedded ideologies about organizational roles, and require changes in power structures and relationships. This is clearly the case in settings where employees and/or union representatives take on partnership and/or co-management roles, such as at Saturn. Even in more limited forms, power relations are altered as middle managers lose power relative to lower-level participants and as information systems are redesigned to provide information to frontline employees. This information was heretofore available only to top managers and generally used as part of the control systems rather than to support vertical and horizontal communication and coordination needed for effective problem solving. In cases where relations among workers and managers, or other functional groups such as design and manufacturing engineers, are adversarial or differentiated by status, solutions to problems that do not require renegotiation of these relationships are likely to be chosen over those that do (Thomas, 1994). Thus, we believe that the role of politics—that is, the dynamics of decision making in settings involving multiple interests that share power—needs to feature more prominently

in the study of organizational learning and diffusion of quality practices, and the organizational transformations in which they are embedded.

The Distributional Effects of Quality and Organizational Transformations

So far, this review has mirrored the dominant focus of both the theory and the empirical literature on quality practices, human resource innovations, and organizational transformations. We have focused largely on the effects of these innovations on firm performance and ignored who benefits from these innovations. Yet concern about the distribution of economic benefits is gaining increasing attention in society in the wake of a decade of improvements in the productivity, profitability, and competitiveness of American industry that coincided with a decade of stagnant real wages, increasing income inequality, increased job insecurity, and the downsizing of large firms. The coincidence of these developments has led many to argue that the social contract in employment relations (Heckscher, 1996; Reich, 1996; Kochan & Rubinstein, forthcoming) has broken down. What, then, are the relationships among these innovations in organizational practice, employee welfare, and the social contract? We believe that this is the central intellectual and perhaps the key public policy question facing human resource and organizational researchers today. Unfortunately, we have little hard evidence available at this point to bring to bear on this question. Instead, the best we can do at this point is to use the evidence from more macro labor market studies to suggest several hypotheses for future micro, firm-level investigation.

Three major facts dominate the labor market outcomes of the past decade: (a) Wage distributions among workers grew more unequal, (b) returns to education increased, and (c) involuntary permanent layoffs increased, especially for white-collar managerial employees (see Cappelli et al., 1997, and Freeman, 1997, for comprehensive reviews of this evidence). Although labor market specialists will continue to debate the relative importance of different market, trade, technological, institutional, and labor supply causes of these developments, we need to ask, What, if any, effects have the quality and other organizational innovations and transformations had on these labor market outcomes? Three hypotheses seem reasonable.

First, those organizations that implemented these innovations produced organizational performance improvements faster than they could expand demand for their products, thereby providing the impetus for downsizing in the face of improving organizational performance. Indeed, one careful case study (Sterman, Repenning, & Kofman, 1997; also see Chapter 9) documented exactly such an effect. If this effect dominates, we would expect that the survivors of downsizing in a transformed organization might share in the benefits through greater job security and perhaps increased wages paid both to compensate them for their increased investments in training and to share in the increased profitability of the firm. If this is the dominant effect, then the net effects of the quality practices and related transformations are to increase income inequality and to increase the variability in job security (and probably thereby increase the number who are worried about job insecurity) in the American economy.

A second hypothesis is also plausible. Given the ability to compete with other lower-cost competitors by using quality and related organizational innovations, more jobs that would otherwise be outsourced to lower-wage countries or to firms in the United States paying lower wages might be created and maintained. If this effect dominates, and if firms continue to reinvest the profits produced in market-expanding endeavors (such as research and development of new products or investment for capacity expansion), then the potential for mutual gains between employees and employers is enhanced.

A third hypothesis relates to the changing role of labor market institutions in general and unions in particular. Specifically, part of the increase in earnings inequality is due to the declining presence and influence of unions. Over the long run, unions have been a major force in reducing earnings inequality across occupations, between entry-level and high-skill work-

ers, and across industries (Freeman & Medoff, 1984). Therefore, although most labor market researchers agree that the long-term decline of unions accounts for part of the increase in earnings inequality, there is no consensus over the relative importance of union decline compared to other market or technological changes. One of the reasons for this is that we have few empirical studies of the effects of union decline in actual organizations. Nor have we explored the effects of alternative forms of worker participation and representation built into quality improvement initiatives for their effects on employee welfare. Yet we observe in cases like Saturn that new models are evolving in which employees are represented in ways that give them a direct voice in both the production and distributional decisions that affect their interests. The union contract at Saturn, for example, calls for a risk-reward payment system based on investment in training and performance targets with respect to quality, productivity, and profitability. As a result, employees have shared in Saturn's performance. Thus, we need to explore more carefully the range of models for worker participation and representation that are present in organizations today. Alternatively, greater attention needs to be given to the long-term effects on the workforce and society if the decline in union representation continues.

Clearly, we need to do a better job of assessing the effects of quality practices and other organizational innovations on the range of outcomes of concern to employees as well as those of concern to firms and their shareholders. But given the highly normative nature of quality literature from its inception, we need to also shift from the top-down, managerial orientation of the theory and empirical research in this field to one that takes a broader approach that considers the effects of these practices and innovations on the full range of affected stakeholders.

Implications for Future Research

Both practice and research on the relationship of human resources and quality improvement evolved in directions not anticipated. Research and experimentation started as far back as the early 1980s among those interested in understanding a simple question: How might the use of Quality Circles and other forms of employee participation aimed at improving organizational effectiveness be introduced as supplements to existing human resource practices and labor-management relationships? Gradually, however, both research and practical experiences led to the conclusion that quality improvement efforts will be successful and sustained over time only if embedded in a broader set of rather fundamental changes in organizational processes, structures, and perhaps even governance systems. If this is correct, it suggests a research agenda for the future that will require organizational researchers to ask some fundamental questions about the role of the corporation in society and its relationships with a range of multiple stakeholders, particularly with employees and their representatives. Moreover, to understand whether or not the transformative effects of quality practices will be widely diffused across organizations and sustained over time will require a more focused understanding of the politics of the learning and diffusion process and a shift in the type of models that guide work in this area to better incorporate issues of power, conflict and conflict resolution, interest articulation, and institutions.

More specifically, we believe that we are at a point in the study of quality and related human resource innovations where it is time to do the following:

1. Shift the emphasis from a top-down, management-driven theory of the change process to a more horizontal, network model of change and coordination.

2. Give equal emphasis to the distributional effects of quality and related innovations as to the impact on firm performance.

3. Give greater attention to the ways that employees gain a voice in the decisions affecting their role in the innovation and change process, especially in an era of declining unionization.

4. Examine more closely the changing nature of supervision (who does it and how it is done) in team-based organizations.

5. Consider the role of organizational governance and alternative conceptions of the role of the corporation in American society that allow experimentation with stakeholder models of the firm.

6. Give greater weight to the political aspects of the organizational learning and diffusion process.

7. Shift from an organizational focus to a focus on the social contract as the unit of analysis for evaluating the full range of effects of quality and other organizational innovations.

If human resource and quality researchers take up this broader and more ambitious agenda, we will collectively have something to contribute to the organizational and public policy debates that are likely to emerge in the next decade, and we are likely to add new intellectual spark to the literature on these subjects. Absent progress on these issues, we agree with Hackman and Wageman's (1995, p. 338) conclusion, namely, that TQM is likely to lose the prominence it now enjoys and to fail to reach its full potential as an instrument for organizational transformation.

References

Aoki, M. (1988). *Information, incentives, and bargaining in the Japanese economy.* New York: Cambridge University Press.

Aoki, M. (1990). Toward an economic model of the Japanese firm. *Journal of Economic Literature, 28.*

Baker, W. (1992). The network organization in theory and practice. In N. Nohria & R. Eccles (Eds.), *Networks and organizations: Structure, form, and action.* Boston: Harvard Business School Press.

Batt, R. (1995). *Performance and welfare effects of restructuring: Evidence from the telecommunication services industry.* Unpublished doctoral dissertation, Massachusetts Institute of Technology.

Bluestone, I. (1981). *The union and the quality of worklife process.* Scarsdale, NY: Work in America Institute.

Cappelli, P., Bassi, L., Katz, H., Knoke, D., Osterman, P., & Useem, M. (1997). *Change at work.* New York: Oxford University Press.

Cole, R. E. (1989). *Strategies for learning: Small group activities in American, Japanese and Swedish industry.* Berkeley: University of California Press.

Cole, R. E. (1999). *Managing quality fads: How American business learned to play the quality game.* New York: Oxford University Press.

Cutcher-Gershenfeld, J. (1991). The impact on economic performance of a transformation in workplace relations. *Industrial and Labor Relations Review, 44*(2).

Dean, J. W., & Bowen, D. E. (1994). Management theory and total quality: Improving research and practice through theory development. *Academy of Management Review, 19,* 392-418.

Dunlop, J. T., & Weil, D. (1996). Diffusion and performance of modular production in the U.S. apparel industry. *Industrial Relations, 35,* 334-55.

Feigenbaum, A. V. (1961). *Total quality control.* New York: McGraw-Hill.

Freeman, R. B. (1997). *When earnings diverge.* Washington, DC: National Policy Association.

Freeman, R. B., & Medoff, J. L. (1984). *What do unions do?* New York: Basic Books.

Gittell, J. H. (1996). *Paradox of coordination and control.* Working paper, Harvard Business School.

Goodman, P. S. (1979). *Assessing organizational change.* New York: Wiley.

Granovetter, M. (1973). The strength of weak ties. *American Journal of Sociology, 78.*

Granovetter, M. (1985). Economic action and social structure: The problem of embeddedness. *American Journal of Sociology, 91.*

Granovetter, M. (1992). Problems of explanation in economic sociology. In N. Nohria & R. Eccles (Eds.), *Networks and organizations: Structure, form, and action.* Boston: Harvard Business School Press.

Guest, R. (1979, July-August). Quality of work life: Learning from Tarrytown. *Harvard Business Review.*

Hackman, R. J., & Wageman, R. (1995). Total quality management: Empirical, conceptual, and practical issues. *Administrative Science Quarterly, 40,* 309-342.

Heckscher, C. (1996). *White collar blues.* New York: Basic Books.

Ichniowski, C., Kochan, T., Levine, D., Olson, C., & Strauss, G. (1996). What works at work: Overview and assessment. *Industrial Relations, 35.*

Ichniowski, C., Shaw, K., & Prennushi, G. (1995). *The impact of human resource management practices on productivity* (Working Paper No. 5333). Cambridge, MA: National Bureau of Economic Research.

Ishikawa, K. (1982). *Guide to quality control.* Tokyo: Asian Productivity Organization.

Ishikawa, K. (1985). *What is total quality control? The Japanese Way.* Englewood Cliffs, NJ: Prentice Hall.

Juran, J. M. (1964). *Managerial breakthrough.* New York: McGraw-Hill.

Juran, J. M., & Gryna, F. M. (Eds.). (1988). *Quality control handbook* (4th ed.). New York: McGraw-Hill.

Katz, H. C., Kochan, T. A., & Gobeille, K. R. (1983). Industrial relations performance, economic performance, and QWL programs: An interplant analysis. *Industrial and Labor Relations Review, 37,* 3-17.

Katz, H., Kochan, T., & Weber, M. (1985). Assessing the effects of industrial relations and quality of working life on organizational performance. *Academy of Management Journal, 28,* 509-527.

Kelley, M. R. (1996). Participatory bureaucracy and productivity in the machined products sector. *Industrial Relations, 35,* 374-399.

Kochan, T., & Cutcher-Gershenfeld, J. (1988). *Institutionalizing and diffusing innovations in industrial relations.* Washington, DC: Government Printing Office.

Kochan, T., Katz, H., & McKersie, R. (1986). *The transformation of American industrial relations.* New York: Basic Books.

Kochan, T., & Rubinstein, S. (forthcoming). *Toward a stakeholder theory of the firm: The case of the Saturn partnership.* Unpublished manuscript.

Landers, R., Rebitzer, J., & Taylor, (1996). Rat race redux: Adverse selection in the determination of work hours. *American Economic Review, 86,* 329-348.

Lawler, E. E., & Mohrman, S. A. (1985). Quality circles after the fad. *Harvard Business Review, 63,* 65-71.

Locke, R., & Jacoby, W. (1995). *The dilemmas of diffusion: Institutional transfer and the remaking of vocational training practices in Eastern Germany.* Working Paper 3846-95-BPS, Massachusetts Institute of Technology.

MacDuffie, J. P. (1995). Human resource bundles and manufacturing performance: Organizational logic and flexible production systems in the world auto industry. *Industrial and Labor Relations Review, 48.*

MacDuffie, J. P., & Krafcik, J. (1989). Flexible production systems and manufacturing performance: The role of human resources and technology. *Academy of Management.*

MacDuffie, J. P., & Krafcik, J. (1992). Integrating technology and human resources for high performance manufacturing: Evidence from the international auto industry. In T. Kochan & M. Useem (Eds.), *Transforming organizations.* New York: Oxford University Press.

MacDuffie, J. P., & Pil, F. K. (1997). Changes in the auto industry employment practices: An international overview. In T. A. Kochan, R. D. Lansbury, & J. P. MacDuffie (Eds.), *After lean production: Evolving employment practices in the world auto industry* (pp. 9-44). Ithaca, NY: ILR.

Nonaka, I. (1991, November-December). The knowledge-creating company. *Harvard Business Review.*

Osterman, P. (1995). How common is workplace transformation and who adopts it? *Industrial and Labor Relations Review, 47,* 173-187.

Piore, M. J., & Sabel, C. F. (1984). *The second industrial divide.* New York: Basic Books.

Rubinstein, S. (In press). The impact of co-management on quality performance: The case of the Saturn Corporation. *Industrial and Labor Relations Review.*

Senge, P. M. (1990). *The fifth discipline.* New York: Doubleday.

Shimada, H., & MacDuffie, J. P. (1986). *Industrial relations and humanware.* Working paper, Massachusetts Institute of Technology.

Sitkin, S. B., Sutcliffe, K. M., & Schroeder, R. G. (1994). Distinguishing control from learning in total quality management: A contingency perspective. *Academy of Management Review, 19,* 537-564.

Spencer, B. A. (1994). Models of organization and total quality management: A comparison and critical evaluation. *Academy of Management Review, 19.*

Sterman, J., Repenning, N., & Kofman, F. (1996). Unanticipated side effects of successful quality programs: Exploring a paradox of organizational improvement. *Management Science, 43,* 503-521.

Thomas, R. J. (1994). *What machines can't do.* Berkeley: University of California Press.

Trist, E. (1981). The evolution of socio-technical systems: A conceptual framework. In A. van de Ven & W. Joyce (Eds.), *Perspectives on organizational design and behavior.* New York: Wiley Interscience.

U.S. Department of Health, Education, and Welfare. (1983). *Work in America.* Cambridge: MIT Press.

Walton, R. (1979). Work innovations in the United States. *Harvard Business Review.*

Womack, J., Jones, D., & Roos, D. (1991). *The machine that changed the world.* New York: Harper & Row.

Name Index

Subject Index

414 \ THE QUALITY MOVEMENT AND ORGANIZATION THEORY

short-term, 105, 170, 185-186, 197
See also Improvement
Quality Improvement Teams, 105, 106
Quality management:
    commitment to, 58-59, 61
    ecology of, 58-62
    effectiveness of, 50-52, 76-77, 135-143,
        201-202, 237-270, 388-396
    historical perspective, 388-389
    implementing, 54-55, 158
    key features, 52-56
    mature systems, 107, 109, 111
    new versus old models, 53, 68-69, 81, 302, 390
    problems, 61
    public sector, 131-151
    quality control versus, 53-54, 390
    time required for results, 50
Quality manager, as cop, 82
Quality measurement, 105-106
Quality metrics, 109
Quality movement, early years of, 67-86
Quality practices, embeddedness of, 390-394
Quality system, structural arrangements of,
    192-193
Quantum theory, 162

Rank-and-file employees, rewards for, 38
Rapid product development, 331-344
Rational actors, quality model adoption and, 70-72
Rational choice, 315
Rational cybernetic control approaches, 320
Rationality:
    decision making and, 343
    product development and, 333, 334-335
    sensemaking and, 159, 163
Raw materials, 202
    environmental quality and, 307
    suppliers, 26
Reality/realities:
    multiple, 297
    new definitions of, 301
    sensemaking and, 300
    social, 310
Recognition programs, 111, 374
Recycling, 304, 305, 307
Reliability, learning and, 316-317
Reliability-enhancing processes, 317-328
Requirements, conformance to, 68
Research:
    futuristic, 326
    total quality, 4
Resilience, 326, 328
Resource(s):

diverted to quality management, 59, 61
limited, 207, 324
process improvement, 211
public sector, 135, 147
reallocated, 209
slack, 229
utilizing existing, 206
Resource allocation:
    dual process requirements, 324
    economic logic of, 52
    efficient markets, 71
    goals and, 140
Resource dependence perspective, 15
Rewards, 10
    allocating equitably, 393
    bonuses, 187, 193
    developing programs, 111
    employee effectiveness and, 9
    extrinsic, 37, 43, 350, 370, 374, 376
    gainsharing, 349-350
    incentive pay, 367-384
    intrinsic, 370, 373-374, 376, 382
    pay, 37-38, 40, 43, 350, 179, 367-384
    public sector, 134, 143, 144
    quality achievement, 29
    recognition, 374
    reported quality and, 370
    trinket, 83
Role clarification, 6
Rules, arbitrary, 84

Saturn, 393-394
Schema, understanding organizations using, 103
Scientific management, 4, 36, 286-287, 390, 391
Scientific methods, 26-27, 29, 31, 38, 40, 55, 57
Semiconductor industry, 80
Seniority pay, 187, 298
Seniority rights, 393
Senior management. *See* Top management
Sensemaking, 155-177, 300
    Japanese top management, 295
    product development, 343
    public sector, 147-149
    TQM deployment, 102-103
    uncertain environment, 321
Service(s):
    design of, 276
    public sector, 134, 145, 149
Service factory, 16
Service firms:
    customer focus, 16
    problem-solving teams and, 28
Signetics, 85

About the Contributors

Carole K. Barnett is Assistant Professor of Management at the University of New Hampshire's Whittemore School of Business and Economics. She holds a PhD in organizational psychology from the University of Michigan. She studies learning—in and across individuals, groups, organizations, and industries. She has examined the complex relationships between individual and organizational learning, organizational adaptation and transformation, and culture as an artifact and/or mechanism of learning. She has published two edited volumes, book chapters, and cases as well as journal articles focused on change processes inherent in organizational crises and failures, mergers and acquisitions, and quality systems.

David E. Bowen received his PhD from Michigan State University. Presently, he is Professor of Management at Thunderbird, The American Graduate School of International Management; previously, he was on the faculties of Arizona State University, West and the University of Southern California. His research, teaching, and consulting interests focus on the organizational dynamics of delivering service

quality and the effectiveness of HR staffs and HR practices. He coedited *Academy of Management Review*'s special issue on Total Quality Management, and his book, *Winning the Service Game,* coauthored with Ben Schneider, has been translated into four languages.

Larry D. Browning (PhD, Ohio State University) is Professor of Organizational Communication in the Department of Communication Studies at the University of Texas at Austin. His research interest is studying how organizations use cooperative strategies to create and implement procedures. This interest is represented in a book he recently coauthored with Judy Shetler titled *The Early History of SEMATECH: How Inter-Firm Cooperation at SEMATECH Changed the U.S. Semiconductor Industry* that analyzes the selection and retention of standards.

Kim S. Cameron is Dean of and Albert J. Weatherhead, III Professor of Management at the Weatherhead School of Management, Case Western Reserve University. Prior to this appointment, he served on the faculties of Brigham Young University, where he was also

Associate Dean of the Marriott School of Management; the University of Michigan, where he served as department chair in the Michigan Business School and director of several University of Michigan executive programs; the University of Wisconsin—Madison; and Ricks College. He also organized and directed the Organizational Studies Division of the National Center for Higher Education Management Systems in Boulder, Colorado, during the early 1980s. He received his BS and MS degrees from Brigham Young University and his MA and PhD degrees from Yale University. His research on organizational downsizing, organizational effectiveness, corporate quality culture, and the development of management skills has been published in more than 70 articles and 6 books. Most recently, his research has focused on downsizing and redesign in private and public sector organizations, on virtues in organizations such as forgiveness and compassion, and on organizational quality and performance in higher education and business enterprises.

Robert E. Cole is Professor of Business Administration and Sociology at the University of California, Berkeley and Lorraine Tyson Mitchell II Chair in Leadership and Communication at the Haas School of Business. He is also Director of the Haas School's Management of Technology Program and an elected member of the International Association of Quality. He is a long-term student of Japanese work organization focusing on organizational learning and a specialist on quality management in the United States and Japan. He has been a member of the American Society of Quality since 1979. His research has focused on the automotive industry and electronics. He is the author of *Managing Quality Fads: How American Business Learned to Play the Quality Game* (1999). His most recent work is on strategies for the transfer of knowledge in multidivisional firms and also on institutional factors affecting new venture for-

mation in the Japanese and American high technology sectors.

James W. Dean, Jr. (PhD, Carnegie Mellon University) is Associate Dean for the MBA Program and Professor of Management at the Kenan-Flagler Business School, University of North Carolina at Chapel Hill. He is the former Program Director for Transformations to Quality Organizations at the National Science Foundation. This program of research on performance improvement was jointly supported by several *Fortune* 500 corporations and the federal government. His research interests include organizational change and performance improvement, strategic decision making, and aesthetic aspects of organizations. He has given talks about his research in Canada, France, Germany, Luxembourg, and Mexico. He has published numerous articles in academic journals (e.g., *Academy of Management Journal, Academy of Management Review, Decision Sciences, Organization Science,* and *Strategic Management Journal*) and business publications (e.g., *Harvard Business Review,* and *California Management Review*) as well as two books. He has served on the editorial boards of several journals devoted to the management of technology, operations, quality, and organizations (e.g., *Academy of Management Review, Journal of Engineering and Technology Management, Journal of Operations Management,* and *Quality Management Journal*). He is a Senior Examiner for the Malcolm Baldrige National Quality Award, with 5 years of experience in the Baldrige Award Program. He has performed research and/or consulting projects with numerous corporations, including ALCOA, Boeing, Corning, DuPont, General Electric, Honeywell, Makino, Nortel, Rockwell, and St. Laurie, Ltd.

George S. Easton is Associate Professor of Decision and Information Analysis at the Goizueta Business School, Emory University. He received a PhD in statistics from Princeton University in 1985. He has formerly been on the faculty of the Graduate School of Business at the University of Chicago and the Faculty of Management at Rutgers University. His research interests are in the areas of quality management and statistics. In quality management, his research has focused on characterizing the quality management phenomenon and assessing its impact on corporate financial performance. In statistics, his research has focused on graphical methods for multivariate data.

Kathleen M. Eisenhart is Professor of Strategy and Organization in the School of Engineering at Stanford University. Her interests center on managing in high-velocity industries such as computing, software, and telecommunications. She is a coauthor of *Competing on the Edge: Strategy as Structured Chaos* (1998). For her ideas on fast decision making, she won the Pacific Telesis Foundation Award. She has also received the Whittemore Prize for her writing on organizing global firms in rapidly changing markets, and the Stem Award for her work on strategic alliance formation in entrepreneurial firms. She has received several teaching honors, including being one of eight professors named to the Stanford Professorial Honor Roll (by student selection), and has been elected a Fellow of the Academy of Management. She received a BS in mechanical engineering from Brown University and a PhD from Stanford's Graduate School of Business.

J. Richard Hackman is the Cahners-Rabb Professor of Social and Organizational Psychology at Harvard University. He received his undergraduate degree in mathematics from MacMurray College in 1962 and his doctorate in social psychology from the University of Illinois in 1966. He taught at Yale until 1986 when he moved to Harvard. He conducts research on a variety of topics in social and organizational psychology, including the performance of work teams, social influences on individual behavior,

and the design and leadership of self-managing units in organizations. He is on the editorial board of several professional journals and has consulted with a number of organizations on issues having to do with work design, leadership, and team performance. He is the author or editor of 7 books and more than 80 chapters and articles. His most recent book is *Groups That Work* (1990). Among the awards he has received are the Sixth Annual AIR Creative Talent Award in the field of "Measurement and Evaluation: Individual and Group Behavior," the Distinguished Scientific Contribution Award of the Society of Industrial and Organizational Psychology, and both the Distinguished Educator Award and the Distinguished Scholar Award of the Academy of Management. He is a Fellow of the American Psychological Association and of the American Psychological Society.

Tomoko Hamada is Professor of Anthropology at the College of William and Mary. She completed her BA in American studies at Vassar College, her MA in sociology at Keio University, and her PhD in anthropology at the University of California, Berkeley. She has taught at Damlin College and the University of Witwatersrand, both in Johannesburg; was Director of Asian Studies at Rose-Rulman Institute of Technology; and, since 1988, has been a member of the faculty at William and Mary. She is the author of *American Enterprise in Japan and Anthropological Perspectives on Organizational Culture,* the editor of *Studies in Third World Societies,* and the author of numerous articles, the primary focus of which is the culture of complex organizations.

Andrew B. Hargadon is Assistant Professor of Management in the Warrington College of Business Administration at the University of Florida. Before becoming an organizational researcher, he earned his BS and MS in Engineering/Product Design from Stanford University and worked as a product designer in the Silicon Valley. His publications and research interests now concern organizational innovation and change, with particular emphasis on new product and process development.

Casey Ichniowski is Professor of Management at Columbia University's Graduate School of Business and Research Associate of the National Bureau of Economic Research. His recent research on the effects of human resource management practices on firms' economic performance has received wide acclaim, including the 1998 University of Minnesota Award for Best Paper on the Employment Relationship. His teaching on human resource management and conflict resolution is informed by his field-based research on human resource management in firms in the paper, steel, retail food, and financial service industries of the United States, Canada, Japan, and Europe.

Sherry L. Jarrell is Assistant Professor of Finance and Economics in the Babcock Graduate School of Management at Wake Forest University. She received a PhD in finance and economics in 1991 from the Graduate School of Business at the University of Chicago. She has been on the faculty at Indiana University (where she received a teaching award), Columbia University, and Emory University, and she has developed original courses on the emerging link between total quality management and strategic financial management. Her research interests focus on empirical research design in financial economics. She has developed two original methods for isolating the impact of economic events on corporate performance and has applied these methods to examine takeovers, management buyouts, and the adoption of total quality management systems. Her ongoing research, funded in part by a National Science Foundation grant in its "Transformations to Quality Organizations" program, explores strategic planning and optimal resource allocation methods at leading U.S. firms.

Linda Kaboolian is Associate Professor in the Kennedy School of Government at Harvard University. She researches and consults about public sector service delivery systems and customer service to diverse communities. She is involved with efforts to infuse innovation into traditional labor-management relations in the public sector. She worked on the Social Security Administration Disability Re-engineering Project, redesigning the process by which initial disability determinations are made. In addition, she has consulted to the Department of Energy; the Environmental Protection Agency; the U.S. Customs Service; the City of Philadelphia; New York City; and a number of state, local, and non-profit organizations. In the private sector, she spent nearly 2 years in a factory studying Ford's Taurus production process, where the introduction of new technology and a new division of labor changed the nature of the social contract on the shop floor.

Thomas A. Kochan is the George M. Bunker Professor of Management at MIT's Sloan School of Management. He came to MIT in 1980 as Professor of Industrial Relations, having previously been at Cornell University, where he was on the faculty of the School of Industrial and Labor Relations from 1973 to 1980. In 1973, he received his PhD in industrial relations from the University of Wisconsin. Since then he has served as a third-party mediator, factfinder, and arbitrator and as a consultant to a variety of government and private sector organizations and labor management groups. He has done research on a variety of topics related to industrial relations and human resource management in the public and private sector. His recent books include *After Lean Production: Evolving Employment Practices in the World Auto Industry* (1997); *Managing for the Future: Organizational Behavior and Processes* (1996); and *Employment Relations in a Changing World Economy* (1995). He is currently president of the Industrial Relations Research Association (IRRA); from 1992 to 1995, he served as president of the International Industrial Relations Association.

David I. Levine is Associate Professor in the Haas School of Business at the University of California, Berkeley. He is also the editor of the journal *Industrial Relations,* Associate Director of the Institute of Industrial Relations, and Director of Research at UC Berkeley's Center for Organization and Human Resource Effectiveness. His research is summarized in several books: *Reinventing the Workplace* (1995); *Working in the Twenty-First Century* (1998); and the edited volume *The American Workplace: Skills, Pay and Employee Involvement* (1999).

John Paul MacDuffie is Associate Professor in the Management Department at the Wharton School, University of Pennsylvania. His research is centrally concerned with the rise of "lean" or "flexible" production as an alternative to mass production, focusing on the world automotive industry. He has investigated the consequences of lean or flexible production for economic performance in manufacturing plants; the diffusion of this approach across company and country boundaries; patterns of collaborative problem solving and knowledge transfer within and across firms; and the implications of these changes for managers, workers, and unions. For many years, he has been one of the core researchers for MIT's International Motor Vehicle Program (IMVP). His current work draws on the second round of IMVP's International Assembly Plant Study, gathered from a sample of 89 plants representing 20 companies and 21 countries.

Nelson P. Repenning is the Robert N. Noyce Career Development Professor at the MIT Sloan School of Management. His research interests include process improvement methods such as Total Quality Management, organizational change, process improvement applied to new product design, and the development of cross-disciplinary management theory. His work draws on a number of modeling methods, including simulation, nonlinear dynamics, and game and contract theory. He is currently working with MIT's Center for Innovation in Product Development, Ford Motor Company, and Harley-Davidson Motor Company.

Saul Rubinstein is Assistant Professor at Rutgers University School of Management and Labor Relations. He is a graduate of Swarthmore College, Harvard Graduate School of Education, and the Harvard Business School. He received his PhD from the Massachusetts Institute of Technology's Sloan School of Management. Through MIT's International Motor Vehicle Program and funding from the National Science Foundation, he has studied the impact of new forms of firm governance and co-management that have resulted from efforts to transform industrial relations and manufacturing systems at General Motors' Saturn Corporation.

W. Richard (Dick) Scott received his PhD in sociology from the University of Chicago. He came to Stanford University in 1960, where he is now Professor of Sociology with courtesy appointments in the Graduate School of Business, School of Education, and School of Medicine. He has served as vice chair and chair of the department and was the founding director of the universitywide Stanford Center for Organizations Research from 1988 to 1996. He is the author or coauthor of numerous books and articles, including *Hospital Structure and Performance* (1987, with A. B. Flood), *Organizations: Rational, Natural and Open Systems* (4th ed., 1998), and *Institutions and Organizations* (1995). His major research interest is the relation between institutional environments and organizational structures and performance. Together with M. Ruef, P. Mendel, and C. Caronna, he has just completed a study of how changes in the institutional context of health care has affected five populations of medical care organizations in the San Francisco

424 \ THE QUALITY MOVEMENT AND ORGANIZATION THEORY

Bay Area. This study, *Institutional Change and Organizations: Transformation of a Health Field,* is due for publication in late 1999.

Kathryn Shaw is Professor of Economics in the Graduate School of Industrial Administration at Carnegie Mellon University, where she has been a professor since completing her PhD at Harvard University in 1981. During her years at Carnegie Mellon, she has published on a range of topics in labor economics and human resource management, and in 1996, was listed as one of the Top 50 Economists worldwide (based on publication record). She has been the recipient of the Minnesota Award (1999) for the best paper on the employment relationship, the Xerox Research Chair, and the departmental teaching award, and she is a Research Fellow with the National Bureau of Economic Research. Most recently, her research focuses on productivity and human resource management and on franchising, with publications in the *American Economic Review, Journal of Political Economy,* and *Management Science.* This work has been funded by the National Science Foundation, the Department of Labor, and the Sloan Foundation.

Sim B. Sitkin is Associate Professor in the Fuqua School of Business at Duke University and Director of Fuqua's Health Management Program. His research examines how organizations and their members become more or less capable of change and innovation. Specifically, his research focuses on how formal and informal organizational control systems affect risk-taking, accountability, trust, learning, and innovation. His articles on these topics have appeared in a number of academic and management journals and books. His coedited book, *The Legalistic Organization,* was published by Sage Publications in 1994.

John D. Sterman is the J. Spencer Standish Professor of Management in the MIT Sloan School of Management and Director of the MIT System Dynamics Group. His research includes systems thinking and organizational learning, simulation modeling, and nonlinear dynamics, focusing on improving decision making in complex systems. He has pioneered the development of "management flight simulators" of corporate and economic systems, tools now used by corporations and universities around the world. In partnership with the National Science Foundation and several leading companies, he is studying the dynamics of quality improvement to help firms design and implement sustainable improvement programs.

Kathleen M. Sutcliffe is Assistant Professor of Organizational Behavior and Human Resource Management at the University of Michigan Business School. She received a PhD from the University of Texas at Austin. Her research program has been devoted to investigating problems that are concerned with the effect of context on organizational members, their units, and organizations. Specifically, her work focuses on how contexts become known; how contexts influence organizational forms and organizational actions/responses; and how organizations and their units can be designed to better sense, cope with, and respond to contextual requirements. She is pursuing these interests through a National Science Foundation grant and a fellowship from the Tauber Manufacturing Institute at the University of Michigan.

Ruth Wageman is Associate Professor of Organizational Behavior in the Management of Organizations Division at Columbia Business School. She received her BA degree from Columbia College in 1987 and her PhD from the Harvard Joint Doctoral Program in Organizational Behavior in 1992. Her teaching and research interests include designing and leading effective task-performing teams, reward system design for groups, human motivation, and structural and individual influences on group and interpersonal behavior. Major publications/papers include "Interdependence and Group

Effectiveness"; "Critical Success Factors for Self-Managing Teams"; "The Role of Competence Information in Reducing Interpersonal Competition"; "Incentives and Cooperation: The Joint Effects of Tasks and Rewards on Group Effectiveness," with G. P. Baker III; and "Effects of Rewards, Achievement Motivation, and Evaluative Focus on Intrinsic Motivation," with J. Harackiewicz and S. Abrahams.

Karl E. Weick is the Rensis Likert Collegiate Professor of Organizational Behavior and Psychology and Professor of Psychology at the University of Michigan. He is a former editor of *Administrative Science Quarterly.* He is concerned with the development of a perspective on human organization that highlights processes of organizing. Central to this perspective is the question of how people make sense of equivocal information when they are under pressure. This question is being explored in the context of wildland firefighting, marine navigation, and medical errors. Concurrent theory development is directed to the topics of organizational learning, collective mind, and theory-practice linkages.

Sidney G. Winter is the Deloitte and Touche Professor of Management in the Wharton School at the University of Pennsylvania. Before joining Wharton in 1993, he served as Chief Economist for the U.S. General Accounting Office. Previously, he was Professor of Economics and Management at Yale University. His current research focus is on the study of corporate strategy and management problems from the viewpoint of evolutionary economics. He coauthored *An Evolutionary Theory of Economic Change* and is a Fellow of the Econometric Society and of the Amercian Association for the Advancement of Science. He received his doctorate in economics from Yale University.